THIS DAY IN MUSIC'S GUIDE TO

THE CLASH

MALCOLM WYATT

This Day in Music's Guide To The Clash

This first edition published 2018 by
This Day in Music
www.thisdayinmusic.com

Email: editor@thisdayinmusic.com

Printed and bound by CPI Group (UK) Ltd, Croydon, CR0 4YY

A catalogue record for this book is available from the British Library

www.thisdayinmusic.com

ISBN 978 1 999592 74 5

Front and back cover concept by Liz Sanchez

Cover design by Oliver Keen

This Day In Music Books
2B Vantage Park
Washingley Road
Huntingdon PE29 6SR

Exclusive Distributors:
Music Sales Limited
14/15 Berners St
London W1T 3JL

CONTENTS

INTRODUCTION 4

THE STORY 15

The Early Days 15
Classic Clash 73
Post-Clash 189

THE MUSIC 235

The Clash's 50 finest 269
Discography 282
Influenced by The Clash 285

CLASHOGRAPHY 287

The Clash's London 289
The Clash in Writing 291
The Clash on Film 297
A Clash Timeline 305
Still Talking about The Clash 319
They Also Served: Clash Conspirators 333

Index 355

0 INTRODUCTION

The Clash were for many the definitive British punk rock band, and arguably the most influential and inspirational. Formed in 1976 as part of the original wave of UK punk, their music incorporated elements of reggae, dub, funk, ska, rockabilly ... you name it. And they were about so much more.

This Day in Music's Guide to The Clash, a conclusive companion to this seminal outfit, details their rise to fame: from their roots in bands such as the 101'ers to their emergence alongside the Sex Pistols; from their CBS deal, the early 1977 release of 'White Riot' and the startling eponymous album that followed to the *London Calling* double-LP that saw them regarded among the finest rock bands of all time, two further innovative long-players that ensured global success, and the internal wrangles that ultimately led to disbandment after just one more record.

Along the way, we tell the stories and appraise the reaction to all their studio product, examine the way they broke America, highlight the many tours and interviews, and shed light on how they fell apart at the height of their commercial success, the demise coming long before their sole UK No.1 hit.

This Day in Music's Guide to The Clash also looks in detail at the band members and how they got where they were, covering in detail their post-split careers and the heartbreak surrounding their frontman's 2002 death, while profiling other key personnel that played a part in the tale. What follows is the ultimate guide to this outfit's enduring legacy: from their outspoken political stance and influential experimentation to the rebellious outlook that inspired so many and ensured their memory lives on, long after the classic line-up – Strummer, Jones, Simonon and Headon – last shared a stage.

My Journey with The Clash

As I was born in 1967, a couple of months after BBC Radio One went on air and the year of so many groundbreaking albums, anyone with a basic knowledge of maths will grasp that I was still in single figures when 1977's incendiary debut single 'White Riot' and the inspirational self-titled album that followed first saw the light of day. But I was a fast learner and by the time *Give 'Em Enough Rope* was released, I saw myself as a proper fan. I may not have looked the part, judging by old photos, and can claim no part in the Paris '68 riots that partly inspired Bernard Rhodes' Situationist political world-view, nor the Notting Hill '76 happening experienced by Rhodes, Simonon and Strummer that fueled The Clash's first 45. But this was a band that spoke to me and would play an important part in my development.

I was a *Smash Hits* reader by '78, and can recall that glossy IPC fo rtnightly magazine printing the lyrics to 'Tommy Gun', as they did with so many key songs that became part of my musical DNA. My brother's record collection and stories from the frontline – not forgetting visits to venues like our local hotspot, Guildford Civic Hall, and Portsmouth Guildhall – also drove me on, his musical tastes quickly drifting from Queen and Wings to things far more cutting-edge. Through my brother and his mates, I got to hear the Sex Pistols, Buzzcocks, The Jam and The Clash, and everything swiftly changed.

Whatever I later read about *Give 'Em Enough Rope* – from the band, critics, and fans – that second LP will forever remain my proper introduction to that world, so I won't be swayed in my own thinking about it. I loved *The Clash* and *London Calling*, fully appreciating the latter even more as years passed, totally understanding the experts' view on their superiority. But it was the record in between that first resonated with me. In that alone, I have to say CBS did the right thing in getting US producer Sandy Pearlman on board. That album introduced the band to a wider audience, and one of those new converts had just celebrated his eleventh birthday in a three-bed council house, deep in Surrey's semi-rural sweet suburbia.

I was soon hooked, and by the time of the fifth album, 1982's *Combat Rock*, I was old enough to be earning from a paper-round and work at a local farm shop to ensure that was the first LP I bought with my own money. At 14, I wasn't big on detail, but there's a diary entry mentioning that purchase alongside other notables such as the Falklands War, the FA Cup Final and its replay (Spurs v Mick Jones' favourites Queen's Park Rangers), and trips to Guildford Civic Hall to see The Stranglers and The Boomtown Rats. I don't think I'd dare play my *Combat Rock* cassette now, but it remains in my collection 35 years on – tracks like the undervalued 'Atom Tan' being another fine example of call-and-response harmonies that had first soared into my musical conscience with 'Safe European Home' three years earlier.

By the late '80s, I was an occasional visitor at the band's old local, meeting friends at the Caernarvon Castle, Chalk Farm Road, downing Guinness and watching Wolfie Witcher 'gum his gob iron' with His Brew. Alas, that pub was eventually converted into a clothes shop, gutted in the Great Fire of Camden one Saturday night in early 2008, then demolished.

I never got to see The Clash live. There, I've said it. The nearest I came was seeing Strummer with The Pogues at the Fleadh in Finsbury Park, North London, in June 1992, a decade after what I and many more saw as the band's last great statement in long-playing form. I didn't even see The Mescaleros; I'm now deeply regretting that, fully appreciating them more than ever. But barely a few weeks go by without a Clash LP, single, or off-shoot project involving former members getting an airing.

They were about more than music. They were a fashion statement, something of a subcultural 'go to' barometer. These Londoners – and John Peel – were more instrumental in inspiring me to dip back and forth between punk and new wave, funk, reggae, rock'n'roll, ska and soul. Nothing was off-limits, if it inspired you, moved you, and was passionately delivered.

This was also a band that made sure it was perceived cool to get involved in left-wing politics and various anti-racist, anti-nuclear, environmentally sound causes. I was already heading that way, my working-class roots and experiences suggesting that path. Now here was a band that not only looked to knock 'the system' but suggested how to go about it. Yes, they were infuriatingly vague or contradictory in some respects, but there was a positive slant, taking on board some of the best elements of the DIY, independent philosophy of punk. And it was never empty rhetoric. Strummer, Jones, Simonon and Headon opened doors. Look deeper and it all seems far more complicated, but that's the essence of their legacy.

Of the early bands on that scene, Dr Feelgood and the Ramones redefined rock'n'roll, while the Sex Pistols were a major wake-up call. Buzzcocks reinvented the short, sharp love song, and The Jam and The Stranglers made me realise local boys really could make good. But it was The Clash who truly inspired so many bands I loved in that second wave (and beyond) to attempt to follow in their wake. They influenced lots of great bands, including many of my personal favourites, not least The Undertones. For that alone they deserve my respect.

I can't honestly subscribe to the CBS line that The Clash were 'the only band that mattered'. But there's no doubting their importance. When the world lost Joe Strummer on December 22, 2002, I was too wrapped up in my world, with two daughters under two, to reflect too deeply on that loss. That dawned later, and having now reached the grand age of 50, I properly realise how much this iconic figure achieved, how cruel it was he had to leave us at the age he was, and just how much he motivated others in a short yet massively full life. As Keith Topping put it in *The Complete Clash*: 'That someone with as much life in him as Joe Strummer should have suffered an old man's death from a heart attack at the age of 50 seemed utterly wrong'. Then again, quoting Pete Townshend, 'That heart of his always worked too hard'.

With Joe's passing went the last hopes of a reunion, and rightly so. Best to leave it there, and arguably not include that sub-standard last LP. As far as I'm concerned, *Combat Rock* was the last great statement. From there on it was more a case of Strummer going solo, Simonon just along for the ride.

On the face of it, there was nothing overwhelmingly new about The Clash that you could easily put your finger on. But isn't that the case for every true revolutionary movement or outfit? There were elements within of so many great bands that came before: glimpses of The Rolling Stones' ability to reinterpret the past; The Who's power and attitude; The Kinks' sense of national identity; and Mott the Hoople's stagecraft and showmanship. The rock'n'roll credence Strummer brought to the party was part Eddie Cochran, part Woody Guthrie, complementing Mick Jones' six-string reinvention of everything he'd infused and inhaled over that past decade.

And make no mistake, this was a proper band. All the members of that classic line-up played a part, with the reggae influence and whole look of the band owing a major debt to Paul Simonon, while Topper Headon added a last piece to the jigsaw, his ability to seamlessly introduce all those other influences helping create the heartbeat that made it all tick.

Here's another thing – if The Clash had

tried to rewrite their debut LP time and time again, they'd perhaps be seen as more of a musical footnote in history, great an album as that was. But they moved on, true to punk-rock ideals, showing admirable progression with every record that followed, whichever one you might class as your favourite. *Give 'Em Enough Rope* opened the door a little wider, *London Calling* redefined the band and truly proved their long-time worth, while *Sandinista* and *Combat Rock* further showed the creative talent and versatility. I'll even put it out there that *Cut the Crap* told an important part of the story.

Then there was the live band. Such an inspiration. I wasn't there, but the footage that survives shines a spotlight on the energy they created. So thanks Joe, thanks Mick, thanks Paul, thanks Topper. To paraphrase the late, great Ian Dury, you were the catalysts that sparked my revolution ... and I'm really glad you came.

Acknowledgements

As Joe Strummer said, 'Without people, you're nothing'. So here's where I thank Neil Cossar for giving me the chance to tell this fascinating story, and Richard Houghton for comparing notes, previous publications and past Clash product, a friendship borne out of great music, and the introductions that got me involved. Then, at the heart of it, there's the unflinching love and support of my better half, Jayne, and our daughters, Molly and Lottie, putting up with me sitting at a computer far too many hours a day for little financial reward.

I need to mention my brother, Mark and friends Alan Hill and Stephan Miles, for helping turn me on to bands like The Clash, my other on-hand unofficial music librarian, Jim Wilkinson, and Undertones guitarist Damian O'Neill for a short-notice interview by way of an introduction to a far more complicated project than I might have imagined. I just hope it lives up to the expectations of dedicated Clash fans like Warren Meadows, Neil Waite and Steve Worrall, and all the others who cottoned on to what I've been working on.

Then there are the band's chroniclers, not least Pat Gilbert, Marcus Gray, Chris Salewicz, Keith Topping, and Clash road manager Johnny Green, for getting this down in print first (and so well), plus Don Letts and Julien Temple for their splendid audio-visual films chronicling an amazing outfit. Similar sentiments go to many more writers and videographers, most of whom I hope I've properly credited. In no way does this replace their endeavours. Think of it as complementary to all that's gone before.

Finally, there's the band themselves for the initial inspiration and all that timeless, great music. I'd love to have convinced Mick Jones, Paul Simonon and Topper Headon over a pint or a cuppa that this wasn't just another Clash book and had something fresh to offer. I'm hoping they'll look kindly on the result, and interviews will follow. Above all, I'd like to dedicate this book to Joe Strummer, his family and friends, and all those sufficiently inspired by the story of The Clash to keep the campfires burning and continue to work for the common good, contributing to the Joe Strummer Foundation.

0 ROCKIN' THE CASBAH

from Derry to Detroit ... and beyond

Not many people can say they were there the night Paul Simonon trashed his bass guitar at the New York Palladium on September 20th, 1979, an iconic moment so memorably captured by photographer Pennie Smith, subsequently used for the cover of classic album, *London Calling*.

Damian O'Neill was though, in the stalls, his band having opened for The Clash earlier that evening, handing over to '60s soul legends Sam and Dave before getting to see the legendary punk outfit that had invited them on to their North American 'Take the Fifth' tour that autumn.

Nearly 40 years on, the London-based guitarist – still occasionally playing with The Undertones as well as That Petrol Emotion spin-off The Everlasting Yeah, and his outfit, the Monotones – re-lived that moment with me, still in awe at being part of an amazing adventure for five lads from Derry, Northern Ireland, living the dream on a run of dates from St Paul, Minnesota (with ex-New York Dolls frontman David Johansen on second), to Toronto, Ontario.

'That was the first of two nights at the Palladium. Little did we know that was going to be the cover of the album. I remember thinking, 'Wow. That's impressive!' It was just so out of the blue, because it was such a great show. It wasn't like he was having a bad time.'

Clash road manager Johnny Green reckoned Simonon's trashing of his Precision bass was more about trying to impress his girlfriend, a New York model, but Paul suggested – in a 2011 video interview for Fender – it was down to venue staff not allowing fans to get up and dance. He said, 'I was annoyed that the bouncers wouldn't let the audience stand up out of their chairs. That frustrated me, to the point that I destroyed the bass guitar. Unfortunately, you always tend to destroy things you love. I wasn't taking it out on the bass because there was something wrong with it. It was a great guitar. I've still got the pieces. Strummer took one and was about to walk off with it. I had to grab it back and say,

Damian O'Neill in 2018

'Actually, that belongs to me!' For the rest of the tour I had to play a really light bass. It just didn't sound the same.'

Somehow, he managed to avoid rock'n'roll cliché in the process. But what would you expect from a fella who was film-star cool personified on a stage, and by then a fair player too. In fact, The Clash, collectively, were so cool that The Undertones were more at ease keeping themselves to themselves in the presence of such punk rock royalty.

'We were really shy. We didn't really get to know them, and only did 10 shows. We were offered the whole six-week tour. I think it was 23 shows. But Billy (Doherty, drums) and John (O'Neill, guitar, Damian's brother) said no, so we compromised.'

It's clearly still something of a regret all these years on that his band didn't take them up on a full run, Damian feeling The Clash's initial offer was partly down to feeling guilty after pulling out of a festival his band were organising in their home city, after Joe Strummer received a threatening letter claiming he would be killed if he appeared (the official line at the time was that they couldn't get the insurance to play, more of which later).

While their hosts were on the verge of releasing their classic third LP, their openers had long been fans, playing Clash covers in an early residency at the Casbah club in Derry, a year before 'Teenage Kicks' set them on the road to success. It was BBC Radio One DJ John Peel who famously broke that single in the summer of '78. Was it on Peelie's show that they first heard The Clash?

'It was either through Peel or the *NME*, of which we were avid readers, probably from around late '76, around the time 'Anarchy in the UK' came out. John went and bought

'White Riot' after hearing that, via mail order. You couldn't get punk singles in Derry at the time. There wasn't even Good Vibrations (Terri Hooley's record shop turned indie label, on which 'Teenage Kicks' was released) in Belfast then.

'John bought a lot of those early punk singles and loved The Clash. And when we heard 'White Riot', we loved it, and the first album, of course. I also remember Tony Parsons' *NME* interview around the time of the first album, with an audio version on the *Capital Radio* EP, given away with the *NME* that April.

'They were supposed to play in Belfast in October '77. I think the council banned them, leading to that incident where all these punks from the area properly met each other for the first time. A lot of people made goods friends for life there. It's probably been exaggerated a little, but it's a nice story. They did come back and play the Ulster Hall in '78 though. And I was there ... up front!

'But I'd say they were at their height as a band when we played with them in America. They were very professional, tight as hell, and Topper was just amazing, top of his game. On that tour we were shocked just how professional they were. They more or less stuck to the same set-list. Strummer even tended to say the same things on the mic. every night. We were kind of aghast, thinking it was all too professional. At the time we were shambolic. Anything goes. We probably didn't even have a set-list.

'It was a learning curve for us, just to watch them, seeing them put 100 per cent into that set, criss-crossing each other on stage. Jesus, they were incredible. I'm not sure I rated Paul Simonon as a player before that tour, and it didn't matter – they were more punk then. But by *London Calling*, he'd mastered his instrument. That was the first time we'd heard 'Guns of Brixton' too, with that great bassline. Out of them all, Paul just looked the handsome one, the iconic '50s rock star. I'd say Joe and Mick were friendliest though. I don't really remember talking to Paul or Topper. The other thing I remember from that tour was Joe coming on stage every night in the dark with a lit candelabra for the first encore of 'Armagideon Time'. Very impressive.'

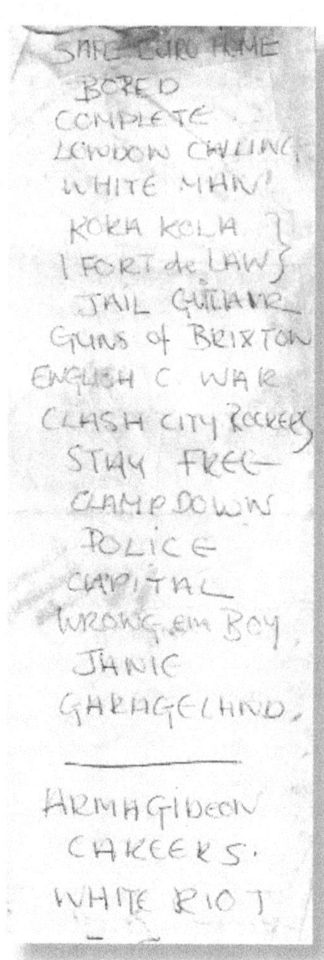

It may only have been a handful of dates, but those appearances with The Clash – including dates in Chicago, Detroit, Boston, Philadelphia, and across the Canadian border in Toronto - clearly resonated with Damian and his bandmates.

'Our first show was in St Paul Civic Center, this big sports arena. I always thought it was 10,000-capacity, but my itinerary said 4,000. You could have driven a bus through the whole arena. It was the biggest place we'd ever played, and as our first show out there it seemed that everything was big in America! There's a great picture of Strummer chatting to Mickey (Bradley, bass) and Billy, taken by Pennie Smith, before the soundcheck that day. I was so jealous. I always wish that was me.

'Joe was very much a father figure and walked the walk as well as talked the talk. He was definitely Mr Nice Guy, very caring. We'd met him before, the time when he came down to Acton Studios while we were recording *You Got My Number (Why Don't You Use It!)*. We first met him at Wessex Studios, when we did the photo opp. for that festival in Derry that never happened. That was amazing as well. We actually interrupted them during the recording of *London Calling*. I don't know what song, but just watching Strummer with his Telecaster, battering the hell out of it ... then they had to stop for this photo. That was great meeting them, even though it was only 10 minutes or so.

'Then Strummer and Jones came to see us, to apologise, personally tell us they couldn't do the show, showing us the (threatening) letter. We should have been upset but were still just star-struck by them coming to see us!

'When it came to the tour, we were going around by station-wagon – five of us and our manager, Andy (Ferguson), driving. Then we had two road crew with the gear in a tiny hire truck. There was a lot of driving. If we'd done the whole tour we'd have probably joined them in the bus though.'

So what Clash covers were they playing back in their Casbah days?

'In the early days, we'd play 'White Riot', 'Garageland', 'Janie Jones' and '1977', probably phasing those out by the time we moved on from there. Unfortunately, there's no recordings of us doing Clash songs there, although we've got tapes of us doing Johnny Moped and The Boys, and Iggy and the Stooges. I loved doing 'Garageland'. That was my favourite ... that and '1977'. What a great song. 'No Elvis, Beatles or the Rolling Stones.' What a great statement.'

'I came across Mick Jones and Joe Strummer a few times in later years. I remember seeing Mick in a car in Notting Hill Gate once. I waved, he waved back. He did recognise me. And I kick myself that one time I was at the old Town and Country Club in Kentish Town for some show, and Mick was at the bar, backstage, and I didn't

have the courage to say hello. But I did speak to Joe quite late on. Alan McGee ran this club in Notting Hill Gate, and I was on Poptones at the time. I was really drunk and introduced to Joe again. He was like, 'Yeah! Undertones! 'Teenage Kicks'!' I said, 'Actually I didn't write that, that was John,' and he said, 'Yeah, I know that!' We chatted for a bit, and I was on cloud nine. Again, he was just really, really nice.

'I didn't get to see The Clash live after we toured with them, and while I feel they should have cut down *Sandinista!* a bit, there's some great stuff on there. I liked *Combat Rock* too, again with some great, great songs. I didn't think they were going to break up, but I guess all bands reach their end. It's a shame about *Cut the Crap* really. It was kind of financially stupid to break up when they did, but I think the relationship between Mick and Joe was abysmal.

'I still play *London Calling* a lot. My favourite Clash single's 'Complete Control' though, closely followed by '(White Man)

In Hammersmith Palais'. Brilliant, brilliant singles. And those songs were in the set when we were supporting them. Then there was 'Safe European Home' - another brilliant track. That's typical Mick Jones. A big Mott the Hoople fan, and he loves all those harmonies. He's so melodic in his sense of writing, and the perfect foil for Joe, with those two together. He's a genius for those great backing vocals and call-and-response harmonies.'

At around that point, I think I'm done, and I'm about to say goodbye to Damian. But then he remembers something else, another anecdote that serves as a great illustration of The Undertones' complete lack of pretentiousness.

'My favourite piece of memorabilia is a baseball bat I had signed by The Clash. I think Mickey mentioned it in his book (2016's *Teenage Kicks: My Life as an Undertone*). The first show we did out there, Mickey and I went to Sears' department store. Mickey bought 10 baseball bats, and I bought one. We ended up having to take them all the way around America with us! After our very last show in Toronto, I got them to sign it.'

There's a clip from that day on YouTube, with Topper Headon, Mickey Bradley and Undertones singer Feargal Sharkey interrupting a TV interview with Joe Strummer in Toronto, bursting in with toy guns they'd bought the headliners as a tongue-in-cheek thank you for inviting them, Damian explaining, 'We thought it would be a nice little present. They were dressing like 1920s gangsters at the time, after all.'

Bradley, embarrassed, reckons he can't watch that footage now. but his bandmate – who's clearly had a few beers, but at least keeps quiet on camera – added, 'You've probably seen the footage. It's kind of weird, but kind of good, showing how earnest Joe's trying to be with all that going on.'

He's not finished yet. In something of a homage to Columbo (The Clash were still singing 'I'm So Bored With the USA' to American audiences back then, but there was no denying that their TV had seeped into our collective consciences on this side of the water), there's 'just one more thing'.

'At that last show in Toronto, Joe and Mick came into our dressing room before to say, 'We'd love to play 'Teenage Kicks' with you at the end of your set. Is that ok?' And Mickey said no! At the time we really didn't like bands jamming. It was such a hippy thing. And because he said no, the rest of us had to kind of sheepishly say, 'Sorry'. And to this day ... oh God, I still regret it. Just think! Someone would have had footage of that somewhere.'

There's a pause there from Damian, then a sigh, followed by a resigned, 'Ah well. It was not to be.'

PRE-CLASH

The Early Days

1

"Putting the Beatles back together isn't going to be the salvation of rock'n'roll. Four kids playing to their contemporaries in a dirty cellar club might"

MICK FARREN, *NME*, 1976

PRE-CLASH

1

The Early Days

Let's start with the basics. Formed in 1976 as part of the original wave of British punk, The Clash were at the heart of a musical revolution that quickly spread across the world, one that remains a major influence and inspiration for so many great bands that followed in their wake.

They were no one-trick ponies, their music reaching far beyond punk-rock guitar roots to incorporate elements of dub, funk, reggae, rockabilly and ska. And that was just part of their appeal. They were also about attitude, culture, fashion and politics, each member playing a part in the wider scope of the band. And we're talking scope. The singer always made a big deal of the band's global credentials. West London was what they were about and where they were at, but like the raised arterial route that marked out the centre of their universe, the road went east and west from there.

For most of the recording career of The Clash, the band consisted of Joe Strummer on lead vocals and rhythm guitar, Mick Jones on lead guitar and vocals, Paul Simonon on bass guitar and vocals, and Nicky 'Topper' Headon on drums and percussion. Headon was sacked in 1982, while dealing with drug addiction, and on-going internal friction finally lead to Jones' departure the following year. The group continued with new members, but just one more LP followed, with their disbandment confirmed in early 1986.

They certainly hit the ground running: an incendiary debut single 'White Riot' in March 1977 was followed by a self-titled debut album, the band achieving commercial and critical success in the UK from the outset. The US caught up within a year, with the follow-up LP, *Give 'Em Enough Rope* being introduced stateside just ahead of *The Clash*. But it was the next offering, *London Calling*, which helped ensure a place in music history on its release in December 1979 (in the following month in the US) and which was declared *Rolling Stone*'s best album of the '80s.

That was a hard act to follow, and as ever there was no move to replicate what came before, for better or worse, depending on your standpoint. But after the ambitious, experimental, flawed but wonderful *Sandinista!* triple-LP in 1981, The Clash reached new heights of success with 1982's *Combat Rock*, going on to achieve double-platinum certification in America. That was the last from the classic line-up, with Headon and Jones moving on and one more album following, 1985's *Cut the*

Crap bringing the curtain down eight years after those 'year zero' tracks that set out the band's stall. But their far-reaching influence in the years that followed led, in January 2003, shortly after the death of Joe Strummer, to the band's induction into the Rock and Roll Hall of Fame, including original drummer Terry Chimes.

That's just the bare bones of the tale. So, let's go back to the start, tracing the early years of the three lads on the cover of the debut LP – Joe Strummer, Mick Jones, and Paul Simonon – and following their respective journeys to Bernard Rhodes' Rehearsal Rehearsals base, Camden, North West London, telling the tale of the two bands that ultimately gave rise to this musical phenomenon.

On the Road to Freedom: Introducing Joe Strummer

'Authority is supposedly grounded in wisdom, but I could see from a very early age that authority was only a system of control and it didn't have any inherent wisdom. I quickly realised that you either became a power or you were crushed.'
Joe Strummer, Westway to the World, 2000

The Clash made great capital of the fact that lead guitarist Mick Jones was from a West London council tower block and that bass player Paul Simonon grew up among Brixton's West Indian community at a time of massive political and cultural upheaval in the UK. But there was something of an air-brushing of the fact that their rhythm guitarist, vocalist and main lyricist was the son of a Government official who sent his son to private school at a young age. Considering The Clash's stance on the Establishment, the Empire and class values, it seems odd that the lad who became Joe Strummer came from a world of starchy official soirées and practically everything the band railed against. However, as Clash biographer Pat Gilbert stressed, Strummer's father, Ronald Mellor, 'was neither posh nor a high-flier'; he was, as the frontman himself put it, a lowly clerical officer who was regarded in his department as a 'junior bum'.

Joe Strummer was born John Graham Mellor in Ankara on August 21, 1952, his father a diplomat working in the Turkish capital as a clerical officer in the Foreign Office at the time. Ronald, born in Lucknow, was the son of a British-born official who worked on India's railways, and was raised in an orphanage after his father died. Though his formative years were spent under the Raj, Ronald was, according to his youngest son, 'more English than any Englishman', working hard to win a university scholarship in the mid-1930s, then serving in World War II. Becoming a British citizen in the late-1940s, he married nurse and divorcee Anna Girvan, née Mackenzie, a crofter's daughter from Bonar Bridge in Scotland's West Highlands. Their eldest son, David, was born in early 1951, and the family settled in Paddington before that first overseas posting, part of the Government's response to Turkey joining NATO, amid tensions in the Middle East.

Two years later the Mellor family moved to Cairo, staying until the Suez Crisis, then to Mexico City and, in 1957, to Bonn, West Germany, a time of constant upheaval in which, as Pat Gilbert put it, young John Mellor 'first began to feel like an outsider, a foreigner everywhere he went, including his father's adopted home of Britain'.

In Mexico, the two brothers attended a Spanish-speaking school for two years, with John aged eight when they moved to Warlingham, near Croydon, Surrey, 20 miles from Central London. And when his father was posted to Iran amid growing fears over the Shah's rule, David and John were sent to the City of London Freemen's School in nearby Ashtead Park as boarders, their fees paid by the Foreign Office.

The school was set in 50 acres of parkland, the boys two of around 100 boarders (including girls); John and his older brother got to see their parents once or twice a year for the rest of their school days. He said, 'The Government paid for me to see my parents once a year. I was left on my own and went to this school where thick rich people sent their thick rich kids. Another perk of my father's job – it was a job with a lot of perks – all the fees were paid by the Government.'

In a 1977 *Record Mirror* interview, Strummer recalled an initiation rite: given a choice between being beaten up or lying in a bath of used toilet paper, going for the former. He later revealed how boarding school taught him to be independent: coping with a feeling of abandonment; having 'to pretend my parents didn't exist'; and trying to run away, with an older pupil, at the age of nine.

Asked by Caroline Coon about his roots in a November 1976 *Melody Maker* interview, Strummer said, 'The only place I considered home was the boarding school my parents sent me to. It's easier, isn't it? I mean it gets kids out the way, doesn't it? It was great! You have to stand up for yourself. You get beaten up the first day you get there. And I'm really glad I went because I shudder to think what would have happened if I hadn't gone to boarding school. I only saw my father twice a year. If I'd seen him all the time I'd probably have murdered him by now. He was very strict.' Two decades later, more reflective for *Westway to the World*, he said, 'My father pulled himself up by his own intelligence. He had a very big ethos of, 'You study'. I often think about my parents and how I must have felt about it, because it was like being sent away. I just sub-consciously got to the heart of the thing, which was, 'Forget about your parents and deal with this.''

Paul Buck, alias Pablo LaBritain, drummer of 999 and briefly with a fledgling Clash, told Pat Gilbert, 'I wouldn't say he was a rebel. He was gentle, but with a sort of wit. In his first year at school, Joe had run away from his school's palatial grounds with a fellow pupil, before being captured by a geography master. He disliked sport and by his early teens had become obsessed with rock – The Rolling Stones, The Beach Boys, Jimi Hendrix, and Chicago blues.' Fellow pupil Simon Cowell (not *The X Factor* one) told Gilbert that John was 'shy and extremely nice, but touched with a kind of sadness'; Chris Reynolds described him as a 'hard nut, a handful for teachers'; and Ken Powell saw him as 'very funny and artistic', recalling him writing poems, saying he

1

A fresh-faced, school-age John Mellor

'always came at whatever he did from an original angle'. Powell also said his parents were 'reserved rather than strict', allowing parties at their bungalow for boy and girl boarders.

In 1964, Joe's passion for music was fiercely ignited when he heard The Rolling Stones' 'Not Fade Away' in the school's recreation room. He told the *NME*'s Sean O'Hagan in 1997, 'The second Stones single literally changed my life. I can still remember the first time I heard it blasting out of this old valve radio. I was at a really brutal boarding school, where they filled you full of crap; 'Not Fade Away' sounded like the road to freedom. Seriously, it said, 'Live, enjoy life, fuck chartered accountancy!' They were definitely the first proto-punks. You can hear it all on all those first few albums.'

He soon became a school rebel. Ken Powell told Pat Gilbert, 'Music was more important than lessons. It was all we talked about. Every new Beatles, Dylan, and Stones album was crucial to us.' The youngest Mellor lad also spent time at a cinema in Epsom, queuing to see films such as *Battleship Potemkin*, *Midnight Cowboy* and David Lean's *Lawrence of Arabia*, T.E. Lawrence becoming a role model of a sort to him. He said, 'I must have been about 13. It swept up my imagination. I read everything he ever wrote'. Marlon Brando's *Viva Zapata!* also impressed him, taking him back to his Mexico days, firing a passion for bandits, cowboys and revolutionary heroes. And in 1965, visiting his folks in Tehran, he bought a Chuck Berry EP and discovered black American R&B and blues.

Then came the summer of '68, as he was starting his O-levels. He recalled the time in *Westway to the World*: 'The Beatles, The Stones, The Yardbirds, The Kinks – it was a great year to come of age. The whole world was exploding – Paris, Vietnam, Grosvenor Square, the counter-culture.' Pat Gilbert added, 'For John Mellor, turning on the news to see anarchists, communists and champions of the new left throwing rocks at policemen, while Hendrix and The Doors wailed away behind on the school Dansette, it was the most exciting thing he'd ever experienced. Revolutionary passion welled up inside him.' While much of it was happening not so far away, John was stuck in his dorm, Gilbert reckoning that 'the sense he was missing out on something momentous never left him. His instincts to go charging off into London to throw a few bricks around lay pent up inside him like a time-bomb.' But as Strummer put it in *Westway to the World*, the Stones' 'Street Fighting Man' was 'just accepted as a fantastic song. I don't think we had the faculty to take on board what it was saying.'

He told Robert Hilburn in 1984, 'I only saw my father once a year after being sent to boarding school. He was a real disciplinarian. He was always giving me speeches about how he had pulled himself up by the sweat of his brow, a real 'guts and determination' man. What he was really saying was, 'If you play by the rules, you can end up like me'. I didn't want to. I saw how the rules worked, and I didn't like them.'

Studying A-levels in art and history, he grew his hair and became a hippy, experimenting with substances. He also took to an Excalibur acoustic guitar, a gift from a cousin, once played by Pete Townshend from their shared late-'50s days at Acton Grammar School. He was soon jamming with Paul Buck and Andy Ward, future drummer of prog-rockers Camel, as The Burgher Masters, yet considered himself completely unmusical.

He got into Captain Beefheart, saw Mott the Hoople in Balham and Canned Heat in Croydon, and when his father returned from a final overseas posting in Malawi to settle in Surrey, it was an uncomfortable reunion. As Pat Gilbert put it, he was 17 and 'now versed in sex, drugs and rock'n'roll,' having 'grown emotionally independent and domestically self-sufficient, and his world of rock'n'roll records, girls and pop rebellion had little in common with their stuffy universe of embassy parties, dry Martinis and stiff upper lips'. And that was before Ronald's Buckingham Palace visit, receiving an MBE shortly after John Lennon handed his back, protesting against UK involvement in Biafra and support for the Vietnam war.

In the summer of 1970 he took his final exams and briefly moved into his parents' bungalow, planning to go to art school. He was duly accepted by London's Central School of Art and Design, off The Strand, and moved into a hall of residence in Battersea. For the first time he was mixing with those outside what Gilbert called 'his own privileged middle-class cocoon', yet he was just five minutes from fashionable Chelsea. There he flirted with becoming a professional cartoonist, starting a one-year foundation course. He became part of an art-student clique that included future *Melody Maker* punk writer and Clash associate Caroline Coon and which booked happening bands like The Velvet Underground. New friend Kit Buckler remembered him as 'charismatic, fun, and extremely popular'. He added: 'He was always a lovely person. Everyone congregated around him. He was a very talented painter and had a good eye for art. He was also a bit crazy, always a bit out there.'

Yet behind the mask, John was trying to make sense of the death of his brother David. In early August. David's body had been found close to his Euston Road digs in Regent's Park. A medical student, he had been suffering from depression, grown estranged from his family and had taken a massive overdose. David's suicide profoundly affected his younger brother, who had to identify his body after it had lain undiscovered for three days. John was staying with his parents then, and Tymon Dogg, a musician he soon got to know and who became part of The Clash story, reckoned he 'always had the ghost of his brother around him.' Joe told *Melody Maker*'s Caroline Coon in 1977 that David was into 'weird stuff', not least the occult and extreme right-wing politics, and rather than becoming a unifying experience, it seemed that John grew even more distant from his parents afterwards, retreating into himself and rarely acknowledging his past. It was around then that he told people he was no longer John but 'Woody', a nod to influential US folk musician Woody Guthrie.

Of art school, he described it in *Westway to the World* as 'the last resort of malingerers and bluffers and people who don't want to work.' He added, 'They weren't teaching us to draw an object, they were teaching us to make a drawing that looked like we knew how to draw the object.' Soon, he moved to so-called 'Vomit Heights' in leafy Palmers Green, North London, where the vibe was 'as much pissed-up student as astral hippy,' according to Pat Gilbert. Fellow residents included future 101'ers bandmate Clive Timperley, who had played in groups since 1965 supporting the likes of Medicine Head, and Stephen Murray, aka the aforementioned Tymon Dogg. He had left a printing job in Liverpool three years before to land a deal with Pye Records (as Timon Dogg), and was subsequently courted by Paul McCartney about a potential Apple deal before joining The Moody Blues' Threshold label; then he'd headed off to busk in Europe.

The trio became fast friends in an environment of LSD, booze and a mutual love of Bob Dylan, Tim Buckley, Leonard Cohen, Carole King, James Taylor and Tim Hardin. The newest arrival, John Mellor, soon proclaimed he had a future as a 'pop star'. He joined Dogg's busking sessions on the London Underground, learning tracks by the Stones, Elvis, Chuck Berry, The Beatles, Bo Diddley and Woody Guthrie, and bought a £1.99 ukulele from a shop in Shaftesbury Avenue, thinking it would be easier to master four strings. In *Westway to the World*, he said: 'I spent the greater part of my youth listening to music. It all seemed so complex at the time. It was the era of the great guitarists like Clapton and Hendrix, and it seemed unobtainable really if you were a slow starter like I was.' He added, 'It seemed a mystical world, where only mythical beings could actually play. When I managed to get some chords together I was chuffed.'

Tymon Dogg recalled on 2005's *Viva Joe Strummer* documentary, 'The first song Joe ever learned was 'Comes the Rain', a tune that a Navajo Indian sang, very simple. I just put a tune to the lyric and it only had one chord – G. He had a great sense of rhythm. He was a fantastic rhythm guitar player.' That summer, Mellor dropped out of art school, fed up with an emphasis on life classes and a 'lousy set-up of lecturers chasing after the female students'. He got a seasonal job on a farm in Blandford Forum, Dorset, before returning to the capital, moving with Dogg and others to a flat in Harlesden, which was vividly described by Pat Gilbert as 'squalid and hardcore hippy ... slowly slipping deeper into the upholstery of the counter-culture.'

John began to learn guitar in a bid to supplement a new day-job as a signwriter for Allied Carpets; he was soon playing at Green Park tube, making up to £5 an hour in time from closing-time drunks while learning more songs. But an act of hippy kindness in a local park, taking in a homeless black man, led to their landlord evicting them, with police help. His efforts to read the 1965 Rent Act did him no good then, nor later when staying on Edgware Road – his household was again evicted illegally, and his records smashed. He took a case to Brent Council, but was hustled out of a tribunal for losing his temper with law students taking notes at the back.

John was naturally left-handed but was taught to play right-handed by Tymon Dogg. He later insisted that that held back his development as a guitarist, but it certainly gave him a unique style, one that led to his stage name. He briefly returned to his parents, setting up a second-hand drum kit there before taking that and a bag of clothes to visit a girlfriend at art school in Cardiff. When she sent him packing, he dropped in on more friends at an art school in nearby Newport, moving into future Clash engineer Mickey Foote's flat, becoming part of a local rockabilly scene (with visiting acts including Shakin' Stevens). John also becoming a regular at a club frequented by the Afro-Caribbean community, fueling a love of ska and reggae.

Asked by Caroline Coon in late '76 in The Clash's first *Melody Maker* interview how he first got involved in rock'n'roll, he said it was through owning that drum kit. He recalled, 'Someone gave me a camera, and then I met this guy who had a drum kit in his garage and I had a go on it one day. I thought, 'This guy's going to swap me this little camera for all that kit.' And I said, 'Here you are.' Then I went down to Wales and ran into a band who had a drummer but no drum kit. But I didn't want to play drums because I wanted to be the star of the show, right? So, I said, 'If you use my drum kit you're going to have me as your singer.' They had no option but to accept.'

The rock'n'roll covers band was reborn as The Vultures when Mellor joined; they were won over by his spirit and stage presence, if not his voice. At the time, Alan Jones was playing bass – under the nickname 'Jiving Al', or 'Jiver' – and John shared a flat with him, he drawing the dole and living on 50p a day, apparently 'enough for a pint of beer, an ounce of Old Holborn and a hot refectory meal'. Around half a dozen gigs followed at the students' union bar in late '73, with John sharing vocal and guitar duties with Rob Haymer on rock'n'roll oldies, country rock, Kinks and Who covers, the set ending with 'Johnny B Goode'. Their final gig was at the Granary, Bristol: a typically shambolic affair, Jiver remembers John's transformation into 'a completely different person,' and 'discovering a natural ability to control and excite people.'

The group fizzled out, Woody getting a job tending graves in the town cemetery for the local council, a dark period that fueled his ambition to make it. He also recorded his first song, 'Crummy Bum Blues', soon heading off with Tymon Dogg. Their initial visit to a friend who'd been busted for marijuana and was in a Dutch jail turned into a road-trip across Holland, France and

Germany, busking and playing gigs. John eventually returned to Newport, cutting his hair into a rockabilly quiff then deciding it was time to return to London.

In *Westway to the World*, he paints a vivid picture of what he found on his return. 'In '74 it did seem that life was in black and white, with rows and rows of buildings boarded up by the council and left to rot. That's what gave birth to squatting. And if we hadn't had the squats we wouldn't have had a place to live and set up a rock'n'roll group and practise in them.' John stayed a while at Dogg's flat in Maida Hill before being directed to a spare room at nearby 101 Walterton Road, a few hundred yards from Wilmcote House, where a certain Mick Jones was teaching himself guitar in his gran's 18th-floor flat.

Rock'n'Roll or nothing: introducing Mick Jones

'If you look at Mick's background, you can see it wasn't just about escaping, he was searching for an identity for himself'
Robin Banks

Approaching his teen years, Mick Jones was deeply into football, comics and the magazines his mum sent from America. He also regularly walked the streets of his beloved London, getting to know the city, picking up 'the knowledge' that his absentee father, a taxi driver, might have appreciated, had he stuck around. Jones later told Clash biographer Pat Gilbert it was 'all part of creating a private universe, a defence against the unhappiness created by his parents' divorce.' And by 1968, music was dominating those welcome distractions. Some 35 years later, he told Gilbert, 'Once I discovered music and realised I didn't want to be a footballer anymore, that was it – it was rock'n'roll or nothing. I never wanted a proper job. That wasn't an option.'

He opted for rock'n'roll, telling Caroline Coon for *Melody Maker* in late '76 he felt 'it was much less limiting' and 'more exciting', adding: 'I went to my first rock concert when I was 12. It was free, in Hyde Park and Nice, Traffic, Junior's Eyes and the Pretty Things were playing. The first guitar I had was a second-hand Hofner. I paid 16 quid for it and I think I was ripped off. But, I tell you something – I sold it for £30 to a Sex Pistol!'

Mick belonged to The Animals and The Kinks' fan clubs from a young age and was big on The Beatles and The Rolling Stones too, telling John Robb in 2006's *Punk Rock: An Oral History*, 'I'd spend Saturdays going to Cheyne Walk, standing outside where Mick Jagger and Keith Richard used to live. Then we'd go down Carnaby Street. There was so much happening in London. There was a feeling we were at the centre of the whole thing. It was really exotic to us. We were young kids, saw how the Stones dressed and tried to emulate it a bit, with kind of tie-dyed t-shirt and a funny colour puffy scarf. I went around London on my own from a

very early age. From six or seven I started going to the cinema. I'd get a Red Rover, go all round London. I didn't have the same constrictions a lot of my friends had. I was going all over to see bands. I didn't have any discretion.' By 1968 he was shelling out on records too, buying Jimi Hendrix's *Smash Hits* best-of LP and Cream's *Disraeli Gears*, the rock'n'roll dream already in his sights.

Michael Jeffrey Jones was born in the South London Hospital for Women in Clapham on June 26th, 1955: '1955! The birth of rock'n'roll!' he told *Blitz*'s William Shaw in 1988. He was the only child of Thomas Jones, 26, a South Londoner whose parents settled in the capital from Wales, and Renee Zegansky, 25, who came from a Russian Jewish family who had come to London's East End at the turn of the century. Stella, his grandmother, was born in Whitechapel in 1899 to Jewish parents who'd escaped the Russian pogroms, with Renee being her daughter from a first marriage. At the end of World War II, Renee fell for a GI and stowed away to America, but was swiftly deported, returning to London, finding work selling jewelry and marrying Thomas on his demob from National Service. Mick's father spent the post-war period in Israel, serving in the Military Police's special investigations branch, his son later saying that 'what they did to the locals changed his view about things.' By the time Mick was born, Tommy was driving taxis and they had a flat in Mitcham, later moving closer to the centre, to a 1930s council block where Brixton Hill meets Streatham Hill, where Renee was before she married.

Mick's parents split up when he was eight, and in Don Letts' *Westway to the World* he talks about their rows; his grandmother Stella living with them by then and shielding him from the worst. He said, 'I did my first concert playing a Beatles number with a tennis racket on the front lawn of the block of flats where I lived, with people passing by. Maybe music became an escape for me. My parents used to fight a lot. My Gran used to take me downstairs to a bomb shelter in the basement of the flats. She'd take me downstairs and we'd wait for the 'raid' to pass.' He added, 'I think I've definitely got a built-in self-preservation thing.'

When his parents broke up, Thomas – a South London taxi driver and a betting-shop manager – moved out and Renee moved to America, with Mick left in the care of his grandmother and, at one point, also her sister and sister-in-law – 'three old ladies' as he put it. In 1966, he started at The Strand, an all-boys grammar school a short walk from his Christchurch House base in Brixton, becoming friends with Robin Crocker, later known as Robin Banks, a future key player in The Clash's entourage, two years older but held back a year for disruptive behaviour. They bonded after a heated discussion over the relative merits of Chuck Berry and Bo Diddley (Mick defending the latter) led to a scrap. But a mutual love of music conquered, the lads doing a 'bit of minor league thievery and spending their evenings going to gigs with their gang down Streatham on the bus'. By March 1970, however, Crocker had been expelled and was later jailed for three years for his part in an armed robbery on a South London betting shop.

Back then however, Jones and Crocker were joined at the hip, attending gigs together, including Sunday afternoons at The Roundhouse, Chalk Farm, seeing the likes of Tyrannosaurus Rex, Kevin Ayers and Pink Floyd – shows put on by a committee including Caroline Coon,

1 part of the art-school set that booked The Velvet Underground when Strummer caught them. Mick told John Robb, 'We'd go to the Roundhouse to the big thing on Sundays, 'Implosion', with Hawkwind and a lot of underground groups. This was 1970. Also, we'd go to The Marquee to hear Blodwyn Pig, stuff like that. Fantastic. I always remember how loud it all was. I'd go to school the next day, my ears ringing. I couldn't hear nothing. My hearing's gone now. I suppose I was a hip kid but didn't see myself like that. There was another young kid around, Nick Laird Clowes, who formed Dream Academy. He was Jeff Dexter's little friend. He was about my age and we'd see each other at the Roundhouse, because Jeff was one of the DJs. They'd play underground and imported records from the States.

'There used to be a few record shops in London, in Berwick Street, where they sold import records and you could get new music from America. My hair was really long. It just grew and grew. 'Little Mick', I was known as for a long time. I was hanging out with older guys, and they didn't know why this little younger kid was there. I was a total hippy. I had long hair and used to do idiot dancing. It was so great.'

In 1968 Mick and his grandmother moved to join Stella's sister and sister-in-law in an upmarket private block of flats at the Marble Arch end of Edgware Road, predominantly a Jewish area then. Just as he was when living only with his gran, he appears to have been pampered at home by doting company, compensating for his parents' absence. As with Strummer's middle-class upbringing, that was conveniently later forgotten in favour of talk of the 18th-floor council flat Mick and Stella moved to next. Either way, Pat Gilbert called it a 'latchkey London existence, unsettled, transient, urban, and if anything, most markedly striped by the shadow of his absent parents.' As for the doting part, Jones told *The Guardian*'s John Hind in 2016, 'I don't know if 'pampered' is quite the right word, but I was the only male, that's why they treated me well. I was like 'Spoilt Bastard' in *Viz* comic. I'd tell gran 'Get me a fucking cup of tea'. I didn't have parental control and heard other kids talk like that, so wasn't kind. I'm very regretful now. You should honour your family, but I learned it too late.'

Four decades earlier, Jones told Caroline Coon in November 1976 for *Melody Maker* about his upbringing and absent parents, 'They kind of left home one at a time. I was much more interested in them than they were in me. They decided I weren't happening, I suppose. I stayed with my gran a long time. And I read a lot. Psychologically it really did me in. I wish I knew then what I know now. Now I know it isn't that big a deal. But then, at school, I'd sit there with this word 'divorce, divorce' in my head all the time. But there was no social stigma attached to it because all the other kids seemed to be going through the same thing. Very few of the kids I knew were living a sheltered family life.'

In the summer of '69, with his exams looming, Jones was more interested in London's music scene, telling John Robb, 'When bands would go to Tramp or somewhere in the West End, we'd wait outside. When they arrived, we'd try and slip in with the party. Often, we were frog-marched out but got in with the Stones once, just behind Billy Preston. When they played Hyde Park, there's a photo where I can point myself out in the crowd. Guy Stevens was on stage. I spent all day slowly making my way to the front, got right up to the fence. I'm two feet from the front and was hit by loads of the butterflies that didn't make it. [The Stones released hundreds of them from the stage as a dramatic gesture.] All the African drummers came on for 'Sympathy for the Devil'. It was pretty amazing.

'I also used to go to Parliament Hill School Fields, where they did all-night shows, free concerts – Soft Machine, Taste, Edgar Broughton Band, I was really into all that. Yes, when they were still really good, before *Tales from Topographic Oceans*. These were all representatives of that alternative lifestyle and the underground press. We were looking at America as well, seeing what was there, trying to be a bit like that here, with your coal fire and cup of tea at 12 o'clock when the telly went off.'

In that same interview he also name-checked Humble Pie, Slade and The Winkies, the impact of *Ziggy Stardust*-era David Bowie, and the Faces. He told Robb, 'It wasn't like the Bowie we all knew about – the 'Space Oddity' Bowie. This was different. We took that seriously. We also used to go and see the Faces. We were into Rod Stewart and Ronnie Wood, and used to follow them around as well.'

Seeing all those bands was more than a social occasion. It was more like a study pattern, explaining in *Westway to the World*, 'If I went to a concert with somebody I'd be checking it all out – what the drummer was doing, what the guitarist was doing, if they had any telepathic communication.' By the early 1970s Mick was into glam rock too, recalling, 'I'd been into The Kinks, The Stones and The Beatles, but then got more into the flash end of things.' Clothes were also important. Robin Banks described his band of mates as 'dandies', with some of their threads shoplifted from trendy Kings Road and Carnaby Street boutiques. And all the time they were seeking out new acts.

'I went to see Iggy at the Scala, the King's Cross cinema all-nighter. I thought, 'This is so great!' He'd come out and interact with the audience. That was an amazing thing to see. The full-on quality of The Stooges was great, like flame-throwers. It was really early in the morning. Lou Reed played as well. We'd be speeding off our nuts all night. King's Cross looked like a fairytale castle at dawn. It looked fantastic high on purple hearts. There was a horrible comedown. It was always really bad. You would feel like shit. We didn't even smoke then. I didn't start smoking until I went on tour. We went to Phun City Festival at Worthing to see the MC5. The Pink Fairies too. That was the first time the MC5 had played. My overriding memory was falling into a ditch. A great festival!'

He was soon smitten with Mott the Hoople – whose producer, Guy Stevens, would play an important part in this story – latching on to them long before any commercial breakthrough. In his later school days, he was hanging out with older pupils and their Mott-inspired band, Schoolgirl, introduced by Banks; 'Little Mick' was seen as a cool kid for his taste in music, sci-fi and comics. They travelled far and wide to see Mott, and in 2006's *Gibson Backstage Pass*, Mick said, 'I'd go to Liverpool or Newcastle or somewhere, bunk the fares on the trains, hide in the toilet when the ticket inspector came around. I'd jump off just before the train got to the station and climb over the fence. Great times, and I always knew I wanted to be in a band and play guitar. That was it for me.' The road manager took a shine to them too, smuggling them in through stage doors, Mott priding themselves on a close relationship with fan – one later mirrored by The Clash. They also followed the Faces, again often reaching the dressing room.

He added, 'Mott were very nice, the way they treated us. We used to go all over. We'd sleep on the town hall steps in every town. It was like being on tour without hotel rooms. Ian Hunter's 1974 book, *Diary of a Rock'n'Roll Star*, was like the brochure, telling you about the world of rock'n'roll, of being in a band – what we were going to do. We tried to make it a real thing. More than anybody, we followed Mott. They had their style, but we dressed more like the Faces.

'We were like little kids, fans, really lucky to be around. Seeing it was like, 'Wow, this is what it's like!' We got little titbits from the girlfriends, like, 'Ian likes to have his back washed in the bath'. We were thinking, 'This is the life!' To see these records they had was like the Holy Grail.

'Music changed continually. I became more discerning. From glam I got into American early punk stuff, like *Nuggets*, and after that the [New York] Dolls came along. mum, in America, sent me *Creem* and *Rockscene* on a subscription. I was finding out about groups like the Dolls really early. There wasn't that much you could find out about these groups in England. Rock'n'roll was a lot more unobtainable. After I'd seen Iggy in *Creem*, standing on people's hands, the audience all holding him, I realised there was something different out there.

'When the Dolls first came over, they played with the Faces at Wembley Empire, July '72. The year after, they did that classic *Old Grey Whistle Test* appearance. I really went for it once I saw Johnny Thunders. I was looking a bit more airy-fairy until the Dolls came along. I was into the Underground thing, hippyish, then got into the more stylish side of things like the Faces and Mott, then got into the Dolls, and that was pretty much it until the Pistols.'

In *Westway to the World*, he explains what it was about the New York Dolls that appealed, saying, 'They were incredible. They blew my mind – the way they looked, their whole attitude. They didn't care about anything. They were a group that was more about style.'

Style was increasingly important, Mick adding, 'We'd go to places like *Granny Takes a Trip* and *Alkasura* on the King's Road. One of these shops had half a car stuck out into the street at the front of it. *Alkasura* sold dandy gear, lacy and frilly. We were wearing that kind of thing - a bit like the Faces. For a while we had our hair feather-cut style. It looked funny but compared to what else was happening it wasn't that bad.'

Soon, he was a roadie for Schoolgirl, practising at a church hall close to Battersea Power Station, later becoming Pete Townshend's Rampart Studios – *Quadrophenia was* recorded there in 1973, a year after Schoolgirl's first pub gigs. While retaking his O-levels, Mick shelled out on his £16 second-hand Hofner, Banks showing him his first chords and riffs. Jones told John Robb, 'I definitely wanted to be in a band. I was 16 before I started guitar. I meant to start earlier but didn't get round to it. I started on Stylophone. Then it was drums, then on to bass, then, 'Alright, I can try two more strings'. I could do a bit of backing vocals but didn't want to be a singer. I didn't get any lessons, but anyone who played I was asking how they did it. I must have been embarrassingly naïve. They couldn't understand where this kid was coming from. Coolness comes with age.'

The dream of making music his vocation remained strong, and in *Westway to the World* he recalled, of his school careers' officer, 'I honestly did go in there and said I wanted to be in a band. There wasn't any creative choice. There wasn't like a vegetarian option on the menu.'

When Schoolgirl split, Mick teamed up with Schoolgirl's John Brown, forming The Delinquents while enrolling for night-school, with art school in mind. The pair grew closer, Brown impressed by his awareness of cult cinema, fiction, record shops and those US magazines. In 1973, Mick and his gran moved to that fabled 18th-floor council flat in the Wilmcote House tower block overlooking the Westway, the elevated arterial route into central London that proved so symbolic for his future band. In September, he began a foundation course at Hammersmith College of Art and Building, in Shepherd's Bush, opposite the BBC. His interest in art was more about the music industry though. As he put it in *Westway to the World*, 'That was how I thought you got into bands. I didn't really meet that many musicians. I was disappointed. I was doing it for the grant really, because you could use that to buy equipment or whatever.'

The following July, he bought the first two New York Dolls albums on import from a shop in Soho. Jones told *Mojo* in 1999, 'They were incredible. They blew my mind, the way they looked, their whole attitude. They didn't care about anything. They weren't great sounding by anyone's standards, but that didn't matter.'

He soon switched from bass to guitar, selling rare sci-fi comics to buy a black Fender Telecaster, their set including hip US garage punk covers by the likes of the Flamin' Groovies, the MC5 and The Standells. A four-piece completed by lead guitarist Paul Wayman and drummer Mike Dowling, they described themselves on their first press release as 'loud and punky'. Their live debut was in June '74 at Queen Elizabeth College, Kensington, and two months later a two-song demo was recorded at a studio in Holborn. Promo shots were taken on a bombsite by the Thames, featuring Mick in a tight blouse, with black gloves, long curly hair and shades. He told John Robb, 'We were like a British Dolls. Then we became aware of the Hollywood Brats. I'd seen the Dolls on *Whistle Test* and they blew my mind – the way they looked, their whole attitude. Another band we were all really into was The Sharks.'

After his summer stint as a DHSS clerical assistant in Paddington, that autumn they placed ads in *Melody Maker* looking for management and gigs, with a string of pub dates following. In early '75, Norwegian-born Geir Waade joined on drums, then Dublin guitarist Eunan Brady (ex-Hollywood Brats) and Schoolgirl vocalist Kelvin Blacklock came in. The band was soon taken on by future Sham 69 and Culture Club manager Tony Gordon, and the name changed to Little Queenie, after a Chuck Berry song.

As it turned out, Gordon quickly let them go, but a fresh impetus brought a positive air, Waade being replaced by Jim Hyatt ahead of the band recording a demo in Marble Arch, playing 'Little Queenie' and Frankie Miller's 'Fall in Love'. They were disappointed with the result though, Blacklock deciding to contact a music industry name who'd proved a major influence on them – Guy Stevens.

Stevens had an impressive CV, his connections going back way before his involvement in the creation of Mott the Hoople. A Mod DJ at the Scene club in 1964, he was Island Records' first house producer, signing and producing Free and Spooky Tooth. Word had it he'd got Chuck Berry out of jail once and supplied a compilation tape to The Who that included much of their pre-originals material. He also had a hand in Procol Harum's commercial success, yet after losing Mott the Hoople in 1972, was something of a music industry joke, and by 1975 his 'legendary fondness for speed and booze had taken its toll,' as Marcus Gray put it.

But Stevens remained well connected on both sides of the Atlantic and, hearing Kelvin Blacklock's band were close to a deal with Pye, he was hopeful he could play a part in their success, relaunching his own career. He headed along to a rehearsal in Acton – after a pub visit with the lads and an opportunity to air a few old stories to a doting audience – and then delivered his verdict. Eunan Brady told Marcus Gray, 'He took Kelvin aside and said, 'I think you need keyboards. Brady can handle all the guitar.' In short, he didn't think the 'skinny young guitarist' with the long hair had much of a future. He wanted a new Mott the Hoople, and Mick Jones had to go. The guitarist later reflected to John Robb, 'He didn't know I wrote the songs. The others were keen to get on, so they said 'Alright'. John Brown didn't agree, but they managed to sway him.' Brady felt Jones was 'mega-depressed' by the decision, but the band thought he took it with dignity, not least considering he'd not only been let down by his friends but also considered not good enough as a musician by his favourite band's producer. It didn't help that he was living with a girlfriend in an Archway bedsit above a basement flat rented by Blacklock, where the band continued to rehearse. There was certainly a feeling of guilt for Brown when they bumped into each other there the following week. Word had it that when Blacklock played Jones a demo tape by the band, who were now known as Violent Luck on Stevens' advice, which had produced by their mentor and engineered by Bill Price at Air Studios, Oxford Street, he broke down in tears.

Soon he packed up and left, moving back to his gran's, hooking up with a friend of Blacklock, Tony James, who shared a passion for The New York Dolls and The Stooges. They immediately hit it off, James saying, 'Mick was devastated but instead of giving up he said, 'Right, I'm going to learn to play properly'. He went to Denmark Street and bought a vintage Les Paul Junior, like that played by the Dolls' Johnny Thunders. I remember him at his gran's flat, spending hours picking out the guitar solo to 'You Can't Always Get What You Want'. Mick was determined to make it.'

Jones told John Robb, 'That was the knockback that made me go to my bedroom, lock myself away for months and learn guitar properly. A lucky thing that happened was that when I started to learn guitar, I started writing songs as part of my learning. It helped me. I'd listen to other people's songs and understood what made those songs work.'

By the time his old schoolmate Robin Banks returned on the scene – his custodial sentence having involved stretches at Wormwood Scrubs then Albany on the Isle of Wight – he felt Jones had become a 'brilliant guitarist', adding, 'You can't overestimate the passion and drive of that man. He was single-minded about making it. That was what made him different.'

1

Attention to detail: introducing Paul Simonon

'Paul was essentially The Clash's musical and cultural barometer. He's silent but deadly'
Don Letts

Talking to Clash biographer Pat Gilbert in 2001, Paul Simonon, who quit playing bass for a living in the early '90s to fulfil his pre-band passion as an artist, said, 'I'm not a musician, or at least I didn't *arrive* a musician.' In the same interview, Gilbert reasons that, despite that iconic Pennie Smith cover for *London Calling*, Simonon didn't so much smash his guitars up as 'customise them' to death. 'First, off would come the scratch-plate for a Pollock-style drizzle of coloured paint, then the real work began,' Simonon explained. 'I used to whack lumps out of the body, much to the amusement of the roadies. I used to chip bits out of it just to give it some life. I hated the bloody things. I wanted to be a guitarist like Pete Townshend, not a bass player.'

Of course, Paul became every bit the musician, his basslines an integral part of the band's sound. Yet, as Gilbert stressed, 'It was Paul's presence that ensured The Clash's iconic status and gave them a subcultural edge.' That was a big part of the story. 'It was a skinhead-Mod thing,' said Simonon. 'You dressed to intimidate or for people to leave you alone. I thought we needed that attention to detail when it came to clothes.' That said, he felt Strummer and Jones went too far with the initial paint-splash look. 'I discreetly did the shirt and maybe the shoes, but the others had the shirt, the trousers, the socks, the jackets. You have to have a bit of style. You can't go at it like a lunatic.'

Gilbert wrote: 'Those in and around The Clash stress how important Simonon was in the power structure of the group. His opinion held the same weight as Mick and Joe's and, though he rarely lost his cool, his taciturn and playful front masked a stubborn and passionate core. Mick described his contribution as 'immeasurable'. It's arguable that much of The Clash's hardline posturing derived from his streetwise codes. He was also the emotional anchor of the group, unflappable in times of crisis. Clash associates Johnny Green and Kosmo Vinyl both use the word 'solid' to describe him.'

Regarding background, there were clear correlations between Paul, Joe and Mick, and Gilbert added, 'His background was arty but hand-to-mouth. It combined elements of both Mick's and Joe's early lives – the latch-key inner city upbringing of the former and unsettled peripatetic world of the latter. His experiences imbued him with the richness of London street life, which would later colour the atmosphere of The Clash. Living among the first generation of black immigrants in Brixton and Notting Hill, Paul was submerged not just in the sounds of ska and reggae but also in the culture that produced them. Unlike virtually every other white English rock band from the Stones onwards, The Clash, via Paul, got their injection of black music virtually from source.'

Paul Gustave Simonon was born on December 15, 1955, in a flat in Thornton Heath, South London, rented by his mum, Elaine (née Braithwaite), a 19-year-old librarian. His father Anthony (Gustave Antoine Simonon) hailed from neighbouring West Norwood. In the early '50s, Anthony was posted to Kenya as part of his national service in the Army and what he saw there at the time of the Mau Mau rebellion – a grim episode in post-war British colonial history – had a deep effect on him. Simonon went AWOL at one point, his son explaining, 'I think he saw some bad things, and was haunted by them for a long time afterwards.' On his demob, he ran a bookshop, settling back in London with his family, including Paul's brother, living close to Railton Road, Brixton. The family moved to Ladbroke Grove, where Paul attended infant school. In *Westway to the World*, Paul recalls a childhood surrounded by Jamaican music, with most of his friends black.

In 1959 the family moved to Ramsgate, Kent, and then again within the county to Canterbury, then Bury St Edmunds in Suffolk; Paul saying his dad had 'a hundred different jobs'. His dream was to be a painter and go to art school, but his father insisted he got a job. Paul told Pat Gilbert, 'My father was a Sunday painter and I followed on from him. He only painted on Sundays because he worked the rest of the week.'

Paul regularly attended movie matinees, with his dad at The Astoria – a venue later triumphantly played by The Clash – watching James Bond and war films, which perhaps later influenced the band's military look and stage backdrop and record sleeve images. And by the age of 11, his parents having split three years earlier, he had a passion for spaghetti Westerns too.

When his mum's new partner won a scholarship to study Latin baroque music in Siena and Rome, Paul and his brother travelled with them to Italy; just like John Mellor, he experienced foreign culture first-hand at an impressionable age. 'It was all a bit bohemian, wandering around these beautiful streets by day, and being taught by my mum for a few hours in the evening,' he revealed to Sean O'Hagan in 2008. When it came to education, Paul and his brother refused to go to school in Italy, because of the uniforms they were expected to wear, instead walking the city streets and visiting art galleries. But a year later they were back in cold, dreary South London, Paul enrolling at a comprehensive school near Crystal Palace, a year behind his classmates. Future Clash road-crew member Johnny Green felt his cautiousness stemmed from that, saying, 'He wanted to check you were cool before he opened up.'

For a while, he ran wild with a gang of skinheads, embracing black culture and the style of Jamaican rude boys. As Pat Gilbert put it, 'While Mick was up the Roundhouse swirling his long hair around, Paul and his pals attended the morning discos at Streatham Locarno, which catered for the schoolboy skins with a diet of ska, rocksteady and reggae. After, there were the inevitable shoplifting sprees, and sometimes Simonon would jump the trains to seaside destinations like Whitstable and Rochester in Kent, to take in the sea air and do a bit of robbing.' By then he was bunking off school, finding it a drag apart from English and Art. And then he didn't bother turning up at all in his final term, later recalling tat 'that holiday went on forever.'

By 1970 it was agreed by his parents that he'd be better off with his father, who was by then renting a small flat in Ladbroke Grove. Then a rough area at the wrong end of Portobello Road, it had been described in Colin MacInnes' *Absolute Beginners* a decade earlier as 'the residential doss-house of our city'. His dad ran a stall on Portobello Market. Paul had switched from one multicultural area to another, but this time with a strict parent. 'It was a bit Steptoe and Son,' he told O'Hagan, 'but with discipline.

He set me homework, made me paint every day. I learnt the technical stuff from a mate of my dads who knew how to do glazes and underpainting. It was invaluable, really. He'd hand me a brush and go, 'Here, Paul, I have to go to work, finish off that fox for me''.

Soon, Paul was manning a market stall selling hand-shaped candles, his dad toughening him up and putting his mind on his art. He slept in what was his father's studio, and told Pat Gilbert, 'On the walls were hundreds of postcards and pages torn out of books: Vermeers, Caraveggios, Van Goghs.' Encouraged by his dad, he copied images into sketchpads, refining his lines and fore-shortening.

He also recalled his dad's ideological conversion, telling Sean O'Hagan, 'He suddenly became a Marxist. One minute I was making a papier-mache crucifix scene for Easter, the next I'm selling pamphlets to help liberate the workers. It was all a bit extreme.' He told Pat Gilbert, 'I learnt the value of hard work,' but still managed to get to occasional 'blues' parties, in *Westway to the World* revealing, 'I'd pass a lot of houses where there was West Indian music playing. I was able to come and go as I pleased - playing on the railways, going to people's houses, a bit of robbing ... I remember having a birthday party and my mum saying, 'You could bring a friend'. We were sitting at a table and I looked at the other end and there's my brother, and I looked around and every face was black. That's what made me realise there was something different here.'

In a Caroline Coon interview in November 1976 for *Melody Maker*, Simonon said, 'I get on all right with my parents. But I don't see them very much. They split up when I was eight. I stayed with my mum but felt it was a bit soft with her. I could do whatever I liked and wasn't getting nowhere, so I went to stay with my dad. It was good training. I had to do all the launderette and that. In a way I worked for him – getting money together and that – down Portobello Market and doing paper-rounds after school. It got me sort of prepared for when things get harder.'

At Simonon's all-boys comprehensive in the shadow of the imposing Trellick Tower council block in Ladbroke Grove, most pupils were black, Irish or Greek. Paul knuckled down to pass O-levels in Art and English, then concentrating on a portfolio to get to art school while working in the carpet section of a John Lewis department store. He won a scholarship to Byam Shaw Art School, Notting Hill Gate, with two frustrating years following, in which he re-did his foundation year. He said, 'A lot of teachers were into American abstract art. I was into figurative art. My father taught me to paint using the traditional methods of Leonardo, with glazes and so on. The other students thought my pictures were great, but the teachers used to take the piss.'

In *Westway to the World*, he added, 'Maybe the art-school thing messed me up. I couldn't see myself in a room for the rest of my life doing this stuff. I've got to do something a bit more exciting.' In spring 1976 he took his final grant and left. By then he'd met Mick Jones. He liked the early Stones, The Kinks, The Who and David Bowie, but didn't play an instrument, owned just one LP – an Eddie Cochran 'best of' – and had seen just two gigs, one of them being the Sensational Alex Harvey Band at Hammersmith Odeon in '75. In that late '76 Caroline Coon interview, he said, 'The first live rock'n'roll I remember seeing was the Sex Pistols, less than a year ago. All I listened to before was ska and bluebeat down at Streatham Locarno.'

But as Pat Gilbert wrote, 'Jones and his new manager Bernie Rhodes thought he'd be the perfect recruit for their new project when he turned up at their rehearsal room one day in early 1976 chaperoning a mate.' That was Roland Hot, trying out on drums for the London SS, who went on to feature on a recording unearthed by Tony James 30 years later. Gilbert explained, 'Mick immediately saw Paul had rock-star potential: tall, blond, cool, cinematic looks. Sadly, he had no musical talent whatsoever.' Simonon recalled: 'First time I met Mick Jones was in the basement with the London SS. All I could see was hair. I don't think I even saw his face. He said, 'Sing 'Roadrunner'. I said, 'What's that?' It was a bit of a disaster.

'There was this bloke in the corner. I said, 'Are you the manager?' His immediate retort was, 'What's it to you?' I thought, 'Well, that's fair enough...' Of course, Rhodes and Jones were to play a major part in his life. Reflecting on how Rhodes felt he looked the part, Simonon told Sean O'Hagan in 2008: 'I was a bit Bowie, a bit suedehead. More importantly, I was at art college. Mick liked that. He was always big on pop history. He knew all about Stuart Sutcliffe, Lennon's best mate in the early days of The Beatles, and a proper artist. I remember Mick introducing me to all his mates. 'This is my new bass guitarist, Paul. He can't play but he's a painter.''

Career opportunities, the ones that never knock...

Before there was The Clash, there were the 101'ers and the London SS, two bands making waves around and about the capital. The former outfit, formed in 1974 and fronted by rhythm guitarist/vocalist John 'Woody' Mellor, were causing a big stir on the pub-rock circuit while the latter were a less prominent proto-punk outfit, the key personnel including guitarist Mick Jones.

Mellor already had plenty of miles on the clock, and over time went from his first stage-name to Joe Strummer: the earlier moniker in tribute to Woody Guthrie; the latter referring to his somewhat basic style of guitar playing, maybe with a nod to early days strumming ukulele, busking on the London Underground.

Jones' band had their roots as fans of iconic '70s glam rock trailblazers Mott the Hoople and later first-wave US punks the New York Dolls. They were rehearsing for much of 1975: while Mellor was making his name around the capital, Mick and co were yet to play a live show, recording just one demo anyone has heard. But they were managed by Bernard Rhodes, a figure who would feature heavily in The Clash story, and a factor that proved key to Jones' progress. A close associate of punk impresario Malcolm McLaren, Rhodes was in fashion first and music later. He was keen to get out of his business associate's shadow and he looked to create a competitive response to McLaren's behind-the-scenes crafting and manipulation of the Sex Pistols.

Being part of that same punk-rock scene in the making, Jones soon got to know Sex Pistols guitarists Glen Matlock and Steve Jones, part of a core of hangers-on who auditioned as potential players for Jones' fledgling outfit. Among those who tried out were Paul Simonon (as a vocalist), and drummer Terry Chimes. Neither were successful, but their time would come, of course, in another form. Meanwhile, another drummer, Nicky Headon, made the grade yet lasted just a week before scarpering. The band themselves going

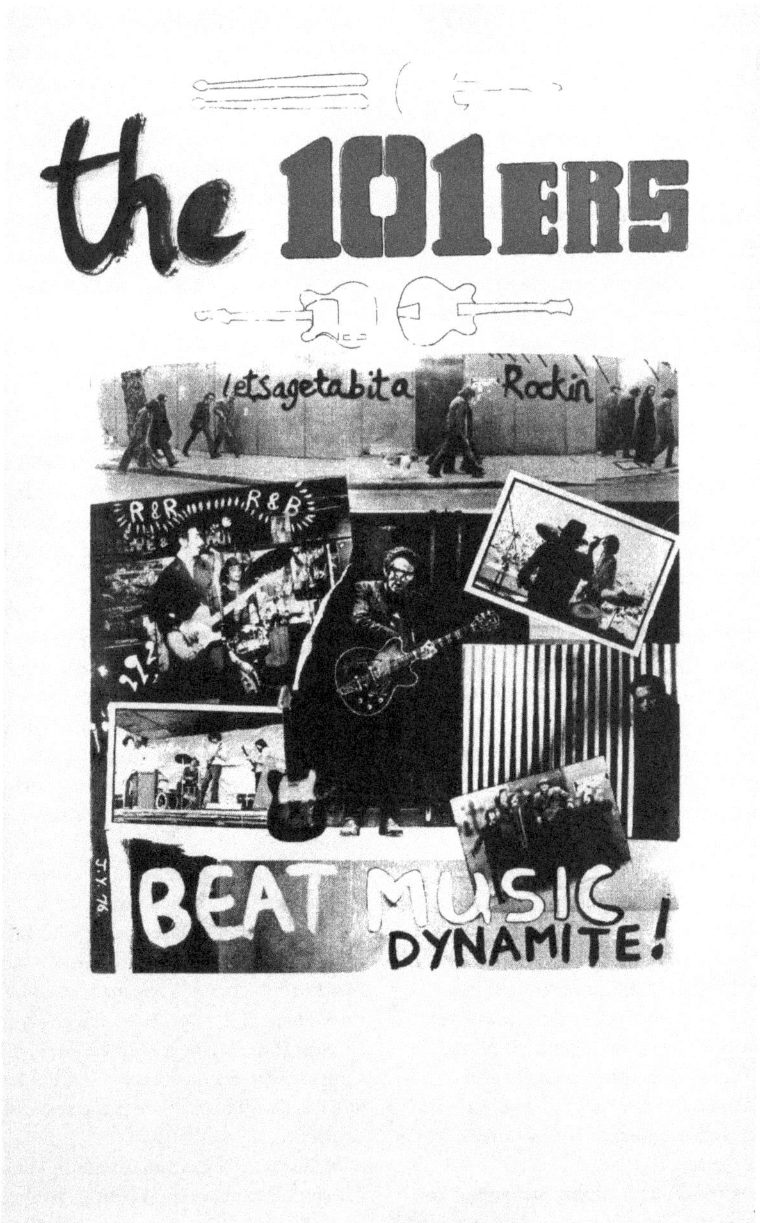
the 101ERS
letsagetabita Rockin
R&R R&B
J.Y. 76
BEAT MUSIC
DYNAMITE!

their separate ways in early 1976, by which time the 101'ers – on the face of it far more successful and with good things likely around the corner – were also reaching something of a creative crossroads.

Straight outta Walterton Road: The 101'ers

'We were like flaming. The place would be packed, and I remember glasses smashing, fights breaking out and dogs running around'
Joe Strummer, Westway to the World, 2000

Listening back 40-plus years on, you can hear Joe Strummer's songwriting potential on the self-penned 'Keys to Your Heart' (inspired by his girlfriend at the time, future Slits drummer Palmolive), 'Sweet Revenge' and several other 101'ers songs. Furthermore, there's power in the band's live and studio recordings, from the Patti Smith-inspired Them cover 'Gloria' to studio cuts like 'Letsagetabitarockin' and 'Motor Boys Motor'.

Those numbers brought out the band's best rock'n'roll sensibilities, and where Van Morrison added soul to 'Gloria', Strummer managed to bring Eddie Cochran, Gene Vincent and Johnny Kidd vibes, as well as the kind of raw, off-kilter qualities that wouldn't have sounded out of place on Lenny Kaye's *Nuggets* compilation. It's where Buddy Holly and the Crickets might have headed if they'd arrived two decades later, a quality also heard on 'Silent Telephone', which would have complemented The Clash's *Cost of Loving* EP alongside their inspired re-imagining of Sonny Curtis' 'I Fought the Law'.

The voice is unmistakably Strummer, an already-weathered troubadour having honed his stage persona and sense of self. The 101'ers were a true rock'n'roll tribute act, channeling the spirit of the originals. There was something of that excitement and verve in a couple of later 1980s revival bands, like The Stray Cats – but the 101'ers came first, bridging a gap between honest rock'n'roll, pub rock and punk. Change was afoot, and while they never pushed on to the next level, the 101'ers set Strummer up nicely for the next part of the story.

Formed in London in May 1974, you could argue that without the 101'ers there would have been no Clash – or, at least, not the classic four-piece that would go on to inspire us. A year earlier, Woody Mellor, as he was known, had joined hundreds of others defying the Criminal Trespass Act, squatting in one of hundreds of abandoned Victorian houses across the capital, the 101'ers being named after the street number of the Walterton Road property in Maida Vale, London W9, where the band were based (although some suggest links to George Orwell's Room 101 in dark dystopian classic, *1984*). Their co-founder, rhythm guitarist and vocalist was not long back from South Wales, and was ready to take on the world.

They prided themselves on a compelling rhythm'n'blues set, making up for a perceived lack of musicianship with live passion that made them a draw on that mid-'70s London circuit. They made their debut on September 7, 1974, at the Telegraph on Brixton Hill, playing a political benefit for Chilean refugees under the name El Huaso and the 101 All Stars – the name soon being shortened.

Mellor was fresh from his South Wales art-student combo The Vultures, while lead guitarist 'Evil' Clive Timperley had played with mid-'60s outfit Captain Rougeley's Blues Band, alongside original Fairport Convention drummer Martin Lamble. The line-up that night wasn't the band's first, their drummer having headed off on his holidays. But Richard Nother had stepped in and was re-christened 'Snakehips Dudanski', the former Salesian College head boy and Chelsea zoology student and bass player Marwood 'Mole' Chesterton being first-time performers, yet quickly creating a live understanding, laying a firm foundation for their bandmates.

As a unit, they bonded from the start, their fired-up frontman later telling *Melody Maker*'s Allan Jones that, 'since '67, music has been chasing itself up a blind alley.' The vocalist was determined to do something about that. 'A naturally-powerful performer given to sudden explosions of passion,' is how Allan Jones described him. Much like his namesake, Alan 'Jiver' Jones, the *Melody Maker* scribe had also got to know Joe Strummer in Newport, and was an invaluable source to this part of the story. They had lost touch for a while, but after his spell busking in the UK and Europe, Mellor was back in London in late '74, by which time Jones was a music writer, and his old friend soon got in touch, enthusing about his new band, which at that point included sax duo Simon Cassell and Alvaro Peña-Rojas.

After graduation, Allan Jones had worked in a stock room at Hatchard's on Piccadilly, but an impassioned letter to an established music newspaper led to a new start. his line '*Melody Maker* needs a bullet up its arse. I'm the gun – pull the trigger' had an effect. He was editing the paper within a decade, and in 1997 was heading up *Uncut* magazine. But he first saw the 101'ers in February 1975 in a room above The Chippenham on the corner of Malvern and Shirland Road.

The Charlie Pigdog Club, as it was known, was handy for the Walterton Road squat and, while Jones was intimidated by many of the punters, he witnessed a band truly focused on their set. They opened that night, as most, with 'Bony Maronie', played in Jones' words 'with an untutored ferocity'. What followed was 'crude, loud, [and] in many respects technically deficient. It relied heavily on covers of classic rock'n'roll and R'n'B, the staple repertoire of what back then was known as pub rock. I thought they were fantastic. After the show, they drove me home to South London in a hearse, which seemed impossibly cool.'

In his review, Jones reckoned the band 'screamed their way through a 20-minute interpretation of 'Gloria', which sounded like the perfect soundtrack for the first apocalyptic days of the Third Reich', while 'opposing factions of (I believe) Irish and Gypsies attempted to carve each other out, bottles were smashed over defenceless heads, blades flashed and howling dogs tore at one another's throats, splattering the walls with blood. No one, I was convinced, was going to crawl out of this one alive.' Yet their charismatic frontman carried on, 'thrashing away at his guitar like there was no tomorrow, completely oblivious to the surrounding carnage. The police finally arrived, flashing blue lights, sirens, the whole works. Strummer battled on. He was finally confronted by the imposing figure of the law, stopped in mid-flight, staggered to a halt and looked up. 'Evening, officer' he said.'

The band also played the nearby Windsor Castle, Maida Vale, and had a Thursday night residency from May 1975 to January 1976 at The Elgin, Ladbroke Grove, just south of the

1

Strummer the 101er

Westway, their public profile continuing to grow. In *Westway to the World*, Mick Jones said, 'Their epic two-and-a-half-hour sets quickly became the stuff of local legends, and a small but loyal following gathered around them'.

Woody was now going by the name Joe Strummer, with Dudanski, Timperley and Mole ever more the real deal, the bass player later making way for 'Desperate' Dan Kelleher. Yet the *Melody Maker* scribe noted 'negligible record company interest' and 'a growing feeling on Joe's part that the band were going nowhere in a hurry'. And by the time 'Keys to Your Heart' was released by Chiswick in May '76, the 101'ers were over.

Chiswick co-founder Roger Armstrong told the www.punk77.co.uk website: 'I'd been at the Elgin one night and there was a very strange band playing in the background, with a weird line-up that included trumpet. Next I heard of them was Ted [Carroll, who started the label with Roger in 1975 as a subsidiary of Rock on Records, shortly joined by Trevor Churchill] coming to the stall saying he'd seen a great band at Dingwalls the night before – the 101'ers. We went to their next gig in a college bar, one of those places that didn't even have a stage. There were a handful of mainly disinterested students, Ted and I. Regardless, Strummer – Woody then – played like his life depended on it.

'We signed them and cut a session at Pathway studio, about the size of a large cupboard. They cut more sessions with Vic Maile and did some sides for the BBC and a self-produced session. In the end, probably because I owned the record company, the Pathway version of 'Keys to Your Heart' came out as the A-side, and the studio sides appeared on a short-lived vinyl in the '80s that drummer, (Richard) Dudanski put together. In negotiating the rights to the

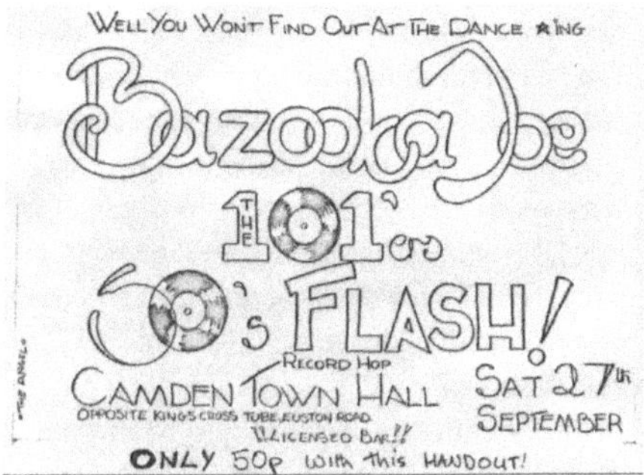

Pathway sides, we got agreement to issue 'Sweet Revenge' as a second single.

'We were about to put out the first single and I was at the Red Cow in Hammersmith meeting someone. I think The Jam were on that night and soundchecking. I was at the bar getting them in, when I got a tap on the shoulder and turned around to face Joe, saying 'Have I done the right thing?' Behind him was a skinny kid who Joe informed me he was forming a band with. What can you say? Great – we're about to put a record out and you go and break up the band! To be fair, it turned out well in the end.'

Allan Jones was there the fateful night the 101'ers were supported by the Sex Pistols at the Nashville, West Kensington, for the first time, on 3 April, 1976 – eight months after Mick Jones had his first date with destiny and Bernie Rhodes at the same grimy venue. Allan Jones was at the bar with Strummer and Dr Feelgood frontman Lee Brilleaux when the support came on. He said, 'Lee and I didn't get them at all, but Strummer looked like he'd seen a future he wanted to be part of. Next thing anyone knows, he'd joined The Clash.' That bombshell arrived eight weeks later, but the writing was on the wall, with Strummer more and more distant from his bandmates. When he finally announced his departure, he invited the 101'ers drummer to join him, but Dudanski said no, finding Bernie Rhodes to be 'odiously domineering and manipulative'. Instead, he went on to The Raincoats, Basement 5 and then John Lydon's Public Image Ltd, while Clive Timperley joined The Passions, best known for UK hit 'I'm in Love with a German Film Star', and Dan Kelleher joined Martian Schoolgirls, then The Derelicts.

Five years after the split, Dudanski was instrumental in the release of the *Elgin Avenue Breakdown* LP, seizing on widespread interest in anything Clash-related. Looking back on those days in a *Melody Maker* review of that March 1981 release, Jones wrote: 'Brash, untutored, they stripped rock to its essential dynamics. Like the later punk bands, they were aggressive, but unlike their successors, they were never bullying. Strummer songs like 'Motor Boys Motor' anticipated the frustrations of punk but betray none of its spiteful impatience or empty rhetoric. While the later punk stormtroopers were still at home in front of the bedroom mirror, miming to The New York Dolls, Strummer and the 101'ers were out there, actually doing it.'

Strummer said, 'I know the 101ers were good. As far as sound and excitement went, we were much better than Eddie and the Hot Rods. The other guys in the group were 25, 26, and played good because they'd spent a few years getting that far. But they were just too old. What I really wanted was to get in with some young yobbos I was more in tune with.'

There were crossovers, despite Strummer's insistence he'd start afresh with The Clash: 'Junco Partner' was reinvented for *Sandinista!* and a re-worked 'Lonely Mother's Sons' became the 'Clash City Rockers' B-side

1 'Jail Guitar Doors', with a Strummer/Jones credit that Dudanski took umbrage at. With that, plus a little animosity over Strummer's distancing from his 101'ers past (on Rhodes' insistence, supposedly), Dudanski got to work on *Elgin Avenue Breakdown*. Rhodes tried to stop it, but by 1981 Strummer had moved out of Rhodes' shadow and supported his old bandmate's endeavours.

In an August 2015 reappraisal of the band, Dudanski told Allan Jones, 'I noticed some people hanging around at the gig, and when Joe disappeare with them, I had a feelin something odd was going on. I think that was two nights before he told me it was all over. I was in bed at the squat in Orsett Terrace, with Joe shaking me, saying, 'Wake up, Snakes. I've got something really important to tell you. This is the end. We' got to talk about it.' I said, 'In the morning, Joe. We'll talk about it then.' I had a feeling something was up. He'd been very taciturn since the Golden Lion. I went downstairs the next morning and there was Bernie, who I remembered from the Golden Lion. He started spewing out this stuff about how crap the 101'ers were and how punk was going to happen, a totally one-way conversation.

'Then he said he wanted me to be the drummer in the new band, stick with Joe. Bernie was the main reason I didn't join The Clash. If there'd been a different manager, I might have thought about it. There was no way I was going to have this guy telling me what to do. I went to see The Clash at The Roxy and couldn't believe how Joe had changed. He was someone else. His identity changed entirely. Some of the things he went on to say were very hurtful. Some of it was just rubbish, like saying we'd taken our name from Room 101 in George Orwell's *1984* to make it sound more political. That was ridiculous, a bit sad. For that first year or two he was in The Clash, he was in another place.'

In the same feature, Dan Kelleher lan Jones, 'That ; Strummer's way of nterpreting the new narrative. Everything that had gone before was crap. We became the fall guys for Strummer having been, as it were, led astray. It must have been especially hard for Clive and Richard, 'ecause they'd been with from the start. Mick Jones is supposed to have said Strummer was brilliant but the 101'ers were crap musically, which was rubbish.'

The last show came two months after they first shared a bill with the Sex Pistols at the Nashville, the 101'ers bowing out at The Clare Halls, Hayward's Heath, on 5 June. Clive Timperley who had left shortly before, unhappy with the direction he felt Strummer was taking them (and possibly been ousted), told Allan Jones in 2015: 'It was all very sad in the end, but I always thought from very early on, Joe had an idea in his mind about where he was going to go and don't think there was much that would have stopped him.' Julian Yewdall added, 'It was like everything came to an end at once. Joe announced the band was over, that he was leaving to join The Clash. At the same time, the whole street where we had our last squat in Orsett Terrace was given its eviction notice. The band was falling apart, the house was falling apart. Previously, we'd always moved as a group. We moved from one squat to another, always together, as a unit. Now it was every man for himself.'

Strummer had already moved on, telling the *NME*'s Sean O'Hagan in 1997, 'The first thing I discovered about punk was that it was more exciting than pub rock. That's where I'd been, where I was coming from. The 101'ers 'Keys to Your Heart' was the first song I'd written. I stand by that song, but it was really a guitar-riff kinda song.'

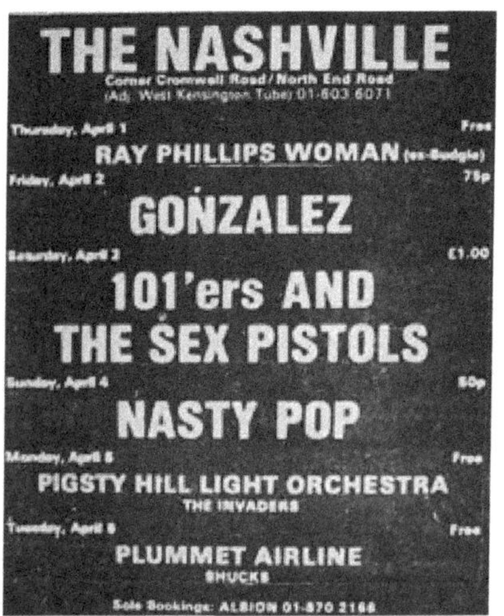

Elgin Avenue Breakdown: an appreciation

Released in Spring 1981, five years after the 101'ers split, *Elgin Avenue Breakdown* comprised a four-song demo recorded by Dr Feelgood producer Vic Maile at Jackson Studios, Rickmansworth; two songs from a BBC Maida Vale session produced by Penguin Café Orchestra's Simon Jeffes; one track recorded by Roger Armstrong for Chiswick Records at Pathway Studio; and five rather raw recordings from The Roundhouse, Chalk Farm, in mid-April 1976, from soundman and future Clash producer Mickey Foote. The Roundhouse songs were from the night the band supported prog-rockers Van Der Graaf Generator (described by Strummer as 'Shakespeare crossed with Uriah Heep'). Strummer had intended a reissue with unreleased tracks, but that only happened after his death, with the help of Dudanski and the blessing of Joe's widow, Lucinda. May 2005's *Elgin Avenue Breakdown Revisited* saw an expansion to 20 tracks, including the original single, plus live numbers recorded at Camberwell Art School, a Rolling Stones cover, 'Out of Time', captured at Wandsworth Prison, and an eight-minute 'Gloria' at Bracknell's Cellar Bar.

On both versions, two Maile recordings provide a dynamic start, with Joe and co. demonstrating some back-from-Hamburg-era Beatles power on a stonking 'Letsagetabitarockin'. While no one can seriously contend Strummer had one of the great rock'n'roll voices, it works well, giving a sense of the 101'ers' live poke.

'Silent Telephone' shares that vibe while showcasing a Johnny Kidd & The Pirates-like rumble, one rarely replicated so well.

Of the live cuts, Chuck Berry's 'Monkey Business' is a straightforward rock'n'roller, reminiscent of The Beatles' revitalising 'Rock'n'Roll Music', while Slim Harpo's 'Shake Your Hips' further displays a rocking surge, and New Orleans standard 'Junco Partner' – 'a rhumba about drug addicts', as Joe put it – dates back to the US Great Depression. The song was revisited in pop-reggae meets roots country mode on *Sandinista!* On YouTube, a user known as 'Monkeytown 1000' claimed in 2011 he saw Woody and the band a few times during his own squatting days, once playing a former bank in Tolmers Square, adding, 'They did 'Junco Partner' and I was impressed – at the time I didn't know anyone else who knew the song. Happy daze of sulphate, spliff 'n Special Brew.'

Bo Diddley's 'Don't Let It Go' is the only Roundhouse survivor on the 2005 version, and closes side one of the original LP; it offers further rockabilly verve, the sort of live cover you'd expect from a frontman with an acknowledged early appreciation of The Rolling Stones' 'Not Fade Away'. Turning over the original LP, we get more Feelgood-esque fare in 'Motor Boys, Motor' – the third of the Rickmansworth cuts and one further suggesting Strummer was ahead of the pack. In places, he's already the fully-formed entertainer; he just happens to be with a different band. And that's not taking anything away from the 101'ers.

'Sweety of the St Moritz' completes the Maile masters, again suggesting a dancefloor pull. When Joe hoarsely encourages 'Evil Clive', with a 'Come on, you've been there, boy!' before a solo, we've a precursor to that wondrous 'guitar hero' call to Mick Jones on 'Complete Control'. It's a floor-filler, with a dynamic suggesting Strummer was a team player as well as a natural out front.

Danny Kelleher's 'Surf City' hardly suggests West Coast America. It's more London inner city but it works well, a real grower with a gravitational tidal pull all its own, like a tripping take on the Stones' 'Let's Spend the Night Together'. That and 'Keys to Your Heart' are both from the BBC session, but I prefer the Chiswick version, pre-dating Jake Riviera and Dave Robinson's vinyl output on Stiff records, but sounding like classic Stiff, as if conjured up by Nick Lowe. There's a touch of the Hot Rods and maybe Elvis Costello, Joe Jackson or Graham Parker too. Was this new wave, before that movement that followed the blast of punk? In the middle section Strummer moves closer to '60s soul bite.

> **'The London SS auditions are the stuff of legend. The fledgling group went through just about everyone on the scene and were equally and fantastically rude to them all. As a way of getting a band together it was a total failure. As a meeting point and catalyst for the emerging punk scene it was perfect'**
> ***John Robb, Punk Rock – An Oral History, 2006***

'Sweet Revenge', from the Pathway session of March '76 and its B-side 'Rabies (From the Dogs of Love)' on the 2005 version - again shows Strummer's versatility, suggesting a timeline back to Ray Davies, via Steve Harley and Ian Hunter. And a cod Caribbean feel adds the kind of reggae influences The Clash would lap up.

Of the further 2005 additions, *Keep Taking the Tablets* is less memorable, and the 'Out of Time' and 'Maybelline' covers add little to the originals, but Strummer originals 'Five Star R'n'R' and 'Hideaway' show strength in depth, and the stand-out of the previously-unreleased tracks is a storming studio take on another fine Mellor composition, 'Steamgauge '99'.

Then they're away with an intense, far longer run through Van Morrison's 'Gloria', as already reinvented by Patti Smith, whom Joe namechecks mid-song. It's raw and unrefined, and if you didn't know the song before you'd have struggled to work out whose name he's spelling. Perhaps he'd have made a better fist of it with his own voice, not some mid-Atlantic hybrid. But a fella by the name of Rhodes was all set to steer him in that direction, insisting Strummer and his new bandmates wrote about what they knew, in their own voice. The remaining traces of that 'Woody' persona were about to bite the bullet.

On all these songs though, the vibe created and power the 101'ers had on audiences make you realise how big a decision Strummer faced when Bernie came knocking. He had a good thing going. I'm just not sure where it was headed. If I'd witnessed the 101'ers live regularly, I'd have been a tad pissed off that they were gone, replaced by something which initially seemed a lesser animal. These boys could play, and it seemed that The Clash couldn't at first. There was more to it than that though, Strummer set to take the 'year zero' route and leave these songs well alone when The Clash formed. He clearly made the right decision, but the 101'ers deserve more than a footnote in the history of rock music.

'Wanted: Martian' Tales of the London SS

Tony James first met Mick Jones at a Heavy Metal Kids gig at the Fulham Greyhound through Jones' bandmate Kelvin Blacklock. Advertising in the music papers and answering other ads, trying to put a band together, James was 'looking for those kind of slightly Stonesy, English rock'n'roll glamorous groups', as he told John Robb. 'I met up with Kelvin in Westbourne Grove, and he said, 'I'm going around to see this mate of mine, Mick, who lives with his Gran.' He takes me round to Mick's house and he's reading *The Tale of Willy's Rats* by Mick Farren and *The Diary of a Rock'n'Roll Star* by Ian Hunter. I had both of these books.

'I went to meet them again in Southwark,

1

where Kelvin was rehearsing with Mick. We were at the rehearsal and they were sort of firing Mick. They had another guitarist and were saying Mick wasn't good enough. Mick and I went home on the tube together to his Gran's. That's how it all started. Straight away we decided to get a band together. When you're young, you go, 'OK, I'll get on with something else.' You don't think your life's in ruins. 'If it's not working, let's do something else.''

In Robb's *Punk Rock: An Oral History*, Jones added, 'I was on the way out of the band and Tony had sort of just come in. I got the feeling it was kind of Kelvin giving me, as a bit of compensation, an introduction to Tony. ... We palled up straight away. We started hanging out together, seriously hanging out. We were into the same things and we talked about it incessantly. We decided to form our own band, using a name that Little Queenie had nearly used, London SS.'

James added, 'You can see why – London SS, New York Dolls, same sort of thing. It positions you in London, has that London vibe. This is the time when you couldn't even buy a pair of dark glasses that looked cool and could only get a leather jacket from a second-hand place if you were lucky, or a motorcycle shop. You had to seek this stuff out. We knew what was going on. We were reading about New York, and knew it was cool, and underground. That was the benchmark.'

'Mick got a job in a bookshop in Camden Town to save up to buy a new guitar. After a couple of months, I went with him to Denmark Street. He'd seen this guitar, the famous brown Les Paul Junior he used in The Clash. We were going out to see every band we could, hoping we could spot something. We would begrudgingly go and see this group playing this pub across the road from Mick's Gran's, the 101'ers. We used to stand at the back, but we liked the singer. We also went to see The Winkies, Ducks Deluxe, and obviously Dr Feelgood.'

If seeing Joe Strummer's band, the 101'ers would prove key in the long term, so would the night they met another major player in the story, Bernard Rhodes. That came about on August 2, 1975, Jones and James at the Nashville Rooms in West Kensington, just another night trying to find out what was happening, checking out up-and-coming Liverpool outfit Deaf School, chancing upon an intriguing character at the bar, a small, bespectacled bloke in a cap, wearing a T-shirt Jones recognised. He said, 'I asked if he was a piano player. I was thinking of Gene Vincent and the Blue Caps. He said, 'No, but you're wearing one of my T-shirts.'' Bought at Let It Rock, that T-shirt read – depending which account you come across – '*One day you'll wake up and know what side of the bed you're lying on*', its slogan accompanied by a list of various hip/non-hip characters, printed by Rhodes for business partner Malcolm McLaren, owner of the Sex boutique on King's Road, Chelsea. Another account suggests '*Too Fast to Live, Too Young to Die*'.

James tells the story with colour, reckoning he asked Rhodes, 'Could you stand over there a bit? You're wearing the same T-shirt as us,' to which Rhodes replied, 'Fuck off! I fucking designed this T-shirt, you cunts!' What have you got going for you?' James told him the pair were forming a band, the London SS, Rhodes' interest growing. James added, 'It was a suicidal name, but had attitude. He seemed impressed and said, 'OK, I'll be your manager.'

According to Pat Gilbert, The London SS was 'merely an idea: raw garage punk dressed up in Nazi chic. The object was to be shocking, musically and visually.' Led by Mick Jones and Tony James, they spent most of their time auditioning potential players, Brian James the only other semi-permanent member.

It was clearly crass and naïve – shock for the sake of it – but there was no Nazi agenda. Jones was partly Jewish after all. The name was thought up, then discarded, by his previous band, supposedly suggested by drummer Geir Waade as The Delinquents looked to change tack. Instead, they settled on Little Queenie, but when Jones started again he and Tony James felt shock value might work. It didn't, but at least it helped garner interest, notably from Rhodes, another major player with Jewish heritage.

Of the first band contemplating that name, John Brown told Marcus Gray in 1995's *Last Gang in Town*, it was 'the result of a general brainstorming session with a dictionary and thesaurus', the London prefix a nod in the direction of the New York Dolls and Hollywood Brats. As for the second part, Waade told Gray, 'I didn't mean like a Nazi thing. It was because we all went on the dole – Social Security.' Gray wasn't convinced, suggesting 'face-saving revisionism', seeing the Nazi reference as 'deliberately tasteless', although conceding it was 'merely another illustration of the mood of the times'.

Jones and James also insisted it stood for 'social security', Jones having a spell working for a Government benefits office in Paddington. But it was a name that would haunt The Clash when they became Britain's premier left-wing political band. Jones, from Twickenham, studying maths at Brunel University in Uxbridge at the time, told Chris Salewicz in his 2007 *Redemption Song: The Ballad of Joe Strummer*, 'We hadn't thought at all about the Nazi implications. It just seemed like a very anarchic, stylish thing to do.'

Chrissie Hynde tried explaining such posturing in John Lydon's 1994 autobiography, *Rotten: No Irish, No Blacks, No Dogs*, saying, 'When the punk kids walked around wearing swastikas and bondage gear, it was their two fingers up at the Establishment. They weren't buying into or in any way associating themselves with Nazism or the National Front or sado-masochism. These were teenagers who were just trying to say, 'Fuck you!''

In John Robb's *Punk Rock: An Oral History*, Tony James gives a vivid example of Rhodes' response to the name, recalling a night he invited the pair to a rough pub in Shepherd's Bush, the Bull and Bush.

'Mick and I nancy-boy in and meet the Bluejean flat-cap man, sitting in the middle of this crowded, dangerous, scary pub. Bernie opens his bag, starts slapping Nazi regalia on the bar – swastikas, badges, Nazi flags, the whole lot. We were saying, 'Bernie, we could get killed here!' He went, 'Alright, you want to be called London SS, you're going to have to deal with it, so wise up!' We went home, like 'Fuck, we never thought of that.' We were saying, 'It means the London Social Security.' We were on the dole-queue rock thing already. Mick worked in the dole office, that's what the name stood for. We never thought any further than that.'

Jones and James were advertising weekly in *Melody Maker* for like-minded individuals into the Dolls, The Stooges and MC5. Jones told John Robb, 'That was enough. If you'd heard of these people you'd be right.' James added, 'We wanted a singer and a drummer into the New York Dolls, Mott the Hoople and The Stooges. That was like asking, 'Wanted: Martian'. Mick and I were such pop culture readers. We were sat in his Gran's one night and said, 'What we need is something like the Two I's coffee bar, like Soho in the '60s.' We got on a bus outside, a No.16, and got off at Praed Street. By the bus stop was a cafe on the corner. We said, 'Here's the place!' like you do. There was a jukebox in the corner. We said, 'Here is our base. We are in!''

Jones recalled, 'Lots of people came down. They had to go through a cafe interview. We put our records on the jukebox and had a little scene going on. It was a pre-check-out before the rehearsal. It depended on a lot of factors – what they looked like, their whole attitude, that was important. It never put us off if you couldn't play, but it might put us off if you were into funny things we weren't into.' James added, 'We were mean to them. We learned from Bernie, who'd be there. Imagine meeting us and you've got Bernie tearing you to bits. We got a tragic letter from Morrissey. Manchester seemed like a million miles away. It would have been really strange if it had happened. People drifted in and out. We were having no joy finding anyone who really understood the music we were digging. Suddenly this café had these hip young guys hanging out in it.

'A couple of weeks later Bernie said, 'I've found a place for you to rehearse.' We came out of the cafe, walked round the back into the Mews, through a door in the basement of the cafe and there was a room with nothing in there, like a dungeon. Bernie comes in and he's got horror film posters, Nazi war atrocity films, all that genre of posters, and puts them on the wall. Little did we know there was a subtle plot to talk us out of the name. It was not a fascist name, Mick was Jewish! We saw it as when you walked into your home with a T-shirt with it on and your parents fainted. You didn't think about the wider issues.'

Jones added, 'I used to spend a lot of the time on the phone talking to people. You had to get past that first. The auditions happened from November '75 till January '76. Loads came down, like Keith Levene, Terry Chimes, Topper Headon, Brian James.' The latter, based in Croydon, was in a group called Bastard, a 'rough rock'n'roll band influenced by The Stooges, the MC5 and the Pink Fairies', at one point based in Belgium. His namesake Tony said, 'He had the look,' while Jones added, 'He played furiously. We liked him.' Meanwhile, Brian saw them as 'a couple of long-hairs ... but they talked about the right people'.

Of the auditions, Brian James added, 'It became like a weekly thing, at Paddington Kitchen, just off Praed Street. There was an endless stream of singers and drummers, all sorts of people would come down or be on the phone. Some didn't have a clue. They must have been living up a Welsh mountain playing to goats, or just come off a steamship doing a cruise gig. All kind of weirdos. It was kind of fun in a way. A few people came down who went on to do other things. There were people into rock'n'roll, not right for us, but it was cool they were doing it. There were a few good guys, but the percentage to bad guys was about 10 to 90!'

French drummer Roland Hot sat in, bringing his mate Paul Simonon, while others included guitarist Matt Dangerfield, Hollywood Brats singer Andrew Matheson and keyboard player Casino Steel, plus Jones' fellow Little Queenie reject Geir Waade. The band were jamming ('fucking about', as they put it) at

Dangerfield's squat in Warrington Crescent, close to Jones' Wilmcote House base. They played rock'n'roll and 1960s R'n'B, yet there were no gigs and just one demo – featuring Jones, Brian and Tony James, and Roland Hot – is known to have survived. Only one song was taken on to Jones' next band, '1-2 Crush on You', eventually recorded as a B-side to 'Tommy Gun'.

Tony James told John Robb, 'When you listen to the demo tape, it's all there. There's only one tape. It's even got a cover and the dates on it. The rarest tape in the world ... and I lost it recently! We promised each other we'd never release it. It's a magical archive. It's got Brian and Roland on it. We recorded it in front of Bernie and Malcolm in the rehearsal room. We ran through our repertoire. We opened with 'Rambling Rose' – a heavier, madder Stooges version – then 'Roadrunner' and a track from the *Nuggets* era, early Rolling Stones tracks, and 'Protex Blue', Mick's first original.' Brian James added, 'Mick had a song called 'I'm So Bored with You'. I preferred it when it was like a little love song. Tony James says he has tapes, but not good quality. Even so, I'd like to hear them. Release them? Nah. Certain things like professional pride would get in the way.'

Of the many others who passed through, Nicky Headon said of his audition, 'I probably looked a right state. I had really long hair and an Afghan coat. My feet are so small I'd wear women's shoes, green platforms. Mick was going, 'Hit the drums like Jerry Nolan.' I got on well with Mick straight away. We respected each other's abilities. But I wanted to earn £25 a week and play something I was familiar with. After a couple of rehearsals, I did a runner and went off to do a soul tour.'

Tony James recalled Paul Simonon's audition, telling John Robb, 'We said, 'He looks good. Can you sing?' and he said, 'I dunno.' He did 'Roadrunner' with us, just went 'Roadrunner, Roadrunner!' over and over. He had no idea really, but he looked good.'

Terry Chimes also failed an audition, and you can add to the 'reject' list punk poet Patrik Fitzgerald and drummer Rat Scabies, whom Brian James left with to form The Subterraneans and later The Damned. Of the others, Tony James joined Chelsea with Billy Idol, the pair later forming Generation X, while Steel and Dangerfield went on to The Boys.

Checking out the Sex Pistols: Denmark Street Competition

'We were still trying to find people in early '76. This wasn't working. Me and Mick didn't fall out. It was not a big deal. Somehow it got lost in the ether. Mick was already off talking to Joe Strummer and I was looking at the 'wanted' ads.'
Tony James to John Robb, Punk Rock: An Oral History, 2006

When they first met, Rhodes explained to Mick Jones and Tony James that he was working with Malcolm McLaren on a band called the Sex Pistols, a new name to the pair at the time. Then, in October, Jones and James responded, intrigued, to another *Melody Maker* ad, which namechecked Johnny Thunders. That ad took them to the Pistols' HQ, McLaren looking for new acts. Two weeks later, Matheson and Steel arranged to meet at their Denmark Street base, Jones and James joining them. Jones recalled to John Robb, 'Everyone had been waiting for a band like the Pistols to happen. I first saw them at a party by Tower Bridge. You knew straight away that was it, this was what it was going to be like from now on. A new scene, new values, so different from what had happened before. A bit dangerous.'

Brian James added, 'Bernie took us down to see the Pistols at Andrew Logan's Valentine's Night warehouse party at Butler's Wharf. Just seeing them playing made me, Mick and Tony aware that there were other people into this kind of music. They were playing The Stooges' 'No Fun'. They weren't the greatest band in the world but had an attitude. They were barking up the right tree. I spoke to John Lydon afterwards and was impressed by his attitude. I moved on at that point. Me and Rat (Scabies) started looking for singers and bass players. I moved to Portobello Road and started hanging out at the Lonsdale pub. There was quite a scene there.'

Tony James, reflecting on the end of the band, told John Robb, 'Towards the end there was a classic Bernie moment. He got me, Brian and Mick into his car. We drove to Madison Terrace, the millionaires' row, one of the poshest streets in London in those days. There's a party going on, we're sat outside in the car, the Stones arrive and it's all very Bohemian. It's like our dream. We were totally on the outside in those days. Guest list wasn't in our vocab. We couldn't believe it. We were in! Bernie gets us outside and he turns around and goes, 'You'll be able to go when you get a great idea.' And he drove us away. 'You're not ready for this yet,' he said. And he was right. We were pissed off at the time, but it was true. He was taunting us.'

Jones added, 'It wasn't getting anywhere. We couldn't find a singer. Me and Tony went our own ways. Bernie said, 'Don't work with Tony, work with Paul Simonon.' Maybe Bernie pulled me away a little bit. Tony lent Paul a bass and Paul started learning the bass.' Tony James said, 'I was living at Mick's gran's flat, Mick was at the Davis Road squat with Sid Vicious and Viv Albertine. Then Brian hooked up with Scabies and formed The Damned and I hooked up with Billy (Idol) in Chelsea. A lot of great people drifted through and went on to do great stuff. Bernie would be there most of the times and would bring Malcolm down. Chrissie Hynde would come down as well, and Mick went off to write with her. It was Bernie who suggested Mick should go and write with her.'

Jones confirmed, 'Me and Chrissie were playing songs in my bedroom and sang together – 'Something's Got a Hold on Me' and Aretha Franklin's 'Every Little Bit Hurts'. I was still a kid and she was quite exotic to me, being from America. She was working for the *NME*, going out with Nick Kent. I was like, 'Wow!' But Bernie pulled me away. He must have had a plan. He didn't think like other people. That was what was interesting about him. He gave me a proper schooling.'

When Jones and Tony James went to Denmark Street to meet Malcolm McLaren, they walked into a rehearsal room and saw 'three kids', as James put it. He told John Robb, 'We were kids as well. But they had short hair and we had long hair. We were the New York Dolls and they were short-haired blokes. We'd grown up with the English underground scene, the kind of freak brother scene where long hair was revolutionary. What Malcolm showed us was that the scene had become bloated. It was the norm now. Suddenly, it was short hair – not skinhead, but short, spikey hair – that was revolutionary.'

The pair became friends with Glen

Matlock, who told John Robb, 'They looked like Mott the Hoople. They all had long hair, stack-heeled boots and snakeskin/tiger-skin trousers. There was a meeting upstairs between Bernie and Malcolm. Mick Jones picked up his guitar and played. There was something about him. I got pally with Mick and guess he realised the way he looked wasn't the way to go.'

Jones said, 'It was about the time John Lydon joined. It was a bit of an eye-opener. I must admit it changed things, the way they looked different. The shock of the short hair. They were so different. We had long hair, tight trousers from Biba, ocelot material.' Matlock added, 'I'd seen Mick out and about. I played bass and Steve played drums while Mick auditioned Chrissie Hynde, long before it was called The Clash. It was a project he was trying to get together. There was a bit of 'hands across the sea', helping people with things. We wanted there to be more bands like us, so it wasn't so lonely out there.'

Back to Garageland: Year Zero

'The day I joined The Clash was very much back to square one – year zero. We were almost Stalinist in the way you had to shed all your friends, or everything you'd known, every way you'd played before.'

Joe Strummer, Westway to the World, 2000

A fired-up Mick Jones was keen to start again, and Bernie Rhodes soon suggested he contact Paul Simonon, encouraging him to learn to play and be part of a new band. That new outfit would involve another face on the emerging UK punk scene, guitarist Keith Levene. There was no regular drummer, the band bringing in whomever they could, including Chimes, although he wasn't keen to stick around.

Jones told John Robb, 'Paul came down with Roland (Hot) and started hanging out a bit. He couldn't play much, so we borrowed a bass off Tony. Things were starting to happen. There was a vibe. Everybody could feel something was going to happen, people wanted to be part of it. It got bigger, more people got into it.'

Keith Levene added, 'I met Mick and we really liked each other. Everyone was a couple of years older than me. When you're 16, that's a big gap. What was going on in West London, which I didn't know about then, was this whole scene with Tony James and Mick Jones, and the 101'ers were around. Mick and Tony were doing London SS and it wasn't really working. Mick thought I was a bass player, so that's what I played. They already had him and someone else playing guitar. What we did was good.

'I picked up an acoustic and started playing, and Mick went, 'Fucking hell, I never heard a bass player play guitar like that!' I said, 'No, I'm a guitarist.' He told me to try one of his tunes. I learned it instantly, playing it better than him. He was really digging it. He said, 'Do you write?' I told him, 'No, I don't, but I guess that's the next thing.' We became really fast friends. He thought I was fucking great on guitar. The next week he invited me down to Portobello Road, introduced me to this guy called Paul and told me, 'This guy comes across as a bit thick, but he's a really great artist. I think he could be the bass player, but he can't play.' I was cool with that. At the same time, we were looking for something. We didn't know what it was. We were just looking to be different.

'Malcolm went away for two weeks and

had Bernard look after the Pistols. The band really improved in those two weeks in which Malcolm was away. This really pissed Malcolm off. They had this real falling out. So Bernard wanted his own band and was working with Mick Jones. I was their absolute brightest find since they'd been together. Bernard was saying, 'I know you're young and you should be in school, but you seem to know about things.' Me and Bernard used to talk all the time, arguing about everything, in a positive way, to make the band better.'

In *Westway to the World*, Simonon says, 'I remember going around to Mick's flat and he was trying to show me this E chord. and after about an hour of complete frustration on both sides, we decided to get hold of a bass.' It involved a fair amount of frustration, but Simonon eventually started to find his way around, with the help of some rudimentary coaching from Jones. He added, 'I thought rather than making it a hard job, I'd just get stickers and write 'A', 'B', 'G', whatever, and just stick them on.'

Moves were soon underway to find a singer, a role Billy Watts ('Billy from Wycombe', as Jones described him, Simonon reckoning 'his look was a bit old-fashioned and we needed fresh input') took first, the band then called the Young Colts. Then came future Pretenders singer Chrissie Hynde's spell out front. But Rhodes soon had his eyes on Joe Strummer, who had impressed both Jones and Levene when they saw him leading the 101'ers at the Nashville Rooms, with the Sex Pistols supporting – the bands' second pairing at the venue in three weeks. Simonon said, 'We needed fresh input and seeing Joe I think it crossed all our minds about nicking him.'

That was on April 23, 1976. Jones' future direction was suddenly clearer after witnessing the Pistols. And it wasn't just the support act that intrigued him. In *Westway to the World*, he added, 'I guess that was the moment we realised Joe was the best guy out there.' Simonon suggests in *The Clash: Strummer, Jones, Simonon, Headon*, that he'd seen Strummer far earlier, recalling, 'The first time I saw the 101'ers was at this dump which had people running about with their dogs and giant hippies stomping around. There was one guy, Dave the Van or something, who wore blue overalls, had a big beard and was jumping around completely sloshed while Joe was on stage. He'd be playing, there was a woman breastfeeding a baby, dogs running across the stage, but Joe was definitely the guy to watch.'

Strummer was ready to move away from the pub-rock circuit as soon as he witnessed the Pistols over those two nights in the spring of 1976, their first show supporting the 101'ers on April 3. Reflecting on those nights to *Record Collector* in 2000, he said, 'I saw the future – with a snotty handkerchief – right in front of me. It was immediately clear. Pub rock was, 'Hello, you bunch of drunks, I'm gonna play these boogies and I hope you like them.' The Pistols came out that Tuesday evening and their attitude was, 'Here's our tunes, and we couldn't give a flying fuck whether you like them or not. In fact, we're gonna play them even if you fucking hate them!'' Reliving that moment in *Westway to the World*, he added, 'Five seconds into the first song I just knew we were like yesterday's papers. I mean, we were over!'

In an overview of that scene, Glen Matlock told John Robb, 'At first there wasn't any other bands, then we heard of a band called The Damned. Then The Jam. We'd already met people like Mick Jones, but not yet as The Clash. Malcolm started looking for a record deal. One of the things I wasn't aware of was that one of the reasons Malcolm and Bernie fell out was that Bernie had been offered this deal by Maurice Oberstein at CBS to set up his own label and radio station, and Malcolm didn't want to know. That's why Bernie went off to form The Clash. He was trying to do the things right that we had done wrong.'

Keith Levene added, 'In early '76 we were getting The Clash together and I was feeling a bit embarrassed about these guys. We had this singer who was this real Mick Jagger imitation and were trying to get rid of him. Joe Strummer had so much fucking energy and was so cool. When he was in the 101'ers he wore this zoot suit and looked late-'50s. The band would play this acceptable, clangy, Telecaster rock, but they'd be quite good. Joe was just fucking mad. He was really, really a great mover. Couldn't sing to save his life but he gave off all this energy and always ended in a total sweat. He was like *the* turn-on singer. The only other guy was John Lydon, but he was in the Pistols.'

Jones, Simonon and Levene saw the 101'ers again at the Red Cow, Hammersmith, on May 12, and the next day a chance meeting between Strummer – who told Jon Savage for *England's Dreaming*, 'By that time Bernie had fallen out with Malcolm over the swastika, because Bernie's mother was a refugee from Europe' – and his two admirers occurred as they collected their dole at Lisson Grove Labour Exchange, north of Marylebone. It was a moment that left a big impression on the three future members of The Clash – two in one queue with Mick's girlfriend, future Slits guitarist Viv Albertine, and the singer in the next.

In *Westway to the World*, Strummer said, 'I was queuing to get my dole. I could see them staring over and didn't realise they'd seen the 101'ers the previous weekend. I ignored them, got my dole and was expecting them to tangle with me on the way to the door or out on the street. I thought I'd punch Mick first. He looked thinner and Paul looked a bit tasty. I thought I'd smack Mick, then leg it!' Simonon added, 'He definitely caught us looking at him. I think he thought he was going to be done over. That moment, he looked really timid, in terror, it seemed.' Jones added, 'We were looking on in awe really.'

Details are sketchy of the next meet, but Pat Gilbert calculated that the next Saturday, on Portobello Road, Strummer bumped into Jones, Simonon and Glen Matlock, who knew the 101'ers singer from their Nashville shows. They exchanged pleasantries, Jones apparently telling Strummer he didn't like his band but thought he was 'great'. And while Strummer didn't say so then, he came away admiring Jones and Simonon's gang-like image, feeling they 'looked like a group'.

In a different version of that encounter, recounted in Caroline Coon's November 1976 interview for *Melody Maker*, Jones and Simonon talked about walking down Golborne Road with Matlock when they bumped into Strummer, who said, 'As soon as I saw these guys, I knew that was what a group, in my eyes, was supposed to look like. I didn't really hesitate when they asked me to join.'

The next part of the tale is equally confused, but it seems that Bernie Rhodes – who possibly heard Jones and Simonon talk about meeting Strummer – approached the singer at a Pistols gig at the 100 Club, on London's Oxford Street, and told him he had some lads he wanted him to meet, with the intention of forming a band like the Pistols. No names were mentioned, with Jones and Simonon unaware of Rhodes' plan, but details were exchanged. Rhodes phoned a number for Strummer the next day, only for 101'ers bass player Dan Kelleher to answer, and Rhodes soon rang off. Instead, Rhodes tried Strummer in person, calling by with Levene at the Golden Lion, Fulham Broadway, at the next 101'ers gig, possibly on Sunday, May 30. It was there that Rhodes delivered his ultimatum for Strummer to decide whether he was up for joining a band that would 'rival the Pistols'.

Some accounts give it as a 48-hour ultimatum, others 24. As it is, Levene denies either version, telling John Robb a more straightforward account: 'Me and Bernard went off to a 101'ers gig one night and talked Joe into coming over to my squat in Shepherd's Bush. I was playing guitar, playing some 101'ers tunes. He went, 'Hey man, I just love the way you play guitar.' I said, 'Will you do it?' He said, 'Yeah', and we got him in The Clash.'

Mick Jones added, 'It's quite an unusual sort of thing to happen – someone comes to your gig and asks if you want to join another band. Obviously, Joe was intuitive enough, already feeling it. He'd seen the Pistols and knew something new was happening. He'd seen us in the dole office and in the street and had seen what we looked like. By that time, I didn't have long hair. So, Bernie gave Joe an ultimatum.'

Whatever the sequence of events, Strummer decided to take that punt, saying, 'I thought about it for 24 hours then rang him back and said, 'OK, I'm in.'' Simonon reckoned that was the spark they needed, adding, 'Once we had Joe on board it all started to come together.'

Another version suggests that Rhodes called back, unable to wait 48 hours, phoning Strummer the next day for a decision. And the following morning, possibly on Tuesday, June 1, Rhodes and Levene turned up at Strummer's Orsett Terrace base, driving Joe back in Bernie's Renault 5 to 22, Davis Road, Acton Vale, where who should be waiting but the two lads he thought were going to jump him two and a half weeks earlier at the dole office. As Strummer put it, 'He (Rhodes) came up to the dressing room after the show and said, 'Hey, come with me. I'd like you to meet some people. I said, 'OK', and we went down Shepherd's Bush to a squat on Davis Road, where Mick Jones and Paul Simonon were waiting in a room.'

Recalling that first rehearsal in 2017's *The Ultimate Music Guide*, Jones said, 'Paul, Keith, myself and a few other people were all there, waiting for Joe. We put egg boxes on the wall of Paul's bedroom. Joe came in and we started working straight away. It was more or less the day we met him. It was quite a move for us because Joe was the lead singer of the 101'ers. We thought he was the best performer out there. For us to even approach him ... we were nowhere at that time. It was to Joe's great credit that he saw the way things were going.'

In that bedroom just off the Uxbridge Road, Levene played Strummer's 'Keys to Your Heart', then the trio ran through Jones' '1-2 Crush on You' and 'Protex Blue'. Strummer was impressed, not least by Simonon's moves and Levene's look. Later that evening, he knocked on bandmate Richard Dudanski's bedroom door, wanting to tell him all about the rehearsal, his decision to leave the 101'ers and why he thought Richard should join him.

Mick Jones recalled in *Westway to the World*, 'We were nervous. I was anyway. We went in this really tiny room. We all sat around with our guitars, then said 'This is one of ours ... 1-2-3-4! I'm so bored with you'.' To which, Strummer reckons, 'I said, 'Never mind all that. Let's write it now – 'I'm So Bored With the USA'. And he went, 'I didn't say that. This is a song about my girlfriend.'' Of course, like most of those key events, that's also disputed, but Jones added, 'Then we went to an ice cream parlour in Edgware Road, all bought ice creams and then wrote 'I'm So Bored With the USA' on the window with ice creams. We were always talking about how there were too many McDonald's, although we'd been brought up with American TV shows and all that. There was still too much of an American influence.'

Reliving that first rehearsal, Jones told John Robb, 'It was a really natural thing. Straight away we clicked. We started playing one of our tunes. It was just like that. He had little bits to put in. It worked straight away.'

At that stage, Jones and Simonon were regulars at Davis Road, hanging out in what was described in one account as a one-bedroom maisonette. It was five minutes from Mick's art college in Lime Grove. The guitarist was living with his gran but staying over at Davis Road with his girlfriend, Viv Albertine, future member of The Slits, a fellow art school student he'd befriended at a Roxy Music show the previous year. That address played host to many key players on London's pre-punk scene, including John Lydon's friend John Ritchie, soon to be better known as Sid Vicious. Mick Jones told Pat Gilbert, 'Sid and Paul would go shoplifting to get us food. We would be sitting there starving, so they'd go out to buy a packet of cigarettes and come back with a couple of tins of beans. They were like the hunters, scavenging for our dinner.'

Gilbert also recalled that Simonon cycled over from Notting Hill every day for his lessons. Jones was now teaching him bass, having abandoned the idea of Paul playing guitar after much frustration, and borrowing the new acquisition from Jones' friend Tony James. Keith Levene was also a regular, having met Jones at his Warrington Crescent base, one of many practice locations, which also included Riverside Studios, Hammersmith and the Pistols' Denmark Street HQ.

Along for the ride with Strummer was old school friend Pablo LaBritain, who sat in on drums during the following rehearsals before joining 999. At that point Terry Chimes joined The Clash, even though Mick Jones said in *Westway to the World*, 'I don't think Terry was officially hired or anything. He'd just been playing with us.' Besides, according to Phil Strongman in 2007's *Pretty Vacant: A History of Punk*, Chimes didn't take a shine to the band's poached lead singer, saying, 'He was like 22, 23 or something that seemed old to me. And he had these retro clothes and this croaky voice.'

Strummer himself told Jon Savage for *England's Dreaming*, 'For about a week we were the Psychotic Negatives, then the Weak Heartdrops, after a Big Youth lyric. Then Paul thought of The Clash.' And as the bass player put it in a 1991 MTV interview, 'It really came to my head when I started reading the newspapers and a word that kept recurring was the word 'clash'. I thought, 'The Clash – what about that?' And they and Bernard, they went for it.'

These were key moments for the band, Strummer embracing the idea of getting back to basics, taking that fabled year-zero approach, and upsetting a lot of old friends, blanking old mates – hence that 'almost Stalinist' quote. And as Jones put it in *Westway to the World*, 'He didn't want to do any of his stuff. He really wanted a clean break,' to which Simonon adds how the focus was on 'getting a unity between us'.

Simonon recalled, 'When Joe came to see us at Davis Road we went into the little room to practise, and me and Mick started throwing our guitars about, jumping around. I think Joe enjoyed it. He didn't get that from his other band, where everything they did had to be perfect. With us it was just bash it out, and with me it was pot luck whether I hit E or G, which is why I painted notes on the neck. Mick would say 'G', then I could just go to the G. Mick called it the 'Paul Simonon School of Music' method.'

Strummer added, 'Our equipment was pretty rudimentary. We only needed three amps and cabs. Bernie bought us a PA and three microphones. One of our mics came from the English National Opera. I had a job cleaning the toilets there before joining The Clash. I noticed a microphone high above the stage on the top gantry, for the man up there to talk to the wings or spot operators. One day when there was no one around I climbed up this ladder to the very top with a pair of wire cutters in my overalls. I got hold of the mic, cut the wires, stuffed the mic down the front of my trousers, climbed all the way down again. I was kind of sweating with the excitement, and as I walked through the back corridor, the manager walked towards me. I thought, 'He's sure to notice this microphone down my trousers,' but he just walked straight past. We used that mic in the early days.'

He told a similar tale to Allan Jones, this time involving the Royal Opera House, where he had to 'carry out the rubbish'. He said, 'I only had to work two hours of the day. There was this hole in the basement, where I'd creep off to play guitar. The manager found me and fired me. He gave me £120 to get out as soon as possible. So, I went out and scored an AC30. I was working in Hyde Park and met this South American chick who wanted to get married, to stay in the country. She paid me a hundred quid, so I quit the job and got a Telecaster to go with the AC30.' The woman was Pamela Moolman. Strummer helped her obtain UK citizenship, and spent the money she offered him on his trademark Fender, originally in three-colour sunburst with white pickguard, later painted black.

Part of the band's need to express themselves followed the concept explored in 'I'm So Bored With the USA'. Rhodes encouraged them to write about what they knew, and as Strummer explained, 'We were trying to grope in a socialist way towards some future where the world might be less of a miserable place than it is.' Strummer told Jon Savage in 1992, 'Bernie would say, 'An issue, an issue. Don't write about love, write about what's affecting you, what's important.' As Tony Parsons put it, 'Mick lived in a tower block with his granny, looked down on the Westway, and you wondered what was going to happen to your life and your town and your country. Tower blocks and urban alienation, and disaffected youth, and all that – that all came from somewhere real.'

That unity came partly through the band adopting Mick's gran's Wilmcote House flat, and partly through the setting up of the band's rather basic HQ in Camden Town, on the first floor of a former railway goods warehouse let to Rhodes, known as Rehearsal Rehearsals. (Jones says in *Westway to the World*, 'I don't know why it was called Rehearsal Rehearsals. I always thought it was a kind of Jewish thing.')

'Rather basic' is a major understatement, as can be seen in Julien Temple's BBC Four film, *The Clash: New Year's Day '77*, built around early footage of the band. Simonon says in *Westway to the World*, 'There was a one-bar heater. I'd spend a lot of time huddled over it, gobbing on it.' Two prominent members of the road crew had their own take on those grim surroundings. Steve Connolly, rechristened 'Roadent' by the band, told Jon Savage, 'We stole electricity from next door. We had a one-bar electric fire, three sheets and one blanket, and there was me, Paul and Joe staying there. Fortunately, Joe didn't have a sense of smell. The sheets never got washed. We'd get turns with the sofa. It was uncomfortable, but you don't remember things like that.' Meanwhile, Barry Cain, reliving his days writing for *Record Mirror* and getting to properly know the band at their Chalk Farm Road base, told of 'a tumbleweed connection stuffed with bravado'.

Roadent's successor, Johnny Green, paints a vivid picture in *A Riot of Our Own: Night and Day with The Clash*, remembering a desolate landscape where Paul and Topper rode 'up and down the tunnels behind the railway track, goofing around' on a 'little pop-pop moped ... like the kids that they were'. Of one typical day, he wrote, 'It was cold and damp, as always, and the strip lighting made it seem colder. There were electric fires, but we might as well have just lit matches for all the effect they had. There was no daylight in the rehearsal room, just a row of barber chairs that were too damp to sit on. These stood against the back wall, on which Paul had painted a bleak mural of the Westway and a car dump. There was a jukebox, with an eclectic range of music, from the earliest Elvis to obscure ska and reggae, but to everyone's frustration, it didn't work anymore. The room was tiny, but all the gear was laid out as if on stage. I didn't realise until other roadies came round to see me that other bands rehearsed quietly and comfortably. To me, and The Clash, it seemed natural to rehearse at full pelt, as if doing a gig.'

Joe Strummer backstage at The Roxy on New Year's Day, 1977

On that jukebox, Jones recalls favourites like 'Pressure Drop', 'Two Sevens Clash' and 'MPLA' by Tapper Zukie playing, songs which the band would then tackle in rehearsals. Meanwhile, Strummer mentions in *Westway to the World*, 'Paul was practising bass to reggae songs and the first Ramones album, which was seminal. It can't be stressed how great the first Ramones album was to the scene because it gave anyone who couldn't play the idea that it was simple enough to be able to play. We all used to practise along with it. Paul and I spent hours, days, weeks playing along to the record. Anyone could see where the notes went. It gave everyone confidence.

It was the first word of punk, a fantastic record.'

At that stage it was really about the four of them. Paul saw himself as 'the bloke who jumped up and down and threw his arms around'. Levene was also in the mix, and Strummer said, 'Mick could always play really great and I could hack into that. We didn't have a drummer really. It was all new, all built from the ground up.'

That said, Terry Chimes became a regular player, if not officially hired, and in *Westway to the World* said of the band he sat in with, 'There was something different about them. I didn't particularly like them, but there was something about the way they did things. They were saying, 'We mean business. We are going to get there. Nothing's gonna stop us.'' Yet Strummer felt Chimes 'was a bit freaked out by our kind of lunatic, overboard Stalinist type of behaviour.' Simonon added, 'We used to have a lot of political discussions about our lives and how things affected us. I think that concerned Terry.' Dismissing the assertion that he'd only 'got into music so he could get a Lamborghini sports car', as Strummer put it, Chimes recalled, 'I don't remember the Lamborghini. I think it was an E-Type Jag actually! The point was that I wanted one kind of life and they wanted another, so why are we working together if we want completely different things?'

One thing was certain, Strummer enthused, 'We were like sticks of dynamite. We could go off any minute.' Simonon recalled how Keith Levene's approach 'was always from another angle to Mick's, and it really made an interesting sound'. Yet that wasn't to last much longer. Jones reckoned, 'Keith left because he couldn't be bothered to come to rehearsals. Then Joe said, 'Don't bother coming at all then!'' That too is disputed, but Levene would nevertheless be around a bit longer. Simonon, though, was not content to wait around in the wings. As the fledgling bass player put it, 'Bernie would say, 'Paul – you stand further back over there.' I'd ignore him and said, 'Not if I'm gonna be Pete Townshend.' I would stick up the front. I suppose when Keith left that was probably quite handy for me. I had my spot.'

Sex Pistols/The Clash, the Black Swan, Sheffield, July 4, 1976

'Things went wrong during the evening, and Mick had to come over and tune my guitar, but it didn't bother me. I just wanted to jump around, but Mick wanted it to be in tune.'
Paul Simonon, The Clash: Strummer, Jones, Simonon, Headon, 2008

If it seems odd that two rival bands, not least with the perceived needle between Pistols manager Malcolm McLaren and Clash manager Bernie Rhodes, should set out on a 300-plus-mile-round trip to South Yorkshire for a one-off concert, it's worth noting the undeniable feeling within the UK punk rock scene and the idea of creating a revolutionary force within the industry. As Strummer put it in *Westway to the World*, 'You had to be in league with each other. There were so many enemies.' This was about camaraderie, despite the obvious competition simmering beneath the surface.

Known locally as the Mucky Duck, and later becoming The Boardwalk (closed in 2010), the Black Swan on Snig Hill, Sheffield, was a regular stop-off point for London pub rockers like Brinsley Schwarz, Ducks Deluxe and Dr Feelgood. That was before punk took off, and in the long, hot summer of '76, the venue played host to a Sex Pistols/Clash show. In the process Mick Jones beat fellow ex-London SS bandmate Brian James to the stage by two days, with The Damned supporting the same headliners at the 100 Club. The Clash's live debut – the first of an estimated 600 or so gigs – was to be their only appearance that month – Rhodes' idea by all accounts. There were probably only a handful of people present, although eyewitnesses reported a sizeable crowd amid that summer's sweltering drought conditions. On the same day that the United States celebrated the bicentennial of its revolution against the British, tensions were already building in both band camps, and that night a disaffected Keith Levene approached the singer known as Johnny Rotten with a view to joining forces if the Pistols broke up, something they would do within a couple of years when Lydon launched Public Image Ltd.

Jones told John Robb's *Louder Than War* website, 'We went in the back of a removal truck, with the gear piled next to us. We all sat in the back. It had a gate on the back, open like an old army truck. It was quite hairy! The gig was in the back room of a pub. There were 50 people there, a couple of punks. It was interesting. Wherever you went, you could see a couple of them in the early times, then you'd see more all the time. They would tell their friends. It was a big thing. Very often people got it completely wrong, but in a way, you couldn't get it wrong. It wasn't formed. We were just starting to find out what it could be. When you're young you think about it after in the post-match analysis! By the time everyone had sussed it, it was already over.

'We were dressed in black and white. A couple of us had ties on. Black and white shirts with suity bits. It was punky style. Not good suits. A bit ripped, tight, slightly different. We would dress fairly straight and well behaved in a way. Maybe a little rip here, splash of colour here, a couple of pin-type things. Not safety pins. The look was still formulating. There was a bit of paint dribbled here and there. It had come off when we had to paint the rehearsal room. We got the paint from the car-spray place just over the road. Bernie was involved in garages. He used to go down there and get spray. We started spray-painting all the amps pink, and as we were painting everything we were getting covered in paint.

'I guess that was our first look. Also, Glen (Matlock) has a claim to this as well, because he had a pair of trousers that were paint-splattered, à la Pollock. So, he should take a bit of credit for it. The style thing came naturally through Paul. We were all into the style, especially Paul and I. Joe not so much, but we would always encourage each other.'

Paul Simonon, in *The Clash: Strummer, Jones, Simonon, Headon*, said, 'It was the first time I ever played on stage. The night before it felt frightening but once we were on the way I began larking about. I tied one of Keith's shoes to a piece of string and hung it out of the back of the van. The door had to be open anyway so we could breathe. There we were, sitting with all the amps and luggage, with a plimsoll bouncing around behind us, all the cars behind us slowing down to avoid it. But the moment we walked out on stage it was like I was in my own living room. I felt really comfortable.'

In *Westway to the World*, the band mention Simonon messing up the instrumental intro of 'Listen' due to nerves, leading to an on-stage crack-up, his bandmates unsure where to come in. And Strummer, using the microphone he'd made that death-defying climb to liberate from the English National Opera two years earlier, gave an account to Jon Savage for *England's Dreaming*, saying, 'It was a Sunday, but 200 people turned up. They were very receptive.'

Keith Levene added, 'I remember John (Lydon) sitting miles away from the rest of the band members, looking miserable. And there's me sitting in another corner away from all my band members, looking miserable. I walk over to Lydon and talk to him. We knew each other, but don't *know* each other because we're the rival bands. We're both in the same scene but knew we were the best bands on the scene at the time. I said, 'I'm out of here after this gig.' Turns out I was, a few gigs later, after The Roundhouse show. 'Do you want to get a band together if the Pistols ever end? Though it doesn't look like it at the moment. It looks like you could be the next Beatles. But if it ever changes. And there's no way I'm going to be in a band with Steve Jones.''

The Clash played around a dozen songs, including the 101'ers 'Rabies (From the Dogs of Love)' and Mick Jones' 'Ooh, Baby, Ooh (It's Not Over)', neither of which would feature in their live show again. A fortnight later, there followed a review in the *NME* in the form of a letter from Reg Cliff – although there was speculation suggesting it was written by someone in the band's immediate circle to drum up publicity. It read, 'I went to see the Sex Pistols and Clash (formerly 101'ers) for the first time. I was very, very disappointed. Both bands were crap. It's enough to turn you on to Demis Roussos. Clash were just a cacophonous brigade of noise. The bass guitarist had no idea how to play the instrument and even had to get another member of the band to tune it for him. They tried to play early '60s R'n'B and failed dismally. Dr Feelgood are not one of my favourite bands but I know they could have wiped the floor with The Clash.' Yet, he added, 'The Sex Pistols were even worse.'

Lydon had his own take on the gig in the 1994 autobiography *Rotten*, saying, 'Strummer and the rest of them had a horrible attitude at that gig. Keith Levene was in the band and was the only one who could actually hold a decent conversation with us. Malcolm and Bernie were competing, so Bernie was revving this band to take a very anti-Pistols stance – as if they were the real kings of punk. I've never liked The Clash. They weren't good songwriters. They'd run out of steam halfway through their gigs, because they would go so mad at the beginning. The Sex Pistols learned dynamics on stage. I credit Paul for that. He could break the tempo down. Strummer would start everything off and from there on in it was just full-on speed. That's not good enough, because you're not saying anything just by being fast. You can't dance to it, and you can hardly listen to it. It's unpleasant after half an hour.

'To me The Clash looked and sounded like they were yelling at themselves about nothing in particular – a few trendy slogans stolen here and there from Karl Marx. The Clash introduced the competitive element that dragged everything down a little. It was never about that for us. We never saw ourselves as being in a punk movement. We saw ourselves as just the Pistols. What the rest of them were up to was neither here nor there. Quite frankly, they weren't there in the beginning. They laid none of the groundwork. They just came in and sat on our coat tails.'

While mellowing in certain respects, Lydon still had little praise for The Clash when he spoke to Barry Cain in 2007 for *77 Sulphate Strip*, saying, 'I always thought The Clash were a rip-off of Bernie Rhodes vs Malcolm McLaren and nothing to do with the bands. I loved The Clash as people, and always will. Just wonderful people. But it didn't mean I had to like their music. It was political sloganeering. I thought it was wrong for them. Mick Jones was someone I knew anyway from The Roundhouse. He was one of the kids who used to bunk in. Mick was Jimmy Page. He actually tried out to be the Sex Pistols' guitarist. Mick Jones was always around. I remember turning up at The Roundhouse when Osibisa were playing and Mick Jones got in because he was part of the Osibisa crowd. I thought, how the hell did he do that?'

He added, 'Joe had this ridiculous cockney accent that wasn't quite right. He used to really drive me crazy. What the hell are you talking about, Joe? This is where Joe Strummer ended up in a house in the country as a lord. He did everything wrong. Joe became the landed gentry, and that was irrefutably wrong. It's nice to earn it, but it's not nice to buy it. Beyond that little world or schism, it was really ridiculous. There'd be Joe Strummer running around with all the posh towels, the steel towel rail people. It was awful trying to get past their middle-class sensibilities. We'd still be banned in clubs where the likes of Joe was accepted because he had, what, ambassador credentials?'

'One, Two, Three, Four...' – the Passion and the Fashion

'We used to take jackets to the car spray shop in the railway arches around the corner and say, 'OK Pete, give us a spray."
Joe Strummer to Jon Savage, England's Dreaming, 1991

On the same night The Clash debuted in Sheffield with the Pistols, 150 miles further south another pivotal moment in the punk story was taking place. New York's Ramones played their biggest gig to date, their first UK show, at The Roundhouse, Chalk Farm, supporting the Flamin' Groovies. Their next was the following night, less than half a mile away at Dingwall's, Camden, the audience including Marco Pirroni, The Damned's Captain Sensible and Rat Scabies, Subway Sect's Vic Godard, and The Stranglers' Jean-Jacques Burnel, who ended up in a fight with Paul Simonon, back from Yorkshire.

Burnel told *Louder Than War*, 'There was that incident with Paul Simonon at Dingwall's, which didn't help with us and the punk elite. The other bands were a bit pissed off we'd been chosen to represent London at the July 4 bicentennial gig. We were the first to play with the Ramones and Patti Smith, and that pissed a few people off. We were out of the inner circle after that. That did us immense favours in the long term. We evolved on our own, as if we'd been in Australia for millions of years, like weird animals.'

Vic Godard told John Robb, 'That was an important gig. I remember Joe Strummer being right down the front. Talking Heads were the support and we were there to see them mainly. McLaren came up and said,

'You look like you are in a band.' We were wearing Oxfam clothes dyed dark grey to make it all look really drab. It was our look. The big influence were these Polish films that had post-war grimy look about them. McLaren told us to form a group.'

Back at nearby Rehearsal Rehearsals, Strummer and Jones were hard at work, the latter putting Strummer's words to music, sometimes in the office above their base. Most of the time, Strummer provided lead vocals, but occasionally they shared those duties or Mick led. Meanwhile, Simonon was playing his part, not least working on the look. As he explained, 'I got some gloss paint, got my shoes and splashed a bit here and there, took it a bit further, got this black shirt, did a bit on that with a different paint. It was all about a wealth of textures, all that arty stuff. It became sort of a Rauschenberg thing.'

Part of that style involved slogans – some of the more politically motivated examples taken from Strummer's lyrics – picked out by stencils and spray-on paint. As the lead singer put it in *Westway to the World*, 'Like trousers, like brain. That was the difference from the flared look, kind of a hangover from the '60s, and the new look, which was more fast and trim and going places.' It did bring conflict though, Jones recalling, 'I was being chased by some Teddy Boys and one of them whacked me over the back of the head as I was fleeing.' But as Simonon stressed, it was a DIY enterprise: 'The thing with The Clash was we didn't have any shop to rely on. The Pistols had it already sewn up for them ... literally!'

But Strummer told Jon Savage for *England's Dreaming*, 'All the stuff about Pollock was a veneer. What happened was that Bernie rented that British Rail warehouse in Camden Town, and we painted it. We didn't have any overalls, so got covered in paint. It was a good way to put together something to wear on the stage, as we didn't have the back-up of the Sex boutique. We had to adapt what we could find in the second-hand shops, which was really horrible.'

Vic Godard, whose band Subway Sect would soon be sharing Rehearsal Rehearsals, told John Robb, 'The Clash looked really good. The first time we saw them was not at a gig but watching the Sex Pistols. They walked in and looked really good. The only one we knew was Joe, and we knew this was Joe's new band. Paul Simonon didn't have all the painted gear then. He just looked like a really good version of us – the same sort of clothes that we wore. You could tell they were a band from the way they looked. Same with the Pistols – they looked like a band.'

Mick Jones added, 'It was never a planned look. It was much more of a natural thing. Bernie gave us the right outlook. That's the best way to describe it. Bernie had a hand in everything. Not the lyrics. He didn't help with the lyrics. He didn't tell us not to write love songs, as the myth goes. That's kind of a simplified version of it. He told us to write about what we knew about. Joe came from a squat background. He was always questioning things anyway. But Bernie helped us put it in the right context. Bernie helped us formulate ourselves.'

Don Letts also recognised Rhodes' influence, adding, 'Malcolm and Bernie were of the same ilk. They had a knowledge of counterculture. That's why these people are important. They could see the idea manifesting itself before its musical expression. That's why you get all this thing with Malcolm and the Situationists. That's where he got a lot of his ideas and sloganeering. You can't just write these people off. They gave punk depth, a bit of bollocks. It wasn't just the rantings and ravings of angry youth. There was a method behind it and it manifested itself in different ways. Whoever said the Pistols made you want to smash your head against the wall and The Clash gave you a reason for doing it, was so right.'

Caroline Coon, in John's Lydon's 1994 autobiography, *Rotten: No Irish, No Blacks, No Dogs*, was less convinced by Rhodes, saying, 'Malcolm and Bernie were anti-intellectual. That's why they went into Situationist politics. Situationist politics is merely sloganeering, second-rate sloganeering at that, all pulled out of the '60s dustbin. There was a positive side, it being graphically quite interesting. Yet it was also incoherent.'

The early look was truly showcased – although Mick Jones suggested there were hints at Sheffield – when the band played a second gig on August 13, an invitation-only set arranged by Rhodes to present The Clash to booking agents and press at Rehearsal Rehearsals. Three journalists showed – *Sounds*' Jonh Ingham and Giovanni Dadomo, and *Melody Maker*'s Caroline Coon – all of whom became early champions of the band. The Clash took the opportunity to unveil their Pollock-/Rauschenberg-influenced paint-splashed stage gear. Strummer said, 'We sprayed guitars, amps, jackets, trousers, shoes. We came out and must have looked fairly striking ... if not somewhat ridiculous.'

Dadomo was certainly impressed, describing them as a 'runaway train ... so powerful, they're the first new group to come along who can really scare the Sex Pistols shitless'. He also mentioned the image, 'as much the antithesis of the bearded be-denimed latter-day hippies as Mods were to Rockers. Clash have plenty of that old Mod flash too.' With Simonon's car dump mural as the backdrop, the gig made for a memorable occasion, with many more following. The band were soon championed by Mark Perry's *Sniffin' Glue* fanzine as well as garnering interest from the more tuned-in writers of the established music press.

Ari Up, who went on to co-form The Slits, was at Rehearsal Rehearsals that day, telling John Robb, 'After that I was never the same. I realised how important it was for them to spray their clothes. I came round, cut up and sprayed all my clothes. I had all these hippy schoolgirl clothes. I looked like a tidied-up hippy with long hair, and thought, 'Fuck, I really look corny putting on my first set of punk clothes.' I made them myself. I didn't do it very sophisticated.'

The Clash's third show – the first public appearance in their home city – was on August 29 at the Screen on the Green arthouse cinema, Islington, with the Pistols headlining. A recording later came to light of this 'Midnight Special' event, organised by Malcolm McLaren with Nils Stevenson to showcase the Pistols to the press, and advertised by the first Jamie Reid-designed hand-bill, featuring silhouettes of John Lydon and Mick Jones. Seen as a dry run for the 100 Club Punk Festival, the groups played after the evening's film screenings. Kenneth Anger's *Kustom Kar Kommandos* and *Scorpio Rising* were followed by The Buzzcocks, making their London debut, The Clash, then the Pistols. Both supports were beset by sound problems, which improved during the Pistols' set, Glen Matlock among those who later suggested sabotage.

There was little punk camaraderie, Strummer admitting his band were 'mean' to the Buzzcocks, whose manager, Richard Boon, told Jon Savage, 'The Clash went out into the alleyway to get dressed, so no one could see they were wearing slogans and paint splatter. There was that urge to secure their turf.' Savage added, 'Guided by a Bernard Rhodes in hot competition with McLaren, The Clash were being carefully groomed for stardom.' But Strummer said, 'We weren't very good that night, because we'd been up very early, up and loading the scaffolding and building the stage.' To add to their woes, they were savaged in an *NME* review by Charles Shaar Murray, who wrote, 'The Clash are the sort of garage band that should be speedily returned to the garage, preferably with the motor still running.' It was a review that hit a nerve and would ultimately inspire one of their finest moments.

Future Adam and the Ants guitarist Marco Pirroni was there; he told John Robb, 'I thought The Clash were great, completely different from the Pistols, who were slower. The '1-2-3-4-rah-rah-rah' thing hadn't happened yet. They were menacing whilst The Clash were manic. The Pistols were more of a sneer. I think I preferred the sneer really, although I liked both sides – the sneer and the boredom. At that time, boredom was the big pose, not being angry – everything is boring.'

Don Letts added, 'I didn't know what the fuck they were saying. The PAs were really bad, but it was this fucking energy. It was a revelation, hearing The Clash's 'Janie Jones' and all this stuff. I was transfixed. It was looking into the Ark of the Covenant. All these guys I'd seen sloping around in my shop, facing me off, were up there doing it, and it don't seem that big a leap.'

Vic Godard was also impressed, telling Robb, 'Lots of bands work to a blueprint. I used to like The Clash when they played the same speed as bands on *Nuggets*. When they heard The Ramones, their songs speeded up overnight. I got a brilliant tape of them at Screen on the Green with the Pistols on the other side. Both bands sound a lot better. All the Clash songs were much slower than on the album, and there are some good tunes that never made it onto their album. Keith Levene in that era was great. When they got rid of him they changed dramatically. I like that '60s garage sound they had, more like The Seeds and Shadows of the Night. They got into a heavier sound after that. Same with the Pistols. They were much better before they bought their first proper amps. They always had crappy equipment when we used to go and see them.'

Creating a Riot of Their Own

'Chaos was breaking out all over the Grove. Ladbroke Grove was lined with rebels, and cop cars were speeding through. These were Rover 2000s being pelted with rocks and cobblestones and cans as they came through. It was like a bowling alley.'

Strummer to Jon Savage, England's Dreaming, 1991

The following day, August Bank Holiday Monday, marked an event that inspired a Clash classic and proved a major milestone for the band, with Strummer and Simonon caught up in the disturbances that marred the final day of the Notting Hill Carnival. On a hot day towards the end of that summer's drought, tensions were running high, in large part due to the Metropolitan Police's 'stop and search' policy. With an estimated 1,600 police officers – eight times the usual number – assigned to the carnival, the spark came when officers attempted to arrest an alleged pickpocket near Portobello Road. Carnival-goers – black and white – came to his aid and within minutes the incident escalated. Some witnesses said the presence of white fascist gangs also contributed to the mayhem. Strummer and Simonon were with Bernie Rhodes, 'under the Westway, checking out all the sound systems', when things took a turn, according to Simonon. Most of the visitors had gone by 5pm, leaving a hardcore of youth. When the police moved in to make the arrest, all hell broke loose, in the first major riot mainland Britain had seen since the riots in 1958. It saw 456 injured and 60 arrests. As Strummer saw it, a 'conga line of policemen came through the crowd', a shower of missiles following, first 'paper cups' and 'then cans', according to Simonon.

Strummer said, 'We were there at the very first throw of the very first brick. All hell broke loose, and I mean hell. The crowd parted, and we were pushed onto wire fencing.' Simonon added, 'There was police everywhere, and they literally just charged. Bernie's glasses went over there, I was over here, and Joe was chucked upside down.' After ducking into The Elgin for a drink, then returning, seeing Simonon throwing a plastic cone at a police motorbike, Strummer was questioned by fellow rioters, soon realising all the white faces had gone. In *Westway to the World*, he added, 'This was one time that people said, 'We've had enough and we're going to say so, now!' That's what gave rise to the song 'White Riot', because we participated in the riot, but I was aware all the time it was a black people's riot. They had more of an axe to grind, and they had the guts to do something physical about it.'

It was already clear that the influence of West Indian culture was an important part of what The Clash were about, not just the reggae they were hearing in the capital, but the visual aspects of various records coming from Jamaica, such as Big Youth's *Screaming Target*. That summer – not least at Notting Hill Carnival – Junior Murvin's 'Police & Thieves', co-written with future band associate Lee 'Scratch' Perry, really resonated with the Clash, leading to their decision to later cover that track.

The following day, The Clash supported the Pistols at Oxford Street's 100 Club. There, during a pause between songs while Keith Levene replaced a broken string, Strummer switched on a transistor radio 'bought in a junk shop for 10 bob' and, without talking to the audience, held it up to the microphone, soundman Dave Goodman adding heavy dub echo as a news report discussed an IRA bomb scare. Talking to Q magazine in 1999, Strummer recalled, 'It sounded like a Radio 4 discussion at the end of the world. To this day Julie Burchill and Tony Parsons refuse to believe it wasn't a setup.'

Then There Were Four: Keith Levene's Exit

'It was a really exciting time in London, a proper buzz. This was my first indulgence in some sort of scene; somewhere between pub rock and punk and the remains of an old hippie happening.'
Rick Buckler, That's Entertainment: My Life In The Jam, 2015

Keith Levene's final show with the band was on September 5 at The Roundhouse, supporting the Kursaal Flyers. On a bootleg tape of the gig Strummer can be heard ranting at the audience, 'I suppose you think you can pay your £1.50 and just come in and sit down as if it's a fucking TV set. Get off your denims. You might wear them out!' As Keith Topping pointed out in *The Complete Clash*, 'Despite being only The Clash's fifth gig, this was a thoroughly tight performance. Significantly, it also demonstrated Strummer's efforts at engaging an, if not openly hostile then at least pretty indifferent, audience.'

In 2001, Levene recalled of his time in that version of the band, 'I was contributing to the

1

ANARCHY
IN THE U.K.
PUNK
special
100 CLUB
100 OXFORD ST.
Monday SEPTEMBER 20
SEX PISTOLS
CLASH
SUB WAY SECT
SUZIE AND THE BANSHEES
AND FROM FRANCE
STINKY TOYS
OPEN 7 PM LATE BAR
ADMISSION £1.50
(£1.00 NUS ETC.)
7P.M LATE BAR
Sex Pistols

helter-skelter factor, to the velocity of how the songs were played.' Tony Parsons and Julie Burchill suggested in *The Boy Looked at Johnny* that Levene was too involved with a heroin habit to continue, something he has always denied. Meanwhile, Strummer claimed Levene's speed intake was a factor, saying, 'His weekend would go on until Tuesday and he wouldn't show up for rehearsals, so he kind of walked out by himself. I thought Keith was brilliant but I realised he had other eggs to fry.' Again, Levene denied that, telling John Robb, 'It's always said, 'Keith got thrown out of The Clash because of drugs.' That's bollocks. The reason I left was because I was too depressed being in the band. They were just too lame for me. I'd start turning up at rehearsals and really being a miserable git. I wasn't saying anything, just playing the numbers fine. When Mick wasn't there, we'd work out something of mine, then the next rehearsal we'd get there, and it would be a completely different version. That version could have been another song. We could have kept the one I'd worked on, kept what they worked on and called it something else. There seemed to be a 'my way/your way' of doing things.'

Whatever the truth, one thing both parties agree on is that the final straw appeared to be Levene refusing to come in the day Strummer told him they were rehearsing their new song. Strummer told Jon Savage, 'He rang up when we were doing 'White Riot' and said, 'What are you working on? 'White Riot'? Well, there's no need for me to come up then, is there.' I said, 'Make that never, man!' Bernie was shocked, but Mick was pleased. Keith and he were in competition about who was going to be the lead guitar player.' Levene confirmed to John Robb, 'I said, 'I'm not fucking singing "White Riot'. You're joking!' That line, 'No Elvis, Beatles or the Rolling Stones' in '1977' was bad enough for me. We were just about to make the first record. There was a rehearsal where they're in one room and I'm on my own in another. I wasn't on any drugs or anything. I was being real miserable, giving off a bad vibe. They'd say, 'What the fuck is up with you?' I said, 'If you really want to know, it's as simple as this – this band is either Mick's band or my band. You either do it my way or Mick's way. I think I've got to leave this band, because you're already doing it Mick's way, and that's fine. The band's really getting me down.'

'When it came to drugs, yeah, we were doing a bit of speed. I could handle my comedowns. Joe used to have terrible comedowns. But it wasn't about drugs. They weren't the band I wanted them to be. I didn't like the clothes they wore. I liked Bernard, I didn't like any of the tunes on the first album, even the one I wrote, 'What's My Name' – it wasn't hard enough. So, we had this little vote, very quickly. Mick said, 'I want him out.' Joe said, 'I want him in.' Paul just went with the flow of the band, so I was out. Terry Chimes for some reason didn't get a vote.'

On September 20, The Clash strode out on stage at the 100 Club in Wardour Street, Soho, as a four-piece for the first time – Strummer, Jones, Simonon and Chimes – for the opening day of a 'punk special' also featuring the Sex Pistols, first-timers Siouxsie and the Banshees – with Sid Vicious on drums and Marco Pirroni on guitar – and Subway Sect, the latter now also under Bernie Rhodes' wing and sharing Rehearsal Rehearsals. McLaren's latest attempt to interest record companies in the emerging scene attracted an estimated 500 intrigued punters. Don Letts filmed some of the festival, and a brief clip appears in *Westway to the World*.

A *Trouser Press* review read, 'Clash sound quite promising. They have the required attack and energy, but the content is too disparate at the moment, and no clear identity comes across. They play mostly original songs, which aren't as strong as they might be. Hopefully after a few months' gigging they will have gotten over this.' *NME*'s Geoff Hill wrote about a 'powerful, tight and varied set. Their numbers are short and to the point, and they perform as if they actually dig rock music. If they stick together they'll soon be looking as hopeful as the Hot Rods.' There was a stand-off between debutants Siouxsie and the Banshees and Bernie Rhodes at one stage, the latter rightly taking exception at Siouxsie and Sid wearing swastikas. Then, on day two of the festival, Vicious was again the centre of attention after throwing a glass which shattered on a concrete post and caused several injuries. Unproven press reports later suggested that a girl lost an eye as a result. It would be 24 years before Strummer returned to play the same venue, for an emotional sell-out show with The Mescaleros.

Recalling the event in *England's Dreaming*, Jon Savage wrote, 'From his grandmother's flat on the Warwick and Brindley estate, Clash guitarist Mick Jones had an eagle-eye view of a whole stretch of inner London, Harrow Road, North Kensington and Paddington, dominated by the elevated Westway and blocks like the massive Trellick Tower, that looms over the whole of Portobello Road and Ladbroke Grove. This was their stretch, marked where the Westway passes over the Harrow Road by a graffito, 'The Clash', that remained there, fading slowly for years after the group's vigorous life was over. The Clash's urban hyperrealism was quickly overlaid by a more conventional sense of social relevance. By the time of the Punk Rock Festival, the songs about school and love went out and in came 'Career Opportunities', 'Janie Jones' and 'I'm So Bored With the USA', their set framed by brand new songs, '1977' and 'White Riot'.'

The reviews kept coming, and on October 9 the band played a leisure centre in Leighton Buzzard. Jones' old mate, fellow Mott the Hoople follower Kris Needs, wrote in *ZigZag*, 'The Clash taking the stage was like an injection of electricity into the smoky air. They charged head-long into 'White Riot' with a shattering energy, strutting and leaping like clockwork robots out of control.' A week later, they played an unlikely support slot for Shakin' Stevens and the Sunsets at the University of London, where the student audience was complemented by Teds gatecrashing the show to see the main act. Legend has it that part way into The Clash's performance, a large greaser approached the stage and held up a five-pence coin, saying, 'Here's your bus fare home.'

Earlier that day, The Clash had seen the first London performance by their future competition, The Jam, who played an outdoor set at Soho Market. It wasn't the first time The Jam had met Strummer, drummer Rick Buckler saying in 2015's *That's Entertainment: My Life in The Jam*, 'We did come across the 101'ers once, and this was because The Jam were booked to play at the same venue as them. I think it was at the Hope and Anchor. Once they turned up, the promoter told us we had to go home, explaining that they had been booked first. Back then, there were so many bands that promoters could book two on the basis that if one didn't turn up the other could play. This way the venue would always have a band. Some of these promoters thought nothing of telling a band to fuck off once they arrived, no matter how far they had come. Although we were pissed off that we couldn't play, we reloaded our gear back into the van, but we did stay to hear the 101'ers' soundcheck.

'SNIFFIN' GLUE...
AND OTHER ROCK'N' ROLL HABITS,
FOR THE NEW-WAVE! (4) OCT'76.'

What,this isn't a joke,if you want something funny buy MAD.Anyway,this issue is priceless.

THE CLASH

BUZZCOCKS ✱ SAINTS ✱ PATTI SMITH NEW LP.

I remember having a conversation with Joe Strummer, but at the time he was just another musician from another band, and one who had nicked our slot too.

'Next time I saw Joe was at Soho Market when The Jam set up our gear and played a few songs in the street. Joe and two other members from The Clash, Mick Jones and Paul Simonon, ambled down to see us play. We thought by doing the Soho thing it would achieve either one of two things. We would get mentioned in the music press or we would get arrested.' As it was, the police just listened, but a press mention followed, including a plug for a 100 Club date on November 9. Buckler added, 'What the Soho thing did was give us all more of an appetite to get more involved with what was going on in London. We had seen The Clash and the Pistols and we saw that it was something we wanted to move into.'

'A Night of Pure Energy' followed, with The Clash headlining London's ICA Theatre. *NME*'s Barry Miles likened their 'spiritual intensity' to The Ramones, but with 'far superior lyrics'. But he devoted more space to an incident involving future Pogues frontman Shane MacGowan and fellow punk Jane Crockford and an incident that – according to Caroline Coon – involved too much alcohol, lots of blood, broken glass, teeth and, as she put it, 'a calm, but no less macabre, love rite'.

In Coon's November 1976 *Melody Maker* interview with The Clash, the model, '60s activist, feminist and artist-turned-music writer gave her account, revealing how the headliners were far from happy with Crockford and MacGowan stealing the headlines. She remembered Strummer telling the crowd, 'All of you who think violence is tough, why don't you go home and collect stamps? That's much tougher.' With that they slammed into 'White Riot', 'played with the force of an acetylene torch'. She added, 'To hammer home their impact, The Clash play with enough committed force to bring down the walls of Babylon, Jericho, Heaven and Hell if necessary,' while conceding, 'their aim is to shake audiences into channelling their frustrations into creative outlets.'

That evening of general chaos even stretched to Patti Smith invading the stage to dance with the band. She told Coon, 'That's what a fan does. I was really excited about The Clash. I thought they were great.' Simonon admitted in *Westway to the World* that he wasn't sure who Smith was when she joined them. It didn't stop him going back to her hotel later though. Mark Stewart, of Bristol punks The Cortinas, and later The Pop Group, told John Robb his band supported Smith at The Roundhouse and took her to see The Clash that night, recalling seeing Simonon 'with little Letraset stickers on his bass telling him where to put his fingers'. He added, 'It's not the arrogance of power, it's the power of arrogance. It's the arrogance to think you don't have to stand there and tip your forelock to people in control. It was the arrogance of Paul Simonon doing that that gave us inspiration. And that inspiration goes down the line.'

NME photographer Red Saunders, later a leading light in Rock Against Racism, added, 'They would collapse after the gigs, exhausted physically and mentally, bleeding hands, blistered fingers, lost voices, covered in job.' Three days later, they played Birmingham nightclub Barbarella's, supporting the Suburban Studs, Jonh Ingham noting, 'Every song is pared to the minimum required to get it across with maximum energy and zero flab.' Another rave review followed from fellow *Sounds* scribe Giovanni Dodomo on October 29, when The Clash supported Roogalator and The Vibrators at Fulham Town Hall. There was also said to be an October '76 gig in Guildford, at a pub disco run by Marmalade's ex-bass player. Strummer told Robin Millar in 1980 that the audience consisted of one lone drunk refugee from the disco below, 'where the bouncers were having the shit kicked out of them by a bunch of squaddies'.

Heading towards Punk's Big Break

'One day you'll wake up and know what side of the bed you're lying on'
T-shirt printed by
Bernie Rhodes, 1976

There was further chaos at the Royal College of Art's Night of Treason on November 5, 1976. The night was marred by violence, 'long-haired types' hurling abuse and glasses at The Clash, prompting Sid Vicious – recently released from Ashford Remand Centre after the glass-throwing incident at the 100 Club – dived into the crowd to lash out, followed by Strummer and Simonon, on a night when the stage was littered with broken glass.

Jon Savage added a philosophical take on the punk scene at the time in *England's Dreaming*, writing: 'Punk began to develop a sociology of its own. The most visible examples of this process were The Clash. The Sex Pistols were located in Soho with a dash of Chelsea, but The Clash were rooted in North Kensington. The Sex Pistols uncompromisingly set themselves apart, while The Clash were warmer and more of the people. If the Sex Pistols implicitly then explicitly advocated the destruction of all values, The Clash were more human, closer to the dialogue of social concern and social realism, more in the world. While the Sex Pistols had been put together the previous year and reflected their time with a sound that was often muddy and sliding, The Clash were brand new that autumn, pin-sharp, straight off the product development line.' He added, 'The Clash began as a classic Mod group: angry, smart, mediated pop. They speeded up the heavily chorded, stuttering sound of The Who and The Kinks and added new variations: the massive galloping beat of Terry Chimes, a minimum of guitar solos, and the plentiful use of 'dropout' – where all the instruments drop away, just leaving the beat – borrowed from the dub reggae you could hear in Shepherd's Bush or Portobello Road markets. And with Joe Strummer they had a great frontman: energetic, tough, humorous, yet compassionate. ... 'London's Burning', '48 Thrills' and 'Protex Blue' were ambiguous celebrations of a new urbanism, as up against the wall of Monday morning, The Clash sped 'up and down the Westway, in and out the lights'. Here was a new map of London, drawn with an innocence and a relish that the Sex Pistols never had.'

Mark Perry, whose *Sniffin' Glue* fanzine backed the band early on, echoed Savage's sentiments while talking to *Uncut* in 2015. He said, 'All that stuff about the Westway, I mean Mick Jones actually lived in a flat overlooking the Westway, so ('London's Burning') just reflects the tension of living in London at that time. Skyscrapers, having the motorway running past your house, y'know what I mean? Literally, London's burning with boredom. It's superb. The Clash had these rallying calls which I think the Sex Pistols would have loved to have had. Apart from 'Anarchy in the UK' and 'God Save the Queen', I don't think the Pistols were that good at describing what it was like to be young, bored and frustrated in London. The Clash did that perfectly with 'London's Burning'.

Caroline Coon was quick to assert the band's political nature, their edge and the highly charged atmosphere that followed them, in her November '76 interview for *Melody Maker*, but made it clear that this was no po-faced outfit, detailing their in-house humour and banter. She wrote, 'Laughter's a cheap luxury when, like The Clash, you never have the money for a square meal and when, like Joe, you live in a squat – or like Paul, you 'crash' in your manager's vast unheated, rehearsal room with no hot water or cooking facilities.'

Reflecting on his decision to join The Clash, Strummer told Coon, 'Yesterday I thought I was a crud. Then I saw the Sex Pistols and became a king and decided to move into the future.' A few months later, he told her, 'As soon as I saw them, I knew rhythm 'n' blues was dead, that the future was here somehow. Every other group was riffing their way through the Black Sabbath catalogue. Hearing the Pistols, I knew. I just knew. It was something you just knew without bothering to think about. It's the music of now. And it's in English. We sing in English, not mimicking some American rock singer's accent. That's just pretending to be something you ain't.'

Mick Jones, speaking on the subject of punk rock, added, 'It's the only music which is about young, white kids. Black kids have it all sewn up. They have their own cultural music. Basically, young white kids are relying on a different time to provide for their kids.' Strummer pointed to a 'Hate and War' slogan – the hippy motto reversed – hand-painted across the shoulders of his boiler suit, saying, 'The hippy movement was a failure. All hippies around now just represent complete apathy. There's a million good reasons why the thing failed. I'm not interested in why. I'll jeer at hippies. That's helpful. They'll realise they're stuck in a rut and maybe get out of it.'

There was conflict within the ranks though. As Coon revealed, 'One of the reasons drummer Terry Chimes is notable for his absence is that he's having a serious argument with Joe. Terry wants to 'get out' of the country while there's still time. Joe thinks he should stick around to see it – the political chaos they see as inevitable – through.' Strummer added, 'There's nowhere to go. Nothing to do. The radio's for housewives. Nothing caters for us. All the laws are against you. Whoever's got money's got the power. The Rent Act's a complete mockery, a big joke. I have to fuck off into the night for somewhere to sleep.'

Simonon added, 'At the moment what the Government should do is put licences on clubs so kids can have somewhere to go. But they're clamping down on that. But it's great, because there's going to be kids on the streets. And they're going to want something to do. And when there ain't nothing to do you wreck up cars and that. The situation beginning to happen now is their fault. If we end up wrecking the place, it's the Government's fault. They'll bring back National Service and we'll all be sent down to South Africa or Rhodesia to protect white capital interest. Then we'll all be slaughtered.'

Questioned by Coon as to why – despite knocking the Establishment – they were still drawing dole, Strummer added, 'We

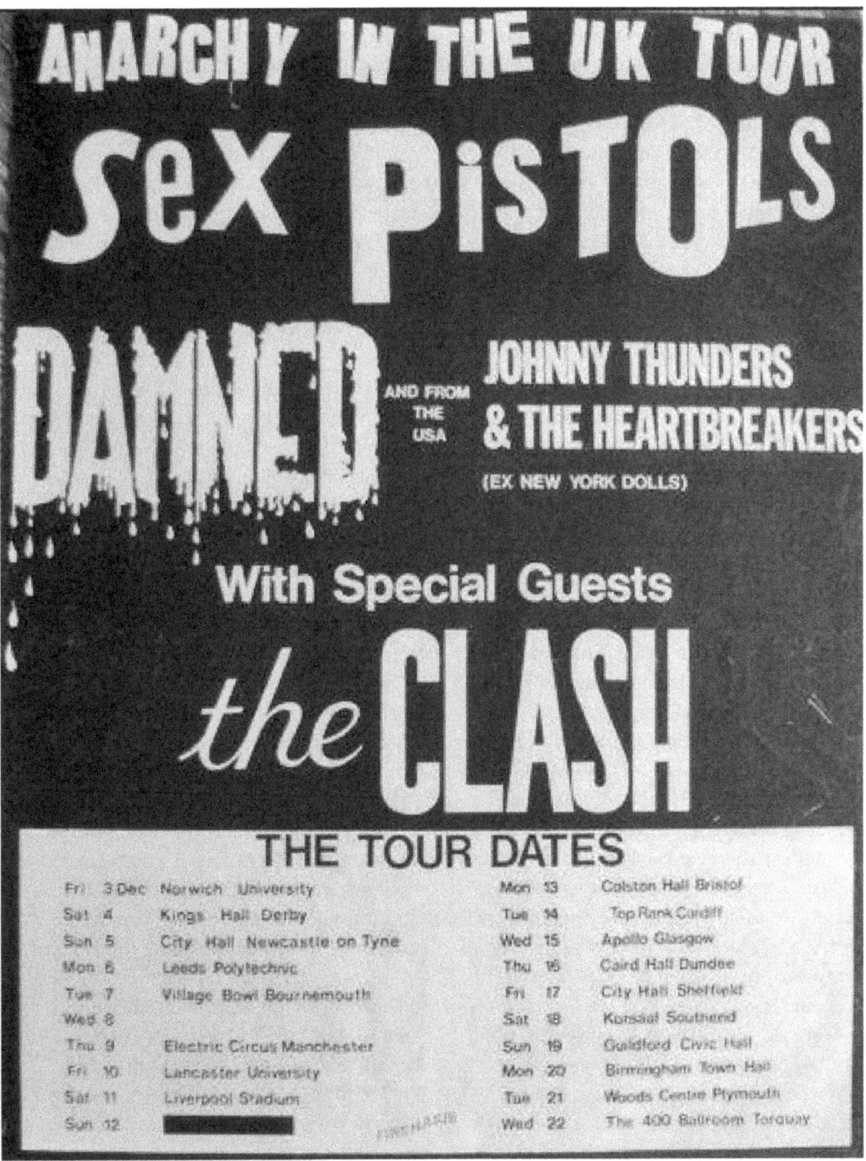
ANARCHY IN THE UK TOUR
SEX PISTOLS
DAMNED
AND FROM THE USA
JOHNNY THUNDERS & THE HEARTBREAKERS
(EX NEW YORK DOLLS)
With Special Guests
the CLASH
THE TOUR DATES
Fri 3 Dec Norwich University
Sat 4 Kings Hall Derby
Sun 5 City Hall Newcastle on Tyne
Mon 6 Leeds Polytechnic
Tue 7 Village Bowl Bournemouth
Wed 8
Thu 9 Electric Circus Manchester
Fri 10 Lancaster University
Sat 11 Liverpool Stadium
Sun 12
Mon 13 Colston Hall Bristol
Tue 14 Top Rank Cardiff
Wed 15 Apollo Glasgow
Thu 16 Caird Hall Dundee
Fri 17 City Hall Sheffield
Sat 18 Kursaal Southend
Sun 19 Guildford Civic Hall
Mon 20 Birmingham Town Hall
Tue 21 Woods Centre Plymouth
Wed 22 The 400 Ballroom Torquay

get a little freedom from social security. Otherwise I'd have to spend 40 hours a week lifting cardboard boxes or washing dishes, or whatever I done in the past. But because we're on the dole – £9.70 a week – I can get a rock'n'roll band together. If I got up at 4am and went to Soho and joined a queue I could get a job as a casual washer-upper. That's the other opportunity I've got. Or the opportunity to work in a factory! There's a social stigma attached to being unemployed. Like 'Social Security Scroungers' every day in *The Sun*. I don't want to hear that. I cheer them. You go up north and the kids are ashamed they can't get a job.'

Simonon chipped in, 'It's the most immediate way we can handle it. We can inspire people. There's no one else to inspire you. Rock'n'roll is a really good medium. It has impact, and, if we do our job properly, we're making people aware of a situation they'd otherwise tend to ignore. We can have a vast effect!' Strummer added, 'You learn by mistakes. The Rolling Stones made mistakes. I want to do something useful. I'm not going to spend all my money on drugs. I'm going to start a radio station with my money. I want to be active. I don't want to end up in a villa in the south of France watching colour TV.'

Simonon continued, 'Bands like the Stones and Led Zeppelin took everything without putting anything back. But we can put money back into the situation we were in before and get something going for the kids our own age.' And Strummer added, 'We make a loss at every gig. It's the promoters who we want to attack. I bet you can only name one or two who really care about music. I'm amazed there isn't one that really cares about what's happening. We're really having to get down on our knees and grovel for venues.'

Summing up, Coon concluded, 'They are more politically motivated than The Damned, perhaps more musically accessible than the Pistols. Their lovingly painted clothes (the same on and off stage), acrylic-spattered with the ferocity of a Jackson Pollock action painting, have started one of the most creative fashion crazes of the year. And their acute awareness, and ability to articulate the essence of the era which inspires their music, will ensure their contribution to the history of rock is of lasting significance.'

Three more shows followed that month. An estimated 25 fans were there at Ilford's Lacy Lady, including future *NME* writer Adrian Thrills, who wrote in the first issue of Clash-inspired fanzine *48 Thrills*, 'The disco audience didn't know how to react.' The next was at the Nag's Head, High Wycombe, with another small crowd. Kris Needs blamed the counter-attraction of a televised Miss World competition, but added, 'The Clash are now firing with more compressed energy than a flamethrower at full blast. They play with almost frightening conviction and intensity.' Then, on November 29, the band supported the Sex Pistols again, this time at Lanchester Polytechnic, Coventry, in what was set to be Terry Chimes' last show. This was the day after The Clash's first TV appearance, having been interviewed by Janet Street-Porter for *The London Weekend Show*. As it was, their 'ability to articulate the essence of the era' – as Coon put it – seemed lost on the masses for now, and they were to be upstaged by a TV interview with the Pistols that ensured the first year of UK punk ended in chaos. The Clash, playing a support role – with Rob Harper on drums – on the Pistols' Anarchy tour, were caught up in the resultant storm.

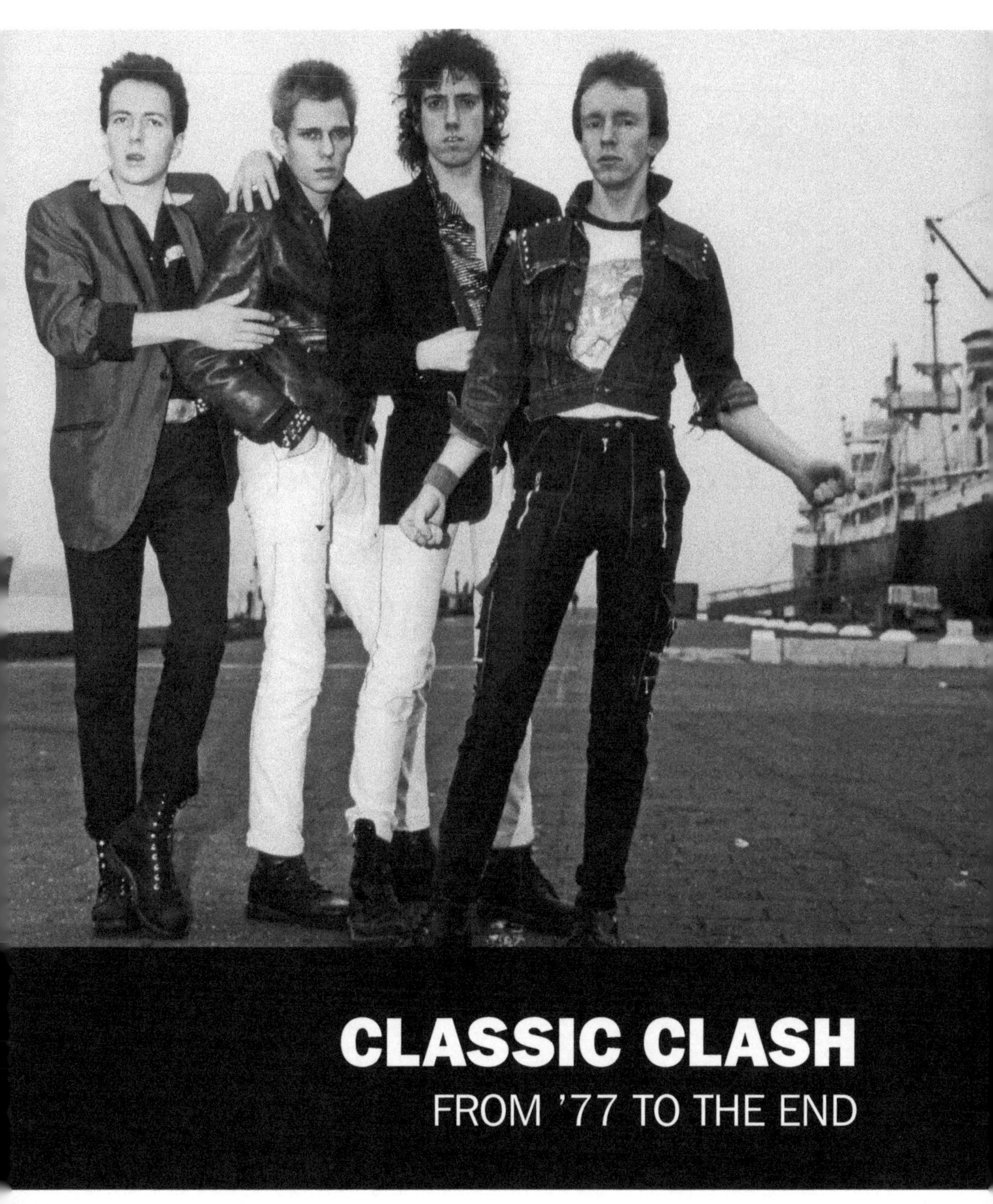

CLASSIC CLASH

FROM '77 TO THE END

2

"I think people ought to know that we're anti-fascist, we're anti-violence, we're anti-racist, and we're pro-creative. We're against ignorance."

JOE STRUMMER, 1976

2

CLASSIC CLASH

FROM '77 TO THE END

On December 1, 1976, The Clash were rehearsing at Harlesden's Roxy Theatre with the Sex Pistols and The Damned. The Anarchy tour was due to begin two nights later, and The Heartbreakers were flying in later that day. But then the Pistols got a call to go to the Thames Television studios at Teddington Lock, to appear on the regional news programme *Today*, presented by Manchester-born 53-year-old Bill Grundy...

All Aboard the Anarchy Express

Some 14 years earlier Grundy had introduced The Beatles on Granada TV, but this time his involvement with a musical phenomenon would effectively end his TV career.
Queen had been due to appear on the 6pm show that Wednesday, December 1, but had cancelled at short notice and were replaced by the Pistols, with their 'Bromley Contingent' entourage in tow. The show was broadcast live and uncensored, and from the beginning Grundy seemed to provoke his guests, soon suggesting, 'They are as drunk as I am!' What started as mocking but innocuous comments from Glen Matlock led to the presenter chiding the band, speaking to his viewers instead of them, challenging what he saw as the hypocrisy of their punk philosophy.

Asked about a reported £40,000 the band had received from their record company, guitarist Steve Jones responded, 'We fuckin' spent it, ain't we!' Grundy didn't respond, but when John Lydon replied, 'tough shit' to his next question, the presenter mocked him, pulling the band's entourage into the interview. A sarcastic comment from Siouxsie Sioux about 'always wanting to meet him' led to Grundy offering to 'meet afterwards'. Steve Jones responded by calling the interviewer a 'dirty sod' and a 'dirty old man'. Grundy, rising to the bait, suggested they 'say something outrageous'. Jones responded by calling him a 'dirty bastard', 'dirty fucker' and 'a fucking rotter', leaving Grundy mouthing, 'Oh shit', as his interviewees danced during the closing credits.

While only a regional programme for London, the interview went national after being picked up by the tabloids. Its presenter was suspended for two weeks and *Today* was cancelled two months later. *The Daily Mirror*

2

> **'They said he had too much to drink**
> **They said that he just could not think straight**
> **He set them up then they knocked him down**
> **Where's Bill Grundy now?'**
>
> ***Television Personalities, Where's Bill Grundy Now?, 1978***

splashed on it, with the headline, 'The Filth and the Fury', one of numerous examples of 'frothing tabloid outrage', as Keith Topping put it in *The Complete Clash*, adding, 'Driven by two days of further negative headlines and articles salaciously detailing many of the more lurid and disturbing punk stories that the tabloid stringers could find in back issues of *NME*, *Melody Maker* and *Sounds*, concert cancellations began in earnest.' Mass hysteria followed, venue after venue pulling shows. Mick Jones told John Robb, 'All the bands were at Harlesden rehearsing for the tour when the Pistols went off to do the Bill Grundy. Then all hell happened. The tour started a couple of days later. All the bands met at Denmark Street and set off. It was meant to be a full tour, but there were hardly any dates left. It seemed like every gig we went to was cancelled.' Strummer recalled, 'I think only nine out of 30 dates were left. We weren't going to play a gig where the Pistols were cancelled. The Damned decided to play a gig anyway, and that caused the first rift. But it really put punk on the map. Every truck driver and builder, and your grandmother, and your uncle now knew what punk rock was about.'

The opening night at the University of East Anglia, Norwich, on December 3, was the first cancellation – axed despite a sit-in protest by students. At Derby's King's Hall the next day, the council were prepared to let the three support bands play, but not the Pistols, unless they auditioned for the leisure committee. McLaren refused, with The Damned soon thrown off the tour amid accusations of selling out when they offered to play despite the Pistols' ban (although they appeared to feature at Leeds).

Sheila Ravenscroft, continuing her late husband's autobiography, *Margrave of the Marshes*, revealed how legendary DJ John Peel was among those who missed out on seeing the Pistols. She wrote, 'John drove to Derby to see them play on a bill that also included The Clash and The Damned. He had gone to see them before this, at the 100 Club on May 11, but left half-way through the opening number because they insisted on being dreadful naughty boys, not starting until late, by which time he had to hotfoot it to Broadcasting House for his show. That night in Derby, he was also unlucky. He thought this was splendid, much more in keeping with the spirit of punk than if it had gone ahead.'

A Newcastle City Hall gig on December 5 was also scrapped, the tour finally getting underway at Leeds Polytechnic on December 6. The audience included future members of Soft Cell, The Cult and Gang of Four, most of these bands forming as a direct result. Julien Temple, on tour with his video camera, talked to Jon Savage about that show, saying: 'There was this pent-up volume of gob, because everybody had read about spitting at punk groups. It was volleys of gob hitting, and they were leaning into it. John looked fantastic with all this snot and gob all over his hair. The Damned were on first, then The Clash, then the Sex Pistols. That was where the ranking of those bands was confirmed. The Damned were like this Radio 1 punk group, and The Clash were very well meaning in a Labour sense. The Sex Pistols were absurd, anarchist theatre.'

After further cancellations, the tour reached Manchester's Electric Circus on December 9, with The Buzzcocks replacing The Damned. Future Joy Division and New Order members Bernard Sumner and Peter Hook were there, the latter soon inspired to adopt Paul Simonon's low-slung bass style. The audience also included future Smiths frontman Morrissey – one of many performers who had failed to get the nod for Mick Jones' pre-Clash outfit – and impressed artist, future *NME* cartoonist and *London Calling* designer Ray Lowry, who said the band performed like, 'They were wired into the mains'. Future Inspiral Carpets star Clint Boon was there too, and in 2015 he told *Uncut*, 'It was a turning point in my life. The Clash struck such a chord with me, not just the songs but the image. It was like, 'Fucking hell! People like me making music.' Before that, people like me didn't make music. It was a massive inspiration, that whole punk scene. A lot of people of my generation still live by that ethic.'

Five days passed before the next show, a hasty replacement for a cancelled Cardiff gig rustled up at the Castle Cinema, Caerphilly, on December 14. Welsh TV footage was later picked up by Temple for *The Great Rock'n'Roll Swindle*. A local newspaper dubbed the Pistols 'Satan's children', and a crowd gathered to sing hymns outside.

On December 19, the tour returned to Manchester's Electric Circus, Peter Hook remembering 'literally a riot' and 'football fans and lunatics throwing bottles from the top of the flats. It was really heavy – a horrible night.' One more gig followed, on December 21 at Plymouth's Woods Centre. Pistols soundman Dave Goodman told *Mojo*, 'The Clash put on one hell of a set and refused to finish until Johnny Thunders enticed them off by waving a huge joint at them from backstage.'

John Lydon, recording his thoughts on the tour in his autobiography *Rotten*, recalled, 'The so-called *Anarchy* Tour was a hilarious affair. Malcolm did most of the details. An agency booked the whole tour and it was great fun having all the bands on the same bus. We got along like a house afire – The Damned, The Heartbreakers, The Clash. There was a falling out with The Clash because they wanted better billing or some bullshit. They decided to travel separately. Then The Damned decided they were the greatest thing since sliced bread. Egos made it fall apart. The only reason The Heartbreakers stuck it out was because they were utterly without egos. Thunders was so out of it on drugs, nothing mattered.

'As a manager, Malcolm could have tried a little harder. What was the point in setting all this up, calling it a tour, then sending us up North, to drive from town to town, spend two nights in a hotel, do one gig, then drive around for a week with nothing to do? There were no escape hatches or alternatives and, again, no money. It's difficult with 200 journalists with cameras following you around.'

Prior to the tour, The Clash entered a recording studio. Polydor A&R man Chris Parry was keen to sign them, and brought them in to Stratford Place studios, near

Oxford Street, with Guy Stevens – who Bernie Rhodes knew from the '60s and was already well known to the band – as producer, and house engineer Vic Smith at the controls. They demoed five songs – 'Career Opportunities', 'Janie Jones', 'White Riot', '1977' and 'London's Burning' – yet Chimes recalled that Parry and Smith had little time for Stevens. The results were not a success. As Strummer put it, 'The results were kind of disappointing. We had quite an energetic unit and it sounded very flat.' It didn't help that, according to Strummer, Stevens was 'too pissed to work'. Also, Smith requested that Strummer pronounced his lines better, seeing as his lyrics were deemed so key to the band's appeal; the singer later told Tony Parsons that the results made him sound like Matt Monro.

Parry's efforts were wasted anyway, with CBS getting in first, making him all the more determined to get his next 'discovery' one board. The Jam subsequently joined Polydor in March '77, Parry later going on to start Fiction Records and launch The Cure to success. But 1976 had been a defining year for punk rock, and there was much more to come in 1977, not least for The Clash, who started on a high, opening The Roxy in Covent Garden on New Year's Day, and rarely pausing for breath from there.

1977 (Danger stranger)

As the songs on the Rehearsal Rehearsals jukebox suggested, The Clash were never about just one thing. And from day one, Strummer, Jones and Simonon's influences were worn on their sleeves – probably stencilled on. But this wasn't just about punk sloganeering. Strummer brought rock'n'roll and R'n'B cool to the party, Jones brought those '60s and '70s guitar bands into the equation, and Simonon brought the sounds of the street from his own manor. What's more, there was soon a firm alliance with British-born Rastafarian DJ Don Letts, with punk rock moving on from the 'Filth and the Fury' headlines to something more constructive. Maybe that's unfair on John Lydon, who was also massively into reggae, but the Pistols' own music hardly hinted at such appreciation.

Much is made of the link between Jamaican culture and punk rock's coalface in Julien Temple's 2014 BBC Four documentary, *The Clash: New Years' Day '77*, and one song above all others seemed to provide the soundtrack for what was simmering below the surface as 1977 dawned: Culture's 'Two Sevens Clash'. Recorded the previous year, the title track of this Jamaican roots reggae outfit's debut LP was produced by Joe Gibbs at his studio in Kingston. It referenced July 1977, and an apocalyptic prediction by early twentieth century black nationalist Marcus Garvey. The Pan Africanism movement leader warned that judgment would follow and past injustices would be avenged when the two sevens clashed on the seventh day of the seventh month of the year 1977. The prophecy caused a stir in Jamaica that summer, with many schools and businesses closing on the day.

While no such apocalyptic event came to pass, a more positive alliance was forged on another level. Joe Strummer recalled for *Westway to the World* how clubs like The Roxy, opened by The Clash on the first day of '77, offered hope – two cultures clashing for good. Strummer said, 'This was the first club for punk groups and their followers, and we agreed to kick it off on New Year's Day. It was a good place to hang out and also a punk/Rasta interface, because the DJ at the time was Don Letts. He'd play a lot of reggae records we hadn't any chance to come across. That gave us a lot of new information. That Rasta/punk crossover was really crucial to the whole scene. It would have been piffle without that.'

Jon Savage talked glowingly in *England's Dreaming* about that Covent Garden appearance, writing, 'They were the true victors of the Anarchy tour, benefitting from the publicity, not embroiled in controversy. They were *the* group to watch. To celebrate, Strummer specially customised a white shirt with a massive '1977' on the front.'

What's more, in what turned out to be their last live outing for two months – as well as disillusioned drummer Rob Harper's last with them – The Clash debuted two reggae covers in their set, Bob Marley's 1966 song, 'Dancing Shoes', and Notting Hill Carnival's most recent anthem, 'Police & Thieves'. This was the year that saw the band not only add the latter to their first album, but hire its co-author, Lee 'Scratch' Perry, as a producer on their feted third single.

As Savage put it, 'The Clash had learned about more than instrument dropout from West Indians. Anybody looking through music that reflected a society in crisis had to look no further than Jamaica and its latest rhythm. By 1975, Chris Blackwell's decision to market Bob Marley and the Wailers as rock stars was finally paying off. Not only were they having hits, but they brought reggae into the open. Stimulated by dreams of crossover success and an expanding English Black market, reggae poured out of Jamaica. The Clash had seen how reggae had acted as a soundtrack for social resistance at the Notting Hill Carnival. And with their use of dropout and stencilled slogans they were attempting to create their own white Rasta in punk, a new cultural resistance.'

Madness lead singer Suggs recalled that year and that venue in his 2013 autobiography, *That Close*, saying, 'I'd seen the words, 'The Clash' sprayed in 10-foot-high letters across the smoked glass of the Capital Radio reception, so I was intrigued when I saw them on the cover of the *NME*. They were going on about how all the records these days were made by old farts. Which was sort of true. But it was the picture of them that caught my eye. They looked good, they were young, they had short hair and straight trousers. The picture showed them with their backs to the camera and their hands on the wall, like they'd just been nicked. The rest of the paper was full of old geezers in capes, or middle-aged brickies in glitter and stack-heel boots.

'The Roxy was where all the kids were headed to check out this new scene they were calling punk. It was 1977 and I was 16 years old. As we piled down the dingy stairs covered in homemade posters and into the dark basement, I couldn't believe my eyes. The place was full of kids, kids my age, all wearing gear that wasn't the status quo or indeed worn by Status Quo.

'There was a fella in an undertaker's outfit with green hair, a couple in matching boiler suits which had the words 'Fuck' and 'Off' on the back. Kids were dressed in all sorts of weird and wonderful homemade get-ups. Don Letts with his long dreads was in the DJ booth pumping out the bass-heavy 'Two Sevens Clash' by Culture. I went to the bar and even the barman had blue hair. I got a pint and suddenly there was what sounded like an explosion. I nearly dropped my beer.

It was a band called Eater striking up the first chords of their set. They started leaping about on stage like lunatics, their average age 14. I'd never seen or heard anything like it. The bands I liked (Roxy Music, David Bowie, Cockney Rebel, Alex Harvey, etc.) all had edge, but this was a new dimension. Everyone in the room was jumping up and down.'

That January, the initial five Clash songs recorded by Polydor were re-recorded, along with 'I'm So Bored With the USA', by soundman Mickey Foote – a technician for the band's live shows who went back to Strummer's Newport days – at Beaconsfield's National Film and Television School, with Julien Temple pulling strings to get them in for free. The version of 'White Riot' they recorded that day made it onto the debut LP, and soon they were back in the studio again, having signed for CBS and been dispatched to Whitfield Street's Studio 3.

Signing on the Dotted Line

'The most important rock band in the world as far as I was concerned at the beginning of '77, and they go and sign to CBS. To me that was a complete disaster.'
Mark Perry to John Robb, Punk Rock: An Oral History, 2006

The Clash signed to CBS Records at Soho Square on January 25, a worldwide deal for £100,000 giving the label an option to release their records overseas. They band had played barely 30 shows by then, few of those as headliners. How did they celebrate? By paying £1.50 each to see Jack Smight's US war film *Battle of Midway*, starring Charlton Heston and Henry Fonda, at a cinema in nearby Leicester Square.

Mickey Foote recalled that all the members – earning £25 a week at the time – received a £1,000 signing bonus, which Jones used to buy a guitar and pay for his gran to visit his mum in America. They were also given a chance to order free records from the label. Jones snapped up Bob Dylan's entire back catalogue, while roadie Roadent chose Abba. Meanwhile, Rhodes bought off-the-shelf company Nineden to administer publishing royalties, so The Clash owned all their songs.

As it was, the deal wasn't for five albums, as they'd understood, but gave CBS an option to pick up as many as 10, or even more. The band had to fund from the advance all living and recording costs, and wages for the rarely paid entourage, until a second LP was ready. They were also expected to underwrite tour costs, pay lawyers and accountants, and buy equipment, strings and clothes, while Rhodes got a 20% cut and income tax liability, and had agreed to cover shared losses from the Anarchy tour with Malcolm McLaren.

Meanwhile, the band were having to justify their deal to the music press and fans, especially after Mark Perry wrote for influential punk fanzine *Sniffin' Glue*, 'Punk died the day The Clash signed to CBS.' To which, Strummer later reflected, 'I remember thinking, that's nice for you, but we were never your toy to begin with.'

Looking back on that period, Perry told John Robb, 'I was never one to toe the line for any punk thing and was outraged when The Clash signed for CBS. I thought that was ridiculous. The most important thing that punk could have done at that point was to stay independent, because economic independence is the most important thing. To sell out to an American company! I did

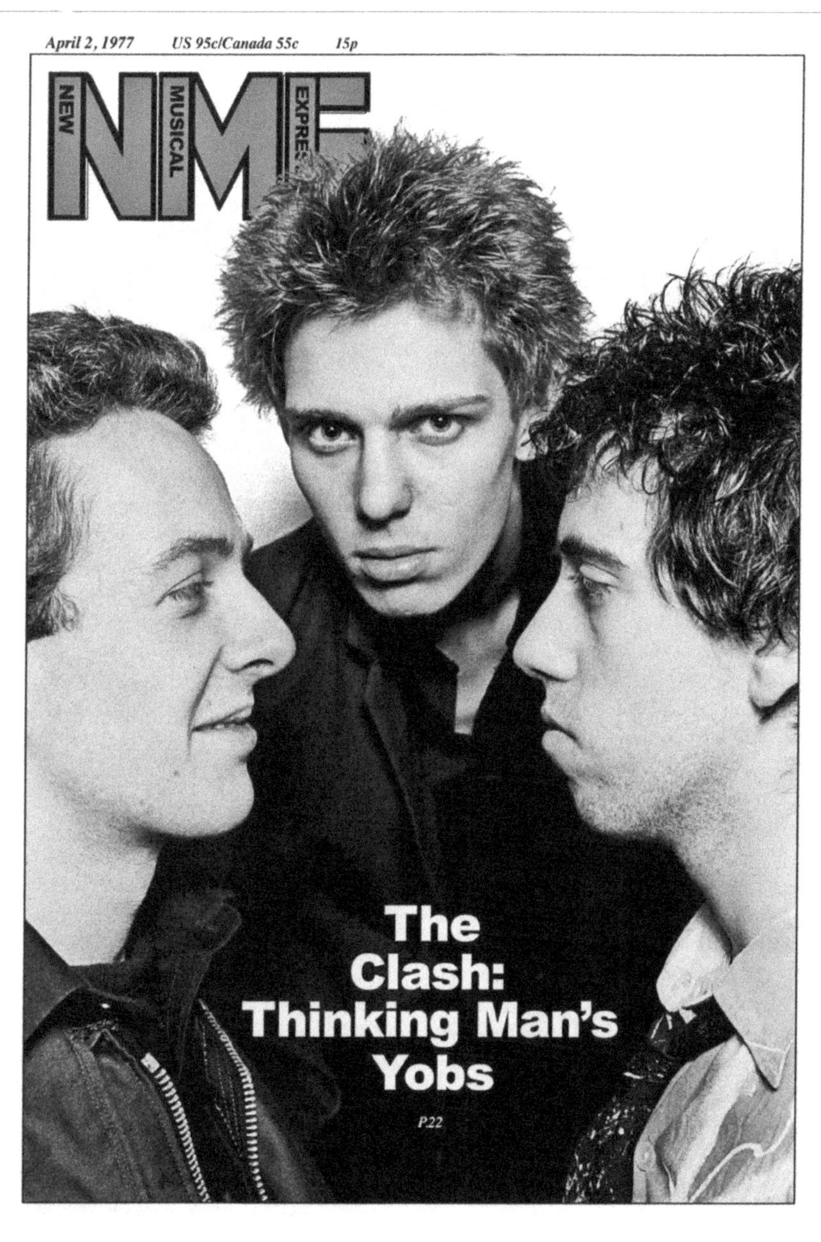
April 2, 1977 US 95c/Canada 55c 15p

NME NEW MUSICAL EXPRESS

The Clash: Thinking Man's Yobs

P22

a TV interview and said punk died the day that The Clash signed to CBS, and they were like, 'How dare he say that about us. We're still punk!'

'I went to a gig to see Japan and Ian Hunter at Hammersmith Odeon and Mick Jones was backstage. Sometimes he's a very sweet, gentle guy, but he tried to come on all heavy. It was all a bit silly. I think they were just embarrassed really. Let's face it, two singles down the line, CBS put out a single The Clash didn't want out. The Clash soon found out how independent they were. They could have had money given to them. You had a few bob around the punk scene. You had Jake Riviera, Geoff Travis had just started Rough Trade, you had the Rock On guys. They were all independent and 100% into it. Imagine the first single or an EP of the best Clash songs coming out on their own label, like UB40 did a few years later. It would have inspired all those other bands to

MOMENTS IN TIME PART 1: APRIL 1977

We're talking less than six minutes in total, yet it's a mighty three-song salvo that remains as fresh today as the day it was recorded in a film studio in Dunstable, Bedfordshire, barely 45 miles north west of the band's spiritual home in West London. That live performance of early tracks from the Strummer/Jones stable proved to be something of a cultural call to arms, resonating well beyond the 'Garageland' this band had just so memorably written about.

It carried in its essence much of what those lucky enough to witness The Clash those first few months experienced live. Come to think of it, it embodied much of the spirit that largely remained throughout the five years in which the band's classic four-piece line-up existed.

This was never a group to stand still or try to re-record the same songs time and time again. But when it came to that original punk consciousness, it's fair to say The Clash rarely, if at all, lost its initial spirit, despite the many highs and lows, trials and tribulations en route.

I was surprised when I realised that this historic footage of first single 'White Riot', its B-side '1977', and 'London's Burning', showcased barely a week after the release of incendiary debut LP, *The Clash*, featured not only Joe Strummer, Mick Jones and Paul Simonon, but also new boy Nicky 'Topper' Headon. I get the impression the filmmakers had been told not to focus on him. He was, after all, just the latest inhabitant of that revolving drum stool, joining a week earlier. How were they to know this slight 21-year-old was the final link in making The Clash the band they truly became? You get the odd glimpse of Topper, but not really enough to make a positive ident.

One thing's for sure though. You get real insight into everything about those other three fellas. Let's face it, Bernie Rhodes might have bided his time and ultimately chosen better musicians, but that was never what it was about. And as it turned out, musical competence came with time. It was about presence, attitude and spirit, and that front-line trio had it in spades from day one: the resultant electrical charge is there to witness all these years on in this revealing footage.

For me, '1977' really stands out. It may just be because I've heard the other tracks so many more times over the years, but something draws me. It seems to be the stronger track, although perhaps the band felt they were sailing too close to the wind regarding that riff being a wholesale 'reimagining' of The Kinks' 'All Day and All of the Night'. But what power!

do the same thing. But The Clash sign up, so all those other bands sign up – The Jam with Polydor, Buzzcocks with UA, Siouxsie and the Banshees to Polydor.'

Those sentiments were echoed by Factory Records' Tony Wilson, who said, 'Independent distribution was available because of Rough Trade. It was wonderful. The independent ethic was so much part of the punk ethic. Punk, though, was never an attack on the corporates: the Pistols signed to EMI, and the first time I heard of The Clash it had a CBS sticker on it. The Buzzcocks signed to United Artists the night Elvis Presley died. It was always about major labels. The indie labels were a way of getting your band signed to a major label.'

Meanwhile, John Lydon told John Robb, 'The likes of The Clash, those boys took the wimpy way out with their Marxist nonsense. They had a university kind of rocky attitude. What were they challenging? Really, when

---

Apparently the audience consisted of the camera crew and an impressed *NME* reporter Tony Parsons, who famously rode the Circle Line with the band a month earlier, his amphetamine sulphate-fired interview later being released in vinyl form as part of a free single issued by his employers.

The backdrop to that stark studio set was a blow-up by Sebastian Conran – the son of design guru Terence and an associate of Strummer's since late-'75 – of the Rocco Macauley shot gracing the back cover of *The Clash*. Lindsay Clinell, who directed this short film, also included interview clips with Parsons and the band around a pool table. I'm not sure how many plays the film got that year though, and while it was played at the Virgin Records store in Marble Arch, Clash biographer Marcus Gray felt that 'the few dozen record purchases this possibly inspired hardly justified the expense,' in his *Last Gang in Town* book.

The track timing on those three songs comes to less than 350 seconds but was all that was needed to show the world that here was an inspirational band helping lead that punk-rock charge. Who knew how long it would last? It didn't matter. Who could see the potential of the band from those songs and the fact that, within two years, they'd have written the highly-acclaimed *London Calling* LP? Who knows.

As it was, five years and one month later it would be as good as over for that classic line-up, with Headon sacked four days before the release of fifth album, *Combat Rock*, the most commercially successful of all their studio LPs. And within 16 months, the unthinkable happened – another key member was off on his way.

With all that in mind, Strummer's year-by-year count-up at the song's climax seems somewhat prophetic. Life imitating art and all that. After the departures of Headon and Jones, The Clash Mk. II properly surfaced in January 1984, and there was still a chunk of the tale still to come, but it was never the same, however much of a thrill those busking shows as a reconstituted five-piece may have seemed. When Joe snarls out '1984', there is a suggestion of Orwellian portent as the guitars, bass and drums cut out and it's all over. As he put it in 2000's *Westway to the World*: '1984 and we were gone really. It was all over bar the brushing out the room.'

it boils down to it, it was meaningless and nice. The Pistols took the brunt of it, and then they all jumped in on it, with no effort at all, and have all gone on to make enormous record sales and have very nice, cosy positions in the record industry for themselves. That's punk rock, is it? I'm very pleased all these bands found a home. They're all cluttered together in the same dustbin.'

The CBS signing appeared to be something of a last-minute affair, conducted in true Bernie Rhodes fashion, the band kept in the dark. Strummer, talking to Sean O'Hagan in 1997, said, 'Originally, we went down Soho to sign to Phonogram, but Bernie had done some nifty footwork and we ended up down at CBS.' Yet label boss Maurice Oberstein obviously felt it important enough to be personally involved. In *Westway to the World*, Strummer reflected, 'He was prepared to stick his neck out and sign one of those damn punk groups. All that was needed from us was to sign the damn thing. They weren't going to talk about clause 95b with us, were they? We signed for £100,000. At the time that seemed like a fortune, but later we found out that what we thought was a five-record deal, in fact in the small print – like in every corny story – was a 10-record deal.' Jones mused on the speed of it all, adding, 'It was so fast that Bernie couldn't think of a big stunt to celebrate it.' The guitarist concluded, 'I guess Bernie went off to bank the cheque.'

CBS were an American-owned company with an English branch able to take independent A&R decisions to develop UK talent for the world market. In 1976 its market share was 16% of singles, second only to EMI, and 9% of albums, third behind EMI and Polygram. Word has it that Oberstein took part in the deal because of A&R man Dan Loggins' hostility to punk, the company's MD telling Jon Savage, 'When the Sex Pistols and The Clash came along there was a level of hysteria within the industry that this is a music we shouldn't be involved in. There is an inherent fear of the unknown. I'd done 15 to 20 years in the business before punk came along, managed to survive every trend, so strangely enough it was easier for older, more experienced record people to contemplate taking on punk than the contemporaries of punk in the record companies. We failed to sign the Sex Pistols and ended up signing The Clash. Our attitude was that they had a uniqueness. I wasn't interested in The Clash as a social phenomenon. We were just making records. They weren't particularly different or difficult. All I did in the beginning was take a gamble that they had a sound and a noise they wanted to make. They simply went into the studio with a producer, an engineer of our choice, and made an album. That was their album. I could see that our approach to making a good album wasn't necessarily making a good punk album.'

Accordingly, Mickey Foote was hired to produce the debut album, with Terry Chimes drafted back in for the recording. The LP was preceded by the release of debut single 'White Riot', inspired by the previous August bank holiday's Notting Hill disturbances. Recorded in February and released on March 18, it went on to reach No.38 in the UK charts on April 9. And what a single. Not just the A-side either – the wondrous '1977' was every bit as good.

Its cover photograph had been taken by Caroline Coon the previous November at Rehearsal Rehearsals, inspired by dub act Joe Gibbs and The Professionals' similar 'up against the wall' cover for their 1976 *State of Emergency* LP. The original shot featured the phrase 'Hate and War' on the back of Strummer's boiler suit, but was airbrushed for the released version and replaced with the B-side's title, '1977'.

Strummer, talking to the *NME*'s Sean O'Hagan in 1997, said, 'I think there was a lot of misunderstanding of some songs. Like the line about 'Sten guns in Knightsbridge' (in '1977'), which Tony Parsons and Julie Burchill took up as a war cry – y'know, we're gonna run through Knightsbridge shooting the rich. I'm going, 'Oh yeah, after we just signed for CBS.' In that song I saw the Sten guns pointing at me. The lyric was about being caught up in a terrorist action and being blown away. I swear those guns were pointing at me. Parsons and Burchill and Jimmy Pursey saw it as some kind of punk call to arms.'

In March 2005, Q magazine placed 'White Riot' at No.34 in its '100 Greatest Guitar Tracks'. The song has been covered many times since, by artists including Angelic Upstarts, Sham 69, Camper Van Beethoven, Audioslave and Rage Against the Machine. Celebrating its thirtieth anniversary in *The Guardian* in 2007, Caroline Coon recalled taking the sleeve photograph on a 'typically dank afternoon' while Strummer, Jones and Simonon were 'keeping warm huddled around one bar of an electric fire'. She added, 'Aside from battered instruments scattered about, there were pots of paint and brushes that The Clash used to stencil reggae-inspired words on their clothes.'

She wrote, 'The band had performed in public only a handful of times – enough to be sure of their explosive potential – but excitement was tempered by the heavy manners needed to break through. We were having not so much an interview as a heated 'reasoning'. The atmosphere of the times had soured from psychedelic optimism into oppressive monochrome. Demonised youth, especially black youth, were frequently stopped and searched on the streets under the despised 'sus' law. To capture something of this in a black-and-white image, I asked Joe, Mick and Paul to stand against the studio wall in the arrested 'Hands Above Your Heads' position that had become so familiar. The moment I saw Joe had painted 'Hate and War' on the back of his boiler suit I understood the punk movement to be essentially, in style and content, a negative of the hippy 'peace and love'.'

Paul Simonon, reflecting on that debut single with *Uncut* in 2015, said, 'It was just that thing of, when we were gonna do the encore, thinking, 'Are we gonna give them what they want or are we gonna take it to another level?' Generally, it was 'White Riot' they wanted. Everything would go haywire. Guitars would go out of tune. There'd be no way you could play another song afterwards.'

And Mick Jones added, 'I loved it when we first did it, I loved the single. I said we should have people running around on the solo, so there was five or six of us stomping round this microphone during the guitar break.'

Writer and broadcaster Robert Elms enthused, 'The joyous machine-gun rattle of this battle call is still the ultimate Clash thrill for me. I was at the Carnival in '76 when Joe was inspired to write this. I first heard it at Harlesden, and it all came back. I saw at least half a dozen gigs on the White Riot tour, and this tune always kicked off. The classic time was at The Rainbow, when it literally turned into one and the Art Deco

2

Melody Maker

PRIL 23, 1977 15p weekly USA 75 cents

Marley talks of his roots PAGE 47

QUEEN – full tour dates PAGE 5

Neil Diamond on his fame PAGE 30

Clash tilt for the top

THE new wave comes to London's Rainbow theatre next month when the Clash headline a special show also featuring four other young bands.

The concert, on May 9, comes mid-way through Clash's [illegible] British tour and is the biggest indication yet of the new wave's growing importance.

Other bands on the bill are the Jam, whose debut single, "In The City" is available this week, Buzzcocks, Subway Sect and the Prefects.

Support bands for the 27-date tour have yet to be announced, but for the concerts in Edinburgh, Newcastle, St Albans, [illegible], Stafford, Cardiff, Brighton, Bristol, [illegible] [illegible], Canterbury and [illegible], the other groups will be the Jam, Buzzcocks, Subway Sect and the Slits.

For full details of the tour, see page 3.

● JOE STRUMMER of the Clash, see special profile on page 29.

● The Jam, talking about their [illegible]: page 8.

roof nearly came off the house.'

On the subject of the B-side, Paul Weller told *Uncut* in 2015, 'What I really liked about '1977' was the fact it was only one minute 40 seconds or whatever. I was really impressed with that, how powerful and short it was. I mean all that 'No Elvis, Beatles or the Rolling Stones' was fucking nonsense, really. I'm sure Joe didn't really mean it either when you think about all those old artists who'd influenced them as well. I mean, one of the things I really liked about The Clash was how they got Lee Dorsey and Bo Diddley to support them on tour. All that ground-zero nihilism stuff, I dunno how much of that they really believed. They were all very aware of rock'n'roll history and English pop culture. One of the first things that really struck me about Joe when I met him was him saying he liked my haircut, and recognising that it was supposed to be like a mod cut. I thought that was pretty cool.'

Sniffin' Glue fanzine's Mark Perry added, 'It's under two minutes and it's just this amazing statement. All those images, like Sten guns in Knightsbridge. You knew that was never going to happen, but it was just the idea of it. It was a real rallying call. That refrain – 'No Elvis, Beatles or the Rolling Stones' – is just genius. I think it's their best riff ever. The way it starts, it's so tense. Unbeatable.'

Don Letts enthused in the same feature, 'Have you ever heard a tune that comes in at just under one minute and 40 seconds that has so much bollocks? The cheek of these young whippersnappers to rail against the old, heralding in the new. Sheer bollocks, man, you gotta take your hat off. Even though I believe that when Joe first came up with the line 'No Elvis, Beatles or the Rolling Stones', he felt a little embarrassed. But '1977', the sheer balls!'

And what about Paul Simonon's take on it, all these years on? 'It's got a certain swagger, that don't-give-a-damn attitude that I really like. At the time it summed up that thing of 'let's wipe the slate clean'.'

Riding the Tube with The Clash

'They'd got rid of their drummer, so it was the three of them. From the outside it looked like Paul was the pin-up, Joe was the leader and Mick the music, but really they were three leaders.'
Tony Parsons, The Guardian, 2016

In another chronicled key moment from that period, just before the first album landed, Tony Parsons, writing for *The Guardian* in July 2016, recalled the day in the spring of 1977 that he spent riding the London Underground with The Clash, the Essex music writer turned bestselling author then just a new *NME* recruit. He wrote, 'I'd been hired to write about punk, but there wasn't much around at the time. Mainly you saw bands play live; there wasn't much vinyl. The culture moved more slowly than it does now. I went to meet The Clash just before their first album came out.'

'We met on the Circle Line. I remember standing on the platform with Chalkie Davies, the photographer, when we saw Joe Strummer stick his head out of the carriage and invite us on board. We met in the morning and spent the whole afternoon going round and round the line, drinking Foster's and taking amphetamine sulphate. It's hard to imagine that happening today with a journalist, but there was an understanding back then. We felt like we were all part of a scene, all at the start of our careers, and the band trusted me not to stitch them up. Nobody had any money and we were all living in odd places – I was in a bedsit in Crouch End that I'd got off Rat Scabies, Mick was living with his nan, Paul was in West London with his girlfriend, and Joe was in a squat.

'They argued a lot, but they were like brothers, or mountaineers, joined together by this absolute belief in their project. A proper band. They were convinced that they were going to become bigger than the Rolling Stones in about 10 minutes. It didn't happen quite like that, but it wasn't far off. It was that early period, when everything was still ahead of us, before the drugs became a problem.

'At Liverpool Street we piled into a photo booth to take more speed. A policeman must have seen four pairs of Dr. Martens sticking out and tried to pull the curtain open while we laughed and laughed until we wept, like you do when you're a child. When night fell we decided we wanted to go to a rock'n'roll club. We tried to go to The Speakeasy, but they wouldn't let us in because we weren't cool enough. In the end it was the perfect punchline to a perfect day. I remember seeing all these people going in with Rod Stewart feather-cuts and velvet flares, just thinking, 'You have no idea what's about to hit you.''

Record company advance or not, it clearly remained a hand-to-mouth existence for now. Reflecting on that period with John Hind for *The Guardian* 40 years later, Mick Jones recalled, 'In Wimpole Street, where we were making the first Clash album, Spaghetti House was the place to go for spaghetti, risotto and mushrooms. We were writing in Joe's squat, a disused ice-cream factory. Sometimes Paul would leave the studio to go to KFC for chicken legs – getting just potato wedges for me – and by the time he'd get back Joe and I would've recorded a new track without him. In the early days, when we spent evenings flyposting for our gigs, Paul would mix flour and hot water to make the poster paste and afterwards he'd eat the remainder. But I never actually lived in a squat, eating baked beans, with Viv Albertine, as is written. I just visited, while still living with my gran. During art college I'd decided moving out would impede what I wanted to do. Once the Clash were a success I got my own home.'

Barry Cain was another writer who got to know the band in those days, while with *Record Mirror*, and in *77 Sulphate Strip*, his excellent 'eyewitness account of the year that changed everything', he talked about his first visit to Rehearsal Rehearsals, just after the release of 'White Riot'. He'd quickly been won over, having first reported on the band at Harlesden Coliseum, soon declaring, 'They send shivers down my spine when they get it right, and they get it right nearly all the time. 'Janie Jones' hits a spot I never knew I had.' In an interview centred on Mick Jones – memorably described as having 'five O-levels and a degree of uncertainty' – and Joe Strummer, his first feature on the band gives something of a detailed sketch of the chief songwriters' mindset back then.

Of Jones, he wrote, '(He's) currently being hailed as the new Keith Richards. He's got the hair and he's got the stare, but does he have the dare? He keeps stopping midway through sentences, throws looks at the other two, smiles, and continues.' A mighty volley of inspirational verbal intent follows from The Clash guitarist, Jones telling Cain, 'There's still the deaf-aid of rock'n'roll. It takes a lot to overcome it. Like 10 years ago in America, when comfortable college kids were coming home from Vietnam in wooden boxes. People like Phil Ochs started singing about it. Everyone took LSD. People who are frightened of us will take what we sing about as major political statements. All I know is what we're in, what we understand. We still have the code of the street.

'A lot of people feel very angry about us, because they can't identify with what we play. Some guys followed us home after a gig and threw a brick through our window. Things like that are always happening. That's just because they don't know what's going on. But I think they'll hear it soon. 'White Riot' is a good rock'n'roll record. It's never worried us that they might not hear our words.

'Young white guys need an identity. We're talking to kids like us who don't have anything. Those who remember 1955 were lucky. They had their own music. We ain't looking for swastikas, just rock'n'roll. Before, it was only authors who made important statements. Music has always spoken to me. The only difference between us and the music of the '60s and '70s is that now we're saying it plainer, more coherently. I'm selling most of the records I ever bought, because listening to them now is a waste of time. The Clash work on a purely emotional level. We recorded our album in a few weeks. It took ELP two years to do their last one. Wow, they must be wondering what on earth's happened now. All we're saying is, question what you're doing and if the answer doesn't satisfy you then fucking do what you want. It's not preaching. I fucking hate that. It's just encouragement.'

In comparison, Strummer's words seem more focused on the bigger world picture, straight out of the Bernie Rhodes handbook, but he later adds a few compelling lines of his own, telling Cain, 'The Clash can't change people – we can only create an atmosphere. If people want to change, they will. I have a great time banging guitars and shouting. People can read too much into that, and it makes me sick. All this talking about how people can gain from what we do makes me puke. Lawrence of Arabia was my only hero, because I thought it was real smooth, him just coming out of England and leading the Arabs.

'I find myself in a void, and it's a good void. I've always known what to do, always known what I'm doing it for. I'm smart, I'm lucky, and luck is a dominant factor in life. You make your own luck by grabbing opportunities, and I grab opportunities by following the Cherokee Indian way. When they have to make a decision, they choose the most reckless course of action. I always like to have my hands on the steering wheel.

'I suppose I'm like this because people have walked all over me in the past. When they do that I'm interested – I want to know why, so they won't do it again. When I was nine, I went to a boarding school. On the first day I was surrounded by a bunch of boys who frog-marched me to the bathroom, where I was confronted by a bath full of used toilet paper, a smear of shit on each fucking sheet. They said I had to get in. If I refused they'd beat me up. I got fucking beaten up.'

Whatever their motivations, it was clearly a productive time for the band, with their self-titled debut LP following. And as John Robb put it, 'Already moving quickly to challenge for pole position in the punk rock hierarchy amidst the Sex Pistols' inertia in the first half of 1977, The Clash found themselves as the flag-wavers of the punk rock consciousness.'

The Clash: An Appreciation

While *The Clash* opener 'Janie Jones' namechecks a '60s cabaret performer turned '70s brothel-keeper, what we really have is the band's take on the drudgery of the nine-to-five world and a bid to leave all that behind, make it big, have the time of your life and tell the boss where to go. Yet our subject knows he needs money to get by, run his Ford Cortina and see his girl. Janie is just symbolic of his fantasy life. It's an age-old conundrum – Eddie Cochran's 'Summertime Blues' springs to mind – but we can identify with the theme and Mick Jones' defiant call to 'let them know'. The tune and chorus came to him on a number 31 bus from Harrow Road to Rehearsal Rehearsals, and newly appointed lead singer Joe Strummer contributed to the lyrics. As Strummer put it to the *NME*'s Sean O'Hagan in 1997, the song 'was a reference to the scandal, which seemed impossibly glamorous to anyone in a city job'.

Janie, a tabloid regular, was jailed for seven years in 1973 for running a brothel and perverting the course of justice. Released early, around the time of the LP, she contacted the band, becoming friends with Strummer, who in 1983 penned the madam her own single, 'House of the Ju Ju Queen', credited to 'Janie Jones and The Lash'. Discussions over Simonon's one-note bassline suggest boredom or a rudimentary grasp of his instrument. But for me, it's what was needed, uncomplicated, and the call-and-response vocals are the right side of terrace chanting. The song remained a live favourite during the band's lifetime.

Written by Jones after the Anarchy tour, the band virtually disowned 'Remote Control' after CBS chose to put it out as their second single – released on May 13 '77, backed by a live 'London's Burning' – without consulting them. They had told *Melody Maker* that the next 45 would be 'Janie Jones', and were irate when they were undermined. That release became a symbol of everything they were fighting, and the incident inspired the next single, 'Complete Control'. Written after the Anarchy tour, mention of a 'meeting in Mayfair' refers to one for EMI shareholders that took place in late '76, which effectively withdrew all support for that tour. A weak choice, but it works as a '70s timepiece, summing up the frustration of the time at pubs closing early and having nowhere to go, with the police on your case, and bureaucrats and big business in league with careerist politicians. Musically, again, there's underlying terrace menace, but Terry Chimes recalled Strummer's initial excitement at Jones' 'mini-opera' and its time signature complexities, on an ambitious number.

The history of The Clash brings up several conflicting versions of events, especially where an alternate take makes for better reading, and 'I'm So Bored With the USA' provides a classic example. In *Westway to the World* you get the notion that it started as an anti-love song, 'I'm So Bored With You', Strummer's twist changing the thrust and condemning the rise of Americanisation in the UK. The original was played by Jones at the initial Davis Road meetings with Strummer in early June '76, the implication being that Strummer misheard the words and improved it, adding lyrics on the spot. Yet live recordings from as late as September '76 suggest that it existed in its first form for longer. In 1999, Jones said, 'Although we'd been brought up on American TV shows, there was too much of an American influence on Britain in the '70s. There were too many McDonald's.' The song became a live favourite, opening sets on three successive US tours, a mischievous Strummer suggesting, 'We wanted to find out if they had a sense of humour in America.'

'White Riot' was deemed to be Strummer's rewrite of the Stones' 1968 statement, 'Street Fighting Man', drawing on the spirit of The Ramones in a short, intense two-chord punk anthem, inspired by Strummer and Simonon's part in Notting Hill Carnival's riot in August '76 – the drought coming to an explosive end, simmering resentment at heavy-handed policing in London's West Indian communities boiling over. Strummer said, 'We were there at the very first throw, the very first brick,' describing a 'conga line of policemen coming through the crowd under the Westway, up by Ladbroke Grove', where 'all hell broke loose'. By all accounts, Bernie Rhodes cowered while Simonon threw bricks and Strummer failed in his attempt to set an abandoned car alight. He added, 'The Notting Hill riot was a black riot, a spontaneous expression of 'We ain't taking this anymore.' 'White Riot' in its clumsy way was saying white people had to become activists too or else they'd get plastered over in society.'

The single used a later session, adding police siren, smashing glass, alarm and stomp effects, while the UK LP take was from the pre-CBS Beaconsfield demo. For me, Jones' buzz-saw guitar takes it to the next level. The live version, even faster, debuted at the 100 Club in September '76. Beyond 1979, it was played more sparingly, usually as a late encore, but when Jones departed it returned, Strummer continuing to play the song in later days.

Written in November '76, 'Hate & War' fit neatly with punk's anti-hippy line, voicing despair at where late '60s optimism had led in grim mid-'70s England. Strummer told *Uncut* in 1991 that he wrote the song in a disused ice cream factory off Harrow Road, scribbling the words by candlelight, taking them to Rehearsal Rehearsals the following day, where Jones added a melody. Marcus Gray suggested in *Last Gang in Town* that the song was written to back the band's media pronouncements on creative violence. Musically, there are also hints of reggae influences in Strummer's backing vocal and chop-guitar.

An explosive 'of the moment' punk classic, with hints of The Buzzcocks' 'Spiral Scratch', 'What's My Name' was the only song on the first LP part-credited to early member Keith Levene, although he said he had a hand in all the songs from that period, something Strummer told *Mojo*'s Sean Egan in 1991 was the 'demented outpouring of an overexcited mind'. The band said the song was principally written by Jones and Levene in May '76 at Riverside Studios, their pre-Rehearsals base, but Levene claimed he wrote it in Sheffield at the time of the first show, showing it to future PIL bandmate John Lydon first. Responding, Strummer said, 'I put in a couple of verses to keep the choruses apart.' Either way, several changes were made. The track, which was introduced at the Screen on the Green in '76, tackles domestic violence and how to survive it. Whatever its origins, there's no doubting Jones' powerful intro and Simonon's brooding bass.

On another track evocative of The Clash's London, the main riff of 'Deny' suggests The Who's 'The Kids Are Alright'. Written by Jones before Strummer joined, and set around the early London punk scene, it mentions the 100 Club, and concerns Jones' then-girlfriend and a struggle to deal with drugs – Keith Topping feels that 'its patent horror of the needle and the damage done shouldn't be underestimated'. There's also a correlation with the Sex Pistols' 'Liar', which Jones would have known through his friendship with Glen Matlock. Jones said Chrissie Hynde helped with part of the song, which underwent a further shift through Strummer to be more in line with Rhodes' 'reality' manifesto. Early on, 'Deny' was a regular live opener.

Drugs were the subject matter on 'London's Burning' too, in this case the punk staple, speed. Strummer recalled in *Westway to the World*, 'One of the few things punks had for recreation was amphetamine sulphate, which was cheap and value for money in that its effects lasted. I decided quite quickly the up wasn't worth the down.' Talking to Sean O'Hagan in 1997, he added, 'It was pretty true to the life we were leading. We'd take amphetamines and storm around the bleak streets, where there was nothing to do but watch the traffic lights. We didn't have no trendy club to go to.'

Asked how important speed was to the scene in the same *NME* interview, Strummer replied, 'Incredibly! A real part of the way we looked at things. All we'd do was take blues and snort loads of cheap sulphate and get out there and live all night. I stopped early because my metabolism wasn't strong enough for my lifestyle. Some people can handle it, but I'd have these comedowns where I'd want to bash my head in with a hammer. What we were doing was next door to Vim – cheap and nasty.'

The track was also inspired by the view from Jones' eighteenth-floor flat at Wilmcote House. Strummer would look out at the Westway towards his Orsett Terrace squat, writing the words when he got home. And while the myth might suggest that tower blocks featured heavily in the band's early material, it was the only Clash song with a direct reference. Either way, Tony Parsons felt they dealt with urban alienation better than anyone else, before or since. The song took its title from the nursery rhyme referencing 1666's Great Fire of London, though others cited MC5's 'Motor City is Burning'. Also notable for Jones' far from minimalist guitar solo, 'London's Burning' was first performed at Screen on the Green in August '76, a live version from a Dunstable gig on the White Riot tour featuring on the B-side of 'Remote Control'.

Suggested as a title by Paul Simonon while flicking through the *Evening Standard*, 'Career Opportunities' also alludes to the Hughie Green-fronted talent show, *Opportunity Knocks*, in a respect the *Britain's Got Talent* of its day. Jones reckons the LP's side two opener was knocked off within half an hour at Rehearsals, yet Strummer said he wrote much of it while the others were getting potato croquettes from KFC. Like 'Janie Jones', the main theme concerns a dead-end job or one of no interest, part-inspired by Jones' clerical role at Praed Street benefits office, Paddington, at a time when the IRA were using letter bombs. (Jones contended that it fell to him to open the mail during a time of high alert for Government departments.) Its live debut was in October '76, and the song was still being busked by the last line-up nine years later.

Regularly played on the White Riot and Get Out of Control tours, 'Cheat' was written just before the band recorded the LP and regarded by Strummer as a filler. Its solo was somewhat influenced by Mick Ronson's riff on David Bowie's 'Suffragette City', with state-of-the-art phasing effects added.

Sung by Jones and dating back to his London SS days, 'Protex Blue' namechecked a '70s condom brand sold in the Windsor Castle toilets' contraceptive vending machine – hence the 'Johnny Johnny!' outro. Like the Pistols' 'Bodies', it was a trademark punk anti-love song, complete with matter-of-fact imagery of loveless sexual encounters. Recorded in early '77, and despite shades of The Stooges, Keith Topping reckoned a close listen 'reveals the main riff is nothing less than a fast version of Led Zeppelin's 'Kashmir'.' The song featured at the band's first show, possibly as the opener.

Junior Murvin and Lee Perry's account of life and political conflict in Jamaica, 'Police & Thieves' – an anthem among London's West Indian communities in the summer of '76 – was heard by Strummer and Simonon at Notting Hill Carnival. Mick Jones told the BBC in 1996, 'In the way '60s bands covered contemporary R'n'B classics, we covered the latest record from Jamaica. We had some brass neck to do that!' But as Strummer added in 2002, 'It wasn't like a slavish white man's Xerox of some riff. It was like, 'Give us your riff and we'll drive it around London!'' And Simonon told Eddie Izzard a year later, 'The Clash's idea was to take reggae music, put it on a number 31 bus, send it up to Camden.' It worked out far better than the band could have imagined, Strummer praising Jones' 'genius' arrangement skills for this late addition.

There's a real band feel too, not least with those ska guitar chops, Chimes and Simonon's work in the engine room – the latter truly finding his way on bass – and falsetto backing vocals. It's not a moment too long at the other side of six minutes, sounding just as fresh 40 years on. Introduced into the live set in April '77, several adlibbed lyrics and improvised moments followed, the song lasting up to 10 minutes, often segueing into the Ramones' 'Blitzkrieg Bop' or Ray Charles' 'Hit the Road, Jack'.

In 1997 Strummer told the *NME*'s Sean O'Hagan that the song was his idea: 'We used to sit down, us and the Pistols, and discuss whether we should cover reggae songs. Rotten would lay down the law, because he was a reggae fanatic. He thought we should leave reggae alone. Anyway, we did it punk style. It weren't bink-bonk reggae. It had balls.'

Jones reckoned it only took 24 minutes to

write '48 Hours', the debut LP's penultimate track, at another productive Rehearsals session. The Clash's take on the tried and tested theme of cramming everything into your weekend, the line 'Monday is coming like a jail on wheels' brings Fats Domino's 'Blue Monday' to mind, or The Easybeats' 'Friday on My Mind'. First aired live at the Screen on the Green in August '76, the song inspired the title of punk fanzine *48 Thrills* and arguably The Jam's 'Here Comes the Weekend'.

Song introductions don't get much more startling than on *The Clash*'s glorious finale, 'Garageland', the band's inspired response to that damning review from the *NME*'s Charles Shaar Murray of the Sex Pistols support slot at Screen on the Green, in which the ex-Oz writer described them as 'the kind of garage band who should be speedily returned to the garage, preferably with the motor running'. The interviews that followed suggested that Strummer took the comments personally, and he told Gavin Martin in 1999, 'He was saying our whole work of art was so piss-poor we should be executed immediately, pretty severe criticism, don't you think? At least he was clear-cut. There was no fucking around with poncy intellectual bollocks. He said what he meant. But so did we.' By '79, however, Shaar Murray was describing them as the greatest rock band in the world, and a friendship was soon forged.

Keith Topping suggests a debt to Mott the Hoople and 'stepping back into rock history from the badlands of punk's 'the past is dead' propaganda'. He added, 'The contracts had all arrived, the groups were contemplating wearing suits, the punks had all come out of the garage and gone into the studio, thereby castrating the DIY ethic of their origins.' At the same time, it was a bold statement as to the band's ambition. As Jones told Kris Needs, ''Garageland' had to be the last song because it indicates where we're moving to next.' What's more, Chimes' drum roll seems to have been taken on by Topper Headon in 'Tommy Gun' on the next album. First aired live at Harlesden Coliseum in March '77, the song remained a permanent fixture, often as an encore.

Receiving the Punk Makeover: Introducing Topper Headon

'We must have tried every drummer that then had a kit. I mean every drummer in London. I think we counted 205. That's why we were lost until we found Topper Headon. He played funk, soul ... reggae didn't faze him. That's really why The Clash became an interesting musical unit in its future, because we had Topper Headon on the kit.'
Joe Strummer

Terry Chimes didn't stick around after the first LP was recorded. He left before the cover shot was snapped, later reflecting, 'I wanted one kind of life, they wanted another and, like, why are we working together, if we want completely different things?' Accordingly, he was credited as 'Tory Crimes' on *The Clash*, in something of a public fit of pique by the others. The time had come to find a permanent replacement, the search carrying on throughout March 1977. While Strummer reckoned they totted up more than 200 potential candidates, Clash biographer Pat Gilbert suggested a few dozen responded to a *Melody Maker* advert stressing 'no jazz, no funk, no laidback', that description somewhat ironic considering the eventual successful candidate's abilities.

Chris Bashford (later in Chelsea) and Jon Moss (later in Culture Club) were among the unsuccessful applicants. Then on March 24, The Clash went to see The Kinks at The Rainbow and Jones bumped into Headon at the bar. Despite the ad, the 21-year-old – capable of playing jazz, funk, soul, absolutely anything – was asked to call by Rehearsals the following day.

Nicholas Bowen Headon was born on May 30, 1955, in Bromley, Kent. His parents were from Wales and they were both musical, enjoying singing and playing piano. The family were based in Orpington until Nicky was 12, when they moved to the outskirts of Dover, his father, a headmaster, having been appointed head of a grammar school there, which Nicky also attended. Describing his school life, Headon explained, 'When your father's headmaster, to be accepted you have to be a lot more naughty than the other kids. I got into trouble to show I wasn't the teacher's pet.'

Nicky taught himself piano and began playing drums at school, inspired by Buddy Rich, Billy Cobham and Man's Terry Williams. 'I listened to rock, but used to play trad jazz every Sunday at the Louis Armstrong pub,' he said. A band engagement followed with the Marines Band at Deal's nine-piece outfit, Force 9, Nicky getting by despite not being able to read music.

He left school with three A-levels, then worked for a year as a shipping clerk at Dover

Topper, Mick, Paul and Joe get edgy for the camera

Docks. He was remembered by colleagues there as 'a quiet, friendly boy who was very nervous'. His band played around Dover, Nicky getting to know future Clash associate Steve Barnacle, before moving to London, marrying his girlfriend, Wendy, and securing work with Canadian rocker Pat Travers. But he was sacked – apparently for not hitting the drums hard enough. It's also documented that he played in 1973 for cult prog rockers Mirkwood, appearing with them for a year and a half, and supporting major acts such as Supertramp.

There was also Headon's audition for the London SS. This time he got the job but decided to jump ship, instead heading off on a tour of US Air Force bases with the GI's soul group. That band also got to open for soul legends The Temptations, something Headon would make the most of mentioning when auditioning for The Clash. Before that, there was a stint with London-based Canadian band Fury, but Headon was again booted out for not hitting the drums aggressively enough. With that in mind, when he tried out for The Clash, he told himself, 'Whatever happens I'm going to knock shit out of those drums. As a result, I had to re-learn my style.' What's more, a little white lie about The Temptations might have helped impress his new employers. Headon admitted in *Westway to the World* a misleading choice of words when recalling his soul covers tour, saying, 'I told everybody I played with The Temptations, but I never. I played for a band that supported The Temptations.'

Either way, he got the job – recruited on £25 a week, like his bandmates – and a punk makeover followed, Nicky being given a short haircut, bespoke fatigues, monkey boots and a copy of *The Clash* so he could learn the songs. He was also rechristened 'Topper' by Paul Simonon, who thought he looked like Mickey the Monkey from the *Topper* comic, because of his sticky-out ears. In *Westway to the World*, he recalled, 'I thought I'd join, stay with the band a year, get my name known, then move on to something good. To me it was so different, I didn't have the foresight to believe it would actually work.' Yet, talking to Caroline Coon for *Melody Maker* the year that he joined, he said, 'I really wanted to join The Clash. I want to give them even more energy than they've got – if that's possible.'

Headon made his live debut at The Roundhouse on April 10, 1977, another two weeks' intensive rehearsals following before warm-up gigs in France for the 28-date White Riot UK tour. Even then he had doubts, staying overnight at Rehearsals in Camden waiting for an early morning coach to Dover. He said, 'I felt quite alone laying there, thinking I don't really know any of these people. I was scared. I thought, 'Shall I do a runner while I've got the chance?''

From Palais des Glaces to Mont-de-Marsan, via Eric's and The Rainbow

'They pay 5p on the buses and they never use toothpaste, but they've got £2.50 to go and see The Clash ... tonight.'
'Part-time Punks', Television Personalities, 1978

Headon decided to stick with it. *Record Mirror*'s Barry Cain was at the Palais des Glaces in Paris on April 27, one of three shows billed as Les Nuits Punk at the Faubourg-du-Temple venue. The Tyla Gang, The Damned and The Stranglers were also involved that week, while Subway Sect supported Strummer and co. Cain didn't actually spot the new Clash drummer until part way into the set, something he classed as a positive sign on another revelatory night, judging by his entertaining review, complete with schoolboy French, as relived in Cain's *'77 Sulphate Strip*.

He wrote, 'Nothing flash, just a casual stroll on and straight into 'Londres est en Flammes', wherein Paul Simonon breaks a string on his bass. The light show is limited but effective. Strummer's 3,000cc voice is encased in soft green, red and white body shells. He slams on the brakes at the penultimate second of the song and introduces the band. 'We Are Les Clash.' While Paul fixes the string, Strummer continues. 'So, you are *les punks de* Paris? You look like a bunch of fucking hippies to me.' His shoulders flap Cagney-style as he walks and his voice has a kinda John Wayne intonation. We're in for a Strummer summer.

''1977' is next up. Mick Jones sandwiches every slice of meat that right-on axemen have dished up through the years, from a Marriott crisscross walk to a Townshend leap, but he covers it in his own unique Rockfort dressing. He's the antithesis of Strummer's on-the-spot throbbing, burning up every inch of the stage, slipping and a-sliding on his own sweat. At times he and Paul look like a pair of grossly distorted Chinese bookends. 'Toots Chute Sepressurisée' is a strange choice which succeeds mainly because of Paul's thunderous bassline. Then there's 'Je M'en Fous Telement De I'USA'.

'Hey, I've just remembered – they've got a new drummer, again, haven't they? Of course. Ol' wassisname, again, Nicky

Headon. That's a tribute. It's taken me 45 minutes to realise there's a different drummer in their midst. He's blending well, like he's been with them for years. But he looks so ill. 'Haine et Guerre' has Mick at the mic. The Frenchman in the next seat nudges me in the ribs. 'They are good musicians, but they are not playing music.' Shut up and stop breathing garlic over me. I flash a friendly smile. After all, the guy could be another fucking pickpocket.

'After 'Tricheur' we're treated to 'Flics et Voleurs', only the second time the Junior Murvin song from the album has been performed live. It's a slightly different version from the record and it works like a dream. 'This is a song for the intelligentsia, *les* intellectuals,' says Joe.

'Holes are dug in the music of The Clash,

2

holes scratched deep by fingernails into which words are poured by Strummer. In the years that follow they'll dry into bone-hard relics of a frustrated generation. '48 Heures' and then one for the girls, if there are any, 'Dis Moi Non' and new song 'Radio Capitale', included on a special EP about the famous London radio station, which, folly upon folly, has already banned it. 'Controle de Loin' and 'Opportunite de Carriere' are fired in quick succession and a big cheer for the anthem 'Emeute des Blancs' with Strummer screaming, '1968' before tearing into the hit single. Favourite for the next single, 'Janie Jones', the most insanely commercial song from the album, is given the all-important pole position in the finale. Two encores – 'Band de Garage' and a re-blast of 'Emeute' first, '1977' and 'Londres est en Flammes' second. The band are treating this gig, and indeed all others in this short European tour, as a warm-up for the all-important nationwide stint, which kicked off in Guildford last Sunday. If this is a warm-up, I want an Eiffel of their hot nights, because they'll be unbelievable. The overwhelming success the gods have in store for The Clash will be totally justified. In the recording studio and live, there are very few bands around that are anywhere near them.'

Cain goes on to mention a post-show happening 'in the dark streets where the prostitutes scream', Strummer and Jones joining forces with The Damned's Captain Sensible and Rat Scabies, 'jamming together before a handful of people on the stage of an incredibly depressing disco on a dirty boulevard in a grubby part of town on the wrong side of shit', playing 'Louie Louie' and 'White Riot', where the makeshift quartet 'embrace like football players'.

The tour proper kicked off at Guildford

Civic Hall on May 1, with support from The Buzzcocks, Subway Sect, The Slits and The Prefects. The Jam were also set to feature, but a fall-out followed between Rhodes and John Weller, The Jam's manager and Paul Weller's father. While it was The Clash's second punk package tour, this time they were headlining. And as Robin Banks put it, recalling that first night, 'We couldn't believe what was happening to us. We

looked out into the auditorium at all the people packed in there. Suddenly it was like the dream of becoming rock stars had come true.'

Buzzcocks lead singer Pete Shelley, talking to Jon Savage, said, 'It was the first proper roadshow. Because the Anarchy tour hadn't managed to do that, its notoriety went ahead of it like a leper's bell. The Clash played everywhere with The Slits, Subway Sect, and us. It was great. everyone got on with one other. It was actually working. There was something there, and it was outside the established music business.' Buzzcocks guitarist Steve Diggle, talking to *Uncut* in 2015, added, 'They were an amazing live band and I don't think they released a single duff track. On the White Riot tour, I'll never forget the shivers I used to get every time they played 'London's Burning'. I used to stand at the side of the stage and watch the audience go crazy every time Joe hollered the opening lines. It was like witnessing the rebirth of rock'n'roll through a punk perspective.'

The Jam hung around that opening night, despite not playing, and Bruce Foxton and Rick Buckler looked back on that night in Guildford in 1993's *The Jam: Our Story*, saying, 'Although the musicians involved mixed quite happily, there was some antagonism between the band and Clash manager Bernard Rhodes, who wanted the signed bands – The Clash and The Jam – to subsidise the other acts. However, with The Jam having to pay for the use of The Clash's PA and buy their way on to the tour, John Weller decided there was too much money coming out of his pocket, particularly as they were only getting second billing.'

In an interview with me in early February 2018, Buckler added, 'The fall-out was really on a managerial level, silly things like ... well, they never really got together before to say, 'How is this going to work?' We were just thrown into this scenario. I think it would have been good if John (Weller) had that bit of foresight to talk about swapping nights as headline acts, because we were starting at level pegging.

'Bernie Rhodes had hired the PA, that was another issue. It wasn't big enough for the venues we were doing, and there wasn't enough equipment. He cheap-skated on a lot of it, one reason for the friction, with the headlining another part. It was ridiculous really. We should never have got into that situation. It was an idea put forward, I think, by the record company, to try and make it work financially, as both bands were hard

2

pushed for cash.'

The Jam would soon go back to Polydor – for whom they had signed that February – to look at financing a tour of their own. As Buckler explained, 'Somebody had to step in and say, 'Look, we've got to do this properly,' and we just went out, did our own tour. It was a situation we probably should never have been put into.'

Wherever they went, The Clash drew admirers, many inspired to form bands of their own. One such example was on May 5 at Eric's in Mathew Street, Liverpool – 14 years after the Beatles' last dates at the nearby Cavern Club – in what proved a major catalyst in the formation of three key bands in that next wave of post-punk: Echo and the Bunnymen, The Teardrop Explodes, and Wah! Heat (later simply Wah! or The Mighty Wah! among other variations). Yet it was The Crucial Three that formed first, a legendary Liverpudlian outfit that barely lasted a few weeks and never played a gig.

According to Julian Cope in 1994's *Head-On: Memories of the Liverpool Punk Scene and the Story of the Teardrop Explodes (1976–82)*, it was Duke McCool's (Echo and the Bunnymen frontman Ian McCulloch) eighteenth birthday when the White Riot tour came to the city, although it was not as if Cope knew McCool or his friend Pete Wylie at the start of the evening.

Cope had watched The Clash's progress from afar until that evening, writing, 'The first single was just a tinny glitter-stompf and football-fan vocals. I was disappointed. I expected something more but didn't know what. There was tremendous peer pressure to like The Clash. They'd been around ages but played nowhere. The album came out mid-April. You had to buy an early copy to get the red sticker. You sent the red sticker to *NME* and they sent a limited 'Capital Radio' single with no sleeve. It seemed like every week you had to dig deep to find cash for some record no one could be without and maintain any credibility. Peer pressure. All the bloody time. It put me off *The Clash* album. How could you enjoy something when you had to have the free accessory that took weeks to come? The Stranglers had done the same thing and been royally slagged off for it. But The Clash were different from everyone else. I could see that, but it still pissed me off.'

Of that night at Eric's, he recalled, 'Mathew Street was awash with brand-new punk rockers, people we'd never seen before – weekend punks, greasers, bikers, Teds, even hippies with make-up and Union Jacks painted on their faces. It was the first real event. It felt like the public had heard too, but that was OK because it was for The Clash and they didn't really suit the underground. Somehow it was even better if young kids got into The Clash, because they had this heavy moral side to them. They were like Cromwell's New Model Army marching into battle. I loved The Clash when Strummer was angry, but when they occasionally became good time, I'd automatically bleep it out of my mind.'

He mentions further regulars Pete Burns (later of Dead or Alive) and Paul Rutherford (later of Frankie Goes to Hollywood), and another character, 'a bit of a loudmouth' he'd noticed in Probe Records and described as 'so animated', wearing 'a black leather jacket and black combat pants' with 'a Clash T-shirt under the jacket, zipped halfway', his hair 'natural black and gelled into a boyish quiff, the 'most enthusiastic person I'd ever seen ... and on his leather was a homemade badge, it said 'Rebel Without a Degree''.

The Clash
JOIN US ON THE WHITE RIOT – '77 TOUR
MAY
Sun. 1st
Mon. 2nd
Tues. 3rd
Wed. 4th
Thurs. 5th
Fri. 6th
Sat. 7th
Sun. 8th
Mon. 9th
Tues. 10th
Thurs. 12th
Sun. 15th
Guildford, Civic
Chester, Rascals
Birmingham, Barbarellas
Swindon, The Affair Ballroom
Liverpool, Erics.
Aberdeen, University
Edinburgh, Playhouse Theatre
Manchester, Electric Circus
London, Rainbow
Kidderminster, Town Hall
Nottingham, Palais
Plymouth, Fiesta
MAY
Mon. 16th
Tues. 17th
Thurs. 19th
Fri. 20th
Sat. 21st
Mon. 23rd
Tues. 24th
Wed. 25th
Thurs. 26th
Fri. 27th
Sat. 28th
Sun. 29th
Mon. 30th
Swansea, University
Leeds, Polytechnic
Middlesborough, Rock Gardens
Newcastle, University
St. Albans, City Hall
Stafford, Top Of The World
Cardiff, Top Rank
Brighton, Polytechnic
Bristol, Colston Hall
West Runton, Pavillion
Canterbury, Odeon
Chelmsford, Chancellor Hall
Dunstable, California Ballroom
... now out + THE LP + The CLASH

That, it turns out, was Wylie.

Of the headliners, Cope added, 'There was no intro, no music or anything. The Clash walked on and just went 'Fuuuck Offff!' It was so funny. I started laughing at them. They were totally brilliant. It was just as cartoony as The Ramones but blazing with colour. And they all moved in rigid formation. Joe Strummer was a maniac, on his knees and bawling his head off at the front row. As he got lower, the guys at the front also went down with him, and from behind you could see everything. It was this weird tableau, one guy performing to about four guys, all of them crouching as low as they could get. I noticed something particular about the audience. You could get lost in it, let yourself get carried anywhere you wished. The crowd was like a field of corn, swaying and dipping. It felt so good.

'I sunk deeper into the centre and The Clash whirlwind blew across us and took our heads off. This group was like one of those old Eastern European wind-up train sets. You turn the key, put the engine on the track, the engine scurries down and picks up a truck, then the two of them zoom into a depot and pick up their load, just some lithographed cylinder. Meanwhile there's a little factory mill in the corner that also started the minute you switched on. The doors open and inside is a click-click-click-click. You peer in and there's a two-dimensional tin man sawing the same piece of tin wood endlessly. In a far corner a signal gantry stutters its stop, go, stop, go. And all this from one wind-up. That was The Clash. Strummer was the engine, Mick Jones was the truck, both zooming round doing their own thing but each picking up the crowd, zipping it round then dropping it back down. In his corner, Simonon endlessly sawed the same piece of wood.

'During Subway Sect I stood still and watched. The Slits made you move, like a skank but more graceless than reggae. The Clash, however, suggested unlimited nuclear war. You needed a dance that described fire fights in the Mekong Delta or the napalming of homeless children.'

As the band tore through their set, Cope reckons he 'bounced ass off for about 40 minutes', regularly careering into Wylie, concluding, 'The Clash were epic. Totally fucking epic. My favourite music was always the weirder shit, but this was so upfront and such hard showbiz I fell for it pretty much all the way. They did loads of encores, made loads of effort, then were gone. The club burned on free energy for the rest of the night. All the right-on guys loved Strummer, all the women wanted to fuck Simonon, all the secret rock stars wanted to be Mick Jones. It was just garble, garble for the rest of the night.'

The Jam were back for the May 9 date at The Rainbow, but Alex Ogg, in *The Jam: Our Story*, said that proved the final straw. 'Unable to soundcheck, The Jam's sound was awful, and there were rumours that this may have been caused by deliberate tampering. The Jam took the decision to pull out with eight dates to play. A decision was quickly taken to sort out a tour on their own terms, now their fan base had swelled sufficiently to accommodate this.'

However, he added, 'The eye-opening Clash debacle at least offered some comic moments. At The Rainbow, security decided to disrobe the audience of anything that could be construed as being a weapon. Punk fashion of the time incorporated ammunition belts, motorcycle boots and studs, all of which had to be left behind outside the auditorium. Hence many viewers had to pogo their way through the night in their socks. In Rick's words, 'The Rainbow foyer looked like a 10ft-high third-world munitions dump.''

Buckler reflected on this in February 2018, telling me, 'There was all sorts of ridiculous things going on, where you would have stuff confiscated from you. There was almost an overkill of paranoia about punks turning up with machetes or bullet belts or all sorts of things that could be used as weapons! The whole violence thing was completely overdone, mostly in the press.'

Paul Weller recalled those days in a 2016 interview with Barry Cain for an updated version of *'77 Sulphate Strip*, saying, 'The world needed punk. There was a really boring drab scene at the time and I didn't relate to any bands apart from the Feelgoods. It was all arena rock, Fleetwood Mac, REO Speedwagon. I'd never seen The Who and wasn't into what they were doing in the '70s. I wasn't into concept records. I liked short, sharp three-minute stuff, something like 'Substitute' meant much more to me than any number off *Tommy* or *Quadrophenia*, all that concept gear. I just didn't understand it. 'I Can't Explain' was much closer to how I felt.

'When I first saw the Pistols, then later The Clash, I thought that was the warning shot, the blazing flare announcing to the world it was our time. We all missed out on the '60s, cos we were just too young. I was into the music, but not old enough to be involved. Then we had Bowie and Bolan in the early '70s, and that was cool, but was followed by a grey numbness until punk happened. It got a lot of kids, me included, back into something, out of our bedrooms, into clubs, creating fanzines, seeing bands, making our own clothes. Punk was so much more than just music. It was a cultural revolution but became a ridiculous sad pastiche after a short space of time. It was one big explosion, then everyone went off and did their own thing.

'I was very inspired by The Clash, especially in the early days. The first time I saw them was when they had the paint-splattered clothes. Keith Levene was playing guitar. They really touched me and made me want to say something important, make some kind of social statement. My early attempts were really naïve and ridiculous, but then I was naïve and ridiculous. I soon learnt how to approach writing and by *All Mod Cons* I hit my stride. I loved the early stuff, but once they started to get too stylised, they just turned into an ordinary rock band. Once they went to America they turned into an ordinary American rock band. First time I met Joe Strummer was at the 100 Club. He'd been to see us at the Windsor Castle in Harrow Road, and he turned and said, 'You're a mod, ain't ya!' He was the first geezer that realised what we were trying to do. A nice fella. He didn't exactly take us under his wing but was that bit older. We stayed in a squat with him one night, just chatting and smoking draw. He was really nice.'

That show at The Rainbow was certainly eventful for The Clash, Paul Simonon recalling 'people ripping up seats, piling them on the stage, stuff going all over', while Strummer added, 'That was unheard of for punk rock groups to play. The Rainbow Theatre was like the Madison Square Garden of London. For punk rock groups filling that stage it meant there was no stopping it now. Like the dam burst!'

Buzzcocks frontman Pete Shelley added, 'I heard them play 'Janie Jones' every night on the White Riot tour in '77. We'd never toured outside the North West before and were all blown away how incredible they were live. They'd play 'Janie Jones' straight after the opening number and I remember people ripping out the seats when they played The Rainbow. The Clash were very much a London band and always got a phenomenal response in London. We never bothered how well we played, but I remember they would come off stage and be shouting, 'You missed that bit' to each other, regardless of how well each set went. They were always trying to be tighter and better and harder and faster.'

Billy Bragg was also there. As he told John Robb, 'We saw The Prefects, Subway Sect and the Buzzcocks. When The Jam came on it seemed like the place was too big for them. They didn't come over as well as they did at The Red Cow and The Nashville. But The Clash just blew us away. We didn't know their stuff but to see them play there, they just had everything. We'd seen the Stones at Earl's Court in 1975 and The Who at Charlton (Athletic) FC the same year, really big venues, but The Clash were our age.

'To see The Clash on the White Riot tour and realise they were doing exactly what we loved the Stones for doing, throwing all the same shapes, using the same equipment and making great noises, but they were our generation. It was a great moment. It was like discovering how to be a rock star. You just did it yourself. You didn't wait for someone to discover you. That was the most important thing that came out of punk. There was something about The Clash that you didn't get from other bands. Also, there was a riot at the gig. Instead of being on the outside looking in, I was right in the centre of it. We came home and cut our hair and bought skinny trousers. It was year zero. That was the moment for me.'

Four nights later a Clash show at Leicester's De Montfort Hall was recorded by BBC Radio 1 for *In Concert*, followed by dates in Amsterdam, Plymouth, Swansea and Newcastle, the latter inspiring Angelic Upstarts frontman Mensi, who told John Robb, 'I was working down the pit, when I saw two bands that changed my outlook on life. One was The Clash at Newcastle University (May 20), the other The Jam at Seaburn Hall (June 17). Absolutely phenomenal, both of them. With The Clash there were two support bands who at the time I thought were absolute garbage, The Slits and Subway Sect. I thought, 'If they can be up there playing, there's no reason why I can't.' It was more The Slits that set us off. I could never aspire to being as good as The Clash. The Jam at the time I'd seen them on the In the City tour had all the energy of the punk thing. That was enough. After The Clash, I formed a band the next day. I knocked on everybody's door.'

The following night, after a show in St Albans, Strummer and Headon were taken to a police station to be interrogated, following complaints about the previous night's rowdy affair at a hotel in the North East. They subsequently confessed to stealing 11 pillows and a room key. Then came dates in Stafford, Bristol and Chelmsford, and a tour finale in Dunstable, filmed by Don Letts. A replacement show for a cancelled punk festival in Birmingham came next, back at Barbarella's in June, before the band recorded a new song for their next single, 'Complete Control', at Sarm East Studios, Whitechapel. Then, in August, came their first European tour.

Barry Cain was on hand for that tour's

August 5 opener at Mont-de-Marsan Festival, in a bullring near Landes, southwest France, 90 miles from the Spanish border. The Clash appeared on a bill including The Damned, The Jam, Dr Feelgood, Eddie and The Hot Rods, and The Boys. They debuted 'Complete Control' and further new tracks, 'Clash City Rockers', '(White Man) In Hammersmith Palais' and 'The Prisoner', the *Record Mirror* reporter reckoning each sounded, 'as good as, if not better than, anything they've ever done before'. Cain added, 'Weeks of devout rehearsing have made the songs Clash-sharp. And that's sharp.' He declared that appearance 'the longest Clash set in history – one and a half hours', yet Strummer reckoned he failed that night 'to click with the fans and when that happens, he's dead'. That said, the *Record Mirror* reporter added that, 'even when they're bad The Clash are better than most.'

The Jam, it turned out, didn't feature. Rick Buckler told me in February 2018, 'I think it was down to John (Weller), another dispute, silly because I think the bigger picture was that we should have played, as it was one of the first punk festivals.' In fact, Cain's report suggests Weller Snr took umbrage at the promoters bumping them back to appear after Dr Feelgood, and refused an early-hours closing-night slot.

As for The Clash, Topper Headon's first few months at the punk rock coalface proved a blast. Another festival date followed in Liège, before the band's continental tour properly started at Amsterdam's Paradiso in late September, from there taking in dates in France, Switzerland, Germany and Sweden. As Headon put it, 'The initial thing about punk, what the hell, do what you wanna do, play what excites you. And we lived it and tried to do that.' But as he stressed in 2005's *Viva Joe Strummer*, 'We constantly progressed, changing our look all the time, and stopped dressing as punks after the first album.'

Establishing the Strummer/Jones Partnership

'They're no garage band anymore – they're a multistorey car park.'
Barry Cain, '77 Sulphate Strip, 2007

It was a time of great creativity for the band, Joe Strummer and Mick Jones truly finding their feet in a productive songwriting partnership. Jones recalled, 'For the first album we'd say we need another song and he'd rush upstairs, knock something out. Later on, we'd get good as a partnership. He'd sit at one end of the table, type out the lyrics, knock them out just like that, sitting there like a newspaper man, pull it out of the typewriter, hand it over to me at the other end of the table, and I'd knock out the tune. Just like that. It would take half an hour. Later, when you kind of reassess things and all the time that's passed since, it's become a magical partnership, but we weren't really aware of it at the time.'

Reflecting on that same writing masterclass, the band's road manager, Johnny Green, who took over from Roadent as the band's main roadie late in '77, told Rod Kitson for *The Quietus* website in 2012, 'It worked on affection and competition. While they were really fond of each other and close to each other, like the best love affairs it could spark up with passion at times. It could spill over in any direction – it was strong emotions. It wasn't cool and calculated.'

The first Clash single featuring Topper

Headon was the explosive 'Complete Control', released on September 23 and rightly seen as one of punk's greatest singles. It was something of a wake-up call from a band angry at CBS releasing previous single 'Remote Control' without consulting them, the band suggesting that any guarantee of artistic freedom had proven a lie. The title was a Bernie Rhodes phrase, Strummer saying in 1991, 'Bernie had a meeting in The Ship in Soho after the Anarchy Tour. He said he wanted complete control ... I came out of the club with Paul (Simonon) collapsing on the pavement in hysterics at those words.'

The song was written in Jones' Wilmcote House bedroom that summer, Strummer seeing no need to change his fired-up lyrics, in what turned out to be the first of an amazing run of 45s, the first three all non-album singles. That said, Tony James told Pat Gilbert, 'I have vivid memories of Joe turning up with a bunch of lyrics, and the pair of them going upstairs to his bedroom for an hour and writing 'Complete Control' on acoustic guitar. I could see it would take them to another level. It was more sophisticated than anything they'd done before.'

Jones' rant also highlighted the band's run-ins with police and their bid to get fans into gigs for free. The group were perhaps desperate to convince themselves that signing with a major was the right call, allowing them to fight the corporate system from within, their punk ideals intact. Early champion and influential DJ John Peel wasn't so sure though, suggesting they must have realised CBS wasn't 'a foundation for the arts'. But Jon Savage felt that, 'Instead of a piece of cynicism, 'Complete Control' becomes a hymn to punk autonomy at its moment of eclipse.'

Assisted by Mickey Foote, Lee 'Scratch' Perry co-produced the track, the revered reggae innovator a fan since hearing the cover of his Junior Murvin co-write, 'Police & Thieves', and moved enough to have a picture of The Clash on a wall of his Jamaican studio. When they learned that he was in London producing Bob Marley and the Wailers, he was invited along. Word had it that during recording he blew out a studio mixing board attempting to get a deeper sound from Simonon's bass, while in a 1979 *NME* feature Strummer and Jones said Perry reckoned the latter played guitar 'with an iron fist'. His contribution, however, was toned down, the band going back and bringing the guitars out more, playing down the innovative producer's distinctive dub echo touches. But whatever they did worked a treat.

Paul Simonon told *Uncut* in 2015, 'It's a bit difficult for me to say about Lee Perry because by the time he was there I had really bad flu. I recorded my bass part, only saw him for half an hour then had to go and lie down. Missed the whole thing.'

In the same feature, Primal Scream's Bobby Gillespie recalled seeing the band for the first time in October '77, and said, 'They were breathtaking. 'Complete Control' had just been released as a single and they played the most scorching version I've ever heard. Bob Dylan has that line about 'the ghost of electricity', and that's exactly what it felt like that night. The whole set had this sensational impact that stayed with me for weeks. They came back to Scotland two months later and played an equally amazing set at the Glasgow Apollo with Richard Hell and The Voidoids.'

Pete Wylie added, 'If I could go back in

time and pick any song to see live in any setting, including Elvis' first gig, The Beatles at The Cavern, Happy Mondays at The Hacienda... if I had to choose just one more song to see live I'd pick 'Complete Control', anywhere, any venue. It's the definitive Clash record. When they played Deeside on the On Parole tour, I had me plus 20 on the guest list. So that line 'On the last tour, my mates couldn't get in', that was literally me! As a fan, when that song came out, life was better and it always is when I play it today. It's a raw record and an absolutely combustible performance. It screams out at you. I was playing it last night, in me living room, shouting the song out, and halfway through I remembered that Joe was dead. All of a sudden it hit me. How can somebody who does this not be here, y'know? For me, 'Complete Control' is just their finest hour.'

Steve Diggle enthused, 'The production sound is completely all over the place, but it's still one of the best fucking tracks I've ever heard. It's got a killer chorus and the lyrics reinforce the fact The Clash weren't prepared to take any prisoners. They might have signed to a major label but it was definitely on their terms: they knew you had to work hand in hand with the devil to get anywhere back then.'

Roddy Frame added, 'I always thought the singles they brought out around then were much more juicy and exciting-sounding than the first album. The message of 'Complete Control' was a bit confusing to me at the time, but more than anything I just thought of it as a great rock'n'roll record with a great riff. I remember learning it, sitting with a little amp, trying to work it out. I think it's the song where Mick Jones came into his own as a sort of Keith Richards of his generation.'

Mark Perry said, 'I still see The Clash as the closest a band can be to the urban terrorist guitar slinger. Without a gun, but with a guitar. That's the early Clash to me. I was the one who actually said that the day The Clash signed to CBS was the day punk died. It sounds dramatic, but at the time The Clash meant so much to us. More than the Pistols, they were *our* band, y'know. So I wondered how you could reconcile something like '1977' with being on one of the biggest record companies in the world? I thought, 'What's all that about?' But looking back more realistically, they were a very ambitious group, they just wanted to be rock'n'roll stars like any band does. I was probably a bit too earnest to appreciate that. So when they did 'Complete Control' I thought it was brilliant, for The Clash to actually be able to tell people that they'd signed to a label who'd released 'Remote Control' as a single without their consent and make a song about that whole dilemma. That was one of the enduring qualities of The Clash, that if they'd made a mistake they'd be able to talk about it.'

Don Letts reflected, 'When they signed to CBS there was all this stuff about selling out – but the way I saw it, if The Clash hadn't done what they did, punk rock wouldn't even be a fucking movement. God bless the Pistols for starting it all off, but it was The Clash who really gave the thing its bollocks, its depth. They took it upon their shoulders to take it on to the next level because they didn't want to be stuck with this fucking three-chord thing. That ended at the bottom of their street. They were ready to take on the world.'

Lyndon Morgans contended that, 'This vies with 'God Save the Queen' or 'Anarchy in the UK' as the supreme expression of

2

what that particular moment in British music was all about. It's a squall of manic energy, a cocksure roar of satisfaction from a band who just knew they were in perfect sync with their times. And their place. And it's funny too – Joe's, 'You're my guitar hero!' a few bars into Mick's solo. And the dropouts near the end are brilliantly done.'

Finally, broadcaster Gideon Coe added, 'For those interested in pointless arguments about the relative merits of records, this is the great punk rock single. It also gives a lie to that hoary old utterance on the part of '76 stalwarts that 'punk rock died the day The Clash signed to CBS'. Without them putting pen to paper with the big boys and then getting pissed-off over the proposed release of 'Remote Control', they might never have delivered this. How would we have survived without hearing that intro, Jones' guitar solos and Strummer barking out, 'This is Joe Public... speaking!' As a measure of just how magnificent this record is, I find it very hard to write about it without immediately wanting to hear it. Again and again.'

The single reached No.28 in the UK, the highest position thus far. It was also No.16 in the *NME*'s 1977 writers' poll and *Rolling Stone* rated it No.361 in its 2004 list of the 500 Greatest Songs of All Time. The B-side was 'City of the Dead', another Jones song from a productive if not dark period for the lead guitarist, who was somewhat disillusioned that summer by the way the punk scene was heading, the negative aspects picked up on by the tabloids exaggerated by an air of violence at several shows, and factors such as the ignorance of the idiots spitting at the band, thinking it was the done thing.

The Inspirational Touch: Home and Away

'Politics and religion weren't mentioned, and a kind of blueprint was set for the local punk scene. Barriers were being broken down and friendships formed.'

Guy Trelford to John Robb, Punk Rock: An Oral History, 2006

Those gigs were something to behold, for the best and worst of reasons. As Johnny Green put it in the *Viva Joe Strummer* documentary, 'Live performances with The Clash were never predictable. It was just mayhem from the word go. Running, jumping, all action.' Mick Jones added, 'Sometimes I'd be going so fast I'd fall off the end of the stage.' Unfortunately, the spitting would remain a problem for quite some time, idiots in the crowd thinking it was part of what the scene was about. Green said, 'You couldn't play a gig in the punk years that was not covered in gob. From the moment you stepped from behind the amplifiers to the stage, you were covered in it. It didn't matter who you were, but it was especially good if you could gob on The Clash.'

Then there was the violence. Strummer chipped in, 'When you see someone being kicked by 30 other geezers, you've gotta stop. We'd all stop and sort the ruck out. Then we'd kick it right back in again.' The tensions weren't just between band and audience, the spark that made this band so special also ensuring added on-stage and in-the-studio tension at times, not least between the bass player and lead guitarist. Paul Simonon said, 'Me and Mick had an argument. I just snapped and went to punch him, got him in the ear. Next thing, Topper and Joe are trying to hold my elbows. I was thrashing and trying to get hold of Mick. Then we ended up in the studio – Mick's over there, I'm over there, and Joe has to go back and forth to tell me, 'Oh, it's E now. Oh, now it's C.''

You've got to remember just how young they were though. At times, Johnny Green felt it was like being in charge of kids on a school trip. Recalling his days driving the band, as memorably relived in his memoir *A Riot of our Own*, with fellow roadie 'The Baker' following in a van with the gear, he told Rod Kitson for *The Quietus* website in late 2012, 'Who sat in the front seat? Always Mick Jones. He had a reputation in those days, and the others would laugh and call him a diva. It was like a group of unruly children. I was three years older. I was the old man – mid-20s. They would be joshing, getting bored very easily, wanting to stop at the services, mess about, drink cups of tea. It wasn't a wild rock'n'roll lifestyle. They'd take it in turns to play music on the stereo, educating each other about new music they'd discovered, always talking, reading the newspapers and swapping stories. It was a pretty interesting place to be.'

There was also a sense of the band taking on what Mick Jones had experienced for himself as a fan following Mott the Hoople a few years before. Green recalled for 2005's *Viva Joe Strummer: The Clash and Beyond*, 'Because it's a democratic band, because it's a thinking band, and because they actually practised what they preached, people came back to the hotel every night. So, people who followed the tour were put up on people's floors, whoever's got space, people travelling to the next town could kip down. But not if you were fools, right, cos this isn't a church outing.' And as Pat Gilbert put it in the same documentary, 'They managed to get through to people what ordinary rock music doesn't. That's why they were so important. That's why they were able to change culture.'

They were clearly on a creative and performance high, having taken the high ground first scaled by their early punk rivals, the reaction on the live circuit and to the recordings taking them to new heights. Gilbert wrote, 'By autumn 1977, The Clash had become the most important new rock group in Britain. The enforced inactivity of the Sex Pistols, banned from playing most UK venues, transformed them into punk's chief ambassadors. Under the tutelage of Bernie Rhodes, The Clash had brought a strong political dimension to punk that chimed with the mood of unrest in mid-'70s Britain. Asked their position on issues such as racism, housing problems, Northern Ireland and terrorism, Joe, Mick Jones and Paul Simonon would often exasperate journalists with their hardline punk rhetoric. But the music press loved them, or more accurately loved to spar with them, as did the public.'

Soon, they were back on the road, for the Get Out of Control tour, set to open in Northern Ireland. And the reception in Belfast was wild, Guy Trelford telling John Robb, 'I was a huge fan. I remember how excited my mate and myself were. This was the first major punk event to take place in Northern Ireland. On the night of October 20, hundreds of punks converged on Belfast city centre and made their way to the Ulster Hall, but the gig was cancelled. The punks were angry. Windows were smashed in the venue. The punks laid down across the road and stopped the traffic. The riot police arrived, busted a few heads, scooped a couple of kids, confiscated cameras, destroyed film.

'The incident subsequently became known as 'The Riot of Bedford Street'. Admittedly, compared to the vicious riots we were used to seeing in Northern Ireland, this was pretty minor. But there was one huge difference. Here we had kids from the two opposing traditions, Protestant and Catholic kids standing side by side, taking on the authorities out of sheer frustration at not being allowed to see their favourite band. At that time, if Protestant and Catholic kids came into contact it was usually to throw bricks and bottles at and kick the shit out of each other. While waiting to see what was happening, the punk kids got chatting about The Clash, punk, other bands, etc.

'In the end, The Clash never got to play, but the whole event became the catalyst for igniting the Ulster punk scene. Joe Strummer promised the band would be back soon as the crowds began to drift away. At least they had the balls to come here in the first place, unlike the Pistols, The Jam, Sham 69, and countless others. And all was soon forgotten and forgiven when the band kept their promise to return.'

That Belfast return was on December 20 at the Ulster Hall, tagged on to the end of the tour, the last live engagement of a highly eventful 1977. The band received a rapturous reception, Trelford adding, 'For a lot of us present that night it still ranks as the most exciting and inspiring gig ever.'

In a 1999 interview with Strummer, Stuart Clark recalled that initial visit, saying, 'The City Council, God bless 'em, forced the eleventh-hour cancellation of The Clash's Ulster Hall gig. The riot that resulted from the RUC's heavy-handed treatment of the punks outside remains a part of local rock'n'roll folklore and led to them being given the benefit of the doubt when they posed for pictures in front of the Long Kesh cages. People were altogether less forgiving when a couple of months later their hero took to wearing an H-Block T-shirt. Forget the cause, there was huge resentment over The Troubles being co-opted into The Clash's guerrilla chic. This is our everyday reality, the reasoning went, not the latest Vivienne Westwood creation.'

Defending himself, Strummer responded, 'If I go to Spain, I'm going to stand in front of an El Greco hamburger stand. If I go to Belfast, I'm going to stand in front of one of those cages. To me it's all about showing people what's going on. You think everybody in the world knows what's going on in Belfast? No, they don't. We didn't construct that cage on the corner or have it flown in. We just fucking walked up to it and stood there. This is reality, let's have it out. No way, in 1978, would that picture have appeared on the front of *The Daily Telegraph*. Y'know, 'We can't be showing that to the people of Tiddlesborough or Braintree, Essex.' I had no trouble with that at all. If we were in Sardinia now I'd get out and stand in front of the Sardinian Office of Sardines, or whatever.'

That said, he admitted the furore taught him a lot, adding, 'If you don't know all the details, shut up. This is a conflict that's been going on for over 700 years, and we've only been alive a microscopic amount of that time. The one thing I'd like to say in relation to Northern Ireland, is that whatever we did there was always well-intentioned. I know I'm contradicting myself all over the shop, but I never saw our actions as being exploitative.'

Guy Trelford added, 'Getting involved in Northern Irish politics is a dodgy business,

Mick, Paul, Joe and Topper working on the rider

as Joe found to his cost when he received death threats from Loyalist paramilitaries, resulting in a planned Clash gig in Derry being cancelled. Understandably a lot of young punks, especially those from the Protestant community, were quite disturbed and angry at their hero's apparent support for Irish republicanism and the IRA. Just over a year before Joe had basked in the glory of 'uniting Protestant and Catholic kids with punk rock' and now our hero was seen to be taking sides in the conflict.

'Statements like Joe's made life even more difficult for punks who lived in the Protestant/Unionist community when some Loyalists mistakenly began to suspect all punks of being left-wing Republican sympathisers. Fuck, they didn't half make life difficult for some of us! I didn't agree with Joe on these points, but still had a lot of respect for the man. He still had the balls to bring The Clash back to Belfast after the death threats a couple more times over the years. While some of my mates completely disowned The Clash, I went back to see them in Belfast, because despite their flaws and contradictions, which only served to make them more human like the rest of us – hell, we all make mistakes – they were undoubtedly one of the greatest rock'n'roll bands of our generation.'

In an interview for my writewyattuk.com website in 2017, Tom Robinson – whose band TRB also played Belfast in 1977, performing at the Whitla Hall, Queen's University – was quick to react when I suggested the public perception was that The Clash were the first punk band to play Northern Ireland. He said, 'They didn't play – they turned up and used it as a photo opportunity in front of all the graffiti and barbed wire and soldiers in uniform, then went back to London. We were there in '77 and went back and played the Ulster Hall, then got Stiff Little Fingers to support us in the UK, the first band to get them over. I'm really proud of that, because there was a lot of attitude, posing and posturing about the politics of Northern Ireland, but ... it was lovely how kids from both sides of the divide would turn up to gigs, the punks hated by both sides!'

Stiff Little Fingers frontman Jake Burns was certainly inspired by that initial Clash visit, telling John Robb, 'We'd already formed the band. But we decided once we heard The Clash where we were going. Henry Cluney (SLF co-founder) came up to my parents' house with every punk record at the time. I bought a couple of things and a lot of it was fantastic. Henry sat me down and we had an evening saying, 'Now we're in a punk band, let's learn some songs.' By the end of the evening I was completely convinced by punk rock and thought, 'Let's do something completely original instead of just copying.''

In a piece for *Uncut* in 2015, Burns added, 'After Joe died, I was asked to write a tribute. I was trying not to be too gushing a fan, even though I am, and mentioned that I did find some of his political ideas somewhat naive. I was specifically referring to that terrorist chic, Joe wearing the Brigate Rosse T-shirt, things like that. I find all that dangerous anyway, anyone who does that. I know nobody back home in Northern Ireland was particularly impressed when they came over to Belfast and had their picture taken outside a British Army base. On that particular trip they didn't even play, so it was a bit like a cheap holiday in other people's misery. But everybody's allowed to make mistakes.'

The Undertones' Mickey Bradley told *Uncut*, 'They could have disappeared after 'White Riot' and would still get talked about a quarter of a century later. Being in Derry, I found it amazing that there were riots in London. Did people get their bowler hats knocked off? Interviews with The Clash explained things. Paul Simonon's bassline is still almost impossible to play.'

Jake Burns added, 'The Clash were absolutely vital to the formation of Stiff Little Fingers. They were singing songs about their own lives, which struck a huge chord with me. I thought, 'Well, if they're fed up growing up in West London, how fed up do they think I am growing up in Belfast?' Up until 'White Riot', I quite liked what I'd heard of the punk movement, but it had just struck me as a bit of fun, nothing particularly important. But The Clash came along and they were singing serious songs, but in an exciting fashion. It was electrifying. To me, 'White Riot' was as exciting as it must have been for someone in the '50s first hearing Elvis Presley. Especially since I'd grown up in Belfast where rioting was a way of life.'

The night after the Riot of Bedford Street, The Clash did get to play in Ireland, south of the border at Trinity College, Dublin, where the audience included the awestruck members of U2. In a 2003 interview with Elton John, marking the first anniversary of Joe Strummer's death and published on the *Epitaph* website, Bono recalled, 'The Clash were the first rock'n'roll band we ever saw perform. It was on the Get Out of Control tour. In fact, we wrote a tune called 'Out of Control' after seeing that show. I was 17 and remember being frightened. There was a lot of aggression at the gate. But I was also elated. I was in awe at the sight of their clothes – they were wearing militant guerilla style, art-attack gear – and there was an atmosphere in the crowd that felt like something was going to happen, like somebody could die or a revolution could start. It was one of those nights that just turn your world upside down.

'When I was a teenager, some of the punk rock stuff that was kicking around was kind of daft, a little bit silly – middle-class kids pretending they were working-class. But Joe seemed to sing from a different place – the kind of place I suppose Bob Dylan sings from, or John Lennon sang from. He was part town crier and part storyteller. The Sex Pistols were punk, and I loved them because of the sort of Richard III character John Lydon was playing, and just the sheer noise of the guitars. But what The Clash did was more like roots music. They were a garage band, but hey, were also fucking around with reggae, rockabilly and bluegrass. Joe just put all these different ideologies into the blender. There was this idea that came across in their music that it is possible, as Patti Smith later said, to 'wrestle the world from the fools', that the world is much more malleable than you think.'

Bono's bandmate, The Edge, speaking at 2003's Rock and Roll Hall of Fame induction ceremony, said, 'In rock'n'roll terms, The Clash are *the shit*. I know this because I saw it back in 1977 in a small hall in Trinity College, Dublin, and it actually changed my life. Bono was there, Adam and Larry, all the local bands. We were like 16 at the time and the first thing I noticed were the road crew. They looked so incredible, like they'd come from some Vivienne Westwood show on acid, and there seemed to be hundreds of them. They weren't doing anything, but they were just kind of wandering around on the stage. We were completely mesmerised.

'When the lights went down, the place just exploded. It was like they were possessed. They went into 'White Riot', and it was just the most intense thing anyone in that building had ever seen. The rage, the commitment ... It was years later that someone explained to me about something called amphetamine sulphate, but whatever was going on, it went way past being a rock'n'roll show. It was truly shamanistic, and by the end of the night Dublin was a different place, because for

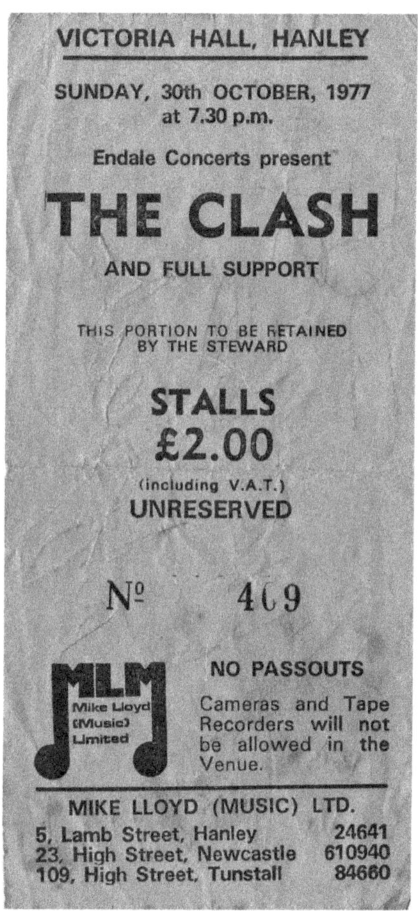

VICTORIA HALL, HANLEY

SUNDAY, 30th OCTOBER, 1977
at 7.30 p.m.

Endale Concerts present

THE CLASH

AND FULL SUPPORT

THIS PORTION TO BE RETAINED BY THE STEWARD

STALLS
£2.00
(including V.A.T.)
UNRESERVED

Nº 469

MLM
Mike Lloyd (Music) Limited

NO PASSOUTS

Cameras and Tape Recorders will not be allowed in the Venue.

MIKE LLOYD (MUSIC) LTD.
5, Lamb Street, Hanley 24641
23, High Street, Newcastle 610940
109, High Street, Tunstall 84660

2

everyone there that show was a kind of awakening. We all caught a glimpse of something, something distant but now attainable, a sense of possibilities, part political, part musical, part personal, but all completely inspirational. The revolution had come to town.'

Taking a Fresh Approach ... to the Limit

'Our attitude was, 'What? What do you mean, 'second album'?"

Joe Strummer, Westway to the World, 2000

The next part of the tale can be picked up at Manchester's Elizabethan Hall in November 1977, as relived by Pat Gilbert in a 2003 feature for *Mojo* marking the twenty-fifth anniversary of the second album, *Give 'Em Enough Rope*. That was the night American producer Sandy Pearlman entered the scene, over from New York on Concorde to see The Clash and contemplate working with them. Word was that on his arrival at the venue, the soundman signalled to Strummer, who announced, 'I'd like to dedicate this next song to Ted Nugent, Aerosmith, Journey, and, most of all, to Blue Oyster Cult,' before the band 'tore into a scorching version of 'I'm So Bored With the USA'.' Gilbert contends that 'loud jeers greeted Strummer's roll call of the leading lights of American AOR, the kind of acts punk was supposedly on a mission to destroy, and which in received punk wisdom represented everything excessive and self-indulgent about the mainstream music industry.' But as Pearlman reflected, 'After seeing that, I was ready to do the project. I thought such venom deserved my personal touch. I went backstage and said, 'I'm up for it – let's start straight away!'

The assumption was that CBS wanted a producer who would make a record with a cleaner sound, and one that would sell in America, *The Clash* having been denied its US release at that stage due to its raw production. As Mick Jones saw it, 'They feared it wasn't fit for human consumption.' But Pearlman denied that was his brief and that he was a safe choice. Joe Strummer said Bernie Rhodes merely selected Pearlman off a list presented to him by CBS, and Jones contended, 'We weren't concerned about who did it, because it was going to be great whatever. Producers make a great contribution, but it wasn't number one on our list of things to think about.'

Strummer said, 'We weren't ready to make a second album. It took so much out of us to make the first.' In a 1991 interview, he said of the man brought in to make the LP, 'The first time I heard of Pearlman was in Bernie's Renault. He was checking out Blue Oyster Cult. I thought he'd gone bonkers.' Yet there may be elements of Clash mythology here, if you're to believe Pearlman's assertion in *Mojo* in 2003 that when he first met the band they told him they loved the sound of his production work.

After his Elizabethan Hall drop-in, Pearlman met the band at CBS in Soho Square, saying to Gilbert, 'They told me they wanted to record with me, and loved the sound of 'Godzilla' and '(Don't Fear) The Reaper'.' He recalled the band watching San Francisco new-wave outfit The Dictators, also produced by Pearlman, at The Roundhouse that night, later having a word with them. He added, 'It wasn't CBS that hired me, it was The Clash. It wasn't to create an American sound, it was to create

SKYNYRD / PISTOLS / HILLAGE / IGGY / BEBOP
SPARKS / SHAM 69 / JAGGER

sounds

Clash City Rockers

2

an extreme sound. And I did. I resent the idea that I lamed them out.'

By the time they made their first public appearance of 1978 at the Rock Against Racism event in East London in late April, most of the songs for the new LP had been written and rehearsed. Strummer and Jones' had embarked on a 10-day writing trip to Jamaica in December, financed by CBS – according to Mick Jones, it was Bernie Rhodes' idea, with recording sessions planned for the following spring – and this had led to resentment from the reggae-obsessed Paul Simonon, who accordingly headed to Moscow and Leningrad with his girlfriend, Caroline Coon. He said, 'I felt really pissed off with the whole situation. When I found out Joe and Mick had spent most of the time in their hotel, I felt a lot better. I remember saying, 'Why didn't you get in contact with Lee Perry?' Culturally, they weren't quite there, but at least they came back with a great song, 'Safe European Home'.'

The Jamaican trip also inspired further album cut, 'Drug Stabbing Time', but it was 'Safe European Home' that truly hit the spot. Their Jamaican experience clearly wasn't what they expected, Jones saying, 'We must have looked a strange pair to the locals.' Strummer told Sean O'Hagan in 1997, 'Kingston, the toughest city in the world. We came out of the Pegasus Hotel all togged up in our punk threads, me and Mick. I tell you, we were like two punk tourists on a package tour, completely naive. We knew Lee Perry, sort of, but couldn't find him, so was on our own. The only reason they didn't kill us is because they thought we was merchant seamen off the ships. We walked through Kingston, down to the docks to score some weed. I tell you what happened. This dubious looking dread comes up, says, 'You want some weed?' He says he's going to have to go and get it, and disappears with our money, which I handed over. Mick's going, 'You fool! You pillock!' I'm saying, 'Have some faith in human nature, Michael!' After about half an hour, when I'm thinking, 'Screw human nature', the guy turns up with a bag of weed.'

Strummer reflected in *Westway to the World* on the same subject, 'I don't know how we weren't filleted and served up on a bed of chips.' The song was written back at their Kingston hotel, Strummer recalling in 1990, 'We went to the pictures a lot. It was like *The Harder They Come* – not on the screen but in the audience. They were much more fun than the films.'

Indie record label boss Laurence Bell enthused to *Uncut* in 2015, 'It's a juggernaut of a rock'n'roll song that really taps into that thing of a white boy wanting to be cool, wanting to be black. Here was Joe, arguably the coolest singer with the coolest band in the world, but he was vulnerable enough to say, 'I could never be as cool as these guys.''

Pete Wylie added, 'It still sounds fresh. In the movie *Rude Boy* when they're doing 'Safe European Home' live, if you pause the DVD, you can see me in the wings when I roadied for them. I'm wearing a pink shirt, white jeans, looking longingly at Mick Jones. That was my movie debut, but I missed the premiere.'

Across the Atlantic, Jesse Malin and Steve Wynn were also enamoured, Malin recalling, 'I had it on vinyl and when I put that needle down, the thing just exploded. I love the outro, that dub thing when it rolls out at the end and comes up again with Topper's drum rolls through the tom. That's Sandy Pearlman's production.' Wynn added, 'I

REMOTE CONTROL FROM THE CIVIC HALL...

...or how about Guildford's Burning ? It doesn't really matter, except that this was the first gig on the White Riot Tour thats making May a great month for the nation.

The trouble when a band is exciting live as The Clash are, is that if a gig is anything less than brilliant, it seems a let down. This one took place only hours after the groups return from France (they played gigs in Paris, Le Mans and Rouen) and that could be the reason why something vital was missing. It took until 'Police and Thieves' near the end before things really started to burn.

It was nothing like that great event in the Paki flea-pit at Harlesden a few weeks back, but it must still have been the best rock n roll Guildford has seen in ages.

As usual, they hit the stage with London's Burning, following it with most of the tracks from the album (What's my name and Protex Blue were the only exceptions).

Hearing Police and Thieves live for the first time was an experience. They played the full six minutes and it looked great against the backdrop of the coppers running under the Westway. Strummer spat out the words, screwing up his face and twisting himself around the mikestand. At one point he fell backwards onto the stage and just kept on singing lying flat on his back ...pol-eece...pol-eece...pol-eece... It was incredible.

Almost as good was 'Pressure Drop'. (Originally by Toots and the Maytals and part of the great soundtrack to 'The harder they Come')

Capital Radio was introduced with the words; "This is from an e.p. I haven't got my copy yet...but I know John Peel has". The song is built around a typically sharp Mick Jones riff and has a great "In tune with Nothing" chorus (more scandal about the e.p. later on).

Deny("for all the women in the audience") still sounds good live - better than it does on the album. Career Opportunities was dedicated to all the kids not at Guildford University, but why did Strummer sing the second verse twice?.

photos by legendary fanzine lensman WALT DAVIDSON

L-R: Jones, Strummer, Simonon. (Roxy, Jan 1st)

Fred Pipes' Guildford fanzine Barbed Wire's verdict on The Clash

2

loved the sound and power of the second Clash album and this song in particular. At the time, it was seen as a sell-out, but I just saw it as taking the anger and power and humour of the first album and spreading it out in full, widescreen technicolor. It was huge, and the kind of leap that allowed them to move on to the incredible *London Calling* one year later. This song rocks impossibly hard, then hits its stride with the exciting and innovative rock dub moments at the end.'

The songwriters having survived their Jamaican ordeal, the band began kicking their new material into shape that January at Rehearsal Rehearsals, including 'Tommy Gun', 'Safe European Home' and 'Last Gang in Town'. Road manager Johnny Green recalled, 'They were moving with real purpose at this point. Paul was upstairs with the headphones on, trying to learn the basslines. Topper Headon, the drumming whiz who'd been with the band only nine months, was working hard and beginning to contribute ideas. The energy levels were right up.'

Pearlman – supposedly not a fan of Strummer's voice and thus ensuring that the drums were mixed louder than the vocals on the album – returned to the UK to hear the new songs at specially arranged secret gigs in the Midlands, including one at Lanchester Poly, near Coventry, that have become part of Clash mythology. Green remembered, 'Somebody had the bright idea of putting Robin Crocker on the door of the dressing room. Pearlman was trying to get backstage, but Robin wouldn't open the door to anyone. So, Pearlman pushes the door open and Robin whacks him. He goes down, blood everywhere.' Simonon added, 'Then to make it more dramatic, Mick shouts, 'Oh no, you've hit the producer!'' Jones chipped in, 'Bernie was very much the one mopping him up, with a big handkerchief. It was really just par for the course. We all stepped over him and went on stage. There was nothing malicious in it. I think he understood that'.

Pearlman was still riled by that version of events 25 years later, insisting to Pat Gilbert, 'He took a swing at me and I took a swing at him. He cut my cheek. Jones and Strummer were appalled. So was Bernie Rhodes, who thought they'd really fucked up. He thought CBS would think they were all a bunch of idiots. But my nose wasn't broken, and I was not beaten up by The Clash. They were incredibly apologetic.'

It was shortly after the band's late January dates, probably because of the excessive spitting at punk gigs, that Strummer succumbed to hepatitis, with demo sessions at CBS's Whitfield Street studio postponed. While the rest of the band continued to rehearse at Camden HQ, Pearlman headed home, the sessions put back to May, by which time the group had already recorded several tracks on their own, including '(White Man) In Hammersmith Palais' and covers of Booker T & the MGs' 'Time is Tight' and Toots and the Maytals' 'Pressure Drop'.

It was around then that 'Clash City Rockers', first aired live at Mont-de-Marsan the previous August and recorded that autumn at CBS, was chosen as the next single. It was released in mid-February, backed with 'Jail Guitar Doors', a reworked version of a 101'ers song. With the A-side's central riff reminiscent of The Who's 'I Can't Explain', seemingly reworked again for 'Guns on the Roof' on the second album, its theme was partly borne out of a conflict that never seemed to go away – Strummer acting as middle-man and peacekeeper amid sniping between Jones and Simonon, in this case at a gig on the Get Out of Control tour. But the single is also remembered for Mickey Foote's decision, encouraged by Rhodes, to increase the speed for the finished master as it sounded flat, his 'varispeeding' technique rendering the track a semitone higher in pitch. Jones was reportedly riled when he heard it on his return from Jamaica and realised what Foote had done, the engineer consequently banished from studio duties and the original version soon reinstated.

Seen as the band's first attempt at self-mythologising on vinyl, 'Clash City Rockers' revisited themes already common to a band determined in its opposition to the concept of accepting dead-end career opportunities. Its middle-eight also garnered interest, the 'Oranges and Lemons' nursery rhyme revamped to namecheck The Move, The Groove, David Bowie, Prince Far I and Gary Glitter, the inclusion of the latter no doubt regretted in view of his later notoriety.

Sonic Youth's Thurston Moore told *Uncut* in 2015, 'The Clash produced dozens of brilliant songs, but 'Clash City Rockers' was the one that actually made you feel part of the band. The fact they used their name in a song – like Bo Diddley used to – was very exciting back then.'

Buzzcocks' guitarist Steve Diggle added, 'The opening chords are electrifying and the whole song just has a ferocious energy to it. I've been listening to it for half my life now and I'm still not tired of it. The Clash were the greatest punk band in the world.'

And The Undertones' Mickey Bradley asked, 'How many other punk bands could get away with Bo Diddley's trick of putting their name in a song title? A song which you loved when you'd never even heard it, having only read the title in the *NME* months before it was recorded. Again the words make it ... A London band, a London song. For a 17-year-old who'd never been to London, you could smell the fumes just by listening to this single.'

When Pearlman arrived back in London he encountered a new problem, Simonon and Headon having to report daily to Kentish Town Police Station following arrest in March for downing pigeons with an air rifle, something that part-inspired the second LP's 'Guns on the Roof'. The incident itself came about when two of Topper's friends called at Rehearsals with a high-powered rifle they intended to sell on. Along with Simonon and roadie Robin Crocker, Headon and his mates went up to the roof for a few practise shots, taking out what they later learned were prized racing pigeons owned by a mechanic working nearby. The shooters were spotted by British Transport Police officers and reported, the boys in blue believing they were dealing with terrorists targeting the main line to Euston. Road manager and witness Johnny Green described what followed as looking 'like a scene from the Sweeney', as the Metropolitan Police's armed anti-terrorist squad raided the building, the guilty parties subsequently charged with criminal damage, and Simonon and Headon later fined £750.

Pearlman booked the band into Utopia Studios in Camden, but they were forced to move on after a few hours. Pearlman told Gilbert, 'The engineer I worked with, Corky Stasiak, a kind of surfer dude, introduced the band to American-grade ganja, which they weren't used to. On the first night I heard a strange noise coming from outside the studio. I opened the door and saw Simonon had upturned an old plant pot and he and Topper had created a track for his trials bike in the lobby. We knew we wouldn't be welcome there again, so literally recorded the whole set that night, and left.'

The operation moved to Basing Street Studios, off Portobello Road, for the beginning of what Pat Gilbert labelled 'a gruelling series of sessions that would continue in various locations until the end of September, which none of the band recall with enthusiasm'. It was Pearlman's meticulous approach that rankled, the producer insisting songs were played again and again until deemed perfect takes. As he put it, 'For a group used to leaping around on stage, playing their instruments with an overload of energy and passion, this was a tall order. The Clash member who suffered most was Simonon, who with no musical experience before joining the band was still the least technically proficient.' He recalled in Don Letts' *Westway to the World* documentary, 'Recording that album was the most boring situation ever. It was just so nitpicking, such a contrast to the first album ... it ruined any spontaneity.' It's been insinuated that his basslines were later overdubbed by Jones, as suggested by the road crew insisting that one of their jobs was to take him home early. Yet Pearlman insisted that Simonon played everything on the record.

Headon, however, was spurred on by Pearlman's approach, and told Gilbert, 'It was the first album I'd ever worked on. It was a real buzz. Sandy was very complimentary. He called me the human drum machine. In those days I just didn't make mistakes. Everything was done in the first take.' Pearlman backed that up, telling Gilbert, 'Topper was unbelievable. After we'd finished 'Tommy Gun', I said let's try and play the drum part backwards. There was a lot of space in the arrangements and I thought this would make it amazing. So, he did it in two takes – inconceivable! Nobody else has ever been able to do that since. I could only do it now with technology.'

Pearlman's drawn-out regime led to lots of hanging around, the rhythm section often playing pool upstairs with Robin Crocker. At one point the band failed to show for days, having neglected to tell Pearlman they had a gig in Paris. Mick Jones told Gilbert, 'The other guys played Sandy up quite a lot. I just remember him sitting there all day eating cashew nuts.' Johnny Green added, 'Paul wasn't welcome after a while. Pearlman pretended to have a sense of humour, because all producers want to get on with their subjects and be one of the boys. But he wasn't. The more Paul twigged on to this, the more relentlessly he directed his humour at him.'

Jones, however, was more agreeable, 'exploring the experience of being in a top studio to learn the finer points of producing', according to Simonon, who told Pat Gilbert, 'Mick was there every minute, looking over his shoulder. It was a good learning curve for him, to be working with someone so professional. It helped us enormously after that.'

That April, the band also started work on a session for legendary Radio 1 DJ John Peel. But it was never completed. Peelie was a fan of the band, and Michael Heatley, in 2004's *John Peel: A Life in Music*, argues, 'The Clash should by rights have taken their appointed place between John Cooper Clarke and the Climax Chicago Blues Band in the roll call of legendary Peel sessions. But it never happened. Not for want of trying.

They started a session but decided halfway through that the equipment they were using wasn't up to the expected standard, so declined to complete it.'

Heatley added that Peel considered such an attitude, 'unbearably pretentious, especially for a so-called punk band', and 'never forgot the slight'. He continued, 'He'd even given Joe Strummer his first pre-fame exposure on the national airwaves, playing the 101'ers' 'Keys to Your Heart', a fact that must have made this knockback all the stranger, though he continued to play Clash records.' In Peel's *Margrave of the Marshes* autobiography (completed by his widow, Sheila Ravenscroft), he recalled, 'They actually got as far as recording the backing tracks but were so out of their heads they couldn't finish it and decided the BBC's equipment wasn't good enough. It was one of those things where you thought, 'How do you argue with stupidity on this level?' Not a very punk attitude, I thought.'

For the First Time from Jamaica

'I knew the moment we came up with the music, it was gonna be a big number. Then taking it home after we'd finished it and listening to it the next day thinking, 'Wow!''
Mick Jones, Uncut, 2015

However, that spring at London's Basing Street Studios – in Pearlman's absence – they did record what many considered their finest track, '(White Man) In Hammersmith Palais'. It was released on June 16 in four different colour sleeves, produced by the band with Simon Humphries, but left off the album that followed. It was the first sign of a new direction for the band, taking a leaf from Jones' innovative arrangement of 'Police & Thieves' on the first LP, a powerful guitar intro dropping to a slower ska chop, something of a surprising departure to the band's early fan base. As Joe Strummer put it for *Westway to the World*, 'We were a big fat riff group. We weren't supposed to do something like that.'

The track starts as an account of an all-night reggae showcase Strummer attended with Don Letts and Roadent – headlined by Dillinger, Leroy Smart and Delroy Wilson. He had expected 'roots rock' rebellion but got 'UK pop reggae', the majority of punters seemingly not on the same page. What follows is his commentary on the state of the UK in 1977, the promise of that previous year's rioting seemingly broken, Strummer – like Jones – showing frustration at the punk and social scene becoming more mainstream. The jibe at an unnamed group wearing Burton suits was seen as a jibe at rivals The Jam, but Strummer claimed in the *NME* that his targets were the power-pop bands hyped by journalists as the next big thing, but only in it to be rich and famous.

Paul Simonon told *Uncut*, 'It was such a change from what we'd been doing, from what the audience was expecting. They thought we were just gonna charge along with another bunch of numbers. Then we came out with this. It's like a couple of songs in one. Same with 'Complete Control' and 'Clash City Rockers'. They're almost like mini operas. It's got that reggae element, but it's also a rock song. It's not a punk song but then again it is. It's a combination of all those elements.'

A startling track, it proved not only a fan favourite but also Strummer's, even being played at his funeral. Ranked No.8 by the *NME* writers in '78 and appearing at No.430 in *Rolling Stone*'s 2004 list of the 500 Greatest

2 Songs of All Time, it surely should have been much higher, as some of the following comments from *Uncut* suggested when it was voted the No.1 Clash track in a 2015 all-star poll.

Norman Cook: 'This was very influential on me; the way the Clash used reggae but were never a cod-reggae band. I also identified with being the only white face in a crowd. It came absolutely out of nowhere, it was like nothing I'd ever heard before.'

Moby: 'With a lot of bands, people's choice of favourite song tends to be very subjective, but with The Clash I feel there's almost a universal consensus among friends I talk to as to what that best song is. And it's '(White Man) In Hammersmith Palais'. It's like, you get a bunch of Clash fans together, at the end of the day and, after one or two minor rows, everyone will probably agree that's their finest hour. It's definitely their most epic song. If anything, it's almost like a weird prog-rock number. In the sense that it begins one way, develops another way, and ends in another way again. It just has so many different facets. It starts out kinda light-hearted, then gets very intense and emotional, then has this big build, then ends quite, well, delicately. And it tells a great story.'

Roddy Frame: 'It's the obvious classic Clash song. People like my brother, who was 10 years older than me and he hated the whole punk thing – even he liked '(White Man) In Hammersmith Palais'! It was the first time The Clash had actually been well recorded. The first album was a bit tinny, but by the time they did this, they'd got their head round the recording process a bit better. It was so melodic, it had harmonies, a middle eight, a reggae beat. It was much slower than any punk record I'd ever heard up till then. It wasn't really a punk record, but it seemed to encapsulate everything about The Clash and what they were gonna do.'

Clint Boon: 'The thing is that after Joe died, it seemed to become more poignant. It was the mood of the track. The week he died, that was The Clash record that I used to play out in the clubs. I'd stick it on at the end of the night. It was like 'Fookin' hell' – hairs on the back of your neck, y'know? It was like we all realised we'd lost somebody really important. Certain people you don't imagine ever dying, and Joe was one of them.'

Gary Crowley: 'An incredible record, and one that always makes me think of being at school just off the Edgware Road. It was mainly all black kids so when we used to go away on organised trips, they'd bring their reggae albums and I'd bring some punk records to play 'em, and they really liked 'White Man'.'

Pete Wylie: 'The dynamic of the song, it's almost like a novel. And that last bit – 'I'm the all-night drug-prowling wolf' – the lyrical imagery is great. Strummer could sing the telephone directory and throw in one line that made it stunning. In some ways, it sums up The Clash in one record. The reggae, Joe bringing in his Dylan thing with the bit with the harmonica, Strummer's great yowl and Mick's great backing vocals. A microcosm of everything there is to love about them. And what great lines. 'If Adolf Hitler flew in today, they'd send a limousine anyway' – you could take them out and have them on Quote Of The Week on bloody Teletext.'

Jake Burns: 'This isn't just my favourite Clash song. It's my favourite song, period. It's the perfect record and I'd have killed to have made it. Because it's unorthodox, because it's a weird structure it holds your attention all the way through. I mean, there isn't even a chorus as such, but it still manages to be big and anthemic. Even now, just that little guitar click at the beginning before they've even started playing and the 'One, two, a one-two-three-four', it just sends the hairs on the back of my neck shooting up. The lyrics are fantastic, they really evoke that whole era. I know exactly what he means because even though I never went to the Palais, I did go and see Dennis Brown at The Rainbow and I felt like the only white guy in there. The whole thing was so obviously written from the heart, y'know. And that was The Clash's big strength. That honesty, that commitment.'

Mark Perry: 'Musically, it's just brilliant, that whole stuttery rhythm. Again, it's great that they're creating their own mythology, Strummer writing about being down the Hammersmith Palais at a reggae show. Lyrically it's self-effacing, it's humorous, it's about a dilemma which we were all suffering at the time.'

Johnny Green: 'A good tune always wins out and a good tune with a good message is always, always gonna win out. It was a kind of crummy recording to do when we made it. The studio was behind The Marquee, so we'd be slinking around in the dark, trying to avoid the crowds queueing up outside, crouching behind cars so as not to get noticed. But out of that came this terrific song. The way Joe turned what was a conversational anecdote into a song that touches everybody is a remarkable testament to the man. I thought it was very nice when they played it at Joe's funeral, too.'

Adam Sweeting: 'Most of the Clash's DNA was encoded in 'White Man' – it was drenched in their West London roots. Musically, it was a perfect mix of garage-band racket and ramshackle reggae – the punks-meet-rasta lyrics amounted to a Clash manifesto, and it even has a classic '1-2-3-4' intro from Jonesy. Strummer, as usual, sang as though he'd got a Red Stripe bottle wedged in his oesophagus, but you couldn't miss those blinding images.'

Jon Langford: 'A great-sounding, great-looking punk rock seven-inch I spied in the window of Jumbo Records in Leeds, took home on the bus and played to death at the threshold of aural pain. Around that time, The Mekons were doing gigs with Misty in Roots, The Ruts, local reggae bands and sound systems at the R.A.R. club at Leeds Poly, the West Indian Centre and Roots in Chapeltown, and for a while the whole punky reggae party thing made perfect sense, crystallised in the grooves of this single.'

Alan McGee: 'Maybe the greatest song ever written by white men. The greatest lyrics ever. It's why The Clash were a religion to people from Scotland or any other shithole the Government has forgotten about.'

Jesse Malin: 'Phenomenal. It's so raw, the guitars are so nasty. And the idea of mixing a reggae feel with a punk thing is just fucking genius. When I saw Joe play it, that was a special moment. But that was what Joe was all about.'

Mickey Bradley: 'Part of a trio of brilliant singles – along with 'Complete Control' and 'Clash City Rockers' – released within the space of exactly nine months – a run that only the Sex Pistols could match.'

Bobby Gillespie: 'A lot of bands pretend to be anti-authority and anti-capitalism, but they don't actually do or say anything political. The Clash made a deliberate stance

2

against the system and tracks like '(White Man) In Hammersmith Palais' remind people what a horrible, racist country '70s Britain was. The Clash were – and still are – one of the genuine outsider bands, and their music was a force for good.'

Robert Elms: 'I'd grown up a reggae fan on a northwest London council estate, my mum and dad met at the Hammersmith Palais, I'd been the white boy at loads of reggae gigs and it just felt as if this song was part of me, the bassline of my life.'

Don Letts: 'This song is particularly poignant to me because I was the one that took Joe to Hammersmith Palais on that night. Like it says, he was the only white man in the house. He went there expecting to see a roots reggae show, not realising that all the people down the ghetto in Jamaica, what are they trying to do? They're trying to get out and be glamorous! So when he went there, instead of this roots ghetto rebel show, what he saw was more Las Vegas glamour, which I think threw him. That was his own misunderstanding, I think. As I often say to people, the ghetto isn't something you get into, it's something that you get out of. That whole ghetto chic thing is a misconception for a lot of people, so I think it was an eye-opener for him. It was a brilliant evening for me, because I was there to see all my reggae heroes like Dillinger, Jah Stitch and Leroy Smart. But Joe was going through a bit of a dilemma about what he was expecting and what he was seeing, which I think was something he came to understand later on, obviously. It was so unexpected for a band to do something like 'White Man'. The groove was slower, it had that reggae feel, it was a complete left turn to what everyone thought they would have come out with, which was another great thing about The Clash. But, literally, when I hear this song I get goosepimples, every fucking time.'

The A-side was backed with 'The Prisoner', recorded at Marquee Studio, Richmond, in March. It was inspired by the cult late-'60s TV series of the same name, Mick Jones reliving the band's latest brushes with authority. And while it was quickly dropped from the set, their night in the cells in Glasgow in June '78, as told in *Rude Boy*, made them realise its impact, fellow internees singing it through the night. But that was still some way off. First, the band were set to join the fight against a rising tide of right-wing nationalism.

Rock Against Racism, Victoria Park, Hackney, April 30, 1978

'The Clash absolutely annihilated Victoria Park that afternoon. It marked their graduation from underground cult status to fully fledged rock stardom.'
Ian Fortnam, Punks, Nazis, Skins, and The Clash's Finest Hour, 2017

Initially planned as a one-off concert in Hackney, East London, Rock Against Racism became much more, its response to the alarming growth of white nationalist groups in the UK from the mid-'70s – notably the National Front – leading to a series of concerts, as pop, rock, punk and reggae artists staged shows with an anti-racist theme, aiming to discourage young people from racism, and partly responding to NF support from established artists such as Eric Clapton.

Rock Against Racism was just an idea from Red Saunders and Roger Huddle until the summer of '76, when, at a gig in Birmingham, Clapton made his notorious drunken declaration of support for former Conservative minister Enoch Powell, known for his anti-immigration 'Rivers of Blood' speech. Clapton told his audience the country had 'become overcrowded' and it was time to stop Britain becoming 'a black colony' and 'get the foreigners out, get the wogs out, get the coons out', the former Yardbirds, Bluesbreakers and Cream guitarist then repeatedly shouting NF slogan, 'Keep Britain White'.

Huddle, Saunders and two members of Kartoon Klowns wrote an open letter to the *NME*, suggesting his comments were 'all the more disgusting' considering he had his first hit covering Bob Marley's 'I Shot the Sheriff'. They called for support for a Rock Against Racism movement, the idea gaining more of a groundswell of support after David Bowie expressed support for fascism and perceived admiration of Hitler in three key interviews, including *NME* and *Playboy*, saying, 'Britain is ready for a fascist leader ... I think Britain could benefit from a fascist leader,' 'I believe very strongly in fascism', 'Adolf Hitler was one of the first rock stars,' and 'You've got to have an extreme right front come up and sweep everything off its feet and tidy everything up.' Bowie later retracted and apologised, blaming among other factors excessive drug use, insisting 'I am not a fascist.' But on ITV's *The South Bank Show* in 2007, Clapton said he still supported Powell, and didn't view him as a racist.

In spring 1978, 100,000 people marched from Trafalgar Square to London's East End, an NF hotspot, for an open-air music festival at Victoria Park organised by Rock Against Racism and the Anti-Nazi League, slamming a growing wave of racist attacks in the UK. As well as the Tom Robinson Band and The Clash, other acts included Steel Pulse, X-Ray Spex, The Ruts, Sham 69, Generation X and Patrik Fitzgerald, with Southall-based reggae band Misty in Roots leading the march from the back of a lorry, in an event Tom Robinson labelled 'the punk Woodstock'.

A second march and concert followed at Brockwell Park, South London, featuring Stiff Little Fingers, Aswad and Elvis Costello, while 40,000 visited Manchester's Northern Carnival, its bill including the Buzzcocks, Graham Parker and The Rumour, and Steel Pulse, tied in with Deeply Vale Festival's Rock Against Racism day. The following year, Acklam Hall, Notting Hill – which would play its own part in The Clash's story – played host to a bill including Crisis and The Vapors.

Comedian, broadcaster and writer Mark Steel talked about the importance of those events in his 2001 political memoir, *Reasons to be Cheerful*, recalling, 'The punk scene, which had started as an anarchist tantrum, even flirting with fascist insignia in an effort to cause outrage, was developing as an opposition movement.' He missed out on Victoria Park, but was at Brockwell Park, and told me in February 2018, 'That was my first event of any kind like that. I thought it was amazing, hugely important. So many times, you hear accounts from well-known people or others in their fifties and sixties now, black people in East London or wherever, and they'll say that transformed their way of thinking. They suddenly felt they were part of the world and part of London and didn't have to hide anymore.'

Anti-Nazi League co-founder and former Labour minister Peter Hain called the events 'a complete watershed, a fusion of popular culture and politics that had not been achieved before and only came close with the Free Nelson Mandela concert at

Wembley a decade later'. He felt it was a 'critical blow against the National Front' that 'mobilised a generation of young people – students, schoolchildren and others, especially working-class kids'.

For their part, The Clash, Ian Fortnam wrote in 2017's *Punks, Nazis, Skins, and The Clash's Finest Hour*, 'were on fire, feeding off an ecstatic audience, premiering unrecorded material like 'Tommy Gun' and 'Last Gang in Town'. The show was a revelation; other than the cheap speed blur of the first album, the only hints as to The Clash's (and therefore punk's) future had come in the shape of 'Complete Control' and 'Clash City Rockers', two solid chunks of self-mythologising. 'Last Gang in Town', meanwhile – sophisticated and decidedly non-punk as it was – sounded like more of the same, in that it was clearly all about The Clash. Even the crap PA couldn't hide that. Nor could Mick Jones's cap hide the fact that he'd grown his hair. He looked more like Keith Richards than ever, and it looked deliberate. Paul Simonon's jacket was a dazzling peacock blue, and a million miles from paint-splashed overalls.'

Fortnam felt 'Tommy Gun' 'coordinated perfectly with Strummer's headline-grabbing terrorist chic T-shirt'. Strummer said of his decision to wear the Red Army Faction insignia, 'I didn't think they were getting the press coverage they deserve. It's vicious and they're murdering people – they go around killing businessmen and the people they see as screwing Italy up. I think what they're doing is good because it's a brutal system anyway. People get murdered by the system every day and nobody complains about that.' As the writer countered, 'Not precisely the message of tolerance and unity the organisers were after.'

After thrashing through 'White Riot' with guest shouter Jimmy Pursey of Sham 69, The Clash's time was up. TRB's roadies, fearing an encore would eat into the headliner's stage time, pulled the plugs, while David Mingay, shooting live footage for *Rude Boy*, encouraged his film's star, Ray Gange – a few drinks worse off – to address the crowd. Gange later told Fortnam, 'I grabbed the mic and just started shouting. It had been so exciting, I thought whatever was going to follow was going to be drab in comparison. I couldn't conceive that the crowd weren't prepared to storm the stage to make sure it continued. Why would you want that energy to stop? At that moment I just wanted it to continue for the rest of my life.' Large parts of the crowd felt the same way. As Fortnam added, 'While a principally punk audience embraced them as conquering heroes, it also marked the day The Clash left punk behind forever. They had essentially grown out of it.'

Tom Robinson's version of events differs, however. As he told me in 2017, 'They were on before us and fuming that they weren't topping the bill. But the organisers said TRB have played lots of shows for us, their songs are about what we're about and we want them to close it. They'll have the right vibe, rather than be about the greater glory. As it was, The Clash wouldn't come off. After they'd over-played by 10 minutes and we could see our set-time dwindling away because of the curfew, my manager got the roadies to pull the plugs. But in the revisionist history version, we got jealous of them, almost provoking a riot.'

Billy Bragg, also there, was inspired by The Clash and TRB. He told John Robb for 2006's *Punk Rock: An Oral History*, 'I listened to political music like Bob Dylan. I was listening to personal politics, but the thing about The Clash was instead of saying how lame things were in interviews, they said, 'We're doing this Rock Against Racism gig.' We thought this was the greatest thing ever. We were knocked back by the power of the National Front, but here were bands determined to do something about it. It's telling that the most revolutionary track on the first Clash album is their version of 'Police & Thieves'. How incendiary it is, what it does with the song rather than the lame version of reggae that The Police did later. It really did just blow me away. And I suppose it allowed us white kids to finally meet the black culture that we had admired for so long, with reggae as a common ground. In the same way that The Beatles, the Stones and The Who had taken black music in the '60s, they truly assimilated not just the music but the power of what the lyrics would be saying. You had The Clash mixing the two together.'

Johnny Green suggested in 1997's *A Riot of Our Own*, 'The Clash were good, but it took a big event to make them realise just how big they had become.' The band were a late addition, approached by co-organiser John Dennis, of whom Green added, 'His angle was flattering. He said the whole event would have more clout if the Clash were involved. The band agreed to do it but were worried about the pure practicalities of playing to a huge crowd in a flat field in the middle of the afternoon – something we hadn't done before. We were very careful to be in control of the music and how it was presented.'

Concerned that the organisers might not be up to such a major task, and worried about becoming associated with the Anti-Nazi League, endorsing their politics, Bernie Rhodes asked Green, 'Are they sure they know what they're doing? Do they really want to be knocking about with these student types? Isn't it all a bit safe and cosy? Aren't they preaching to the converted? And what's it going to achieve?' But Strummer was up for it, telling Green, 'Tell Bernie people have gotta walk before they run. If people get out of their bedsits for the day, it'll have achieved something. If they think about politics just enough for 'em to know they hate fascists, that's something.'

Green reckoned all Rhodes was interested in was the band's huge stage backdrop, featuring a fighter plane, 'the bane of mine and The Baker's lives on the road, and a source of hilarity to The Clash. Not only was it heavy to lug into position on awkwardly shaped stages, we had to cover it with black polythene sheeting, and, seconds before the band came on stage, balance precariously behind it on whatever we could find, ready to unwrap it, like the Queen unveiling a plaque at a hospital, just as the applause started – usually while Mick and Joe screamed for last-minute adjustments to their guitars.'

Days before the show, Rhodes asked Green to get hold of a 'cheap van' to take a film crew along, going on to find 'the cheapest I could find in Greater London, from a company known to us as Avawreck. It broke down three times on the way from Rickmansworth via Camden to Hackney, the backdrop tied on the roof because it was too big to go inside.' As it was, Green and The Baker – aka Barry Auguste, Subway Sect roadie-cum-Clash drum tech and general dogsbody – set up the stage and picked up an excited band, and as they drove in through the crowds, 'It started to sink in that this was big –

not just big, but huge. It was different to anything we had ever done before. There were columns of cops, blokes with collecting buckets, blokes selling *Socialist Worker*, giant trade-union banners, leather jackets, tweed jackets, green hair, no hair.'

Green recalled a 'feeling of unity' backstage', saying Dave Mingay and his film crew's agenda as they started filming for *Rude Boy* was 'the last thing on my mind', suggesting it was a 'shambles' backstage, 'like a huge student gig, except for the professional entourage of the Tom Robinson Band. They were a pro outfit. As far as they were concerned it was the Anti-Nazi League starring the Tom Robinson Band.'

Introduced by Dingwalls DJ Barry Myers, The Clash 'ran on stage, fast as always, no twiddling with amps, straight into the first song'. Green added, 'I watched their faces closely, looking for any signals that they needed something. I saw their looks of delight freeze into fixed grins at the sudden realisation of the size of the crowd, filling the park as far as the eye could see, heaving and bobbing to the music. The Clash's set was remarkable.' Yet Green became more and more aware of the TRB crew 'looking at their watches, shaking their heads, as cold as ice. Then, suddenly, the music stopped. Joe, Mick, Paul, all looked round at me. I didn't know what had happened. I was afraid. I knew nothing about electrics. I would have to go on stage in front of a crowd of 80,000 and try to fix ... whatever it was that was wrong. I saw the Scottish TRB road manager standing threateningly over the plug board. I knew immediately what had happened. I ran on stage to Strummer saying, 'They've pulled the plug,' then back to the road manager. I shaped to hit him, then dived under him and replaced the plug. I grabbed Steve English, Johnny Rotten's mate and minder, and asked him to guard the plugs. No one would dare move him.

'Jimmy Pursey came on stage, dressed like a reject from Billy Smart's circus, to join the Clash in singing 'White Riot'. The crowd roared once more. Pursey's band, Sham 69, were notorious for their skinhead following. The audience saw his appearance on stage at this gig as nailing his colours to the mast. I heard Jack Hazan, filming for Mingay just behind my shoulder, mutter, 'Unbelievable. The hair's standing up on my neck.' He'd grown mischievous. As I cleared our gear from the stage, he said to Ray Gange, whose part in *Rude Boy* was to be filmed as a Clash fan: 'You don't want to hear the Tom Robinson band. I bet the crowd don't either. Why don't you ask them?' So, Ray ran on stage and started geeing up the audience. 'We want more Clash!' Tom Robinson's road manager said, 'Get this idiot off.' And he was bundled away.

'There was a slight sour taste in our mouths, but it soon disappeared in the jubilation backstage. We had done our set as arranged, and it wasn't our fault it had overrun. But the enormity of the event was such that a little egotism couldn't spoil it. Driving home with the band, everyone was delighted, excited and chattering. It was one thing to sell out a gig in a 1,500-capacity hall, another to play before a crowd of 80,000, all going crazy. It began to sink in that The Clash were big. And Bernie's only input into the show had been quibbling about the backdrop.'

As it was, Rhodes was off within a month, although he'd return within a couple of years, invited back into the fold by

Strummer, who told Don Letts for *Westway to the World*, 'Bernie was manoeuvred from the managerial chair in a power struggle. And whatever The Clash was, it was something to do with Bernie Rhodes and The Clash, that's what I always maintain ... for better or for worse.'

Communication between Rhodes and the band, and even Johnny Green, was sporadic by then, and often bizarre. Headon recalled, 'It got to the point that he never paid me. I said to him one day, 'Bernie, I'm skint. I haven't been paid for three weeks.' He said, 'If I was your bank manager, would you expect me to live in your wardrobe?' He never made any sense. I'd go away without any cash, totally bemused with what he said.' He added, 'Paul and I didn't have to do as much as Mick and Joe. We had loads of time on our hands and messed around. If you put two 22-year-olds together with a few bob in their pockets and nothing to do, they'll do silly things.'

It's well documented that around then, Jones was into cocaine, Pat Gilbert feeling he was, 'unashamedly living out his teenage rock star fantasies, cutting a dash around town in his long black curly hair, living it up off the Portobello Road in a supposedly flash pad. 'I turned up to see them rehearse near the 100 Club on Oxford Street, and they're all mad at Mick. All of a sudden, he's out of the band for a few days. Steve Jones from the Sex Pistols was playing guitar. 'Why's Mick out of the band?' Maybe it's because he wanted to be Mott the Hoople and the others didn't.' Steve Jones had been turning up at venues on that summer's Out on Parole tour to join the encores of 'White Riot' and 'Garageland', his namesake apparently 'very curious'.

The Specials' Neville Staple has great memories of that tour, with his band featuring as support, not least because he had been hooked by the band at a young age back in his home city, Coventry. He told John Robb, 'I was in a youth club doing my DJ stuff, playing reggae at the time, and The Specials used to rehearse in the room next door – Jerry (Dammers), Horace (Panter) and Lynval (Golding). They asked if I could go out on the road and help them as a roadie. The punk scene hadn't really started at the time. That was just coming up. We were called The Automatics, playing reggae and ska. I used to see the punk bands when they came through Coventry. We saw The Clash a lot. When The Specials got going we did the Out on Parole tour. That was fucking brilliant.

'That was the first time I'd seen so many kids jumping and spitting. You should have seen the fucking spitting. It was like fireworks, man. What the fuck is going on here? Punk made us speed our music up. Playing in front of those kids made it more energetic. I used to really like The Buzzcocks. But it was The Clash who we were very close to. They were a great band. The Bernie Rhodes connection came through Jerry Dammers. We were living in Coventry, and Jerry had all the contacts and knew where to go. We used to rehearse at Rehearsal Rehearsals – it was a fucking pit, man! We used to sleep there in sleeping bags, and there were rats all over the place.'

The live footage used in *Rude Boy* brilliantly illustrates the power of the band at that stage, and for me the clip of 'Complete Control' recorded at Camden's Music Machine in July '78, is all you need to understand that track's sheer, awe-inspiring power and the reaction to it from such a

In happier times: Mick 'n' Paul 'n' Bernie 'n' Joe (pic: COLONEL CAROLINE COON)

CLASH SACK RHODES

THE CLASH, who have added 18 more concerts to the Sort It Out tour, have sacked Bernard Rhodes as their manager, ending one of the stormiest manager/band relationships to blossom within the new wave.

The friction that led to the split started a year ago, but grew more pronounced when the band decided — against Rhodes' advice — to team up with producer Sandy Pearlman to record and mix their new album in America.

Rhodes has now started legal proceedings against the band for the recovery of money he claims the group owes him. On Tuesday he asked the High Court to freeze the band's earnings, and they have counter-claimed saying that his financial accounting amounted to a breach of his duties as manager.

The group's management has now been taken over by a team of lawyers and accountants plus CBS, the Clash's record company, assisted by rock writer Caroline Coon, who lives with Clash bassist Paul Simonon.

The full tracklisting of the band's album, "Give 'Em Enough Rope," set for release on November 10, is: Side One — "Guns On The Roof," "Drug-Stabbing Time," "Stay Free," "Cheap-Skates," "All

"Safe European Home," "English Civil War," "Tommy Gun," "Julie's Been Working For The Drug Squad," "Last Gang In Town."

The tour dates are: Middlesbrough Town Hall (November 17), Leeds University (18), Sheffield Top Rank (19), Leicester De Montfort (20), Bristol Locarno (21), Bournemouth Village Bowl (22), Manchester Apollo (23), Derby Kings Hall (24), Cardiff Top Rank (26), Exeter University (27), Coventry Locarno (28), Stoke Victoria Hall (29)

devoted fan base. In fact, it's difficult to know where the band finish and where the crowd start, such is the massed choir on the chorus. You almost feel the lives of those that were there changing.

Completing that difficult second album

'They became visiting dignitaries, ambassadors to the SF punk scene. It was happening there. They'd come to the right place'

Sandy Pearlman, in Pat Gilbert, Passion Is a Fashion, 2004

Soon, Sandy Pearlman relocated his operation to the Automatt studio in San Francisco, and in August Strummer and Jones flew out for three weeks of overdubbing, their first taste of 'reaching the Promised Land', as Pat Gilbert put it. Jones told him, 'We'd always dreamed of going there. We never wanted to be a parochial band. It was great to get there. We missed the others, definitely. We were based in Chinatown and having a party. It was like a hangover from the '60s. Country Joe and the Fish were playing. Early on, we made friends with people like Mo Armstrong, the singer of Daddy Long Legs, a Vietnam vet. We had a lovely time. The Automatt had a great jukebox, with 'I Fought the Law' on it and stuff like '(Sittin' On) The Dock of the Bay.'

Simonon's response? 'Was I bothered? I'd have rather gone to Jamaica. Anyway, I'd have only argued with Mick about the level of the bass.' Meanwhile, Strummer told Don Letts, 'When you've been into American music for as long as I have, to go there is a trip. To ride across the country, even better on a bus, is another trip. It was fantastic. I got endless amounts of inspiration from it.' Jones added, 'Constantly, looking out of a window, it's like watching a movie.'

However, the band's chief songwriters remained focused, and Pat Gilbert added, 'For three weeks, Mick and Joe knuckled down to a period of intense guitar overdubs and backing vocals. Mick flourished under the hothouse conditions. Sandy would later boast, 'There are more guitars per square inch on this record than in anything in the rest of Western civilisation.' After three weeks, Mick and Joe – exhausted and missing the others – decided to go on strike. It was agreed that they both take off a week and reconvene in New York, where the final mixing was due to take place at the Record Plant.

Strummer headed off on a Kerouac-style road trip across the States with new friends. Jones flew to LA to see Blue Oyster Cult at the Coliseum, reconvened at the Tropicana, went to the gig, met The Go-Go's. The following Saturday, they both arrived in New York – Jones on a plane, Strummer in a Ford pick-up, enthusing about all the different places he'd been, including Memphis, and the colourful characters he'd met. The next week, mixing began in a small room on the tenth floor of the Record Plant, the air thick with the fug from 'potent Polio pot, sourced from local East Coast surfers'.

Gilbert wrote, 'The final touches to the album were recorded in a glass-walled vocal booth, with panoramic views of Manhattan,' adding, 'With thousands of dollars spent in three expensive studios, there was no going back. *Give 'Em Enough Rope* was a Sandy Pearlman production, and no one was getting out of there until the guitar tracks glistened and the performances were as damn near perfect as they could be.'

It was during that period that Jones got a call from Nancy Spungen, asking him to back Sid Vicious, recently relocated to New York, at a gig at Max's Kansas City, his band including 'various New York Dolls, Heartbreakers and Idols'. Mick was eventually persuaded, telling Gilbert, 'We just about managed five songs – five songs for five bucks. It was a nightmare between shows, full-on. Me and Joe kept looking at each other. We couldn't believe it. The people there were as out of it as you can be without actually being dead. We weren't heavyweight drug guys. We had more than that to share.'

In late September, Simonon and Headon were flown to New York to hear the final mixes, Gilbert suggesting, 'The record they heard together was tough, big and loud – a slick but powerful rock album that took in everything from the cauterising blasts of 'Tommy Gun' and 'Safe European Home' to the New Orleansy-jolly of 'Julie's Been Working', the rock'n'rolly 'Last Gang in Town' and the nostalgic teen reminiscences of Mick's 'Stay Free'. Those who wanted a reprise of *The Clash* were shocked by the scope and freight of the record, which cranked up Joe's parochial Westway vignettes on the first album to a prophetic vision of international terrorism, Third World poverty and the trials and tribulations of being reluctant rock'n'roll heroes, all with guitar overdubs as thick and sweet as treacle, and memorable Strummer ad libs. There was, however, no sign of the more rootsy, punky reggae direction that the

2

glorious 'White Man' had promised on its release as a single earlier that summer.'

As it was, by the time the LP was released, the band had already moved on. In fact, Paul Simonon told Pat Gilbert, 'After we got back from America, our look changed. Johnny Thunders always wore those cool boots, and as soon as we got to New York we bought some. We started growing quiffs and getting that look, then we started working up 'I Fought the Law' into a Clash song.'

Give 'Em Enough Rope – an appreciation

Strummer and Jones' visit to Jamaica may not have been what they envisaged on leaving London, but it inspired one of The Clash's greatest moments in 'Safe European Home', the opening salvo of an explosive opus. Written in Kingston's Pegasus hotel, it set a perfect tone, the story of the 'Martian arrival' of two white boys, far from home and keen to just see out their stay and get safely home, suggesting a correlation with 10cc's 'Dreadlock Holiday', released three months after it was recorded.

Opening the Sort It Out tour, it remained a live favourite, and in 2003's *The Complete Clash*, Keith Topping highlighted Topper Headon's contribution, feeling he 'underpins Jones' powerful Mick Ronson-style heavily tracked riffing with staccato bursts of machine gun fire', adding praise for Jones' 'finest backing vocals since 'Complete Control'' and 'some exquisite harmonies, a much-overlooked part of The Clash's oeuvre'. He concluded, 'It reflects the final and most pointed isolationist tirade from a group who even by the song's release were already making rapid strides towards true and lasting internationalism. By the time of the next LP, The Clash were no longer bored with the USA. They'd be busy conquering it.'

A high-octane start continues with 'English Civil War', a guitar-driven, contemporary rewrite of Irish-born Massachusetts Unionist Patrick Sarsfield Gilmore's American Civil War folk song 'When Johnny Comes Marching Home', itself derived from Irish anti-war song 'Johnny I Hardly Knew Ye'. Strummer transported England's own mid-seventeenth-century Civil War to an era when right-wing political groups like the National Front were on the rise, the band warning against all things uniformed and sinister.

Strummer told *Record Mirror*'s Terry Lott after the song's Victoria Park debut, 'War is just around the corner. Johnny hasn't got far to march. That's why he's coming by bus or underground,' going on to mention a recent race riot following an incident in Tower Hamlets, and warning that fascism could take a hold given the chance. Within two weeks, a young Bengali was stabbed to death in London in a racist attack, prompting a series of demonstrations, one leading to Asian protesters rioting in Brick Lane that June.

The second single from the LP, released on February 23, 1979 (charting at No.25 in the UK and No.28 in Ireland), backed with

Toots and the Maytals cover 'Pressure Drop', the artwork of English Civil War was a still from John Halas' 1954 animated adaptation of George Orwell's dystopian novella *Animal Farm*.

Put out as a single a fortnight after the LP, on November 24, backed by Jones' '1-2 Crush on You', 'Tommy Gun' saw Strummer suggest that terrorists loved all the publicity about their killings. And while he'd already spoken out on politics in Germany, Italy and Northern Ireland, this wasn't so much about taking sides as questioning extremism and violence itself. He told Gavin Martin, 'I was saying us rock'n'rollers are all posers and egomaniacs. But we know terrorists are as bad or worse than we are. They definitely love to read their own press. They dedicate their lives to a cause but are always posing for pictures.' And he told Sean O'Hagan in 1997, ''Tommy Gun' was an anti-gun song, a slagging of the guy holding the gun.'

Keith Topping saw Topper Headon's 'machine gun drum-fills' and the 'awkward start-stop structure' as the band's 'first significant foray into sonic assault, a cacophony of controlled feedback containing Jones' Morse code guitar solo and Headon's finest hour, beating out a military tattoo on his skins, The Clash at their most vicious'. Introduced live at The Rainbow in December '77, It became the group's first top-20 UK hit, its promo video filmed by Don Letts at a Harlesden Roxy soundcheck on October 25.

Amid Topper Headon's gangster-like rapid-fire snare hits and those distorted guitars and feedback, Strummer hoarsely barks out lines described by The Libertines' Carl Barat in the *Singles Box* liner notes as 'a product of the volatile climate of the late '70s – all those references to terrorist organisations like Baader-Meinhof and the Red Brigades. It's like a punk rock adaptation of The Beatles' 'Revolution'.'

Strummer's retelling of an elaborate police drugs bust in early 1977 – Headon's jazzy, shuffling beat augmented by Blue Oyster Cult's Al Lanier on piano – 'Julie's Been Working for the Drug Squad' tells of an undercover policewoman who helped net 1.5kg of LSD microdots, some of the purest acid ever produced in Britain, most from a Welsh farmhouse, which was thought to be the largest LSD production ring. The song also references The Beatles' 'Lucy in the Sky with Diamonds', Strummer recalling in 1991, 'The only way for the cops to bust them was to put in some hippies of their own, who had to take acid repeatedly to remain undercover. The song's about tripping policemen.' After the raid, in which 17 defendants pleaded guilty and were sentenced to an accumulative 130 years inside, LSD prices more or less doubled in the UK.

One of the first songs written for the LP, first performed at The Rainbow in December '77, 'Last Gang in Town' alludes to bank holiday scraps between Teddy Boys and punks in UK resorts, but also every other inter-factional, tribal youth conflict of that era. Keith Topping noted that Mick Jones 'throws in every Ronnie Wood and Mick Ronson lick in the book, and a few that aren't, during his two extended solos, while the bassline includes a rousing variant on The Move's 'Fire Brigade', itself a bastardisation of Duane Eddy's 'Peter Gunn' theme. The song features the best bass playing on *Give 'Em Enough Rope*, although whether this was in the hands of Simonon or Jones remains a subject of considerable debate.'

It's easy to assume that side two opener 'Guns on the Roof' – credited to The Clash and first played live in Victoria Park – is a retelling of the late March '78 incident when Headon and Simonon were arrested at their rehearsal base. But in the wider sense, Strummer gets on to global terrorism, war and corruption. Working on a further 'I Can't Explain' type riff – as on 'Capital Radio' and 'Clash City Rockers' – its lyrical content covers all manner of issues, such as torture, oppression, assassination, justice, corruption, the global arms trade and military operations.

Also dating from Strummer and Jones' Jamaican adventure, 'Drug-Stabbing Time' was premiered live during the On Parole tour and first demoed at Rehearsals in December '78, with Gary Barnacle on sax. This is another police drug bust tale, but loses some of its impact through common knowledge of Jones' cocaine use at the time, something Clash biographer Marcus Gray reckoned would serve 'inevitably to bring down yet more accusations of hypocrisy on their shoulders'.

An unexpected wistful departure into nostalgia, 'Stay Free', which tackles enduring friendships, saw Mick Jones taking the mic, providing what *Rolling Stone*'s Greil Marcus saw as 'a lovely Keith Richards-like vocal', in a poignant career highlight. The Rumour's Bob Andrews added Booker T-style organ to a track that remained a live favourite for much of Jones' time with the band. 'Even the skinheads cry! It really moves them,' he told *Trouser Press* in 1979.

Based on his friendship with schoolmate and Clash roadie Robin Crocker, Jones asserted, 'It wasn't totally about him. That was the starting place. What happened to him happened to a lot of people.' By March 1970 Crocker had been expelled from school and was later jailed for his part in an armed robbery on a betting shop in South London, serving three years inside. But the pair got back in touch, Crocker initially becoming Jones' guitar tech and later writing for *ZigZag* magazine under the name Robin Banks.

When Mick sings, 'I practised daily in my room,' adding that Mott-like guitar lick, I'm pretty much gone. It encompasses the high emotion of 'The Saturday Gigs', but something else I can relate to – Jones' application to his craft in a bid to escape a lesser life, desperate to make it. Being given his marching orders from the London SS was what he needed to buckle down and start again.

He's not judgmental, but there's underlying commentary about life choices. You often hear it among boxers – insisting sport was their salvation, and if it wasn't for their application and discipline, they might have taken the wrong path, become another crime statistic. Jones could have gone down that road. Thankfully, he stuck at it, his rock'n'roll dream becoming reality. There's something of that 'what might have been' in The Jam's 'Saturday's Kids' too, Paul Weller also determined not to follow the wrong path.

Seen as a put-down of Clash manager Bernie Rhodes, rumours suggested that Strummer was also having a dig at Mick Jones on 'Cheapskates'. He denied that, claiming it was directed at press criticism of the band. There are elements of filler though, and the song soon dropped from the live set. Jones told Gary Bushell, 'The song was written during a period of heavy drug-taking. The lyrics are meant to be a satire on that.' Keith Topping described it as 'the most sloppily recorded song on the album', and saw a correlation with Sandy Pearlman's best-known production credit, Blue Oyster Cult's '(Don't Fear) The Reaper'.

Its title suggesting a nod to David Bowie-penned Mott the Hoople hit 'All the Young Dudes' and Ian Dury's debut LP, *New Boots and Panties!!*, LP finale, 'All the Young Punks (New Boots and Contracts)' was seen as the band's own take on the cut-throat music business, perhaps 'Complete Control' part two, or maybe Ian Hunter's *Diary of a Rock'n'Roll Star* updated in song form. Jones' guitar solo was compared to that of Eric Clapton and the track itself described as 'not unlike an outtake from *The Who Sell Out*' by Keith Topping. Recorded at Basing Street Studios, Strummer is seen in *Rude Boy* recording an impassioned vocal. The song debuted live during the On Parole tour but soon dropped. The US issue was initially titled, 'That's No Way to Spend Your Youth'.

Again, there's a feel of Mott the Hoople when the duelling guitars kick in halfway through. The Clash were about progression, but with a magpie-like quality of taking what had come before, choosing the best elements, albeit unconsciously. We are what we're made of, and Jones' DNA had all that. To quote Maya Angelou, 'You are the sum total of everything you've seen, heard, eaten, smelled, been told, forgot – it's all right there.'

Reaching out to America – Clash style

'America was the promised land for Joe Strummer, because it's the home of rock'n'roll. When I first took up with him, in Camden Town, the whole rockabilly thing was really big and Joe loved to get out of town, jump in the motor, go see one of the big rockabilly jobs up in St Albans or somewhere. He loved to dress up, put all the gear on. He was a natural for a quiff. Joe's record player reflected America.'

Johnny Green, Viva Joe Strummer: The Clash and Beyond, 2005

The next Clash release was 'The Cost of Living' EP, recorded in early '79 in Highbury, North London, and released in a gatefold sleeve on May 11. The record was produced by the band with Bill Price and marked a major sea change, bridging the intensity of the band's earlier punky sound with more US-influenced rock'n'roll, as taken on for *London Calling*.

Lead track 'I Fought the Law' was a 1958 Sonny Curtis song, released two years later when he led the post-Buddy Holly era Crickets, although it was the 1966 Bobby Fuller Four version that became a top-10 US hit, one Strummer and Jones picked up on while recording overdubs at the Automatt, having heard it on one of the

San Francisco studio owner's collection of classic jukeboxes. By the time they returned home, they could play it. The song later featured on the US edition of *The Clash*, and it also gave them their first taste of US radio airplay, becoming their stateside debut single in late July.

'I Fought the Law' would remain in the live set for much of The Clash's career, Strummer performing it with later bands too, including The Pogues. A live recording from the Lyceum Theatre in London on December 28, 1978, features in *Rude Boy*, and is seen as the film's thematic title song.

Music writer Adam Sweeting told *Uncut* in 2015, 'Choosing cover versions is a fine art that most bands never master. The Clash did this one so well that hardly anybody realised it wasn't one of their own, since the outlaw sentiment felt so intrinsically Clash-like and the song's terse, taut verses and singalong chorus felt like they'd come straight out of the Strummer/Jones operator's manual.'

The EP also included two others tracks showcasing the band's new direction, 'Groovy Times' and 'Gates of the West' – describing the band's first awed encounter with the US – plus a re-recorded version of early freebie 'Capital Radio', the band's attack on what was then London's only legal commercial music radio station, for its mostly mainstream playlist.

Strummer said at the time, 'They say 'Capital Radio, in tune with London'. Yeah! They're in tune with Hampstead. They're not in tune with us at all. I hate them. What they could have done compared to what they have done is abhorrent. They could have made it so good that everywhere you went you took your transistor radio. They could have made the whole capital buzz. Instead Capital Radio has just turned their back on the whole youth of the city.'

While America was about to wake up to The Clash, their highly polished second album and subsequent US tour had nearly bankrupted the band. As Topper Headon recalled, 'We had to get someone in to rescue us from the mess. We were told by our accountant we were something like a quarter of a million pounds in debt.' Among those called in was Peter Jenner, who in *Westway to the World* said, 'What we helped to do was find a way the world could talk to The Clash and that business could relate. I think that's why (*London Calling*) is such a great record, because of the spirit without the deadening musical limitations of punk.' That said, Paul Simonon felt the band's new 'regular management' had 'none of the excitement Bernie had'.

As Johnny Green put it in *A Riot of Our Own*, 'CBS weren't really interested in another Clash album at that time. They were releasing a revised version of *The Clash* in America and didn't really want another Clash product muddying the waters. But it had found a Clash manager it liked in Caroline Coon. For The Clash, the music they were making at that point was the way forward. For Coon, America was the way forward. She was always formulating action plans, targets, setting agendas; and The Clash let her get on with it. It was nothing to do with what they were doing. She went spinning off to New York. CBS had hooked someone from The Clash camp they could do business with, but when they reeled in the line, all they found was Coon on the end. The Clash had unhitched.'

Back to work: from

THE CLASH
"GIVE 'EM ENOUGH ROPE"
1ST AMERICAN TOUR 1979
ON EPIC RECORDS & TAPES
THE CLASH

2

Vanilla to Wessex

'There was a point where punk was going narrower and narrower, painting itself into a corner. We thought we could just do any kind of music.'
Mick Jones, Westway to the World, 2000

Having separated from Rhodes, the band left his rehearsal studio in Camden. Green and The Baker were tasked with locating a new rehearsal base, and found Vanilla Studios behind a garage in Pimlico, near Vauxhall Bridge. Prior to that, Strummer and Jones had experienced writer's block, and with no new songs written from scratch in over a year, the band arriving at Vanilla in May 1979 without a single track prepared. Once there, however, the group began performing covers in a variety of genres, from rockabilly and rock'n'roll to R&B and reggae. For the first time, the band kept those sessions private, barring hangers-on and hoping to rebuild confidence without worrying about the reaction, a disciplined afternoon routine broken only by late-afternoon games of football then drinks at a local pub and a second rehearsal session in the evening.

The band gradually rebuilt their musical and songwriting confidence that summer, their choice of covers setting the template for the diverse material that followed, encouraged by a growing appreciation of Headon's drumming, already way beyond the initial punk rock remit. Songs were written and recorded as demos, Jones composing and arranging much of the music and Strummer generally writing the lyrics. Their first US tour aided the shift, not least because they got to watch up close R&B giants like Bo Diddley, Sam & Dave, Lee Dorsey and Screamin' Jay Hawkins, as well as neo-country artist Joe Ely and punkabilly outfit The Cramps, helping to define a fresh rock'n'roll vibe. And the story of those sessions became part of Clash folklore, a 'lost tapes saga' explained in detail by Johnny Green in his highly entertaining 1997 memoir. That story was re-examined online by the *Green and Black Music* website in 2017, where it was noted that fans had questioned whether the tapes even existed before Mick Jones' 2004 'discovery'.

Strummer first hinted at the existence of self-made tapes in a 1979 interview, proposing that 'bands could avoid expensive studio bills by recording on simple Teac machines'. Verification followed with Green's book and his detailed account of those early sessions. As the *Green and Black Music* site feature put it, 'Necessity brought the band to Vanilla Studios. This was no professional music space, but an old factory refurbished as an auto-repair shop. The benefit of using the unorthodox space was total isolation from the punk scene. Without the distraction of hangers-on, The Clash focused their energies on music. In the summer of 1979, the songs that comprise *London Calling* organically came together amid broken cars and exhaust fumes. Inside their new home, they installed a four-track tape machine. Practices were recorded, and cassettes made for band members. Each musician could monitor progress, reflect on their individual contributions.'

As Green put it, 'It soon became apparent that the new material was taking shape so fast that we needed to slap it down on tape. The Baker and I realised we had to do it, but neither of us had a clue of how to go about it. Bobby Pridden of The Who helped enormously. We had used a rental company set up with The Who's millions, hiring stage gear in the past. Pridden, a small, bearded and balding bloke with smiling eyes, who resembled a pot-bellied garden gnome, was happy to share his expertise, which was rare in the roadie world. He came in one morning from Shepperton to take a look and was appalled at the seediness but told us what we needed. Over a weekend, me and The Baker set up a Teac four-track reel-to-reel with a Portastudio. The Baker learned how to get the sound balanced and spent a lot of time with a cheap notebook, studying the tapes, working on the equipment.

'Up to this point, The Baker, me and Battersea (Headon's dog) had been the only audience. Only we knew how good this music was. But with the tapes, The Clash were able to sit back with a spliff, listen to themselves, confirming what they felt while playing it – it was good. They knew it had to be put onto record urgently. Joe wanted to do it at Vanilla. 'Let's do it ourselves. Fuck CBS if they don't like it! Here, it's got rawness. We want the dynamism, the vibrancy.' But try as The Baker might, we were never going to get a good enough sound there. Mick said, 'We'll get as close as possible. We'll use Wessex.'

'We liked Wessex, it had the right rough feel and the right privacy. Only one band at a time could use it. It was perfect. Mick was aware he knew enough to produce an album himself but we knew CBS would not buy it. They needed someone in charge, someone responsible for the budget, someone to put his neck on the line. They didn't trust The Clash, because The Clash didn't play ball with them. CBS wanted a big-name, big-budget producer. But when Mick named Guy Stevens, there was no contest in The Clash camp. When talking about ambience, feel, greatness, as opposed to the technical nuts and bolts, there was only Guy. But he was off the musical scene and supposedly off the rails. Joe said he would track him down and went off in search. 'I found him in a boozer in Soho,' he announced three days later. 'He was interested but wants to hear what we're doing first. Make him a tape, Barry. And Johnny, get him a cassette player. He ain't got one.'

'I hadn't met Guy, but I'd heard of him. I couldn't believe a record producer didn't have a tape deck. I went off on the Tube to Tottenham Court Road, brought a little mono player. It was all we could afford. That night we were delighted. The Clash were producing the music they wanted. We had the man we wanted, and the studio we wanted. We had a few beers. On the way home, I had a kip on the Victoria line and ended up in Seven Sisters. It wasn't till I reached home that I realised I had left the cassette player and the tape on the Tube. Unfortunately for bootleggers, The Baker had labelled the tape 'Val Doonican'. I phoned left luggage the next morning, but no joy. There was nothing for it but to own up. All I got for my confession was, 'Wanker', and the band made Guy another tape. He loved it.'

That part of the tale might have ended there if not for Jones. In 2004, he said he was preparing to move into a new residence when he discovered the *Vanilla Tapes* inside a forgotten cardboard box, coinciding with the twenty-fifth anniversary of *London Calling*. Columbia Records subsequently released a deluxe edition of the landmark LP with the *Vanilla Tapes* included as a bonus disc.

As the *Green and Black Music* site put it, 'Exploring the *Vanilla Tapes* offers a unique insight into a band pushing the boundaries of punk rock. The songs exist in various degrees of completion. Fragments of undeveloped ideas coexist beside completed

2

Paul Simonon onstage at The Palladium in New York on September 20, 1979

songs. Some tracks are performed as instrumentals while others have distinctively different lyrics. There are four original songs that never made *London Calling*, a rehashing of 'Complete Control', even a Bob Dylan cover ... Hearing The Clash in a raw, stripped-down form is intensely satisfying.'

The tapes included 'Paul's Tune', an early instrumental take on 'The Guns of Brixton', built around its bassline. As the site author put it, 'Considering the *Vanilla Tapes* were made weeks before recording *London Calling*, the incomplete 'Paul's Tune' reveals just how quickly The Clash were writing songs. In those feverish final weeks before entering Wessex studios, The Clash worked to refine their new batch of songs. The *Vanilla* version of 'I'm Not Down' shines light on how the band continued to revise lyrics until they were satisfied.'

There are many more such examples of a masterful work in progress; 'The Right Profile', for example, was an instrumental titled 'Up-Toon', suggesting lyrical content was non-existent then. And the band continued to tweak those songs until the last minute, as was the case for the title track. As the *Green and Black Music* site put it, 'The anthem would undergo a dramatic rewrite. In the original version presented on the *Vanilla Tapes*, most of the lyrics are unrecognisable.'

In August 1979, the band entered Wessex Studios to begin recording with Stevens producing. This was much to the dismay of CBS, because of Stevens' unconventional methods and mounting alcohol problems. They had a point – during one recording session he swung a ladder and upturned chairs in a bid to create a more rock'n'roll atmosphere. But the band got along well with the maverick producer, Simonon finding him helpful and productive to both his playing and their recording as a band. Explaining Stevens' role, in *Westway to the World*, engineer Bill Price said, 'Guy used to believe his job as producer was to instil the maximum emotion in a record. He would do this by a process he would call 'direct psychic injection'. He'd inject his personality into the musicians, face-to-face, as they were playing the master.'

The resultant mighty double album was recorded over five to six weeks, involving 18-hour days, with many songs recorded in one or two takes, in what was seen as the first post-punk double LP. Again, there was definite progression, many of those infused influences reflected on a record hailed from that point on as the band's most

2

März 3/79
DM 3.- · SF 3.30 · ÖS 24
C 6858
Sounds
The Clash
Henry Cow
Keith Richard
Jim Morrison
Joe Cocker

accomplished long-player.

When all was down on tape, the band left Price to mix the album, Stevens overseeing. Yet this wasn't any textbook production, Simonon telling Don Letts, 'We looked over in the control booth and there were two grown men wrestling over the mixing desk. We looked closer, Guy was wrestling with Bill Price.' Price explained, 'He just got so excited, but I just used to hold him down with one hand and carry on the manual mix with the other.'

Returning to the States – on a Career High

'Joe Strummer was on stage, talking about how great country music radio stations were in America. It was a soundcheck in the St Paul Civic Center and The Clash already sounded like they'd invented rock'n'roll.'

Mickey Bradley, Teenage Kicks: My Life as an Undertone, 2016

With the new LP complete, it was time for the band to get back on the road, returning to the US with Northern Irish punks The Undertones joining them for part of their travels. That invite followed The Clash's decision to pull out of a free festival the Derry five-piece were planning for their hometown, which Strummer and co. had agreed to participate in. As awestruck bass player Michael Bradley put it in *Teenage Kicks: My Life as an Undertone*, 'While we were in London it was decided we should do publicity shots with The Clash to let the world know about what was going to be called The Derry Dance. We were taken to Wessex Studios, where *London Calling* was being recorded. We didn't know it was going to be their best LP, otherwise we'd have been hanging around, waiting to hear what they were doing. We weren't that fussed about its predecessor, so weren't exactly holding our breath. No one was. But they were still the band that did 'White Riot' and 'Garageland'.

'The Clash were very warm, welcoming and well dressed. Did I say well dressed? I meant to say that they looked like sun-kissed gods who'd just stepped out of a Marlon Brando movie in order to meet the extras from a public information film about the dangers of poor nutrition and bad haircuts. We stood beside them, trying to blend in. We didn't. Five minutes of talking, posing and occasional pushing passed. That's pushing in the old playground sense. The photographer had his pictures, so we went back to The Marquee while they resumed making *Rolling Stone* magazine's eighth best LP of all time. The Clash must have liked us, as they not

Topper, Paul, Joe and Mick cross the border

only agreed to play in Derry but also invited us to support them on their September tour of America.'

Yet at Eden Studios a week later, with The Undertones recording their fifth single, 'You've Got My Number (Why Don't You Use It!)', the band were visited by Strummer, 'letting us know that The Clash would not be coming to Derry after all'. Bradley explained, 'He had received a death threat from the Red Hand Commando. If they were German, with a name like that, you would imagine they'd be a fashion inspiration for The Clash, a nice bit of stencilling on a white shirt to go along with 'Hate & War'. But they were from Northern Ireland, they were Loyalist, and no, they didn't own any Clash records.'

The death threat followed a short piece Strummer did for the *NME* for the 1979 UK General Election, including support for the withdrawal of the British Army from Northern Ireland. Bradley said, 'Not the most radical policy doing the rounds of the left wing in England at the time. I read the piece and paid it little heed, but someone else in Derry wasn't as relaxed. I don't know who it was, but they got out the Basildon Bond and put their thoughts down on paper. No, they didn't, they tore a page out of an exercise book and scrawled on it that if Joe Strummer set foot on Ulster soil he would be assassinated. Signed, Red Hand Commando, Londonderry. Joe took it seriously. 'Sorry,' he said, 'but we won't be playing in Derry.' We sympathised, but I had to admit I wanted to tell him that the letter was obviously not from an actual Red Hand Commando or anyone connected with them. The real RHC would have phoned a journalist if they were intending to threaten someone, especially if they didn't know where they lived. Either that or they would have left a statement in some newsroom. I didn't say that though.'

Soon though, The Undertones were supporting their heroes during the The Clash Take the Fifth US tour. Bradley added, 'I recognised some of the songs, 'I Fought the Law' and '(White Man) In Hammersmith Palais', but some of the others were new to me. After they'd finished, Joe came over to talk to me and Billy (Doherty, Undertones drummer). We were sitting out front, waiting, watching and wondering how we ended up in the middle of America listening to The Clash. Joe was a good guy. I can't remember what we talked about but I'm sure he did his best to make us feel welcome. And we were, throughout the tour. We didn't exactly hang out with The Clash but didn't really hang out with anyone but ourselves.'

Billy Doherty, in a writewyattuk.com interview in late 2016, told me about that conversation with Strummer, adding, 'There's a great photograph I have, taken by Pennie Smith, of Michael and myself in some auditorium, with Joe talking and us hanging on every word! He was really protective of us, as was John Peel, who I think having championed the band, felt concerned that we might be spat out very quickly by the industry, wanting to protect our honesty.'

Meanwhile, Mickey Bradley wrote, 'Thankfully, The Clash still had a bit of punk rock pioneering spirit left. They were as good as you would have imagined them to be in 1979. They'd just recorded their best LP and had yet to sack Mick Jones. They even did 'White Riot' at the end. After the show they got on a tour bus. We got in a car. It was an American car, so we all fitted in, (manager) Andy Ferguson driving.

'Our last show with The Clash was Toronto, September 26. Afterwards, they had a party for us. We bought them some gifts – woolly hats and toy machine guns. Yes, we were slightly mocking them, but they didn't mind. We even crashed a TV interview Joe was doing with an earnest presenter from a local station in the dressing room after the show. Damian (O'Neill), Feargal (Sharkey), Topper Headon and I jumped in with those toy guns and pretended to shoot the interviewer and interviewee. I only hope Joe didn't think the Red Hand Commando had followed him to Canada. About 30 years later the footage was resurrected. I can't watch it now. Not out of sadness at Joe's early death but embarrassment at my younger self and what I can only describe as showing off. No call for it.'

Soon, The Clash would release the only UK single from the new LP, its title track, 'London Calling', finished in November and released on December 7. Strummer delivered his celebrated apocalyptic message over Simonon's booming bass and mighty percussive electric guitar, the song's title alluding to the world-renowned BBC radio ident, and its lyrics reflecting concern over

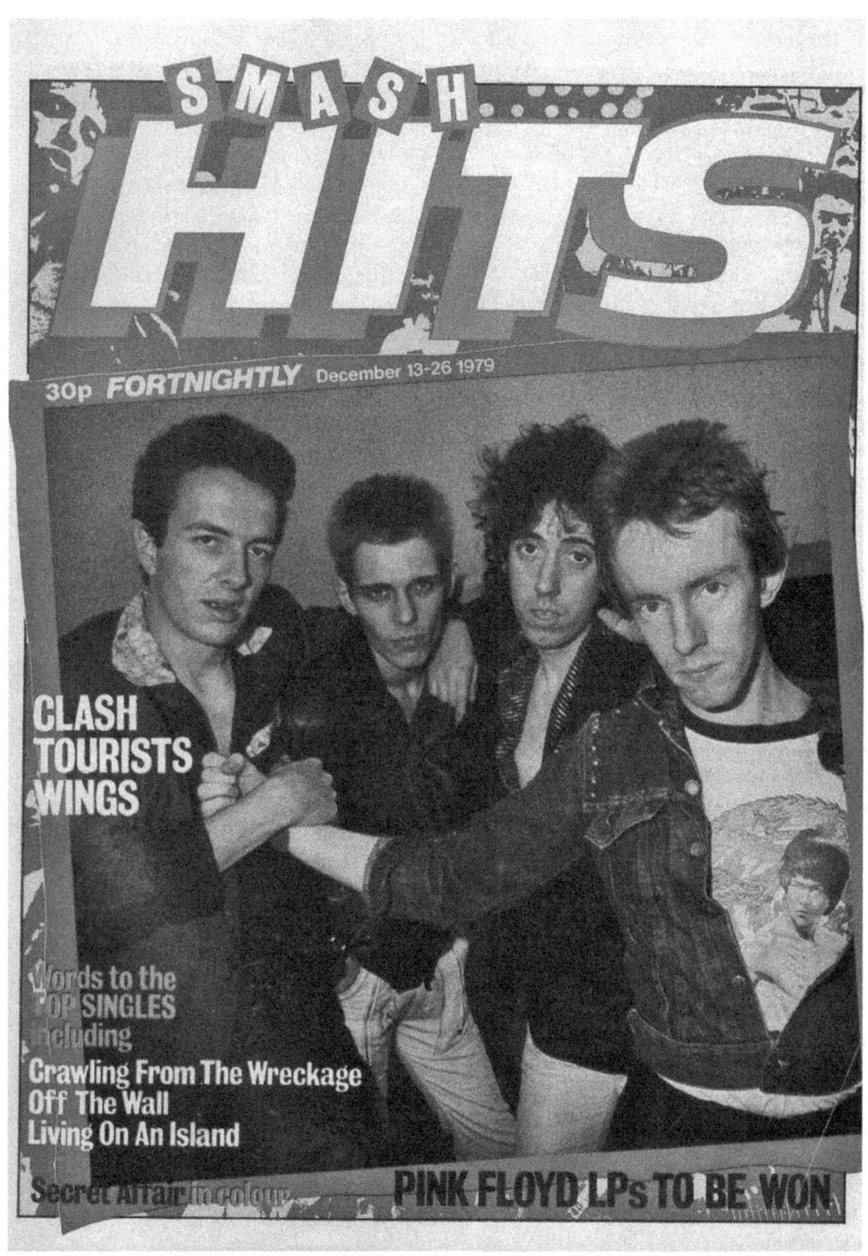
SMASH
HITS
30p FORTNIGHTLY December 13-26 1979
CLASH
TOURISTS
WINGS
Crawling From The Wreckage
Off The Wall
Living On An Island
PINK FLOYD LPs TO BE WON

the threat of 'a nuclear error' like that year's Three Mile Island disaster. Strummer recalled, 'We felt we were struggling, about to slip down a slope or something, grasping with our fingernails. And there was no one there to help us.'

He takes it all up a notch by referring to a double-whammy amid environmental fears that the River Thames would flood the city, leading to the construction of the Thames Barrier, completed in 1982. Elsewhere, there's talk of police brutality and the band's management and knock-on financial woes, and an underlying plea to the public not to expect any great answers to the world's woes from their latest perceived spokesman for a generation.

The single was accompanied by Don Letts' video, the band playing the song on a boat at Festival Pier, next to Albert Bridge, Battersea Park, on a cold, rainy December evening. Letts confessed to *Uncut* in 2015, 'I'll tell you a secret: it was all done by mistake. Because it was the first one I'd ever done, I was sort of making it up as I went along. We went down to the Thames to shoot the bloody thing but didn't know the Thames had a tide. You're talking to a man who can't swim here! We got there and the river had gone down 10 feet. Then we had to fill things on the boat to get it up. Then it started to piss with rain, all by chance. But if those things hadn't happened, it wouldn't have been the video that it was. Like everything with punk rock, we made our problems our assets.'

Over the years, that track became regarded by many as the band's finest moment and proved to be just their first show of strength, their punk, reggae, ska, rockabilly and rock'n'roll influences coming to the fore on a mighty long-player chock-full of an energy many felt was missing from Sandy Pearlman's more polished, *Give 'Em Enough Rope*, a new decade starting in style for The Clash.

What's more, it was released as a double-A-side, with cult reggae number, 'Armagideon Time', a cover of a 1978 song by Jamaican singer Willie Williams, recorded at Wessex in early November. It was a superb bass-heavy, dub reggae production, of which Pete Wylie, speaking to *Uncut* in 2015 about his DJing days at Eric's in Liverpool, said, 'We'd play it three or four times a night. People would still go back and dance to it every time. Liverpool sometimes picked on a certain track over others. Maybe it was a perverse bullshit thing, but 'Armagideon Time' was the one. It's spooky and it's taking reggae and making it their own thing. An ominous record.'

Like the album that followed, the single was produced by Guy Stevens and engineered by Bill Price at Wessex Studios, a former church hall in Highbury, North London, previously used by the Sex Pistols, The Pretenders and the Tom Robinson Band.

As would be continued with the retro Elvis Presley debut album-inspired *London Calling* LP cover, the front and back sleeves of the single were based on old Columbia 78 rpms, the artwork designed by Ray Lowry. The teenage models featured are listening to The Beatles' *Please Please Me*, the Sex Pistols' *Never Mind the Bollocks*, The Rolling Stones' debut LP, *The Clash*, Bob Dylan's *Highway 61 Revisited* and *Elvis Presley*.

The single had several issues, all with different covers, including four that first year, and reached No.11 in the UK, the band's highest charting single while they were together. In America, it would be the following album's uncredited extra track which would crack the singles market.

Pete Wylie told *Uncut* in 2015, 'If it was the only song The Clash ever did, they'd still deserve a special place. The fluke, though, was they had millions.'

Roddy Frame agreed, adding, 'It's writ big. It's cinematic. It ranks alongside the best Rolling Stones stuff or whatever. It's just a classic record. The musicianship's great – I know you're not supposed to say that when you're talking about The Clash – and it's got that ominous feel, that juice at the beginning. It was them coming back and establishing themselves as the British rock band, the only serious contenders for that crown. I just like it because it's world class.'

Film director Alex Cox felt, 'It suggests the possibility of revolution, which is tremendously enticing. 'English Civil War' does too; it's definitely a rallying call for something, but 'London Calling' is a bit more advanced – the war is about to take hold.'

Jake Burns said, 'Such a fantastic song. It's the whole construction of the thing, the rhythm of it, everything. It's proved to be incredibly enduring.'

Mark Perry added, 'It's just a superb opener to a classic album. It was that moment when they matured, when they grew out of being a UK punk band. When I heard 'London Calling' I thought, literally, this is the best band in the world.'

And Butch Vig gave the picture from across the Atlantic, adding, 'I first got it when I'd just graduated from college and used to play all four sides back to back non-stop for months. There was a huge buzz about The Clash in the US at the time and I remember driving over to Chicago with six of my buddies to see them play The Oregon Ballroom. The atmosphere was so charged you could feel the electricity in the air. Everything they played sounded amazing that night, but when they played 'London Calling', the audience just exploded. A lot of other musicians I know went to see that show and they remember it being just as mind-blowing.'

Over the years, 'London Calling' has come to be regarded by many as the band's finest song, and *Rolling Stone* rated it No.15 in its 2004 list of the 500 Greatest Songs of All Time, the highest of any punk single (with four other Clash songs listed: 'Should I Stay Or Should I Go' – 228, 'Train in Vain' – 292, 'Complete Control' – 361, '(White Man) In Hammersmith Palais' – 430). It was also ranked No.48 in the magazine's 2008 list of the 100 Greatest Guitar Songs of All Time, and appeared among the Rock and Roll Hall of Fame's 500 Songs That Shaped Rock and Roll. What's more, the LP that followed would go even higher.

London Calling – an appreciation

With its short-sharp-shock guitar, hammering drumbeats and expressive, almost questioning bass, the third album's title track, 'London Calling', signalled a startling return, an SOS to the world from a band unshackled from their past yet looking to truly break free and branch out.

London Calling's title track wasn't Joe Strummer evoking the desert island vibe of The Police's late '79 chart hit 'Message in a Bottle' or reinventing Martha and the Vandellas' invitation across the nation 15

2

years earlier for 'Dancing in the Street'. This was more a yelp for help from a financially hit band set to start again amid widespread political and social upheaval, a new right-wing Government in power. As the writer himself put it, 'We felt we were struggling, about to slip down a slope or something, grasping with our fingernails. And there was no one there to help us.'

As the struggle threatened to drown them, The Clash were defiant, fighting end-of-the-world trials with grim determination to succeed against the odds, fired up by Guy Stevens' belief in them, ready to battle on, in synch with each other more than ever before, Joe wrestling with images of that March's 'nuclear error' at Three Mile Island, transporting that horror to his home city, wondering what will get him first – nuclear annihilation or a risen Thames.

Word was that the song was born from a discussion about the plight of the world between Strummer and fiancée Gaby Salter, in a taxi back from the Pimlico rehearsal rooms to their flat at World's End. Strummer told *Uncut*, 'There was a lot of Cold War nonsense going on. We already knew that London was susceptible to flooding. She told me to write something about that.' There were several drafts before completion, Strummer placing himself in the winter of the apocalypse, a reluctant spokesman for a

MOMENTS IN TIME PART 2: AUGUST 1979

There's some grainy black-and-white footage, filmed during the recording of *London Calling* and belatedly released with the album's expanded 25th anniversary edition, that captures legendary Clash producer Guy Stevens in his unhinged pomp. It's barely 14 minutes long, caught on home video during sessions at Wessex Studios, but it packs a punch. Stevens is clearly 'loaded', repeating the phrase 'local gymnasium' while bouncing in his seat in a bid to inspire Joe Strummer to deliver the ultimate take on the song 'Four Horsemen'. He's soon right in Strummer's face, encouraging the lead singer, telling him: 'Nearly there, Joe. Come on, Hold on to this. Hold on to this motherfucker!'

You can't quite work out what he's asking him to grab, but Strummer tells him to be careful, fearing a breakage, hoping his producer doesn't cause himself an injury. Stevens is seemingly oblivious of any danger, asking Bill Price on the desk to roll the tape.

In the next short clip, Stevens – the Arsenal fan with his beloved Liam Brady scarf, as ever, round his neck – tells Strummer to 'just come off the vocal properly'. It could well be 'Death or Glory' they're working on. He's gently encouraging rather than bullying, but so pissed that he sounds like Phil Cornwell's CHECK animated version of Mick Jagger from *Stella Street*. Then there's an emphatic, 'Now I'm producing, right!' as if he's reminding himself what he's actually doing in that Highbury studio, having no doubt arrived that morning by taxi via a stop-off at the Arsenal Stadium, where arrangements have been made for him to walk to the centre-circle each day and – while the meter's running – summon up the spirit of the Gunners and take that inspiration into work.

As the next clip kicks in, we witness Mick Jones and Paul Simonon jamming on an instrumental take of 'The Right Profile', possibly still in its 'Up-Toon' format: Jones noodling with some rather splendid blues guitar and Topper with his cans on, fag dangling from his lips as he keeps time. Soon we catch Stevens in the act again, leading a wooden ladder to the studio piano, propping it up low,

generation, insisting he didn't have all the answers. There's even a 1956 reference, in keeping with the Elvis connotations of the sleeve, with the song playing out on a line from Guy Mitchell's 'Singing the Blues'.

That vibe continues with 'Brand New Cadillac', one of three covers and perhaps the most symbolic of the move from punk to traditional rockabilly. Vince Taylor's 1959 tune, the band's initial warm-up song before recording, was given new life 20 years on, driven off at erratic speed to Stevens' manic encouragement, Taylor's tune a perfect vehicle for the band. The London-born US rock'n'roller had also influenced fellow homegrown talent David Bowie, forming part of the inspiration behind *Ziggy Stardust*. Paul Simonon brought the song in, via a 1976 Chiswick reissue, and it was the first song finished for the album, nailed in one take. Introduced live in July '79 at The Rainbow, Strummer was still playing it with the Mescaleros two decades later.

The band's obsession with Rude Boy culture took a twist with 'Jimmy Jazz', a quirky number in which their wider musical sensibilities seemed to expand amid a broad base of Irish Horns brass, blues and jazz, Strummer narrating the tale of a young Rasta turned underground fugitive on the run from the law, following a high noon showdown with Jimmy Dread. There's even Django

climbing it and then jumping off for maximum crash effect, giving a cacophonous burst of ivory-bashing. He picks up the ladder and throws it across the studio, walking off with a determined 'Keep filming', collecting a plastic chair from a stack at the back, then returning with it and rotating it, as if locating its best sound.

Next, he's there in the epicentre of a Clash jam session, pogoing in his own inimitable way. In fact, it's more like a kangaroo-hopping session; he's looking like he's contemplating the long jump rather than a vertical motion, the spirit of Neanderthal man apparent as he shows appreciation of a run through 'Louie Louie'. He's in Jones' face again then, as Jones riffs away on his Stratocaster, Stevens running around in front of the other bandmates, with studio hands trying to move dangerous objects out of his path. He finally throws his plastic chair to the ground with some force, Topper's dog Battersea barking in the background.

Then we see Headon give a good account of himself on guitar. I can't make out who's on drums, but I'm distracted by a balding, bearded madman following them around with a mic stand, trying to capture the essence he's unleashed on the proceedings. There's further tension as assistant engineer Jerry Green tries to wrestle a wooden pole from Stevens, the band suggesting he just leaves him to it. Green's clearly not so sure. It is, after all, his job to hand the keys back later. But as he reluctantly gives up, that pole is also launched across the floor. Finally, we hear Simmo patiently plead, 'Come on, let's get started,' to which Stevens responds, 'Right, let's go!' – as if it was his idea, not the bass player's. Stevens adds a terse, 'I've been ready for about two hours!' as the footage ends. It's an experience to behold and comes at least some way towards a visual explanation of just what it must have been like, working with this maverick producer. Absolute mayhem, Guy Stevens style. But what a result!

Reinhardt-style acoustic guitar from Jones. The song first aired live in Minneapolis, as a tour opener.

'Hateful', first aired at Vanilla. On the face of it, the song is a seemingly bright and breezy number, but it warns about junkie culture, detailing the debilitating nature of helpless heroin addiction, Strummer's line, 'This year I lost some friends,' denoting Sid Vicious' death that February.

As the Rude Boy returns, Strummer's lyrics on 'Rudie Can't Fail' chronicle the life of a young man failing to act like a responsible adult in a pop-soul reggae collision. The song originated at Vanilla in spring, Strummer arriving on the No.19 bus each day, no doubt late. There are elements of Desmond Dekker's '007 (Shanty Town)', and Keith Topping notes Paul Simonon's 'bone-shaking ska bassline', Topper Headon's 'rhythmic rim-shots' and Jones' 'most successful solo vocal to date', on a track tipping a pork-pie hat to the 2 Tone explosion, not least recent live support The Specials, who namechecked Bernie Rhodes on debut single, 'Gangsters'. Recorded at Wessex in July '79, and first tried out live that month in London, it also closed the film *Rude Boy*.

Don Letts told *Uncut* in 2015, 'It just sums up that moment when we were turning each other on to our respective cultures. I think it was written in the summer when Joe and Paul were going to a lot of reggae shebangs and blues dances, partaking in herb and brew and generally being turned on by West Indian culture. At the same time, me and my mates were being turned on by them. We became closer by understanding our differences and not trying to be the bloody same. Joe's description of the Rudie character too – 'drinking brew for breakfast' and the 'chicken skin suit' – it's a great song. A classic.'

'Spanish Bombs' was also inspired by a conversation between Strummer and fiancée Gaby, this time while travelling home from Wessex late one evening, discussing Spain's Basque separatists and holiday resort bombing on the Costa del Sol, drawing parallels with the Spanish Civil War six decades earlier. That said, Strummer told Sean O'Hagan in 1997 there was a link to past love interest Palmolive of The Slits, who was from Andalucía. He added that it was 'another complex lyric, drenched in García Lorca. It moves back and forth through time, from Spanish history to package holidays ... it's a kind of love song.'

The subject was sparked by Johnny Green's interest in the Spanish conflict and George Orwell's *Homage to Catalonia*, the band's road manager lending Strummer books on the subject. Written from the viewpoint of learning from history, not making the same mistakes again, Keith Topping noted that it contains some of Strummer's 'most beautiful imagery', where 'the colours of red and black run through the song like rivers, ripped out of time, transported to the present day with references to DC10s, disco-casinos, shattered hotels and burning buses'. Tom Carson in *Rolling Stone* was similarly enamoured, noting 'jangling flamenco guitars and a lilting vocal meshing in a swirling kaleidoscope of courage and disillusionment, old wars and new corruption'. Elegant guitar from Jones added to the picture.

Strummer, fascinated by Golden-Age Hollywood, penned 'The Right Profile' after reading a book lent to him by Guy Stevens about US method actor Montgomery Clift, who was facially disfigured after a

Paul, Topper, Mick and Joe take the Far East by storm

car accident in 1956 (yes, that year again), leading to part-paralysis and a subsequent request to be directed via his right profile. Clift later slid into alcohol and barbiturates, and Green saw the song as much a tribute to Stevens' own battle with the bottle as Clift's. Again, the Irish Horns add real soul, but without their input, it was never played live.

Sung by Mick Jones, 'Lost in the Supermarket' was Joe Strummer's take on adolescence, disguised as a study of consumerism, delivered with emotion. Jones felt it was about his own Harrow Road upbringing rather than Joe's spell in suburban Surrey. It was the first time he'd tackled that period, writing with regret rather than anger at being sent off to boarding school. The supermarket metaphor suggests depersonalisation, a nation of lonely people checking out the aisles, desperate to find connections. The song was conceived in the early hours in a store beneath the flats Joe and Gaby shared with her family. Musically, Headon was inspired by seeing Taj Mahal's percussive playing style, while Simonon added 'layered, neo-funk basslines', as Keith Topping put it.

John Bramwell simply called it, 'The greatest Jam song Paul Weller didn't write', while US producer Butch Vig told *Uncut* in 2015, 'One minute they'd be playing around with rock and blues, the next ska and reggae. 'Lost In The Supermarket' brings a lot of these different influences together with a really hypnotic chorus. It also demonstrates Mick Jones' unique guitar techniques and the way he would produce really hooky leads. I used to get into arguments with Kurt Cobain about The Clash because he would say they didn't have as much energy as the Sex Pistols and I would say the Sex Pistols only had four or five killer songs and that most of their material was really one-dimensional. It was just a light-hearted thing, but we'd argue for hours about this and other classic rock debates like The Beatles vs The Stones.' And fellow US musician and singer-songwriter Matthew Ryan added, 'The first song I wished I'd written. I was inspired by their wonderful marriage of truth-telling, vulnerability and being pissed off. It was my first moment of absolute envy, and an important point in my interior life as a writer.'

Following a Spike Milligan-esque, 'What are we gonna do now?', we're in classic Clash territory on 'Clampdown'. Strummer paints a picture of the world at the abyss on a Jones composition with the guitars turned back up, decrying a system grinding you down the minute you're old enough to work. Road-tested at Vanilla as Jones' instrumental 'Working and Waiting', Strummer's lyrics again touch on the Three Mile Island nuclear meltdown, the world's worst atomic accident at the time.

Johnny Green reckoned it was about wheel-clamping, a London feature by the late '70s and a 'metaphor for mean-spirited authority, literally ball and chaining people's freedom'. But Strummer also took in religious indoctrination, fascism, and the power of the judiciary, politicians and more or less anyone wielding power, breeding a nation of robots too afraid to voice discontent. The suggestion is that those willing to work for the clampdown ultimately get what's coming to them. The answer? Resistance is not only possible, but an obligation.

Paul Simonon, talking to the *LA Times*, spoke about the opportunities available to him on leaving school, saying, 'They took us out on trips to give us an idea of what jobs were available. But they didn't try to introduce us to anything exciting or meaningful. They took us to the power station and the Navy yards. It was like saying, 'This is all you guys could ever do.' Some of the kids fell for it. When we got taken down to the Navy yards, we went on a ship and got cooked dinner and it was all chips and beans. It was really great. So some of the kids joined up – the food was better than they ate at home.'

In the same interview, Strummer added, 'I'm not like Paul or the others, I had a chance to be a 'good, normal person' with a nice car and a house in the suburbs – the golden apple, whatever you call it. But I saw through it. I saw it was an empty life. I only saw my father once a year. He was a real disciplinarian who was always giving me speeches about how he had pulled himself up by the sweat of his brow: a real guts and determination man. What he was really saying to me was, 'If you play by the rules, you can end up like me.' And I saw right away I didn't want to end up like him. Once I got out on my own, I realised I was right. I saw how the rules worked and I didn't like them.'

With its roots in a mighty Paul Simonon reggae riff, we get the bass player's take on life in a police state on 'The Guns of Brixton', in which *The Harder They Come*'s Ivan lands in South London for a brush with the law, Met Police style, in a song chock-full of violent imagery. It was the first Simonon track the band recorded and the first to have him sing lead. His monotone delivery works so well, the music he grew up around and lived with oozing from the finished product.

Initially seen as an instrumental, Simonon soon added a set of lyrics, which Strummer branded 'fantastic' but insisted the bass player sing. After a few days building up courage, he did. What's more, his riff returned in March

1990, Norman Cook's Beats International fusing it with an S.O.S. Band dance hit for UK chart-topper 'Dub Be Good to Me'.

Don Letts, discussing the track for *Uncut* in 2015, wrote, 'I'm a South London guy, I was in the Brixton riots and all that stuff. In fact, y'know that dread walking up to the policemen on the cover of *Super Black Market Clash*? Well, that's me! It was actually taken in Notting Hill, but not a lot of people know that. Anyway, this song just captures the mood of what was going on in Brixton with the SUS laws and everything. Another South London thing, but one that was particularly poignant to black people.'

A cover of Jamaican rocksteady outfit The Rulers' 'Wrong 'Em Boyo' – itself a take on Lloyd Price's R&B standard 'Stagger Lee' – saw a blues and ska blend on an 1895 tale of Stagger Lee and Billy Lyons, whose deadly altercation in a St Louis bar became American Deep South folklore. The C. Alphonso-penned original was a Simonon favourite on the Rehearsal Rehearsals jukebox, but Strummer had tackled Price's version with the 101'ers, and added lines from that, this infectious, skanking version introduced live in Boston that September.

Strummer's tongue-in-cheek take on the punk scene and youth culture, 'Death or Glory' looks at how rebel rockers eventually grow up, mellow out and end up 'making payments on a sofa or a girl', risking becoming 'just another story'. Again, Simonon's bass stands out as Strummer reflects on time changing everything, following a teenage hood's drift into domesticity. The song also touches on domestic violence, the notion of selling out and the importance of perseverance, and Guy Stevens apparently threw chairs around the studio during recording to create extra tension.

The LP's fastest, most punky cut, 'Koka Kola' examined drugged-up advertising execs and the products they convince us we need. The song is more amused than angry, although it also slams the evils of hard drugs, Keith Topping feeling it had 'one of the best sets of lyrics Strummer ever wrote', satirising 'yuppie cocaine culture' and casting 'a jaundiced 'been there, done that' eye at New York's young execs and their paranoid world of sex, drugs and money'. It often featured live in a medley with 'I Fought the Law'.

Deemed too complicated to attempt live, the band recorded each part twice to create a 'sound as big as possible' on 'The Card Cheat', a Phil Spector-like epic following a lonesome gambler as luck finally deserts him. Jones pushes the band on, suggesting Mott the Hoople in their pomp, as well as Spector's wall of sound. Strummer produced further striking imagery in a vivid tale of death and renewal on one of the last tracks recorded for *London Calling*, the Irish Horns again adding depth.

Alluding to the smooth reggae going down well at the time, Strummer offered instructions on how to 'treat your lover girl right' for 'Lover's Rock'. Its take on birth control earning criticism, this Rude Boy tale is seen as rather dated and sexist regarding unwanted pregnancies and the comparative prowess of black and white males.

The Clash had already gone down the ironic self-referential route with 'Clash City Rockers', and on 'Four Horsemen' they opted to ride us out of the impending apocalypse. As Keith Topping put it, 'Strummer's lyrics take the biblical imagery of Revelations chapter six and give it a Monty Python twist, presenting The Clash as hard-drinking, hard-drugging, hard-loving prophets, and they're coming to your town.'

He'd had his troubles, but Mick Jones was not to be beaten, and 'I'm Not Down' is about battling on, determined not to fall victim to 'that kind of day when none of your sorrows will go away'. Looking for a way back after a break-up with Viv Albertine and a burglary at his flat that saw many cherished possessions lost, and suspecting that good times were not far away, his reference to Judgment Day seems apt after the 'Four Horsemen'.

Soon we reach 'Revolution Rock', a celebratory Danny Ray and the Revolutioneers cover, with Jackie Edwards' 'Get Up' as its foundation, tackling freedom through the medium of dance, the Irish Horns again on form as 'El Clash Combo' promise 'requests now on the bandstand!' at 'fifteen dollars a day'. Meanwhile, Strummer suggests you 'smash up your seats and dance to a brand-new beat'. An instrumental version featured on the *Rude Boy* soundtrack, offering a carnival-style finale, Strummer advertising, 'El Clash Combo – weddings, parties, anything ... and bongo jazz a speciality'.

Then we're away on 'Train in Vain' (Stand by Me)', Mick Jones getting the last word on a late arrival that didn't even get track-listed, Strummer's guitar hero looking to convey to his departed girl that he's going to somehow get through. Jones recalled, 'The track was like a train rhythm, and there was, once again, that feeling of being lost.' Bill Price added, 'It was the last song we finished after the artwork went to the printer. It wasn't intended to be hidden. The sleeve was already printed before we tacked the song on the end of the master tape.'

It was interpreted by some as a response to The Slits' 'Typical Girls' and how they 'stand by their man'. Jones had recently split with Slits guitarist Viv Albertine, who said, 'I'm really proud to have inspired that, but often he won't admit to it. He used to get the train to my place in Shepherds Bush and I would not let him in. He was bleating on the doorstep. That was cruel.'

It's the kind of simple love song you'd expect Bernie Rhodes to have rallied against, ushered in at the end of the platform by Headon's slick beat, Jones' lovesick lyrics written the night before they were recorded. Yet it became the band's first US top-30 hit when released there as a single. It was also released in mainland Europe on 33 rpm, with extra tracks 'Bankrobber' and 'Rockers Galore... UK Tour', and later pressed as the next UK single.

It was originally down to be a flexi-disc freebie issued with the *NME*, but that deal fell through, and the track was described by Keith Topping as a 'last-minute triumph, a caustic PS to all those who had written off The Clash for having lost their way'. Written, rehearsed and recorded in less than 24 hours, and introduced live over Christmas '79 in London, it remained a set fixture until Jones left. Don Letts filmed a promo video at Lewisham Odeon in February '80, in which Strummer invites us to 'take the soul train from platform one'.

Around the turn of the year, the band members attended a special private screening of a new film, *Rude Boy*, the partly fictional documentary film telling the story of a Clash fan who leaves his job in a Soho sex shop to become a roadie for the group. It featured plenty of great live tour footage, including clips from their Rock Against Racism appearance, and shots of the band in the studio recording *Give 'Em Enough Rope*. Yet the band weren't impressed by the storyline and distanced themselves from the finished product. They'd move on long before.

By then, The Clash were touring the UK again, and among those enthralled by the experience was future BBC Radio 1 DJ Andy

Joe, Mick and Paul onstage, 21 May 1980

Kershaw, at that point a student booking bands at Leeds University. As he recalled in his 2011 autobiography *No Off Switch*, 'I'd seen The Clash before, and their earlier scratchy fury was itself impressive, if limited. But by the 16 Tons tour they'd matured into something magnificent. They'd rejected their previous tactical but silly 'year zero' approach to any music that came before punk.

'Now, live, just as they had on record with *London Calling*, a radical departure from earlier releases, they were finally allowing their collective musical enthusiasms and their immersion in rock'n'roll history to enrich gloriously their performances on stage. Not just evident now, but celebrated were the elements of R&B, roots reggae, Keith Richards, country, soul, rockabilly, and dub. The Clash of January 1980 had also accumulated those almost indefinable qualities necessary for elevation to the status of greatness. To embellish those musical components (and naturally their playing had only improved over time), they had the look, the charisma, the élan. In the refec that night, they were the fully rounded finished article, and utterly riveting. I stood agape. I was not, however, witnessing the future of rock'n'roll, nor strictly speaking the end, but both the alpha and the omega. After that gig I came to realise anything that followed in the name of rock music was by definition, at best second-rate, and probably pointless.'

According to Kosmo Vinyl, the band aimed to release a double LP, and a single every month for a year, starting with 'Bankrobber'. He said, 'As one dropped out of the charts, we'd release another. We delivered it to CBS, but they wouldn't release it. They said it sounded like all of David Bowie's records played backwards at once.'

On 'Bankrobber', the band's reggae influence again showed up well, on a track only initially available in the UK on import – part of the European pressing of 'Train in Vain' – yet reaching No.12 in the charts, and doing well in Ireland and New Zealand too. What did CBS really object to? Did they see this brooding ska track as advocating violent crime? Surely not. It's just another take on the quintessential Clash 'don't settle for a dead-end job' theme – 'A lifetime serving one machine / Is 10 times worse than prison' – and a great one at that, not least thanks to Simonon's heavy bassline and Jones' bottleneck guitar riff.

2

The band filmed a low-budget promo video of themselves recording the song while chief roadies The Baker and Johnny Green – bandanas covering their faces – performed a bank heist in Lewisham, during the filming of which they were stopped and questioned by police. B-side 'Rockers Galore... UK Tour' was a reworking of the A-side, with Mikey Dread singing new lyrics about touring with The Clash, and there was also 'Robber Dub', on a 12-inch record the label refused to release. Incidentally, future Stone Roses frontman Ian Brown was at the recording session, as told to John Robb in *Stone Roses and the Ressurrection of British Pop*.

As it turned out, the fact that CBS struggled to comprehend where the band were at with 'Bankrobber', proved to be something of a dress rehearsal for what followed as The Clash brought out a momentous fourth album, and this time it was spread over six sides.

Sandinista! – an appreciation

The scope of what's to come is soon apparent on opening track, 'The Magnificent Seven', recorded at NYC's Electric Lady Studios in April 1980 and released as a single a year later, reaching No.34 in the UK. The song was a ground-breaking take on rap, inspired by a number of New York hip-hop acts. As Strummer recalled, 'Mick stumbled upon a music shop in Brooklyn that carried the music of Grandmaster Flash and the Furious Five, the Sugarhill Gang ... these groups were radically changing music and they changed everything for us.'

His lyrics involve what Keith Topping called 'an acerbic stream of consciousness ... free association that slips from one image to the next, suggesting the sound equivalent of TV channel surfing'. Taking its title from John Sturgis' 1960 Western, it's more about the drudgery of humdrum working days and the rise of soulless multinationals, Strummer's subject looking to earn cash to buy goods for a girlfriend seduced by TV ads. But the song also namechecks Marx and Engels at a checkout in a 7-Eleven store, Martin Luther King and Mahatma Gandhi facing a heavy defeat in a football match, as well as Socrates, Plato, Richard Nixon and Rin Tin Tin, the five-minute mark crossed with no end in sight before 'vacuum cleaner sucks up budgie'.

Mick, now carrying a boom box around, was quickly won over by the emerging New York hip-hop scene. The track was built on a funky bass loop from The Blockheads' Norman Watt-Roy, with Strummer adding the words on the spot, as was the case with further *Sandinista!* rap track, 'Lightning Strikes (Not Once but Twice)'. Considered the first attempt by a rock band to write and perform original rap – not least with political and social content – it predated Blondie's 'Rapture' by six months. The single failed to chart in America, but proved an underground hit, with heavy play on underground and college radio, and various dance remixes, including B-side 'The Magnificent Dance'.

Jones' homage to early Motown, 'Hitsville UK' involves Mickey Gallagher's gospel organ, vocals shared between Jones and partner Ellen Foley, and even a glockenspiel played by the lead guitarist. Strummer's lyrics celebrate musical independence – namechecking several UK indie record labels – while dissing the 'mutants, creeps and musclemen' of the major labels with their 'expense accounts' and 'lunch discounts', making 'AOR' and fixing the charts. It was recorded at Wessex in August 1980 and chosen as the album's second single in mid-January 1981, yet never performed live. The UK single was backed with 'Radio One', Mikey Dread's take on the music scene.

Strummer performed Robert Allen's traditional blues number, 'Junco Partner' with the 101'ers, and here gave it a makeover at Channel One in Kingston, Jamaica. The original lyrics concerning alcoholism and life on the streets, Strummer added his own slant and namechecked girlfriend Gaby. The track is seen as Mikey Dread's most extreme production for the band, with plenty of dub echo and Strummer's piano. Overdubs at Wessex included scratchy violin, and the song was wheeled out live as late as '84. The song is reprised in a different format three tracks from the end of this mighty opus with Dread's 'Version Pardner' dub version, completed at Wessex late on, with plenty of extra squeaky sound effects, put through an echo box. Another great dance number, on an album rammed with them.

Joe proves it wasn't just Mick seduced by New York City's street life

Headon's first songwriting credit, 'Ivan Meets G.I. Joe', saw him write the music and add his first vocal on a disco tune namechecking New York's Studio 54 and Paris club Le Palace, paving the way for 'Rock the Casbah'. The lyrics cast the world's superpowers as contestants in a bizarre dance-off – Frankie Goes to Hollywood's later No.1 'Two Tribes' springs to mind – and references atomic and chemical warfare, Stalin and, conversely, Marvin Gaye's 'Hitch Hike'.

Where from there? A rockabilly rumble about newspapers and falls from grace, of course, 'The Leader' inspired by tales of the early '60s Profumo affair. Its rocking strut and Jones' chugging guitars saw it fit neatly into the live set for April '81's Radio Clash tour, remaining there for much of the next two years.

The Clash's take on music hall, 'Something About England' was something more likely tackled by Ian Dury or Madness, deemed too complex to play live. Keith Topping saw it as Strummer 'deliberately attempting to nullify some of the American influences on the New York material, writing his lyrics about deliberately parochial English subjects', yet 'patriotic without being xenophobic and wistful and nostalgic without becoming mawkish or trite'. Focused on racism and poverty through the ages, Jones added piano and Gary Barnacle, his father Bill and military bandsman David Yates added brass. The track segues into dream-like, experimental number 'Rebel Waltz', Mick Jones combining Byrds-like guitar with 'chiming bells and brass band flourishes', as Topping put it.

Mose Allison cover, 'Look Here', recorded at Electric Lady and overdubbed at Wessex, was another example of the band's expansive vision, with Topper Headon's jazzy percussion, Mickey Gallagher's piano, and Lew Lewis's harmonica complementing Jones' fine fretwork.
Often seen as Simonon's 'The Guns of Brixton' sequel, 'The Crooked Beat' shares a South London location and his trademark delivery, but otherwise has little in common. Taking lyrical inspiration from a nursery rhyme, there are references to 'the tower blocks of my hometown' on one of the last tracks recorded for the album – laid down at Wessex in September – the song followed by Mikey Dread's echo-saturated dub version, complete with authentic Trenchtown patois.

During the early '80s, Strummer was approached by Jack Nitzsche, who was scoring Al Pacino movie *Cruising*, asking him to provide a heavy rock song for the soundtrack. That night, the car park attendant at the block of flats where Strummer was living in World's End was stabbed over £5, and Strummer was subsequently inspired to write about such a pointless crime. Jones sang one of his most complex tunes on 'Somebody Got Murdered', layered with synth, recorded at Electric Lady and completed at Wessex, Headon's dog Battersea adding vocal embellishments. Strummer never heard back from Nitzsche, but the song found its place.

Primal Scream frontman Bobby Gillespie told *Uncut* in 2015, 'The Clash have had a huge influence on us and the way we approach music. Everything they did had an emotional impact and they really tried to push themselves as a band and experiment with different sounds. I don't think it's as mind-blowing as *Give 'Em Enough Rope* or *London Calling*, but I'm a big fan of *Sandinista!* and particularly 'Somebody Got Murdered'. It's a really brutal song with a lot of depth and passion behind it.'

'One More Time', an Electric Lady reggae tune referring to Marvin Gaye's 'Can I Get a Witness', was inspired by Strummer's interest in US Civil Rights, Martin Luther King's Alabama segregated bus protests, the '65 LA Watts riots and life in the ghetto. And soon after *Sandinista!* was released, riots followed in several British inner cities. Mikey Dread's version, 'One More Dub', followed, credited separately.

Taking on the premise of the LP's opener, Strummer rapped over another fine Watt-Roy bassline on 'Lightning Strikes (Not Once but Twice)', the band absorbing New York City life while walking several blocks from hotel to studio every day during the transit strike of March 1980. The song namechecks everywhere from Harlem to Brooklyn, but the Westway and Hounslow too.

Jones' attack on the 'towers of London', 'Up in Heaven (Not Only Here)', was written after a return to his gran's council flat following a number of flash NYC hotel stays, the imagery taking us back to the urban alienation of the debut LP's 'London's Burning', but more personal this time, lashing out at the powers responsible for the capital's crumbling high-rises, on a track given added resonance after the horrors of the 2017 blaze at Grenfell Tower, barely a mile and a half further west.

Headon's military-style drumming is at the heart of 'Corner Soul', a UK roots reggae groove that again hinted at the riots that would follow in Britain's inner cities the following summer. It also references Enoch Powell's notorious 'Rivers of Blood' speech, at a time when the National Front was stoking distrust within urban communities across England. Meanwhile, Strummer shone a light on Trinidadian steel band calypso with 'Let's Go Crazy'. But beneath a feelgood track were underlying allusions to slavery and ongoing distrust of the police

Paul, Joe, Topper and Mick scrub up nicely

among black communities.

The band embraced further new-found 'outside the box' creativity and New York spirit on 'If Music Could Talk', a Bob Dylan-like talking blues broadside over instrumental backing track, 'Shepherd's Delight', recorded with Mikey Dread at Pluto two months earlier. Strummer's stream-of-consciousness lyric, is again packed with vivid imagery and metaphor on what Keith Topping saw as 'one of the most interesting pieces of music on the LP'. Among wider references and name-dropping – from Bo Diddley to Errol Flynn via Buddy Holly and Jim Morrison – are references to the band themselves, Headon's growing heroin habit and even Strummer's in-studio 'Spliffbunker'. Gary Barnacle added jazzy sax, the song overdubbed at Wessex, its backing track dominated by Headon and Simonon.

Keith Topping saw 'The Sound of the Sinners' as 'the least likely gospel song since the Rolling Stones' 'I Just Wanna See His Face'', its 'twin themes of sin and temptation' driving an 'infectious pseudo-gospel jam' which affectionately 'lampoons its religious subject matter' yet offers 'real conviction in the song's evocation of the forthcoming tidal wave of Armageddon'. Amid the biblical allusions there's an attack on the Church's need to raise its own funds, on a track that largely baffled, yet which Strummer reckoned was Elvis Costello's favourite Clash song.

Recorded at the Power Station (Simonon later adding bass at Wessex), The Equals' 'Police on My Back', written by British-Guyanese guitarist Eddy Grant, was a tour-bus favourite, and Kosmo Vinyl was tasked with getting a vinyl copy of their *Explosion* LP from London so The

Clash could learn the lyrics. A guitar solo live showcase for Jones, the track was introduced on the Far East tour in 1982, and later handled vocally by Nick Sheppard in the Mark II era.

Revival outfits like Matchbox and the Stray Cats in the early '80s set the scene for a re-emergence of Strummer's interest in rockabilly, not least on the hard-ball, rather cynical 'Midnight Log', including Simonon's slap bass. Meanwhile, we have more bass-heavy reggae on 'The Equaliser', which sees Strummer in posturing mode, issuing a further call to arms to the oppressed workers of the world, yet with far less substance than 'Clampdown'.

'The Call Up' was the first track from the new album publicly aired, released as a single on November 28, 1980, a fortnight ahead of the album. Featuring additional guitar from The Voidoids' Ivan Julian, the track opens and closes with a US Marines marching chant. While the US ended the military draft in 1973, the Congress reinstated a requirement for 18- to 25-year-old men to register with its Selective Service System in 1980, the subject topical again. Jones noted in 1991, 'The registration for the draft in America affected a lot of our fans. I remember going to a demonstration on the Upper West Side.'

Recorded at Electric Lady Studios, New York, it tackled not only the draft, but war in general, the line 'It's 55 minutes past 11' referencing the Doomsday Clock and our proximity to global disaster, on a track also dealing with the long-time Clash theme of accepting dead-end jobs, the anti-establishment rhetoric given a more laidback vibe in defiance of its call to arms.

Don Letts filmed the track's accompanying black and white video in a warehouse owned by '60s singer and military collector Chris Farlowe, the band dressed in a bizarre range of apparel, with Simonon as cowboy and Second World War pilot, and Jones in Mountie hat and leopard skin. The single was backed with 'Stop the World', an anti-nuclear track initially intended for a CND compilation LP.

As close as we get to a title track, 'Washington Bullets' is Strummer's take on world politics, citing conflicts and controversies far and wide, siding with popular leftist movements or governments while criticising the American, Chinese and Russian elites for a new brand of imperialism. A *Rolling Stone* review saw this plus 'The Equaliser' and 'The Call Up' as being at 'the heart of the album', and Keith Topping viewed it as the 'key song to understanding the concept', offering a 'jaundiced view of America's influence on the outside world that was, in terms of popular awareness, a decade ahead of its time'. Strummer made a point of talking to various underground political groups in the US, and through San Francisco second-hand record store owner and Vietnam veteran Mo Armstrong, learned about Nicaragua's Sandinistas, consequently drawing attention to links to right-wing dictatorships in Central and South America.

He also highlighted Russia's invasion of Afghanistan in 1980, China's suppression of Tibet two decades earlier, and Britain supplying mercenaries and arms to some of the world's worst trouble spots, as well as the murder of a 14-year-old Jamaican in a Kingston drug deal during their stay. The track is reprised in radical format four tracks from the end, Wessex-recorded 'Silicone on Sapphire' taking the backing track to 'Washington Bullets', adding phasing effects then a spoken-word vocal and more than a touch of brooding electronica, Keith Topping seeing a parallel with Hawkwind on a rather 'unnerving' number, like 'the soundtrack to an undistinguished sci-fi movie'.

'Broadway' was seen as the closest The Clash got to jazz, and it's a track steeped in New York City imagery. *The Clash on Broadway* sleeve notes explain, 'We stayed at the Iroquois. Outside was a heating vent. There was always this one particular bloke, standing or sleeping on it. One night we came back from the studio, about four in the morning, and Joe was looking at this guy quite intently. I always thought 'Broadway' was about him.' Meeting a tramp who 'testifies' with his life story, it's a beautifully observed, vivid portrayal amid misty rain-covered streets and bright lights, something you'd more likely hear from Nick Cave, Shane McGowan or Tom Waits, its burnt-out boxer metaphor suggesting Martin Scorsese's *Raging Bull*, filmed in New York the previous year. The song itself segues into Mickey Gallagher's young daughter's off-kilter run through *The Guns of Brixton*, over Dad's basic piano.

Author and journalist Simon Goddard told *Uncut*, 'Joe's Strummer's brilliant lyrical monologue' was 'a proper performance in every sense of the word. It's like *On The Waterfront* meets 'Rhapsody In Blue' or something, fucking genius.' He added, 'I admit it's pretty lonely being in the *Sandinista!* fan club, but I love every inch of the bastard.'

He's not alone, BBC 6 Music presenter Gideon Coe seeing it as his favourite Clash album, 'a sprawling, flawed masterpiece of a record that just happens to be one-and-a-half sides too long'. But, he adds, 'Broadway' is one of the reasons for forgiving them its excesses. Strummer's on top form and his Grove-meets-Lower-East-Side drawl is honed to perfection for this tale of a bum who's down on his luck. The Clash are full of delightful paradoxes, one being the way America puts fire and anger in their bellies while at the same time firing their imagination. They may have been bored with the USA but they also bought into its mythology and romantic imagery big-time. That's what you get with 'Broadway'. And the band sounds great. Start to finish.'

Joe rekindled his friendship with busking pal Tymon Dogg after a chance meeting in New York. An invite to Electric Lady followed, with Strummer persuading the band to back Dogg on his own composition, 'Lose This Skin', which was released as an independent single in June before being added to *Sandinista!* There's an almost John Lydon-like vocal to Tymon's violin-led Irish jig, and the guest frontman later rejoined Strummer in his final days with the Mescaleros.

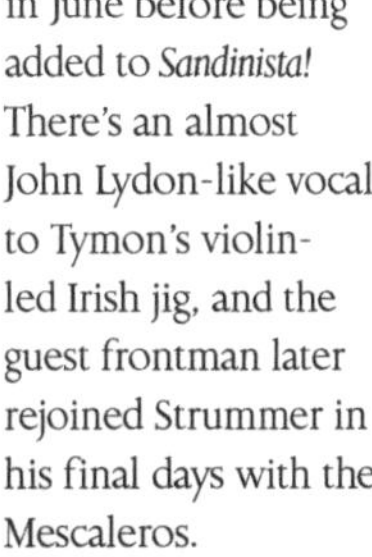

In February 1980, Strummer told *Sounds'* Robbi Millar of his obsession with Francis Ford Coppola's *Apocalypse Now*. 'It doesn't leave you. It's like a dream.' Taking its title from dialogue by Robert Duvall's surf-obsessed US cavalry officer Colonel Kilgore, 'Charlie Don't Surf' sees Mick Jones take the lead role, portraying a Viet Cong soldier there to 'keep the strangers out', in a song taking a look at US cultural and military imperialism in South East Asia, imposing its own religion and belief systems on others, by whatever means.

'Mensforth Hill' has the air of The Beatles' 'Revolution 9' but is in fact 'Something About England' played backwards, with added 'haphazard instrumentation, synthesisers and voice sample-snippets' from Strummer. It's something of a trip, described in the LP sleeve notes as 'the title theme from a forthcoming serial'. Meanwhile, Strummer seems to hone in on Headon for 'Junkie Slip', tackling the drummer's escalating drug addiction, on another New York track, before 'Kingston Advice' takes us back to the band's latest Jamican sojourn, Joe looking at increasing gun use among teenagers in another state of the nation address, advising us to look to the sky for signs of change, his voice drowned in echo and dub effects, over a soundtrack of two-chord reggae, Jones having fun with a guitar solo.

Keith Topping saw 'The Street Parade' as 'one of the most underrated songs on the LP', and 'a gorgeous syncopated band arrangement', with Jones' 'graffiti-like guitars playing off a sweet floating horn section and stabs of Caribbean marimbas'. The track celebrates the ability to lose yourself among the throng – as per The Jam's 'Away from the Numbers' and 'In the Crowd' – something Strummer seems to have taken to the next level with his Paris disappearing trick further down the line.

With Mick Jones' harmonica and Headon's train-rhythm percussion, 'Version City' offers a fresh take on a long line of American railroad tracks, so to speak, Strummer conjuring up the image of an engine that can 'pull you through to better days', as per Elvis' slant on Junior Parker's 'Mystery Train' in 1953, itself revising 1920s gospel standard 'This Train'. Allusions to a 'lonely soul at a crossroads' give a nod to 1930s delta blues legend Robert Johnson, Strummer also referencing Fender and Gibson while Mickey Gallagher pitches in on piano on a song recorded in New York and finished at Wessex.

Recorded in New York in March 1980, 'Living in Fame' was Mikey Dread's put-down of the UK ska revival, suggesting bands should live up to the name or 'die in shame'. The Specials, The Selecter, The Beat, Madness, The Blockheads and Shane MacGowan's pre-Pogues outfit The Nipple Erectors get a pasting before Dread praises The Clash. With sax from Gary Barnacle and Jones' echo-treated guitar, the track is seen as something of a filler.

Often perceived as a karaoke-like take on the debut LP's side two opener, for my money this version of 'Career Opportunities' was an imaginative reimagining, orchestrated by Blockheads keyboard player Mickey Gallagher and employing his sons, Luke and Ben, singing amended lyrics referring to school rules. Recorded at Wessex in 1980, and arguably intended as little more than a band in-joke, it was included all the same, and works nicely.

Piano and acoustic guitar-led instrumental 'Shepherd's Delight' offers a surprising finale. Recorded with Mikey Dread at Pluto in February 1980 during the 'Bankrobber' sessions, and 'not unlike the incidental music from some anonymous BBC2 documentary about homelessness', according to Keith Topping, it is complete with 'disturbing wailing noises', its producer playing with a squeaky toy, then manipulating the tape speed. Train and aircraft noises are added, with plenty of heavy dub echo, 'an experiment in musique concrete … as unlike The Clash as it's physically possible', providing 'a slightly sinister and downbeat end to a remarkable under-appreciated work'.

From Fort Bragg to Times Square, Paris and the Far East: On the Road to Destruction

'It was the first time since Frank Sinatra that Times Square had to be blocked off. It was incredible. It wasn't down to us. We just went to play seven nights and were told we couldn't. The establishment, by trying to stop us, made it huge, made conquering

the States a lot easier for us.'
Topper Headon

Following 1980's triple album offering, Joe Strummer felt the group were 'drifting' creatively, Paul Simonon agreeing with his dissatisfaction at the 'boring' professionalism of The Clash's then managers Blackhill Enterprises. The pair convinced their bandmates to reinstate original manager Bernie Rhodes in February 1981, in an attempt to restore the 'chaos' and 'anarchic energy' of The Clash's early days. But it wasn't a decision welcomed by Mick Jones, progressively estranged from his bandmates. As he put it, 'Although Bernie was really 100% working on ideas for the group, he wouldn't share them with the rest of us. We wouldn't know what was going on.'

Meanwhile, Topper Headon's heroin and cocaine problems escalated, occasional drug usage now costing him £100 per day and undermining his health. His drug addiction would later force his bandmates to fire him from The Clash, after the completion of *Combat Rock*.

Returning to London in 1981 after a spell with Joe Ely in America, Johnny Green felt there had been a shift in the way Strummer was perceived, telling Rod Kitson for *The Quietus* website in 2012, 'People were already seeing him as some kind of spokesman. He wore that hat very reluctantly – he didn't want to be that sort of bloke. He wanted to be in a successful band, of course, but still wanted to have his regular life, he didn't want to be isolated from that.

'In many ways he was a more opened-up man, because he'd done more. But he didn't just want to play the rock star. People were trying hard to not let him be grounded. They'd treat him like a star wherever he went, and he didn't particularly want that, much as he wanted them to like his music.'

The returning Rhodes soon made his presence known, organising a run of shows in Times Square, New York City, starting in the last week of May '81. As it was, The Clash went on to play 17 concerts at Bond's International Casino – a former department store converted into a large second-floor hall – supporting the *Sandinista!* album, with several shows recorded for either CBS or radio, which subsequently appeared on many bootlegs and the 1999 *From Here to Eternity* live album.

2

And what a reaction from the American public. With that residency seen as a major milestone in the band's popularity stateside, the initial eight shows planned over nine days from May 28 expanded to more than double that. With a legal capacity of 1,750, tickets were blatantly oversold from the first night, and the city fire department cancelled the Saturday, May 30, show. The band hit out at the promoters while promising to honour every single ticket, and the original dates were extended through June. Simonon remembered, 'We turned up and they said, 'There's too many people. We'll have to close you down.'' Strummer added, 'We were presented with a situation which escalated beyond control. We were on the news. Check into New York and you're on the evening news. That was fantastic. However many tickets had been put out, we were going to play. But there's something strangely monotonous about getting up, going to the same hall, playing a gig, doing that many nights in a row. It nearly killed us.'

The safety concerns ensured the gigs were relatively small, adding to the intimate nature of the shows. Audience members clambered on stage to join their heroes in singalongs, with the likes of New York musician Pearl Harbor taking on DJ spots alongside Andy Dunkley. The gigs were seen as the band's emergence as a major force rather than a cult band in America, the shows also including high-profile support acts, including cult Salford outfit The Fall; Jamaican maverick producer and performer Lee 'Scratch' Perry; and breakthrough US acts as diverse as Grandmaster Flash and the Furious Five, Bad Brains, and the Dead Kennedys. And while some of the featured hip-hop acts were booed off, Strummer was quick to berate his audience when the headliners took to the stage.

A new single followed on November 10, 'This is Radio Clash', which was first publicly aired on Tom Snyder's US show *Tomorrow* in June, issued in 7-inch, 12-inch and cassette formats with extra tracks, backed with 'Radio Clash', 'Outside Broadcast' and 'Radio Five'.

US critic Eric Schafer retrospectively saw it as a 'magnificent, daring, challenging record … years ahead of its time; one of the great rock records of the 1980s, it has never been given its just credit.' In 2009 he contended that if it were released again, 'It would still burn up the radio.'

By the time that was out there, the band had started on their fifth album. But they weren't in a good place. With a new album set to take shape and tour dates booked in Europe and North America, the relationship between Strummer and Jones was increasingly strained, with Headon's drug problem spiralling.

After initial recording sessions in London, the new LP – with the working title *Rat Patrol from Fort Bragg* during the recording and mixing stages – the group relocated to New York, Jones living with his girlfriend, Ellen Foley, while Strummer, Simonon and Headon were at the Iroquois Hotel, with recording sessions at Electric Lady Studios booked for November and December 1981. After finishing the NYC output, they returned to London for most of the following month, then between January and March embarked on a six-week tour of Japan, Australia, New Zealand, Hong Kong and Thailand. But as Strummer put it, 'Topper's health was going. He'd got addicted to heroin. If you try and imagine a group, and the drummer is falling apart, then no matter what you're putting on top, it's going to fall apart. That was the beginning of the end really.' Pennie Smith added, 'What he was up to made a mockery of what the group was about and what Joe was writing about.' The man himself concurred, adding, 'Looking back, I was out of control. He was saying, 'How can I write all of these songs, anti-drug, when you're stoned out of your head behind me?' There was a lot of friction building up over a period of time.'

What's more, before *Combat Rock* saw the light of day, Strummer went into hiding. It was actually the band's management that suggested he should 'disappear', returned manager Bernie Rhodes feeling the pressure after slow ticket sales for the Scottish leg of their April and May UK shows, concocting a publicity stunt in which he would 'vanish' for a few days. Strummer recalled for *Westway to the World*, 'Bernie said, 'Look, we're starting the tour in Scotland, the tickets are not selling that well. You'd better disappear or something, I need an excuse to cancel the tour.' Like a fool, I went, 'Alright.' I should never have listened to that. I went to France and just dicked around for a while.'

In secret, Strummer was set to head to Texas to stay with his friend, musician Joe Ely, but uneasy with the idea, decided to genuinely disappear. After a phone interview on April 21, promoting the Scottish shows, he crossed the Channel and made for Paris, meeting girlfriend Gaby Salter and generally keeping his head down. That said, while there he ran the Paris Marathon, claiming his training regime consisted of 10 pints of beer the night before. Strummer would later regret his disappearing act, though, tensions within the band leading soon enough to the end of that classic line-up. As Strummer reflected in an interview later used in *The Future is Unwritten*, 'I thought it would be a good joke if I never phoned Bernie at all. He was going to be thinking, 'Oh, where's Joe gone?''

When Strummer didn't report back, Rhodes began to worry. And as it turned out, fans were even less inclined to buy tickets now he was missing. The *NME* ran updates, asking for leads, with concerts cancelled and the UK tour postponed. But by the mid-May release of *Combat Rock*, rumours started to spread about possible sightings of a bearded Strummer in Paris. Soon, Kosmo Vinyl was dispatched to France, and on May 18 one such tip-off led to him finding his prey, greeting him with a cry of 'Fidel!'

Explaining his departure to the *NME*, Strummer said, 'It was something I wanted to prove to myself – that I was still alive. It's very much being like a robot, being in a band. Rather than go barmy and go mad, I think it's better to do what I did, even for a month. I think I would have started drinking a lot on the tour, maybe, started becoming petulant with the audience, which isn't the sort of thing you should do.'

Instead, Strummer returned in time for a band engagement in the Netherlands at the Lochem Festival. As it was, several of the punters had already left, expecting another cancellation. But The Clash duly performed, in what turned out to be Headon's last appearance with the band.

Combat Rock – an appreciation

Kicking off the fifth album in style, 'Know Your Rights' sees Strummer grab the attention, as he had with 'London Calling', this time backed by stark, metallic, stomping percussion, rumbling bass and rockabilly guitar. It became a highlight of the later live set, introduced during September '81's Paris residency, having been written a few weeks before at Ear Studios. Our narrator takes us through our basic human rights – 'all three of them' – Strummer on a playful, sarcastic high as he points out that it's been 'suggested in certain quarters that these are not enough'.

The assertion that murder is a crime 'unless it is done by a policeman' seemed to refer to the deaths of Sunderland boxer Liddle Towers in Gateshead in 1976 and New Zealand schoolteacher Blair Peach in Southall, West London, three years later. Issued as a single on April 23, 1982, three weeks before *Combat Rock* saw the light of day, it was later covered by the likes of Primal Scream and Pearl Jam. The B-side, 'First Night Back in London', was another contender for the original *Rat Patrol from Fort Bragg* version of the album, with disco and reggae influences to the fore.

First recorded with 'This is Radio Clash' and 'Sean Flynn' at Marcus Music in April '81 and completed in New York that December, 'Car Jamming' references included Agent Orange and Lauren Bacall, the track also featuring Ellen Foley on backing vocals.

Written in Autumn '81, rehearsed at Ear Studios, and released as a single with 'Straight to Hell' on September 17, 1982, 'Should I Stay or Should I Go' was Mick Jones' highly successful 'attempt at writing a classic', as he put it. A 1991 advert for Levi's jeans saw it top the UK charts nine years after an initial top-20 placing. Inevitably, the lyrics suggest Jones was contemplating his future in the band, a theory he never fully discounted. 'Maybe it was pre-empting my leaving,' he told Stuart Bailey in 1991, but added that the song mostly concerned 'a personal situation', taken to refer to his relationship with Ellen Foley. Elsewhere, he added, 'It wasn't about anybody specific and wasn't pre-empting my leaving The Clash. It was just a good rockin' song, the kind of thing we used to like to play.'

Strummer reckons he decided on the spur of the moment to add backing vocals in Spanish, with tape operator Eddie Garcia calling his mother in Brooklyn Heights so he could read the lyrics over the phone for translation – hence the fact that the lines voiced by Strummer and Joe Ely are in Ecuadorian Spanish. Ely got involved after running into the band again in New York. Explaining Jones' cry of 'Split!' he recalled, 'Me and Strummer snuck up behind and jumped out at him in the middle of singing and scared the shit out of him. He looks over and gives us the dirtiest look. They kept that in the final version.'

The track was first aired live in Paris in September '81, remaining in the set until Jones left, then sung by Nick Sheppard. Don Letts' video featured an October '82 performance at Shea Stadium, NYC. In November 2004, the song was ranked No.228 in *Rolling Stone*'s 500 Greatest Songs of All Time, and in 2009 at No.42 on VH1's *100 Greatest Hard Rock Songs*.

BBC Radio London presenter Gary Crowley told *Uncut* in 2015, 'The fact that it was used on a jeans ad doesn't put me off at all. When I first heard it I thought, 'Jesus! What's that!' It's such a great riff, really dirty, almost like The Kinks. It's one that makes me want to jump straight on the dancefloor or get out the old air guitar.' And Buzzcocks guitarist Steve Diggle added, 'The Clash were incredibly prolific. They put out a lot of great albums and made a conscious decision to fuck with the formula, take themselves and their fan base on a journey. Not everything they did worked, but the fact they tried their hand at writing rock, punk, reggae and blues is amazing. People bang on about Radiohead and how eclectic they are, but they've never written a song as immediate and infectious as 'Should I Stay or Should I Go?' It's incredibly simple – just vocals, drums and guitars slowed down and speeded up – but it captures the whole essence of The Clash and what they were about in three minutes.'

Largely written by Topper Headon and recorded in 1981, 'Rock the Casbah' was based on a piano part the drummer was working on while waiting for his bandmates to show up, progressively taping drum, piano and bass parts, and recording the bulk of the song. On arrival, the others were impressed, feeling it essentially complete. However, Strummer had already come up with an idea and headed to the studio's toilets to write something matching the melody.

Released as a single on June 11 in the UK, with instrumental remix, 'Mustapha Dance', it reached No.30. It also became the band's biggest US hit, reaching No.8 in the Billboard Hot 100 and dance chart. Strummer told Richard Cromelin in 1988, 'The true genius of 'Rock the Casbah' is Topper. He banged down the drum track, then ran over to the piano and then the bass. This is, like, within 25 minutes.' The Baker added in 1991, 'Every time we would go into a studio and there was a piano, he would always play this riff. I told the engineer to put the tape on.' Headon, for *the Clash on Broadway* sleeve notes, said, 'I only played it twice around the houses. They said leave it. I said, 'We can't, there's only two verses and a middle bit. There should be four verses.' So they spliced the tape and doubled the length of the song.'

Jones added guitar, Strummer's lyrics following a remark by Bernie Rhodes, after hearing the longer, original version of 'Sean Flynn', generally bemoaning an increasing tendency to perform lengthy songs, asking, 'Does everything have to be a raga?' Strummer arrived back at the Iroquois Hotel and got to work, soon switching attention to a story he'd been told: 'That you got lashed for owning a disco album in Iran.' He was soon away on images of oil wells, sheikhs in Cadillacs, jet fighters dropping bombs between the minarets and Bedouin nomads defying the local Sharif. The result celebrated the power of music over religious fundamentalism, Keith Topping feeling, 'The song's greatness lies in its ability to comment on serious ethical issues with humour, but without racism.'

Strummer was dismayed to hear in 1991 that during Operation Desert Storm, the track was the first broadcast by Armed Forces Radio across the area. And in 2007's *Joe Strummer: The Future is Unwritten*, a friend of the singer revealed that he wept when he heard that 'Rock the Casbah' was written on a US bomb dropped on Iraq during the 1991 Gulf War. The track was also frequently requested on the British Forces Broadcasting Service during the Iraq War.

Don Letts' accompanying video – 'about breaking taboos' – was filmed in Austin, Texas, in June '82, Topping feeling that the band were 'almost outperformed by an armadillo'. He added, 'The irony is that it's Terry Chimes behind the drum kit and sitting beside the swimming pool on the video, the song's composer having been fired from the band a month earlier.'

Norman Cook told *Uncut* in 2015 that the song was, 'A personal favourite for the simple reason it made me realise a white rock band could make dance music. In those days dance music was black music, so the fact they attempted to make songs that fused rock with elements of dub and reggae was a real revelation. Getting Grandmaster Flash to support them on tour was another brave move that introduced the whole concept of hip-hop to thousands of teenagers, including myself.'

In the same feature, Clint Boon simply called

it 'the all-time definitive punk-pop record', while Andrew Weatherall said, 'Whenever I hear 'Rock The Casbah', it brings back really vivid memories of going to warehouse parties and nightclubs in the early '80s. It also reminds me that The Clash helped me get out of a few dilemmas. As a teenager, I couldn't decide whether to be a mod or a rocker and as a young man I couldn't decide whether to be a punk rocker or northern soul boy. Hearing The Clash weld brutal rock'n'roll with dub, reggae and ska made me realise I didn't have to make the choice – I could listen to everything and be everything.'

Inspired by the New Year's Day, 1982, murder of Frankie Melvin, a member of New York City subway vigilantes the Guardian Angels, by a policeman, 'Red Angel Dragnet' also quotes Martin Scorsese's 1976 movie *Taxi Driver*, Kosmo Vinyl having recorded dialogue from main character Travis Bickle – played by Clash fan Robert De Niro – who sports the mohawk hairstyle adopted by Strummer for the *Combat Rock* tour.

Written by Strummer, the song was sung by Simonon in what Jones later described as his 'Jamaican Marlene Dietrich style', referencing Jack the Ripper, Alcatraz and Roger Miller's *England Swings*. Keith Topping noted, 'On the surface a cynical, vicious diatribe about the sick, venal underbelly of America, it's actually more about Hollywood's vision of the same subject.'

When Strummer sings of a 'volatile Molotov' thrown at Puerto Rican immigrants in Alphabet City as an encouragement to leave, he is referring to arson that claimed buildings occupied by immigrant communities – notably Puerto Rican – before the area was subject to gentrification.

The song's distinctive drumbeat was described by Topper Headon as 'basically … a bossa nova'. Strummer said just before the take, Headon told him, ''I want you to play this,' and he handed me an R White's lemonade bottle in a towel. He said, 'I want you to beat the bass drum with it'.'

The *Combat Rock* version comes in at five and a half minutes, edited down from almost seven, the original featuring extra lyrics and more prominent violin. The full, unedited version can be found in the *Clash on Broadway* and *Sound System* box sets.

Moby and Heather Nova covered the song in 1999 for Clash tribute album *Burning London*, while in 2007 M.I.A. sampled the track for Paper Planes, which also tackled immigration. The song was also refashioned by Mick Jones with Lily Allen for the *War Child: Heroes* album in 2009, and Jakob Dylan and Elvis Costello covered it around the same time for the *Spectacle: Elvis Costello with D* show.

One of the recurring themes on *Combat Rock* is the impact and aftermath of the Vietnam War, and the subject matter of 'Straight to Hell' includes abandoned children fathered by GI's to Vietnamese mothers. But a song Pat Gilbert described as saturated by 'colonial melancholia and sadness' also highlights scenes of a broken, divided UK, drugs culture in America, and the plight of immigrants around the world.

Released with 'Should I Stay or Should I Go' as a double A0-side on September 17, 1982, Keith Topping saw it as a 'Desolation Row for the 1980s', which 'contains many of Joe Strummer's finest lyrical images with an austere clarity that haunts the listener', and says 'more about the reality of working-class Britain of the era than any number of *Play for Todays*'. By the time we reach the last verse, Strummer reminds us that it could be 'any frontier, any hemisphere', and, 'King Solomon, he never lived round here.'

The backing track was recorded at Electric Lady on December 30, '81, Jones' guitar-led

2

29 May 1982 US $1.95 (by air) 30p ISSN 0028 6362

NME
NEW MUSICAL EXPRESS

STRUMMER
WHY I RAN OUT ON THE CLASH

EXCLUSIVE INTERVIEW BY CHARLES SHAAR MURRAY

DEFUNKT
ANTI-NOWHERES
FUNKAPOLITAN
DEAD or ALIVE
FARREN on ROBOTS
ROXY·BLONDIE·BLUES

track taking many forms before Headon took it to another level. He said, 'You couldn't play rock'n'roll to it. I started messing around on the snare. Basically, it's a bossa nova.'

Strummer's lyrics followed on New Year's Eve – just before the band were set to fly home – and were quickly recorded. For 1991's *Clash on Broadway*, he wrote, 'I'd written the lyric staying up all night at the Iroquois Hotel. I went down to Electric Lady and just put the vocal down on tape. We finished about 20 to midnight. We took the E train from the Village up to Times Square. I'll never forget coming out of the subway exit, just before midnight, into a hundred billion people, and knew we had just done something really great.'

Later, Glyn Johns removed a verse about New York's Latino drug dealers, shaving off a minute, the song later adopted by Strummer for his stint in The Pogues then The Mescaleros. There was a commendable cover by Moby and Heather Nova in 1999 on the *Burning London* tribute album, the song also tackled by Mick Jones with Lily Allen for *War Child: Heroes*, and by Jakob Dylan and Elvis Costello around the same time for the latter's *Spectacle* TV show.

Mick Jones told *Uncut* in 2015, 'The lyrics are great. I think part of 'Straight to Hell' was what was going on in El Salvador at the time. It was gonna become like Vietnam. The US were sending advisors in and all that stuff so we were aware of everything. That Latin feel it's got is probably a subconscious thing cos of what was going on in Central America. Not even thinking of it but just being tuned in to things. We never had 'world music' in those days.' And Don Letts saw it as, 'A good example of how Strummer moved the lyrical goalposts of what rock music could deal with. Joe's lyrics, man – any two of his rhyming couplets had more content than most people's fucking albums. Seriously, what The Clash could do in three minutes was a fucking trip.'

Roddy Frame called it, 'A beautiful, beautiful record. They were always a bit ahead of the game; they were always pushing forward. For me it's a personal thing because I can just remember touring in 1982 with Aztec Camera and we listened to *Combat Rock* over and over on headphones and just hearing all these lovely things that were happening in the music. Lyrically, it's just great and very kind of personal – it just showed the whole punk thing could go somewhere else. In the wake of The Clash and the Sex Pistols, there were about a thousand daft punk bands but they were never going to go anywhere other than that three-chord trash. 'Straight to Hell' is just a beautiful piece of music – it transcends the whole punk thing.'

Music writer Adam Sweeting saw it as, 'An audio version of *Apocalypse Now*, as Strummer intoned his weird panoramic lyric about American expansionism, British post-imperial decline, rotting ghettoes, rampant drug cartels. Slightly mad, admittedly, but the clattering pseudo-Asian percussion and treated fiddle sounds conspired with Strummer's bleak vocal to create something authentically chilling.' And radio presenter Gideon Coe insisted, 'The edit on *Combat Rock* is mighty fine, but after you've listened to the full version on *The Clash On Broadway*, that's the one ... It may be the sound of a band falling apart, but it's a beautiful record.'

Strummer's gripe at the often-banal lyrics used in dance music, 'Overpowered by Funk' was recorded at Ear Studios in September '81. As Keith Topping put it, 'Funk becomes a fractured metaphor for the obese greed of capitalism feeding on itself.' Again, there are references to Vietnam and a critique of

America's re-emergent debate on capital punishment, plus namechecks for Edgar Rice Burroughs and Benny Goodman. Finished at Electric Lady in December 1981, it featured a rap by Futura 2000, and keyboards by Poly Mandell. And despite entering tricky dance territory, it's a brave attempt at crossing into yet another genre.

Never performed live, yet another great example of the band's call-and-response vocals, this time with a guitar-led, soulful chop-guitar strut, 'Atom Tan' was recorded at Electric Lady in November '81, its rather puzzling lyrics seemingly stream of consciousness but touching on suicide, sexual violence and the ever-expanding influence of TV on our lives ... possibly.

'Sean Flynn' was another song looking at the impact of the Vietnam War, this time centred on the photojournalist son of actor Errol Flynn, who disappeared in 1970 while covering the war with Dana Stone, the pair leaving Phnom Penh in Cambodia on rented motorbikes to find the frontline, only to be stopped and led away by the Viet Cong or Khmer Rouge. The CIA later indicated that they were executed by their captors. A decade later, Strummer was fascinated by that era's South East Asian conflicts and how key films exposed America's collective guilt complex over being there in the first place. The track was written at Vanilla Studios during rehearsals for the 1981 European tour and recorded at Marcus Music in April. Gary Barnacle said Headon was largely responsible for the Oriental feel, which he then improvised over with Strummer and Jones. Keith Topping called it one of the band's 'most spectacular sounding recordings', saying, 'You can almost feel the clammy heat of the Cambodian jungle in the LP's grooves.' Almost halved by Glyn Johns during the mixing, Topping saw the

released version as a 'fierce piece of musical experimentation, but it only tells half the story'.

Featuring legendary US beat poet Allen Ginsberg, who performed it on stage with the band during their Bond's residency, 'Ghetto Defendant' was written and rehearsed in September '81 at Ear Studios, at that stage a mid-paced reggae tune featuring Jones on harmonica. Its lyrics tackled New York's spiralling drug crisis. Kosmo Vinyl recalled that when Ginsberg came to the studio, 'He wanted The Clash to back him on a record but ended up on ours instead.' Strummer invited him to be the voice of God on the song, the poet writing his own words on the spot, including 'a litany of international areas of confrontation in 1981 – Guatemala, Honduras, Poland, El Salvador, Afghanistan', and a plug for his favourite existential-symbolist poet, Arthur Rimbaud.

Mick Jones attacked the notion of 'just following orders' on 'Inoculated City', Keith Topping feeling the template may have been XTC's 1980 UK hit, 'Generals and Majors'. The track slammed 'the futility of conflict and the crassness of politically motivated interference in such matters'. Rehearsed during the Ear Studio sessions, it showed Jones' growing interest in sampling, part of a TV toilet cleaner commercial included, later removed from some US imprints until a settlement was reached with the advertisers.

'It's about the way we all queue up at the cinema to see someone get killed,' Strummer told Roz Reines in 1982 on the subject of closing track, 'Death is a Star'. 'These days the public execution is the celluloid execution. I was examining why I want to go and see these movies.' Half spoken, mainly acoustic, with crickets chirping, Keith Topping called it a 'damn strange way to end *Combat Rock*'s tour of The Clash's vision

MOMENTS IN TIME PART 3: OCTOBER 1982

If ever a piece of film footage suggested The Clash had broken the North American market, it was Don Letts' promo video for 'Should I Stay or Should I Go', and additional footage of 'Career Opportunities' from the Shea Stadium in New York City in late '82. Okay, so the band were supporting The Who over those two nights, in on-off 45-minute hits sets. But it doesn't look like crowd indifference to me. To misquote one of Mick Jones' musical heroes, Ian Hunter: 'It's a mighty long way down the dusty trail from the Westway, W10, to the New York Shea.'
This was stadium rock at its grandest, and I'm not sure it quite suited an outfit 'all the way from Ladbroke Grove', as self-styled Clash consigliere Kosmo Vinyl put it in an excitable on-stage introduction. This was a band that truly came alive in more intimate venues. Paul Simonon, talking to Clash biographer Chris Salewicz, later recalled those US dates, saying: 'It felt a bit like miming, because there were so many people there. The audience weren't very close, so you didn't get the same reaction from them … in clubs, the group and audience would feed off each other.' Similarly, Joe Strummer mentioned feeling some unease: 'It's like playing, if you can imagine, to the grand concourse at Central Station. With 90,000 people in the house, at least an eighth of them are going to be going for burgers or a beer or to take a leak. That's 10,000 people constantly moving around.' Mind you, compared to The Beatles' appearance at the same venue in August 1965, you could at least hear the band play.

Three days before that two-night stint at the Shea, the band played 'Should I Stay or Should I Go' – recorded not so far away at Electric Lady Studio, NYC – and 'Straight to Hell' on high-profile NBC show *Saturday Night Live*. And as Letts shows on screen, they arrived at the stadium in Queens in a white '56 Cadillac. Yet while Strummer was decked out in Davy Crockett-style raccoon-skin cap and antique fur-coat, word was that they were half-frozen on arrival. It was a little late in the year for that – The Clash were clearly still capable of masterclasses in rock'n'roll posturing, for all the escalating tensions in the camp.

An even bigger show followed, the Us Festival in San Bernardino at the end of May '83, by which time it was even clearer that their days were numbered. Sure enough, the bombshell came

2

of the American Gothic experience, yet conceptually it's a cornerstone of the LP. All the recurring themes are present and correct: references to Americana, the movies, drug culture and war – particularly in the jungles of Vietnam.' Piano, Spanish guitar and snare brushes 'manage to carry the song through, despite the stop-start format, towards a vaguely structured conclusion', on a 'striking if rather solemn and downbeat end to the often-bombastic, radio-friendly world of *Combat Rock*'.

The End of the Story of The Clash Mk. 1

'We were just so tired. Tired of each other, tired of the road, tired of the studio. We were burned out. It had been a lingering death.'
Joe Strummer

With relationships in the band increasingly fragile, Headon was asked to leave the band just before the release of *Combat Rock*, his heroin addiction having taken its toll on his health and his playing. It was a huge loss, and with a popular band member gone, friction within the ranks was further exposed, Jones and Strummer continuing to feud on dates where they opened

three months after that incident-packed Californian date, with Jones fired in the first week of August. As it was, The Clash as a unit would hobble on for another two and a half years. One more studio album followed, but it was panned by fans and critics alike, hardly beginning to compare to that previous seven-year campaign after Strummer joined Jones and Simonon at the end of May '76.

But although Headon had been replaced by the returned Terry Chimes, they still had it in '82, and 'Career Opportunities' has the fire of earlier performances, with an added poignancy. As Strummer put it on *The Essential Clash* DVD: 'It was fun to play 'Career Opportunities' in a situation like that. Who'd have thought four years previously, when we'd written it in Camden Town, that we'd be playing it there? But these are the things that make the world so interesting ... and amusing.' Actually, it had been six years since its first airing at Barbarella's in Birmingham, the song written 'in half an hour at rehearsals', according to Jones, Strummer finishing the bulk of the lyrics while Jones and Simonon went to Kentucky Fried Chicken for potato croquettes. The track was first recorded – with stressed enunciation – as part of their Polydor demo sessions in mid-November '76, a certain Guy Stevens producing.

Strummer (wearing shades and sporting a Travis Bickle-style 'rockin' mohawk') barks out the lyrics at the Shea, including the topical reference 'I don't wanna die, fighting in the Falklands'. It's not obvious that Mick (in beret) and Paul (baseball cap) are barely on speaking terms as they pitch in on backing vocals and dart around the stage – the old electrical charge still in evidence.

For 'Should I Stay or Should I Go', Mick (red shirt, red trousers, almost like the old boilersuit) is out front, with Simonon and Strummer backing him and Chimes (sleeveless denim jacket) holding it all together, not far off passing on the baton to Pete Howard. Again, there's a poignancy as Jones tells us, 'This indecision's bugging me'. And you can't help but feel that cry of 'split!' part-way through had added meaning. The end was nigh. As it was, that song's biggest commercial moment was yet to come, its use in a Levi's commercial seeing it belatedly top the UK charts in 1991, becoming their sole No.1, albeit long after The Clash were gone. Oh, the irony.

for The Who on their final US tour, including that milestone show at New York's Shea Stadium.

Strummer was quoted as saying Headon's drumming skills were vital to the band, yet tensions with band members rose due to his addiction, and he was sacked on May 22, 1982, at the beginning of the *Combat Rock* tour. The band covered up the real reason, claiming it was due to exhaustion. In his interview for Don Letts' 2000 documentary *Westway to the World*, Headon reflected on and apologised for his addiction, speculating that had he not been asked to leave, the band might have lasted longer.

Asked by Scott Rowley in 1999 how it felt when Headon was ousted, Simonon recalled, 'A bit empty. I mean, we didn't realise you were supposed to go on holiday and have a break from each other. We just worked non-stop really, from day one onwards. Inevitably it's gonna catch up on you.'

With Headon gone, Terry Chimes returned for a run of North American dates, then a rescheduled series of UK gigs that summer, the success of 'Should I Stay or Should I Go' and 'Rock the Casbah' ironically leading to some of the band's biggest shows. But there was no mistaking that The Clash as a band were on something of a downward spiral.

Reflecting on his departure, Headon said, 'Joe did an interview in the States where he said, 'Well, we had to get rid of Topper, he was a heroin addict.' And my life just fell apart. The only reason I was keeping any semblance of order for myself together was The Clash. When they went, I just nose-dived. When the band sacked me, I promised I'd stop misbehaving and taking substances. If I'd have kept my act together, I could have seen the band still being together today. I'd like to apologise to them for letting the side down, for going off the rails. But I think if it happened again I'd probably do the same thing. I'm just that kind of person.' Headon, still battling his demons at the time, later reflected on that last line, telling *The Independent*'s Mark Lucas in a 2009 interview, 'I was trying to explain that when you're a heroin addict you don't choose to fuck your life up, it's inevitable.'

Trying to convince himself about that fateful decision, Strummer explained, 'You need to have everyone firing on all cylinders if you're going to take things to new levels or in new directions. You can't have any passengers on board. It slows the whole thing down. You slow it down, you lose spirit and you grind to a shuddering halt.' He added, 'Whatever the group is, it's the chemical mixture of these four people that makes a group work. You can take one away and replace them with whoever you like, or 10 men, and it's never going to work.' Headon later revealed, 'I met Joe a year after I'd been sacked and he was carrying my picture around in his wallet. He felt so guilty.'

The band made a final TV appearance on October 9, 1982, performing 'Straight to Hell' and 'Should I Stay or Should I Go' on *Saturday Night Live*, then three days later played the first of two consecutive appearances at New York City's Shea Stadium. Strummer later mused, 'It was fun to play 'Career Opportunities' in a situation like that. Whoever would have thought four years previously when we'd written it in Camden Town we'd be playing it at Shea Stadium? But these are the things that make the world so interesting.'

As it was, by early 1983 Chimes had once again quit. He was replaced by Pete Howard – previously with Bath-based Cold Fish – for the Us Festival in California, playing what would turn out to be Mick Jones' final gig with The Clash. The band were co-headlining a three-day event along with David Bowie and Van Halen. (A country bill followed the next weekend, headlined by Willie Nelson.) But it was an event rife with problems as far as the band were concerned, with arguments between Bernie Rhodes, The Clash and the promoters over inflated ticket prices leading to threats to pull out unless a large donation was made to a local charity.

The Clash topped a 'New Wave' bill on May 28, in front of an estimated 140,000 crowd in San Bernardino, at an event that was the second such festival of its kind (a reprise of a Labor Day weekend success the previous September, another with many big names involved). The Us Festival was the idea of Apple co-founder Steve Wozniak, who saw the '70s ethos as being about a 'me' generation, and aimed to instil a more community-oriented approach for the '80s, while combining new technology with rock music. The 'reprise' event was run by Colorado-based promoter Barry Fey, over Memorial Day weekend, with the opening night also involving fellow UK bands The Beat, A Flock of Seagulls and Stray Cats; Australian outfits Divinyls, INXS and Men at Work; and homegrown acts Oingo Boingo and Wall of Voodoo, at a new open-field venue with state-of-the-art temporary stage. Overall attendance was said to be 670,000, the festival losing $12m.

In a telling remark that seemed to pitch that moment against the band's past squabbles and illustrate the fact that – irrespective of the size of venue – the problems were in front of their faces, Simonon said on *Westway to the World*, 'Like we were on stage was like we were backstage – Mick was all the way over there, I was over here, and Joe was in the middle, and that's how it was. Me and Mick didn't talk.' Yet despite all that animosity, there was still kinship between this band of brothers. Jones was caught up in an altercation as they came off stage with the event's security, or as he put it, 'a bit of a scuffle at the end that was symbolic of the whole mayhem'. Simonon explained, 'I remember looking over, seeing some bouncer hitting Mick, so went over and started laying into this bloke's head, cos I just thought it was unfair. Mick's not muscles or whatever.'

Following a break, the band reconvened that June for rehearsals in London. About a week in, tensions that had been present within the group throughout the year re-emerged, reportedly due to a musical difference of opinion brought about by guitarist Jones' use of a synthesiser he'd recently acquired. Another point of contention was his frequent tardiness and absences. By that point, he and songwriting partner Joe Strummer had difficulty communicating with one another, new drummer Pete Howard saying, 'It got to the point where Joe was posting lyrics through Mick's door. He thought the music that Mick was putting to them was a pile of shit.' At the same time, Jones refused to sign a new contract presented by Rhodes without taking legal advice. One Clash associate commented that Rhodes was angered by that, and 'twisted Joe up about it', asking Strummer if he really wanted to be in the band with the guitarist. The rehearsals eventually ceased.

In August 1983, The Clash arranged to reconvene to discuss plans for their follow-up to *Combat Rock*. Speaking of the tension between Strummer and himself, Jones said, 'By then, our relationship was ... *bad*. We weren't really communicating. The group was dissipating.' Their relationship was already past a point of retrieval, Simonon adding, 'Me and Joe had been talking about it and got to the point where we said, 'We're grown men. I can't take any more of this.'' Jones concurred, saying, 'We lost communication with each other, even though we were in the same room. We were sort of looking at the floor.'

The bullet arrived within four months of the Us Festival, back at Rehearsal Rehearsals, of all places. And in a moment of bizarre timing, it just so happened that Topper Headon was visiting his old workplace that day, ending up on Pete Howard's kit, having a quick jam with Jones. He said, 'I was in Camden Town at the end of August '83 and thought, 'I'll go and see The Clash.' I went to Rehearsals and Mick was there, saying, 'I don't know where the others are. I'm normally last.''

Jones soon found out. Simonon recalled, 'Joe said, 'Mick, we want you to leave.' Mick said to me, 'What do you say?' I said, 'Well, yeah.'' Jones later told Chris Salewicz, 'I put my guitar in my case, picked it up, and walked out. Bernie ran after me, trying to give me a cheque – like giving you a gold watch when you retire. I was in shock, and furious.' Headon added, 'Like me, he had no idea he was going to be sacked.'

A week prior to the official statement of Jones' ejection, Strummer, Simonon and Rhodes met Howard in a pub, who reckoned Strummer aggressively told him, 'I've just fucking sacked Mick Jones. He's a fucking cunt. You have to make a decision: are you with us or him?' Howard elected to stay.

Explaining his decision, Strummer said, 'Mick was intolerable to work with by this time. No fun at all. He wouldn't show up, and when he did it was like Elizabeth Taylor in a filthy mood.' Jones didn't deny that, adding, 'I was just carried away really. I wish I'd had a little more control, and you wish you know what you know now.' Seeing it the same way, Strummer concluded, no doubt with a heart heavy with regret, 'It only happens like that in hindsight. It never happens like that when it's actually going on, cos things are moving so fast you don't have the time to stand back and have a view.'

Asked by Scott Rowley in 1999 about that move, Simonon said, 'Me and Joe were just pretty much sick of waiting for Mick to turn up and problems with his reliability and we just said, 'Well, sod it.' And that was it – we just asked him to leave. But it was interesting in a way, cos one time in rehearsal, Joe got a piece of chalk and drew a line on the floor and said, 'On this side there's the musicians, and on this side there's the entertainers.' And it was Topper and Mick on one side and me and Joe on the other. It was like: so there's a few wrong notes – who cares, really? We want to see some people jumping around, we wanna see some excitement, we wanna be entertained, not us all standing dead still getting it all right. You may as well listen to the record.'

Chris Salewicz called the band's decision 'unthinkable', reflecting in *Mojo* in 2006, 'A collective madness seemed to have overtaken the group, and many felt this was being driven by Bernard Rhodes.' And while Jones felt insulted by Rhodes following him out of the old BR depot that day with that cheque, he cashed it all the same, soon co-founding General Public along with members of The Beat, another band who split after that San Bernardino event.

There followed the band's infamous 'Clash Communique', announcing that their co-founding guitarist had followed drummer Topper Headon out of the door. The official statement, dated September 10, was brief and to the point, reading, 'Joe Strummer and Paul Simonon have decided that Mick Jones should leave. It is felt that Jones drifted away from the original idea of the group.'

Chris Knowles, in a 2005 feature for *Classic Rock*, believed, 'Jones had become obsessed with the New York hip-hop scene and was growing tired of his second-banana role in the band. On stage, Jones had reinvented himself as the Clash's co-lead singer. Off-stage, he spent his time messing around with beatboxes and synthesisers while his Les Paul collection gathered dust in the corner. On Jones' insistence, a brief holiday break in 1982 stretched into a nine-month indolence. Not only was nothing being worked on, but the boys were not on speaking terms. The Clash's only activity in 1983 was a mini-tour leading up to an appearance at the mammoth, three-day Us Festival in California.'

According to Knowles, most recent addition Pete Howard, then 23, was soon to discover his 'dream gig was more like a nightmare – The Clash's ongoing, behind-the-scenes dysfunction was not going to make his job an easy one.' Howard told Knowles, 'After the auditions, they basically just said, 'Go away and learn everything.' Not 'these songs' – everything. We had some rehearsals in Notting Hill, and basically Mick wouldn't turn up. If he turned up at all, he would turn up three hours after everyone else had. The tension between Mick and Joe was palpable.' What's more, after the Us Festival, the band did very little. Howard added, 'I didn't get a phone call for four months. Then all of a sudden, I got this incredibly fucking vitriolic phone call from Joe, saying 'I fuckin' sacked the stoned cunt! Whose side are you on, mine or his?' And I was like, 'Uh-uh-uh... yours, Joe, yours!''

Whatever the real chain of events, Strummer and Simonon soon recruited again, and that October the band began posting anonymous advertisements in *Melody Maker* seeking a 'young, hard guitarist (under-25, over 5ft 9)', with auditions – during which the identity of the band remained a secret – held at Camden's Electric Ballroom. One of the first to reply was Nick Sheppard, 24, previously with Bristol punk band The Cortinas, and he was the first taken on.

Marathon rehearsals were held and over a dozen new songs were worked on. Strummer told *Jamming*'s Ross Fortune in May 1984, 'I didn't want to record until we'd got the group into a unit.' The original intention had been that The Clash would record at Lucky Eight Studio, newly built on the site of their old Rehearsal Rehearsals base in Camden. Sheppard recalled, 'At one point I was given a tape of songs numbered one to five. They had no lyrics, just Joe playing mad riffs over a drum machine. They made no sense whatsoever.'

Sheppard told Chris Knowles, 'It was more a back-to-basics approach, after the excesses of Mick's last days.' He saw Strummer's new songs as 'far more of an eclectic bunch of tunes than we ended up with', incorporating, 'lots of world music influences – Latin, African grooves – that kind of thing'.

But that wasn't what Rhodes had in mind, and that 'back to basics' approach was soon upgraded to 'rebel rock', as Strummer saw it. After a couple of weeks of rehearsals, new guitarist, Greg 'Vince' White, a physics and astronomy student described by Chris Knowles as a 'middle-class boy from a wealthy family', joined, yet clearly had to win over his acquired bandmates. Apparently, the newest arrival took new first name 'Vince' because Simonon refused to play in a band with someone named 'Greg'. Nick Sheppard added, 'He was told he had to change it because it wasn't cool enough. Paul said, 'Name me one cool guy called Greg,' to which Vince instantly replied, 'Gregory Isaacs'. That shut everyone up!'

With Strummer set to play less, Sheppard took over rhythm guitar duties, the new band practising early and new three- and four-chord Clash songs. They then booked a brief tour of the US West Coast for January 1984, prompting Mick Jones to inform concert promoter Bill Graham he was planning to tour there with Topper Headon as 'The Real Clash'. Subsequent legal action soon had earnings from the Us Festival and *Combat Rock* frozen, leading to Strummer writing, 'We Are the Clash', one of the first tracks to be aired live, along with further new tracks, 'Three Card Trick', 'Sex Mad Roar' and 'This Is England'.

The Clash Mark II was up and running, Pete Howard continuing on drums on their self-financed Out of Control tour, with the band a three-guitar outfit for the first time since Keith Levene's departure in 1976. But as Chris Salewicz pointed out, by firing Mick Jones the band had removed the person who'd written virtually all the music before. As Clash associate Kosmo Vinyl later admitted to Chris Salewicz, 'We didn't think. 'Anyone can write a punk song!' That was our mistake.' As it was, unknown to the band at the time, Bernie Rhodes' solution was to take control of the music by writing it himself.

The Story of the Clash Mk. II

'Mick was pushed out by a power struggle. Bernie convinced me and Paul we should get rid of him. But even Mick will tell you he was being extremely uncooperative. So we thought we'd try and carry on without him, which obviously proved a mistake.'
Joe Strummer to Chris Salewicz, Redemption Song: The Definitive Biography of Joe Strummer, 2006

The story of the new band was retold by Chris Salewicz for *Mojo* in 2006, guitarist Nick Sheppard telling him, 'They got Vince (White), the second new guitarist, in so Joe wouldn't have to play guitar on stage. But Joe's a fantastic rhythm guitarist. He has such vigour, and a very clean sound.' White added, 'The early days were brilliant. We'd go out drinking. Joe was very warm. We got on really well. It was solid up to the point where we went to go to America in January 1984.' And Pete Howard recalled, 'Bernie sent us off on a three-and-a-half-month tour of the US in a real Greyhound bus, without a proper toilet. He thought it would bring something out of us middle-class boys.'

White told Salewicz, 'We had quite a few new numbers – 'Three-Card Trick', 'Dictator', 'We Are The Clash', 'Are You Ready for War?' – But we were pretty much told what to do, how to play. There was a lot of bullying going on. It's hard to deal with. Paul Simonon was amazing. Nothing touched him.' Howard chipped in, 'There would be band meetings. 'You're not happening,' was Bernie's favourite phrase. By the end of it, someone yet again has been reduced to near-tears.'

What Chris Knowles described as a 'rowdy new batch of face-punching rants' was eventually chosen to be played on tour. Also including 'Jericho', 'Are You Ready for War?', 'Sex Mad War', 'Glue Zombie' and 'This is England', it saw 'rockabilly, funk, reggae, surf

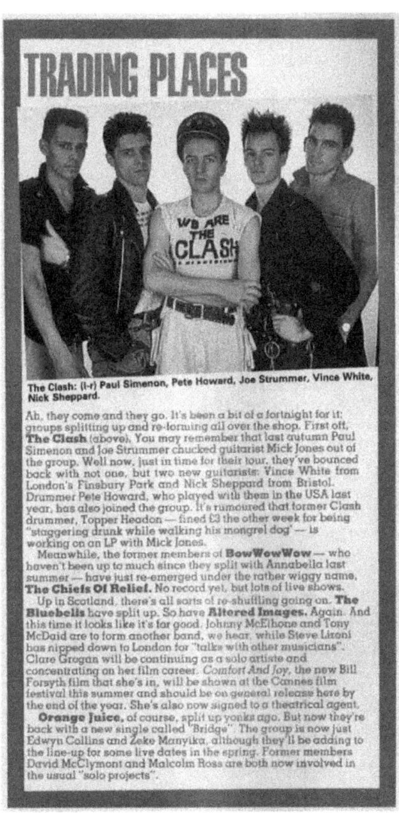

TRADING PLACES

The Clash: (l-r) Paul Simenon, Pete Howard, Joe Strummer, Vince White, Nick Sheppard.

Ah, they come and they go. It's been a bit of a fortnight for it: groups splitting up and re-forming all over the shop. First off, **The Clash** (above). You may remember that last autumn Paul Simenon and Joe Strummer chucked guitarist Mick Jones out of the group. Well now, just in time for their tour, they've bounced back with not one, but two new guitarists: Vince White from London's Finsbury Park and Nick Sheppard from Bristol. Drummer Pete Howard, who played with them in the USA last year, has also joined the group. It's rumoured that former Clash drummer, Topper Headon — fined £3 the other week for being "staggering drunk while walking his mongrel dog" — is working on an LP with Mick Jones.

Meanwhile, the former members of **BowWowWow** — who haven't been up to much since they split with Annabella last summer — have just re-emerged under the rather wiggy name, **The Chiefs Of Relief.** No record yet, but lots of live shows.

Up in Scotland, there's all sorts of re-shuffling going on. **The Bluebells** have split up. So have **Altered Images.** Again. And this time it looks like it's for good. Johnny McElhone and Tony McDaid are to form another band, we hear, while Steve Lironi has nipped down to London for "talks with other musicians". Clare Grogan will be continuing as a solo artiste and concentrating on her film career. *Comfort And Joy*, the new Bill Forsyth film that she's in, will be shown at the Cannes film festival this summer and should be on general release here by the end of the year. She's also now signed to a theatrical agent.

Orange Juice, of course, split up yonks ago. But now they're back with a new single called "Bridge". The group is now just Edwyn Collins and Zeke Manyika, although they'll be adding to the line-up for some live dates in the spring. Former members David McClymont and Malcolm Ross are both now involved in the usual "solo projects".

and Brazilian influences wrapped up in an iron-hard blanket of guitar aggro that strongly recalled second album *Give 'Em Enough Rope*.'

Sheppard told Knowles, 'I felt a similarity of intent between the new songs and that era, although it was never specifically mentioned. I think the twin-Les Paul sound lent itself very well to that style, and songs from that period translated very quickly to the new setup. Bernie was adamant we both play Les Pauls. He wanted the Pistols' guitar sound.' Knowles added, 'After rehearsals, Joe would subject his new band to marathon pub sermons. He was a man on a mission to save the world from Ronald Reagan and Duran Duran. *Combat Rock*'s success had done nothing but bolster Strummer's messianic complex. The mandate of the new Clash was nothing less than total revolution.'

A mini tour was booked in Southern California, a few weeks after the new line-up was confirmed. Despite touring without record company support, the dates received substantial press attention, adding to the pressure on Strummer to make it all work. Knowles added, 'The credit or blame for the new Clash would fall solely on his shoulders, and he was touring with a band unaccustomed to large venues. Of the new members, only Howard had played to more than 200 people. As if there wasn't enough pressure to begin with, Mick's zealous legal team harassed the new Clash at every turn, seemingly just out of spite.'

Howard said, 'The pressure on Joe was big. I mean, fucking hell, Bob Dylan came back to see him after we played. And Joe – he was crying. There was a lot to take on. In that respect, I can understand why he had to see himself as being in fighting form. He believed in Bernie as his trainer, very much like a boxer.' Sheppard added, 'I always thought we should have done some commando-style secret club gigs before we played any halls or arenas. If you've never played those big stages, there's a lot of adjusting to do.'

With no record to promote and no corporate advertising, most gigs were not on the scale of the 1982 US tour, except in San Francisco, where they played to a 10,000-plus capacity crowd of 'gone-apeshit fans', according to Chris Knowles. He added, 'San Francisco was chafing under Ronald Reagan's rule and the new Clash were treated as conquering heroes. It should come as no surprise that a Clash-influenced punk scene emerged not long after in the Bay area.'

After California, the band flew to Europe

and found they were front-page news in the music press there, headlining larger venues than they were used to. Then, in late February, while preparing to play the first of two nights at Milan's Palasport stadium, Strummer received news that his father had died. Howard recalled, 'When we were in Milan, Joe was fucking mental. He stayed up for about three days drinking bottle after bottle of brandy, berating everyone around him for their weaknesses, and just really fucking losing it. We had a couple of days off or something and didn't see him. And then he came back.

'We were all soundchecking and Vince was moaning, saying, 'I can't hear my fucking guitar in the monitor.' It led to an argument. Bernie was going, 'Look at you. You're so fucking pathetic. You're so middle-class, you're so fucking weak.' He said, 'Look, this guy here's just fucking buried his father, and you don't hear him talking about it, do you?' I remember that time very clearly as being among the worst.' Sheppard added, 'He didn't know us that well, so I guess he didn't feel comfortable sharing his hurt with us.' He did however recall, on March 2, Strummer flying from his father's funeral to a gig in Scotland. He told Chris Salewicz, 'No leniency was shown to him. It was ridiculous. The gig should have been cancelled.' It would be some time before Strummer publicly acknowledged that period, but he told Jon Savage in 1988, 'When The Clash were really happening, my father – for the first time in my life – was really proud of me. But you can't heal a lifetime's... just because your records are selling. I think not having had that final conversation with him...'

In the UK, pressure was even more intense, not least from the music press, the *NME*'s Gavin Martin dismissing one Brixton Academy date as 'the heaviest and most orthodox rock show I've ever seen The Clash play'. And it was at that show that Strummer took umbrage at being spat at from the audience, rounding on one such brainless culprit, and shouting, 'Listen! I'm prepared to murder someone tonight! I don't give two fucks! I want some fucking human respect – when I clear my throat, I do it on the floor! I'm serious! I'm prepared to kill someone! I don't give a fuck anymore! Blood – if you want it, let's have it! Let's get down to it! And fuck the lot of you!'

The band returned to the US for a relentless two-month jaunt, and as Pete Howard recalled, it wasn't a happy time for the most part. He told Chris Knowles about the 'no girlfriends on tour' rule, musing, 'I do understand where that comes from, because if you're going to look at yourself in the world arena, you have to be up for the competition.' But he found Rhodes' approach far harder to deal with, saying, 'He'd ask questions like 'What would you do with a million dollars?' to which every answer proved you were an idiot. I stared at his 'new' nose and said I'd have my ears pinned back. It was like being hauled into the headmaster's office and served as much purpose.' Howard backed him up, saying, 'It was constantly, every day, 'Right, tonight you're going to wear sunglasses.' Then after that show, it was like, 'You look like a wanker in sunglasses. Never wear them again.' I remember having an argument with Kosmo Vinyl once. I was saying, 'This is like being in the fucking Moonies. You've got this fucking dwarf Buddha standing up there handing out dictums, and you have to follow them. I don't think like that, I don't want to live that way.' And he just said, 'That is how it is. You take it with Bernie or you don't take it at all.' Then he went on to tell the story about Bernie turning Joe from a nothing to a something. And he said, 'If you don't believe that Joe is an iconic figure, then that's your issue. But most of the world who know of him do believe that, and Joe believes Bernie made him that."

As the tour progressed, Strummer introduced subtler tracks from *Sandinista!* and *Combat Rock* into the set, Knowles feeling a 'once-ragged band had matured into a raging, razor-sharp, rock'n'roll leviathan'. Sheppard added, 'We were definitely a heavier, more hard rock proposition than the previous incarnation. Our versions of 'Broadway', 'The Magnificent Seven' and 'Rock the Casbah' didn't mess about.'

Knowles added, 'The band's entrance into the mainstream had brought a younger audience whose approval was often displayed through acts of mayhem. Near-riots broke out at venues in Philadelphia, Chicago and Providence. But as the tour progressed, nerves began to fray. Like the original Clash, the new band soon discovered Rhodes' Spartan ideals didn't apply to himself: he flew between gigs, while the band spent 'three months in a fucking Greyhound bus because we were so fucking middle class we were used to luxury'.

Howard concluded, 'That doesn't make you into an elite, mean killing machine. It just makes you angry. We were at a soundcheck at a gig and Bernie said something that was just one thing too fucking far, and I just left and packed my bag. One of my biggest regrets is I didn't leave at that point. I would have liked to have fucked Bernie over, for him to have to cancel gigs. But he actually curled around my legs like a fucking cat: 'You know, you've got to understand the pressures, we really value you being in it, blah blah blah.' Two days later, he was being exactly the same all over again.'

But Sheppard stressed that there were good days too, not least a night off, seeing Black Flag in Atlanta, and days off in Chicago, Kansas City and Detroit. He added, 'Shopping, eating soul food, watching protest marches, being taken out by great-looking girls – I've had worse jobs, believe me.'

And despite Paul Simonon's loyalty to Bernie Rhodes, Howard reckoned he 'enjoyed his time with the new Clash and acted as a mentor' to the new members. He added, 'Everybody was sort of muttering, 'If Joe could get away from Bernie, this thing could be really good.' And Paul was very much of that party. He'd never really stick his neck out about it but was one of us mutterers who were going on about Bernie the whole time.'

The band returned from America ready to go into the studio. But then came news that Joe Strummer's mother was diagnosed with terminal cancer, so soon after his father's death. Chris Knowles suggested, 'The news sent Joe into an emotional tailspin and The Clash's back was broken for good. Joe left the band to fend for themselves. A mini tour of Italy in September was undertaken without Joe rehearsing with the band,' with 'Joe's sole preoccupation in the second half of 1984 ... tending to his dying mother. The Clash withered without his involvement.' Knowles believed that while Strummer was otherwise preoccupied, Rhodes seized 'complete control', booking a studio in southern Germany to record the new album. And at one of the band's two striking miners' benefit shows, Scargill's Christmas Party, in December 1984, it was announced that an album would be released within a month.

Former Clash road manager Johnny Green gave his verdict on The Clash Mk. II in 2005's *Viva Joe Strummer: The Clash and Beyond* documentary, saying, 'I drove up from Kent, watched a show and thought it was awful. Terrible. I went backstage after, but Bernie was back there, manager again. He shouted, 'Who let him in?' So, I felt really welcome. Joe came out of the dressing room. We stood in a draughty corridor by the back door. He looked at me. I had an awful suit on. I bought it the week before for a cousin's wedding. He said, 'That's a terrible suit, Johnny!' And I said, 'Yeah, it is pretty awful, innit, but it's not as bad as your band, is it?' And he cried. I felt, I wish I hadn't said that, but it was the truth, and Joe would never ask anything other than ... one of his great phrases was, 'You would tell me, wouldn't you?' He never said what that meant, but to me that meant if it was crap, you'd tell him. You'd level with him.'

The subsequent recording sessions were chaotic, with Rhodes and Strummer working in Munich and most of the music played by anonymous studio musicians, Nick Sheppard and later Vince White flying in to provide guitar parts. Chris Knowles noted that they were 'using the very synthesisers and drum machines that led to Mick Jones' dismissal', with Pete Howard replaced by a drum machine, and Sheppard and White 'stunned to discover the album was nearly complete'.

Inevitably, Strummer and Rhodes soon fell out, the latter taking the master tapes from the Munich sessions and disappearing, and Strummer, 'boxed in by his new contract', powerless to stop him. At that point, he tracked down Mick Jones in the Bahamas, begging him to rejoin, only to be rebuffed. Knowles added, 'The album was one of the most disastrous ever released by a major artist and a complete failure artistically and commercially.'

Vince White told Chris Salewicz, 'The biggest mistake was to let Bernie in the studio and let him think he could produce a record. A drum machine was used all the way through. Nick had gone out and laid out most of the rhythm guitar. Norman Watt-Roy did the bass.' Sheppard added, 'I met Joe in a coffee shop across the road from the Munich studio. He didn't want to hear what I felt about the sessions. He had to keep believing.'

Soon, the band reassembled, going on a UK city 'Busking Tour' that May, playing acoustic versions of their hits and popular covers, Strummer as good as back to his musical roots. Recalling that tour, Strummer said, 'All the group agreed to meet at midnight in Nottingham station one day in May and we just busked it from there. That was it. No expectations, just three acoustic guitars, me singing and Pete drumming on chairs with his drumsticks. We had the time of our lives. I never felt so close to the audience.' Simonon added, 'The most exciting time was when we arrived in York (May 9). We marched through the town with our guitars, singing with this crowd of 200 people. Because the audience knew all the words, it became one big sing-song.'

The band hitchhiked and busked around the North of England, at one point following The Alarm from gig to gig. Asked by Scott Rowley why them, Simonon replied, 'Why not? Just to wind them up, really. It was just being playful. We didn't ever speak to them – they were probably very pissed off. Their bouncers were trying to get rid of us, red paint was chucked at us – it just made it more exciting. It was the last thing we should have done, really, but we had a lot of fun – it was as exciting as the Anarchy tour. You didn't know where you were going to go next or what was gonna happen. I really enjoyed that.

'I think the last show we played was in Greece at some festival. That was really great. We had three guitars by that point, so it gave me a bit more space in some ways. I'd been practising breakdancing for some reason and in the middle of 'The Magnificent Seven', I took the bass off and started spinning around. We were just so comfortable on stage by that point, it didn't matter – it just mattered that people got a good show.'

White recalled, 'After Munich Studios in

April, we did some work on the album at Eel Pie Island and Southern Studios in Wood Green.' Sheppard added, 'Joe walked out at Wood Green, then disappeared.' The game was nearly up, Sheppard telling Chris Salewicz, 'We played Roskilde Festival in Denmark that summer (June 29). On the bus to the site I saw Joe looking at Bernie with such hate. I thought, 'This is over.'' Strummer later reflected, 'I hadn't understood what the game was. Bernie had decided to become an artist. Malcolm McLaren had begun releasing albums and Bernie wanted some of that. He stepped in once Mick was no longer there and stupidly allowed that to happen. That's what destroyed the group.'

Strummer was soon laying low in Spain and was there when the first single from the album, 'This is England', was released, to mostly negative reviews. As he later put it, 'CBS had paid an advance for it, so they had to put it out. I just went, 'Well, fuck this,' fucked off to the mountains of Spain to sit sobbing under a palm tree, while Bernie had to deliver a record.' The single was championed to a degree in later years, as opposed to the rest of the album, which had been drastically re-engineered by Rhodes, with synths and football-style chants added to Strummer's incomplete recordings, and drum machines used for most of the percussion tracks. It was all a bit of a mess.

Sheppard mused, 'My experience of being in The Clash was tarnished by the record. It's unforgiveable. The awful thing for me, Vince and Pete was that we got the lion's share of the blame and had nothing to do with it.' Meanwhile, Vince White was more succinct, telling Salewicz, '*Cut the Crap* was fucking dreadful. I was horrified.'

Strummer called a band meeting in October, and Pete Howard remembered, 'We sat down, and Joe said, 'It's over.' He gave us a thousand pounds each. I said, 'You followed Bernie's advice, and this is where it got you.' He said, 'Yeah, I know.'' Vince White and Nick Sheppard gave a different date and circumstances, White suggesting, 'We met at Paul's place, late in November, after the album had come out. Nobody really said anything. Nobody really tried to persuade Joe not to break up the group,' while Sheppard added, 'The next day in a drinking club in Soho, we were each given a grand.'

However, word has it that Bernie Rhodes was still keen to get a new line-up together, White telling Chris Salewicz, 'After Joe left, Bernie was going to make Paul the frontman. One of us was going to play the bass. But Paul wouldn't go for it. So, we got Nick to audition new singers. It was going to be a Clash without any of the original members. Bernie was blaming Pete Howard for the break-up. I thought, 'If I'm going to regain my life and my sanity, it's better to let go of it all, get a job.'

Asked about The Clash Mk. II by Sean O'Hagan in 1997, Strummer said, 'The best time we had was when we left Bernie and Kosmo and did that busking tour. After Greece, I'd had enough. See, Bernie's idea was to see if the original ideal of The Clash would still stand up in the '80s. I thought the ideal was still impressive, but it didn't work out in practice.

'Man, I felt burned out, real burned out. I had a terrible time with Bernie in the end. In a nutshell, in order to control me he destroyed my self-confidence. I shouldn't have let it happen, but I did ... I dunno why. I didn't realise his full motives until it was too late and the whole thing had gone too far. It was too late to stop. The Clash Mk. II was a big fuck-up. It was a very heavy scene in my mind. It took a long time – the last few years – to get over.'

Simonon gave his thoughts on that lacklustre finish when he spoke to Scott Rowley in 1999, saying, 'I suppose the end really came when

Mick was out of the group. Cos with drummers we always had this sort of: they were there, and then they weren't. But when Mick was out that was a big change because the musician of the group had left. Then again, after Mick left, we had a pretty good time. We did loads of shows around America with these new guys, and we did the busking tour, which was really exciting.'

As it was, after a Mescaleros appearance in Australia in 2001, Joe Strummer hooked up with Nick Sheppard and healed old wounds. Sheppard told Chris Knowles, 'Joe apologised for what happened. I told him I didn't regret a moment. I know we were never the 'classic' Clash, but I've moved on, made some great music, and have a great life.'

Pete Howard didn't get that chance but talking to Chris Knowles for that 2006 *Classic Rock* interview, at which point he was with indie outfit Queen Adreena, he said, 'Before he died, Joe said something in an interview. He said, 'I felt really sorry for Pete, Vince and Nick, because you had a chemistry between four people that worked really well, and there was no way anyone could have replaced that.' And I felt somewhat exonerated by that. Because I was limping, mentally, for a while.'

Cut the Crap – an attempted appreciation

This has the potential of being the shortest piece in the book, but rather than concentrate on the mess that was *Cut the Crap*, I'll start by examining what might have been, using as my basis the ragged but rather promising 14-track 'Out of Control' tapes from Camden Town's Lucky 8 Studios, a 47-minute demo from two years earlier, recorded in November 1983, featuring Joe Strummer, Paul Simonon, Nick Sheppard and Pete Howard.

Forget the internal politics for a moment and see those tapes as evidence that, at least at face value, this was a band that still had something to offer. It was never likely to be one of their finest LPs – it needed Mick Jones for that – but should never have been as bad a mess as it turned out. As demos go, there's something there to work with. Here, it seemed, was a back-to-basics approach. Whatever you made of *Combat Rock*, it's fair to say Strummer was looking to start again and strip the band down to its roots again. There's certainly a rock'n'roll feel, one a number of producers and engineers could have worked with, maybe using a template of Gene Vincent, Eddie Cochran or Sun-era Elvis Presley. That '50s vibe suggests a whiff of the spirit of *London Calling*'s 'Brand New Cadillac', and there are some neat lead and rhythm guitar touches. What's more, as per every Clash demo, it's fair to surmise Joe would have honed his vocals and lyrics along the way.

So what's missing? Well, I touched on the absence of Jones, but maybe it's just a sprinkle of magic, something the production team might have remedied. It could have been fairly promising, and maybe the next LP by The Clash Mk. II might have been better still. Instead, we got murder by synthesiser, the spirit of the live shows and busking sessions that helped galvanise this new unit and those earlier raw demos lost to the world accordingly. What a shame, not least for

Howard, Sheppard and Vince White – the latter only getting to add guitar on the CD bonus track – all missing out on a chance to be proud of brief stints in The Clash.

Listening back nearly three and a half decades on, I surmise that if I'd seen this band – let's just call them Strummer and Simonon's side project, because they aren't The Clash – play in a sweaty club somewhere, I'd have spotted their potential and waited to see what else they had to offer. But it wasn't to be. Can the finger of blame be pointed solely at Bernie Rhodes? It's possible, not least as Strummer was in a bad place at the time, and really needed a powerful presence on his side, someone who could be trusted to take creative control rather than complete control. Simonon was also seemingly out of the loop in those later stages, and the new members hadn't been around long enough to have any real influence. As a result, The Clash were hurtling *Out of Control*, the spectacular car crash that followed somewhat inevitable.

When it came to the finished product, opening track 'Dictator' set the tone, experiments with new synths and samples – with added waves of pseudo jazzy brass – instantly dating the product in what soon becomes a sonic mess, killing off any imagery Strummer's trying to get across, while next cut 'Dirty Punk' sounds like a cry for help from our Joe, full of leaden, tired, American imagery, the underlying guitar riff falling on the wrong side of hairy-arsed rock.

After the promise of 'We Are The Clash' on the demo, I feel robbed by the end product, which evokes the spirit of a pastiche of the Sham Pistols (or maybe even the Sham Rejects or Cockney 69) rather than the Sound of the Westway, high on football terrace chanting, low on real substance. What all those punk rockers, hip-hoppers, Britpoppers, showstoppers, beboppers and hair-droppers would learn from seeing this bastardised version of the band, I can't say. To quote Paul Cook and Steve Jones, 'Oh, you Silly Thing, you've really gone and done it now.'

With 'Are You Red.. Y?' it's difficult to even understand the question, and I can't imagine how anyone felt this clichéd take on world conflict might shift units as a single. Thankfully, it was only released in Australia, ending up buried Down Under. Think of the band attempting 'Overpowered by Funk' without Topper Headon and Mick Jones' musical nous.

On 'Cool Under Heat' the Sham Rejects are back again on another half-arsed tale of a rebel rocker. Didn't they get the message to not bother dropping in for this Clash tribute night? Again, there's electronic effect overload. Then – just when you thought it impossible – side one reaches an even lower ebb with 'Movers and Shakers'. The chorus is just horrible, and I wonder at what point those in the control room thought this lacklustre tale of getting by through taking on any job going (the antithesis of 'Career Opportunities', surely) was worth keeping.

Side two opener 'This is England', the LP's lead single, was at least innovative and somewhat inventive, conveying the spirit of the time. It's Thatcher's Britain nailed in four minutes, worthy of accompanying the end credits of a film reflecting such desperate times. The guitars are raw enough in the mix to rise above the drum machines. Even the terrace chanting works, to a point. But one good song does not an album make.

It was traditional to include a reggae track, and from 'Police & Thieves' onwards it served The Clash well. Not here though, 'Three Card Trick' leaving us with nothing more than ska tissue from self-inflicted wounds. But it at least sounds like it has something to say. However,

2

The Clash terrace choir are back again on 'Play to Win', and I can only guess that their woeful season has continued with a further 7-0 thumping. Strummer and Simonon – up front together – seem oblivious, mind, perhaps still sloshed from their pre-match lager intake.

Is it possible that we reach a further nadir with 'Fingerpoppin'? Slap bass, faux brass, repetitive strain injuries from Rhodes' drum machine programming, Strummer's lacking vocal... What's not to like? Erm, everything. From tales of Jimmy Dread to just plain dreadful in three albums. How the mighty had fallen. Three minutes 25 seconds rarely seemed so long.

Sheppard and Strummer shared vocals on 'North and South', but neither could deflect blame. Imagine a half-cocked karaoke version of Tiffany's take on 'I Think We're Alone Now'. Tame is the kindest word I can use for this diatribe about youths grasping power amid the UK's regional divide. And then the finale, where 'Life is Wild', apparently. Yep, the terrace mob's back, and now and again you hear more slap bass and wonder if the band's resident Blockhead sessioneer was trying to escape from the building and recover his pride. A more positive line? Its message is fairly upbeat and it's the only track under three minutes. But those who bought the CD got one more, 'Do It Now', a closing-time mess, best forgotten, like this entire album. Do It now? Do what now? I'd suggest switching off and calling it a day.

Beyond The Clash

'There was talk about The Clash reforming before he died. But there had been talk for years and years about them reforming. They'd been offered stupid amounts of money but were very good at keeping the moral high ground, saying no. But I think it would have happened. It felt like it was in the air.'
Jazz Mellor, discussing in 2013 how her late father, Joe Strummer, had contemplated a Clash reunion

When Joe Strummer contacted Mick Jones in an effort to reform the Clash, he found he was already ensconced on new project Big Audio Dynamite (BAD), with their debut album released in 1985. The pair did work together again the following year though, Jones helping with two songs Strummer wrote and performed for the Sid and Nancy soundtrack, while Strummer co-wrote a number of tracks on BAD's second album, No.10, Upping St., which he also co-produced.

Soon, Strummer moved on to various solo projects and screen acting, while Paul Simonon formed Havana 3am, and Topper Headon recorded a solo album before a further gruelling round in his battle against drug abuse. Meanwhile, Terry Chimes drummed with a succession of acts. Then, in March 1991, a reissue of 'Should I Stay or Should I Go' gave The Clash their first UK No.1 hit, in the year Strummer reportedly cried on hearing that 'Rock the Casbah' had been adopted by US bomber pilots in the Gulf War.

By 1999, Strummer, Jones and Simonon

were back in tow, helping compile live LP, *From Here to Eternity*, Don Letts' video documentary *Westway to the World* following year later. Then, in November 2002, news broke that The Clash were to be inducted into the Rock and Roll Hall of Fame the following March, that announcement followed by Strummer and Jones sharing a stage on November 15, performing three Clash songs during a London firefighters' benefit show by Joe's band, the Mescaleros.

Word had it that Jones and Headon were up for a reunion show to coincide with the induction, but Simonon felt that playing at such a high-priced event wouldn't have been in the spirit of The Clash. As it turned out, it wasn't an issue, as Strummer died from a congenital heart defect on December 22, 2002.

In March 2003, the Rock and Roll Hall of Fame event took place, with Terry Chimes inducted alongside the classic line-up of Joe Strummer, Mick Jones, Paul Simonon and Topper Headon at the Waldorf Astoria, New York City. U2 guitarist The Edge introduced the award, speaking in awed tones about the recipients, telling the assembled, 'I love this band and to me without doubt they are, next to the Stones, the greatest rock'n'roll band of all time,' going on to recall that first night he and his bandmates saw The Clash in 1977 'in a small hall in Trinity College, Dublin, and it actually changed my life', as part of his own tribute.

Then, with Terry Chimes, Paul Simonon and Lucinda Mellor at his side, Mick Jones briefly talked about Joe Strummer, telling the audience, 'He had so much integrity and inspired us all, and was the real thing.' He also namechecked Kosmo Vinyl, Johnny Green, Baker Glare and Robin Banks, adding, 'I'd like to accept this honour on behalf of all the garage bands that never may have dreamed of this type of moment.'

Chimes, next to speak, said, 'I loved those early songs on the first album. I love them still, but I had no idea back then the extent to which the band would develop and diversify. In fact, when I re-joined five years later it was a bit of a shock to have to play all those different styles. Much of the credit for that goes to Topper, I think, not just because of his unbelievable skill as a drummer but also because of his contribution on the creative side, helping with some of the songwriting, for example on 'Rock the Casbah'.'

Paul Simonon added, 'I was 18 years old and studying at the Byam Shaw School of Art. A year later, by a chance meeting with Mick Jones and Bernie Rhodes, I was suddenly in the group that became The Clash. From 1976, the next eight years were exciting and explosive, both on and off stage. Mick, Joe and me were like the Three Musketeers, brothers-in-arms fighting to get our message across. On achieving international recognition, we disbanded and went our separate ways. I'd like to acknowledge the important contribution that Bernard Rhodes played in the make-up of the Clash. Some would say, 'No Bernie, no Clash.' I sadly miss my older brother, my big brother Joe, who I shared my most life-changing experiences as well as his dole cheque.'

Simonon also namechecked, 'Topper, Terry Chimes, Kosmo, Johnny Green, The Baker and Guy Stevens ..., and Tricia Ronane for keeping it together after The Clash had split up', before Lucinda's short but emotional address, saying, 'Joe was very proud and honoured to be inducted, and on his behalf I accept his award.' Just before they left the stage, Jones added, 'I just want to say a big

2

shout to the Sex Pistols as well.'

Five years later, Headon performed on stage with Jones for the first time in more than a quarter of a century, joining the latter and his former London SS bandmate Tony James at London's Inn on the Green with their band Carbon/Silicon, the start of a six-week residency, Topper performing on 'Train in Vain' and encore, 'Should I Stay or Should I Go'.

A year later they were back together again, recording 'Jail Guitar Doors' with Billy Bragg to honour a Bragg-founded charity named after the song, giving musical instruments and lessons to prison inmates. Jones, Headon and Bragg were backed by former inmates during the session, filmed for tie-in documentary Breaking Rocks. Meanwhile, Simonon and Jones featured on the title track of 2010 Gorillaz album Plastic Beach, the first time they'd worked together in more than 20 years, the pair later joining Gorillaz on their world tour.

In September 2013, a 12-disc box set celebrating the band, Sound System, was released, featuring remastered studio albums and various demos, non-album singles, rarities and B-sides, along with a DVD with previously unseen footage by both Don Letts and Julien Temple, original promo videos and live footage, an owner's manual booklet, reprints of the original Armagideon Times fanzine and a new edition curated and designed by Simonon, plus merchandise, including dog tags, badges, stickers and a new poster. Both Jones and Simonon oversaw the project, including the remasters, the box set coming in a package shaped as a 1980s ghetto-blaster. It also included a five-album studio set containing all the LPs bar Cut the Crap, and a 33-track, double-CD best of, The Clash Hits Back, sequenced to copy the set played by the band at the Brixton Fair Deal – later renamed the Academy – on July 19, 1982.

To tie in with that, Jones spoke to *Rolling Stone* magazine and discussed the reunion, suggesting it wouldn't have happened, adding, 'There were a few moments I was up for it, Joe was up for it. Paul wasn't. And neither, probably, was Topper, who didn't wind up even coming in the end. It didn't look like a performance was going to happen anyway. I mean, you usually play at that ceremony when you get in. Joe had passed on by that point, so we didn't. We were never in agreement. It was never at a point where all of us wanted to do it at the same time. Most importantly for us, we became friends again after the group broke up, and continued that way. That was more important to us than the band.'

Jones added that the *Sound System* box set was the last he would be involved with, saying, 'I'm not even thinking about any more Clash releases. This is it for me, and I say that with an exclamation mark!' That month, Jones, Simonon and Headon reunited for a BBC Radio 6 Music show to promote their legacy and the release, while in an October 2013 interview with the radio station Jones confirmed that Strummer had intentions of a reunion, with new music being written for a possible album. In the months prior to Strummer's death, Jones and Strummer had worked on new material for what he thought would be the next Mescaleros album. Jones added, 'We wrote a batch. The idea was that he was going to go into the studio with the Mescaleros during the day, then send them all home, I'd

POST-CLASH

B.A.D., Mescaleros and more

"We started as punk, but we developed into all sorts of things. We didn't have a barrier, like, 'you can't do this!' We wanted to do a different album every time, not the same one over and over."

MICK JONES, 2013

POST-CLASH

3

B.A.D., Mescaleros and more...

Joe Strummer

'He was trawling the bars of Notting Hill, wandering about the pubs. I'd see him bemoaning the fact that he'd let the greatest band in the world slip through his fingers. Mentally and emotionally it took him 10 years of doing films and having a stab at a solo career, while watching Mick go on to achieve with Big Audio Dynamite. Joe would never have come back with The Mescaleros if it hadn't been for Richard Norris and Roger (Goodman). He never would have made a return or left that final statement.'

Kris Needs, Viva Joe Strummer: The Clash and Beyond, 2005

As Pat Gilbert put it in *Mojo* in 2006, 'Without Bernie Rhodes to cajole him and Paul Simonon to stand firm behind him, Joe struggled to find a meaningful immediate post-Clash role.' But that's not to say he was ever idle. Far from it. And within a year of The Clash breaking up, Joe Strummer was coaxed back into writing songs by English film director Alex Cox for 1986 biopic *Sid and Nancy*, then reunited with Mick Jones to feature with Big Audio Dynamite's second album, co-writing most of the songs as well as producing the album with Jones.

The following year, he starred in another Cox film, a spaghetti Western of sorts with a Clash title, *Straight to Hell*, also featuring London-Irish folk/punk band The Pogues as actors and soundtrack contributors, as well as Elvis Costello and young unknown Courtney Love. Pat Gilbert wrote, 'His character, Simms, inspired a new Joe identity that would carry him through the late '80s – a sort of scuffed-up mariachi figure dressed in crisp black and white and propping up a Spanish bar somewhere, entertaining folk with tales of the old days.' 'He was a method actor,' Cox told Gilbert. 'And kept his cards close to his chest. He always wore his black suit and shoulder-holster. The prop man made him give his gun back at the end of the day. He slept in the desert for the first week. Then, having become romantically involved, returned to the hotel, where he could shower. Joe took acting seriously but was having a bit of a laugh as well.'

Strummer also played a small part in a 1987 Cox film, *Walker*, an anti-imperialist allegorical tale of American adventurer William Walker's invasion of Nicaragua in the 1850s, also writing and performing on the film's soundtrack. His part was extensively cut, but his soundtrack is widely regarded as one of his post-Clash musical high points, cited by Cox as, 'The point Joe realised where his real talent lay – in creating great music'. As Stephen Dalton put it in *Classic Rock* in 2017, 'It was with the soundtrack that he struck gold: the lush score for *Walker* remains the finest of his career.' Cox agreed, saying his scores eclipsed anything he did on screen, adding, 'His impact was as a composer. *Walker* has the best soundtrack of any film I've done.'

Strummer joined The Pogues for a 1987/88 tour, with Philip Chevron unwell, the guitarist revealing that he 'taught him all the guitar parts in an afternoon and was on tour in the USA as deputy guitarist the next day'. He added, 'Joe wrote all the tabs in his meticulously neat hand on a long piece of paper, which he taped to the top of the guitar, so he could glance down occasionally on stage.' It would be the first of several collaborations with the band.

His next film score was for Marisa Silver's low-key 1988 suicide drama, *Permanent Record*, to which he contributed five songs. Strummer used the core of the group that played on *Walker*, his new combo named The Latino Rockabilly War Band, also performing with them on a Rock Against the Rich tour, benefitting radical organisation Class War. The standout cut was 'Trash City', which Stephen Dalton called, 'A terrific clatter of Springsteen-esque power folk'. And while neither film nor album made much commercial impact, he kept the band together, studio album, *Earthquake Weather* following in 1989. Though its commercial failure resulted in the loss of Strummer's Sony contract, Dalton suggested that was because he was, 'still a little lost without Mick Jones, with his flair for sharp arrangements and melodic hooks'. He added, 'Or maybe the singer's poetic blend of beatnik poetry and jukebox Americana simply sounded outmoded in a rock era that was dominated by dance music, thrash metal and grunge.'

He kept busy with film appearances, and in 1989 appeared in Jim Jarmusch's *Mystery Train* as a short-tempered, drunken drifter named Johnny. While Stephen Dalton felt, 'Increasingly, the films were low-budget cult affairs, often going straight to video or simply disappearing altogether,' Jarmusch told him, 'Joe was a really fine actor. Musicians are performers, but that doesn't mean all of them translate into good actors. He was so observant of details and human nature, and he was also empathetic to other people, which you certainly know from his music.'

Following roles included a cameo in Aki Kaurismäki's 1990 film *I Hired a Contract Killer*, as a guitarist in a pub, performing 'Burning Lights' and 'Afro-Cuban Bebop', released as a limited 7-inch single credited to Joe Strummer and the Astro Physicians, who were in fact The Pogues. That year, Strummer also produced the fifth Pogues album, *Hell's Ditch*, the last to feature Shane MacGowan, later stepping in as his replacement after the band were forced to tour the LP without him. But, Dalton suggested, 'The tour became a kind of career finale for Strummer. Locked in a legal dispute with Sony, his public profile fading, he drifted away from music to focus on his young children and turbulent private life.'

It was a rough time, Strummer soon splitting from long-term partner Gaby Salter and leaving London, moving to a rented cottage in rural Hampshire, beginning a new romance with Lucinda Tait, who in time became Lucinda Mellor. Strummer first married South African citizen Pamela Moolman in 1975, so she could obtain British citizenship, and had been with Gaby for 14 years, since shortly after her 17th birthday, the couple having two daughters, Jazz and Lola. They never married, as Joe was unable to locate and divorce his first wife.

Alex Cox told Stephen Dalton, 'The weird thing about Joe was for the longest time he didn't do anything. He did have crises of confidence that lasted a long time. That's the mystery of those years when he retired to the countryside and didn't produce anything, because he had such torrential creative flow going on in the years I knew him. It's hard to imagine that ever dried up.' Lucinda later told Dalton, 'I think it was lack of confidence. He felt *Earthquake Weather* had been totally unsupported by his record label. It just left him disheartened, doubting himself and his abilities.'

In April 1994, Strummer joined Czech-American band Dirty Pictures on stage in Prague at a 'Rock for Refugees' benefit concert for those displaced by the Bosnian war, and that year The Clash were offered a multimillion-dollar figure to reform for alt-rock touring festival Lollapalooza. They debated the idea but declined. Five years later, Strummer told Dalton, 'It was five million dollars for 50 gigs or something. But you can't put something together for money that was originally for an idea. We could probably knock up a few gigs but it's not going to do anything for the world, is it? Creatively you're really The Searchers on a chicken-in-a-basket tour. If you're confronted with a choice: take one million dollars for the death of an artist, or you can live as an artist forever – maybe – you're gonna take the second option.'

Johnny Green, reflecting on Strummer's post-Clash days with Rod Kitson for *The Quietus* website in late 2012, said, 'You might call them lost years. But he kept his hand in. Quietly he was always helping other musicians, which never really comes out.'

On what Kitson called an 'alcoholic fug' he couldn't shake off until his Mescaleros days, Green said, 'It did make him emotional. Drink makes you lose your inhibitions, and when you're confused they come out. Joe was aware of what had happened, and in his view, he'd blown it. He thought he made The Clash fall apart, that's how he saw it for a long, long time. For the rest of his life, in fact.

'Joe was a flawed character. He struggled at times to make sense of his own private life, his relationships didn't always go swimmingly, and he wasn't always that clever about the decisions he made in his own career – look at The Clash's history, and the major part he had to do with its collapse. I'd go around to his house and he'd be beating himself on the chest like Tarzan, calling himself an idiot, saying it was all his fault. Joe said after that they might have just taken a bit of time out, cooled down a bit, because they worked frantically. They never went on holiday. It was non-stop.'

On Strummer's ability to reinvent himself and his determined approach, Green added, 'He tried to become the man he wanted to be. None of us can choose the life we're born into. Joe believed that rock'n'roll – right back to Gene Vincent and Elvis – is the medium of reinvention. Joe was very tough, back to '76 in saying they weren't a druggie band. The thought that he might have someone on his hands who might be that way brought shame on the inner Joe.'

Green also acknowledged that Strummer knew he 'was not a top-notch musician', adding, 'He had to work at it. I think he was always self-conscious about that. If you play day-in, day-out alongside Mick Jones, a consummate musician, it will do that. And Joe wasn't a very organised man. He had this knack of crawling behind amplifiers or strange bits of venues before the doors opened, scribbling away on little bits of paper. He'd write ideas down as soon as he got a moment, then stuff them into plastic bags – he never carried a case. He'd get into a hotel room with about six supermarket carrier bags, tip them all out on the floor and then root through them like some bag man going through a skip, saying, 'Where did I put that bit of paper?''

Strummer later described that period as his 'wilderness years', but soon turned his life around, marrying Lucinda in May 1995 in a low-key ceremony at Kensington and Chelsea Register Office. And while previously only an occasional festival-goer, he became an enthusiastic convert, setting up makeshift 'Strummerville' camps backstage at Glastonbury and WOMAD, initiating communal campfire gatherings with friends, old and new, including Mick Jones, comedian Keith Allen and his daughter – emerging pop star – Lily, artist Damien Hirst and his partner Maia, Happy Mondays' Shaun Ryder and Bez, Primal Scream bassist Mani, and many more.

Pat Gilbert painted a vivid picture of that period in *Mojo* in 2006, recalling a summer's evening a decade earlier around a campfire in the garden of Strummer's tumbledown country cottage near Hook, Hampshire, with various friends, family and musical collaborators, including Bez and Kermit of Happy Mondays offshoot Black Grape, plus 'their twilight entourage of gangsters, dealers and vibe merchants'. After experimentation with a natural hallucinogen derived from Brazilian tree bark, Gilbert recalled things became a little 'bendy', future Mescaleros bandmate Pablo Cook finding Strummer in the woods, having been tripping for two days. 'I got very low,' he told Gilbert a year before his death. I took an 11-year breather and reckon about halfway through I thought, 'Shall I hang my guitar up?' I know I wasn't getting anywhere.'

'There was talk of a nervous breakdown,' Cook told Gilbert, 'But it didn't seem any different from any painter and decorator thinking, 'Right, I'll fuck off somewhere for a couple of years.' I knew Joe very well, and think if there was something really bad happening, he'd have said'. As Strummer told Gilbert, 'Rather than have a nervous breakdown, or hit the booze, I'd rather sit down with a few joints and a glass of wine. That was always The Clash's method. That kept me chilled.'

Within three years he re-emerged, 'looking and sounding like the man who two decades earlier had led the punk charge from the front', according to Gilbert. Roger Goodman, part of an inner circle as Joe set about getting his life back on track and key in setting up the Strummerville charity, said in 2005's *Viva Joe Strummer* documentary, he was 'Very, very happy. He was newly wed to Lucinda, and there was no happier man I could see.' And it was his new campfire lifestyle that drew him back towards performing, experimentation with ecstasy leading to immersion in dance music, a scene that had a familiar pull on Strummer to a past conversion. He told Stephen Dalton, 'As with punk, two mad geezers in a room could do it. Like Karl Marx said, let the workers have the means of production, then we'll see the world change. That's why dance music is fucking great – anyone could get into it.'

A love of world music blossomed, and at Peter Gabriel's Real World Studios, near Bath, he met players from all over, bonding with Richard Norris of techno outfit The Grid and Black Grape percussionist Pablo Cook, and collaborating on Euro 1996 football anthem 'England's Irie' with then Keith Allen project Fat Les. In 1997 he scored the *Grosse Pointe Blank* film soundtrack, collaborated with Pablo Cook, wrote and performed the soundtrack to Robert Wallace's *Tunnel of Love*, and reunited in New York City with Lee 'Scratch' Perry to mix Clash and 101'ers reissue dub material. He also bought a farmhouse near Taunton in Somerset, with Damien Hirst and Julien Temple both close, with Dalton suggesting,

'This new pastoral hippie phase ultimately re-energised him.'

By 1998 he was on his way back to a more prominent public life, even guesting on animated TV hit, *South Park*, and appearing on a tie-in album. He was still in a legal dispute with Epic though, a disagreement that lasted nearly eight years and ended with the label agreeing to let him record solo records with another label – unless The Clash were to reunite, in which case they would have to record for Sony. Yet he also helped raise his profile through a BBC World Service presenter's role, his memorable half-hourly weekly programme London Calling going out to a global audience of 40 million.

Richard Norris, for 2005's *Viva Joe Strummer*, said, 'His sort of epiphany and realisation that dance music was pretty good, I'm sure, came from the Glastonbury experience. I just kind of hooked up with Joe straight away, and we recorded all kinds of surreal nonsense, with whoever we could grab and get into the studio. Joe would be shaking maracas, encouraging people.'

As Lucinda Mellor confided to Stephen Dalton, 'Glastonbury and the whole campfire thing was so good for him. He had been pottering around in his own studio and not associating with likeminded people. Going out to Real World Studios opened a new world to him. He met people involved in techno or world music and got really enthusiastic and excited about everything again. He felt he had something to offer.'

And as Rod Kitson, for *The Quietus*, put it in 2012, 'Forming The Mescaleros in 1999, Strummer went full circle and reconciled the 'Year Zero' manifesto that had seen him turn his back on everything and everyone from his life pre-1976.'

The Mescaleros

'I've had the full experience, from hero to zero. My ambition is screwed on one particular target, which is to break the record even, then you can make another record. I'm more about fighting for survival than worrying about going off to the top of Mount Olympus again.'
Joe Strummer, Let's Rock Again, 2004

'It was very important for Joe. He'd severed all links with people from before he got into punk. Anyone from before then, he didn't want to know, cut everybody dead. As part of his Joe Strummer reinvention, he didn't acknowledge the man he'd been before that. Eventually he came to realise they were good people. It was time to pick up and make up. That was an important factor. He was more of a reflective man at that time. He was still feeding the inner man – reading, thinking, talking – and that period gave him the chance to do that, and work on his music. He was delighted to be back in music.'
Johnny Green, to Rod Kitson, The Quietus, 2012

'By the end, he was enormously reconciled with his inner man.'
Robin Crocker, Viva Joe Strummer, 2005

Strummer's initial idea was for an 'acid punk' combo, alongside Richard Norris, Pablo Cook and Bez, telling Stephen Dalton in 1999, 'We made some brilliant tracks, but the cultural collision was too much.' Norris and Strummer eventually parted company, but earlier co-wrote a clutch of tracks that later featured on the first Mescaleros album. Meanwhile, Strummer met Antony Genn, sometime member of Pulp and Elastica, who he first spotted dancing naked onstage at Glastonbury in 1995. Genn ordered the singer to put a new band together, Strummer telling Dalton, 'That was the call I'd been

3

waiting for. I'd had a loss of confidence. It's hard, like a car that hasn't run for years. You think it's never going to run, as you stand around kicking the wheels. But with a bit of goosing and some gasoline in the carburettor... I just needed someone to pull my sleeve and say: 'Come on!''

Genn was installed as co-producer, co-writer and guitarist. His heroin addiction was a problem for Strummer, but they recruited a band, including guitarist Martin Slattery, bass player Scott Shields and drummer Steve 'Smiley' Barnard, eventually settling on their name, after a Native American Apache tribe. Recorded in his latest 'boozy, flag-draped spliffbunker' in North London, an LP was completed in early 1999, but Strummer's initial hawking to record companies was somewhat dispiriting until US label Hellcat, run by Tim Armstrong of arena punk veterans Rancid, offered a generous one-album deal worth $250,000. In Britain the album was licensed by Mercury.

The first gig was that June at the Leadmill in Genn's native Sheffield, with reviews generally positive, Strummer dropping several Clash songs into the set. The album, *Rock Art and the X-Ray Style*, followed in October, its cave painting sleeve design by Damien Hirst, and the LP received mostly encouraging reviews. As The Mescaleros toured Europe, America, Japan and Australia, it went on to sell 150,000 copies.

Strummer was in philosophical mood with Stephen Dalton for *Classic Rock* that year, feeling he'd spent much of the past decade 'running into brick walls', but told him, 'I've enjoyed my life because I've had to deal with all kind of things, from failure to success to failure again. That has made me a better person. I don't think there's any point in being famous if you're an arsehole, or if you lose that thing of being a human being. You ain't gonna be happy living in some mansion somewhere.'

Dalton was certainly sold on some of his new material, and while the project was still in its infancy, he felt that, 'The soulful sandpaper rasp in his voice and newly spiritual scope of his lyrics suggested he was maturing into a kind of English Bob Dylan or Johnny Cash.'

Stuart Clark interviewed Strummer in 1999 for *Hot Press*, unintentionally joining the Mescaleros on a Larne–Stranraer ferry following a Belfast Limelight show. The previous night he'd witnessed the band live south of the border, where, 'Strummer, obviously on a course of monkey glands, had treated Dublin Olympia to the most athletic display of rock'n'roll showmanship since Steven Tyler was last in town. The crowd responded by refusing to go home, even though the house lights had gone on, the bouncers' famously sunny disposition in danger of clouding over. The whooping and hollering continued for 15 minutes until Joe, showered and changed into civvies, emerged from behind the security curtain and announced if we promised to bugger off after, he'd do 'London Calling'. The deal brokered, it was 1979 all over again as 1,300 pairs of feet pogoed in perfect unison.'

As it was, Charles Shaar Murray – the writer who had inspired 'Garageland' with his 1976 Clash assassination, by then with *The Sunday Telegraph* – got in before Clark, who was more than happy to wait till the next day to be 'given another opportunity to see the man who changed my life'. He wasn't alone in that thinking, those present at the Limelight including Northern Irish musician and producer David Holmes, and Ash drummer Rick McMurray, Clark saying both looked 'like five-year-olds on Christmas morning'.

Shaar Murray recalled his own interview after that Dublin show for a *Mojo* tribute in early 2003, remembering asking Strummer about the worst mistake he'd ever made. His response? 'Could I have two for the price of one? Firstly, to fire Topper Headon, and secondly to fire Mick Jones.' The writer added, 'What he'd realised too late was that The Clash was one of those perfect groups in which no one could be replaced without ineradicably altering the nature of the beast.'

In that same interview, Strummer said, 'When I think of The Clash, I think of Paul Simonon slamming the bass. I've seen 10,000 bass players using the same moves, and when all's said and done about the songs and the lyrics, I always think of Paul Simonon smashing that thing around. That says it all. I'd like to think The Clash were revolutionaries, but we loved a bit of posing as well. We were revolutionaries on behalf of punk rock. It was pretty dark in '74/'75. It all seems grey when you look back. I think of it in black and white. There was no MTV, no radio. It was a hard job to break it in America, and we did it playing every shithole between Kitchener, Ontario and the Everglades. Now it's all fucking business. We may as well be in the business of making cheap plastic clips they hang curtains off. That's what rock'n'roll really is.'

Asked by Clark what he'd been doing in the eight years since he was with The Pogues, Strummer said, 'I decided to watch and learn from household flies. I began to draw the patterns they make when they crisscross and circle the room, and eventually realised it's a language. Y'know, the fly's not just randomly flying around the room like we think it is but making statements that in its own tiny corner of the world are very deep and profound.

'I have three girls – two from my first marriage, 15 and 13, and a step-daughter, aged seven – who needed their tiny corner of the world to include a dad. Once you're enthralled to your ego in a relentless pursuit of world domination, shoving your boring personality down the throats of as many globe inhabitants as possible, you don't have time for anyone else. In my book, that's not living or being a human.

'My five years with The Clash were just too intense. After releasing 16 sides of long-playing vinyl in that time, I'd had my say. Imagine it was a party and I'd been talking for five days and five nights straight. At the end of that anybody would go, 'Wooo, I need a breather.' When you're young and your group takes off, you don't really have any life experience. I'd had a bit more than the others. I'd worked as a gravedigger and a toilet-cleaner. But there were times when I forgot what the world outside rock'n'roll was like. When we supported The Who in America in '82, I remember looking at them, thinking, 'God, any day now this is going to be us.' I was also worried that no matter how hard I tried not to, I was going to become a phoney. How can you impart things to other human beings when you're not one yourself? There was a point around the time of *Combat Rock* that if we'd been prepared to become just another conveyor-belt rock band, we could've been huge. On one hand there was our dignity, and on the other, Aerosmith.'

Recalling his Pogues days, he added, 'The only reason I ended up playing with them is that I'm a soft touch. Phil Chevron, a better rhythm guitarist than I'll ever be, fell ill before they were due to go to the States and they asked me would I fill in. The Clash had just exploded, so I thought Fuck it, why not? I did my bit depping for him, then later on when Shane got sick I received my second SOS. They couldn't afford to cancel a tour. They had 17 people with wives, mortgages and expensive sexual fetishes to maintain. So when Jem (Finer) said to me in Los Angeles, 'Er, would you dep for Shane on this world tour, thanks,' what could I do other than learn the fucking lyrics? I know you're dubious about this, but anyone can get into 'Dirty Old Town' and 'The Broad Majestic Shannon'. They're such great songs.

'Then it came to recording *Hell's Ditch* and every producer in London town turned them down because they were frightened. Five days before they were meant to start working on it in Rockfield, Frank Murray rang and said, 'Look, all these bastards have given us the bum's rush. The studio's booked, will you save our arses and do it?' I tell you, we had a ball! It was the middle of summer, so we had the doors open and half the gear set up on the grass. Most of it was done live, with even fucking Spider getting his act together. I defy any proto-folk punk band to better it!'

At that point in their interview, the Mescaleros' tour manager informed the party they were to make a dash for a 2.30 Seacat, Clark encouraged to hitch a ride on their tour bus to the ferry terminal. That was the plan, but he was so wrapped up in the interview and the band's rider that he ended up sailing with them, not realising until they were off the coast of Antrim, Stranraer getting closer.

Strummer, asked why after 10 years turning down megabuck offers, he'd decided to record again, told Clark, 'I've run out of money. I still live off my songwriting, but you can't cut your cloth according to your means cos you don't know what your means are. There's a Clash live album out in October, which'll probably mean I receive a big cheque in 2001, but I've no idea what I'm due this year. The other reason I'm back doing this again is that I'm fed up paying £14.99 for CDs that get spun a couple of times, then begin to work their way into the back-room. I want to make a record that's worth having.'

At that stage, 'Straight to Hell', 'Brand New Cadillac', '(White Man) In Hammersmith Palais', 'London Calling', 'Bankrobber', 'Tommy Gun' and 'I Fought the Law' were in the set, Clark adding that, 'Of the eight new songs unveiled in Dublin and Belfast, at least half have the same Latino rockabilly groove that made the latter-day Clash so irresistible.'

Asked if he was having as much fun in 1999 as in 1979, Strummer replied, 'More. Because when you're young you dissipate your energy too much. As a veteran, who kind of understands the patterns of the world, I can almost predict what's going to happen next. I've been to Bologna. I've been to Kitchenou, Ontario. I've seen everything it's possible to see go down and survived it. Which is all a very rambling way of saying nowadays I reserve my energy for the good stuff and do my best to ignore the crap.'

Was there a chance of reforming The Clash? 'Never in a hundred million fucking years. You heard the crowd tonight shouting for 'Cheat' and 'Police & Thieves'. It'd be the easiest thing in the world to put The Clash back together again, but like shagging an old girlfriend, I'd regret it the moment we went on stage. Don't get me wrong, I love Paul, Mick and Topper, but we had our moment in time together.'

And was Strummer proud of what The Clash achieved? 'As proud as a gnarly old lion. I tell you, what I'm going to have on my gravestone: 'Here, not of his own volition, lies Joe Strummer. He could've lived his life differently, but he couldn't have lived it better. Apart from doing the Fat Les single, that is.''

Pat Gilbert alluded to Clark's interview in his 2006 *Mojo* feature, writing, 'With the success of The Mescaleros, Joe re-established himself as a creditable and vital musical force. He also seems to have enjoyed himself like never before, impishly luring tipsy Belfast journalists onto ferries bound for Scotland and scampering off into the night like a naughty schoolboy when on the instructions of Mrs Joe, his road crew were trying to steer him home.'

As recording sessions for a second album loomed, Genn's heroin habit led to him missing shows, Strummer reluctantly sacking him in July 2000. When Barnard also left, he installed Luke Bullen on drums, Simon Stafford on bass and former Clash cohort Tymon Dogg on fiddle, broadening the band's Celtic-reggae folk sound, the band clearly maturing.

Dogg, for 2005's *Viva Joe Strummer*, stressed, 'He was really enjoying it. Of all the gigs I did with him for the last two years, I think he enjoyed virtually every single one.' And as Mick Jones put it to Stephen Dalton, 'I liked them. It was a thing that was developing in public, he was actually out there doing it. I would have developed it in private then come out. It's two different approaches. Everybody changes as their journey continues.'

However, former Clash road manager Johnny Green stressed to Rod Kitson in his 2012 interview for *The Quietus* that while the Mescaleros were a form of catharsis, there was no suggestion that Strummer found peace in his last years. He added, 'I'm not sure he was a very peaceful sort of guy. He was always pushing himself in different directions. He was musically curious, philosophically interested and politically motivated.'

What's more, the crowds at Mescaleros gigs inevitably wanted to hear Clash songs, and over time that proved to be another dilemma. Green told Kitson, 'He struggled with that. When he was playing with the Mescaleros and people were shouting out for Clash songs. He was always in two minds. 'People want to hear that stuff,' he'd say. 'But on the other hand, I'm out here making music with my new band and want the public to hear it. This reflects me as a slightly older man.' In the end he recognised those songs were part of his persona.'

The Mescaleros appeared on BBC TV's *Later with Jools Holland* in 2000, Strummer joined by Warren Zevon and Tracy Chapman and an ensemble cast for finale, 'I Fought the Law'. And in late 2000, almost two decades after asking The Clash to open for them, The Who offered Strummer's new band a support slot on their UK arena tour. And between shows, Roger Daltrey dropped added backing vocals on the title track to the upcoming second Mescaleros album, *Global a Go-Go*.

The second album was released in July 2001 to positive reviews and supported by a 21-date tour of North America, the UK and Ireland, including festivals. The band's set included 'London's Burning', 'Rudie Can't Fail', '(White Man) In Hammersmith Palais' and classic reggae and ska covers, The Mescaleros regularly closing with the Ramones' 'Blitzkrieg Bop'.

Strummer also summoned *Straight to Hell* co-star, film-maker Dick Rude, to shoot a documentary of the band's global exploits in 2001 and 2002, released as *Let's Rock Again*, Rude telling Stephen Dalton, 'I think there was enough momentum and chemistry with that band. It had finally reached its solidarity, musically, the songs were poppy enough to get people's attention. Had Joe been around to promote that last record I think he could have crossed back over into the Clash category of recognition.'

In the US, shows attracted famous friends like Blondie's Deborah Harry, actors Matt Dillon and Steve Buscemi, Talking Heads' Chris Frantz and Tina Weymouth, and film director Jim Jarmusch, who saw three of the five nights in Brooklyn, stating, 'The Mescaleros were so good that last time I saw them. He had really whipped them into a fine band.'

That year, the band's 'Minstrel Boy' appeared on the *Black Hawk Down* film soundtrack, and it turned out that during the LP sessions, Strummer had sent lyrics to Mick Jones, hinting that he wanted to make an album with his old writing partner. Assuming the lyrics related to the Mescaleros, Jones worked them into songs, but didn't hear back. Intriguingly, Strummer later told Jones they were for 'the next Clash album'. Whether he was serious, Jones never found out.

Pat Gilbert pointed out in *Mojo* in 2006 that while rehabilitating himself during his 'woodshed years' with Pablo Cook, Bez and Richard Norris, Strummer was in regular touch with Jones and Paul Simonon, and one evening in '96 or '97, 'something quite extraordinary happened – they drunkenly planned a Clash reunion'. Cook told Gilbert, 'I said, 'Let's get a tribute band together, The Clish or An Afternoon with The Clash, or something.' That was going to happen at the Amersham Arms in South London. Paul was up for it, Topper was obviously too mashed at that point, Mick was up for it, and I was going to play drums.' But it was never to be, Gilbert feeling a quote in a mid-'90s issue of *Ray Gun* magazine 'perhaps hinted at the deeply personal reasons why', Strummer telling the interviewer, 'I get on with (Mick), but if we have a session, about five in the morning he'll say, 'You cunt – you fucking sacked me!' while I'm on the sofa, rolling my eyes.'

Gilbert also brought up the subject of Strummer's relationship with his 'alter ego' John Mellor, recalling how in a 2001 Mojo interview, he had typically sidestepped the question, replying, 'I do (this) because I'm half-crazy. (Being Joe Strummer) allows you to do stupid things like write ditties on the back of fag packets. I really think it's a sin to bore people. I don't really like to talk about myself.'

In the spring of 2002, Strummer recorded a version of Bob Marley's 'Redemption Song' with Johnny Cash at Rick Rubin's house in LA. And on the West Coast tour that followed, he wrote 'Coma Girl', inspired by his 16-year-old daughter, the band also filming a live special for cable network HBO, while Strummer was offered his own VH1 music show. Drummer Luke Bullen told Dalton, 'He seemed really happy with the final line-up. He was very creative, always scribbling lyrics. I never got the sense it was a finite thing; he was just following his instincts and seemed really excited about working with young musicians. He never gave anyone the impression of being the boss.'

Touring in the UK that autumn, The Mescaleros played a benefit for striking firefighters at Acton Town Hall in West London on November 15, 2002, in what turned out to be their final London show. Mick Jones was in the audience and found himself drawn onstage to play on 'Bankrobber', followed by encores 'White Riot' and 'London's Burning' – the pair's first time playing live together in 19 years. In the *Viva Joe Strummer* documentary, Jones said, 'I just went to support him. I didn't have any intention of going on stage. But I felt compelled when I heard the first notes of 'Bankrobber', I sort of went, 'Hold my coat!' and went up. It was just so good and atmospheric. I just felt totally compelled to get up there. I went up and Joe went, 'Play guitar now!' He was quite pleased to see me. It was really nice, and we played this number and (for) the next number, he didn't tell me what it was. It was 'White Riot'. We used to have that bit of a problem sometimes over whether we should play it. He went to the 'A' position, the first chord, and went, 'You know it,' went, '1-2-3-4!' and we went into it. Then we played 'London's Burning', appropriately enough as the last number. It was wonderful. Joe's driver told me he was driving him back that night, and he said, 'So what did you think of Mick getting up then?' And the driver said, 'Oh I thought it was great!' And he said, 'Bloody cheek!' But he was just kidding!'

As Rod Kitson put it in *The Quietus* in late 2012, 'That Strummer and Jones should encore with 'White Riot' was telling. The only time Strummer ever used his fists came 20 years earlier, when his writing partner refused to go on stage to perform the same song, citing its racist misinterpretation by some of the less intellectual sections of the crowd.' Johnny Green told Kitson, 'That was the only time I ever saw Joe use violence, and he did smack him a thumper in the dressing room. It was at the Sheffield Top Rank. But doesn't it say a lot about teamwork that within a minute Mick had dabbed himself up, strapped his Gibson back up and was out there?'

Film-maker Julien Temple mused on the Strummer/Jones relationship in those later years in an interview with Edward Douglas for comingsoon.net in 2007. He said, 'There was certainly a time where they weren't friendly, but it didn't last that long. I think you have the perception that they were more estranged for longer than they were. Joe produced the Big Audio Dynamite album for example, and their kids had grown up together. They were friends, but hadn't played together onstage until, ironically, 10 days before Joe died.'

Green missed out on that final hook-up, but told Rod Kitson 10 years later, 'It certainly wasn't planned, it wasn't orchestrated. It was instinct and impulse. One of Strummer's great phrases was 'instinct not intellect'. I'd been with Strummer about a week before, in Hastings. He played down on the end of the pier, and I thought for no good reason I'd go. I remember that gig for being a bit of a shit-hole. I spent the afternoon with Joe and save for the gig in the evening that was the last I saw of him.'

Strummer's final regular gig was with The Mescaleros at Liverpool Academy on November 22, and his last performance was two weeks before his death, at The Palace, in Bridgwater, Somerset, near his home.

A couple of nights before Strummer died, Jones spent a drunken evening with him at the Groucho Club in Soho. Pat Gilbert wrote, 'After several hours putting the world to rights, Joe hugged Mick goodbye and ascended to his rented room upstairs while Mick toodled off home.' A shaken Jones told *Mojo* a fortnight later, 'It was kind of cinematic. Him, ascending, and me walking out of the door.' But even at the end, Joe remained an enigma. His friend Julien Temple said, 'Was he happy at the end? I don't know. He was talking about blasting out from rock'n'roll, doing something different. But he was also quite infuriating. He talked in the end about respecting Margaret Thatcher. He was always self-questioning. Happiness and contentment with Joe were a contradiction in terms.'

Shortly before his death, Joe Strummer and U2's Bono co-wrote '46664' for Nelson Mandela as part of an AIDS awareness campaign in Africa, with Strummer set to play Mandela's SOS fundraising concert on Robben Island in February 2003. But it wasn't to be, 50-year-old Strummer dying on the afternoon of December 22, 2002, at home in Broomfield, Somerset, the victim of an undiagnosed congenital heart defect, one that could have claimed him at any time.

Long-time friend Chris Salewicz talked about the funeral that took place at the West London crematorium on Harrow Road on Monday, December 30, 2002, in 2006's *Redemption Song: The Definitive Biography of Joe Strummer*, publishing his diary account of the funeral, in which he described the sky that day as 'a slab of dark, gravestone grey; rain belts down in bucketfuls, leaving enormous pools of water on the roadside. Thomas Hardy funeral weather.'

He goes on to describe his arrival at the 2pm service and conversations with Chrissie Hynde and Jeannette Lee (formerly of PIL, co-managing director of Rough Trade, a punk-era girlfriend of Joe), plus music journalist Charles Shaar Murray and girlfriend Anna Chen, outside, the rain pouring down, adding, 'I take a half-spliff out of my jacket pocket and light it, take a few tokes, and hand it to Charlie. Out of the hundreds of hours I spent with Joe, I don't think I had been with him on a single occasion when marijuana had not been consumed, so it seems appropriate, even important, to get in the right frame of mind to be with him again.'

Salewicz also mentions the massed ranks of firemen, 'two ranks of a dozen, standing to attention in Joe's honour'. The fellow attendees he names including Bob Gruen, Don Letts, Jim Jarmusch, Johnny Green and 'the stick-thin Stan Laurel-like figure of' Topper Headon. Inside the chapel he describes 'an acoustic guitar, covered in white roses, really beautiful. In its hollowed-out centre is a message, 'R.I.P. Joe Strummer, Heaven Calling 1952–2002'. A large beatbox, next to it, is similarly covered in white roses. All the seats in the chapel are full.'

He adds, 'The sound of bagpipes sails in through the door, lengthily, growing nearer. (Later I learn that the music is 'The Mist-covered Mountains of Home', also played at the funeral of President John F. Kennedy.) At last Joe's coffin slowly comes in, held aloft by half a dozen pallbearers. It is placed down at the far end of the chapel. Keith Allen, the actor and comedian, steps forward and positions a cowboy hat on top of it. There's a big sticker on the nearest end: 'Question Authority', it reads, then in smaller letters: 'Ask me anything'. Next to it is a smaller sticker: 'Vinyl Rules'. On the sides of the coffin are more messages: 'Get In, Hold On, Sit Down, Shut Up' and 'Musicians Can't Dance'. Around the end wall of the chapel are flags of all nations. More people are ushered in, like the kids Joe would make sure got through the stage door at Clash gigs, until the place is crammed. In the crush I catch a glimpse of Lucinda, Joe's beautiful widow: she carries herself with immense dignity but – hardly surprisingly

– has an aura of almost indescribable grief, pain and shock. People are standing right up by the coffin. The aisle is packed: suddenly a tall, blonde woman, looking half-gorgeous, a Macbeth witch, is pushed through the throng, to kneel on the stone floor at the front of the aisle – it's not until later on that I realise this is Courtney Love.

'The service begins. I don't know who the MC is, a man in his late fifties, a vague cross between Gene Hackman and Woody Allen. He's good, tells us how much love we are all part of, stresses how honoured we are that our lives were so touched by Joe, says that he's never seen a bigger turnout for a funeral. (There is a sound system outside, relaying the proceedings to the several hundred people now there.) Then he says we'll hear the first piece of music, and we should turn our meditations on Joe: it is '(White Man) In Hammersmith Palais'.

'Paul Simonon gets up to speak. He tells a story about how when The Clash first formed in 1976, he and joe had been in Portobello Road, discussing the merits of mirror shades, as worn by Jimmy Cliff in *The Harder They Come*. If anyone shows any aggro while you were wearing such a pair, Joe decided, then their anger would be reflected back at them. immediately he stepped into a store that sold such sunglasses. Paul didn't follow: he was completely broke, having been chucked off social security benefits; Joe, however, had just cashed that week's social security cheque. He came out of the store wearing his brand-new mirror shades. Then they set off to bunk the tube fare to Rehearsal Rehearsals in Camden. As they walked towards Ladbroke Grove tube station, Joe dug into his pocket. 'Here,' he said, 'I bought you a pair too.' Although Joe was now completely broke and with no money to eat for three days, he'd helped out his mate. This story increases the collective tear in the chapel.

'Maeri, a female cousin, gets up to speak. Joe's mother had been a crofter's daughter, who became a nurse and met Joe's father in India during the war. Joe's dad liked to have a great time: a real rebel himself, it seems, not at all the posh diplomat he's been made out to be, a man who called himself up by his bootstraps. We're told a story about Joe as a 10-year-old at a family gathering: he is told that he can go anywhere but 'the barn'; immediately he wants to know where 'the barn' is. Then another female cousin, Anna, reads a poem, in English, by the Gaelic poet Sorley MacLean.

'Dick Rude, an old friend of Joe's from LA who has been making a documentary about The Mescaleros, speaks. Keith Allen reads out the lyrics of a song about Nelson Mandela, part of an AIDS charity project for South Africa organised by Bono of U2, that Joe had just finished writing. A Joe demo tape, just him and a guitar, a slow blues-like song, is played. And The Mescaleros' tune, 'Willesden to Cricklewood'. The MC suggests that as we file past the coffin to leave, we say a few words to Joe. 'Wandering Star' begins to play. 'See you later, Joe,' someone says. Yeah, see you later, Joe.'

Charles Shaar Murray, in a tribute for *Mojo*, also painted a vivid picture of that day, writing, 'On the day of his funeral, the skies opened over the Westway. It seemed only appropriate as the sound of '(White Man) In Hammersmith Palais', Joe's favourite of his Clash songbook, fought the weather head on while former bandmates, family members, contemporaries like Chrissie Hynde, Glenn Matlock, Patti Palladin and Nicky Tesco turned up to pay their respects.

'The Fire Brigades Union, for whom Joe

3 and Mick Jones had played together at a recent benefit concert, provided a guard of honour, the flags of many nations flew above the doors of the West London Crematorium, Keith Allen read the lyrics from Joe's last song, Joe Ely and Jim Jarmusch flew in from the US, and Courtney Love provided a moment of pure farce by throwing herself on the sticker-bedecked coffin, as if someone entirely different was inside it.'

Many tributes followed, Sean O'Hagan in *The Guardian* on December 29, 2002, and Billy Bragg for *BBC Online* on January 2, 2003, beautifully setting the tone.

Sean O'Hagan: 'Even when the venue was wrong, or the sound was shit, or the bouncers were in full-on psycho mode, what you got from a Clash gig was pure passion. They hit the stage running and did not let up until the last encore, Strummer up front, flailing at his guitar, or wrapped around a mic stand, howling out his words like some unholy cross between Eddie Cochran, Lenny Bruce and someone in the throes of an epileptic fit. You left feeling wrung out and exhilarated, feeling like you had felt the full force of some primal rock'n'roll energy that had its source way back in Memphis or Chicago rather than West London.

'This, though, was the fabled Sound of the Westway, in all its guttural, frenetic, inchoate glory. It was a kind of white boy blues, a kind of protest; the sound of primal rage and racial tension, of inner-city boredom and sheer frustration, all channelled into this pent-up noise that at times threatened to consume the singer. The titles alone gave ample warning that this was not a music for the faint-hearted or the purist.

'For an all too brief time, the Clash were the greatest rock group on the planet. Anyone who tells you different is lying, or a pop-swat who sat out punk on the sidelines, taking notes and formulating theories, while everyone else surrendered to the noise and the chaos. Nowadays, the original meaning of punk has all but been buried under a surfeit of mostly transatlantic pseudo lit-crit theorising, and while the Sex Pistols are seen as the true heirs of the Situationists – despite the fact that three-quarters of the group couldn't even spell the word, never mind absorb the politics – the Clash have received short shrift.'

Billy Bragg: 'The Clash were the greatest rebel rock band of all time. Their commitment to making political pop culture was the defining mark of the British punk movement. They were also a self-

mythologising, style-obsessed mass of contradictions. That's why they were called The Clash. They wanted desperately to be rock stars but also wanted to make a difference. While Paul Simonon flashed his glorious cheekbones and Mick Jones threw guitar-hero shapes, no one struggled more manfully with the gap between the myth and reality of being a spokesman for your generation than Joe Strummer. All musicians start out with ideals but hanging on to them in the face of media scrutiny takes real integrity. Tougher still is to live up to the ideals of your dedicated fans. Joe opened the back door of the theatre and let us in, he sneaked us back to the hotel for a beer, he too believed in the righteous power of rock'n'roll. If he didn't change the world he changed our perception of it. He crossed the dynamism of punk with 'Johnny Too Bad' and started that punky-reggae party. He drew us, thousands strong, onto the streets of London in support of Rock Against Racism. He sent us into the garage to crank up our electric guitars. He made me cut my hair.

'The ideals that still motivate me as an artist come not from punk, not even from The Clash, but from Joe Strummer. The first wave of punk bands had a rather ambivalent attitude to the politics of late '70s Britain. The Sex Pistols, The Damned, The Stranglers, none of them, not even The Jam, came close to the radicalism that informed everything The Clash did and said. The US punk scene was even less committed. The Ramones, Talking Heads, Heartbreakers and Blondie, all were devoid of politics. Were it not for The Clash, punk would have been just a sneer, a safety pin and a pair of bondage trousers. Instead, the incendiary lyrics of The Clash inspired 1,000 more bands on both sides of the Atlantic to spring up and challenge their elders, and the man we all looked to was Joe Strummer.

'He was the White Man in Hammersmith Palais who influenced the 2 Tone movement. He kept it real and inspired the Manic Street Preachers. And he never lost our respect. His recent albums with The Mescaleros found him on inspiring form once again, mixing and matching styles and rhythms in celebration of multiculturalism. At his final gig, in November in London, Mick Jones got up with him and together they played a few old Clash tunes. It was a benefit concert for the firefighters' union. One of the hardest things to do in rock'n'roll is walk it like you talk it. Joe Strummer epitomised that ideal and I will miss him greatly.'

The Mescaleros – an appreciation

We had a dress rehearsal for Joe Strummer's final triumphant return on the wondrous 'Trash City' from the *Permanent Record* soundtrack in 1988 and the following year's *Earthquake Weather* LP, backed by the Latino Rockabilly War, showing us just what might lay ahead further down the well-worn road,

Strummer carrying on where he'd set out in his Alex Cox film years with his work on *Walker*. We were still some way off in terms of musical rehabilitation, but a decade later Joe was well and truly out the other side, ready to embark on the next adventure, the first fruits of that new alliance heard on 1999's *Rock Art and the X-Ray Style* with new band, The Mescaleros. The album was produced by Antony Genn (and elsewhere by Richard Norris), Strummer seeing the old century out with a promising return to form. There was still a sense that he wasn't quite there, and there's a fair amount of soul-searching on that 10-song opus, but things were definitely coming together.

As with all three Mescaleros albums, this was a world music affair, fusing folk rock with dance, reggae and much more, Strummer building on all he'd lived and experienced since his arrival in Ankara in 1952. What's more, this was no solo project, with a real band feel from the off, as heard on second single 'Tony Adams', the Arsenal and England captain namechecked in a fantasy kick-about on a number which had the feel of a jam committed to tape. Here we had Joe on his travels, searching for the morning sun while Pablo Cook set down a bass drum foundation for those trademark ska guitar touches and BJ Cole's pedal steel flourishes.

'Sandpaper Blues' keeps that vibe going, that world music feel at the heart of a hand-drum-led number, the African chanting and underlying dance feel neatly complemented by Strummer's vocals and those guitars, in almost Beats International style. With the scene set, Joe moved into the heart of the LP – campfire style – on title track, 'X-Ray Style', Cook's percussion and Martin Slattery's Spanish guitar proving perfect accompaniment for a typically descriptive narrative from the main man, albeit an artist still seemingly out to find his way.

But we're soon back on our feet, a safe distance from the flames, for the album's first big statement on 'Techno D-Day', Strummer and Genn letting lose on guitars in a rousing anthem to free speech. We're back with more tales of the open highway on 'The Road to Rock'n'Roll', Scott Shields' bass and Cook's percussion perfect vehicles for a song written for Johnny Cash. There's a Bob Dylan meets The Blue Aeroplanes feel to 'Nitcomb', Strummer in reflective mode on a slow-building masterwork, 'singing to all the torn betting slips flying around my feet', and 'talking to all the chewing gum that's stuck everywhere on the street'. And if that was Dylan-esque, 'Digging the New' is Tom Petty, Bruce Springsteen and Neil Young rolled into one, on a forward-looking rock blast that seems rather ironic when half of his audience would be shouting for Clash requests each night.

'Forbidden City' is more of a curiosity, Joe in pensive mode again, Shields' upfront bass setting the tone and Slattery adding Hammond touches, acting as a bridge towards the LP's big flourish on lead single 'Yalla Yalla', described by its author as, 'an ancient British folk song... written in the year 1999', and another album cornerstone, underlining Strummer's search for understanding. He's still questioning everything, his 'vision of a homeland' relevant the world over, the electro touches adding to an impressive band feel.

And then we're home on 'Willesden to Cricklewood', and it's personal. As our man puts it, 'We're alive and that's the one,' expressing a little inner peace and providing a rare glimpse of Joe the family man, this citizen of the world digging his local scene over expressive piano and keyboard noodling from co-writer Genn, who revealed on *The Future is Unwritten*, of a song which later featured in Strummer's funeral service, 'Maybe that night I wrote a song with John Mellor.' It's a lovely, laid-back yet deceptively powerful number, which truly stirs the emotions. And as Aztec Camera frontman Roddy Frame said of that track, 'Only someone who really loved London could write this.'

It would be a year and three quarters before we got the next chapter, but 2001's offering *Global a Go-Go* was well worth the wait, and set out its sense of ambition with wondrous opener (and sole single) 'Johnny Appleseed', Strummer seemingly suggesting across this album that he'd now sussed just what this journey was about, his starting point nailing his environmental theme and pan-global spirit of communication to the mast, its imagery gorgeous, the harmonies and band top-drawer and tighter than ever. And while Antony Genn appeared on just one song and Richard Norris was gone, Tymon Dogg was back with his old busking pal, alongside mainstays Martin Slattery, Scott Shields and Pablo Cook.

Again, this was no formulaic trip, and 'Cool'n'Out' took us in a different direction, where 'Punk rock's what it's all about,' amid a melding of musical styles by a band confident enough to branch out and fill your aural senses, their barrage of big sound including a saxophonic assault from Slattery. The title track was next, 'Global a Go-Go' shining further light on the key theme, Joe's World Service bulletins used as an illustration of the need to keep the bigger picture in mind, with music the hand of friendship across the world, those broadcasts later revisited on *Streetcore*'s 'Midnight Jam'. In a sense, it was the message of 'Rock the Casbah' 20 years down the line, extolling the virtues of music's powerful reach and the need to use it for good. Roger Daltrey helped out on vocals, on a track also including stirring Russian-style choral touches.

Strummer often mastered the story-song, and excelled himself on 'Bhindi Bhagee', a hymn to the joy of diversity, ethnic flavour and open community spirit, Joe giving us a tour of the 'humble neighbourhoods' over bodhran, flute, guitars, violin, Wurlitzer and much more. It proved to be a perfect depiction of The Mescaleros, this esteemed 'bunch of players' who were 'really letting go', through an inspired modern twist on Shakespeare's assertion, 'If music be the food of love, play on.'

'Gamma Ray' was an atmospheric curiosity, Strummer's imagery all over the shop but often top-notch, not least that line about there being no guest list tonight at the Memorial Hall, but, 'Cher got in cos she's so thin'. And then, Strummer 'took a tram into the fourth dimension' for the evocative 'Mega Bottle Ride', his glorious tangent – 'We've gone Balkan anyway' – giving off a Faces and Rolling Stones vibe, which I guess points to a Ronnie Wood influence. It's another song from the road, and surely only Joe could paint a romantic picture of the Ilminster bypass. Talking of travel, 'Shaktar Donetsk' followed an Eastern European refugee entering the UK, amid a suitably rich Eastern bloc soundscape. Then we had the gently lilting picture postcard, 'Mondo Bongo', Strummer seemingly returning to the Western soundtrack game, Dogg's guitar and violin giving us the feel of a chapter from a Laurie Lee Spanish novella.

Then, as our man says, 'Before you know it you'll be in 'Bummed Out City' in a cloud of dust and rust, and all the dogs biting on your exhaust pipe.' Again, such detail, Strummer on top form, bringing us neatly to 'At the Border, Guy', a reggae skank of sorts and a perfect play-out for this global adventure, Slattery coming into his own on melodica, Hammond and piano, the low hum of The Mescaleros' choir adding an African feel on a track that builds and builds. And then we're away, after making the most of the last heat from the campfire with an instrumental take on traditional Irish jig, 'Minstrel Boy', the tracklist suggesting Martin, Pablo and Tymon did all the work while Joe added 'off-stage voices' and Scott 'just sat there, staring off into space'.

That might have been it of course, but Strummer was well underway with the follow-up, and thanks to Martin Slattery and Scott Shields on production, arrangement and playing duties, with help from Joe's widow Lucinda, we got the wondrous *Streetcore*, 10 months after his passing, this 10-track epitaph a fitting tribute to a performer who had truly found top form again, building on two previous acclaimed works and going out in style, sad as it was to even contemplate that there would be no more Joe Strummer records.

This time Luke Bullen took over from Pablo Cook, and Simon Stafford added bass, guitar and more. Many of Strummer's contributions were first takes, but that just adds to the honest, emotive feel of the finished product, as perfectly illustrated by the initial adrenaline rush of 'Coma Girl', enough to make you head straight down the front one more time, a rousing rock'n'roller that shook off any nagging doubts that this might not work, the song later covered by Bruce Springsteen.

Again, The Mescaleros weren't for hanging around, and headed off elsewhere, finding Joe at the mountaintop for 'Get Down Moses', looking down on a 'prairie full of lost souls' in a mighty reggae/ska jam, before they brought the tempo down for a raw but atmospheric acoustic stroll through Johnny Cash tribute 'Long Shadow' (co-written and performed with Smokey Hormel), one which probably said just as much about our Joe, for whom, 'Somewhere in my soul, there's always rock'n'roll.'

It's difficult to pinpoint the emotional heart of this album, with so many contenders, but there's arguably no more fired-up moment than 'Arms Aloft', not least the moment the first chorus kicks in just before the minute mark, Strummer and co reminding of us of that scene, where 'the spirit is our gasoline'. It's a tribute to everyone who ever stuck by Joe, kept the faith and was duly rewarded by those later Mescaleros live shows. So powerful, and later adopted by Pearl Jam.

On an LP seemingly full of tributes, 'Ramshackle Day Parade' counts as a moving commemoration of the victims of the terrorist attacks on September 11, 2001, just one example of the kind of songs that made this a deeply spiritual record, Strummer's focus truly found, three years into his Mescaleros' journey. And while it seems almost a slight to the original to say this is my preferred version of 'Redemption Song', the pure understated emotion in Joe's voice takes it to new heights. In a way, it's the centrepiece around which the LP is built – its streetcore, if you like – and every bit as much about Strummer's journey as Bob Marley's. Rick Rubin's trademark production hit the right tone too. Three and a half minutes of sonic perfection.

We're far from done though, 'All in a Day' getting us back on our feet. Written by Strummer with Danny Saber, its throbbing *Revolver*-esque bassline and pure punk rock energy is thrilling, the 'hey hey' bhangra-flavour chanting harking back to the previous album's more global ethos.

By now, I'm as good as gone, finding it hard even completing this review, Martin Slattery's searing guitar lines and stirring strings from around the two-and-a-half-minute-mark leaving me floored on exquisite Strummer/Slattery/Shields number, 'Burnin' Streets'. Here was a journey started in 1976 with 'London's Burning', Joe, Mick and Paul looking down over the Westway from the 18th floor. Since then, Joe had taken us around the world many times, and we're back again, having seen, heard and learned so much. And there's a reminder of that wider-world focus when we hear Strummer in DJ mode on instrumental number, 'Midnight Jam', his bandmates adding the perfect accompaniment in a truly emotional jam around Joe's broadcasts.

Then we're done, Bobby Charles' 'Before I Grow Too Old' (its co-writers including Fats Domino) given the Strummer treatment on 'Silver and Gold', for what proves to be a perfect endpoint, the sheer poignancy of those simple but effective lines striking you. There's also closure in the fact that it's Tymon adding the violin, a busking partner to the last, helping change the world through the power of music.

It's so easy to overcompensate in the circumstances and make this out to be something it wasn't meant to be, but the sheer strength of the songs, the musicianship and the vocal delivery on 'Streetcore' mean it can be nothing other than a stunning epitaph, put together with so much thought, an album that does Joe's memory true justice.

Before I Grow Too Old: Remembering Joe Strummer

On the Inside

'I think about him every day. It's sort of like Einstein or someone dying. There was so much there, and it's never going to be repeated anywhere else. It's so original.' (Mick Jones, *Viva Joe Strummer: The Clash and Beyond*, 2005)

'It's taken Joe's death to make me realise just how big The Clash were. We were a political band and Joe was the one who wrote the lyrics. Joe was one of the truest guys you could ever meet. If he said, 'I am behind you,' you knew he meant it 100 per cent.' (Topper Headon, 2002)

'It's great that Joe still means something to people down the years. He told it straight, he said what he thought. He didn't try and couch what he was trying to say for his own public image. Particularly in the early days what he said was not always acceptable, and I think people respect honesty and truth. His legacy is that he showed people you can have a bash at whatever you try: don't feel intimidated by it, give it your best shot, whatever your dream is. Secondly, he always thought you should question authority, think for yourself, figure it out. What he really said – and what was printed on his coffin was, 'question everything'.' (Johnny Green to Rod Kitson, *The*

Quietus, 2012)

'There were a lot of other frontmen. But he had something special. It was a bit like watching what one would imagine Eddie Cochran to be. The way he moved around the stage and his complete dedication to what he was doing.' (Mick Jones, *Viva Joe Strummer: The Clash and Beyond*, 2005)

'He always had a corner to fight. He always had someone to stick up for. He had that fantastic haircut, with the quiff, and the way his leg just pumped. He had his sneer and always did downstrokes on his guitar, so looked like a pneumatic drill when he was playing. When I first joined he didn't have any teeth left. He had them done later. He gave this impression he was dangerous, you know. He was a force to be reckoned with.' (Topper Headon, *Viva Joe Strummer: The Clash and Beyond*, 2005)

'It was his joy of life, he loved doing what he did. He was great company. Before a show, after a show, and even during a show he was so alert. Never bored with what he did, and thus a very good man to be with.' (Johnny Green to Rod Kitson, *The Quietus*, December 2012)

'I've never seen a man work the crowd so well, as a frontman of a group.' (Long-time Clash associate Robin Crocker, *Viva Joe Strummer: The Clash and Beyond*, 2005)

'I'm not too big a man to cry. Yeah, I can cry. I miss him. He enriched my life and I'd have done anything for that man. I'd have killed a man for him if he'd have asked me at that point. I was hook, line, and sinker in there with him.' (Johnny Green, *Viva Joe Strummer: The Clash and Beyond*, 2005)

'Joe never had any effects on his guitar. It was like, 'Turn it up, let's fucking get on with it!' And we did get on with it.' (Mescaleros bandmate Pablo Cook, *Viva Joe Strummer: The Clash and Beyond*, 2005)

'I think it was a burden to Joe that people expected him to change the world. I don't think he expected to change the world and I think there were times when it was a very exhausting business, being the man about to change the world. His take on it would be that he was interested in changing the way people think about the world, and there's a difference in that. He didn't shy away from the problem of being the figurehead of that change, but if you're asking for a saviour or a Messiah or a Fuhrer, he wasn't the man, and didn't want it. He liked time out, he was just a human being. Fuck it, he was just a rock'n'roll singer.' (Johnny Green, *Viva Joe Strummer: The Clash and Beyond*, 2005)

'There was a public persona and he was the frontman of The Clash. But that was enormously at odds with the real John Mellor, a very private person and in a lot of ways a very shy person.' (Robin Crocker, *Viva Joe Strummer: The Clash and Beyond*, 2005)

'I always found Joe a paradox between being a very private man, alone with his thoughts, and being a very open man, sharing them. There was no way of knowing which way that was going to go. I would say right to the end I knew him very well but didn't know him in the same breath. He was a man who could just shut down, alone with his thoughts. I was always amazed at his patience, particularly on tour and in a strange town. He was always curious. What did people do? How did people live their lives? What went on in this place? He was a good listener. For a man that had the verbals, he'd listen well. But when it came to being offloaded on, and 'What are you gonna do about it, Joe?' I did think he was patient, but he got it non-stop.' (Johnny Green, *Viva Joe Strummer: The Clash and Beyond*, 2005)

The Artists as Fans

'I still think of Joe every time I see the Westway. The night he died, my daughter was

NME
NEW MUSICAL EXPRESS
JOE STRUMMER AT 60
A PUNK ICON
REMEMBERED
HIS GREATEST LYRICS, CHOSEN BY BOBBY GILLESPIE AND MORE
THE NEXT GENERATION KEEPING HIS SPIRIT ALIVE
BLUR
HYDE PARK SPECIAL!
FRONT ROW AT THE WARM-UPS
+FREE POSTERS
"I'M NOT INSANE!" ARIEL PINK PROTESTS
WHAT'S THE BEST CRIBS TRACK? JOIN THE DEBATE INSIDE
"DON'T WRITE SLOGANS. WRITE TRUTHS"
JOE STRUMMER
PUNK. REBEL. REVOLUTIONARY

coming home from Australia for Christmas. I was staying with a mate in London so I could pick her up from the airport the next morning. About two in the morning the phone goes. My mate John McGee, who'd just worked on the Mescaleros tour, said, 'Joe's dead.' I was baffled. I thought, 'Why would anyone make such a stupid joke?' I was absolutely in bits. A few hours later I met my daughter at Heathrow and was overjoyed, I hadn't seen her in two years and was ecstatic. But mixed in with all that jubilation was that thing of, 'One of my mates has died.' On the journey home, we made a detour so we could go along the Westway. It was so poignant, there in the car with my daughter, the morning after Joe died, driving along the Westway, singing 'London's Burning' to myself in this half-broken, shocked way. It's still a bloody shock, when I think about it.' (Pete Wylie, *Uncut*, 2015)

'He was very nice to me, and nice about me, though it must have been irritating for him. We were a really young, gauche, unsauced group when we started off. With U2, I always felt we had a lot going wrong, but ultimately had something special. Lots of bands around us were much better looking, better players, better songwriters. They had everything. But we had the 'it' – whatever 'it' might be – and built around that. That idea comes from the Clash – that you could come out of the audience, get up onstage, grab the microphone, and if you had something to say, you have a valid reason for being there. That idea changed my life: It's the reason U2 exists today.' (Bono, U2, in a 2003 interview with Elton John, published on the *Epitaph* website)

'Whatever he sang affected you because it was just so raw. His voice reeked of hurt and anger. Take his version of 'Redemption Song' on *Streetcore* – just him alone, with an acoustic guitar. He just makes it his song.' (Elton John, in a 2003 interview with Bono, published on the *Epitaph* website)

'People didn't really realise how important Strummer was. It only kind of popped out when he was no more. He really was a great artist.' (Film director Alex Cox to Stephen Dalton, *Classic Rock*, 2017)

'He was my first hero. I was 15 and starting to write songs with Nick (Wire). We saw The Clash on TV playing 'What's My Name' and 'Garageland' and they seemed so vital, brutal and intelligent. He didn't seem to have a switch-off button when he was on stage. It was like a religious fervour. I admired him for that.' (James Dean Bradfield, Manic Street Preachers, *Mojo, 2003*)

'He was like an older brother or father figure. I painted a picture of Joe on my bedroom wall, so from the ages of 14 to 19, until I moved out, Joe watched over as I slept. When my Dad redecorated, he tore that piece off the wallpaper and I still have it. I listen to that first Clash album more than any other. I can't imagine what things would have been like without it.' (John Squire, The Stone Roses, *Mojo*, 2003)

'I don't know if Joe was religious in any way, but 'Redemption Song' is a kind of hymn, and if there was a hymn Joe could sing, that would be the one. Those are such beautiful lyrics, and so prescient right now as these are very nervous times. Hearing Joe sing that, in his voice, means a lot. It's infuriating to realise the most maddening of clichés has come to be true – *Streetcore*, Joe's last record, is probably his best. I hate the sound of that as it comes out of my mouth, y'know – 'Fuck off. Why didn't you tell him the last Mescaleros record was great?' There's some great stuff on his other albums with them, but on this one it all comes together.' (Bono, U2, in a 2003 interview with Elton John, published on the *Epitaph* website)

'The Joe Strummers of this world don't come along very often, but when they do, they shine like beacons because of what they have to say and the passion with which they say it. Even though Joe sounds contented on *Streetcore*, I don't think he ever stopped searching for new sounds, new ideas.' (Elton John, in a 2003 interview with Bono, published on the *Epitaph* website)

The Writers Remember

'The contradiction at the heart of The Clash was ultimately the contradiction at the heart of Joe Strummer. He longed for his band to be the biggest, flashest, craziest, most powerful, full-on rock'n'roll experience in the world. At the same time, he wanted The Clash to be the voice of a global underdog and a positive force for good in the world. The conflicting imperatives of flashy success and collective personal integrity have pulled apart many bands, but never a better one.' (Charles Shaar Murray, *Mojo, 2003)*

'It took the death of Joe Strummer for the mainstream to finally recognise the brilliance of The Clash and Joe's iconic status.' (John Robb, *Punk Rock: An Oral History*, 2006)

'I never got to know Joe that well. I had no idea how he lived, if he liked tea better than coffee, if his shit was more thick than thin, if he cried over spilt milk, or laughed at Morecambe and Wise. But his honesty shone through his voracious music, and when he spoke, that odd glutinous voice resonated with integrity.' (Barry Cain, *'77 Sulphate Strip*, 2007)

'It was like he was plugged into the mains. Y'know, his left leg was going.' (Kris Needs, *Viva Joe Strummer: The Clash and Beyond*, 2005)

'As a performer he was the best. When he went on that stage he wasn't a human being. He was something else. He was born to be a rock'n'roll star.' (Pat Gilbert, *Viva Joe Strummer: The Clash and Beyond*, 2005)

Into the Great Unwritten Future

Eight months after Joe Strummer's death, on August 21, 2003, on what would have been his 51st birthday, a celebratory concert took place in the hills above Granada, Spain, with Mick Jones, Tymon Dogg, The Pogues' Jem Finer and the 101'ers' Richard Dudanski 'among those who played into the warm night', as Chris Salewicz put it.

In 2006's *Redemption Song: The Definitive Biography of Joe Strummer*, Salewicz wrote, 'Afterwards, down in San Jose, Jazz and Lola took their portion of their father's ashes along the coast to a cliff of gnarled white rock, a beautiful, perfect spot. Behind it, in the desert, was the bikers' bar where Joe would enjoy Toxico, the marijuana-infused tequila drink. As well as his two daughters, there was a small party present, including Jem and Marcia Finer, Lauren Jones and assorted children.

'They were responding to a dream that Gaby had. From a pottery urn made by Pockets, Jazz tipped Joe's ashes over the cliff towards the sea. 'I'd never seen them before,' said Jem. 'I was amazed how fine they were, like particles. It was beautiful to see them drifting out in the breeze, like white, sandy rock. They dispersed towards the sea, the mountains in the background. That's my last memory of Joe, drifting off across the sea and mountains. Very beautiful.'

'Jazz still clutched the urn. 'Shall we keep it?' she asked Lola. As Lola was replying in the affirmative, it flipped out of Jazz's hands, as though grabbed by a gust of wind, and hovered in the air above the cliff edge before smashing down onto a rock below. The urn's broken

fragments were gathered and thrown out to sea.

'It was weird,' said Jem. 'Mischief from the other side. You don't stop, Joe, do you?'

'Get on with it!' Joe would have barked.'

When Strummer died, he'd already started work on what would become that third and final Mescaleros album, *Streetcore*, released in October 2003, and as Stephen Dalton wrote in *Classic Rock*, 'Cruelly, Strummer died on the cusp of a major career comeback, his profile higher than at any time in the previous 15 years. Back in Somerset in 1999, Joe seemed to have found some kind of contentment. He had become a kind of punk King Arthur, ruling over his campfire Camelot under the widescreen skies of Rebel Wessex. The best thing about his new rural kingdom, he told me, was the sky.

'Whatever he did musically, Strummer was never likely to eclipse his glorious heyday in The Clash. But his midlife reinvention with The Mescaleros helped liberate him from the long shadow of his legendary past in the same way as Robert Plant and Paul Weller escaped theirs. Tragically, he was cut short, cheated out of his third-act comeback.'

His estate, valued at just under £1m, was left to his wife Lucinda, and in his memory, friends and family established the non-profit organisation Strummerville, later renamed The Joe Strummer Foundation, giving opportunities to musicians and support to projects around the world, creating empowerment through music. The foundation also holds an annual festival.

In addition, Strummer was instrumental in setting up Future Forests, later rechristened The Carbon Neutral Company, which is dedicated to planting trees in various parts of the world to combat global warming. And he was the first artist to record, press and distribute his records in a carbon neutral way through the planting of trees.

After his death, not only was there the 2003 induction of The Clash into the Rock and Roll Hall of Fame and the Grammy Awards the following month – at which Elvis Costello, Bruce Springsteen, Little Steven, Dave Grohl, Pete Thomas and Tony Kanal performed 'London Calling' – but also another tribute to Strummer that month at rock club Debaser in Stockholm, which saw various Swedish artists performing Clash songs, followed by Swedish punk band Ebba Grön reuniting, aided by Mick Jones on guitar.

On the first anniversary of Strummer's death, there was a tribute show and benefit at Irving Plaza, New York City, with The Slits' Ari Up on the bill, while Belfast punks Stiff Little Fingers recorded a 'Strummerville' tribute for their *Guitar and Drum LP*, one of the first of many tribute tracks from bands around the world.

On February 12, 2005, Class 47 railway locomotive 47828 was named Joe Strummer, its nameplates unveiled by his widow, Lucinda, in a ceremony at Bristol Temple Meads station. That July 22, she also unveiled a plaque on the house in Pentonville, Newport, where he lived from 1973 to '74 and made his first foray into recorded music, 'Crummy Bum Blues'. Later that year, Bob Dylan played a shortened 'London Calling' for an encore at Brixton Academy, while Springsteen would go on to cover 'Coma Girl' and Pearl Jam would tackle fellow Mescaleros song 'Arms Aloft'.

In June 2009, there was a further Springsteen tribute, this time with the E Street Band, opening a set at Hyde Park, London, with 'London Calling', while five years later he opened his 'High Hopes' tour set with 'Clampdown'. Then, The Pogues, Badly Drawn Boy, Frank Turner, Roots Manuva, Billy Bragg and KT Tunstall topped the bill at August 2012's Strummer of Love festival in Somerset, a one-off three-day celebration of the singer's 60th birthday and the 10th anniversary of his death, including contributions from Don Letts and Glen Matlock.

In conjunction with the Strummer estate, there's even a guitar manufactured in his honour, the Joe Strummer Tribute Telecaster, an attempt at recreating the road-worn finish of his 1966 Telecaster, which he used until his death. Meanwhile, in November 2009, Tonara in Sardinia dedicated a street to him, and barely three years later he had a plaza named in his honour in the Spanish city of Granada, Strummer having lived in Almeria in the '80s and '90s.

Closer to his former stomping ground, in June 2013 a mural of Strummer was unveiled on the corner of Portobello Road and Blenheim Crescent, attended by a number of friends, including Mick Jones. Also that year, another mural outside Niagara bar in Manhattan's East Village, New York City, was destroyed due to construction, but it was replaced, a new version unveiled that September, with Jones again on hand.

Mick Jones

'I liked Mick. He was the closest thing to an actual rock star that punk ever threw up. He looked great on stage, sang compelling songs in a cool Rasta Sta-Prest voice, and played a guitar that got inside your head via your arse.'

Barry Cain, '77 Sulphate Strip

Looking back on his time with The Clash and subsequent dismissal from a band he co-founded for 2005's *Viva Joe Strummer* documentary, Mick Jones said, 'It took a long time to get over it, for all of us. But we all did and became friends soon after. We didn't get back together again but became great friends and remained so throughout the whole time. We didn't feel the need to get back together again, which is probably a good thing.'

What's more, Jones was the member who had the most success straight after leaving. After his exit, he initially became a founding member of General Public with members of The Beat and The Specials but, while listed in the credits of the band's 1984 debut album *All the Rage*, he left part-way through the recording and was replaced by Kevin White, whose picture appears on the back cover. He did play on several tracks though, including the single 'Tenderness'.

In 1984 Jones formed Big Audio Dynamite with Don Letts, who directed various Clash videos and went on to make 2000's Clash documentary, *Westway to the World*. Letts said of the band, 'Big Audio Dynamite's secret was really rock'n'roll guitar, reggae basslines, sort of hip-hop drums, and the whole dialogue-sampling thing that was going before they could slap a lawsuit on you.'

The band's début LP, *This is Big Audio Dynamite* was released in 1985, singles 'Medicine Show' and 'E=MC2' both becoming UK hits. Letts told John Robb: 'After The Clash split, Mick was moping around. I went round, saying, 'Mick, what the fuck are you going to do? You're not going to be a milkman.' Next thing I know, he asked me to join the band, and I said, 'Mick, I can't play anything'. He said, 'Don, it's punk – come on!' I said, 'I've got a few ideas up my sleeve''.

'I was thrust into the whole sample thing from watching movies and things. We were probably the first band to have a hit with major sampling. I couldn't play an instrument. It was the punk rock way to create or recreate sound. I didn't write a lot of the lyrics. I wrote most of the songs with Mick. I had a filmic approach, more Nic Roeg, more abstract. It's the people who know the least about an art who come up with the best ideas. They don't know the restrictions. I was always surrounded by people who can play instruments, but their ideas sucked. I'd be on stage with BAD with these keyboards that had coloured stickers on them. And I didn't care. I'd lift up the keyboard, show the audience, basically saying, 'If you've got the balls, fucking come here and do it!''

For Big Audio Dynamite's second album, *No. 10, Upping Street*, Jones reunited with Strummer to write several songs, Strummer also co-producing. This reunion didn't last though, the pair not working together again for some time. But in October 1986, Jones and Strummer featured in the first Q magazine, interviewer Chris Salewicz looking back 'over 10 years of back-stabbing and blurred ideals'.

Salewicz recalled a previous visit to Sarm West Studios, Notting Hill, in July '85, when Jones told him, 'At first Joe and I used to write everything together. Then we wrote sitting in separate parts of the same room. Then we got to the stage where we were sending lyrics over to each other through our manager.' Yet barely a year on, the pair were working together again on the second BAD album, at Trident Studios, Wardour Street. Salewicz wrote, 'For those who believed in some sense of divine justice, the success of BAD was heartening news, combating the preposterous ill-judgement that led to Mick Jones being unceremoniously dumped from The Clash in August 1983, on a charge of being 'ideologically unsound' (essentially meaning he was no longer in line with manager Bernie Rhodes' spurious left-wing ideals).' But in philosophical mode, Jones told the writer, 'Not many people get a second chance, like I've had. I see this as an opportunity to avoid making all those mistakes again. I won't throw any wobblers this time, though sometimes I'm still a bit late!'

At that stage, BAD had scored top-30 hits with 'E=MC2' and 'Medicine Show' from a successful first album. What started as cult appreciation grew way beyond that, and the LP had soon sold more than 100,000 copies. By the time they'd completed their first UK tour they were, as Salewicz put it, 'widely considered the most innovative of all contemporary British groups'. Then, in Trident Studios on June 26 – Jones' 31st birthday – Strummer turned up, just as his former bandmate was recording his new album, telling Salewicz, 'We need some rock'n'roll'. The writer described Strummer then as an 'integrated, whole human being, as opposed to the man rent apart by internal crises that he had been a year previously'.

Salewicz felt, 'The pair were always a double act ... and the very real pain both went through for two years from that day in August 1983 undoubtedly made them stronger, better human beings, in addition to being unquestionably major artists.'

Days after Salewicz and Strummer's drunken night out, it appeared that Strummer and Jones bumped into each other in the street – the first time they'd seen other since Jones was fired. Strummer told him what he'd realised, and 'a reconciliation of sorts was achieved.'

With work on the first BAD LP soon complete, Jones and his family flew to Nassau for a holiday, Strummer getting on a plane and going looking for him on the island, intent on persuading him to rejoin The Clash. Salewicz wrote that 'Plain-speaking has always been one of Joe's commendable virtues. Sometimes however, a measure of tact could well be used to dilute this. This does not seem to have been particularly in evidence when Jones played him in Nassau the tapes of *This is Big Audio Dynamite*. 'I don't like it. There aren't any songs. You need me,' was his response. Not necessarily the best way to re-establish a working alliance.'

But in subsequent months the friendship strengthened and old bandmate Paul Simonon, by then busy as the painter he had trained to be at Byam-Shaw Art College, also returned to the fold. In the 'Medicine Show' video, both made cameos as Southern cops, 'Strummer simulating down to the last grunt the part of Rod Steiger in *In the Heat of the Night*,' as Salewicz put it. Meanwhile, Jones added guitar to, and helped restructure, 'Love Kills', Strummer's single from the *Sid and Nancy* movie.

Salewicz continued, 'One lunchtime in Wardour Street, Strummer ran into Don Letts on his way into Trident, and together they joined the *10 Upping Street* sessions.' Strummer never left, taking on the role of co-producer and helping out with lyrics, approaching the task 'with the obsessive loving dedication of old, working 36-hour stretches, as Mick Jones was, and sleeping on the floor or under the old grand piano.' Strummer told Salewicz, 'Once the rest of BAD realised I don't get involved with anything unless I do it to the max, it worked out fine.'

Salewicz added, 'The situation was mutually advantageous. Strummer's creative block vanished and songs started to pour out of him. Of his part in the process, Strummer said, 'I've figured why all the BAD songs are a minute too long – because so many of the parts are programmed on to tape, and no one remembers to stop them. I'm getting them to roughen up the sound and lose that Radio 2 tendency Mick has. Mick isn't going to know what's happened when this record gets going in the mix.'

They mixed the album in New York, working 'for 20 days and nights before I went to a bar,' according to Strummer. 'It went even greater once Joe was on board', added Jones. 'Everything sounds so great. I can't remember a time when I've felt so over-awed or was so happy with what I was doing'. From there, Strummer flew back to London and the next evening to Almeria, southern Spain, to join the cast of Alex Cox's film *Straight to Hell*.

Had Strummer joined BAD at that point? 'Are you kidding? The BAD LP's brilliant because me and Mick were involved, but I'm going to make an album of my own when I've got something really good. I'm just about ready, and I'm looking forward to working

3

with Mick again, because we're going to do it together. It'll be called *Throwdown* and it'll be completely the opposite of everything else that's being made now – just three instruments and the cheapest studio. Everyone'll hate it, except the hipsters and flipsters. I just promise to make a good record when I can, and not to tour, and not to foist any shit on the public. And never to make another video. It's the performance and the content that counts. I'm 33, and no offence, but I don't want to be Huey Lewis. It ain't rock'n'roll anymore. It's just wallpaper. Now is the time when you've got to look for things, as it was in the days of beatniks existing in straight society, when the good stuff was hard to find, but was even more valuable when you discovered it.'

While Strummer was out of the picture from there, Big Audio Dynamite's third album, *Tighten Up, Vol. 88*, featured a cover painted by Paul Simonon. Yet following its release, Jones developed chicken pox and pneumonia and spent several months in hospital, going on to release just one more Big Audio Dynamite LP, 1989's *Megatop Phoenix*, before a revamp, returning as Big Audio Dynamite II for 1990's *Kool-Aid* then 1991's *The Globe*, from which they enjoyed an international No.1 hit with 'Rush', topping the US Billboard rock charts and seeing similar success in Australia and New Zealand. That was also the year The Clash finally got their first UK No.1, with the Levi's ad-inspired 'Should I Stay or Should I Go' single.

In 1990, Jones also featured on the Aztec Camera hit, 'Good Morning Britain', duetting with long-time Clash fan Roddy Frame. By 1994, the BAD line-up had undergone anopther reshuffle, the album *Higher Power* released under the name Big Audio, followed a year later by *F-Punk* under the original band name. One more LP followed in 1997, *Entering a New Ride*, an internet-only release due to a dispute with their label, Radioactive Records, although a successful reunion finally followed in January 2011, with a UK Spring tour including two sell-outs at Shepherd's Bush Empire before a number of festival dates, among them Coachella and Lollapalooza appearances in America, shows in Serbia, Spain and Japan, and a June visit to Glastonbury.

Big Audio Dynamite – an appreciation

When you listen back to Big Audio Dynamite's first album, it's no wonder Joe Strummer lost confidence in his own ability in his 'lost years'. Here was a brutal reminder that Mick Jones wasn't just the fella who turned up late and pranced around 'like Elizabeth Taylor in a filthy mood'. I guess we knew that, deep down. From the moment The Clash came together, it was Jonesy's musical know-how that laid the foundation upon which his songwriting partner could showcase that impassioned delivery and vital turn of phrase. But it must have hurt Joe to find himself floundering around with a broken format while his old mate so effectively set out on the next phase of his musical journey.

He'd done it before when The Delinquents cast him out, Jones taking himself back home and starting again – as partly recalled in 1978's 'Stay Free'. This time, too, he focused and raised his game, leading to major commercial success and a fair amount of critical esteem during a period when the old industry was struggling to adapt and Strummer seemed unaware of how to tackle it.

After something of a false start with Top

Risk Action Company (T.R.A.C.) – including a commendable attempt to give heroin addict Topper Headon a chance to get clean and return to the party – Jones got back to the drawing board, keeping Leo Williams but bringing in old pal Don Letts plus Dan Donovan and Greg Roberts: the first fruits of that alliance showcased on October '85's *This is Big Audio Dynamite*. And what a statement it was, albeit a slow-boiler commercially, taking until April '86 to make ground, its eventual success coming on the back of the wondrous 'E=MC2'.

It's hard to get into my own mindset at 17, hearing that LP for the first time, taking in its visionary samples and loops, but a sense of euphoria still grabs me on opening track, 'Medicine Show', in retrospect not so far off where Jones was headed on *Combat Rock*. And the experimentation worked more times than it failed, not least the Sergio Leone snatches. What's more, while Strummer was seen as the wordsmith, lines like 'If you ain't ill, it'll fix your car' gave me hope.

As for 'E=MC2', it's as fresh now as on early listens, the borrowing from Nic Roeg's *Performance* being inspired. I might have sequenced 'The Bottom Line' as the opening track, a worthy show-starter, with Jones' anti-poverty comment welcome in an era when music couldn't afford to be about escapism if it was to remain relevant. No escapism maybe – but cool all the same. And while I considered Jones a reluctant frontman, Don Letts – a non-player thrown in the deep end – was on hand, crucial to the image and the aesthetic. Like Simonon in The Clash, I suppose.

As for the show-stopper, 'BAD' was close to six minutes yet every inch a winner, with a groove replicated in the clubs five years later at the hands of bands like The Farm. I was also partial to the B-side 'This is Big Audio Dynamite' when I bought 'E=MC2', a mash-up of the LP's finest moments (but no 'Stars on 45'). I'd seen the future and I was impressed. And while it's easy now to snigger at the baseball caps, hip-hop threads and layers of loops and technology, writing it all off as a fad, if you check out the band playing 'BAD' on ITV's *Night Network*, you'll see that here was a band with balls on stage as well as in the studio. Jones' guitar was still very much in evidence, and us old punks were ready to move into clubland anyway. What's more, he still created killer hooks and melodies.

By the time of *No.10 Upping Street* in late '86, Strummer was on board, albeit just for the time being, yet that second album didn't seem to grab me the same way. Joe co-produced and co-wrote five of the songs, but the previous dynamic seemed to have been disrupted. Jones and Letts' opener, first single 'C'mon Every Beatbox', worked well, not least that Bo Diddley-like riff over the drum machine, but the overall feel of the LP soon dated. Of the Strummer/Jones tracks, 'Beyond the Pale' – Mick's pro-immigration tale, telling of his grandparents' escape to London for a better life – and second single 'V.Thirteen' might have made for quality Clash B-sides, but what the best songs gained in structure they lacked in fire, the element Strummer had boasted would take the band to another level. If this was Jones expanding on the formula of the debut LP, more technically-adept in what he set out to achieve, I felt he'd lost the fresh, experimental vibe. And while LP finale and third single 'Sightsee MC' was a step in the right direction, its John Barry sample just made me want to dig out the original *From Russia with Love* soundtrack instead.

familiar but still impressive, 'The Battle of All Saints Road'. In fact, Letts' 'Wah Do Dem' section suggested they were having lots of fun, while 'Hip, Neck and Thigh' channeled the spirit of Buddy Holly. Then the first single 'Just Play the Music' saw us out, the most radio-friendly number showing Jones take a pop-soul turn and proving he hadn't lost his touch. It cried out for the Irish Horns, mind – the brass being a little too sequenced.

One more album followed from the first incarnation, 1989's *Megatop Phoenix*, made for old time's sake with Bill Price at Konk Studios, Jones somewhat rejuvenated after a touch-and-go chicken pox and pneumonia scare. By then he was properly embracing the emerging acid house scene, re-examining his long-hair psychedelic experimental years, in the way Strummer embraced a similar scene half a dozen years later and set himself back on track. *Rewind* led the charge this time: Letts to the fore, the creative vibe at play again on 'Union Jack', visionary in its focus, taking sampling up a level. Here was fusion at its finest, that track leading neatly into acid-dance-rocker and second single, 'Contact', including its Who 'Can't Explain' riff. It led to out-on-the-floor territory on the splendid 'Dragon Town', Jones' vocal supremely suited to his new direction as we made our way across

Strummer had returned to the desert by the time of 1988's *Tighten Up Vol. 88*, by which time Jones and co. seemed to be looking for hits but were prepared to take the project in new directions too, as seen in the transition from the promising 'Applecart' to rock'n'roll tribute 'Esquerita'. There are far less samples and synth touches, and tracks like second single, 'Other 99', showed Mick at his melodic best again, throwing the original BAD premise to the elements. There was little in the feel of a Trojan Records tribute, despite the title, but I liked the oddly-

the floor towards lead single, 'James Brown' and its host of fevered references to the Godfather of Soul. As for the samples, we had everything from *A Matter of Life and Death* to *Listen with Mother*, via *The Great Escape*, *Stalag 123* and *Withnail and I*, with George Formby, Alfred Hitchcock, Bernard Cribbins, The Pretty Things, The Rolling Stones and Noel Coward thrown in. Audacious.

The following year the revitalised Jones re-emerged on the limited-edition UK-only eight-track LP, *Kool-Aid*, now trading as Big Audio Dynamite II, joined by Nick Hawkins, Gary Stonadge and Chris Kavanagh, who would stick around until 1995's *F-Punk*. Five of those songs were reworked for the next worldwide release, *The Globe*, released in the summer of '91 on the back of The Clash's posthumous UK No.1 with a re-released 'Should I Stay or Should I Go', at the height of the Madchester indie/dance scene. In a way it's hard to separate those albums, but I'd say that, between the 13 tracks represented overall, this was their finest in-your-face pop period, every bit as much a statement as the BAD debut six years earlier.

Startling opener 'Change of Atmosphere', complete with 'Baba O'Riley' sample, was reworked for a big hit outside the UK as 'Rush' on an album seen as Jones' most diverse outing yet, his original stop-gap model of acoustic ballads, acid-dance techno-rock and electronica finely honed and finally appreciated. Tracks like the infectious 'party time' title-track 'The Globe' (the yelp on 'Should I Stay Or Should I Go' met with a 'bless you') made major headway, and the latest BAD combo clearly were having fun, tapping into rave culture to great effect. But it wasn't just about hits, Jones bearing his soul again on the powerful 'Can't Wait'. All those years after 'I'm

Not Down', here he was, peddling 'better times' optimism, his coke days behind him, rediscovering a lust for life.

And while the use of samples is inspired, from Harold Melvin on *Kool Aid*'s 'Kickin' In' (a remix of 'Free' from the *Flashback* soundtrack, unfortunately left off *The Globe*) to Phil Collins on the picture-sharp 'Innocent Child', the songs are still there, with new arrival Gary Stonadge proving a worthy co-writer for Jones on this evidence. While certain aspects of *The Globe* work better than others, I prefer the studio version of 'Can't Wait'.

After that, it was all too easy to suggest the band had lost their dynamite, following a rebrand as Big Audio, and there are indications that 1994's hour-long *Higher Power* implied the old format was wearing thin for Jones. The band now included Andre Shapps and DJ Mickey Custance, with guitar riffs replacing some of the hip-hop like touches. But we were ready for that, and 'Harrow Road' seemed to signpost a new direction for the likes of Blur, that track later given a mighty ska remix (included on the *Planet BAD* compilation). It didn't help that sole 45 'Looking For A Song' seemed to be Jones admitting how hard it was to find inspiration. Yet his melodic hook was still intact, as seen on at least half of the album, not least 'Modern Stoneage Blues'. I quite like 'Slender Loris' and 'Moon' too (was the latter's F.R. David riff another way of suggesting, 'Words don't come easy'?). 'Lucan' (was Mick contemplating a Joe-like disappearing act?) seemed to channel Pink Floyd rather than P-Funk and 'Light Up My Life' suggested a content family man had more important priorities than cutting reviews. Album-closer 'Hope' was pure Faces. All fine by me, but I'm not quite sure who the band-leader was appealing to. Under the name 'Mick Jones' it would have made more sense. His new direction didn't seem to fit the mood of a buying public, either side of the Atlantic, and you wondered if nine years was his maximum band term.

If you felt that was the least BAD album in Jones' post-Clash catalogue, what about the following year's *F-Punk?* With its cover boldly referencing *London Calling* and Elvis' 1956 debut, Jones' first LP for Radioactive saw the name revert to Big Audio Dynamite, but there was little hint of the early albums. At first, Jones seemed to know where he was headed, with an energetic, punchy start and year zero approach on 'I Turned Out a Punk', grabbing the attention in wryly autobiographical mode. But with the benchmark down, they meandered from there on, getting no closer than 'Psycho Wing', with a Television Personalities meets The Who vibe, the guitars to the fore. Around half a dozen songs roughly fit the bill, but there's a feel of a demo, and for the first time all bar two songs are just credited to Jones (one of those with his daughter), again suggesting more of a solo venture.

One more album followed – 1997's free, download-only release *Entering a New Ride*, Jones' response to a fallout with Radioactive, and one of the earliest Internet-distributed albums. The Beat's Ranking Roger was heavily featured, with only Jones, Shapps and Hawkins still around from *F-Punk*. If anything, this is more *F-Punk* than its predecessor, not least 'Taking You to Another Dimension', hinting at The Strokes. Dare I suggest this is what *Cut the Crap* might have sounded like if Strummer's original vision had been realised?

There's certainly an air of a band determined to prove themselves. In fact, the opener sounds more like a reunion of the original BAD. There's a euphoric post-dance feel across the tracks, and maybe it should have been named *Self-Preservation Society* in honour of *The Italian Job*'s coach party chorus. Some of the vocals seem like Jones was holding bonding sessions on the terraces at Loftus Road, or at least back-from- the-pub singalongs. But it works, the rave/dance undercurrents pulling it all together in the manner of The Prodigy or Underworld, in what proved a better epitaph than the previous album would have: Jonesy quitting while he was ahead before re-immersing himself in various Clash reflection projects then starting the new century with old pal Tony James in Carbon/Silicon, not returning with BAD until 2011.

After '97, a couple of compilations reflected on the whole adventure. And what a 12-year ride it had been. Whether Jones was ever likely to get back on board with Strummer remained a talking point, and I felt it was almost inevitable. Joe hit top form with The Mescaleros, but there was at least one Strummer/Jones offshoot project pencilled in.

That's beside the point though. BAD were clearly influential, with so many new bands taking on their vision and coming up with their own variation on this new rock-dance model. That in itself had its drawbacks, but I like to think of Jones' outfit as an influence on the likes of Gorillaz rather than the EMFs of that late 1980s/early 90s scene. All in all, Mick Jones can be proud of his output from that 1985 BAD debut onwards, and many of these songs remain with us. Follow the line, and you'll see his progress towards the genial elder statesman we now feel we know. What's more, he never lost that knack for knocking out a great tune, taking on board the best influences around and reinterpreting them, from the 1950s right through to electronica and dance fusion, embracing new technologies as he went but never forgetting the power of the song beneath it all.

Into the new millennium with Mick Jones

'Maybe we'll make some money by playing live dates, or maybe it'll come in another way. We've gotta eat, you know. We have three albums, and they're all available on the Internet.'
Mick Jones to Tom Lanham, Magnet, 2007

Jones had always kept his hand in as a producer, going right back to 1981's LP by then-partner, Ellen Foley, *Spirit of St Louis*, co-writings songs for the album with Strummer and Tymon Dogg, with The Clash and The Blockheads playing on the record. That same year Jones also co-produced former Mott the Hoople front-man Ian Hunter's *Short Back'n'Sides* LP, with David Bowie associate Mick Ronson providing guitar and vocals on several songs. And Jones also produced Theatre of Hate's debut LP *Westworld* in 1982, then *Aria of the Devil* for the same Kirk Brandon-led outfit.

Then, 20 years later, in 2002, he was back in the public eye, producing The Libertines' debut album, *Up the Bracket*, and its follow-up, a No.1 in 2004, critical and commercial success, *The Libertines*, plus lead singer/guitarist Pete Doherty's next band Babyshambles' first album, 2005 top-10 hit, *Down in Albion*.

It was in 2002 that Jones teamed up with his former London SS colleague, Generation X and Sigue Sigue Sputnik guitarist Tony James, forming Carbon/Silicon, described by Creation founder Alan McGee as 'The Stones jamming with a laptop' on account of their embrace of music technology. They toured on both sides of the Atlantic and performed a number of anti-fascist benefit concerts, with their LPs *A.T.O.M*, *Western Front* and *The Crackup Suite* all made available online for free, the band encouraging fans to share their music on P2P networks, while allowing audio and video-taping of shows.

Talking to Tom Lanham for online magazine *Magnet* in 2007, an enthused Jones said, 'The great thing about what we're doing is the minute you finish your track, you can put it out. You can upload it. Everybody can hear what you're doing right now, with no six-week wait or whatever. Tony [James] is really big on it. He thinks it's the future, and in a way, I agree with him. 'MP Free' was our first single, and that's also the name of our label. I think file-sharing is great. Just like I used to collect bootlegs of the bands I liked, and also Clash bootlegs when they came along. There were many, and I don't think they did anything but enhance our reputation. They did us no harm at all. People who think they should be suing their best customers need to rethink that.'

But how, Lanham asked, did they plan on getting paid? 'Well, we haven't completely worked this out yet. But we're hoping to have a regular release in the future. And we're gonna come and play.' And they did. On seven consecutive Friday nights in early 2008, Carbon/Silicon played a series of gigs at the Inn on the Green, under the Westway between Ladbroke Grove and Portobello Road, their special guests including Topper Headon, former Clash associate Tymon Dogg, and Sex Pistols pair Paul Cook and Glenn Matlock.

Jones' 21st-century credits also included guitar and vocals on a track by Los Fabulosos Cadillacs, a score for Nick Mead's contemporary dance film, *Dice Life – the Random Mind of Luke Rhinehart*, and stage appearances with Primal Scream in 2007 on '(White Man) In Hammersmith Palais', later reuniting with Paul Simonon to play on 2010 Gorillaz album *Plastic Beach* and playing live with the band, including headline shows at 2010's Coachella, Glastonbury and Internacional de Benicassim Festivals.

A year later, he collaborated with Pete Wylie and members of The Farm as The Justice Tonight Band, promoting awareness of the Hillsborough Justice Campaign for various shows, and collaborated with The Wallflowers as a guitarist/backing vocalist on 2012 album *Glad All Over*. He was a featured guest on Rachid Taha's *Zoom* album in 2013, along with Brian Eno, the pair also joining Taha's tour.

It was that year that Jones got behind The Clash's 2013 box-set, *Sound System*, Jones, letting on that he had no further plans to work on the band's music, having also spoken on the issue during The Clash's Rock and Roll Hall of Fame induction a decade earlier.

By the time of an interview with John Hind in *The Guardian* in August 2016, with an emphasis on his vegetarianism, Jones talked about his mother and how she'd been based in America for half a century at that point, based in Ironwood, Michigan, where he occasionally visited.

Meanwhile, on November 11, 2017, Jones was closer to his old band's spiritual home, on a stage under the Westway for a benefit show tied in with the 15th anniversary of his good friend Joe Strummer's final London gig, at Acton Town Hall, that fabled night when Strummer's guitar hero stepped up to join The Mescaleros.

That night he made a number of emotional guest appearances with a band called the Rotten Hill Gang, as well as Clash tribute band Take the 5th, and the Portobello Love Choir at another Fire Brigades Union (FBU) benefit gig, this one at the Maxilla in Ladbroke Grove, London W10, in the shadow of gutted Grenfell Tower (its survivors being beneficiaries on the night), so close to where The Clash story had started 40-plus years before. And this too was a big night, with long-time associate Tymon Dogg also delivering a short set, Chris Salewicz reading from his 2006 Strummer biography, and *Rude Boy* actor Ray Gange DJing.

Jones played five songs, four of them Strummer's, including 'Jimmy Jazz', 'London's Burning' and the 101'ers 'Keys to Your Heart'. Collared for an interview by Gregg McDonald, filming that night, the 62-year-old said, 'It seems very natural for me to come out; I only come out for special occasions. I'm retired really. But yeah, it was important. It has symbolism maybe, this part of the Westway. There's a nice connection between the past and the present. I can't believe how fast time flies. The last few weeks I've been thinking about it, to tell you the truth, and how fast it's gone. And how I miss Joe. That's why I played Joe's songs tonight. I wanted to do that.'

Paul Simonon

'You could tell the Clash were art-school punks from the start, what with those shirts stencilled with slogans and that paint-splashed bass guitar.'
Sean O'Hagan, The Guardian, 2008

Despite claiming in a post-Clash interview to be occupied by paintbrushes, motorbikes and books on bull-fighting, Paul found time to appear on Bob Dylan's *Down in the Groove* album in 1988, taking part in a session also involving former Sex Pistols guitarist Steve Jones. He later resumed full-time musical service with Havana 3am, releasing a self-titled LP – recorded in Japan – with them in 1991, leaving two years later. But work as an artist was starting to take precedence, his two worlds occasionally coming together: he designed covers for Mick Jones' Big Audio Dynamite LP, *Tighten Up Vol. 88* and the first of his Damon Albarn collaborations, The Good, The Bad and The Queen, also playing bass with that band. Simonon then featured on Albarn's Gorillaz's third album, *Plastic Beach*, joining his former Clash bandmate Jones in the group on their tie-in world tour.

The youngest Clash band member was barely in his 30s when that final split came about in 1986, yet it was his work as an artist – Simonon's first love – that finally coloured his direction, leading in time to several gallery shows, alongside those occasional music projects. In 2011, he spent time aboard Greenpeace vessel *Esperanza* incognito as 'Paul the assistant cook', campaigning against Arctic oil drilling in Greenland, earning two weeks in a Greenland jail after illegally boarding a Cairn oil rig. He later joined Damon Albarn and other members of The Good, the Bad and The Queen in a London show celebrating Greenpeace's 40th anniversary.

Simonon's passion for painting began as a child, spending a lot of time in his father's studio, often sleeping there. There, surrounded by books and pictures pinned to the walls, he first encountered the works of 19th and 20th century masters, from impressionists to cubists and beyond. Introduced to an artist friend of his father's, he assisted him on projects at an inner-city London school, learning the basics of using paint, supplementing those skills by teaching himself at home. Taking up a scholarship at the Byam Shaw School of Art in Kensington (later part of Central St Martin's College of Art and Design) he left before his studies ended to play with The Clash, but on days off when on tour continued to visit museums and galleries.

As well as his love of late 19th century French modernist painting, which took him to the islands of French Polynesia on the trail of Paul Gauguin, his painting has been heavily influenced by 20th century realism, particularly the work of the American Ashcan school and Kitchen sink school of painters of 1950s post-War Britain, specifically documentation of working-class living conditions.

In 2015's *Wot no Bike* exhibition at the ICA Nash and Brandon Rooms, he exhibited a series of new oil on canvas paintings depicting his own everyday personal effects, including biker paraphernalia such as jackets, boots, helmets, and gloves, alongside cigarette packets and books, his personal exploration of British subculture and counterculture in the post-war decades. To accompany the exhibition, he published a limited edition hardback publication of the same name, featuring 24 of his paintings.

In an in-depth interview with Simonon for *The Guardian* in March 2008, Sean O'Hagan went into detail about how the former Clash bass player had returned to art, and how, with a solo show opening in London's West End, his figurative paintings were now expected to fetch up to £30,000 each.

Meeting outside Westbourne Park tube station, Simonon walked O'Hagan to his studio underneath the Westway, and when asked what it was like to walk through his 'own history and his own mythology' every time he goes to work, responded, 'Most of the time, I don't really think about it. But I guess it's kind of poetic that this is where the Clash started out and this is where I've ended up.'

More than 30 years after his band took off, he described himself as 'a painter who occasionally dabbles in music', even though his most recent bout of 'dabbling' had led to a No.2 album through that Damon Albarn-orchestrated supergroup, The Good, the Bad and the Queen. He said at the time that project was 'done and dusted', but later revealed the group were in negotiations to play a benefit for the re-ignited Rock Against Racism campaign, exactly three decades after the Victoria Park event that helped nail The Clash's colours to the anti-racism message.

In fact, that album was certified gold within a week of its release, and followed two UK hit singles, October 2006's 'Herculean' (No.22) and January 2007's 'Kingdom of Doom' (No.20), while the band's appearance at the Love Music Hate Racism Carnival at Victoria Park, Hackney, on April 27th, 2008, also featuring Mick Jones, the Buzzcocks and The Libertines.

Simonon told O'Hagan, 'I can dip in and out of music when I feel like it, but it's not my life any more. There was a point after the whole intensity of The Clash finally subsided when I just found that painting grounded me in a way that music didn't.'

He'd been painting seriously since 1986, when he returned from a stint in LA and was startled by the British weather, telling his interviewer, 'I saw the beauty in it for the first time – the clouds, the rain, the cold and even the grey skies. It suddenly seemed rich compared to the sameness of Los Angeles. I went out in the rain and drew the gasworks by the canal. That was the turning point.'

He also started visiting museums again with his sketchbook, drawing 'faces, hands, feet, whatever took my fancy', and in 2002 had a show, *From Hammersmith to Greenwich*, at a gallery in Green Park, featuring several big London riverscapes, each selling for around £4,000.

His interview for The Guardian was to help publicise an event at Thomas Williams Fine Art on Old Bond Street, Simonon unveiling a series of figurative paintings inspired by the bullfights he witnessed in Madrid in the summer of 2003, as well as still lives. The interest in the show was reflected in the prices too, ranging from £5,000 to £30,000 for the larger canvases. Thomas Williams told O'Hagan, 'Paul is not in any way a dilettante. He has the dedication of the true artist. He lives and breathes art and is constantly thinking and talking about painting. We already have an incredible amount of interest in the show. As far as I'm concerned, his musical career was a brief interlude in his artistic one. He's an artist. It's the music that's the aberration, not the painting. Paul's not a conceptualist who parades his intellectual pretensions. He really belongs to an older English tradition, to Augustus John and the Edwardians.'

O'Hagan described Simonon, 52 at the time, as 'always the most dapper member of the group,' and he 'remains a snappy dresser, decked out today in a tailored coat, pinstripe suit and silk scarf. When he smiles, you can see traces of his younger self, the angular cheekbones and sullen good looks that made him punk's premier pin-up. He has long since shed the rude-boy attitude that was a prerequisite of those angry times, but still looks like he could hold his own should the circumstances arise. These days, though, people tend to want to shake his hand rather than throw a punch at him, like they did back when punk gatecrashed the mainstream following the Sex Pistols' expletive-strewn appearance on prime-time TV in the summer of 1977.'

Simonon told O'Hagan, 'It was intense back then. People wanting to fight us, jumping on stage to punch us. If you had short hair and looked at all like a punk, you wouldn't get served in many pubs. Then, you had the Teds, who really took it all personally. I remember walking down Shaftesbury Avenue with a girl and seeing this blur of movement out of the corner of my eye. It was this big Teddy Boy running through the traffic to have a go. Mad.'

Reflecting on what he saw as his 'non-musician background in the days of punk, he added, 'I always had the painting to fall back on. That's what pulled me through the so-called wilderness years. I never wanted to go back and relive the glory days, I just want to keep moving forward. That's what I took from punk. Keep going. Don't look back.'

Chris Salewicz, in his Joe Strummer biography, *Redemption Song*, described Simonon as 'essentially quite a shy bloke, but also a bit of a prankster', telling O'Hagan, 'Paul was a bit of a bad boy back then, but that may just have been what was required at the time. The way he managed to move from rock'n'roll back to painting with such ease is quite remarkable when you consider how diametrically opposed the two are in terms of artistic endeavour. Then again, he's always been self-contained; someone who, you suspect, is very much at ease with himself, and with the solitary nature of painting. He's definitely a bit of a thinker.'

Describing the scene at his sub-Westway studio, O'Hagan wrote, 'Simonon's studio is brightly lit, cluttered but comfortable, a pair of two-bar electric fires throwing out some much-needed heat. There are newly finished canvases stacked in rows, tables full of reference material – postcards, books on bullfighting and art, holy pictures. One wall is partially obscured by stacks of boxes from his recent house move. A bottle of Whyte & Mackay whisky and a jar of instant coffee stand side-by-side by a kettle for those winter mornings when he needs a kickstart.

'Underneath the light streaming in from the high windows stands an easel on which a nearly-completed painting rests. It depicts a huge bullring and a parade of toreadors. Like his Thames paintings, the scene has been painted from life, and from somewhere high above the action. Simonon is essentially a figurative painter, concerned as much with the application of paint as with the subject. It is obvious from the work, and the real sense that this is a working studio, visited daily, that he is not just another rock star who paints as a hobby.'

O Hagan added, 'As a teenage art student, Simonon had little interest in being contemporary or cutting edge in his painting, preferring the likes of Constable and Sickert to Warhol and De Kooning. He won a scholarship to Byam Shaw but lasted a year-and-a-half, dismayed by the teachers' total espousal of American abstraction. He points to a painting on the wall of his studio, an angular urban landscape that, were there elongated figures in it, might have been painted by Edward Burra. 'That was the last painting I did at art school. The students loved it, but the teachers hated it. I'd had enough by then.''

Simonon was seen as the 'conceptualist' in The Clash camp, and as O'Hagan put it, 'The one who paid most attention to the visuals, the image. He painted the backdrop to the Clash's rehearsal studio, and designed some of the later stage sets, including the dive-bombing Stukas that echoed their often-explosive performances.'

Explaining that approach, Simonon said, 'That was the art student in me trying to find a look that would make us stand apart from the Pistols. The Buzzcocks were very Mondrian, and we were Pollock. As a painter, though, I'm essentially old-fashioned. Conceptualism just doesn't do it for me. I love Walter Sickert, Samuel Palmer, Rubens and Constable. That's just the way I am. I love putting paint on canvas, getting lost in the process of painting.'

O'Hagan also revealed how Simonon had 'a passion for the sheer physicality of the job', explaining how he'd carried huge canvases up on to the roofs of various high buildings along the Thames and often had to rope them to railings to stop the wind carrying them off. Simonon added, 'I was on top of the Shell Mex building for weeks. I think I entered a trancelike state up there. A bit like Blake. Hours would go by and I'd suddenly realise I was bloody freezing.'

He also revealed how he'd been given access to a prime apartment overlooking the Thames by Jeffrey Archer, still a Tory MP then, staying for a week, adding, 'I think he got a bit pissed off with this hulking great bloody canvas in his kitchen every morning, but, I have to hand it to him, he didn't go back on his word and chuck me out.'

He reflected on his younger days painting toy soldiers on pieces of paper, musing, 'Whether I'm in a good or a bad mood, painting takes me out of myself. And I've realised lately it often resolves things for me.'

In late 2006, Simonon split up from his wife Tricia Ronane, embarking on a new relationship with their friend, Serena Rees, co-owner of Agent Provocateur, who was married to Joe Corre, her business partner and the son of Vivienne Westwood and Malcolm McClaren. He was unwilling to talk about his personal life in 2008, but stressed he was 'happy' and had a 'good relationship' with sons Louis, then 16, and Claude, then 14.

O'Hagan added, 'For all the domestic upheaval and constant flitting from place to place, Simonon seems to have come through remarkably unscathed. He is certainly the most grounded punk survivor I have met in a long time.' Simonon added, 'I suppose my upbringing made me resilient in some way. What I remember most, though, is that feeling of always being the new boy at school. That was kind of tough. I have absolutely no friends from school, no connections from back then. I was always moving on. I gained a certain independence from that experience. Funnily enough, all the members of the Clash had it, too. We all came from broken homes – even our manager, Bernie Rhodes.'

Simonon was 21 when he joined the Clash, and 31 when Strummer finally brought the band to a halt – Topper Headon and Mick Jones already long gone. He reflected to O'Hagan, it was 'a heightened state of alert throughout' and 'total life experience', 'working and living and being the Clash, 24-7'. Then, as suddenly as it had started, the 'heightened state of alert' ended, Simonon finding himself sat at home, bored and brooding, telling O'Hagan, 'It was a weird time. I guess I was a bit dazed. Bewildered. The thing was, Mick lived just around the corner and had formed Big Audio Dynamite. I'd see his tour bus heading off, and I wasn't going anywhere. It was tough, after all those years of the constant Clash agenda. That's really what sent me back to painting. It was the only thing that kept me sane.'

Reflecting on Strummer's sudden death in December 2002, he added, 'Me and Joe were tight, you know. We were very close throughout the early days, living on the street, sharing dole money. And then he stayed at my house a lot after the band broke up. So it was tough. Really tough. First, it's like you are shocked so much you don't even know you're in shock. Then, you have to find some way of making sense of it.' Had he made sense of it since? 'I think so. Yeah. Finding out that Joe had a congenital heart condition helped, in an odd way. I mean, it could have happened at any time along the way. It's great in a way that he crammed so much in. He used his allotted time to the full.'

He also revealed that he'd received a text message from Strummer the day before he died, saying, 'Come on, Paul. Give it a try. You might even like it,' referring to a possible Clash reunion for a one-off gig to celebrate their imminent induction into the Rock and Roll Hall of Fame. But he was having none of it. He added, 'Joe was up for it, and so was Mick and Topper, but I wasn't. I was the one who always said no. In this instance, I really didn't believe it was the right moment. A big corporate event like that, two grand a seat. Nah, that wasn't in the spirit of the Clash, was it?'

He did go to the ceremony though, to celebrate Joe Strummer's legacy and support his widow, Lucinda. He told O'Hagan, 'I wasn't comfortable, though. I just hate all those bloody awards ceremonies. There's too many of them and they really don't mean a lot to me. It's that looking back thing again. It's not what The Clash were ever about, and it's not what I'm about.'

In September 2003, Simonon made a far more personal tribute, a pilgrimage of sorts to the remote Hebridean isle of Raasay, where Strummer's ancestors came from, having been commissioned to paint Joe's grandmother's old house by the Scottish Herald. He was accompanied by Chris Salewicz, who recalled, 'It was absolutely extraordinary. We spent days finding this derelict cottage miles from nowhere in this stunningly beautiful setting. Then Paul carted this big canvas up there and started painting. Suddenly the heavens opened, and the wind started up and his boots are so waterlogged he's taken them off and he's painting barefoot on this canvas lashed to a big stone. He was like a madman on the deck of a ship in a storm. Just incredible.'

It was, Simonon told O'Hagan, 'a healing moment'. He continued painting there alone for a few days, then placed a Clash album inside the chimney breast of the old cottage, had a drink to toast absent friends, and rang Joe's cousin, Iain Gillies, based in Texas. 'I told him where I was, in this house that Joe's great, great, great-grandfather had built. We were both brought to tears. It was quite powerful, really. That put me at ease with a lot of stuff, helped me move on.'

Topper Headon

'When the band sacked me, I think it was like tough love in a way. I think they were hoping things would happen and I'd get myself together. It's said that they looked me up shortly after. I was still out there, using, so they couldn't get me back. I think they were hoping I'd get my act together, which I did ... about a year ago! It was like a comedown. It left such a hole in our lives. Not just the music, but the friendships, the life, everything. When it ground to a halt it was like, 'What do we do now?' And for me the depression after the band was intense. My answer to it - which wasn't an answer – was to take more drugs.'

Topper Headon, Viva Joe Strummer: The Clash and Beyond, 2005

Royalty disputes over 'Rock the Casbah', a battle with heroin addiction and a prison sentence ensured Topper Headon had little connection with his band-mates in the immediate years after his sacking from The Clash in 1982. Initially considered for Mick Jones' Big Audio Dynamite, he then played in short-lived group Samurai with Blockheads keyboard player and former Clash 'fifth member' Mickey Gallagher, former Pretenders bassist Pete Farndon, guitarist Henry Padovani (an original member of The Police) and vocalist Steve Allen (Deaf School).

He released a solo single for Mercury in 1985, tackling Gene Krupa instrumental, 'Drumming Man', and the following year the same label released an album, *Waking Up*, including the singles, 'Leave it to Luck' and 'I'll Give You Everything', his band including Gallagher. Recorded at Wessex Studios, Headon took on production duties alongside Jerry Green, who worked with The Clash on *Combat Rock*. The album was dedicated to Pete Farndon, who played on the first two Pretenders LPs before being sacked due to his own drugs problems. He died in April 1983, aged 30.

In a retrospective review for the

AllMusic website, Ralph Heibutzki wrote, 'Left to his own devices, Headon cut this sleek-sounding album with first-rate help from guitarist Bob Tench (of Jeff Beck fame), ex-Clash session keyboardist Mickey Gallagher, and vocalist Jimmy Helms, who sounds appropriately gritty without being overbearing. Musically, the album offers few surprises from The Clash's resident soul-jazz buff, falling comfortably into unhurried jazz, R&B, and soul grooves; just compare his relaxed take on the Stax classic 'Time Is Tight' to his former band's more urgent treatment. Highlights include the swirling pop-funk of 'Got to Keep on Going', one of several songs addressing Headon's addiction; 'Pleasure and Pain', a hard-hitting showcase for Tench; and 'Just Another Hit', whose poppy drive belies its clever metaphor for stardom, professional killing, and drug addiction. Unfortunately, Headon's lyrical agility is less spectacular elsewhere ... Such material may have been the best he could offer at the time but made no impression even among the old Clash crowd, an issue later rendered moot by Headon's 1987 imprisonment for drug-related offenses. In hindsight, *Waking Up* is best appreciated as enjoyable, but unspectacular, journeyman fodder.'

In the year he launched his solo career, Headon also produced albums for New York band Bush Tetras and in 1989 contributed drums to punk rock band Chelsea's *Underwraps*. Headon was extensively interviewed for Julien Temple's *Joe Strummer: The Future is Unwritten* 2007 documentary, relating his experiences with the band, his heroin addiction and band tensions. In January 2008 he performed with Mick Jones' Carbon/Silicon at London's Carbon Casino Club, *for* 'Train in Vain' then an encore of 'Should I Stay or Should I Go', his first appearance with Jones since 1982. Settling back in the Dover area, Headon's contribution to the band was described by American novelist Scott Kemore as 'tremendous', while 'his drumming remains an undiscovered treasure for too many.'

Rather poignantly, on 2005's *Viva Joe Strummer: The Clash and Beyond*, former Clash road manager Johnny Green mentioned how he was with Topper Headon when the pair heard about Joe Strummer's death on December 22nd, 2002. Green recalled, 'At that moment, Topper walked in the door and the phone rang. Topper was standing there. He picked the phone up. I realised it was Mick Jones on the phone. I watched Topper, a small man, just dissolve into his fitted carpet, and shout 'Oh no', turn round, throw the phone right at his mantlepiece and throw himself on his settee.'

Headon revealed in the same documentary, 'My first thought when I heard Joe had died was, 'Fuck, that should have been me.' If anyone in The Clash was gonna die a premature death ... I was lucky enough to see him play the Shepherd's Bush Empire a couple of months before his death, and it was great to see him. The only sad thing was that backstage he said, 'What's that you're drinking?' It was beer, and he knows I'm an alcoholic. I really wish that the last time he'd seen me, that was a Coke, y'know. That's kind of my one regret.'

Speaking to Mark Lucas for *The Independent* in late June, 2009, Headon recalled his darker days, including painful memories of how a mini-cab driving job in Fulham, West London, in the late '80s to fund his addiction became too much for him and he took to busking with a set of bongos on the London Underground, telling Lucas, 'Every hundred people who passed, there'd be one who'd stop and ask, 'Are you Topper Headon from The Clash?' I'd have to say, 'Yeah, this is what I do now.' It was so humiliating.'

But 20 years on, Lucas, who knew from his own cab-driving days, reported his friend 'transformed' and in good shape when collected at Dover railway station by Headon, then 54, 'small and slim ... dressed in jeans, a striped shirt and trainers, he wears wire-rimmed glasses and his greying, spiky hair is receding,' with 'charming smile, lengthy anecdotes and frank admissions'.

By then Headon was making up for lost years, working with local music charities, drumming with various bands, being a spokesman for the Hepatitis C Trust, a virus he'd recently beaten, and about to donate his beloved Mini Cooper to be raffled by the Strummerville Foundation.

But Lucas reflected, 'Months after being in one of the world's biggest rock'n'roll bands, Headon was living in a freezing, windowless squat in Fulham, while The Clash were performing stadium shows in the US in support of 'Rock the Casbah', a song largely written by Headon. He made various attempts to continue his musical career. Friendship with Pete Townshend nearly landed him the job of drumming for The Who ... Headon scuppered it in characteristic style. In full stage gear he climbed a 25ft drainpipe, ran across a roof and jumped off the other side, waking up in hospital with a broken leg and a policeman, who charged him with attempted burglary.'

Of his days playing with Pete Farndon, he told Lucas, 'We got Rob Stoner, a heroin addict, from Bob Dylan's band and Pete Townshend, a heroin addict with one foot in recovery, to produce us. Then we went to Farndon's funeral. It's not funny, but within two months of forming the band the bass player's died. I mean, that was selfish, and Pete (Townshend) comes up to me and says: 'You're next.''

When Jones was sacked from The Clash, the guitarist went in search of Headon, taking a roadie to Fulham to 'kidnap' him and get him back to his flat before putting him into the Priory for treatment. He was enrolled into Big Audio Dynamite, and. 'It was while they were returning from rehearsals one evening that Jones told Headon the good news: they were each about to receive £200,000 in royalties from The Clash.' Headon added, 'I went, 'See you, Mick!' Who wants to stay clean when you've got £200,000 in the bank?' The money lasted less than 18 months, at which point Headon was declared bankrupt. He added, 'My dealer used to come round and say, 'I'll take the rug,' and a big Persian rug would walk out for a gram. When I went to his, I thought, 'Fuck me! This is my house!'' Meanwhile, 'Headon was left sitting on the floor of his empty, remortgaged Abbey Road flat watching a black-and-white television.'

His 1986 album 'Waking Up' was his attempt to finance his addiction, Headon also remarrying, his wife Catherine working in the music industry. Six months after the LP's release, he was arrested on charges of supplying heroin and received a 15-month jail sentence, served at Standford Hill open prison in Kent, his career effectively over and 'what little energy he had ... used in the pursuit of heroin.' Lucas added, 'When we drove together ... he would only appear for as long as it took him to earn the £25 he needed to buy drugs.'

When *Westway to the World* was released, Johnny Green reckoned there was a gasp from the audience when Headon came on screen, the drummer 'hesitant and his speech slurred, he weighed seven-and-a-half stone, an appearance emphasised by the oversize shirt Jones lent him when Headon arrived for the interview in a T-shirt full of cigarette burns.'

With a second marriage behind him, he found himself in a homeless hostel, yards from the Westway, 'living on cans of Special Brew supplemented by twice-daily visits to soup kitchens'. Lucas added, 'He returned to Dover, becoming the local drunk, cornering people in pubs and shouting at cars in the street until his doctor told him his liver was 'waving the white flag'.' Headon had, not uncommonly among intravenous drug users, contracted hepatitis C.

He returned to heroin, before his doctor stepped in again, convincing him to move in with his parents before going back into the Priory. He'd been through rehab 13 times, but this time it worked. Asked why, he replied, 'I don't know. Something happened. I started feeling part of life again. I've been clean ever since.' He launched a Narcotics Anonymous group in Dover and set up a hepatitis C support group, and the year before the interview had that on-stage reunion with Mick Jones.

Lucas added, 'Today, Headon feels he's finally over the five years he spent in The Clash. He has borne the brunt of the blame for the band's break up, compounding the problem by making the widely misunderstood statement in

Westway to the World that if he had his time over, he would do it all again.' Headon added, 'I was trying to explain that when you're a heroin addict you don't choose to fuck your life up, it's inevitable.' But Lucas concluded that Headon looked 'remarkably well ... keeps fit and his kitchen cabinets are crammed with health supplements,' his interviewee later claiming, 'I'm just a middle-aged man by the sea.'

THE MUSIC

The albums, the influence, the greatest tracks

4

"I knew that rhythm and blues was dead, that the future was here somehow."

JOE STRUMMER, 1976

THE ALBUMS

4

THE CLASH

Side one: 'Janie Jones', 'Remote Control', 'I'm So Bored with the USA', 'White Riot', 'Hate & War', 'What's My Name', 'Deny', 'London's Burning'; Side tswo: 'Career Opportunities', 'Cheat', 'Protex Blue', 'Police & Thieves', '48 Hours', 'Garageland'

All songs written by Strummer/Jones, except 'What's My Name' (Strummer/Jones/Levine) and 'Police & Thieves' (Murvin/Perry).
Personnel: Joe Strummer: lead/backing vocals, rhythm guitar (lead guitar on '48 Hours'); Mick Jones: lead guitar, backing/lead vocals; Paul Simonon: bass guitar; Terry Chimes (credited as 'Tory Crimes'): drums; Mickey Foote: production; Simon Humphrey: engineering; Kate Simon: cover art; Rocco Macauley: back cover photo

'The big watershed was the Clash album – that was go out, cut your hair, stop mucking about time, y'know. Up to that point we'd still been singing about bowling down California highways. I mean, it meant nothing to me. Although The Damned and the Pistols were great, they were only exciting musically; lyrically, I couldn't really make out a lot of it. To realise that The Clash were actually singing about their own lives in West London was like a bolt out of the blue.'
Jake Burns, Stiff Little Fingers

Released on April 8, 1977, through CBS, *The Clash* is widely celebrated as one of the greatest punk albums of all time, and according to *The Times*, it was, alongside *Never Mind the Bollocks*, 'punk's definitive statement'. Recorded and mixed over three weekend sessions in February at CBS' since-demolished Studio 3 in Whitfield Street, the tapes were delivered to the label at the start of March, at a cost of £4,000.

Studio 3 was only a tiny room at the top of the building, but it was also the same location at which The Stooges had recorded *Raw Power* with David Bowie four years earlier, helping the band get over the fact that it was so 'very sparse, like a long oblong', with 'hessian wallpaper and drab 50s décor', as it was described in the *Clash on Broadway* booklet. There were teething problems, however. Engineer Simon Humphrey recalled to Pat Gilbert,

'They refused to shake my hand because I was a hippy.' The 21-year-old engineer was no novice, having previously worked with ABBA, Gary Glitter, Hot Chocolate, Mud and Smokie. But the suggestion was that he was chosen as he was the youngest in-house engineer, his only remit to get them in and down on tape before the punk bubble burst.

That sense of urgency seemed to be reflected in the fact that within three days of signing, the band had recorded their first single. And as Mickey Foote put it, his perceived task was simply to 'set up and keep the overdubs to a minimum', with it all done and dusted within 12 days, after three straight Thursday to Sunday sessions up to February 27. It was claimed that Mick Jones was sketchy during the sessions because of his speed intake at the time, but many years later he told John Robb, 'We recorded it very fast. They always say I don't remember making it, but I do. We'd play a song, have a quick break, play the next one, shout at each other, then do another song. Joe would give me the words and I'd make a song out of them. The words would have such a great rhythm to them. Everything would come together really fast.' He added in *Westway to the World*, 'I like that album best. I like that kind of sound it has overall.'

Looking back on that period, he added, 'There was a lot of struggling with instruments at the start. And it was that struggling and learning to play that made it alive, made it real, made it something that wasn't like anything else.' Yet despite that modest appraisal, Humphrey – who reckoned the LP 'was recorded almost live' – said he felt the lead guitarist was in charge from the start, not least 'teaching Paul what to play'. Joe Strummer agreed, saying, 'Any guitar of note on the record is Jonesy.'

The cover art was designed by Polish artist Roslaw Szaybo. Its main image of Simonon, Strummer and Jones was by US photographer and friend of the band Kate Simon, taken on the trolley ramp of the old tack room opposite the front door of the Rehearsal Rehearsals building in Camden in late '76, by which time Terry Chimes had moved on. The picture of the charging police on the rear, shot by Rocco Macauley, was taken during the Notting Hill Carnival disturbances of August '76 – the inspiration for 'White Riot'. Art-wise, there are ripped-effect edges, Xeroxed images, flashes of fluorescent spray paint, a distressed band logo and a typewritten tracklisting, all as evocative as Jamie Reid's pieces for the Sex Pistols.

Released on April 8, the album entered the UK Top 40 at No.12 on April 30, and stuck around for eight more weeks. As Humphrey explained, 'Everybody at the record company was shocked when *The Clash* went straight into the charts. They hadn't realised the extent of what was happening.' Meanwhile, Tony Parsons wrote in *NME* that the band 'chronicle our lives and what it is to be young in the stinking '70s better than any other band, and they do it with style, flash and excitement'. *Sounds*' Pete Silverton more or less agreed, writing in a five-star review, 'The Clash are the essentials of street London personified.'

Barry Cain enthused about the album in *Record Mirror*, writing, 'This is the best debut album any British band has ever produced. Forget the sociological quagmire predictably promoted by crawling confederates. Forget the patronising 'whatever they lack in musical ability, they more than make up for in sheer gut political energy'. Forget all the new wave regalia that haunts every toilet paper periodical like computer data. The

Clash pull the chain on all the crap that's preceded them with a stunningly conceived record. If you've got ears, the message is, 'We'll smash your face in soon enough, but don't be impatient. Just savour the rest of the deal, because it's straight from the top of the pack.' There's no such thing as a highlight on this album. Every track has an identity, a concrete and clay beauty. Strummer and Jones have written all the songs, except Junior Murvin's 'Police & Thieves'. Reggae? The Clash? White boys don't sing reggae. But they do if they make it white-boy reggae decked with white-boy aggression and white-boy attitude. Its inclusion is genius. At a masterstroke they've punched their way out of the punkweight division, successfully taking the 'h' out of Clash and replacing it with an 's'. I never knew phasers could be so effective. 'Cheat' is a track that actually needs the often-superfluous Frampton device. There's also a remix of 'White Riot' and it sounds far superior to the single. The production is sometimes a little oblique, but Strummer's heavy artillery voice, Jones' maniacal/ disciplined guitar and Paul Simonon's all-embracing bass blast criticism into kingdom come. Oh, and 'Janie Jones' is a work of art.'

Talking of 'Janie Jones', Aztec Camera's Roddy Frame told *Uncut* in 2015, 'I had *The Clash* on cassette, and this tiny cassette player, and just remember everyday coming home from school and playing 'Janie Jones'. It was so exciting, like hearing Chuck Berry coming out of a jukebox. I can see now that a lot of the stuff Strummer was doing came from his rock'n'roll schooling in the 101'ers. It kind of boogied. That's something the Sex Pistols didn't really do because they were rooted in that whole New York Dolls sleazy thing. But in The Clash you could hear those elements of rockabilly and almost boogie guitar – it had its roots in something much older.'

And Pete Wylie added, 'Just the start with Terry Chimes' drums. He sometimes gets a hard deal, but his drumming is amazing. I'd never heard anything like it. It was the same the first time I heard 'Anarchy in the UK' or 'Starman' or 'Wrote For Luck'. The first time you hear it you think, 'Fuck me, what's happening?' It was sparse, then intense, then sparse, then intense again. It summed up The Clash for me. From the first three seconds you knew that first album was gonna be fantastic. Those lyrics, about this guy working in a crap job and then the glamour of singing about Janie Jones. To have the bollocks to start with a song that good, y'know?'

As for 'Police & Thieves', Stiff Little Fingers frontman Jake Burns enthused, 'The thing that really impressed me was that they weren't actually trying to play reggae. The guitars still sounded like white-boy rock guitars, and they didn't make any concessions to try and sound Jamaican in any way. I thought that was really honest. I hadn't heard the original when I bought *The Clash* because, with regards to reggae, Belfast in the mid-'70s was very much a backwater. You heard Bob Marley on the radio and that was it. The Clash opened my ears to all that. I like the original but prefer The Clash's. It's a lot more edgy, a lot more urban.'

Meanwhile, DJ and producer Andrew Weatherall added, 'Hearing that song encouraged me to go and check out people like Lee 'Scratch' Perry and Big Youth. When John Lydon started doing reggae stuff a few years later, that was the final seal of approval for me and my mates, and we spent a lot of time actively seeking good reggae and dub records.'

Pete Wylie is similarly animated on the subject of the last song on the album, 'Garageland', seeing it as 'a statement of intent'. He said, 'The first time I saw The Clash, there's a phrase that's never left me head and that's that they had 'a roar of defiance'. And it was like a roar, a fucking animal sound. When I was 18 it was a lot more intense and serious, but 'Garageland' is also funny. 'There's 22 singers – but one microphone' – that's funny! It was an anthem.'

Broadcaster Gary Crowley added, 'It just sums up that whole first album for me and brings back all the memories of those early gigs, seeing The Clash at The Rainbow, The Lyceum, Nôtre Dame Hall. That three-pronged attack of Paul, Joe and Mick in a line along the front and Topper at the back. Such an incredible live band.'

Paul Simonon told *Uncut*, 'In a way, that

song does pronounce that the next step is about to be taken. To me that song almost, I dunno, it puts an exclamation mark at the end of the punk period. I mean, we signed to the record company and, like the song says, my mates have got new boots, that's what it was like.' Mick Jones added, 'We were very steeped in that garage band thing as well. We loved all the stuff on *Nuggets*, that late-'60s American stuff. We really saw ourselves as a garage band.' And Terry Chimes enthused, 'More than anything I just love the sound. We never thought it was going to be an anthem because we never thought about the future. We were very much a band of 'now'. I mean we thought we were going to be famous, but we never really considered the implications of that. I was always the one who thought the punk 'sell-out' thing was nonsense anyway. You have to have a record label; you have to have money coming in. I was a realist, whereas the others used to fight against it. We used to argue all the time about that stuff.'

Melody Maker's Michael Oldfield wasn't so enamoured with *The Clash*, calling it 'a tuneless repetition of choruses at breakneck speed' that 'should go down well with the Blank Generation' and adding, 'Thank God I'm 'Too Old' to have enjoyed it.' But time was on The Clash's side, and in 1993 the *NME* – its writers originally ranking the record No.7 in its '77 poll – ranked it No.13 in its Greatest Albums of All Time, and No.3 in its Greatest Albums of the '70s, praising its 'speed-freaked brain of punk set to the tinniest, most frantic guitars ever trapped on vinyl', and adding that 'lives were changed beyond recognition by it'. And in December 1999, Q magazine wrote that The Clash 'would never sound so punk as they did on 1977's self-titled debut', adding that it 'still howled with anger'. It also placed *The Clash* at No.48 in its list of the 100 Greatest British Albums Ever in 2000.

In 2003, *Mojo* ranked *The Clash* No.2 in its Top 50 Punk Albums, citing it as 'the ultimate punk protest album. Searingly evocative of dreary late '70s Britain, but still timelessly inspiring'. John Harris, in a retrospective interview for the same magazine that year, wrote, 'For all the talk about *Never Mind the Bollocks* being the quintessential punk album, *The Clash* has an arguably greater claim, both in terms of its lo-fi buzz-saw ambience and its overarching sense of place. For an instant portrait of pre-Thatcher England, listen to the fury of 'Career Opportunities', Hate & War' and 'Janie Jones'. Best of all is their rockified take on Junior Murvin's 'Police & Thieves', an apocalyptic view of Kingston, Jamaica, refracted on to '70s London.'

Talking of 'Career Opportunities', Buzzcocks frontman Pete Shelley told *Uncut* in 2015, 'It doesn't sound as good on record as live, but it's probably one of my favourite songs. It has a real energy and intensity, and the lyrics are about not wasting your life working nine-to-five in a job you hate. That was what Joe was best at really – writing songs that people could relate to on different levels.'

The same year, Keith Topping wrote in *The Complete Clash*, 'The freshness and power it had in 1977 may have dissipated slightly, but thematically it's still an absolute barometer of its time. And, perhaps, of other times too.' And in a thirtieth anniversary BBC online review in 2007, Susie Goldring compared the band to the Sex Pistols, feeling, 'The Clash had just as much raw energy, but a lot more to say', as a 'well-mannered, socially aware' outfit that 'raged about injustice and poverty for the sake of revolution'. She added, 'The band wrote about what they knew: clashes with police, clashes between black and white, clashes with each other. They couldn't have come from anywhere other than London. The Clash sums up what it was like to be young in London in the 1970s.'

John Robb, in *Punk Rock: An Oral History*, enthused, 'There isn't a duff song. It was a rough and ready collection of direct action rock'n'roll street anthems that perhaps more than any other album of the time totally connected with the lives of its audience, detailing perfectly the punk rockers' frustration and anger, setting the blueprint for the sound and soul of what punk rock would be about. Scratchy machine gun guitars drive along the songs, which have great sing-along choruses. Strummer's lyrics perfectly capture the aspirations and anger of the dole-bound generation floundering around in the shabby UK of the late '70s. Mick Jones' years studying rock'n'roll hadn't been wasted. The songwriting is spot on, and the arrangements clever. Their cover of Junior Murvin's 'Police & Thieves' also combines the key rebel musics of the late '70s, punk and reggae, into one cool whole. The Clash were utterly inspirational, utterly positive, and offered a million possibilities. For many they were the ultimate band from the punk generation.'

For all that, CBS denied the record a US release, feeling it too raw, and a North American version was not forthcoming until the second LP *Give 'Em Enough Rope* saw the light of day there – and even then with a different tracklisting. By then, however, the original version had become the bestselling import album of the year stateside. Epic, the US branch of the label, famously dragged its feet over the release, until finally its hand was as good as forced by the fact that the record had sold around 100,00 copies on import. Joe Strummer suggested in *Westway to the World*, 'The audience was already way beyond them, far more than the executives knew.' Epic finally put out its own version in July 1979, opening with additional track 'Clash City Rockers' and adding the singles 'Complete Control', '(White Man) In Hammersmith Palais' and 'I Fought the Law', plus B-side 'Jail Guitar Doors', and leaving out 'Deny', 'Cheat', 'Protex Blue' and '48 Hours', while a re-recorded 'White Riot' replaced the Polydor demo.

In 2015, US fan Paul Dougherty published on his *Punk Before Punk* blog a November '77 response from Epic Records A&R executive Bruce Harris to his frustrations at the LP not having received a stateside release by then. In it Harris explained his reasons for not signing the band, writing them off as an 'amateur act'. He stressed he was a fan, but wrote, 'My responsibility is not to release records I like but rather records which I feel will bring profit into this company. The album for all its quality is not at all matched by the level of production, an enormous drawback. The band's live performance is many times better than what is on this record and one has to question the artistic integrity of creating an inferior-sounding album. I believe The Clash can make better records and those are the records we should choose to bring to the American marketplace.'

When that release finally followed, it proved a critical success stateside, with *Village Voice*'s Robert Christgau describing it in '79 as 'the greatest rock'n'roll album ever manufactured anywhere'. Meanwhile, *Rolling Stone*'s Tom Carson said, 'Perhaps more than any other album ever made, *The Clash* dramatised rock'n'roll as a last, defiantly cheerful grab for life, something scrawled on the run, on subway walls. Here was a record that defined rock's risks and its pleasures, and told us, once again, this music was worth fighting for.' In 2003, the US version was ranked No.77 in *Rolling Stone*'s 500 Greatest Albums of All Time and No.12 in its 100 Best Debut Albums of all time, stating, 'Youthful ambition bursts through The Clash's debut, a machine-gun blast of songs about unemployment, race, and The Clash themselves,' and adding, 'Both UK and US versions distill their radical vision with a crystal clarity.'

Stephen Thomas Erlewine, for www.allmusic.com, wrote, 'The Clash's debut album was pure, unadulterated rage and fury, fueled by passion for both rock'n'roll and revolution. Though the cliché about punk rock was that the bands couldn't play, the key to The Clash is that although they gave that illusion, they really could play – hard. The charging, relentless rhythms, primitive three-chord rockers, and the poor sound quality give the album a nervy, vital energy. Joe Strummer's slurred wails perfectly compliment the edgy rock, while Mick Jones' clearer singing and charged guitar breaks make his numbers righteously anthemic. Rock and roll is rarely as edgy, invigorating, and sonically revolutionary.'

Elsewhere, Australian music blogger Bruce Jenkins' fortieth anniversary appraisal for www.vinylconnection.com.au read, 'Holy shit, what a debut. Smashing out angry rock songs full of piss and vinegar, The Clash showed both that they really *could play and that they were no one-trick ponies. There is a clutch of memorable street-savvy songs here, adding up to an album spurting energy, sweat and conviction. The US version replaced no less than five songs from the UK original with tracks that are, frankly, stronger. 'White Riot' howls, 'London's Burning' snarls, and 'Career Opportunities' stamps its feet, while the surprising 'Police* & Thieves' presages later work. Add another cover on the US version, 'I Fought the Law', and the chest-thumping 'Clash City Rockers', and you have a kick-down-the-door arrival.'

But for me, the final quote on the subject perhaps deserves to go to Sean O'Hagan, the former *NME* writer, who on December 29, 2002 – a week after Joe Strummer's death – wrote in *The Guardian* about that first album, 'If you want to hear British punk at its most pared down and powerful, The Clash's eponymous debut album still sounds more singular and ground-breaking than *Never Mind the Bollocks*, not least because it avoids the heavy metal guitar roar that, alongside Rotten's enervated sneer, was so much a part of the Pistols' signature. I still remember the first time I heard 'Janie Jones' exploding out of my speakers at breakneck speed, a thrill so new I was not even sure I understood it, much less liked it.'

GIVE 'EM ENOUGH ROPE

Side one: 'Safe European Home', 'English Civil War', 'Tommy Gun', 'Julie's Been Working for the Drug Squad', 'Last Gang in Town'; Side two: 'Guns on the Roof', 'Drug-Stabbing Time', 'Stay Free', 'Cheapskates', 'All the Young Punks (New Boots and Contracts)'

All songs written by Strummer/Jones, except 'English Civil War' (Trad. arr. Strummer/Jones) and 'Guns on the Roof' (Strummer/Jones/Simonon/Headon). Personnel: Joe Strummer: lead/backing vocals, rhythm guitar; Mick Jones: lead

4

guitar, backing/lead vocals; Paul Simonon: bass guitar, backing vocals; Topper Headon: drums. Also featuring: Allen Lenier: piano on 'Julie's Been Working for the Drug Squad'; Stan Bronstein: saxophone on 'Drug-Stabbing Time'; Bob Andrews: keyboards on 'Stay Free'
Production: Sandy Pearlman: producer; Corky Stasiak: recording, mixing, engineering; Paul Stubblebine – mastering engineer; Dennis Ferrante, Gregg Caruso, Kevin Dallimore and Chris Mingo: sound engineers; Gene Greif: cover designer; Hugh Brown: concept designer, cover photograph

'It needed to break out and reach America and be kind of global. And somebody had to take that bull by the horns.'
Joe Strummer, Westway to the World, 2000

The second studio album by The Clash was released by CBS on November 10, 1978, peaking at No.2 in the UK. Its cover was designed by Gene Greif, based on a Chinese communist postcard titled *End of the Trail*, photographed by Adrian Atwater and featuring Wallace Irving Robertson, showing a dead cowboy being picked apart by vultures. Side one tracks 'Tommy Gun' and 'English Civil War' were released as singles either side of Christmas, reaching No.19 (the highest position for a Clash single so far) and No.25, respectively, in the UK.

On the subject of 'Tommy Gun', Inspiral Carpets' Clint Boon told *Uncut* in 2015, 'What you learn about politics from bands like The Clash is more important than what you learn at school. You didn't get taught about terrorist factions in school, you learnt about that from records like 'Tommy Gun'.'

Despite rumblings from the critics about its smoother production, *Give 'Em Enough Rope* was fairly well received. That said, CBS' gamble on it being the LP to crack America largely failed, and it stalled at No.128 in the US Billboard chart.

Rolling Stone's Greil Marcus, in late January '79, hailed the LP as a poised, unpretentious record of 'straight English punk with a grip on the future' and 'accessible hard rock', showcasing The Clash's unyielding, humorous 'vision of public life,' and felt it was 'a rocker's assault on the real world in the grand tradition of *Beggars Banquet, Let It Bleed* and *Never Mind the Bollocks*'. However, he reckoned Pearlman's production meant the 'sound seems suppressed: the highs aren't there, and the presence of the band is thinner than it ought to be. The record doesn't *jump*.' He added, 'The Clash's attack is still fast and noisy, but with lyrical accents cracking the rough surface ... Imagine The Who's 'I Can't Explain' as a statement about a world in flames, not a lover's daze, and you've got the idea.'

Marcus appreciated the feel of the album, adding, 'The storm begins with the first note and lets up only in snatches. The reality The Clash convey is that of a world upside down, a world in which no one can be sure of where they stand. Lines are drawn between oppressors and victims, killers and targets, but it isn't meant to be clear who's who, and there's not a hint of self-righteousness, of political purity'.

Robert Christgau wrote in *The Village Voice* that the pessimistic mood and a couple of bad moments made it less listenable than the debut LP but concluded that most songs were as 'effective melodically as anything on *The Clash*, and even the band's ruminations on the star as culture hero become more resonant as you hear them over and over. This isn't among the greatest rock albums

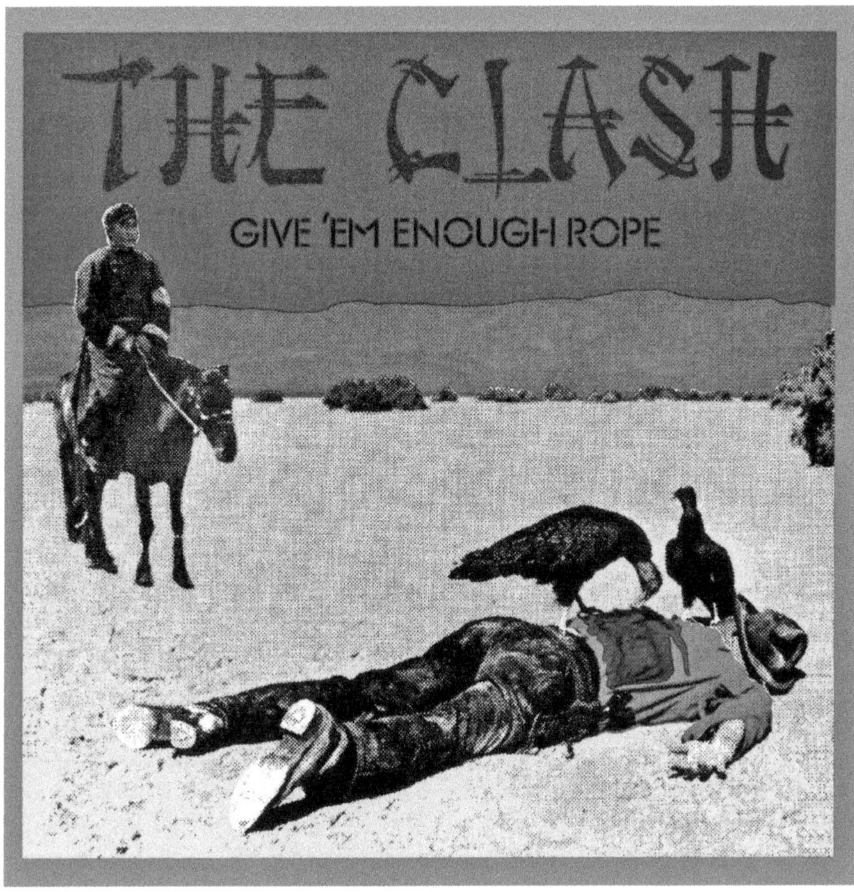

ever, but it's among the finest of the year.' He named it the fourth best album of 1978, while *Sounds* named it the best.

In 1991's *England's Dreaming*, Jon Savage wrote of 'a powerful but baffling record', saying, '*The Clash* took a week. *Give 'Em Enough Rope* took over three months. *The Clash* had been a concept album of trial and tribulation in Ladbroke Grove. *Give 'Em Enough Rope* was about global oppression. The Clash posed in military gear in front of a world map underscored by National Front marches. Inset boxes on the map depicted what was happening, country by country. This was confused to say the least, yet The Clash were adept at recognising their contradictions and expressing them musically. Here, high-gloss production is still fighting amateurism and the whole monolith is given humanity by Strummer's ranter persona. When the group take off together and he launches on one of his rants, like 'English Civil War', The Clash

4

retain the suspension of disbelief that was now necessary, not only for the group to carry off a rhetoric that was bursting at the seams but just to keep together.'

In 1993, *Give 'Em Enough Rope* was named the *NME*'s eighty-seventh greatest album of all time, while Q included it in its 100 Best Punk Albums list. Stephen Thomas Erlewine, for allmusic.com, admitted the sound was 'considerably cleaner', yet 'while the record doesn't burn with the same intense, amateurish energy of *The Clash*, it does have a big, forceful sound that is nearly as powerful. What keeps *Give 'Em Enough Rope* from being a classic is its slightly inconsistent material. Many of the songs are outright classics, particularly the first half and 'Stay Free', but the group loses some momentum toward the end.' He concluded, 'Even with such flaws', it 'ranks as one of the strongest albums of the punk era'. And Keith Topping, in *The Complete Clash*, believed it was an LP 'in need of a major re-evaluation', seeing it as, 'The sound of a band spreading its wings, not having them clipped'.

On the subject of 'Stay Free', Pete Wylie told *Uncut* in 2015 that it was, 'Mick's finest hour,' adding, 'He had a great voice, and even though he only got to sing one or two songs, he made the most of them. 'Stay Free' was a different kind of Clash song, very melodic.' Norman Cook added, 'The Clash were the first band to get into politics and had an equally big effect on the rest of The Housemartins. They talked about important issues in interviews and addressed problems like racism and unemployment in their songs. 'The Magnificent Seven' took a scalpel to factory life, while 'Stay Free' made me realise I shouldn't waste a moment of my life. It was a seminal song on a seminal album and, whenever I see one of my oldest mates, we still sing it to each other.' Meanwhile, broadcaster Gideon Coe, felt, 'It's The Clash at their most wistful. It's as affecting a tale of friendship and lost days of youth as I've ever heard in my life.' While Buzzcocks guitarist Steve Diggle added, 'Stay Free' has to be one of the best Mick Jones compositions ever committed to tape. The whole song is really moving and poignant and it sounds just as good decades later.'

On January 20, 1979, adulation for the band was clear in the *NME*'s Readers' Poll for 1978, '(White Man) In Hammersmith Palais' being voted best single (it was also No.8 in the writers' poll), alongside a 'best group' award, with Mick Jones receiving 'best guitarist' and the LP No.27 in the writers' poll.

A 30-plus-date UK Sort it Out tour followed the album's release, with support from The Slits and The Innocents, as recalled by Siouxsie and the Banshees drummer Budgie, who was with The Slits at the time. He told John Robb, 'That was really amazing, when The Clash came into their own, with a massive following. It was full-on, non-stop. I never experienced anything like it. We travelled in our car, following The Clash's bigger van. It was a proper production, proper rock.'

Then in February came a largely successful first North American tour, Caroline Coon by then caretaker manager, the band having sacked Bernie Rhodes. But as Pat Gilbert noted, 'As they drifted off to sleep en route for San Francisco, news came through from New York that Sid Vicious had died of an overdose. It was the end of an era, the end of punk, the beginning of a whole new phase. The tribulations of the previous year, the interminable recording sessions, the fractious relationships between band members, Bernie's mind games, all had somehow made the band stronger and better. The Clash had a new sense of purpose, and within a year had unleashed their next album, a genre-mixing double album and for many their career highlight.'

LONDON CALLING

Side one: 'London Calling', 'Brand New Cadillac', 'Jimmy Jazz', 'Hateful', 'Rudie Can't Fail'; Side two: 'Spanish Bombs', 'The Right Profile', 'Lost in the Supermarket', 'Clampdown', The Guns of Brixton; Side three: 'Wrong 'Em Boyo', 'Death or Glory', 'Koka Kola', 'The Card Cheat'; Side four – 'Lover's Rock', 'Four Horsemen', 'I'm Not Down', 'Revolution Rock', 'Train in Vain'

All tracks written by Strummer/Jones, except 'Brand New Cadillac' (Vince Taylor), 'The Guns of Brixton' (Simonon), 'Wrong 'Em Boyo' (Clive Alphonso; originally performed by the Rulers), 'The Card Cheat' (Strummer/Jones/Simonon/Headon) and 'Revolution Rock' (Jackie Edwards, Danny Ray; originally by Danny Ray and the Revolutionaries).
Personnel: Joe Strummer: lead and backing vocals, rhythm guitar, piano; Mick Jones: lead guitar, piano, harmonica, backing and lead vocals; Paul Simonon: bass guitar, backing vocals, lead vocals on 'Guns of Brixton'; Topper Headon: drums, percussion. Also featuring: Mickey Gallagher: organ; The Irish Horns: brass
Production: Guy Stevens: producer; Bill Price: chief engineer; Jerry Green: additional engineer; recorded at Wessex Studios; Ray Lowry: design; Pennie Smith: photography

'One of the greatest rock'n'roll experiences I've ever had was attending a Clash show in New York in early 1980. I was at the side of the stage watching from the wings, standing between Joey Ramone and David Bowie, when The Clash played 'Hammersmith Palais' and 'London Calling' back to back. I was so giddily caught up in the transcendent emotional and sensual power of the moment that I didn't even say hello to Bowie or Joey. The Clash in their classic incarnation of Joe Strummer, Mick Jones, Paul Simonon and Topper Headon could do that to a person.'
Charles Shaar Murray, Mojo, 2003

If one Clash album is held up to the light more than any other as a sign of the band's worth, it is *London Calling*, which is, according to *The Times*, 'one of the most influential rock albums'. In *Rolling Stone*'s 2003 list of the 500 Greatest Albums of All Time, it was ranked No.8, the highest entry by a punk band (*The Clash was at 77 and Sandinista! 404*). *The NME* – whose writers ranked it No.8 LP and the title track No.3 single in 1979 – went on to rank the album as the sixth greatest of the '70s. And in 2007, the LP was inducted into the Grammy Hall of Fame's 'collection of recordings of lasting qualitative or historical significance'. It was also included in BBC Radio 1's 2009 Masterpieces series, described as 'one of the most influential albums of all time', 30 years after its original release.

This was a mighty opus incorporating a range of styles, tackling social displacement, unemployment, racial conflict, drug use and adulthood. Its US release – through Epic – following in January 1980, it was released as a double LP in the UK and sold for the price of a single album. CBS initially denied the band's request, instead giving permission to include a free 12-inch single, that becoming a second nine-track LP. On its release, *London Calling sold around two million*

4

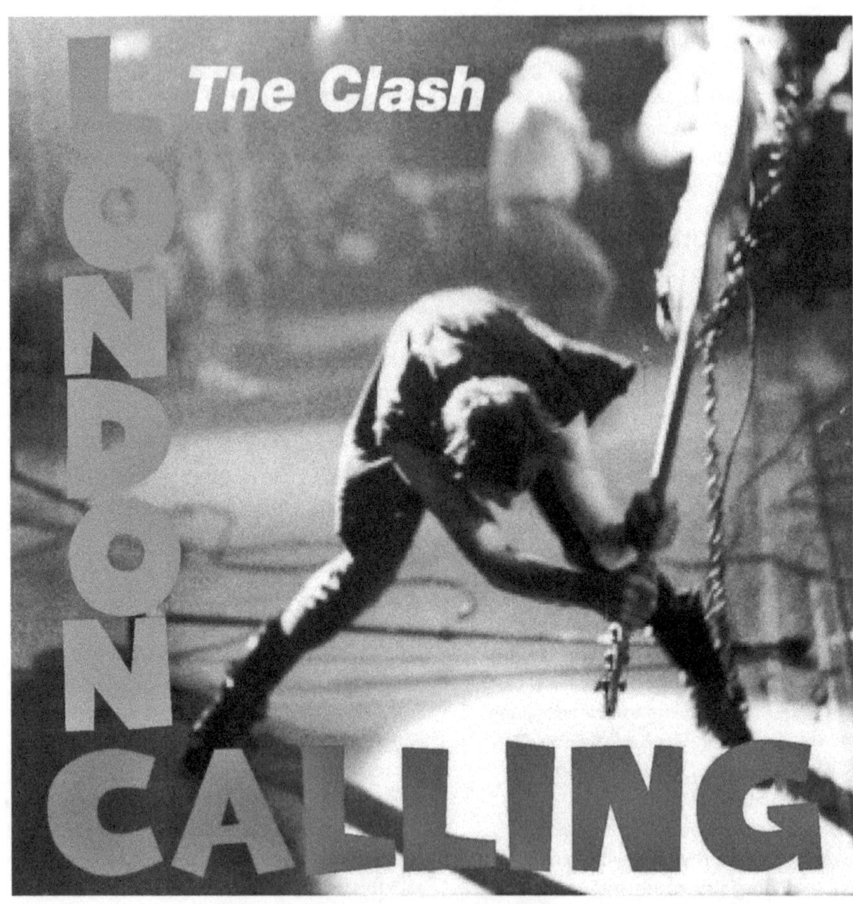

copies, peaking at No.9 in the UK, and was certified gold that month. It also reached No.2 in Sweden and No.4 in Norway and in the US peaked at No.27 on the Billboard pop chart. It went on to sell over five million copies worldwide, and by February 1996 it had been certified platinum in the US.

The album's iconic front cover features Paul Simonon smashing his Fender Precision bass (later displayed at the Cleveland Rock and Roll Hall of Fame) against the stage at The Palladium in New York City in late September '79, during the Take the Fifth US tour. Simonon explained in a 2011 interview with Fender that he smashed the bass out of frustration, as the bouncers weren't allowing the audience to stand up. Pennie Smith, who took the shot, felt it was too out of focus, but Strummer and graphic designer Ray Lowry, the *NME* cartoonist travelling with the band, were insistent. In 2002, her photograph was named the best rock'n'roll photograph of all time by *Q magazine, as 'it captures the ultimate* rock'n'roll moment – total loss of control'. The same magazine also named it ninth best LP cover of all time a year earlier.

That cover was among 10 chosen by Royal Mail for its 'Classic Album Cover' postage stamp sets in January 2010, the Lowry-designed artwork also paying homage to Elvis Presley's self-titled 1956 debut LP, with its pink lettering down the left and green text along the bottom. And in 1995, Mick Jones' Big Audio Dynamite used the same scheme for its *F-Punk* album.

London Calling received widespread critical acclaim on release. In the *New York Times*, John Rockwell felt it finally validated the acclaim received by the band, stating, 'This is an album that captures all The Clash's primal energy, combines it with a brilliant production job by Guy Stevens and reveals depths of invention and creativity barely suggested by previous work.' *NME*'s Charles Shaar Murray agreed, while *Melody Maker*'s James Truman said The Clash 'discovered themselves' by 'embracing American music styles'.

In a 1980 *Rolling Stone* review, Tom Carson wrote, 'By now, our expectations of The Clash might seem to have become inflated beyond any possibility of fulfillment. It's not simply that they're the greatest rock'n'roll band in the world. After years watching too many superstars compromise, blow chances and sell out, being the greatest is just about synonymous with being the music's last hope. While the group itself resists such labels, they tell you exactly how high the stakes are, how urgent the need. The Clash got their start on the crest of what looked like a revolution, only to see the punk movement either smash up on its own violent momentum or be absorbed into the same corporate-rock machinery it had meant to destroy. Now, almost against their will, they're the only ones left.'

Comparing the third LP to its predecessor, he added, '*Give 'Em Enough Rope* railed against the notion that being rock'n'roll heroes meant martyrdom. Yet the album presented itself so flamboyantly as a last stand that it created a near-insoluble problem. After you've brought the apocalypse crashing down on your head, how can you possibly go on?' He went on, 'Merry and tough, passionate and large-spirited, *London Calling* celebrates the romance of rock'n'roll rebellion in grand, epic terms. It doesn't merely reaffirm The Clash's own commitment to rock-as-revolution. Instead, the record ranges across the whole of rock'n'roll's past for its sound, and digs deeply into rock legend, history, politics and myth for its images and themes. Everything has been brought together into a single, vast, stirring story – one that, as they tell it, seems not only theirs but ours. For all its first-take scrappiness and guerrilla production, this two-LP set is music that means to endure. It's so rich and far-reaching it leaves you not just exhilarated but exalted and triumphantly alive.'

He concluded, '*London Calling* is spacious and extravagant, as packed with characters and incidents as a great novel, and the band's new stylistic expansions – brass, organ, occasional piano, blues grind, pop airiness and the reggae-dub influence that percolates subversively through nearly every number – add density and richness to the sound.'

That love for the LP never dwindled. In 2004, 25 years on, Amanda Petrusich wrote for pitchfork.com, '*London Calling* remains one of punk's defining documents,' adding that it was 'their creative apex, a booming, infallible tribute to throbbing guitars and spacious ideology', and 'a quarter-century after its release, *London Calling* is still the concentrate essence of The Clash's unparalleled fervour'.

She also paid tribute to Guy Stevens' part, adding, 'With a frenzied halo of tightly curled brown hair and a penchant for destroying property, Stevens came to rule Wessex Studios, hurling chairs and ladders, wrestling with engineers, and famously dumping a bottle of red wine into Strummer's Steinway piano. Fortunately, Guy was far more concerned with encouraging 'real, honest emotion' than with achieving technical perfection, and consequently, the band's determination at Vanilla, coupled with Stevens' shit-storming, led to *London Calling*'s odd and glorious balance of studied dedication and absurd inspiration.'

And for *BBC Online*, also in 2004, Mark Sutherland wrote, 'If music-loving aliens land and you find yourself, at laser-point, searching for one single example of how rock's supposed to be rolled, you are strongly advised to recommend *London Calling*. This epic double album, from its iconic sleeve to its wildly eclectic mash-up of styles, is surely the quintessential rock album.' He added, 'This was when The Clash came of age, progressing from the brilliant-but-limited punk rock ire to the stage where they could turn their hand to reggae, ska, rockabilly and pretty much anything else they fancied. Yet the record never lacks focus and Strummer and Jones' willingness to experiment is never let down by a lack of great songs. Truly, a record so brilliant you'd have to be from another planet not to love it.'

John Harris, in a retrospective interview for *Mojo* in 2003, wrote, 'On which The Clash shred any lingering notion that they are a punk group, and à la the Stones circa *Exile on Main Street* map out a creditably vast universe. A few examples prove the point. Among *London Calling*'s hubbub lurk the spectres of UK rock'n'roller Vince Taylor and Montgomery Clift, the after-shocks of the Conservative victory of '79, Spanish terrorists and South London outlaws. The fact that Mick Jones can casually drop in a line like, 'From the 100 Years' War to the Crimea' on a Spector-esque 'The Card Cheat', probably says it all. The music is equally diverse, all of it suffused with the passions catalysed by producer-cum-guru Guy Stevens. His historic links with Mott the Hoople give some clue as to *London Calling*'s abiding spirit. But if Mott's love of rock myth was couched in terms of fond nostalgia, The Clash sound like they're soaking up the past in the manner of revolutionary cadets, aware you can't alter history without understanding it.'

And Stephen Thomas Erlewine, retrospectively for allmusic.com, wrote, '*Give 'Em Enough Rope*, for all of its many attributes, was essentially a holding pattern, but *London Calling* is a remarkable leap forward, incorporating the punk aesthetic into rock'n'roll mythology and roots music. Before, the Clash experimented with reggae, but that was no preparation for the dizzying array of styles on *London Calling*. There's punk and reggae, but there's also rockabilly, ska, New Orleans R&B, pop, lounge jazz, and hard rock; and while the record isn't tied together by a specific theme, its eclecticism and anthemic punk function as a rallying call. It is also invigorating, rocking harder and with more purpose than most albums, let alone doubles. Over the course of the record, Joe Strummer and Mick Jones (and Paul Simonon) explore familiar themes of working-class rebellion and anti-establishment rants, but also tie them in to old rock'n'roll traditions and myths. The result is a stunning statement of purpose and one of the greatest rock'n'roll albums ever recorded.'

Word is that The Clash originally wanted to call the album *The Last Testament*, suggesting it would close a chapter in music history that began with Elvis Presley's RCA debut. They scrapped that title but kept the general concept, mimicking the cover of the 1956 album. This was seen as a revolutionary strategy for a group that sprang from the UK punk scene all about disavowing the past, and from a band whose first statement of intent included the 'no Elvis, Beatles or the Rolling Stones' pronouncement of '1977'.

Asked by Tom Lanham in a 2007 Q&A for online magazine, *Magnet*, if he realised when they were making *London Calling* that they'd crafted one of rock's greatest masterpieces, Mick Jones replied, 'Not really. Almost the minute we finished it, we had a playback in the studio with four speakers, a sort of semi-surround sound. We heard it, but it wasn't mixed then, and we went straight away to America. We used to go to America all the time and play continually, every place. They mixed it, then came over to New York and played it, and it was great to hear it. But we never really thought like that. Although we had ambition and drive and wanted to go places, we didn't realise that was gonna turn out to be a big part of our undoing, as well. The more success we got, the more things seemed to get difficult for us, the more strain we were under. There were all these contradictions.'

SANDINISTA!

Side one: 'The Magnificent Seven', Hitsville UK, 'Junco Partner', 'Ivan Meets G.I. Joe', 'The Leader', 'Something About England'; Side two: 'Rebel Waltz', 'Look Here', 'The Crooked Beat', 'Somebody Got Murdered', 'One More Time', 'One More Dub'; Side three: 'Lightning Strikes (Not Once but Twice)', 'Up in Heaven (Not Only Here)', 'Corner Soul', 'Let's Go Crazy', 'If Music Could Talk', 'The Sound of the Sinners'; Side four – 'Police on my Back', 'Midnight Log', 'The Equaliser', 'The Call Up', 'Washington Bullets', 'Broadway' (features an epilogue of 'The Guns of Brixton', sung by Maria Gallagher); Side five – 'Lose This Skin', 'Charlie Don't Surf', 'Mensforth Hill' ('Something About England' backwards, with overdubs), 'Junkie Slip', 'Kingston Advice', 'The Street Parade'; Side six – 'Version City', 'Living in Fame' (dub version of 'If Music Could Talk'), 'Silicone on Sapphire' (dub version of 'Washington Bullets'), 'Version Pardner' (dub version of 'Junco Partner'), 'Career Opportunities', 'Shepherds Delight' (dub version of 'Police & Thieves')

All songs written by The Clash, except 'Junco Partner' (Unknown); 'Look Here' (Mose Allison); 'One More Time', 'One More Dub', 'If Music Could Talk' and 'Living in Fame' (The Clash and Mikey Dread); 'Police on My Back' (Eddy Grant, originally performed by The Equals); 'Lose This Skin' (Tymon Dogg).
Personnel: Joe Strummer: lead and backing vocals, guitar; Mick Jones: guitar, backing and lead vocals; Paul Simonon: bass guitar, backing vocals, lead vocals on 'The Crooked Beat'; Topper Headon: drums, lead vocals on 'Ivan Meets G.I. Joe'
Also featuring: Tymon Dogg (as Timon

4

Dogg) – vocals and violin on 'Lose This Skin', violin on 'Lightning Strikes (Not Once But Twice)', 'Something About England', 'Mensforth Hill' and 'The Equaliser', keyboard on 'The Sound of the Sinners'; Mickey Gallagher (The Blockheads) – keyboards; Norman Watt-Roy (The Blockheads) – bass; J. P. Nicholson; Ellen Foley – co-lead vocal on 'Hitsville UK'; Davey Payne (The Blockheads) – saxophone; Rick Gascoigne – trombone; Band Sgt. Dave Yates; Den Hegarty (Darts) – vocals; Luke and Ben Gallagher – vocals on 'Career Opportunities'; Maria Gallagher – coda vocals on 'Broadway'; Gary Barnacle – saxophone; 'Bill' Barnacle – trumpet; Jody Linscott – percussion; Ivan Julian (The Voidoids) – guitar; Noel 'Tempo' Bailey (aka Sowell) – guitar; Anthony Nelson Steelie; Lew Lewis (Eddie and The Hot Rods) – harmonica; Gerald Baxter-Warman; Terry McQuade; Rudolph Adolphus Jordan; Battersea; Mikey Dread – vocals on 'The Crooked Beat'
Production: The Clash: producers; Bill Price: chief engineer; Jerry Green, J. P. Nicholson and Lancelot 'Maxie' McKenzie – engineers; Mikey Dread: version mix; Pennie Smith: photography; Steve Bell: cartoonist

'I could only say I'm proud of it – warts and all, as they say. It's a magnificent thing and I wouldn't change it, even if I could. And that's after some soul-searching! Just from the fact that it was all thrown down in one go. It's outrageous. It's doubly outrageous. Its's triply outrageous!'
Joe Strummer, Westway to the World, 2000

The Clash's contentious triple album, 'three pieces of long-playing vinyl for the price of one', according to Joe Strummer, was the record that split fans and critics but certainly saw the band seek out new directions; its extended dubs and first forays into rap, for example, ensured they were the first major rock band to go down that road. Released on December 12, 1980, it contained 36 tracks – six songs per side – and predated that decade's move towards world music, featuring a heady mix of influences and genres, not least funk, reggae, jazz, gospel, R&B, folk, dub, rockabilly, calypso, disco and rap. As Mick Jones put it in 2005's *Viva Joe Strummer* documentary, 'I always saw it as a record for people on oil rigs or Arctic stations who weren't able to get to the record shops regularly.'

For the first time, songwriting plaudits were shared across the band, credited to 'The Clash', rather than mostly Strummer/Jones compositions, and *Sandinista!* was produced by the band, with added participation from Jamaican reggae artist Mikey Dread. The LP's title referred to Nicaragua's Sandinista movement, its FSLN1 catalogue number abbreviating the party's Spanish name, and it proved their most controversial album to date – politically and musically – with opinion divided. Yet it sold well, reaching No.19 in the UK, No.24 in the US, No.3 in Canada and New Zealand, and making it into the Norwegian and Swedish top-10. As Robert Christgau wrote in *The Village Voice*, 'If this is their worst – which it is, I think – they must be, er, the world's greatest rock'n'roll band.'

Explaining the general concept, Strummer told David Hepworth in 1980, 'We went into Electric Lady after the American tour. We made some music and it just kept going on and on.' Nearly two decades later, he added, 'Every day we showed up and wrote phantasmagorical stuff. Everything was done in first takes and worked out 20 minutes beforehand. It was the most beautiful time ever. To be in New York, in Jimi Hendrix's studio, everything on a roll. As soon as they'd got a rough mix down, we'd be like, 'Fresh tape on the reel. Let's get the mics out because we're gonna go like this, and this, and this.' And we'd keep doing this day and night. That's why it had to be a triple album, even though it would have been better as a double album, a single album, or an EP... who knows. Fact is we recorded all that music in one spot at one moment, in one three-week blast, for better or worse. That's the document!

'Mick Jones again was the king-arranger and always looking to do the new thing. It was really banging off in New York. Rap was there. It *was* 1980. WLBS was blasting all over the city. We hooked on to some of that vibe and made our own version. We made an instrumental mix of 'The Magnificent Seven' and they played it to death. You couldn't go anywhere in New York without hearing that. And that was *us* – weirdo punk rock white guys doing the kit!'

Speaking about that ground-breaking track, Norman Cook, aka Fatboy Slim, told *Uncut* in 2015, 'The Clash were one of the first rock bands to embrace rap music. That was hugely influential on me – I was blown away that The Clash and, later, BAD, had the bollocks to do rap. I thought it was very brave; it risked alienating a lot of people. But they really embraced it, just like they had reggae – they hooked up with Futura and Grandmaster Flash and brought them over to England and seeing them support The Clash was my first exposure to hip-hop. The dub version, 'Mustapha Dance' was equally ground-breaking – it still gets played in clubs, and a lot of house DJs acknowledge how ahead of its time it was.'

Meanwhile, Primal Scream frontman Bobby Gillespie said, 'I used to work in a factory when I was a teenager, so when I listen to 'The Magnificent Seven' I can totally relate to the words. 'Cold water in the face / Brings you back to this awful place' totally sums up the alienation of work and spending five days a week in an environment you hate. People talk about Dylan and Jagger and The Beatles, but Joe Strummer was an equally talented songwriter. He wrote so many fucking great songs – I'm just an enormous fan.'

But this wasn't just a triple helping of white-boy rap. It was so much more, the band open to new ideas, to extremes, many of which worked, some of which didn't. Strummer explained, 'If someone had come in and said, 'Let's play this with balalaikas,' everyone would have gone, 'Give me the biggest balalaika!' We were open about stuff.'

Few at CBS were convinced, Headon recalling, 'They were horrified by *Sandinista!* To them it was just a mess of different tunes, but a lot of effort went into that.' According to Strummer, releasing a triple LP was the band's way of mocking CBS for resisting their desire to release *London Calling as a double, then releasing Bruce Springsteen's The River* less than a year later. They also insisted that the finished product should retail at less than £6, as per Strummer's 1979 line to Garry Bushell that there would never be a Clash LP above that price. CBS agreed on the condition that the package would count as one LP towards their recently extended 10-record deal, and they would forego claims to performance royalties on the first 200,000 copies sold. To get the LP out in that format, The Clash agreed, Strummer later telling Vic Garbarini, 'To do that, in Thatcher's

Britain, during a recession, was a flamboyant gesture.' Asked by *Rip It Up*'s Duncan Campbell about CBS's response, Jones noted, 'If it had happened in Japan, all the executives would have killed themselves.'

Despite its perceived shortcomings, *Sandinista!* was voted best album of the year in *The Village Voice*'s critics poll, and ranked No.404 in *Rolling Stone*'s 500 Greatest Albums of All Time list in 2003, while in 2012 *Slant* magazine placed it at No.85 in its Best Albums of the 1980s list. It won several 'best of the year' critics' polls at the time, and *Alternative Press* magazine included it on a 2000 list of the '10 Essential Political-Revolution Albums'.

Recorded over most of 1980 in London, Manchester, New York and Jamaica, the band shared production duties (though essentially it was down to Strummer and Jones), while it was recorded and mixed by Bill Price, and engineered by Jerry Green (Wessex Sound Studios), J. P. Nicholson (Electric Lady Studios), Lancelot 'Maxie' McKenzie (Channel One Studios) and Price (Pluto + Power Station Studios). There were also dub versions of some songs, and 'toasting' by Mikey Dread, who first stepped in on 'Bankrobber'. The band carried on from where they had started with *London Calling*, reaching beyond punk, reggae, rock'n'roll and R&B into dub, calypso and gospel too, displaying a Lee 'Scratch' Perry influence, adding a dense, echo-filled sound on even the straight rock songs.

When recording began in New York, Paul Simonon was working on a film and so replaced briefly by Ian Dury and The Blockheads' bass player Norman Watt-Roy. This later caused some bad feeling when Watt-Roy and keyboard player Mickey Gallagher (also of The Blockheads) claimed they were responsible for co-composing 'The Magnificent Seven', the song being based on a tune of theirs. Watt-Roy recalled in 1991, 'Jonesy said, 'We need something really funky, cos Joe wants to do a rap. Joe wrote the words there and then, totally spontaneously. A couple of hours later it was in the can.'

Dread, too, was upset he wasn't credited as producer, although credited with 'version mix'. Other guests included Jones' partner at the time, singer Ellen Foley; former Voidoids guitarist Ivan Julian; ex-Eddie and The Hot Roads member Lew Lewis; and Strummer's friend and musical collaborator Tymon Dogg, who played violin, sang on and wrote the track 'Lose This Skin', later joining Strummer's band The Mescaleros.

Mickey Gallagher's children also appeared, his sons Luke and Ben singing a version of debut LP track, 'Career Opportunities', and his daughter Maria singing a snippet of 'The Guns of Brixton' at the end of 'Broadway'. It's also the only Clash album on which all four members have a lead vocal, Topper Headon making a unique lead vocal contribution on disco track 'Ivan Meets G.I. Joe', while Paul Simonon sang lead on 'The Crooked Beat'.

Four singles were released from the *Sandinista!* sessions in the UK, non-LP track 'Bankrobber' followed by 'The Call Up', 'Hitsville UK' and 'The Magnificent Seven'. The original, three-disc vinyl release also included a tri-fold lyric sheet, *The Armagideon Times, No.3* (parts one and two were Clash fanzines), featuring cartoons by *The Guardian*'s Steve Bell, plus handwritten lyrics. The double CD contained a reduced-size version.

The first *Sandinista!* recording was made in Manchester, instrumental 'Shepherd's Delight' being completed in February 1980 at

Pluto during the sessions for 'Bankrobber'. After the completion of the US leg of the 16 Tons tour, Simonon was required in Vancouver for six weeks, starting on March 11, for his acting role in Lou Adler's *Ladies and Gentlemen, The Fabulous Stains* (aka *All Washed Up*), Nancy Dowd's tale of a female rock'n'roll band. But Strummer, Jones and Headon checked into New York's Iroquois hotel on West 44th Street, inspired by stories of James Dean having stayed there in the '50s, getting Epic to book them in at Power Station recording studios for a few days. The idea was simply to record cover versions and sketch out new songs with Bill Price and Mikey Dread, to be used on the collection of singles they intended to release during 1980. And as Price later put it, Dread 'expanded the range of music from rock'n'roll to what he had to offer, genuine Jamaican dub, which was very exciting'.

'Police on My Back' was recorded first, and after a few days The Clash moved across town to Electric Lady, Mickey Gallagher and Norman Watt-Roy flown in to assist for five days, after which Jones and Strummer shared bass duties 'in Paul's style', as Strummer told *New York Rocker*'s Richard Grabel. A chance encounter with Strummer's old busking partner Tymon Dogg followed, leading to an invitation for him to join them. Gallagher recalled, 'It was an experiment in recording where you go into a studio, with all the pressure on you, without any material. The mood was very creative.' Strummer recalled in *Westway to the World*, 'Mick Jones bringing in the new sound of New York, Simmo with his reggae thing, me with my rhythm and blues thing, and Topper with all his soul chops. We could do that.'

Clash biographer Marcus Gray suggested that the musical direction they took may have been partly responding to harsh press criticisms of the 'retrogressive tendencies' of their 1979 output. Whatever the reason, they barely left the studio over those next three weeks, Strummer, Headon and lighting man Warren Steadman building a sanctuary in the studio with flight cases, what became known as the 'Spliffbunker', in which many songs were written. Strummer said, 'It was a place to retreat for musicians and groovers only. It stops everyone hanging out in the control room. The engineer can't work with all that babble. I wrote nearly all the lyrics on *Sandinista!* in the bunker.'

While in New York, the band – Jones in particular – picked up on the radical new hip-hop sounds coming out of radio stations. 'Jonesy was always on the button when it came to new things,' Strummer noted in 1999. 'That stuff we made the week after he came back from Brooklyn with those Sugarhill records, it still rocks.' Jones remembered in 1991, 'We were writing a lot of material and making it up as we went along. There was a lot of jamming. We always took on the music that was going on around us and made it our thing. I was so gone with the hip-hop that the others used to call me 'WhackAttack'. I'd walk around with my beatbox all the time, my hat on backwards!'

After three weeks in Electric Lady, The Clash – including a returned Simonon – flew with Mikey Dread to Jamaica to use Channel One Studios in Kingston. Simonon had finally reached his promised land, saying, 'That was great. I was there at last!' Strummer recalled, 'We recorded 'Junco Partner' and it sounded great. I was sitting at the piano figuring out the chords for the next song when Mikey tapped me on the shoulder and said, 'Quick, we've got to go, the drugmen are coming to kill everyone.'' It emerged that the last foreigners to use Channel One had been The Rolling Stones, recording tracks for *Emotional Rescue* there several months before. They had ensured they weren't bothered by local drug barons by handing out lots of cash. Assuming every white rock band was similarly loaded, The Clash were perceived as greedy and in need of being taught a lesson. As on Strummer's and Jones' previous visit to Jamaica, they quickly returned to their safe European home – 'less *The Harder They Come*, more Jacques Tati,' as Strummer later noted.

Behind the scenes there was a fourth change of management in four years. 'We're not very organised,' Strummer told *Smash Hits*. 'We're not like The Jam, who've got a tight ship with Dad running things. I'm glad we're the way we are – it's more exciting.' Peter Jenner told *NME*'s Len Brown in 1989, 'It was all getting a bit weird. There were white powders going around in certain quarters of the band. I tried to get the band to do something about Topper. I was told to fuck off and mind my own business.'

Having toured Europe that May and June, the band reconvened in August at Wessex Studios, Bill Price overseeing the backing tracks. Jeremy Green, entrusted with overdubs, said, 'Mick was the one with the overall plan. Every track was written down with every overdub that would be needed. If it was done and acceptable, it was noted in a certain colour.'

One evening, legend has it that The Blockheads – performing 'I Want to Be Straight' on *Top of the Pops* dressed as policemen – decided to visit their old mates. They burst into Wessex and Jones – thinking a drugs raid was in progress – flushed his stash down the studio loos. *NME* reported the prank later, hinting heavily at Headon's blossoming heroin problems, noting he was 'last seen wearing a false beard and reading a paper upside down in the Gatwick departure lounge'. Interestingly, a similar tale is told by Madness lead singer Suggs in his 2013 autobiography, *That Close*, recalling, on the subject of *Top of the Pops* performances, his band hiring uniforms from Camden theatrical costumier Berman's and Nathan's. 'One time we got our hands on these authentic coppers' uniforms,' he wrote. 'Can you begin to imagine the fun the seven of us had out on the streets in those? Especially once we found out The Clash were rehearsing near us. We burst into their rehearsal rooms, kicking the doors open, shouting: 'Nobody move, it's the pigs!' We were greeted by the sounds of doors slamming and toilets flushing! They didn't speak to us for five years.'

Meanwhile, after hearing initial mixes of the NYC sessions, Richard Grabel asked whether the US influence evident represented a betrayal of their British fans. Strummer's surreal response? 'Who gives a shit whether a donkey fucked a rabbit and produced a kangaroo? At least it hops, and you can dance to it!'

With all the tracks assembled, Jones and Price set about the running order. There were 38 songs, but the band's 'six songs per side' obsession meant Dread's 'The Crooked Dub' was included as an extension of 'The Crooked Beat', and Maria Gallagher's 'The Guns of Brixton' singalong was tacked on to 'Broadway'. Some sides were stronger than others, Keith Topping seeing the final side as 'conceptually dazzling and linked by several amusing Strummer soundbites' but 'among the most wilfully anti-commercial bits of vinyl a major rock group has ever released'. And Strummer noted in 1988, 'Only bold men go there.' Several songs were also linked

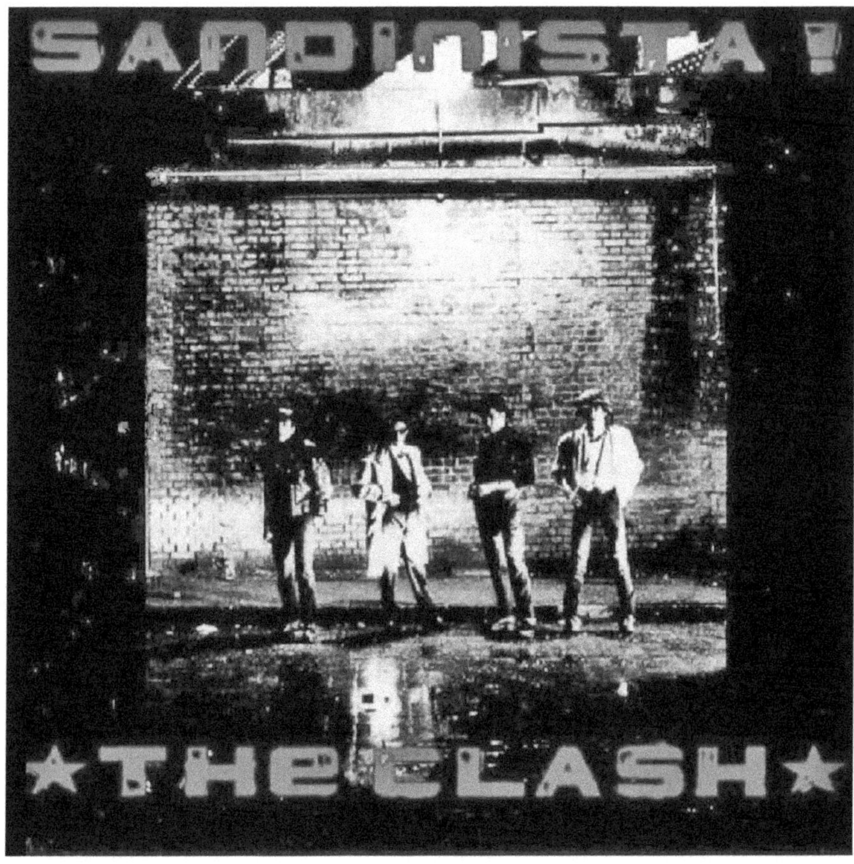

by radio samples and studio chatter. Once completed, the lyrics were given to Steve Bell to illustrate, and the cover featured a moody Pennie Smith shot of the band lined up against a wall behind King's Cross station.

Sandinista! was generally crucified in the UK music press music, albeit with back-handed praise for trying to be different, David Hepworth noting in *Smash Hits*, 'We should be grateful they're let down by ambition.' The *NME*'s Nick Kent considered it 'ridiculously self-indulgent', adding, 'This record is strong testimony that The Clash have temporarily at least lost a grip on their bearings and find themselves parked in a cul-de-sac.' *Melody Maker*'s Patrick Humphries reported on a 'floundering mutant of an album', saying, 'The odd highlights are lost in a welter of reggae/dub overkill.' Yet *Sounds*' Robbi Millar found 'an adventure of diversity and wit, excellence and dross', adding, 'When it is good, it is very good.'

Rude Boy star Ray Gange is definitely a fan, telling *Uncut* in 2015, '*Sandinista!* just blew everything apart. Whatever people were expecting from the next Clash album, *Sandinista!* wasn't it. The variety of stuff was brilliant. I liked the fact that a lot of people didn't get it.'

And *The Complete Clash* author Keith Topping, writing in 2003, felt it had 'aged remarkably well', noting 'an obstinately eclectic collection of world music that was a decade or more ahead of its time' and 'a major influence on the Manchester/baggy dance-rock fusion of the late '80s'. He added that the 'best songs still sound fresh and contemporary'. In *The Irish Times*, Michael McCaughren noted, 'The first time I heard mention of Nicaragua's Sandinista revolution was on the cover of the 1980 Clash album, bought with Christmas pocket money. Five years later I found myself lying in bed with dengue fever in a dusty village in rural Nicaragua, a punk rock political journey inspired by The Clash's magnificent triple album.' And in 1998, *Uncut*'s Simon Goddard praised *Sandinista!* as 'the most innovative rock album ever made'.

Bono, of U2, in an interview with Elton John in 2003, published online by the *Epitaph* website, said, 'The Clash got terrible criticism for *Sandinista!* But were it not for that record, I'd never have heard about Nicaragua or ended up going there and meeting with Daniel Ortega, the leader of the revolution, and Ernesto Cardenal, a minister of culture, or ended up writing 'Bullet the Blue Sky', because my mind was blown by the experience. Those were the kind of doors The Clash, and Joe in particular, opened up for me, and there were worlds behind them.

'I remember we were staying at the Gramercy Park Hotel, New York City, and The Clash, our idols, walked through the door. Paul Simonon, the bassist, looked like somebody out of *West Side Story* crossed with an axe murderer. He had this jacket, and on the back was the name of a local gang. They had been hanging out with some of the gangs, listening to early scratch hip-hop; then they came up with 'This Is Radio Clash', finding in New York that sort of interface between black and white music that they'd found in London. That was a real moment when the Clash were crossing genres. Hip-hop was in at the time, and Chuck D of Public Enemy came out of that scene. I know Elvis didn't mean shit to Chuck D, as he once famously said, but I'll bet The Clash did. They meant something to others as well – Manic Street Preachers, Rage Against the Machine, The Beastie Boys.'

Chuck D, of Public Enemy, in another 2003 Joe Strummer tribute published online by the *Epitaph* website, said, 'The first time I heard The Clash was in 1981. I was in college at Adelphi University on Long Island, and one night went down to this show in Manhattan, one of Kurtis Blow's hip-hop package shows. The crowd was rough. People from different camps were there – the hip-hop people and the punk rock people. They even started throwing tomatoes at Kurtis. That's the type of wild kids who were there. But The Clash completely broke it that night. It was an awakening for a New York cat like myself.

'As I delved more into the music scene, I started learning about how the kids across the water in England were rebelling against the Queen and the aristocracy. Around the same time, Bill Stephney, a friend of mine from Adelphi and one of the original members of Public Enemy, started playing The Clash's records on his hip-hop radio show, which opened up a lot of people's minds. He would reach into The Clash's catalogue, as well as the Sex Pistols', and make those kinds of songs work in the context of a hip-hop show. He was instrumental in exposing a lot of hip-hop cats to what The Clash were doing.

'I had great respect for Joe Strummer. How he used his music – incorporating a lot of black music like hip-hop and reggae – was very different from the guys who invented rock'n'roll. He always paid homage to those who came before him. I admired him for his humility as an artist and for the fact that he dug musical cats, no matter what type of music they played. He was constantly pushing the boundaries of The Clash's sound and of what music could do on a greater level. And Joe was still rebellious. He was speaking about things he saw in his life – the things right in front of his face that no one wanted to talk about – and taking his message around the world.

'Public Enemy is an American group but we address the same issues – political, social, musical – on an international level. We take our conversation worldwide. I learned the importance of that from Joe Strummer. Right now, there's a hunger out there for a musician like that. It's not an easy way to go, but there are people who are doing it in hip-hop right now. That's Joe Strummer's legacy – the idea that you need to stand by your word every step of the way.'

Drawing parallels between *Sandinista!* and its predecessor, Stephen Thomas Erlewine at allmusic.com, said, 'The Clash sounded like they could do anything on *London Calling*. For its triple-album follow-up, *Sandinista!*, they tried to do everything, adding dub, rap, gospel, even children's choruses to the punk, reggae, R&B, and roots rock they were playing. Instead of presenting a band with a far-reaching vision, like *London Calling*, *Sandinista!* plays as a messy, confused jumble, which means its numerous virtues are easy to ignore. Amid all the dub experiments, backward tracks, unfinished songs, and instrumentals, a number of classic Clash songs rank among the band's best, yet it's difficult for anyone but the most dedicated listeners to find them. A few of the failed ideas were worth exploring, but even more weren't even worth pursuing. As the cliché says, there's a great single album within these three records, and those songs make *Sandinista!* worthwhile. Nevertheless, its sloppy attack is disheartening after the tour de force of *London Calling* and focused aggression of *The Clash*.'

John Piccarella, for *Rolling Stone*, mentioning John Lennon's murder in New York four days before its release, wrote, 'Nothing could have helped get me through the unreal mass depression ... other than the release of the Clash's *Sandinista!* Its three records – 36 tracks to get lost in – ask and answer some of the right questions about violence and non-violence, history and the future, crime and the law, revolution and fascism, worldwide angst and hope.' After the 'standard-setting' *London Calling*, he found *Sandinista!* 'a sprawling, scattered smokescreen of styles, with an expanded range that's at once encyclopedic and supplemental', feeling that 'without *London Calling*'s machismo, *Sandinista!* tries harder and goes further'. He also mentioned how its 'odd instrumentation, different production values in different studios, and guest musicians', gave 'the unsettling impression that this isn't necessarily the band you expected to hear when you bought the album', but added, 'There's rarely been an LP this big or far-reaching,' making comparisons with George Harrison's *All Things Must Pass* and Frank Sinatra's *Trilogy*.

4

Piccarella added, '*London Calling* was the Clash's *Exile on Main Street*, *Sandinista!* their *White Album*,' later concluding, 'If the ambition of *London Calling* was to recast the whole of rock'n'roll history, *Sandinista!* wants a place in the cultural traditions of the world. Its lyrics – and its melodies and rhythms – make reference not only to the US and UK but to the USSR and places in Europe, Asia, Africa, Central and South America, and the Caribbean. And the inclusion of lead vocals by women, children, friends and taped voices, as well as by every member of the band, all reinforce that global reach.'

And John Harris, for *Mojo* in 2003, wrote, 'If *London Calling* was expansive, its successor had the dimensions of a planet. The Clash threw themselves into the tumult of early '80s New York, in particular the first stirrings of hip-hop. Given its six sides, 36 tracks and the group's prodigious weed intake, the album got a reputation for being dazed and unfocused. It is, but its borderline lunatic breadth is actually part of its appeal.' Taking on Piccarella's point for *Rolling Stone*, he added, 'Think of it as their *White Album*, both flawed and inspired, testament to minds so supercharged they didn't know when to stop.'

COMBAT ROCK

Side one: 'Know Your Rights', 'Car Jamming', 'Should I Stay or Should I Go', 'Rock the Casbah', 'Red Angel Dragnet', 'Straight to Hell'; Side two: 'Overpowered by Funk', 'Atom Tan', 'Sean Flynn', 'Ghetto Defendant', 'Inoculated City', 'Death is a Star'

All tracks written by The Clash, except 'Know Your Rights' (Strummer/Jones).
Rat Patrol from Fort Bragg (unofficial) tracklisting: 'The Beautiful People Are Ugly Too', 'Kill Time', 'Should I Stay or Should I Go', 'Rock the Casbah', 'Know Your Rights' (extended version), 'Red Angel Dragnet', 'Ghetto Defendant', 'Sean Flynn', 'Car Jamming', 'Inoculated City', 'Death is a Star', 'Walk Evil Talk', 'Atom Tan', 'Overpowered by Funk', 'Inoculated City' (unedited version), 'First Night Back in London', 'Cool Confusion', 'Straight to Hell' (extended version).

Personnel: Joe Strummer: lead and backing vocals, guitar, harmonica, piano; Mick Jones: guitar, backing and lead vocals, keyboards, sound effects; Paul Simonon: bass guitar, backing vocals, lead vocals on 'Red Angel Dragnet'; Topper Headon: drums, piano and bass guitar on 'Rock the Casbah'
Also featuring: Allen Ginsberg – guest vocals on 'Ghetto Defendant'; Futura 2000 – guest vocals on 'Overpowered by Funk'; Ellen Foley – backing vocals on 'Car Jamming'; Joe Ely – backing vocals on 'Should I Stay or Should I Go'; Tymon Dogg – piano on 'Death is a Star'; Tommy Mandel (as Poly Mandell) – keyboards on 'Overpowered by Funk'; Gary Barnacle – saxophone on 'Sean Flynn'; Kosmo Vinyl – vocals on 'Red Angel Dragnet'
Production: The Clash – producers; Glyn Johns: chief engineer, mixing; Joe Blaney, Jerry Green, Eddie Garcia: assistant engineers; Pennie Smith: photography

'When you're struggling it holds you together, cos you're heading for some point. 'We're going to make it. Come on boys, hang in there!' And then 'Rock the Casbah' went top-five. All this has gone down in the space of four years. It had to have a toll on us and I think we should have had maybe a year off. Combat Rock went top-five in America and this is unheard of for us. Our placings had

been like 198 below that. And suddenly it just all blew up.'

Joe Strummer, Westway to the World, 2000

The Clash started work on their fifth studio LP, with the working title *Rat Patrol from Fort Bragg*, in April 1981, for what was originally set to be a double album. Mick Jones produced one cut, but the others weren't happy, in time handing over to Glyn Johns, the album reconceived as a single LP, released as *Combat Rock* the following May. It became their most successful long player, reaching No.2 in the UK and No.7 in the US. But the album's success came at a high price, the new LP as good as finishing The Clash off as a creative force. By the time they were done, Topper Headon had been sacked, and by the time they'd finished touring the LP, Mick Jones had also received his marching orders.

Recorded at Marcus Music, Kensington

4

Gardens; Ear Studios, London W11; and Electric Lady, New York, in April 1981 and January 1982, and released that May on both sides of the Atlantic, *Combat Rock* had its experimental moments – as *Sandinista!* had. Yet it was the more commercial tracks that received the most airplay, including US lead-off single 'Should I Stay or Should I Go', a Jones-fronted number that reached No.17 in the UK but would be re-released and top the British charts nine years later. It got plenty of radio airplay in the States from the start, and further single 'Rock the Casbah', composed by Headon, had just as much impact. In fact, it turned out to be the band's biggest US hit, reaching No.8, its Don Letts-directed video heavily plugged on emerging international music channel MTV.

While Jones was keen to present another grand, visionary work, carrying on where they'd left off with the previous album, his main co-writer was intent on a more back-to-basics rock'n'roll opus, and a single LP this time. Initial recording sessions in April and September '81 led to demos re-recorded at Electric Lady either side of Christmas, but the results were deemed somewhat grandiose in places, and Bernie Rhodes, on hearing a seven-and-a-half-minute take of 'Sean Flynn', asked, 'Does *everything* have to be a raga?' – a remark that inspired the opening of one of the big hit singles, 'Rock the Casbah'.

It didn't help matters when Headon was arrested at Heathrow Airport for heroin possession, appearing at Uxbridge Magistrates Court a week before Christmas. As it was, his solicitor described him as 'a valuable member of a band, recently voted one of the world's top-five drummers', and he got away with a £500 fine, having promised the magistrate he'd clean up his act. But the writing was on the wall.

The LP was due to be completed in early January '82, before The Clash's ground-breaking tour of Japan, Australia, New Zealand and South East Asia. But there was still plenty of work to do, the band well behind schedule for an intended April release, and way over budget.

Tempers reached breaking point when Strummer accused Jones of sabotaging affairs by insisting the album be recorded in New York, describing his partner as 'often acting like Liz Taylor in a filthy mood'. By then the pair were looking to avoid each other in the studio, recording overdubs at different times to avoid further confrontation. Meanwhile, Jerry Green said Paul Simonon's contributions were minimal, with Jones and tape operator Eddie Garcia recording many of his basslines. Then, in late January, Jones presented the rest of the band with a 15-track, 65-minute double LP, which Strummer later referred to as 'a home movie mix', rejecting it. He told Bill Holdship in 1984, 'I don't believe anyone is so great that they don't write crap sometimes. I said, 'Mick, I don't think you can produce,' and it was, 'You bastard, I thought you were my friend!''

With the Far East tour imminent, studio time was booked in Australia, so the band could work on the new mix there. Jones reflected, 'That's where we really ground to a halt.' Headon recalled in 1991, 'We were trying to remix *Combat Rock* after gigs. You can imagine what your hearing's like. They said, 'You have a go at mixing. I tried to be all professional, slide the bass up a bit, so I can't hear the drums. By the time I finished, every fader on the desk was on full.'

Tensions remained, and Simonon said in *Westway to the World*, 'I remember a two-hour argument with Mick about the level of the bass on 'Know Your Rights'. I wanted it louder and deeper, a reggae sound. I think he'd got bored of playing guitar by then. He had equipment that would make it sound like a harpsichord or an orchestra.' Time wore on and still it wasn't ready, The Clash flying to Thailand in March. It didn't help when they were marooned in a hotel, with their money stolen, and when Simonon fell ill, with what was initially diagnosed as a twisted colon turning out to be food poisoning.

It was around then, on a railway siding outside Bangkok, that Pennie Smith took the photo that would end up on the album cover. And in an interview used in the *Viva Joe Strummer: The Clash and Beyond* DVD, she recalled, 'Halfway through the shoot, something just happened. Somehow they just dissolved in front of my eyes.'

With a double album ruled out, the band looked to outside help. Bernie Rhodes' initial suggestion of using Gus Dudgeon was turned down, until he realised – according to Kosmo Vinyl – that he'd got the wrong name, actually meaning former Rolling Stones, The Who, Beatles, Faces and Led Zeppelin engineer/producer Glyn Johns. And while Johns wasn't keen on mixing material he hadn't recorded, he was intrigued by what he heard and took on the job. The Clash booked into Wessex Studios at the end of March, and Johns started by reviewing their New York recordings from three months before.

They'd recorded 18 songs, enough for that possible double album, but while Jones argued in favour, proposing lengthier, dance mixes, his bandmates argued for a single LP and shorter tracks, the subsequent internal wrangling creating further tension. The editing took place in Glyn Johns' garden studio in Warnford, Hampshire, accompanied by Strummer and Jones, with *Combat Rock* cut down from 77 minutes to 46, largely by removing instrumental intros and codas from songs such as 'Rock the Casbah' and the reinstated 'Overpowered by Funk'. Additionally, the trio decided to omit four songs entirely, dropping the final track count to 12. Generally, the drums and bass were pushed up in the mix, and three tracks each lost a verse, including 'Straight to Hell' and 'Sean Flynn', the latter cut to half of its original length. Meanwhile, Strummer re-recorded his vocals for the opener, 'Know Your Rights', as did Jones for 'Should I Stay or Should I Go', with amendments to the lyrics.

'Know Your Rights' was chosen as the album's lead single, released in the UK on April 23. And while that failed to reach the top 40, the LP itself followed on May 14 and reached No.2 in the UK album charts. It stuck around for 23 weeks, only kept off the top by Paul McCartney's *Tug of War*. In the US, *Combat Rock* reached No.7, spending 61 weeks in the album chart. It also reached the top 10 in many more countries.

'Rock the Casbah' would go on to reach No.8 in the US singles chart. Back in the UK, it made No.30, while September's UK double A-side release of 'Should I Stay or Should I Go'/'Straight to Hell' made No.17. The album itself was ranked at No.4 among the *NME*'s top albums of 1982, with 'Straight to Hell' ranked No.20 and 'Know Your Rights' No.30 in its top 50 tracks, while the US certified *Combat Rock* gold in November 1982, platinum in January 1983, and multi-platinum in June 1995.

As well as two tracks focusing on the impact and aftermath of the Vietnam War

– 'Straight to Hell' and 'Sean Flynn' – Clash biographer Pat Gilbert pointed to how many of the songs had a 'trippy, foreboding feel', saturated in a 'colonial melancholia and sadness' reflecting that conflict. The band were also hugely inspired by Francis Ford Coppola's 1979 film about the war, *Apocalypse Now*, as previously referenced on 'Charlie Don't Surf' for *Sandinista!*

With the album released just as Britain went to war with Argentina over the Falkland Islands, the *NME*'s X Moore declared it 'an inadvertent counterblast to the Falklands, too important to be snidely lumped with the other dross, by a band too important to tear themselves apart'. Meanwhile, *Sounds*' Dave McCullough wrote, 'The Clash aren't static anymore, but sailing into their own Heart of Darkness trying to settle those wild contradictions they seemed doomed by.' He praised the lyrics and 'strange musical landscapes' and gave it five stars. Adam Sweeting in *Melody Maker* was unhappy with the 'hard, dry mix' but found the music 'increasingly effective' and picked up on the cinematic imagery.

In America *Combat Rock* was generally well received, and while *Village Voice*'s Robert Christgau lamented further attempts at funk and dub on the album – as per *Sandinista!* – he dismissed any notion that the band were selling out, believing they were continuing to evolve, writing songs at a 'higher level of verbal, musical, and political density', albeit in less 'terse and clear' fashion than on early work. Elsewhere, *Slant* magazine would list the LP at No.80 in its list of 'Best Albums of the 1980s', and Nirvana frontman Kurt Cobain put it in his top 50 albums of all time.

David Fricke for *Rolling Stone* in June 1982, reckoned 'rock's last angry band' had fallen out of fashion in the UK, 'scorned by a cynical press drunk on funk and futurism, and by their own punk progeny, the Oi! bands, for selling out to Yankee commercial interests', in the wake of *London Calling and Sandinista!* while 'in Reagan country', they had 'immortality thrust upon them'. He added, 'The message of *Combat Rock* – a snarling, enraged, yet still musically ambitious collection of 12 tight tracks on a single disc – is 'pop hits and press accolades be damned'. This record is a declaration of real-life emergency, a provocative, demanding document of classic punk anger, reflective questioning and nerve-wracking frustration. It is written in songwriter-guitarists Joe Strummer and Mick Jones' now-familiar rock Esperanto ... and like every Clash record from 1977's 'White Riot' on, it carries the magnum force of the group's convictions in the bold rhythmic punch of bassist Paul Simonon and drummer Topper Headon and the guitar-army bash of Strummer and Jones.'

He added, 'For the most part, Combat Rock is short on practical solutions, long on the horror of the problems,' but contains 'stirring, inspirational rock'n'roll, arranged with good pop sense and shot through in concentrated doses with the imagination and vigour spread throughout Sandinista!' Fricke concluded, 'Whereas most of the false prophets and non-stop complainers washed up by the New Wave await a brave new world, The Clash are battling tooth, nail and guitar to salvage the one we've got, in the only way they know. *Combat Rock* may not have the answers, but it may be our last warning: sign up or shut up.'

Stephen Thomas Erlewine, in a retrospective review for allmusic.com, wrote, 'On the surface, *Combat Rock* appears to be a retreat from the sprawling stylistic explorations of *London Calling* and *Sandinista!* The pounding arena rock of 'Should I Stay, or Should I Go' makes The Clash sound like an arena rock band, and much of the album boasts a muscular, heavy sound, courtesy of producer Glyn Johns. But things aren't quite that simple. *Combat Rock* contains heavy flirtations with rap, funk, and reggae, and even has a cameo by poet Allen Ginsberg – if this album is, as it has often been claimed, The Clash's sellout effort, it's a very strange way to sell out. Even with the infectious, dance-inflected new wave pop of 'Rock the Casbah' leading the way, there aren't many overt attempts at crossover success, mainly because the group is tearing in two separate directions. Mick Jones wants The Clash to inherit The Who's righteous arena rock stance, and Joe Strummer wants to forge ahead into black music. The result is an album that is nearly as inconsistent as *Sandinista!* even though its finest moments – 'Should I Stay or Should I Go', 'Rock the Casbah', 'Straight to Hell' – illustrate why The Clash were able to reach a larger audience than ever before.'

John Harris, for *Mojo* in March 2003, wrote, 'The classic line-up's last hurrah, prepared for release during downtime on the Australasian tour that finished them off. Here, *Sandinista!*'s abiding aesthetic, roughly the notion of an international urban rock music, is fine-honed to the extent that on the back of the majestic 'Rock the Casbah', The Clash managed to break into the American top-10. That song plus 'Know Your Rights', 'Car Jamming' and 'Straight to Hell', prove their talents remained intact, but a good third of *Combat Rock* rings hollow, particularly 'Red Angel Dragnet's attempt to evoke *Taxi Driver*, emblematic of one of their Achilles heels – if you seek to capture the spirit of everywhere you visit, you'll occasionally come off sounding like a tourist. One of its other drawbacks was unavoidable. In the wake of their previous two albums, a mere 12-tracker would always seem like short measure. But financially, *Combat Rock* was their most successful album, receipts belatedly swelled in 1991 by the Levi-sponsored ubiquity of 'Should I Stay or Should I Go'.'

Meanwhile, Keith Topping, in *The Complete Clash*, noted, '*Combat Rock*'s cluttered lyrics and inelegant stubs at outré musical forms render the LP somewhat gauche beside *London Calling*'s ground-breaking and urbane recontextualisation of The Clash's basic sound, and positively anaemic compared to the breathtaking sophistication and depth of *Sandinista!* Nevertheless, there is much to admire.'

A full *Rat Patrol from Fort Bragg* finally appeared, although not officially released, including 'First Night Back in London' and 'Cool Confusion', both discarded from *Combat Rock* but released as B-sides, while some of Mick Jones' original mixes appeared in the *Clash on Broadway* and *Sound System* box sets.

CUT THE CRAP

Side one: 'Dictator', 'Dirty Punk', 'We Are The Clash', 'Are You Red..Y', 'Cool Under Heat', 'Movers and Shakers'; Side two: 'This is England', 'Three Card Trick', 'Play to Win', 'Fingerpoppin'', 'North and South', 'Life is Wild'; CD bonus track – 'Do It Now'

All tracks written by Joe Strummer and Bernard Rhodes.
Personnel: Joe Strummer: lead vocals, guitars; Paul Simonon: bass guitar; Nick Sheppard: guitar, lead vocals on 'North and

4

South'; Vince White: additional guitar on 'Do It Now'; Pete Howard: drums
Also featuring: Hermann Weindorf – keyboards, synthesisers; Norman Watt-Roy – bass; Michael Fayne – drum machines, vocals on 'Play to Win'; Norman Watt-Roy (The Blockheads) – bass; Bernie Rhodes – drum machine programming
Production: Bernie Rhodes – producer (credited as Jose Unidos)
Recorded in Munich and mixed in Mayfair, London, produced by Jose Unidos (Bernard Rhodes) and engineered by Ulli Rudolf and Simon Sullivan.

'That wasn't such a great idea. It wasn't any reflection on Vince White or Nick Sheppard or Pete Howard. I think about those guys sometimes and hope it didn't fuck up their lives too much, because they were good people in a no-win situation.'
Joe Strummer to Sean O'Hagan, NME, 1997

Released on November 4, 1985, in the UK and US on CBS and Epic, respectively, I could argue that we shouldn't even count Cut the Crap, the sixth and final studio album by The Clash. Many fans would choose not to. But it's an important part of the tale.

Manager Bernie Rhodes took over studio production duties under the alias 'Jose Unidos', with the result a critically maligned LP, one generally ridiculed on release by the UK music press. And yet, as Keith Topping pointed out in *The Complete Clash*, *'While every authorised retrospective until 2003 saw Mick Jones' departure in September 1983 as effectively the end of The Clash, at the time it was seen as a new beginning, at least within the band itself.'*

The original title was *Out of Control*, Rhodes believed to have changed the name shortly before the LP's release without consulting the band. In 2000, *Cut the Crap* was remastered and re-released in Europe with bonus track 'Do It Now', but that reissue was unannounced and not promoted. It came after the rest of the band's catalogue had been reissued in December 1999 and January 2000 in the US.

While Pete Howard was an adept drummer, drum machines were used for virtually all percussion tracks, and Strummer always disowned the album, although admitting a liking for 'This is England' and saying 'North and South' was 'a vibe'.

Cut the Crap wasn't mentioned in Don Letts' 2000 documentary, *Westway to the World* and was only briefly acknowledged in official 2008 book *The Clash*, pointedly not receiving an overview as the first five albums had. Furthermore, none of the tracks made it on to the band's official compilations until *The Essential Clash* in 2003, *Singles Box* three years later and 2007's *The Singles* included 'This is England'. The 2013 career-spanning boxsets *Sound System* and *5 Album Studio Set* also missed the album off, as had 1991 boxset *Clash on Broadway*.

Sole single 'This is England', released five weeks earlier on September 30, like the rest of the LP, was drastically re-engineered by Rhodes, with synths and football-style chants added to Strummer's incomplete recordings. The single also received mostly negative reviews on release, including one from the *NME*'s Gavin Martin, who claimed, 'Strummer's rant bears all the signs of aged rocker well into advance senility.' But Dave Marsh later championed it as one of the top 1001 rock singles of all time, and allmusic.com's Stephen Thomas Erlewine called it 'surprisingly heavy' on a record of otherwise 'formulaic, tired punk rock that doesn't have the aggression or purpose of early Clash records'. It was also No.30 in an *Uncut* poll chosen by an all-star panel in December 2015.

Written in late 1983, the track was Strummer's attempt to address the state of his homeland during the early years of the Thatcher administration, addressing inner-city violence, urban alienation, life on council estates, high unemployment, an ailing motorcycle industry, racism, nationalism, police corruption, the Falklands War and a consumerist subservient mindset. And it was described by the man himself as his 'last great Clash song'.

Initially, with attempts made by The Clash and others to ignore the band's final incarnation, 'This is England' was left off several compilations and boxsets and not mentioned in 2000's Westway to the World, giving the impression that the band broke up when Mick Jones was sacked. But by 2003 it was the last track on The Essential Clash and has been included on further collections since.

Don Letts, discussing the track in *Uncut* in 2015, said, 'To deny 'This Is England' is a fantastic song is to not do Joe his full justice. It was a magic combination between Joe and Mick, but this song points out what Joe's part in that relationship was. I'm talking about lyrically and the 'state of the country' thing. It's a fantastic tune. I agree with everybody that The Clash ended when Mick left, but 'This Is England' is a tune that highlights what was great about Strummer. No disrespect to Mick, I even feel like saying 'apologies to Mick', but even he couldn't take 'This Is England' away from Joe as a great Clash record.'

Recording for the album had finally got underway the previous December in Munich, Rhodes choosing that studio mainly, according to Nick Sheppard, because it was cheap. It was also out of the way, an early digital studio, owned by a millionaire who had made his money in construction after the Second World War. The backing tracks were almost entirely recorded by Strummer and engineer Ulli Rudolf, with drums and keyboards added by session musicians Michael Faye and Herman Wagner. Sheppard flew to Munich in January '85 and was subsequently joined by Pete Howard and Vince White. Sheppard told Marcus Gray, 'I'm on all the songs. I would say Vince is as well. Paul wasn't really involved much but did play on a couple of tracks.' Howard's contributions were limited to two songs the five-piece recorded live in the studio one afternoon – 'This is England' B-sides 'Do It Now' and 'Sex Mad Roar'.

Having wrested control of the project from Strummer, Rhodes oversaw mixing in Mayfair with engineer Simon Sullivan. He also received co-songwriting credits on all the songs, even 'This is England', previously credited to The Clash. Strummer told Bill Flanagan in 1988. 'He served as a sounding board for me, but I thought it was a bit cheeky all the same. That's not to say he didn't write anything, but I wouldn't have said it was half and half.'

With its title taken from dialogue in 1981 post-apocalyptic movie *Mad Max 2: The Road Warrior*, Keith Topping, in *The Complete Clash*, felt that 'most of *Cut the Crap*'s songs inhabit the same fantasy universe, shot through with occasional proto-realistic lyrics here and there, but essentially a Hollywood version of life in the urban jungle in the last days of the twentieth century.' By the time it was released, the band were effectively history, Topping adding, 'Any lingering doubts in Strummer's mind about trying to flog a dead horse and keep The Clash going were assassinated by the reviews the LP received.' Critical and commercial reception was certainly poor, Jones and Headon's departure leading most to regard *Cut the Crap* as a Joe Strummer solo LP, despite Paul Simonon's involvement. Yet even the most blinkered fans of the band's frontman – still privately grieving the recent deaths of both of his parents – could surely see his disillusionment with The Clash by that point.

Mat Snow's *NME* review was as harsh a critique as the band ever received, describing the cover as a 'marketing director's idea of Ye Style Punke', feeling their sound had been reduced to 'snub-nosed guitars bullying the trooper and railing at the bastions of privilege'. Adam Sweeting at Melody Maker added, 'Guess what? It's CRAP! And it doesn't cut it. Football chants, noises of heavy meals being regurgitated over pavements, and a mix that Moulinex would be ashamed of... it's painful.' But Sounds' Jack Barron gave the LP four and a half stars, declaring that the band 'don't miss Mick Jones and have finally managed to lucidly stitch together their love of ethnic music with gut-level rock'.

David Fricke, for *Rolling Stone* in early 1986, wrote, 'Too much of *Cut the Crap* is Strummer's angst running on automatic, superficially ferocious but ultimately stiff and unconvincing.' Fricke added, 'There was a time when The Clash embodied all that was noble about punk. They understood the difference between apocalypse and mere anti-style and, as songwriters, Joe Strummer and Mick Jones had the gift of grab. Sadly, *Cut the Crap* sounds like the last nine years never happened. London's still burning; so are Liverpool, Central America and the Middle East. But this album is the sound of The Clash just blowing smoke, thrashing in desperation under Strummer and bassist Paul Simonon's uncertain leadership. In Jones' absence, they have beat a retreat back to buzzsaw basics, abetted by controversial manager Bernard Rhodes, who boldly assumes co-authorship of the 12 songs with Strummer. The three new members are little more than bit players, filling out the sound with dutiful bluster, but rarely kicking it to life.'

It didn't help when Fricke compared the album to Mick Jones' debut with his new band, *This Is Big Audio Dynamite*, released the previous month on Columbia and reaching No.27 in the UK and just outside the US Billboard 100, even if The Clash did slightly outperform that when *Cut the Crap* reached No.16 in the UK and No.88 in the US. Fricke mused, 'If *Cut the Crap* is a cheat, Mick Jones' new band Big Audio Dynamite is an unexpected gamble. 'That old-time groove is really nowhere,' Jones shrugs in 'The Bottom Line', brusquely dismissing Strummer's retro-punk didacticism. Instead, he continues, 'I'm gonna take you to part two,' an intoxicating subversion of '80s dancefloor cool with *Sandinista!*'s dub-funk turmoil.' He concluded, '*This Is Big Audio Dynamite* hardly transcends The Clash's finest hours, but for Jones it is a new beginning. With *Cut the Crap*, one might well wonder if Joe Strummer's at the end of the road.'

In a more positive review, Richard Cromelin, at the *Los Angeles Times*, felt the new band sounded less effective than previous Clash records in light of a tamer political climate and the absence of Jones, but concluded, 'Strummer's singing was still compelling' and 'This is England' and 'North and South' made the album 'more than

passable'. *Village Voice*'s Robert Christgau also added positive notes, writing, 'Most of the songs eventually take effect, some persistent, exuberant, melancholic, and even-keeled, particularly 'We Are the Clash'.'

John Robb, in 2006's *Punk Rock: An Oral History*, reckoned *Cut the Crap* was 'cronked by its bizarre production, turning the latter-day Clash's rabble-rousers into electronic pop waffle'. He did, however, feel that final single 'This is England' stood out, thanks to 'Joe's great lyrics and impassioned vocal, raising the game at the final post', conceding that, 'The rest of the songs sound great on live bootlegs from the time.' He too made negative comparisons with BAD, adding, 'Mick Jones hit pay-dirt and kept moving forward with Big Audio Dynamite, old buddy Don Letts joining him in the band, fusing electro and the emerging flavours of the hip-hop scene to cinematic samples and futuristic Westway rock'n'roll.'

Phil Gibson gave the album a fresh listen for John Robb's *Louder Than War* website in 2012. He was keen to shout from the rooftops about the merits of 'This is England', but couldn't fully defend the rest of the LP. He also compared 1985's offerings by The Clash with that by their ousted lead guitarist and founder member, writing, 'Mick Jones and Big Audio Dynamite came along at the same time and presented their songs well. Clear production brought clarity to their ideas. The irony is that for all their musical differences, Strummer and Jones walked the same path, with 'This is England' utilising samples and keyboards, as did the bulk of *This is Big Audio Dynamite*. That Mick Jones with 'E=MC2' equaled the highest-ever Clash single chart placing of *London Calling* (No.11 in the UK) put it all into stark contrast. The Clash was never solely about chart positions, but Strummer surely must have seen the writing on the wall.'

He added, 'The original title was to be *Out of Control*. Check out the song of the same name and you wonder how it wasn't included on the album. There are bootlegs that give a better reflection of The Clash Mk. II and the fact that they had many songs that could have made *Cut the Crap* a better album or indeed made up a good follow-up album. Check out 'Glue Zombie' and 'In the Pouring Rain'. The Clash Mk. II deserved a better album than *Cut the Crap*, but the reality is this group carried the name The Clash, and that group deserved so much better.' Gibson concluded, 'Is the album cutting edge? Definitely not, but if you take away the amateur production and ridiculous backing vocals, there are the makings of a good album. But to get to those ideas and that more fitting epitaph The Clash so richly deserved you really do need to cut through all the crap.'

Meanwhile, back in 2003's *The Complete Clash*, Keith Topping concluded, '*Cut the Crap* has become a virtual industry byword for a terrible mistake made by a major rock group.' So while Jon Savage, in England's Dreaming, bewilderingly considered it 'an ambitious and moving state of the nation address with innovative use of rap, rhythm and atmosphere', Topping looked to shoot him down in flames, stressing, 'It's actually none of those things or anything even remotely like them, and it beggars belief that a writer as good as Savage could hold this LP in higher regard than *Give 'Em Enough Rope*, let alone *London Calling*.'

Besides, as Strummer himself later reflected, 'When The Clash collapsed, we were tired. There had been a lot of intense activity in five years. Secondly, I felt we'd run out of idea gasoline. Thirdly, I wanted to shut up and let someone else have a go at it.' Furthermore, before it was even released, Strummer had decided he didn't want to carry on with The Clash. And to that end, the NME of November 23, 1985 – less than three weeks after the official release date – carried a brief statement to the effect that 'Sheppard, White and Howard had left the band'.

As writer Kris Needs put it in 2005's Viva Joe Strummer: The Clash and Beyond documentary, 'Joe was the one who gave Topper the word that he was fired. Joe was the one who fired Mick. Joe said, 'My ego told me to get rid of them.' He could carry it on. He couldn't. He carried on the band, but Paul Simonon was hardly in the band at that point. It was Joe Strummer and a cabaret Clash tribute band behind him.'

THE CLASH'S 50 FINEST

Maybe we'll never see eye-to-eye on a 'definitive' list of 50 great Clash songs. Whatever combination of tracks I come up with, there will be disagreement. But you've got to start somewhere, and after a little head-scratching this is the line-up I chose (in vaguely chronological order). If your favourite track's not included, perhaps I feel your pain.

My own list may be different if I restart tomorrow, but the publisher was breathing down my neck ... and you really have to let it go sometimes, with your instincts. When I told Clash fan Neil Waite I was struggling on this top 50, he replied, 'You might as well spend your evening trying to put toothpaste back in the tube.' There are at least a couple of tracks added where over-familiarity breeds less interest, but they're included all the same because of their importance in the scheme of things. And I made sacrifices where I really couldn't justify inclusion. So, with excuses out of the way, here goes...

1 'White Riot'

Single, March '77, and *The Clash*, April '77

Just under the two-minute mark in both studio versions, and as much an assault on the senses now as first time I heard it. Three-chord punk at its most inspirationally-startling. Here was Joe Strummer – admittedly a little naïve then, but always with heart in the right place – tackling class, economics, race and social change, and it was only controversial if you didn't really get it. Strummer's barking vocal plays on that simmering resentment at the state of the nation, encouraging us to follow the example of our black brothers and find a cause worth fighting, while Mick Jones pitches in with searing guitar welts, as if eager to stop himself lapsing into rock power chords. And from that first strangled riff, he's got us.

2 '1977'

'White Riot' B-side, March '77

Turn that first single over and you have another corker, this time barely 100 seconds long but expressing all you needed to hear about punk's 'year zero' approach. Again, only the confused could really took umbrage at that 'No Elvis, Beatles or The Rolling Stones' sentiment, and 'Sten guns in Knightsbridge' threat. From that buzzsaw guitar from Jones to that six-string chop over Simmo's chunky bass, and the Orwellian allusion to 1984 being around the corner that suggested a bleak future was in store. But at the same time there was a feeling that we were all in it together (I know, I was only nine when they came up with this, but the best music is timeless). And while The Kinks deserved at least a percentage for the inspiration behind that awesome riff, Mick Jones took it to a level that suggested respect rather than pure plagiarism.

3 'Janie Jones'

***The Clash*, April '77**

We've all had jobs we've hated, yeah? And what saw us through? Sometimes, just fantasising about something better around the corner, even something impossibly glamorous, will spur you on. Here's Mick Jones dreaming of telling the boss where to go, amid those wondrous terrace-like chants, Terry Chimes' relentless drumming, Simmo's highly-charged bass-line, no-nonsense boogie – all just what was needed. In the same way that the Buzzcocks characterised the punk mood, turning their attentions on 'Boredom', The Clash gave us this, and both inspired you to rise above it all. For 'Janie Jones', read joyous. You're hooked within seconds. What a way to start an album. And what an album.

4 'I'm So Bored With the USA'

The Clash, April '77

Again, confrontation puts the point across. They were called The Clash after all. That generation and many more since had seen America tighten its cultural grip on us, and here, the band tackled the worst aspects of that, while later they would celebrate the better. Or was it more a case of making a frustrated stand and taking pride in their own neighbourhood instead? The raucous Clash choir on the chorus suggests as much. Either way, the fact that they delighted in belting it out to US audiences made it all the better.

5 'What's My Name'

***The Clash*, April '77**

You can almost feel the surge down to the front here. A rough round the edges electron charge. Keith Levine certainly added something to that early formation, but it wasn't to be. The dynamic wasn't quite there. Yet moments like this showed that five-piece Clash's potential. This was where they were at in '76, and it sounded no less relevant when committed to vinyl a few months later, neatly encasing that feeling of claustrophobia, paranoia and a desire to strike back. A manic punk thrill.

6 'London's Burning'

***The Clash*, April '77**

Perfectly encapsulating a time and a place, but with direction thrown in, the location being the Westway, the time the mid- to late-'70s, and the recreational speed intake only blurring the need to get out and make something of your life, at a time when Old England seemed to be going to the dogs. Here was the capital's punk ethos condensed into one short but mighty song, and it was something the suburban kids got too. Punk was about going places, it seemed, and creativity was the vehicle. A group of young lads looked down from an 18th floor flat and sought to find their way out, and expressed it all wonderfully, inspiring so many more to try it for themselves. Incendiary.

7 'Career Opportunities'

***The Clash*, April '77**

If 'Janie Jones' was the fantasy, here was the band railing against the reality on offer, yet both carried an underlying determination to not make do with the first offer on the table. When Bernie Rhodes encouraged his charges to write about what they knew and what was really going on around them, they could see that the alternatives to rock'n'roll were jobs that would ensure they were just working for the weekend. And that's not always enough. In the wrong hands it could have been bleak, but The Clash inspired you to strive for something far better. The fact that they were still playing that song in far grander settings in years to come underlined the premise that they had followed their own advice.

8 'Police & Thieves'

The Clash, April '77

Mick Jones' arrangements and guitar ingenuity, the experimentations with dub echo, off-beat licks and harmonies, Terry Chimes' and Paul Simonon's sterling work in the engine room, and Strummer's impassioned delivery ensured what could so easily have been lame 'white blokes attempt reggae' fare became so much more, providing the template for a raft of great Clash covers that followed. And if they hadn't torn through their own catalogue quite so quickly, it might never have been committed to tape. Later generations of would-be music stars take note – mere impersonation is never enough. You need to fully immerse yourself and understand what you're attempting, yet sometimes that's just down to pure instinct, assimilation and grasping the bigger picture. The Beatles and the Stones reinterpreted R&B, while The Clash looked to a Jamaican vibe and found it in their own backyard.

9 '48 Hours'

***The Clash*, April '77**

Here comes the weekend, and The Clash are ready to party, late '70s style. Banged out in no time by a band truly finding their creative feet, and an honest celebration of seeking out good times in spite of that imposing backdrop of urban alienation and a need to find answers. The ramshackle guitar solo just adds to the vibe. Can I use that world 'inspirational' again? Simply thrilling.

10 'Garageland'

***The Clash*, April '77**

You haven't lived until you've taken on board occasional knock-backs and shown your mettle and true determination to bounce back, and here we have a celebration of that resolute spirit. The message is clear – put The Clash down at your peril. But it's not just about giving your detractors the two fingers and proving them wrong by making it big. It's a celebration of that whole garageland spirit, underground culture, and punk's DIY ethos, with a respectful nod to rock'n'roll's rich past and a statement of intent for a brighter future thrown in. Perhaps inevitably, like many bands before and since, they seemed to misplace that spirit later, but this postcard from time suggests they were all in it together and having the time of their lives. What's more, while Terry adds his late drum tattoo, we can all sing along.

11 'Complete Control'

Single, September '77

Topper was on board now, Lee 'Scratch' Perry was guesting at the controls, and The Clash were ready to take on the wider world, starting with a jibe at their own record company. But this was no small-minded stand. Barely 10 months on from 'Anarchy in the UK', here was a sign that punk's promise wasn't necessarily behind us. Here was a band with no intention of falling by the wayside, and they weren't to be taken for mugs. If ever a song should be met with an open mouth on first hearing, this was it, and it's no less stirring four decades later. Such power, such venom, with those guitars right up in the mix, and on its night surely capable of reviving the deadheads. The audience loved it and every night were part of it, those 'C-O-N-Control' backing vocals while Joe let loose suggesting Team Clash were impregnable, and their determined spirit of independence belied their major label backing.

12 'Clash City Rockers'

Single, February '78

Anecdotes of live performances involving The Clash often include descriptions of the band moving around as if plugged into the grid, giving off a mighty charge. And here we have just one of many early electrical shockers. You didn't have to understand what Joe was on about here to get that, but maybe the tension between band members at the time helped take them to another level. Meanwhile, they're talking about themselves again, but without even a hint of being self-absorbed. This time, it was a Who riff at the heart of it and the middle-eight suggests a punk take on The Byrds' retelling of 'The Bells of Rhymney' rather than any nursery rhyme. But isn't all great rock'n'roll based on a spirit of reinvention?

13 'White Man(In Hammersmith Palais)'

Single, June '78

If the previous two singles proved this was a band not content to just stick with the original Sound of the Westway and concentrate on more of the same, here they showed an inventive ability to move into new directions. Their Junior Murvin cover gave them the balls to attempt a further foray into roots reggae, and here was the next step. Yet they were far from being out of their depth, Strummer and Jones' growing confidence proving justified, and the band defying audience expectations. We're talking lyrical as well as musical invention, Joe proving his potential as a master-storyteller. From day one, they'd tackled the need to unite against a common enemy. Yet he was learning as he went, realising it wasn't that simple, and the world wasn't just black and white. Here, the observations were more considered, better observed. And you can still sing along. From Jones' 1-2-3-4 count-in and that initial crash of guitar, we're hooked, falling away to lolloping bass, Topper's subtle percussive mastery, chop-chords, Strummer's echo-filled vocal and Jones' distant responses. Simply stunning.

14 'Safe European Home'

***Give 'Em Enough Rope*, November '78**

I loved this track before I even knew what the hell it was about. Such a big sound, with those call-and-response vocals and glorious guitars, the drum rolls, its wondrous false ending and that glorious return bringing palpitations, to this day. Hairs up on the back of the neck. It was only later that the humour of the lyric hit me, not least the admission that these two seemingly uber-cool tourists might have been well and truly out of their depth in downtown Jamaica. Turns out that they needed Simmo to pull them through – yep, the one who earlier had stickers on his bass to tell him what to play next. There was a vulnerability there that we hadn't been privy to before, and I loved them all the more for it. Such an explosive start to the second great Clash LP. I know, I'm not supposed to see it as that, but it was two-thirds wonderful, and that'll do for me.

15 'English Civil War'

Single, February '79, and *Give 'Em Enough Rope*, November '78

Again, I'm my 11-year-old self, hearing this for the first time, learning the words from *Smash Hits* and loving it, if not fully understanding why. That's the power of music for you, and that grounding line about arriving by bus or underground had an impact on me even then. I'll refer to my earlier comments about cover versions, the art of reinterpretation and making something relevant, in this case dragging traditional folk into a contemporary post-punk UK landscape and putting modern-day fascists to the sword. All power to you. Hurrah!

16 'Tommy Gun'

Single, and *Give 'Em Enough Rope*, November '78

Having suitably addressed the state of the UK nation in the second half of the 1970s, The Clash were now starting to look further afield, and here they tackled terrorism head on, in their own raucous way, scrutinising extremism, violence, the nature of hypocrisy, and the ideological cause. The point, for those who bothered to get it, was about the posing, and the fact that it was the innocents who got caught up in it all. And while they were loud and proud, there was a little more sophistication in the delivery too, Topper in particular increasing in confidence, leading from the rear.

17 'Julie's Been Working for the Drug Squad'

***Give 'Em Enough Rope*, November '78**

At the risk of overplaying my defence of *Give 'Em Enough Rope*, here was another sign that the band weren't ever likely to make the same album twice, with elements of everything from Cockney Rebel to Mott the Hoople, and on into Stiff territory here. Another story-song that proved Strummer's ability to properly write outside his comfort zone, and one of the first signs that Headon was no two-bit punk sticksman. He had soul, he had jazz, he had flair, and it was rubbing off around him.

18 'Last Gang in Town'

***Give 'Em Enough Rope*, November '78**

Another song that perfectly illustrated a moment in time, in this case – over an Attractions-like bassline from Simonon, starting to show his true potential –

4

Strummer turned his attention to youth culture in '78, and the on-going conflict between the Teds and the punks. And yet, change the fashions, and it's just as relevant to today's gang culture or any other tribal nonsense. Meanwhile, the band's year-zero approach has been well and truly jettisoned, with Joe's guitar hero's true musical DNA now evident for all to hear.

19 'Stay Free'

Give 'Em Enough Rope, November '78

We'd learned not to expect a love song from The Clash, but here we had something different, and every bit as motivational as that which had come before. Not boy-girl fare, more nostalgic, a song about lost youth and enduring friendships. Mick stepped up to the mic. and delivered his finest vocal to date, managing poignancy without over-sentimentality or preaching, in a moving, personal tale many of us felt we could properly relate to. Life was hard and decisions often harder, but there were positive choices to make, and in Jones' case a determination to succeed. Again, there were elements of Mott, but this was no Hoople-by-numbers rewrite, that whole feel just adding to its deeper, reflective nature.

20 'All the Young Punks New Boots and Contracts'

Give 'Em Enough Rope, November '78

From the start, this was a band comfortable reflecting their own experiences on record, and sometimes you got a clearer picture from the lyrics than the spin coming out of their Camden rehearsal space. If 'Complete Control' gave us an angry take on the music industry, here was a summary – albeit with added mythology – of how that kicking back at the system was going, with added rock guitar flourishes from Jonesy (of course). And the conclusion? The Clash had come too far to turn back now, but don't expect them to stick around and go over the same territory either.

21 'I Fought the Law'

The Cost of Living EP, May '79

No longer bored with the USA, The Clash were on the way to conquering the world, and again drew on their mastery of the cover version to find their feet. Seen as a sign of the band's shift away from the post-punk cul-de-sac to rock'n'roll revitalisation, looking back to find the way forward, a healthy obsession with '50s imagery and sound ignited, and adding their own newly-professional but still raw verve to a forgotten moment from a rich past. It was their most commercial sing-song to date, and yet they remained the epitome of cool, the track's outlaw element right up their street.

22 'London Calling'

AA-side Single, and _London Calling_, December '79

A new decade was on the horizon, and we were potentially staring into oblivion, the Doomsday clock ever closer to midnight, the Cold War nuclear threat very real, and environmental concerns firmly to the fore. But Strummer's pain was our pain, and together we were going to get through this, against the odds. The Clash were already seeing their way back from a mini-state of internal crises, and their new togetherness was contagious. Never before had they sounded so accomplished as a band, and on this evidence they were being seen by the critics in 'best rock'n'roll band in the world' territory, something that became all the more apparent the moment the LP of the same name followed.

23 'Brand New Cadillac'

***London Calling*, December '79**

Again, that '50s spirit shone through, with this little-known Vince Taylor rocker revamped and carrying the band to new horizons, the band on a musical high and the world listening intently. In the same way that 'I Fought the Law' suggested they were seeking out new horizons, here was the vehicle to take them on, madcap maestro Guy Stevens cajoling them – in his own inimitable way – and the band soon inspired to enter a fresh phase of sharp songwriting and musical discovery.

24 'Rudie Can't Fail'

***London Calling*, December '79**

It's difficult to pick and choose between so many great non-singles on the band's third album, but here was just one example of how the band's new direction was about so much more than just taking the rock'n'roll highway. And it was some tour bus party, taking in so many influences and giving a Clash spin to them all. Here was an outfit forever with their ears to the ground, be it drawing on the past, present or future, and they were knocking out a fine line in pop-soul reggae, the band's togetherness shining through and all four members raising their game, the Irish Horns adding a further dimension, the excitement of that happening era for 2-Tone and so much more neatly captured in these blues-party grooves.

25 'Spanish Bombs'

***London Calling*, December '79**

Another track that made a huge impression on a lad in suburban Surrey who'd got no closer to Spain than his big sister's holiday snaps at that stage. But – as would prove the case after the band had written about political conflict in South America and South East Asia too – in time I'd be reading Laurie Lee and George Orwell and finding myself drawn to the tales of those from afar who felt compelled to join anti-fascist factions in the Spanish Civil War, and their subsequent disillusionment, my fascination partly drawn from interpretations of Strummer's imagery. And so it was that The Clash turned their attention to the wider world, and so did we. Even as an instrumental this song would have seduced me, but again those combined vocals and Joe's vivid poetry sealed the deal. My only complaint was that this track was over too soon.

26 'The Right Profile'

***London Calling*, December '79**

Before there was even a word added, we had a winner, as suggested by *The Vanilla Tapes*' 'Up-Toon' instrumental, just one example of the product borne out of those initial jam sessions for *London Calling*. Guy Stevens heard enough from those demos to know he wanted to get involved, and in this case his own seed of a suggestion, lending the band his treasured Montgomery Clift biography, led to Strummer stepping in, the end-result seen as much a tribute to Stevens' sad battle with the booze as it was to Clift's. And the Irish Horns made it truly swing.

4

27 'Lost in the Supermarket'

***London Calling*, December '79**

Whether it was the positive reaction to 'Stay Free' that gave him the confidence to step forward, I'm not sure, but Mick Jones was quick to take on Strummer's autobiographical wander down his back years, seeing it as his own life story, and there's real emotion in his delivery. Was this the true John Mellor hiding behind another disguise, in this case his lead guitarist? Who knows, but it worked, the detail in the imagery suggesting Joe's guard was temporarily dropped, Headon and Simonon playing their parts to perfection too. In the same way that I never held with the notion that you either loved The Beatles or the Stones and there was no in between, it was the same with The Clash and The Jam as far as I was concerned. And this was perhaps the closest Strummer and Jones got to writing in the style of Paul Weller. But there was always common ground, that Ray Davies influence apparent, with this just another fine example.

28 'Clampdown'

***London Calling*, December '79**

While the band were moving into uncharted waters, with aplomb, it was something of a relief to hear this number on *London Calling*. Hardly 'familiarity' in the dictionary definition, but this was The Clash we already knew and loved, from the Pistols-like opening to the old-style punk rock charge and compulsion to fight the system. And while the band were seemingly tighter than ever as a musical unit, it turned out that they could still be raw when it came to the crunch. Yet this was no straight-forward thrash. It was (whisper it) complex, and full of twists and turns and glorious nuances.

29 'The Guns of Brixton'

***London Calling*, December '79**

As if to prove the fact that this band had come on so much in barely three years, here was reluctant bass player Paul Simonon venturing forth with words and music and stepping up to the mic. – after some coaxing – for yet another *London Calling* highlight. The band's in-house reggae aficionado delivered in style too, transporting *The Harder They Come* to the mean streets of South London, neatly capturing the feeling of resentment among the communities he'd grown up among, and showcasing his own musical DNA in a cinematic setting, that pounding bass riff and this track's heady atmosphere proving truly influential long after The Clash's time together was over.

30 'Wrong 'Em Boyo'

***London Calling*, December '79**

What 'Rudie Can't Fail' was to reggae, 'Wrong 'Em Boyo' was to infectious ska, Clash-style, The Rulers' rocksteady rubbing off nicely on the Westway Four, as the skanking ghost of Stagger Lee arrived at the cusp of the '80s, the originals regularly spun on the Rehearsal Rehearsals jukebox and something of the spirit of Coventry export The Specials' first album infused through that Camden link. And yet the first 30 seconds are not so much from the home of the Hillman Hunter as the Mott the Hoople front-man who shared that name.

31 'The Card Cheat'

***London Calling*, December '79**

Talking of the spirit of Ian Hunter, it's written large here, with the flavour of Steve Harley and Roy Wood too, a wall of Spector-esque sound taking this grand number into the 'epic' league, with Jones' intricate arrangement – again commendably complemented by the on-loan brass section – matched by Strummer's imagery in this tale of one of life's outsiders, chock-full of cinematic detail.

32 'Revolution Rock'

***London Calling*, December '79**

The sound of 'El Clash Combo' – given extra balls by those horns again – having the time of their life at Wessex Studios, working hard but playing hard too, and I don't just mean their tackling outside the studio in the pre-record kickabouts, on a Danny Ray and the Revolutioneers cover. And just in case you're worried they might be tipping towards a more mainstream approach to music, Joe Strummer is tempering his request for you to dance to a brand-new beat **with added bongo jazz a speciality and even a little cheese-grater by asking you to smash up your seats while you're at it.**

33 'Train in Vain' (Stand by Me)'

***London Calling*, December '79**

The added track on *London Calling* seems to divide opinion, but I guess no one likes to see their group get too big, and the American record-buying public loved this. By the end of this monumental third album, Mick Jones had shrugged off his romantic troubles in some style, and it was close-run choosing between this or the similarly-resolute 'I'm Not Down', cataloguing his frustrations at those cross-town rail trips to see Viv Albertine, by all accounts. And it was great to see a confident post-Bernie Clash go for out-and-out 'My Baby Left Me'-type love songs. What's more, it always pays to have a train-related ditty in the armoury, not least one knocked out so refreshingly quickly, old school style.

34 'Armagideon Time'

AA-side Single, December '79

One thing I overlooked when reading all those edgy, scholarly or politically-charged features and interviews with The Clash in the music press in my youth was that the band had a great sense of humour, something all the more apparent when you look at most of their post-split interviews and band biographies. And among the latter, road manager Johnny Green's memoir made me love this rather spooky but infectious Willie Williams cover all the more. I can't hear this now without imagining a floating candelabra and a torch shone in Joe's face. What a groove too, embracing all the best aspects of bass-heavy, late-night dub reggae production.

35 'Bankrobber'

Single, August '80

When this came out in the summer of 1980, who knew we'd soon be faced with a perplexing six sides of long-playing vinyl for the next release? Word was that this was to be the first of many single releases, but CBS failed to get behind the concept, having not really understood this one (sitting on it for five months). What they didn't get perplexes me (perhaps the outlaw aspect didn't sit well with them), even more than the sight of Legs and Co.'s interpretative dancing to the track on *Top of The Pops*, an unintentionally-iconic moment that rather outflanked the band's decision to rule out appearing on a show where you had to mime your hits. Again, that reggae/ska vibe's to the fore on a slightly menacing but danceable take on the 'don't settle for a crap job' theme, built around Simmo's heavy bass and some groovy effects.

36 'The Magnificent Seven'

Single, April '81, *Sandinista!* December '80

Something of a watermark, this bunch of white boys building on their re-interpretation of roots reggae, applying similar principles to the newest sound on the block, the emerging funk/hip-hop scene. As before, it was a brave move, but worked, breaking down barriers, similarly introducing rap to US rock audiences and relevant rock'n'roll to the hip-hop crowd during their mid-'81 NYC residency, shortly after premiering this track in Europe. Of course, The Blockheads' Norman Watt-Roy deserves much of the credit for this number. What a bass-line. And here was another stream of consciousness Strummer rant, tackling the joyless job where 'the minutes drag and the hours jerk', while helping inspire a new musical direction, spreading the word of the neighbourhood.

37 'Hitsville UK'

Single, January '81, *Sandinista!* December '80

Not only Strummer, Jones and his other half, Ellen Foley paying homage to early Tamla Motown, with commendable backroom support from Headon's hipsville swing, Simonon's soulful bass roll and Mickey Gallagher's swirling organ, but also a celebration of the indie spirit that was taking hold back home. It doesn't sound much like what was coming out of Factory, Mute, Postcard, Rough Trade, Stiff or 4AD, but it was the thought that counted – The Clash embracing a move away from the majors, even though they were still tied into their own contract.

38 'Junco Partner'

***Sandinista!* December '80**

Strummer's link with Robert Allen's blues standard went right back, but here it got an effective Mikey Dread dub makeover, on the band's brief return to Jamaica, and a personal update from this former 101'er. What's more, it had never sounded better, Joe playing the Studio One piano and his old mate Tymon believed to have added the quirky violin back at Wessex, on a track carrying a nostalgic feel of the Harry J All Stars' *Liquidator*, that glorious bass-drenched echo pounding out.

39 'Somebody Got Murdered'

***Sandinista!* December '80**

For 'Stay Free' and 'The Card Cheat' on the last two LPs, add this *Sandinista* number for the poignancy factor, a senseless killing in Camden inspiring heartfelt lyrics from Strummer, neatly translated in the studio by Jones, adding a sense of vulnerability. Lots of synth, but that worked too in another complex arrangement that proved just how far this band had progressed, musically.

40 'Up in Heaven (Not Only Here)'

***Sandinista!* December '80**

Four years after 'London's Burning', Mick Jones was reflecting on his high-rise upbringing, angry at the state of the crumbling council skyscrapers he knew so well. And his passionate delivery leaves you in no doubt that it's personal. The gap between rich and poor was ever more evident in Thatcher's Britain, and here was an illustration of a new frontline, the author no doubt wandering what might have become of him if he hadn't got out when he did. Fast forward three and a half decades, and West London's Grenfell Tower disaster – so close to his former Wilmcote House base – proved how little had changed and that the issue had not gone away, with the fight for residents to be heard stronger than ever.

41 'Police on My Back'

***Sandinista!* December '80**

A tour bus favourite from The Equals got a Clash makeover, and the masters of the cover version were on top form again, with Eddy Grant's original taken into another realm. With Jonesy letting rip on guitar, and the joint soon rocking, there's almost a feeling of elation and celebration, the sentiment as much about togetherness as it was about the underlying defiance, the band's appropriation of outlaw status again to the fore.

42 'The Call-Up'

Single, November '80, *Sandinista!* December '80

A wake-up call for America, still sleepwalking in the post-Vietnam era, seven years after the military draft ended, but in danger of returning under Ronnie's Republicans, the band tying their anti-war colours to the flag, while the US got further embroiled in their far-reaching overseas ambitions. It had been seven years since Nick Lowe had written, '(What's So Funny 'Bout) Peace, Love and Understanding', and the question remained relevant.

43 'Washington Bullets'

***Sandinista!* December '80**

The title track of sorts of *Sandinista!* took the notion of 'The Call-Up' on and took it on a tour of oppressive regimes across the globe, over a glockenspiel rhythm. An era of world music was upon us, and The Clash were leading from the front against the rise of the latest wave of imperialism, Joe's vocal pared back but impassioned all the same, the power in the words beautifully delivered. And the new generation coming through, not least this 13-year-old, sat up, took notice, and was soon headed for the library to find out more.

44 'Broadway'

***Sandinista!* December '80**

Just where had the journey of The Clash taken us now? Another US state of the nation address, but this time a more personal dispatch from the War on Want, seemingly another stream of consciousness observation, Strummer telling the tale – over Mickey Gallagher's piano – of a down-at-heel ex-boxer amid the cars, bars, bright lights and rain-covered NYC streets, on a track that seemed more Tom Waits than Westway. The band's new-found musical experimentation had taken a late-night, early-morning jazz turn, and we didn't really know what to make of it. But in time the dime dropped. What narrative, and what poetic sense of place!

45 'Lose This Skin'

Sandinista! **December '80**

In a sense, this is the least Clash-like song among this 50 (and there are a few contenders for that crown), and ostensibly a vehicle for Strummer's old busking pal Tymon Dogg, but here were the group as a professional backing band, and what a great noise they make behind their stand-in leader's Lydon-esque vocal and violin. I raved about 'Safe European Home' and its false ending, and here was a further awesome example. And all because of a chance meeting between Dogg and Jones in New York while the band were at Electric Lady, a chain of events that eventually led to Tymon ending up with The Mescaleros, sharing Joe's joyous reemergence. Happenstance? Fate? You decide.

46 'Charlie Don't Surf'

Sandinista! **December '80**

Compiling this list led to some tricky choices, and I nearly left this out. But how could I? This Vietnam-based number Illustrates perfectly the band's early '80s fascination with the Far East – memorably taken on with *Combat Rock*'s 'Sean Flynn' and 'Straight to Hell' – and compulsion to highlight damaging US interest in world affairs during that era, something we could do to learn from in frightening times three and a half decades later. Back then, Strummer was hooked on *Apocalypse Now*, and here we have Mick Jones as a VC conscript defending against 'strangers', fighting an enemy out to impose its own belief systems on others, just another example of a planet where seemingly 'Everybody wants to rule the world'. Now there's an idea for a song title.

47 'Know Your Rights'

Single, April '82, *Combat Rock*, May '82

We're on to the final chapter for the classic line-up, and Joe has us by the throat as he issues his latest pronouncement, with tongue firmly in cheek, but his message all the more powerful for that. 'Know your rights – all three of them!' Rockabilly rebellion, inventive metallic percussion, and so much more, the justice system and the Establishment ripped to shreds, Strummer-style, our front-man in born-again preacher mode, working his socks off, his voice stretched to breaking point, lozenges at the ready, and the crowd going wild.

48 'Should I Stay or Should I Go'

AA-side Single, September '82, *Combat Rock*, May '82

For all their political bluster and right-on posturing, The Clash were a rock'n'roll band above all else, and sometimes the history of rock seemed to bleed from Jones' guitar, not least on the mighty riff behind this special moment. It would have been a hit in any decade, proving that with later elevation to chart-topper, the sum of all the parts Mick had played, ingested and reinvented over the years. But while commercial success seemed inevitable, it didn't sit well for a group so washed out after a draining, six years.

What a moment though. Much was made of whether it was about Jones' role within the band, and I'd say there were elements of that. But surely it's just a bloody good Stones-like rock'n'roll love song from an outfit on top form.

49 'Rock the Casbah'

Single, June '82, *Combat Rock*, May '82
While Topper was clearly on the road to ruin, the cracks more than showing, he was still grounded when it came to studio prowess, more so than ever before, on a high as a musician, the confidence in the camp all to hear. Every part of this glorious number was put on a plate for the band, and yet Strummer still added the icing on the cake, having a lyrical ball that ensured the music and lyrics were for all time. By the time Headon and Jones had moved on, the story was as good as over as far as the band's inventive songwriting was concerned. They certainly didn't have the nous to make top-drawer punk dance music without them. Strummer needed someone to rub off on, and it would be some years before he found his next musical foils. But here was the group's last hurrah, and this particular song rightly resonated around the world, starting in the UK and the USA and rippling out. Clearly, it's a track that's been misappropriated in certain circles over the years, but that was not of The Clash's making. They got it spot on. Stonking.

50 'Straight to Hell'

AA-side Single, September '82, *Combat Rock*, May '82
Finally, we have Joe Strummer, Mick Jones, Paul Simonon and Topper Headon on a stirring, poetic, lyrical and musical high, for what was arguably the most hauntingly-beautiful Clash song, on top of Headon's hypnotic, percussive masterclass. Strummer revisited past themes, from the UK to the US and South-East Asia, looking at poverty, militarism, drugs and the human cost of all those factors, but this time with what seemed a beyond-wise and certainly more subtle approach. In a sense he was taking his '(White Man) in Hammersmith Palais' out on the road, three and a half years on, his bandmates instinctively getting where he was coming from, making this such a joy to hear on the headphones, their internal niggles momentarily set aside on an under-stated yet truly powerful moment, the imagery conveyed so evocative.

Now I'm done, you'll note I left off three UK singles, including one that tends to make it on to other polls but I consciously left out. You'll see from my description elsewhere that I agree 'This is England' is worthy of inclusion, but for me that would be bending the rules, like including a couple of dozen Mescaleros songs or a few Big Audio Dynamite numbers. Think of this more as a Clash Mk. I top 50, honouring the Strummer, Jones, Simonon and Headon or Chimes line-up. As I suggested in the introduction, there's never going to be agreement across the board on which tracks are included. As I type this, I can hear in my head, 'What about 'Capital Radio' and 'Death or Glory'?' But I'd like to think the above list at least gives a taste of a 'best of'. Feel free to argue among yourselves though.

DISCOGRAPHY

Studio Albums

The Clash (CBS)
Released: April 8th, 1977
UK charts: 12
US charts: 126 (Epic version, July 26th, 1979)
Others: Sweden 42
Certification: UK & US Gold

Give 'Em Enough Rope (CBS)
Released: November 10th, 1978
UK charts: 2
US charts: 126
Others: New Zealand 15, Sweden 36
Certification: UK Gold

London Calling (CBS, 2LP)
Released: December 14th, 1979
UK charts: 9
US charts: 27
Others: Austria 17, Canada 12, Norway 4, New Zealand 12, Sweden 2
Certification: UK & US Platinum, Canada Gold

Sandinista! (CBS, 3LP)
Released: December 12th, 1980
UK charts: 19
US charts: 24
Others: Canada 3, Norway 8, New Zealand 3, Sweden 9)
Certification: UK & US Gold

Combat Rock (CBS)
Released: May 14th, 1982
UK charts: 2
US charts: 7
Others: Canada 12, Netherlands 29, Norway 7, New Zealand 5, Sweden 9
Certification: UK & Canada Gold, US Double-Platinum

Cut the Crap (CBS)
Released: November 4th, 1985
UK charts: 16
US charts: 88
Others: Canada 59, New Zealand 35, Sweden 30
Certification: UK Gold

Live Albums

From Here to Eternity: Live (Epic, live recordings 1978/82)
Released: October 4th, 1999
UK charts: 13
US charts: 193
Others: France 17, Sweden 47

Live at Shea Stadium (Epic, 1982 NYC show)
Released: October 6th, 2008
UK charts: 31
US charts: 93
Other: Sweden 26

Compilation Albums

Black Market Clash (Epic, 10" LP)
Released: 1980
US charts: 74
Other: New Zealand 15

The Story of The Clash, Volume 1 (CBS, 2LP)
Released: February 29th, 1988
UK charts: 7

US charts: 142
Others: New Zealand 3, Sweden 50
Certification: UK Gold, US Platinum

1977 Revisited / A Collection of Rare Tracks and B-Sides (Relativity/CBS)
Released: 1990
Did not chart

The Singles (Epic)
Released: November 1991
UK charts: 68
Others: New Zealand 2, Portugal 22

Super Black Market Clash (Epic)
Released: October 26th 1993
Did not chart

The Essential Clash (Epic, UK & US versions)
Released: UK April 22nd 2003 (US March 11th)
UK charts: 18
US charts: 99
Others: New Zealand 50, Sweden 22
Certification: UK Gold

The Singles (Sony BMG)
Released: June 4th, 2007
UK charts: 13
Other: New Zealand 36
Certification: UK Platinum

The Clash Hits Back (Sony Legacy, 2CD)
Released: September 9th, 2013 (US September 10th)
UK charts: 13
Other: New Zealand 27
Certification: UK Silver

Box Sets

Clash on Broadway
November 19th, 1991 (CBS/Epic, 3CD)

Singles Box
October 30th, 2006 (Sony BMG, set of 19 UK singles across 19 CDs)

Sound System
September 9th & 10th, 2013 (Sony Legacy, 12-CD box-set – entire studio catalogue minus *Cut the Crap*, plus 3 extra discs, a DVD and other items, 53 in UK charts)

Five-Album Studio Set
September 9th & 10th, 2013 (Sony Legacy, 8-CD box-set – first five studio albums, remastered)

UK Singles / Extended Plays

(Peak chart position in brackets)

1977

March 18th – 'White Riot' / '1977' (38)
April 9th – 'Capital Radio' EP: 'Listen' (excerpt)/ 'Interview Pts.1 & 2 / 'Capital Radio' (NME offer)
May 13th – 'Remote Control' / 'London's Burning' (Live) (did not chart)
September 23rd – 'Complete Control' / 'City of the Dead' (28)

1978

February 17th – 'Clash City Rockers' / 'Jail Guitar Doors' (35)
June 16th – '(White Man) In Hammersmith Palais' / 'The Prisoner' (32)
November 24th – 'Tommy Gun' / '1-2 Crush on You' (19)

1979

February 23rd – 'English Civil War' / 'Pressure Drop' (25) (Ireland 29)
May 11th – 'The Cost of Living EP': 'I Fought the Law' / 'Groovy Times' / 'Gates of the West' / 'Capital Radio' / 'The Cost of Living Advert' (22) (Ireland 24)
December 7th – 'London Calling' / 'Armagideon Time' (11) (Australia 28, Ireland 26, New Zealand 23)

1980

August 8th – 'Bankrobber' / 'Rockers Galore ... UK Tour' (12) (Ireland 14, New Zealand 14)
November 28th – 'The Call-Up' / 'Stop the World' (40) (New Zealand 13, US Dance 21)

1981

January 16th – 'Hitsville UK' / 'Radio One' (56)
April 10th – 'The Magnificent Seven' / 'The Magnificent Dance' (34)
November 20th – 'This is Radio Clash' / 'Radio Clash' (47) (Australia 40, New Zealand 28, Sweden 9, US Dance 17, US Mainstream 45)

1982

April 23rd – 'Know Your Rights' / 'First Night Back in London' (43)
June 11th – 'Rock the Casbah' / 'Long Time Jerk' (30) (Australia 3, Canada 26, Netherlands 21, New Zealand 4, Sweden 16, US Billboard 8, US Dance 8, US Mainstream 6)
September 17th – 'Should I Stay or Should I Go' / 'Straight to Hell' (17) (Australia 37, Canada 40, Ireland 16, US Billboard 45, US Mainstream 13)

1985

September 30th – 'This is England' / 'Do It Now' (24) (Ireland 13, New Zealand 26, Sweden 16)

Re-releases

1988 – 'London Calling' (46)
1988 – 'I Fought the Law' (29) (New Zealand 17)
1990 – 'Return to Brixton' (57)
1991 – 'Should I Stay or Should I Go' / 'Rush' (1) (Austria 5, Belgium 3, France 25, Germany 5, Ireland 2, Netherlands 3, Norway 3, New Zealand 2, Sweden 6, Switzerland 4)
1991 – 'Rock the Casbah' (15) (Belgium 22, Ireland 10)
1991 – 'London Calling' (64) (Ireland 18, Sweden 30)
1991 – 'Train in Vain' (did not chart)

Additional singles outside UK

1979

'Clampdown' / 'The Guns of Brixton' (Australian release) (Australia 33)
1980 – 'Train in Vain'/ 'London Calling' (Canada 62, New Zealand 26, Switzerland 23, US 30)
'Rudie Can't Fail' / 'Bankrobber' / 'Rockers galore...UK Tour' (Dutch release)
'Police on my Back' / 'The Crooked Beat' (Australian release) (Australia 38, US 21)

1981

'Somebody Got Murdered' ('Alguien Fue Asesinado') / 'Hitsville UK' (Spanish release)

1985

'Are You Red..Y' / 'Three-Card Trick' (Australian release)

INFLUENCED BY THE CLASH

4

The band's influence goes without saying really, but deserves coverage, not least the love of ska, reggae and England's Jamaican subculture that helped inspired the 2 Tone movement. I've already mentioned that Billy Bragg and U2's The Edge compared The Clash's inspirational effect to that of the Ramones – both acts giving young musicians the 'sense that the door of possibility had swung open'. The Edge added, 'The Clash, more than any other group, kick-started a thousand garage bands across Ireland and the UK. Seeing them perform was a life-changing experience.' Meanwhile, bandmate Bono saw them as, 'The greatest rock band. They wrote the rule book for U2.'

A whole host of American bands also pointed towards the legacy of this London outfit, including Green Day and Rancid, as was the case for South Welsh outfit Manic Street Preachers, while the band's love and translation of Jamaican influences inspired similar cross-genre projects such as Massive Attack, and the band were credited for laying the groundwork for LCD Soundsystem's 'post-funk'.

Then there was Sweden's The Hives, Australia's The Vines, the UK's Libertines and America's White Stripes. From there, followed the Arctic Monkeys, and those Bruce Springsteen tributes – at the 2003 Grammys with Little Steven , Dave Grohl and Elvis Costello; in June 2009 with the E Street Band, opening at Hyde Park, London, with 'London Calling'; and five years later opening his 'High Hopes' tour with 'Clampdown'.

And you can't give an in-depth portrayal of The Clash without also bringing into it the politics, a key part of this story from day one. While steering clear of party politics, Strummer in particular came over as a socialist, in words and in deeds, while the band were credited with pioneering radical politics in punk rock, questioning the monarchy and aristocracy, yet rejecting the nihilism of many contemporaries. They found solidarity with a number of liberation movements, not least the Anti-Nazi League, playing an important role in April '78's Rock Against Racism concert in Victoria Park, East London, Strummer decked out in a T-shirt identifying two left-wing revolutionary groups.

Politics were part of the music from the moment the band first played 'White Riot', 'Career Opportunities' and 'London's Burning', Caroline Coon feeling such 'tough, militaristic songs were what we needed as we went into Thatcherism'. And the band's political landscape grew from there, the title of 1980's *Sandinista!* celebrating the Nicaraguan left-wing factions that overthrew their national regime, while 'Washington Bullets' and 'The Call-Up' tackled key US overseas military operations. *Combat Rock*'s 'Straight to Hell' further set out Strummer's stall, in what Simon Reynolds called an 'around-the-world-at-war-in-five-verses guided tour of hell-zones where boy-soldiers had languished'.

Closer to home, such sentiments were reflected in resistance to established music industry profit motivations, the band eager to ensure that shows and souvenirs were reasonably priced and double LP *London Calling* and triple LP *Sandinista!* sold for the price of single albums – £5 for the first, £5.99 for the next. The Clash forfeited all performance royalties on the first 200,000 sales to ensure that happened, a policy that ultimately meant they remained in debt to CBS, only starting to break even around 1982.

At the band's induction into the Rock and Roll Hall of Fame, The Clash were said to be 'considered one of the most overtly political, explosive and exciting bands in rock and roll history', their songs tackling social decay, unemployment, racism, police brutality, political and social repression, and militarism. Furthermore, Strummer later supported Rock Against the Rich shows from anarchist group Class War. While the Sex Pistols provided an initial spark, it was The Clash who helped politicise The Jam, Strummer inspiring Paul Weller to write about things that matter.

However, as Mick Jones reflected in a 2007 Q&A with Tom Lanham for the online *Magnet* magazine, with The Clash, 'It was politics with a small 'p'. We never relied on any kind of party line in any way. We just wanted to play some tunes, have a bit of a laugh. To be decent and treat people decently, in a way you'd hope to be treated yourself. Which I learned from following bands when I was younger; Mott The Hoople, especially. They were particularly kind and welcoming, once they got to know you. I was really young when I followed them around and was in the dressing room of the Royal Albert Hall when they played there: a thing you wouldn't imagine being possible but through their good grace.

'I see it as all being part of a big line of music being handed down from people I really liked and admired who influenced me. Then I had my chance to do my bit, and it carried on. We were always decent people; we always treated our fans nicely. They were very important. It wasn't like the bands who came before us. We were much closer to our audience, I think. We didn't leave them as we found them. We left them hopefully inspired. Inspired to do something themselves, maybe.'

Jones expanded on that philosophy in the same interview, telling Lanham, 'We were almost the same as our audience. There wasn't that big barrier there with the groups that came before us. One of our most important things was VFM – value for money. We always thought it was really important, and we did it in our record prices and our ticket prices. It really gave people their money's worth.'

Road manager Johnny Green expanded on that in *A Riot of our Own* in 1997, recalling, 'Fans would ask where we were playing tomorrow. Joe kept a notebook of their names, telling doormen to put them on the guest list. Being accessible was all part of the punk movement, or at least The Clash's version of it.'

But how did Jones feel about his record company still putting out Clash releases, more than 20 years after they split? 'It's strange to get to that level when you're still alive. But I'm happy to be alive. It's nice when people are still interested in what you've done. Maybe they'll be interested in what you're doing now as well.'

CLASHOGRAPHY

Discography, recommended reading & more

5

"In fact, punk rock means exemplary manners to your fellow human beings. Fuck being an asshole"

JOE STRUMMER

THE CLASH'S LONDON

5

25 key locations in the story of The Clash

'The striking thing about the Clash was that, as universal as their appeal grew to be, all the influences in their music could be attributed to a few square miles of London. When I think of them, I think of Ladbroke Grove, West London. I can see the doorways and record shops. I can remember the smell of the Jamaican restaurants. It was a long way from fish and chips!'
Bono, in a 2003 interview with Elton John, published online for the Epitaph website.

1. 101 Walterton Road W9 – the location of the squat where Joe Strummer co-founded the 101'ers, his first London outfit, in May 1974 (later demolished).
2. Nashville Rooms, West Kensington, W14 – where Mick Jones met Bernie Rhodes in August '75, and where the 101'ers supported the Sex Pistols twice in April '76, Strummer seeing his future direction.
3. Paddington Kitchen, Praed Street, W2 – where Mick Jones, Tony James and Bernie Rhodes auditioned potential London SS members in late '75/early '76, including Paul Simonon, Terry Chimes and Nicky Headon, rehearsing in the basement, close to where Jones previously worked in a benefits office.
4. 22 Davis Road, Acton Vale, W3 – location of the first Clash rehearsal in June 76. with Joe Strummer introduced to the rest of the band and the first songs aired. Jones' then-girlfriend, Sydney-born art student and future Slits guitarist Viv Albertine lived there.
5. Rehearsal Rehearsals, Chalk Farm Road, Camden, NW1 – Bernie Rhodes' HQ, a former Gilbey's gin warehouse taken over by the railways, where The Clash practised and occasionally slept from 1976 onwards, later incorporated into Stables Market.
6. Wilmcote House, W2 – Mick's nan's Warwick Estate 18th floor flat overlooked the Westway, a key location for the band in the early days, Jones based there for five years from 1975.
7. The Screen on the Green, Islington, N1 – location of The Clash's first public London show, after the evening's films, supporting the Sex Pistols, with Buzzcocks also on the bill.
8. The 100 Club, Oxford Street, W1 – where The Clash supported the Pistols in late August '76 and again at Malcolm McLaren's September '76 Punk Festival, also marking Siouxsie and the Banshees' live debut.
9. The Roxy, Neal Street, Covent Garden, WC2 – where The Clash headlined the opening of short-lived, legendary punk hangout on New Year's Day '77, the subject of Julien Temple's later documentary.
10. CBS Studio 3, Whitfield Road, W1 – location for the early '77 recording sessions that led to debut LP *The Clash*, with Mickey Foote producing.

11. The Roundhouse, Chalk Farm Road, Camden NW1 – former railway engine shed that played host to Topper Headon's Clash debut on April 10th, '77. Also a regular venue for Mick Jones in his early years.
12. Sarm East Studios, Osborn Street, Whitechapel, E1 – where Lee 'Scratch' Perry sat in on the production of third single 'Complete Control' in the spring of '77, the band and Mickey Foote assisting.
13. The Rainbow Theatre, Seven Sisters Road, Finsbury Park, N4 – scene of the London show in May '77 on the 'White Riot' tour, supports including The Jam and Buzzcocks. Two months before, the band met Topper Headon at a Kinks gig there, Mick Jones inviting him to Rehearsals the next day. Closed in 1982.
14. Victoria Park, Hackney, E3 – where the 'Rock Against Racism' gig was held on April 30th '78, with The Clash second on the bill and Tom Robinson Band headlining, to an estimated 100,00 crowd.
15. Basing Street Studios, Ladbroke Grove, W11 – '(White Man) in Hammersmith Palais' recorded here in the spring of '78, and where Sandy Pearlman got to work on *Give 'Em Enough Rope* with the band. Later renamed Sarm West Studios.
16. The Music Machine, Camden High Street, NW1 – scene of a four-night residency in July '78, with footage included on *Rude Boy*. A Sid Vicious Defence Fund show followed in December. Renamed Camden Palace in 1982 and Koko in 2004. The band also played the nearby Electric Ballroom.
17. Vanilla Studios, 36 Causton Street, Pimlico SW1 – the location where the band put together their *London Calling* set, before switching to Wessex Studios, May '79. No longer there.
18. Wessex Studios, Highbury New Park, N5 – where the band, producer Guy Stevens and engineer Bill Price worked on *London Calling* in August '79, and where part of *Sandinista!* was recorded.
19. Cadogan Pier, Chelsea, SW3 – the location used for the 'London Calling' video, directed by Don Letts in December '79, by Albert Bridge, and overlooking Battersea Park, not far from the flat Joe Strummer and his partner Gaby Salter shared at World's End, Chelsea.
20. Acklam Hall, Ladbroke Grove, W10 – scene of two word-of-mouth Christmas 1979 dates, four years after the 101'ers first appeared there, close to the flashpoint of the 1976 Notting Hill riots that inspired 'White Riot'. Later names for the venue included Bay 63 and Subterania.
21. Hammersmith Palais, Shepherd's Bush Road, W6 – the band played two nights at the iconic venue which inspired 1978's '(White Man) In Hammersmith Palais' (after Joe Strummer attended a reggae showcase with Don Letts and Roadent there) in June 1980 on the '16 Tons' tour. Venue closed 2007.
22. Lyceum Ballroom, Wellington Street, WC2 – scene of an October '81 seven-night residency closing the 'Radio Clash' tour, the band having played in February too. In later years a theatrical venue again.
23. People's Hall, Freston Road, W11 – later rehearsal space for the band and recording studio – Ear Studios – before their Camden return, the focal point of Frestonia's squatters' co-operative community, where the *Combat Rock* album (the 'Rat Patrol sessions') took shape.
24. Brixton Fair Deal/Academy, Stockwell Road, SW9 – The Clash played two shows at the Fair Deal in the summer of '82 on the 'Down the Casbah' tour and returned in the Mk.II era – after the venue had been

relaunched under original name The Academy – in March '84 for a five-night run, returning that December for two NUM benefits.
25. Acton Town Hall, High Street, Acton, W3 – the scene of Joe Strummer's final London appearance, a benefit for striking firefighters on November 15th, 2002. Mick Jones joined the Mescaleros on stage for 'Bankrobber' plus encores '*White Riot*' and '*London's Burning*', *their* first live appearance in almost 20 years, the location a 20-minute walk and barely a mile from the Davis Road squat where Strummer first jammed with his new bandmates in June '76. Six weeks later, John Graham Mellor's funeral was held at nearby West London Crem., Harrow Road, W10, with a guard of honour by the chapel from firefighters.

THE CLASH IN WRITING

Look online and you'll find a wealth of Clash-related published titles, far too many to comprehensively review here. Some are long out of print and hard to get hold of (or just in e-Book format), several are not worth pursuing – either littered with mistakes, poorly presented, woefully written, or all three – and a select few are great, while many more are worthy additions to the Clash canon.

With that in mind I've just gone for a handful, concentrating on the more text-heavy tomes rather than photographic works from the likes of Bob Gruen and Pennie Smith (both out of my price range today), where the pictures tell the story. The following are the ones I've gone back to and flipped in and out of while researching this book. That's not to say the others aren't worth the cover price. Some will be. Let's just say that here are six of the best, listed in order of first publication. There are many more not specifically about The Clash that I've headed to while writing this book, but hopefully they're properly sourced in the text and in the bibliography.

LAST GANG IN TOWN: THE STORY AND MYTH OF THE CLASH

THE CLASH: RETURN OF THE LAST GANG IN TOWN

Marcus Gray (Fourth Estate, 1995/Helter Skelter, 2001)

Respect is due to Belfast-based writer Marcus Gray, for the first properly-recognised, substantial Clash biography, published in 1995. No easy task. There would be contenders later, and improvements and corrections in places (not least in Gray's 'Return of'), but a lot of hard work

5

went into that mighty tome. Fellow Clash biographer Pat Gilbert called it, 'The first roadmap of The Clash's early lives and an excellent overview of their career,' and just a glance at the list of key interviewees acknowledged gives a flavour of the hard slog and thought put in. Gray makes much of the myth-making of The Clash, rightly so, and there's a commendable determination to get at the truth on these pages. My copy of the Return of is in a not-so-great paperback format, with the type too small and too many words on the page – it deserves a better edition, and there may well be one out there. But here I'm just concentrating on the product, and Gray's meticulous, extensive approach deserves praise. As he acknowledged himself in 2003, his approach won't work for everyone, but it's 'a distillation of a decade's work' and one he likes to think will at least be 'considered worthy of a seismic period in pop-cultural history, an incendiary rock'n'roll band, and a recently-deceased, much-loved and highly inspirational man.' It certainly is that.

A RIOT OF OUR OWN: NIGHT AND DAY WITH THE CLASH

Johnny Green & Garry Barker (Indigo, 1997/ Orion, 2003)

With a foreword from Joe Strummer and illustrations by esteemed Lancashire-based artist, cartoonist, designer, satirist, and dedicated Clash fan, Ray Lowry (who died, aged 64 in 2008), here we have a memorable memoir recalling a heady three years at the heart of The Clash machine with the man known as Johnny Green, aka John Broad, Clash roadie, driver and general dogsbody/ valet for three hectic rock'n'roll years from late '77. At times it's funny, at others it delves deeper than most biographies could ever go, and at other times you want to stop him and ask for more detail. But – as per Green's ethos – it's never boring and it's always entertaining. While hugely enjoyable, it's makes for uncomfortable reading at times too. But wasn't that the way The Clash's way?

Johnny was 27 when he joined the entourage, and clearly still had a lot of growing up to do. Yet to the band he was something of an elder statesman, and there was mutual respect, even if they did take the piss at times. In short, we have recollections from the front-line and the backline at a key time for the band, from someone who not only got to know them supremely but also knew instinctively when it was the right time to leave the party. Be aware that there are two versions, the revised edition including 40 extra pages and great black and white shots from Pennie Smith, Barry Myers and Mark Rusher. Even if you bought the original, I'd recommend the update, Green slipping back into his seemingly-effortless narrative to detail various conversations and social meetings with the band, from the end of the old century through to the Rock and Roll Hall of Fame induction. And while there's an element of closure and a more mature outlook, it's far from a safe version of events. Green still had the fire.

THE COMPLETE CLASH

Keith Topping (Reynolds & Hearn, 2003)

Many of the books I've seen advertised online about The Clash claim to list all the recorded output, but you get the feeling that few offer the kind of detail and dedication provided by Newcastle-based freelance journalist, novelist and critic Keith Topping, even if he does class his efforts as an 'unexpected opportunity to wobble on drunkenly about The Clash for 272 pages'. It's an impressive, authoritative work by a proper fan, who first got to see the band in his native North East in late '78. The live section itself is worth the cover price, its 'exhaustive coverage' of 600-plus Clash performances over nine amazing years including his own memorable Middlesbrough Town Hall debut ... although not memorable for the reasons he'd have chosen. There are also in-depth album, TV and film studies, and a weighty A-Z of Clash tracks. Described on the back cover as 'the first book of its kind,' it's fair to say others followed in its wake, but this definitely holds its own. Again, be aware that there are two editions, one with added sections, not least that live section. Like all the titles I've chosen here, it's a labour of love, a lot of hard graft going into its production. But Topping's toils deserve to be appreciated.

PASSION IS A FASHION: THE REAL STORY OF THE CLASH

Pat Gilbert (Aurum, 2004)

If the prime objective here was to expand on Marcus Gray's 1995 premise and 'explain the peculiar and unique relationships' between Strummer, Jones, Simonon and Headon, looking to provide, 'factual detail about what was happening behind the scenes, especially for the second half of their 10-year career,' Pat Gilbert certainly achieved that. It's an illuminating, fascinating read.

The former *Mojo* editor, and *Q* and broadsheet contributor was always a fan of the band, and was close enough to the inner circle to have the impact he aimed for, but toiled hard to achieve that. What's more, he's a great writer, as reflected in the meticulous detail and evocative narrative. When he takes you on a walk around The Clash's London, you're there with him. Again, as with all the main Clash chroniclers, Gilbert found the band, 'weren't the kind of people to give up their secrets easily,' and 'a conspiracy of silence seemed to prevail'. But he delved deep, tracking down key players, the end-result a revelatory portrait, not least of the relationship between band members and with their entourage, plenty of factual detail about what was happening behind the scenes adding to the bigger picture.

I particularly like the interviews carried out closer to publication. And while the band and their close associates seemed more open by then, he continued to treat his overall subject and Joe Strummer's memory with respect. Like Marcus Gray, the list of those interviewed is impressive, in Gilbert's case including all the major players – his *Mojo* features becoming solid foundations for an accomplished work. And despite his admitted Clash-obsession at an early age, this isn't blinkered fan-lit. If anything, his love for the band inspires him to analyse further what made them – not all of it making for easy reading, much as you might love them. And while you might have assumed Joe's untimely death would help build a more straight-forward band biography, with old quarrels swept aside and key characters finally more revealing, it would prove the project all the more complicated. Yet somehow, Gilbert skillfully navigated his way through.

REDEMPTION SONG: THE DEFINITIVE BIOGRAPHY OF JOE STRUMMER

Chris Salewicz (Harper Collins, 2006)

Who better to deliver the definitive

biography of Strummer, but a close friend right back to the days of the first album. And a fine writer too, as those who came across his 1974/81 NME features and subsequent pieces for the broadsheets and music press on pop culture, punk and reggae over the years will know, his other biographies including those on Bob Marley, Mick Jagger and Keith Richards, The Pretenders, Paul McCartney, Billy Bragg, and Jimi Hendrix. He also added text to Bob Gruen's Clash photo-book.

It's as close as you'll get to 'official', backed by Joe's relatives, friends and musicians, that factor affording him the right access to make this truly work. It was never likely to be warts'n'all, but didn't need to be. And it's honest as well as heartfelt. I deliberated over copying Salewicz's words in full about Strummer's funeral and a family and friends' memorial event in Granada that followed in August 2003. But it was a fantastically-sharp, emotional and evocative read, and after much soul-stirring I decided it offered a valuable insight into how Joe was loved by those around him, so used a fair amount. The same went for his account of a pilgrimage that same year to Raasay with Paul Simonon, who was commissioned to paint Joe's grandmother's old house there.

At 650-plus pages in hardback, it's certainly got substance, and the research on before-then untold parts of the story of this enigmatic performer's story make for an invaluable read. As with my other choices, there's a determination here to get to grips with the real story, way beyond the mythical version of the band, reaching the key figures at its epicentre. In a sense I get the feeling that part of Salewicz's personal remit was to try and understand for himself more about his truly-enigmatic subject. In that respect, it's a personal odyssey. He's gone about as close as you can on that front, and that took some doing, revealing the true 'colossal humanity that struck such a chord in the collective unconscious'.

ROUTE 19 REVISITED: THE CLASH AND LONDON CALLING

Marcus Gray (Jonathan Cape, 2009)

We're back to Marcus Gray, 14 years after his first major Clash publication, and this time not only is the pure feel of the book far better, there's real substance too. By the time it was put together, the record at its heart had finally been truly recognised, even gaining Grammy status in 2007, 27 years after a US release. And marking its 30th anniversary, Gray looked in detail at the lauded double-LP that ensured the band's deserved place at rock'n'roll's top table. As the blurb put it, 'Now The Clash's finest hour and five minutes gets a book, telling when, how and where it was made, detailing the stories behind its songs, placing the album in contexts personal, musical and socio-political, noting its impact upon release, and considering the ripple effects since, both in the members' own careers and 'in the culture'.

And the Route 19 link? The clue's not only in the number of tracks on this mighty double-vinyl dealing, but also on side one, track five's joyful, 'Rudie Can't Fail' and Strummer's introductory invitation for his lead guitarist to, 'Sing, Michael, sing – on the route of the 19 bus!' That's the south-west to north-east cross-capital route from Battersea Park to Finsbury Park, Strummer getting on in Chelsea and heading for his dates with sonic destiny at Wessex Studios. As Gray put it, 'This is no random ad-lib:

most of London Calling's songs were indeed conceived, polished and recorded at points along the city's No.19 bus route,' and, 'What Dylan did with the old and the new in the mid-'60s with Bringing it all Back Home and Highway 61 Revisited, The Clash did at the close of the '70s with London Calling. Yes, they took pointers from Dylan, The Beatles, The Stones, Elvis, the Sex Pistols, and all the others who had gone before, but they went their own way. On a literal level, route 19 might have been a bus journey across their hometown; but on a whole other level, it was absolute freedom to go wherever they pleased. This book sets out to recreate the trip.' And that he does, in style. A fitting tribute to a fantastic album.

Further recommended reading

The Clash: Strummer, Jones, Simonon, Headon by The Clash (Atlantic, 2008)
The Rise and Fall of The Clash by Danny Garcia (2012)
Joe Strummer and the Legend of The Clash by Kris Needs (Plexus, 2004)
Out of Control: The Last Days of The Clash by Vince White (Moving Target, 2007)
Joe Strummer and the Mescaleros: Vision of a Homeland by Anthony Davie (Reynolds & Hearn, 2005)
77 Sulphate Strip – Barry Cain (Red Planet, 2016)
Punk Rock: An Oral History by John Robb (Ebury Press, 2006)
England's Dreaming: Sex Pistols and Punk Rock by John Savage (Faber & Faber, 1991)
Pretty Vacant: A History of Punk by Phil Strongman (Orion, 2007)
The Jam: Our Story by Bruce Foxton and Rick Buckler, written with Alex Ogg (Castle, 1993)
That's Entertainment: My Life in The Jam by Rick Buckler (Omnibus, 2015)
Teenage Kicks: My Life as an Undertone by Mickey Bradley (Omnibus, 2016)
Margrave of the Marches by John Peel (Transworld/Bantam Press, 2005)
John Peel: A Life in Music by Michael Heatley (Michael O'Mara Books, 2004)
No off Switch: An Autobiography by Andy Kershaw (Serpent's Tail, 2011)
That Close by Suggs (Quercus, 2013)
Head-On: Memories of the Liverpool Punk Scene and the Story of The Teardrop Explodes (1976-82) by Julian Cope (Thorsons, 1994)
I Was a Teenage Sex Pistol by Glen Matlock (Rocket 88, 2012)
Anger is an Energy: My Life Uncensored by John Lydon (Simon & Schuster, 2015)
Rotten: No Irish No Blacks No Dogs by John Lydon (Hodder & Stoughton, 1993)
Can't Stand up for Falling Down: Rock'n'Roll War Stories by Allan Jones (Bloomsbury Publishing, 2017)
The Ultimate Music Guide: The Clash (IPC Magazines, 2017)
Joe Strummer: The Struggle after The Clash by Stephen Dalton (*Classic Rock*, 2017).
Straight to Hell – The Final Days of The Clash by Chris Knowles (*Classic Rock*, 2005)
The Making and Meaning of 'Hell W10' – Art Imitating Life by 'The Baker' & Derek Goddard (2013) via https://thebaker77.wordpress.com
The Clash – Exploring the Vanilla Tapes (London Calling Rehearsals 1979) by *The Green and Black* music website (2017) via http://greenandblackmusic.com
Julien Temple talking to Edward Douglas (Coming Soon, 2007) http://www.comingsoon.net/
Punk Before Punk – US fan Paul Dougherty's blog, via https://punkbeforepunk.wordpress.com/

5

Clash-related online sources

TheClash.com: a one-stop shop for details of the band's LPs, singles and videos, and including a gallery and gig archive. Also issues a Clash newsletter. Includes an official store. http://www.theclash.com/
BlackMarketClash: a comprehensive biography of The Clash on stage, in the studio and on film, linking to rare recordings. Regularly updated. http://cluster1.website-staging.uk/blackmarketclash.co.uk/
The Clash Site: a photography and in-depth information-led journey through the history of The Clash on a site run by Don J. Whistance, a former schoolmate of Mick Jones. http://www.theclash.org.uk/
The Joe Strummer Foundation: official charity providing opportunities to musicians and supporting projects around the world, creating empowerment through music. http://joestrummerfoundation.org
Paul Simonon: the website for Clash bass hero turned full-time artist and painter, with details of Paul's exhibitions and art news, and including an online shop. http://paulsimonon.com/
The Baker: Scraps and Glimpses: Roadie Barry Auguste, aka 'The Baker': after many years turning down interviews: recalls his days with The Clash. https://thebaker77.wordpress.com
The Great Wen: A London Blog: the online home of journalist Peter Watts, formerly of *The Sunday Times* and a features writer at *Time Out*, including lots of London copy. https://greatwen.com
Green and Black Music: a music blog for obsessed music fans, including album reviews, deconstruction of album art, top-10 lists and 'bloated essays', including music and TV. http://greenandblackmusic.com
Louder Than War: John Robb's award-winning anti-genre music site, not adhering to preconceived rules. Reviews, news, interviews, new artists. Also has its own magazine. http://louderthanwar.com
Pat Gilbert Writer: London-based *Mojo* and Q feature writer/interviewer/editor and Clash biographer, author, screenwriter and musician. https://www.patgilbert.co.uk/
The Quietus: North London-based arts website, speicalising in news, reviews, features and opinions, including music, film, books, art, radio and podcasts, with its own record label. http://thequietus.com/
Retro Man Blog: 'the ramblings of a man who really should have grown out of listening to that sort of music.' Thoughts and photos on music and related paraphernalia. http://retroman65.blogspot.co.uk/
Toppermost: Music fans' favourite tracks by favourite artists; not necessarily the most popular/biggest sellers, but the less celebrated too: 'the toppermost of the poppermost'. http://www.toppermost.co.uk
WriteWyattUK: Lancashire-based Malcolm Wyatt's online site: feature/interviews and reviews, mostly music and comedy. Punk, new wave, pop, rock, soul, from the '60s onwards. https://writewyattuk.com

THE CLASH ON FILM

5

As with books, there are so many Clash-related visual documentaries and film projects that it would be a near-impossible task to talk about them all in detail. As a result, I've gone for a selection – some well known, some acclaimed, others not so, but all key to the overall story and worth documenting on these pages.

RUDE BOY

Jack Hazan and David Mingay, 1980

I've written plenty about blurred lines between fact and fiction in trying to piece together the story of The Clash, and fictional documentary Rude Boy provides a microcosm of that 'taking a liberty with history' approach. More to the point, what a missed opportunity this was. It could have been one of the greatest rock'n'roll films. All for the want of a better script ... or perhaps even just a script.

By all accounts, the project was sprung on the band in true Bernie Rhodes style, road manager Johnny Green – whose on-screen dynamism outstrips that of many around him, despite being dragged into the fray by default – detailing the often-strained relationship with independent filmmakers Jack Hazan and David Mingay – who also made 1973's *A Bigger Splash*, a semi-fictional biopic of British artist David Hockney – in his memoir *A Riot of Our Own*.

It's a paper-thin work of part-fiction, the story following Clash fan Ray Gange in his first and only lead role, drifting between a day-job in a sex shop and a blagged role as a roadie. What the production team were looking to achieve remains uncertain. You get the idea that the film crew were making it up as they went along, although they'd probably use the term improv.

That said, it's fascinating from a fan's point of view, seeing the band at such close quarters, and the live footage saves the day. And in retrospect the film gives a valuable portrayal of Britain on its arse at the end of the '70s, picking up on the social and political malaise that led to Margaret Thatcher seizing power. It certainly captures an atmosphere of racial tension, at a time when the National Front were whipping up ill-feeling among disenfranchised, gullible white youth. We encounter a UK that no longer exists, journalist Peter Watts seeing the film as 'a terrific social documentary of the 1970s,' while Jon Savage suggests in 1991's England's Dreaming, 'If in 1979 Rude Boy was embarrassing, today it is a visual record of a lost era.'

The fact that Gange's character (playing 'Ray Gange' – another blurred line) seems to take the right-wing arguments on board doesn't help empathise with him. You have sympathy at times, but his on-screen character comes over as a bit of a prat, a naïve young South Londoner not understanding the band's anti-racist stance. That's no reflection on the real Ray, recent interviews suggesting a lovely bloke, a far cry from the character Hazan and Mingay loosely scripted. While he gets a part-credit for the script, he's in denial about co-writing, instead seeing himself as a fan exploited by the filmmakers for his friendship with Joe Strummer, asked to take counter-arguments in on-camera discussions. He also insists he was apolitical then, and now. He added in a 2015 interview, 'Making that film changed my life in as much that it gave me money to get out of the country, which I don't know if I'd have been able to do that in any other way. And it opened my eyes to a lot of stuff ... it opened my eyes to the perils of film-making!'

Gange's character spends a lot of his time drinking on set, while the plot-line for the black lad in the film is similarly-flimsy, one-dimensional tosh. Yes, these were dark times, but there's nothing here to inspire other than the band's stage presence. Why not have Gange gradually take on board their message? And why not give the black character more input, perhaps getting into the band after hearing their interpretive take on reggae? Instead, we get hollow clichés and Ray losing it while the black lad lands himself a prison term. The last shots of the band tearing through 'I Fought the Law' at the Lyceum should have been celebratory, but just underlined a depressing outcome.

Understandably the band distanced themselves from Rude Boy, and only Mick Jones properly questions Gange's character's casual racism in the film. There are highlights though, even some of the staged vignettes. Like seeing Strummer lecture Gange on politics in the pub, an elder statesman of sorts, while only in his mid-20s. And although his political thinking is – as it always seemed to be in those days and beyond – rather idealistic and infuriatingly vague in places, you can listen to him and understand the loyalty he invoked in people. Then there's his impassioned vocal at Basing Street Studios on 'All the Young Punks (New Boots and Contracts)' and the charm of the man as he talks to Gange between piano renditions of self-penned blues number, 'No Reason' ('Piano Song'), then Shirley and Lee's 'Let the Good Times Roll', his ironic response to Gange's pessimism.

Then there's Jones giving his all on 'Stay Free' at Basing Street, before Gange spoils the moment in his drunken, gushing praise. Throughout, Jones comes over as stroppy, but I'm with him – those cameras were intrusive at a time when the band were looking to buckle down and find their way out of the punk maze. The Clash had enough mounting problems without having to worry about carrying passengers. We see them struggle with police, bouncers, audiences ... Yet by the end, things are tightening up, their open demeanour giving way to a more professional approach, the band thinking bigger.

We also experience the farcical scenes at Victoria Park at 1978's Rock Against Racism carnival, Jimmy Pursey seemingly dressed as a French mime-artist while barking out 'White Riot' with the band before a rat-arsed Gange – egged on by his director – grabs the mic and incites the audience. The stage-hand who shouts, 'Get this idiot off the stage' possibly has the most pertinent line in the film, the event's spirit of camaraderie lost in the translation as fact meets fiction again.

Paul Simonon, like the benevolent

Strummer, comes over as loveable with a hint of mischief, and you can see the women around him – including Caroline Coon – hooked by that gap-toothed smile and those good looks. Yet Fred Dellar and Roy Carr, reviewing for *Vox: 50 Movies That Rocked the Aisles* in 1991, wrote, 'It's Strummer who really matters. As *NME* commented on his performance at the time of the film's release, 'He has the riveting presence of James Dean or the young Brando. On stage, he is the quintessential rock martyr, frequently unable to control the forces he has summoned.'

As for Topper Headon, he's the bundle of energy you expect, as shown in his kick-boxing training with a punchbag and poor Ray, the latter assailed by the nutter in yellow Bruce Lee replica tracksuit. 'The Baker' also features, and you see why Simonon gave him that nickname when he's off-loading gear in half-mast trousers and white socks one night outside the studio. Needless to say, Rhodes kept well away though, his chaos done, and his days numbered ... for a while.

As it was, the band insisted on over-dubbing the live footage's poor sound quality, at Wessex, then George Martin's Air Studios. And it was worth the hassle. The best moments are those where the band give an impassioned performance at Camden's Music Machine, belting out 'Complete Control', 'Safe European Home' and 'What's My Name', but others come close – 'Police and Thieves' at Barbarella's, Birmingham; a slightly-slower 'Garageland' in rehearsal; '(White Man) In Hammersmith Palais', 'I'm So Bored With the USA', 'Janie Jones' and 'White Riot' on a particularly-riotous night at Glasgow Apollo; 'The Prisoner' in Aberdeen; 'Tommy Gun' in Dunfermline, then that 'I Fought the Law' Lyceum finale.

As Gange put it, 'I can't think that any other live footage of any band I've seen ever comes close to the live stuff of The Clash in that film. Don't Look Back is a really great film, but what's great about that is all the off-stage stuff. What's really great about Rude Boy is that the live stuff is fucking phenomenal. It really does pick out why at the time people were on that scene, your blood would just pump round your body when The Clash were playing, and the hairs on your fucking back would stand up. For that, it's like the best thing ever.'

THE CLASH: WESTWAY TO THE WORLD

Don Letts, 1999/2000

Westway to the World provides the foundation for every subsequent documentary film about The Clash and remains the best of those specifically tackling the band's story. It was the first to get the official treatment and featured all four classic members (plus fellow Rock and Roll Hall of Fame inductee Terry Chimes), telling the story in their own words on camera for the first time, with Tony Parsons, Johnny Green, Bill Price, and Pennie Smith chipping in.

As a friend of the band, long-time Clash associate and band videographer Don Letts was the right choice for this project, and tells the story at pace, with some neat anecdotes and evocative footage along the way. He certainly doesn't over-complicate matters, to the extent that the story more or less ends with Mick Jones' sacking. Yet that air-brushing of the full history is arguably preferable, and doesn't diminish this film's power.

With its premiere at the Coronet Cinema, Notting Hill Gate, on September 21st, 1999, and a TV debut in a 50-minute cut 11 days

5

later on BBC2, Letts' authorised biography is essential viewing for fans and makes for compelling viewing. It's the 85-minute director's cut from the year 2000 that we tend to see now, including extra interviews and a salvaged cutting copy of *Clash on Broadway*, featuring the band's 1982 17-show back-to-back run at Bond's Casino, Times Square, New York City.

The format's fairly straight-forward, but that works too, the on-screen 'talking head' style interviews with the band never over-cooked, handled well (off-screen) by Mal Peachey, and interspersed with great live footage, the basic format proving fresh throughout, as we get to experience the (not often recognised) humour of the band. This is no po-faced tale of political sloganeering and self-importance.

From the individual original members' musical, biographical and art backgrounds (Letts' simple stencil and paint-splash graphics also work well) to the band's emergence in time for London's first summer of punk, the director kick-starts a largely-chronological but effective narrative. Then, Topper Headon comes into the story, his on-screen appearance an effective advert for teaching kids not to dabble with hard drugs (he was still very much a heroin addict at that point, but thankfully pulled through in the years that followed).

I mentioned the live footage, and while much of it pops up elsewhere, it works nicely here, not least moments like the Granada TV film of the band playing 'What's My Name' at Manchester's Elizabethan Ballroom and those priceless Camden Music Machine performances. And just seeing Strummer with his left leg pumping while his right hand attacks that guitar takes us right back.

Of course, there's no Bernie Rhodes interview, but he gets a few mentions, and pretty much every major issue up to Jones' departure is covered. As we near the end, Joe Strummer's contributions are ever-more emotional, the essence of the band's spirit bottled right there by a frontman clearly still struggling to come to terms with the questionable decisions made in those last couple of years before the split. And yet it seems that just the right amount of time had lapsed before tackling those issues – making for more honest, 'benefit of hindsight' musings, the bigger picture put in context.

Footnote: an antidote to Letts leaving out the last chapter is provided in *The Rise and Fall of The Clash* (Danny Garcia, 2012), its Spanish director – a big Clash fan – also credited as co-producer with former Clash roadie Robin Banks. This 90-minute documentary is described as 'the definitive biography of the group's fall from grace after they made it to Shea Stadium,' and concentrates on the band's ultimate collapse. Of course, to many fans that's the part of the story we'd try and pretend never happened. But it's car-crash TV, and you know you're intrigued, not least as so many key names took part, including Mick Jones, Topper Headon and Terry Chimes. There were also Clash Mk. II personnel Pete Howard, Nick Sheppard and Vince White, Blockheads' sessioneers Mick Gallagher and Norman Watt-Roy, fellow scene luminaries Viv Albertine, Vic Goddard, Pearl Harbour, Dan Donovan and Tymon Dogg, and writers Pat Gilbert, Kris Needs and Chris Salewicz. Damien Love wrote in Uncut at the time that it, 'scores because it's about the messy, inconvenient part of the story Letts's great film shies away from. Specifically: the end.' Mind you, the same reviewer described it as 'meat-and-potatoes rock doc stuff, low-budget talking heads interviews, interspersed with archive footage,' before conceding it was 'a useful supplement to Westway to the World'. Interestingly, David Mingay was involved as well, also down as a co-producer, 32 years after the release of his first Clash film, Rude Boy. I'm guessing it's not a film that would have been on Bernie Rhodes' Christmas list though.

JOE STRUMMER: THE FUTURE IS UNWRITTEN

Julien Temple, 2007

Much as I love Don Letts' *Westway to the World*, this for me ranks even higher among the finest rock'n'roll biopics. Released five years after Joe Strummer's death, Julien Temple's stylish tribute to his friend featured award-winning film director Martin Scorsese and big-name actors such as Johnny Depp and John Cusack alongside contemporary artists and later stars, from Mick Jones, Topper Headon and Terry Chimes through to Steve Jones, Tymon Dogg, Primal Scream's Bobby Gillespie, U2's Bono and members of the Red Hot Chilli Peppers, 'all of whom attest to the life-changing power of The Clash,' as Sean O'Hagan pointed out in his review for *The Guardian*.

While we're playing the name game, you can add the afore-mentioned list, Letts, Bez, Mani, Courtney Love, Damien Hirst, Steve Buscemi, Matt Dillon, Joe Ely, John Cooper Clarke, Pogues' manager Frank Murray, and Roland Gift. But the director goes far deeper, the film's real strength in the testimonies of those who were closest to Joe across the years, not only bringing in old flames and friends from his Vultures, 101'ers and art-school past, and those by his side in the Mescaleros era, but the performer's family too. If this was just a celebrity affair, it wouldn't work so well. And while there's plenty of love for the main subject, there's also honesty, Joe's worse aspects examined as well as his humanity, sincerity, and enormous charisma. As Luke Lewis wrote, 'Admirably, Temple makes no attempt to sugar-coat Strummer's various contradictions and hypocrisies – this is an affectionate documentary, but not an uncritical one.'

This two-hour epic documentary includes previously-unissued footage of its main subject, from studio sessions to archive film and home movie footage, and even some quirky animation involving Strummer's personal notebooks and doodles. In fact, there are plenty of touches that leave you in no doubt that this is a Julien Temple film, including occasional classic film clips illustrating the scene, 1954's animated *Animal Farm* and TV adaptation of *1984* looming large, while a scene from *If* plays alongside The MC5's 'Kick Out the Jams' to set the scene of the '68 counter-culture protests. There's even an old Fry's Turkish Delight advert, conjuring up the romance of just one of the faraway places John Mellor lived as a child – his birthplace, Ankara.

The soundtrack also includes Rachid Taha's wondrous 'Rock El Casbah', and evocative snippets of Andres Landeros, Ernest Ranglin, Bob Dylan, Woody Guthrie, Eddie Cochran, Elvis Presley, Nina Simone, Tim Hardin (accompanying the sad tale of Joe's brother David) and U-Roy, the spirit of the times stoked, most of the choices from Strummer's *London Calling* Bush House recordings for the BBC World Service.

But it's the conversations about Joe around campfires in Granada, London, Los Angeles, New York City, and Somerset that define this work, and one that appears to be on the Kent coast, interviewee Topper Headon seemingly in rude health compared to his on-screen haunted look in *Westway to the World* seven years earlier. In fact, the DVD includes an extra 100 minutes of interview footage (with Paul Simonon the only obvious absentee), the most notable exception to the 'campfire' premise being Mick Jones, who had his own spin on the theme, Temple explaining, 'He said, 'I'll do it, but I want to be in front of a three-bar electric fire rather than a campfire.' That's the kind of fire he used to grow up with in his Nan's flat.'

There are certainly some powerful contributions, not just from Joe's widow, Lucinda, step-daughter Eliza, and his ex, Gaby. And in the same way that Strummer's emotional pieces to camera tug the heart-strings in Letts' film, the conclusive moments here leave me broken, not least cousin Iain Gillies' last words, then Joe's stirring 'Without people you're nothing' monologue before the credits roll. All hail the punk rock warlord.

Footnote: For more on the Mescaleros story, I recommend *Let's Rock Again!* (Dick Rude, 2004), an acclaimed documentary following Strummer and his band as they tour the US and Japan promoting the *Global a Go-Go* LP, after its predecessor failed to secure commercial success. Shot by a filmmaker and long-time friend of Strummer in the 18 months leading up to his death in late 2002, it was co-produced with Strummer and his widow, Lucinda. Strummer's link with the director went back to Alex Cox's mid-'80s films, *Sid and Nancy, Straight to Hell* and *Walker*, in which both had acting roles, by which time Rude was also working with the Red Hot Chilli Peppers, directing their promo videos. The DVD version was released in 2006, Mat Snow, for The Guardian, writing, 'Dick Rude joined them in America and Japan to shoot access all areas for what was hoped to be a triumphant comeback. The tour had its highs, but embarrassing lows too, and Strummer was denied a return to the spotlight's fullest beam by his sudden death. What should have been the document of a work in progress turned out to be an epitaph. Inevitably sad to watch now, Let's Rock Again! portrays a star of rare humility, a rock romantic bemused by the times but well-preserved, like a mid-life André Previn, and seldom without an inspirational yarn to gee up the band, though oddly un-snappy in interview for such a vivid lyricist. A fine way to remember him, though.'

THE CLASH: NEW YEAR'S DAY '77

Julien Temple, 2014

A late addition to The Clash's televisual canon, nearly four decades after its initial footage was shot (and soon abandoned), but another winning project from Julien Temple, built around film of the band in the build-up to opening dodgy punk hang-out The Roxy in dilapidated Covent Garden on January 1st, 1977.

The year of the Queen's silver jubilee was also the year punk properly emerged into the mainstream, and Temple skilfully weaves Clash footage from that period around moments from the BBC's '76 into '77 New Year schedule. And from the moment Vera Lynn wishes us the compliments of the season, we're shipped back in time, afforded a glimpse of a long-gone era.

The film makes much of Marcus Garvey's prophesy of calamity, with Culture's mighty 'Two Sevens Clash' key to its soundtrack, images of revelry around the nation building the scene. Then there are the TV discussions about the bleak prospects on offer at the back end of Jim Callaghan's faltering administration, the PM determined to fight on, Mrs Thatcher waiting menacingly in the wings. As fellow Clash filmographer Don Letts, DJing at the Roxy from that first night, put it, '1977 had more of a millennium feel than the millennium did.' And while Garvey's predictions didn't come to fruition in Jamaica, he adds, 'There sure was a lot of chaos in the United Kingdom.'

At that point, the 'Filth and the Fury' headlines that followed the Sex Pistols' *Today* appearance remained fresh in the public consciousness, a nation sitting up and taking notice of a supposed enemy within. Malcolm McLaren suggests on camera that was 'the spark', and we get to see some of the others drawing the flames, from The Damned and The Jam to Siouxsie and the Banshees, The Slits, and The Subway Sect. And what of these Camden-based pretenders to the Pistols' crown? What gets me is how young The Clash look, not least when huddled around a TV excited at scratchy black and white images of themselves, or when Strummer's modifying his stage clobber in next door's vehicle workshop ('Give it a good hammering, Joe!' says Pete the mechanic, taking an approach Guy Stevens would echo in 1979).

And both the live and background footage is fascinating, not least when you hear the band voice their frustration at the opportunities on offer, backed up by Temple's portrayal of a monochrome Britain, the 'no future' protestations of John Lydon given fresh impetus in interviews with a fledgling outfit on their way to delivering an explosive first LP, chock-full of the issues Bernie Rhodes called to be explored. And while the director juggles their impassioned rants with the pop message of bands like Brotherhood of Man, Dr Hook and Sailor, Strummer points out that even old heroes like The Who have lost their way.

Musically, the band remain raw, as seen and heard on a buzzsaw-led 'What's My Name' in rehearsals. When it comes to the Roxy appearance – one of two that night, with their hired PA on the blink – the electrical charge is there from the moment Mick announces 'London's Burning' by way of introduction and they're off, Temple feeding in disturbing operatic imagery (we are in Covent Garden, after all) as the band tear through a key component of the LP that will follow. We also see them looking down over the Westway and beyond from Mick's high-rise.

Next up, 'I'm so Bored with the USA's opening riff seems more 'Pretty Vacant'-like live, its lyrics still being refined by Joe. Work in progress, but what a sound. The same can be said of 'Career Opportunities', Strummer telling the interviewer about his dole office dilemmas, before a raucous roll through 'Janie Jones', Temple adding dancing girl footage while future Pogue Shane McGowan gives his all down the front, Paul Simonon's out of tune bassline all over the shop. Shambolic, yet inspirational.

From there, Marcus Garvey's predictions get another twist with the band's 'White Riot' response to that previous August's Notting Hill disturbances, before the set ends with a dynamic '1977' – the title proudly emblazoned on Joe's white shirt, his tie askew – its count-up climax punctuated by further archive film illustrations before a shuddering halt in 1984, Temple cutting – as also on *The Future is Unwritten* – to an image of Peter Cushing as Winston Smith, where 'Big Brother is watching you'. Powerful viewing all-round, the band repair to the dressing room, soon to get to work on that debut album, while Strummer, *Sniffin' Glue*'s Mark Perry, Rhodes and McLaren surmise just what 1977 may hold in store, the stage set for The Clash's true breakthrough.

Footnote: More of a curate's egg (but so was *Rude Boy*), *Hell, W10* (Joe Strummer, 1983) was another project that fascinated, and not necessarily for the right reasons. Filmed while the band were taking a break from touring, Strummer felt it might be a good idea to bring the post-Headon group together through another movie project. And it's an oddity, a half-hour black and white 16mm silent film with a Clash soundtrack. Paul Simonon plays the key role in a gangster movie Joe later admitted was a disaster, telling *Film Comment*'s Graham Fuller in 1987, 'Luckily, the laboratory that held the negative went bankrupt and destroyed all the stock, so the world can breathe again.' It finally emerged in the early 2000s though, supposedly found on videotape at a North London car-boot sale, becoming a bonus feature on *The Essential Clash* DVD, re-edited by Don Letts. With a 1950s' crime pulp fiction feel, there are intriguing views of early '80s London as we arrive by train at Westbourne Grove, Simonon playing West London gangster Earl, Mick Jones as ruthless white tuxedo-wearing drug baron Mr Socrates ('The Lord of Ladbroke Grove') and Strummer as an armed police inspector with a dodgy moustache, and various other cameos, including those from Pennie Smith, Pearl Harbour, and Kosmo Vinyl. With Simonon and Jones barely speaking by then, their fictional feud here makes for uncomfortable viewing, not least when you consider the latter got the bullet that September. But the soundtrack, including instrumental early mixes of 'Atom Tan' and 'Overpowered by Funk', means you can always play it without watching the screen, doing something more worthwhile with your time. Journalist Peter Watts, writing about the film in 2011, wrote, 'Both Jones and Strummer confess that the band had simply spent too much time in each other's company and should have taken a break; if they had done so, hotheads may have had time to cool. Instead, they made a film. Perhaps if they'd had a summer holiday in 1983 rather than fool around with a camera, the band might have lasted another few years. Still, it looks like they had fun making it.'

Further recommended viewing

Hell W10 (1983)
Viva Joe Strummer: The Clash and Beyond (Mike Parkinson, WHE International, 2005)
The Rise and Fall of The Clash (Danny Garcia, 2012)
The Clash Live: Revolution Rock (Sony, 2008)
The Essential Clash (Sony, 2003)
Let's Rock Again! (Dick Rude, 2004)

A CLASH TIMELINE

5

1952

August 21st – John Graham Mellor born in Ankara, Turkey.

1955

May 30th – Nicholas Bowen Headon born in Bromley, Kent.
June 26th – Michael Geoffrey Jones born in Clapham, South London.
December 15th – Paul Gustave Simonon born, Thornton Heath, South London.

1956

July 5th – Terence Chimes born Stepney, East London.

1970

Autumn – John Mellor starts at Camberwell Art School.
Late '70 – John Mellor, 18, going by the name 'Woody', moves to 'Vomit Heights', Palmer's Green, London N13, his housemates including future bandmates Clive Timperley and Tymon Dogg, the latter inviting him to go busking on the Tube, Woody soon buying a ukulele.

1972

Late '72 – Mick Jones and John Brown (ex-Schoolgirl) co-form The Delinquents.

1973

Summer '73 – 'Woody' Mellor' joins Newport, South Wales rock'n'roll covers band The Vultures, providing shared guitar and vocal duties, and records his first song, 'Crummy Bum Blues'.
September – Mick Jones begins a foundation course at Hammersmith College of Art and Building in Shepherd's Bush, London W12.

1974

May – The 101'ers formed by squatters based at 101, Walterton Road, London W9, with Woody Mellor on rhythm guitar and vocals.
Summer '74 – Paul Simonon wins a scholarship to Byam Shaw Art School, Notting Hill Gate, London W8.
September 7th – The 101'ers' live debut at the Telegraph, Brixton Hill, London SW2, supporting South London reggae band Matumbi at a benefit for Chilean refugees.

1975

February – Mick Jones sees the 101'ers for the first time at The Chippenham's Charlie Pigdog Club in West London.
May – The 101'ers commence an eight-month Thursday night residency at The Elgin, Ladbroke Grove.
April – Tony Gordon takes on Mick Jones' band, The Delinquents, renaming them Little Queenie after a Chuck Berry song.
Summer – Guy Stevens is invited along to an Acton rehearsal of Little Queenie, suggesting

5

they ditch extra guitar player, Mick Jones. Voted out, he returns to his Gran's to sharpen up his playing.
August 2nd – Mick Jones and Tony James meet Bernie Rhodes at the Nashville Rooms, West Kensington, at a Deaf School gig, mistaking him for a keyboard player because of his Bluecaps look.
November '75 – Mick Jones, Tony James and Brian James, guided by Bernie Rhodes, hold first auditions for the London SS in a basement beneath Paddington Kitchen café on Praed Street, London W2. Nicky Headon gets the nod but quits for a soul tour with The GI's.

1976

January – Paul Simonon joins drummer Roland Hot for the latter's audition at Paddington Kitchen with the London SS. He fails to shine but is remembered by Rhodes, later suggesting he's brought back.
April 3rd – The Sex Pistols support the 101'ers at the Nashville Rooms, West Kensington. Strummer sees 'a future he wanted to be part of', according to journalist Allan Jones.
April 23rd – the same bands appear at the Nashville, with Jones and recent recruits Keith Levene and Simonon watching.
May – The 101'ers' 'Keys to Your Heart' is released as a single by Chiswick.
May 12th – Jones, Simonon and Levene see the 101'ers again, this time at the Red Cow, Hammersmith.
May 25 – Bernie Rhodes approaches Joe Strummer at a Sex Pistols gig at the 100 Club, telling him there's 'some boys' he wants him to meet, forming a band 'like the Pistols'.
May 30th – Levene and Rhodes speak to Strummer after a 101'ers show at the Golden Lion, Fulham Broadway, giving him a 48-hour ultimatum to join their new band. He accepts a day later.
June 1st – Strummer is taken by Rhodes and Levene from Orsett Terrace to a squat on Davis Road, Acton Vale, London W3, to join Jones and Simonon for the new band's first rehearsal.
June 5th – The 101'ers play their final gig at the Clare Halls, Haywards Heath, Sussex.
July 4th – The Clash, after weeks practising at Bernie Rhodes' Rehearsal Rehearsals HQ in Camden Town, make their live debut at the Black Swan, Sheffield, supporting the Sex Pistols, the first of an estimated 600 shows to 1985.
July 5th – the band return to London in time for the Ramones' second weekend show in the capital at Camden Dingwall's (after Chalk Farm's Roundhouse the previous night), Paul Simonon and The Stranglers' bass player JJ Burnel getting in a scrap.
August 13th – the band play an invitation-only show for press at their Rehearsals base in Camden Town.
August 29th – The Screen on the Green, Islington, supporting the Sex Pistols. Buzzcocks open the show.
August 30th – Notting Hill Carnival ends in a major disturbance, with Strummer, Simonon and Bernie Rhodes present and inspired to write 'White Riot'.
August 31st – the band play the 100 Club, Oxford Street, supporting the Sex Pistols.
September 5th – support slot at The Roundhouse with the Kursaal Flyers. The last show with Keith Levene in the band.
September 20th – opening of two-day Punk Festival at London's 100 Club, also starring the Sex Pistols and Siouxsie and the Banshees, the latter including Sid Vicious on drums and Marco Pirroni.
October – gig in Guildford, Surrey, referred

to in 1982 NBC TV interview with Simonon and Strummer as having 'only one person in the audience'.
October 9th – Tiddenfoot Leisure Centre, Leighton Buzzard, Bedfordshire, supporting The Rockets.
October 15th – Acklam Hall, Ladbroke Grove, London, supporting Spartacus and Sukuya.
October 16th – University of London – supporting Shakin' Stevens, whose fans offer them 5p for an early bus home
October 23rd – first headline gig at 'A Night of Pure Energy' at London's ICA (Institute of Contemporary Arts), with Subway Sect.
October 27 – first visit to Barbarella's, Birmingham, supporting the Suburban Studs.
October 29th – Fulham Town Hall, supporting Roogalator.
November 3rd – Harlesden Coliseum.
November 5th – 'A Night of Treason', London's RCA (Royal College of Arts), supported by The Rockets, Strummer and Simonon jump in after Sid Vicious – just out of Ashford Remand Centre – gets in a scrap.
November 11th – Ilford Lacy Lady.
November 13th – Birmingham Barbarella's return, supported by Suburban Studs.
Mid-November – the band enter Polydor Studios, London, to record five songs, Guy Stevens producing.
November 18th – Nag's Head, High Wycombe, Bucks, supported by Clayson and the Argonauts.
November 28th – first TV interview, with Janet Street-Porter on *The London Weekend Television Show.*
November 29th – Lanchester Polytechnic, Coventry, supporting the Sex Pistols. Terry Chimes' 'final' gig.
December 1st – rehearsal at Harlesden's Roxy Theatre, with The Damned and the Sex Pistols when the latter leave to replace Queen as interviewees on ill-fated early evening ITV show *Today* with Bill Grundy.
December 3rd – *Anarchy* tour set to get underway at Norwich University, but first of many cancellations, followed by Derby King's Hall (4th) and Newcastle City Hall (5th) dates.
December 6th – Leeds Polytechnic. *Anarchy* tour underway at fourth attempt, filmmaker Julien Temple present, and Rob Harper on drums. Sex Pistols headline, The Damned and Johnny Thunders & the Heartbreakers also supporting.
December 9th – Manchester Electric Circus, *Anarchy* tour. Buzzcocks replacing The Damned. Morrissey and Joy Division in the crowd.
December 14th – Castle Cinema show, Caerphilly, late rearrangement. Protest outside covered by TV.
December 19th – the band return to Manchester's Electric Circus, Peter Hook recalling the punks attending being attacked by locals outside the venues.
December 21st – Plymouth Woods Centre, first of two nights ends *Anarchy* tour. An estimated crowd of 30 on 22nd replacement show after a good first-night turnout.
December 26th/28th – stop/start eventful month aptly ends with three nights at Harlesden Roxy Theatre cancelled, also set to star the Pistols and The Damned, fellow headliners Ramones pulling out.

1977

January 1st – The Clash open the Roxy, Covent Garden, with two sets. Becomes a prime punk rock hang-out. Don Letts as DJ. Last show for Rob Harper as drummer.
January 27th – The Clash sign to CBS at Soho Square for £100,000, after negotiations

5

between Rhodes and label boss Maurice Oberstein.
February – debut LP recorded at CBS Studio 3, Whitfield Street, London.
March 11th – Harlesden Coliseum. Terry Chimes returns for one-off. Buzzcocks, Subway Sect and The Slits support. First airing of 'Garageland'. Filmed by Don Letts for *The Punk Rock Movie*.
March 18th – debut single, 'White Riot'/ '1977' released by CBS, recorded the previous month, going on to reach No.38 in the UK the day after the first LP is released.
April 2nd – the band get their first *NME* front cover, with Strummer, Jones and Simonon pictured, the headline reading, 'Thinking Man's Yobs', Tony Parsons' Circle Line interview inside.
April 8th – debut LP, *The Clash*, released by CBS, the 'Capital Radio' single out the following day, free to readers who sent off an *NME* coupon plus a red sticker on the album.
April 10th – Topper Headon's live band debut at The Roundhouse, London.
April 17th – Lindsay Clinell films a promo for the band at a studio in Dunstable, Bedfordshire, featuring 'White Riot', '1977' and 'London's Burning'. *NME* writer Tony Parsons among the assembled.
April 27th – Paris Frankrike. First gig outside the UK and the first playing reggae covers 'Police and Thieves' and 'Pressure Drop'.
April 30th – *The Clash* enters the UK top 40 album chart at No. 12, Its highest position.
May 1st – Guildford Civic Hall. 'White Riot' tour opens. Buzzcocks, The Slits, Subway Sect and The Prefects as support. The Jam set to play but cancel after a fall-out between the bands' managers.
May 5th – Liverpool Eric's, a mightily-impressed Julian Cope, Pete Wylie and Ian McCulloch – 'the Crucial Three' – meet for the first time and are inspired to form a band.
May 9th – Rainbow Theatre, London. Strummer calls it, 'The night punk really broke.' Billy Bragg there. An estimated 200 seats ripped out. The Jam also play but then decide to quit the tour.
May 13th – Leicester De Montfort Hall, recorded by BBC Radio 1's *In Concert*. Also 'Remote Control'/ 'London's Burning (Live)' released as a single, against the band's wishes, failing to chart.
July – 'Complete Control' recorded at Sarm East Studios, Whitechapel.
August 5th – Mont-de-Marsan, France, near the Spanish border. European Punk Festival, the first of a few European dates, also visiting Belgium, Holland, Switzerland, Germany, and Sweden.
September 23rd – 'Complete Control'/ 'City of the Dead' out, reaching No.28 in the UK.
October 20th – 'Out of Control' tour set to open at Ulster Hall, Belfast, but local council cancel, leading to the 'Riot of Bedford Street'.
October 21st – Trinity College, Dublin, show attended by wide-eyed members of U2.
October 24th – the band play the Kinema, Dunfermline, local band The Skids supporting, with Richard Hell & the Voidoids, and The Lou's. Four days later, the Sex Pistols release *Never Mind the Bollocks*.
November 13th – Southampton Top Rank tour finale after 22 gigs in 25 days.
November 15th – Elizabethan Ballroom, Belle Vue, Manchester. Sandy Pearlman flies in to see the band for the first time. Granada TV's *So It Goes* filming.
December – Strummer and Jones visit Jamaica for a 10-day writing trip, inspiring 'Safe European Home', and on their return

play three nights at London's Rainbow Theatre.
December 20th – the band return to Belfast, to a rapturous reception at a rescheduled Ulster Hall show, for their last show of a busy 1977.

1978

January 24th – Birmingham Barbarella's (as featured on *White Riot* tour). First low-key gig booked to help Sandy Pearlman get to know the set ahead of *Give 'Em Enough Rope* recording sessions.
January 26th – Lanchester Polytechnic return. Rob Crocker punches Sandy Pearlman out at stage door.
February 17th – 'Clash City Rockers'/ 'Jail Guitar Doors' released, recorded the previous autumn at CBS, reaching No. 35 in the UK.
March 30th – Topper Headon's friends Steve and Pete Barnacle arrive at Rehearsals, Camden, with an air rifle. A decision to test it out on pigeons – turning out to be expensive racing pigeons – on the roof leads to a major armed police raid, after a report of terrorists taking pot shots by the main railway route into central London. Headon and Simonon are among those arrested, held and charged for criminal damage.
April – The Clash start a John Peel session for BBC Radio 1 at Maida Vale, but fail to complete it.
April 30th – Victoria Park, Hackney, East London. Rock Against Racism show supporting the Tom Robinson Band. Caught on camera by the *Rude Boy* film crew. Jimmy Pursey joining in on 'White Riot'.
May 20th – Paris Hippodrome show – 10th anniversary celebration of the French capital's 1968 riots.
June 16th – '(White Man) In Hammersmith Palais'/ 'The Prisoner' released (recorded in the Spring at London's Basing Street Studios), reaching No. 32 in the UK.
June 28th – Aylesbury Friars date opens 'Out on Parole' tour.
July 4th – Glasgow Apollo show ends with Strummer arrested outside venue. Simonon piles in and also spends the night in the cells, with mass singing from other interns of 'The Prisoner'.
July 12th – Sex Pistols guitarist Steve Jones joins the band at Birmingham Top Rank.
July 13th – Blackburn King George's Hall show ends with Mick Jones arrested for cannabis possession at the Moat House Hotel after a police raid.
Late July – four-night residency ends tour at Camden's Music Machine, the final show on the 27th. Steve Jones joins them on all four nights, Barry Myers as DJ. Pete Townshend, Ian Hunter and Mick Ronson in crowd, and Paul Cook and Jimmy Pursey join in on 'White Riot' on first night.
August – Strummer and Jones spend three weeks overdubbing at the Automatt, Los Angeles, with Sandy Pearlman.
September – Strummer and Jones fly to New York to hear the new album's final mixes.
October 13th – 'Sort it Out' tour opens at Belfast's Queen's Hall.
October 14th – Top Hat, Dun Laoghaire, Dublin, before the tour moves to mainland Europe.
October 25th/26th – rescheduled Harlesden Roxy dates, the second for 700 ticket holders kept out on first night. Tour then moves on to Holland.
November 9th – tour resumes at Bournemouth's Village Bowl, the first with Caroline Coon as manager.
November 10th – second album, *Give 'Em Enough*

Rope released, peaking at No.2 in the UK.
November 12th – Simonon, Headon and Johnny Green's parents in the box at Canterbury Odeon date.
November 24th – 'Tommy Gun' / '1-2 Crush on You' released as a single, reaching No. 19 in the UK.
December 2nd – Jones and Simonon appear on the NME front cover, with headline, 'C.L.A.S.H'.
December 19th – Camden Music Machine gig for the Sid Vicious Defence Fund.
December/January – tour ends with three nights at London's Lyceum Ballroom. Final date on January 3rd.

1979

January 20th – the band scoop three *NME*'s Readers' Poll awards for 1978, voted 'best group', with '(White Man) in Hammersmith Palais' best single, and Mick Jones 'best guitarist'
January 30th – Vancouver Commodore Ballroom warm-up gig before the 'Pearl Harbour' tour (their first US tour) with Bo Diddley as support, the band fresh from recording the 'Cost of Living' EP.
February 20th – US tour ends with Rex Danforth Theater gig in Toronto.
February 23rd – 'English Civil War' / 'Pressure Drop' released in the UK, reaching No. 25.
May 11th – 'The Cost of Living' EP ('I Fought the Law'/'Groovy Times'/'Gates of the West'/'Capital Radio') released in a gatefold sleeve in the UK (US version follows in late July), recorded in Highbury, North London and reaching No. 22 in the UK.
May – with Rehearsal Rehearsals now off limits, the band seeking new practise rooms, Johnny Green and the Baker finding Vanilla Studios, Pimlico, London SW1, where the *London Calling* LP will take shape.
July 5th and 6th – third anniversary secret gigs at Notre Dame Hall, off Leicester Square, London. First public performances of five *London Calling* songs. Strummer's father present.
July 14th – Southall Defence Fund benefit gig for Rock Against Racism, with Aswad and The Members.
July 26th – US version of debut album, *The Clash*, released, reaching No. 126.
August 4th – Turku, Finland's Restrock Festival, supporting Graham Parker and The Rumour.
August – the band move to Wessex Studios to start rehearsing and recording the *London Calling* album with Guy Stevens and Bill Price.
September 8th – Monterey Festival warm-up gig for the 'Take the Fifth' North American tour, *NME* cartoonist Ray Lowry and photographer Pennie Smith joining them, and Joe Ely jamming on stage.
September 12th – tour starts at St Paul, Minnesota. The Undertones and David Johansen supporting.
September 19th – Boston Orpheum Theatre, supported by Sam and Dave. First appearance for Mickey Gallagher, becoming a regular for the next 18 months on keyboards.
September 20th/21st – New York Palladium, including Simonon's first-night Fender bass-smashing incident, as snapped by Pennie Smith and subsequently featured on the cover of *London Calling*.
October 13th – Kozar Pavilion, San Francisco, supported by The Cramps and Dead Kennedys.
October 16th – final gig of tour at Vancouver Pacific National Exhibition Centre.
December 7th – 'London Calling' / 'Armagideon Time' released as a AA-side

single, a week before the LP of the same name, reaching a highest-yet UK No. 11, its video shot by Don Letts at Festival Pier.
December 14th – *London Calling* is released in the UK, reaching No. 9 (US No. 27 on release in January).
December 25th/26th – London's Acklam Hall, Ladbroke Grove, community centre low-key Christmas gigs. Sparse turn-out on Christmas Day includes Mick's gran, Stella.
December 27th – Hammersmith Odeon benefit gig for Kampuchea (three other nights with other bills).

1980

January 5th – '16 Tons' tour opens in Aylesbury, Ian Dury and the Blockheads supporting first two dates.
January 9th – second night at Brighton Top Rank sees Pete Townshend join in on 'Bankrobber', 'Louie Louie', and 'Garageland'.
January 27th – Strummer punches Jones at Sheffield Top Rank after he refuses to play 'White Riot'.
January 29th – Mikey Dread joins for a first time, for 'Armagideon Time' at Bradford St George's Hall.
Early February – 'Bankrobber' and early *Sandinista!* tracks recorded at Manchester Pluto Studios, before two nights at Manchester Apollo.
February 15th / 16th – Camden Electric Ballroom shows.
February 17th – London's Lyceum Ballroom, with Joe Ely joining on 'Fingernails' and 'White Riot'.
February 18th – Lewisham Odeon show, after Don Letts films Johnny Green and The Baker staging a fake robbery for the 'Bankrobber' video.
February 20th – tour finale six days early after Headon stabbed in hand with scissors in altercation at his home, probably drug-related.
February 27th – Palais des Sports show in Paris filmed for French TV programme, *Chorus.*
March 1st/2nd – '16 Tons' tour part two opens, San Francisco's Fox Theater, Lee Dorsey supporting.
March 10th – US leg of tour concludes at Detroit's Motor City Roller Rink, for the Jackie Wilson Medical Fund, the soul legend's wife attending. Last show with Johnny Green as road manager, deciding to stay on and work with Joe Ely. Meanwhile, Strummer and Jones visit Motown's original Hitsville USA HQ, inspiring new song 'Hitsville UK'.
March 13th – *Rude Boy*, directed by Jack Hazan and David Mingay, starring Ray Gange and The Clash, gets a UK release, without endorsement from the disapproving band.
April 27th – '16 Tons' tour part three starts with a stateside warm-up at a 500-capacity Roxy Club in LA's Sunset Strip, after five weeks in New York recording *Sandinista!* The band return to Europe via Jamaica.
May 13th – European leg of the tour opena at Berlin's Metropole before a riotous night at Hamburg's Markthalle, followed by dates in Sweden, France and Italy.
June 13th – European leg ends in Turin.
June 9th – '16 Tons' tour's second UK leg moves on from Derby Assembly Rooms to Newcastle's Mayfair Ballroom, the last visit to the venue having been cancelled due to previous violence.
June 16th & 17th – two nights at Hammersmith Palais replace shows at Balham and Mile End Library Cinemas.
June 18th – '16 Tons' finale at Stoke's Hanley

Victoria Hall, rearranged for a fourth time.
August 8th – 'Bankrobber'/'Rockers Galore... UK Tour' single released in the UK, reaching No. 12.
November 28th – 'The Call Up'/ 'Stop the World' single released in the UK, reaching No. 40.
December 12th – *Sandinista!* Released in the UK, reaching No. 19 in the charts, and 24 in the US.

1981

January 16th – 'Hitsville UK'/ 'Radio One' single released in the UK, reaching No. 56 (No.53 in the US).
February – Bernie Rhodes returns to manage the band.
March – 101'ers compilation *Elgin Avenue Breakdown* released on the Andalucia label. Mick Jones produces Ellen Foley's *Spirit of St Louis*, featuring all four Clash members, with several Strummer/Jones songs. Jones goes on to co-produce (with Mick Ronson) and play on Ian Hunter LP, *Short Back'n'Sides*.
April 27th – 'Radio Clash Europe' tour opens (aka the 'Impossible Mission' tour) – the first dates in 10 months – in Barcelona, with an emphasis on *Sandinista!* songs and a live debut of 'This is Radio Clash'.
April 30th – 'The Magnificent Seven'/ 'The Magnificent Dance' single released in the UK, reaching No. 34.
May 23rd – European tour ends in Florence, Italy.
May 28th – opening night of what was intended as a seven-night residency at Bond's International Casino, Times Square, New York City. May 30th show cancelled due to safety concerns, the run ending t after 21 dates on June 13th.
September 24th – first of a seven-night residency at Paris' Mogador Theatre, supported by The Beat. First live outings of 'Should I Stay or Should I Go' and 'Know Your Rights'.
October 5th – a short, delayed UK 'Radio Clash' tour opens with the first of two nights at Manchester Apollo, starting with 'Broadway' then 'Know Your Rights'. Other dates include Liverpool's Royal Court Theatre and St Austell's Cornwall Coliseum.
October 26th – final night of a seven-show run at London's Lyceum Ballroom ends the tour.
November/December – Mick Jones staying with girlfriend Ellen Foley while the rest of the band are at the Iroquois Hotel during recording sessions at Electric Lady, New York City.
November 20th – 'This is Radio Clash'/ 'Radio Clash' single released in the UK, reaching No.47.

1982

January 24th – opening night of a Far East and Australasian tour in Tokyo.
February – the band go down a storm in New Zealand (Auckland, Wellington and Christchurch), while Mick Jones is credited as producer on Theatre of Hate LP, *Westworld*, also producing follow-up, *Aria of the Devil*, unreleased until 1998, when frontman Kirk Brandon rediscovered the masters.
February 11th – first of seven nights at Sydney's Capitol Theatre, the band attempting to mix 'Combat Rock' before the Australian leg continues in Brisbane, Adelaide, Perth, ending with two nights at Melbourne's Festival Hall.
February 28th – the tour reaches Hong Kong.
April 21st – Strummer heads to Paris, disappearing, taking up Bernie Rhodes'

suggestion to try and create mystique as ticket sales are slow. He's soon off the radar, but still manages to run the Paris Marathon.
April 23rd – 'Know your Rights'/ 'First Night Back in London' single released in the UK, reaching No. 43.
March 2nd – tour reaches Bangkok's Thamasat University, Thailand.
May 14th – *Combat Rock* released in the UK, reaching No. 2 in the charts, the following year a US No. 7, with 61 weeks on the chart and in time certified multiple-platinum.
May 18th – a bearded Strummer is eventually tracked down by Kosmo Vinyl, returning for the Lochem Festival appearance in Holland two days later, in what turns out to be Headon's last appearance.
May 22nd – Headon sacked at a band meeting in Simonon's London flat.
May 29th – 'Down the Casbah Club' tour (or 'Combat Coast to Coast' tour) opens at Asbury Park Convention Hall, New Jersey, with Terry Chimes back on drums, Strummer sporting his 'mohawk', The Beat supporting.
June 11th – 'Rock the Casbah'/'Mustapha Dance' single released in the UK, reaching No.30 (and No.8 in the US Billboard Hot 100.
June 29th – North American leg of the tour ends in Edmonton, Canada.
July 10th – rescheduled UK leg of the 'Down the Casbah Club' tour opens at Brixton's Fair Deal.
July 14th – first of five nights at Hollywood Palladium.
July 30th – Thomas Jones sees his son Mick perform for the first time on a return to Brixton's Fair Deal.
August 3rd – a second night at Bristol Locarno ends with the band storming off early after a spitting incident. Mick Jones' final UK gig with the band.
August 9th – 'Combat Rock' tour, with Kurtis Blow supporting, the band embarking on a second major US tour of the year, opening at Morrison's Red Rock Amphitheatre.
September 7th & 8th – the tour is scheduled to end with two dates at Boston's Orpheum Theatre, but then the band are offered a lucrative support on an 18-date stadium tour with The Who.
September 17th – 'Should I Stay or Should I Go' / 'Straight to Hell' AA-side single released in the UK, reaching No. 17 (the US version, b/w 'Inoculated City' earlier made No.45 in the US Billboard Hot 100).
September 25th – the band's tour supporting The Who opens at Philadelphia's JFK Stadium.
October 9th – final TV appearance, performing 'Straight to Hell' and 'Should I Stay or Should I Go' on *Saturday Night Live*.
October 12th/13th – Shea Stadium, New York City, with The Who, the second show filmed, as featured in the 'Career Opportunities' and 'Should I Stay or Should I Go' footage.
October 29th – US support role with The Who ends at Los Angeles Coliseum.
November 27th – final gig of 1982 at the Bob Marley Centre, Montego Bay, Kingston, for the Jamaican World Music Festival, taking to the stage at dawn. Terry Chimes' final gig ... again.

1983

May 28th – after a six-month hiatus, the band headline the opening day of the Us Festival in San Bernardino, California, playing to an estimated 140,000 crowd after a short series of warm-ups in Michigan, Wichita Falls, San Antonio and Tucson, stopping over in Las Vegas on the way home.
Late August '83 – Mick Jones is sacked at

a band meeting at Rehearsal Rehearsals. Camden.
September 10th – the *NME* runs an announcement that Jones is no longer with the band.

1984

Early January – The Clash Mk.II's 'Out of Control' tour rehearsals start.
January 19th – the new band's US tour starts with a warm-up at the Arlington Theater, Los Angeles.
January 28th – UK release of *All the Rage*, the debut LP by General Public, fronted by The Beat's Dave Wakeling and Ranking Roger, Mick Jones contributing guitar on at least half of the songs.
February 1st – Fox Theater, San Diego, first US date of the new band's tour.
February 10th – Glasgow Barrowlands – first UK gig, followed by a brief foray to the Continent.
March 8th – a five-night residency begins at Brixton Academy, The Pogues supporting, with Belfast and Dublin shows between, then a return to North America, then Europe.
December – recording gets underway in Munich for what becomes the *Cut the Crap* album, then known as *Out of Control*.
December 6th & 7th – National Union of Mineworkers (NUM) benefit shows back at Brixton Academy, the band announcing a new album will be released within a month.

1985

January – Nick Sheppard flies to Munich and is subsequently joined by Pete Howard and Vince White to work on the new LP.
May 7th – the band's 'Busking' tour opens in Nottingham, ending 10 days later in Glasgow.
June 29th – Roskilde Festival, Copenhagen, Denmark.
July 13th – Rockscene Festival, Guehenno, France, the same day as Wembley Stadium's Live Aid spectacular.
August 27th – the Greek Music Festival at Athens' Olympic Stadium marks the final live show, nine years and eight weeks after that 1976 Sheffield debut, with The Cure and The Style Council also appearing, The Clash on stage late at night amid riotous scenes, and an estimated 40,000 crowd.
September 30th – final single, 'This is England'/ 'Do It Now', released in the UK, reaching No.24.
October – Joe Strummer calls a band meeting and announces The Clash are over, Bernie Rhodes initially intending to carry on and audition a new front-man. Meanwhile, Mick Jones' new band, Big Audio Dynamite, involving Don Letts, release debut LP *This is Big Audio Dynamite*, including top-40 UK hits 'E=MC2' (No.11) and 'Medicine Show' (No.29). The LP reaches No.27 in the UK.
November 4th – final album, *Cut the Crap*, released in the UK, reaching No.16, but panned by the critics.

1986

Joe Strummer records two tracks for the *Sid & Nancy: Love Kills* film soundtrack, the title song, 'Love Kills', and 'Dum Dum Club'.
July/August – Topper Headon working on debut solo LP, *Waking Up*, at Wessex Studios, after the release of single *Drumming Man* in '85, his band including Blockheads/Clash keyboard player Mickey Gallagher.
October – *No.10, Upping Street*, the second album from Mick Jones' Big Audio Dynamite, is released, reaching No.11 in the UK,

including several songs co-written with co-producer Joe Strummer.

1987

Joe Strummer scores a soundtrack for Alex Cox movie, *Walker*.

1988

February 29th – *The Story of The Clash Volume I* compilation double-LP released in the UK, reaching No. 7 (No. 142 in the US).
June – *Tighten Up, Vol. 88*, a third album by Mick Jones' Big Audio Dynamite, is released, reaching No.33 in the UK, with a cover painting by Paul Simonon.

1989

September 5th – *Megatop Phoenix*, a fourth LP by Mick Jones' Big Audio Dynamite, released in the UK, the last featuring Don Letts and last to chart, reaching No.26.
September 20th – Joe Strummer releases solo LP, *Earthquake Weather*, mostly recorded in Los Angeles the previous year.

1990

March 23rd – Big Audio Dynamite II play Amsterdam's Paradiso, a show released as the *Ally Pally Paradiso* album by Mick Jones' band in 1991.
October – Mick Jones duets with Roddy Frame on Aztec Camera's 'Good Morning Britain', reaching No.11 in the UK singles chart.
November 1st – Mick Jones' band are rebranded Big Audio Dynamite II for the *Kool-Aid* eight-track LP.

1991

Paul Simonon features with the band Havana 3am, with co-writing credits with Nigel Dixon and Gary Myrick on a self-titled debut album.
March 9th – reissued 'Should I Stay or Should I Go' reaches the top of the UK singles chart, and stays there another week, after use in a Levi's TV commercial. A subsequent reissue of 'Rock the Casbah' reaches No.15 in the UK on April 20th.
June 16th – *The Globe*, by Mick Jones' Big Audio Dynamite II, a part-rebranded version of the last album, released in the UK (August 6th in the US).
November – *The Singles* compilation released. All 18 UK singles in chronological order.
December 19th – comprehensive triple-CD boxset *Clash on Broadway* released.

1994

November 8th – Mick Jones' band are rebranded Big Audio for new LP, *Higher Power*.

1995

June 20th – Mick Jones' band are back as Big Audio Dynamite for the *F-Punk* album.
September 12th – Mick Jones' Big Audio Dynamite release the *Planet B.A.D.* best of compilation, featuring the band's output from their first decade (under various name variants).

1997

Mick Jones' Big Audio Dynamite return with *Entering a New Ride*, a download-only following a disagreement with the Radioactive Records label.

1999

May 4th – Big Audio Dynamite, Mick Jones' band, bow out with best of LP, *Super Hits.*
October 4th – *From Here to Eternity: Live* album released in the UK, reaching No.13 in the charts.
October 19th – *Rock Art and the X-Ray Style,* the debut LP from Joe Strummer and the Mescaleros is released.

2000

Don Letts' full-length documentary film, *The Clash: Westway to the World,* is released.

2001

July 24th – Global A Go-Go, the second album from Joe Strummer and the Mescaleros is released.

2002

Mick Jones joins forces with pre-Clash bandmate Tony James (Generation X, Sigue Sigue Sputnik) to form Carbon/Silicon, touring the UK and US, and plays several anti-fascist benefit concerts
September 25th – Paul Simonon holds his 'From Hammersmith to Greenwich' exhibition at the Hazlitt, Gooden and Fox art gallery in Green Park, London, SW1, running for 16 days.
October – Mick Jones produces *Up the Bracket,* The Libertines' debut LP, reaching No. 35 in the UK.
November 7th – the Rock and Roll Hall of Fame announces The Clash will be inducted in March 2003.
November 15th – Mick Jones joins Joe Strummer and the Mescaleros on stage at a FBU benefit gig at Acton Town Hall, London, for 'Bankrobber', 'White Riot' and 'London's Burning'.
December 22nd – Joe Strummer dies at home in Broomfield, Somerset, as the result of a congenital heart defect, aged 50.

2003

March 10th – The Clash are inducted by U2's The Edge into the Rock and Roll Hall of Fame at its 18th annual ceremony. Terry Chimes and Joe Strummer's widow Lucinda Mellor join Mick Jones and Paul Simonon on stage at the Waldorf Astoria, New York City.
April 22nd – *The Essential Clash* compilation released in the UK (preceded by a US release on April 22nd) and reaches No. 18 (99 in the US).
October 21st – *Streetcore,* the final album from Joe Strummer and the Mescaleros is released.

2004

August 30th – *The Libertines,* the second LP by the indie-rock outfit of the same name, produced by Mick Jones, debuts at No.1 on the UK album charts, selling more than 72,000 copies in its first week.

2005

November 14th – Mick Jones produces the first album for Pete Doherty's post-Libertines outfit, Babyshambles, the LP reaching No.10 in the UK.

2006

Jul 28th – Mick Jones and Tony James' Carbon/Silicon release debut LP, *A.T.O.M (A Twist of Modern),* available free online.
October 14th- Carbon/Silicon release second

album (again free online), *Western Front*.
October 30th – *The Singles Box released*, a set of 19 Clash singles across 19 CDs.

2007

January 20th – Julien Temple's full-length documentary film and tribute, *Joe Strummer: The Future is Unwritten*, premieres at the Sundance Film Festival.
January 22nd – Paul Simonon features alongside Blur's Damon Albarn, The Verve's Simon Tong and Fela Kuti's drummer Tony Allen on The Good, the Bad, and the Queen's self-titled debut album, which reaches No.2 in the UK album charts and is certified gold within a week of its release.
March 9th – Carbon/Silicon, Mick Jones' project with Tony James, release third album, *The Crackup Suite*, like the first two, againb free online.
June 4th – *The Singles* released – a 19-track version (essentially the 1991 release plus 'This is England').

2008

January/February – Mick Jones' project Carbon/Silicon, with Tony James, play seven consecutive Friday nights at the Inn on the Green, under the Westway, Ladbroke Grove, London, with special guests including Topper Headon ('Train in Vain' and 'Should I Stay Or Should I Go' on the opening night), the Sex Pistols' Paul Cook and Glen Matlock, and former Clash associate, Tymon Dogg.
April 27th – Mick Jones and Paul Simonon (the latter with The Good, The Bad, and The Queen) guest at the Love Music Hate Racism Carnival in Victoria Park, Hackney, East London, marking the 30th anniversary of the original Rock Against Racism concert starring The Clash.
October 6th – *Live at Shea Stadium* LP released (from the 1982 NYC show), reaching No.31 in the UK.

2009

September – Mick Jones and Topper Headon reunite to re-record 'Jail Guitar Doors' with Billy Bragg, the namesake of a charity giving musical instruments and lessons to prison inmates. The trio are backed by former inmates during the session, filmed for the *Breaking Rocks* documentary.

2010

March 3rd – Mick Jones reunites with Paul Simonon on *Plastic Beach*, the third LP by Damon Albarn's Gorillaz. Both feature live with the band, including the Coachella Festival, California, Glastonbury Festival, and Spain's Festival Internacional de Benicassim.

2011

January – Mick Jones announces a Big Audio Dynamite reunion, including a UK tour in March and April (with two sell-outs at Shepherd's Bush Empire), a small number of US dates (including the Coachella and Lollapalooza festivals), shows in Serbia, Spain and Japan, and a June visit to Glastonbury Festival.
April 11th – Mick Jones and Paul Simonon feature on *The Fall*, the fourth LP by Damon Albarn's Gorillaz, on 'Hillbilly Man" (Jones) and 'Aspen Forest' (Simonon), both recorded in October 2010.
Late 2011 – Mick Jones playing Clash songs live again, with Pete Wylie and members of The Farm in The Justice Tonight Band,

promoting the Hillsborough Justice Campaign, joined onstage at different gigs by several other musicians, including Paul Simonon, Billy Bragg and Shane MacGowan.

2012

Danny Garcia's *The Rise and Fall of The Clash* film documentary is released.
October 9th – Mick Jones features on two songs on *Glad All Over*, the sixth album from Californian alt-rock band The Wallflowers, led by Jakob Dylan, Clash fan and son of Bob Dylan.

2013

April 2nd – Mick Jones features on French-Algerian singer Rachid Taha's LP, *Zoom*, along with Brian Eno.
September 6th – Mick Jones, Paul Simonon and Topper Headon reunite for an exclusive BBC Radio 6 Music show promoting forthcoming release *Sound System*.
September 9th – *The Clash Hits Back* double-CD 33-song best of and *Sound System*, a 12-CD box-set featuring the studio catalogue re-mastered (minus *Cut the Crap*) plus an additional three discs, DVD and various other items released (US release dates both a day later), the former reaching No. 13 in the UK and the latter No.53. The same dates also saw the release of the *5-Album Studio Set* eight-CD box-set featuring the first five studio albums re-mastered.

2015

January 21st – Paul Simonon's art exhibition *Wot no Bike* opens at the ICA's Nash and Brandon Rooms in London, running for 17 days, with a limited-edition hardback book also published.

2017

November 11th – Mick Jones plays several Joe Strummer songs with the Rotten Hill Gang, Clash tribute band Take the 5th, and the Portobello Love Choir at a Fire Brigades Union benefit at the Maxilla in Ladbroke Grove, marking the 15th anniversary of Strummer's final London gig. Other guests include Tymon Dogg and *Rude Boy* actor Ray Gange as DJ.

2018

September 28th – Ignition Records releases the Joe Strummer 001 LP/CD/digital boxset, the first compilation spanning Strummer's career outside his recordings with The Clash, including songs recorded with the 101'ers and The Mescaleros, his solo albums, soundtrack work and unreleased tracks.

STILL TALKING ABOUT THE CLASH

5

Since I got the nod to work on this book in the summer of 2017, I've amassed a fair few feature/interviews for the *Lancashire Post* and my own *writewyattuk.com* website, where The Clash pop up in conversation ... sometimes when I least expect it. Admittedly, it's often me bringing up the subject, but it seems that so many of the past couple of generations of musicians and even comedians – Phill Jupitus springs to mind, whose alter-ego Porky the Poet's set once included 'Career Opportunities' – will have an opinion, anecdote or inspirational words about an influential band that left such a rich legacy.

In the last few months, that included a conversation with Belinda Carlisle, inspired by that whole UK punk scene in LA when putting the Go-Go's together. When I told her I heard she was a fan, she said, 'You kidding? I saw them live a few times. One of The Go-Go's' influences and favourite bands for sure. A really, really great band, and Joe Strummer was one of a kind.'

Richard Jobson's personal association went back to October 1977, when The Skids supported The Clash at the Kinema Ballroom in the band's hometown, Dunfermline, and he was back in touch with Strummer over the years. He recalled that night 40 years earlier as 'an amazing night', adding, 'The Clash were one of the few bands that came from the London scene that actually stood by some of the principles of punk and played places like Dunfermline. Others were a bit more aloof. We established a scene, playing here a few times, with a cult following. All of those things together made it a viable place to come, and that was one of the great nights, an amazing evening. The idea that we managed to convince them to come and were their opening act ... even though we were on stage before the doors opened!

'Joe was a good guy, and never changed. I saw him not long before he died, had a coffee. He was always very generous with his time, always very supportive of what I was trying to do. He was a hero!'

I was unaware of the link to Andrew Roachford, best known for late '80s UK hits with Roachford, until delving into his past, learning that he spent his late teenage years as part of a pool of musicians put together by Bernie Rhodes to make the much-maligned *Cut the Crap*. Don't judge him by that though. He got to know Joe Strummer better in later years, and Mick Jones.

He explained, 'When I started music college, Bernie Rhodes was trying to start a record label and needed to get some people into the studio to help, and one thing they wanted was an in-house keyboard player. They found me, and I didn't really know anything about The Clash. When I started at the studio they were away in America, touring, so I didn't see anyone from the band for six months. Then one day they turned up, just after they'd got rid of two members. I was there every day for a year or maybe more while they put that album together.

'Joe was a lovely guy, very intelligent, big-hearted, and that educated me about The Clash. He really felt what he was singing about, really meant it. Even though maybe he came from a nice background, he really was a working-class hero. He'd travel on the Tube every day to the studio in Camden, and never went for all that pop-star status. Last time I saw him was at Glastonbury Festival, with the Mescaleros. He was living in that area and found me, telling me he'd recorded all these jam sessions I was involved with, had all the master tapes but couldn't find a machine to play them on! It was an old eight-track two-inch tape. I haven't heard anything about them. I need to talk to his family about that.

'He was into his rave culture and invited me to this campfire gathering where they were going to be jamming. I turned it down – I was getting a bit cold. It was the end of the evening. I wish I'd gone. Instead, I went off-site. That was the last time I saw him. He had a heart attack that following winter. But we really connected and I really liked him as a person. He also helped when I was still finding myself as a singer, telling me, 'You're great. If I sang like you I wouldn't be in this band! That was his sense of humour. He was also into the whole soul scene and reggae thing. He was great.

'I met Mick afterwards. He's a lovely guy as well. We were both on Columbia. Of course, he knew my Clash connection. And it was great through Gorillaz, seeing Mick and Paul Simonon back together again all those years later.'

Former Fine Young Cannibals front-man Roland Gift was similarly complimentary, telling me, 'They were my 'coming out' band. The Clash were the kind of band I was into at that impressionable age! We (*his first band, Acrylic Victims, later renamed Akrylykz*) supported The Clash at Bridlington, around 1980. Me and some mates went hitch-hiking, following them, then I got a job doing back-drops for them down at the Music Machine. This fella I knew, Roger Hudson, knew their tour manager, Johnny Green, and we'd turn up at gigs and get free passes.

'I was more of a fan than a contemporary. They were the biggest of the bunch really. I just liked being around it. You'd see gigs and people you'd seen at other gigs. You felt some sort of camaraderie. Also, The Clash played reggae. When punk started, people weren't so sure, because of the swastikas and that, with the National Front on the rise. Something like The Clash playing reggae was a good invitation for someone like me to be a part of it.'

Joy Division and New Order bass player Peter Hook painted a vivid picture of the pandemonium during The Clash's 1976 visits – two gigs within three weeks – to Manchester's Electric Circus, supporting the Sex Pistols on the *Anarchy* tour, him and fellow punk attendees having to evade an angry mob after the first Clash appearance there, stoked up by the public furore that followed the Bill Grundy affair.

'Hooky' was of the opinion that The Clash's 'strange image' didn't go down so well with the North West 'homegrown grass-root punks,' but added, 'I think musically they were a far better group, without a shadow of a doubt.' He told me about a later Strummer link too, saying, 'I liked The Mescaleros. I only met Joe once, in Groucho's in the late '90s. He was a little the worse for wear. He took us over to Soho House. He was a member and took us in ... then went home! So I didn't really get much of a chance to talk to him, but he was a hero to a lot of people.'

In early 2018, I talked to ska-punk guitarist Roddy 'Radiation' Byers, with The Specials from 1978-81 as well as in later spells, his song credits including 'Rat Race', 'Concrete Jungle', and 'Hey Little Rich Girl'. He was with the inspirational 2 Tone act from the start, including a tour with The Clash. What's more, his band worked with Bernie Rhodes, at one stage also running out of Camden's Rehearsal Rehearsals.

As Roddy put it, 'I've said before, I always wanted Mick Jones' job! Actually, Paul came to see the Skabilly Rebels recently, and we had a nice chat about the old days. And Joe always asked how my bands were doing when I saw him, always knowing what the current band was called. Our first UK Tour was supporting The Clash, so we drew inspiration from them in many ways.'

Regarding Rhodes, he added, 'Bernie made us realise we had to conform to a certain image and sound to succeed. As Horace (Panter, bass) says in his book (*Ska'd for Life*) – working with Bernie and supporting The Clash was like rock'n'roll boot camp! But when you're young it all seems like fun, even if we didn't always eat, or have a bed for the night.'

Byers was in a mid-'70s glam-rock and rock'n'roll covers band before discovering punk, saying, 'A friend moved to London and told me about these bands he thought I'd like. I went down and he introduced me to Joe Strummer and I got to see the Sex Pistols, The Clash and The Damned in 1976. I was going to move and join a punk band, but stayed in Coventry, eventually joining what became The Specials.

'The scene at the time was in general about older musicians looking down on up and coming young players, but when punk came along it didn't matter if we weren't great players. In fact, image and being young and not caring what people thought was more important. And I never bought into the racist crap! I didn't get into ska and reggae until I discovered Bob Marley, but that got me into Jamaican music and led me to join the early Specials.'

Then there was Mark Chadwick, frontman of the Levellers, who recalled in our conversation in late January 2018 his band's main inspiration. He told me, 'In 1988 when we formed, there wasn't a lot of lyrical content in music. Brighton had quite a thriving music scene, with a few indie bands and rock acts, but it was all very leather trousers and big hair. But we were both into The Clash, wanting to do something in that vein, where something was actually being said. That was the basic germ of the idea – get together and create music that's got lyrical content.'

He got to work with Strummer too, in 1995, proudly telling me about him playing honky-tonk piano on the band's top-20 hit, 'Just the One', calling him 'a really nice guy' and The Clash 'a gregarious bunch'. He added, 'So was Joe. He was instantly relaxed in our studio, totally cool. He did what we wanted, had a laugh, stuck around a few hours, and we saw him at a few festivals from there to say hello.' He was, I suggested, coming out of a rather dark period then, trying to re-find his way. 'Yeah, he'd been fairly quiet for a while, and I think he was quite remorseful about the way The Clash had ended.' That said, he wasn't one to commit if he wasn't interested fully. When he did get involved, he'd throw himself into it. 'He really did. We got this boogie-woogie piano in, so he could play it, and he certainly had a go!'

That cross-section might not seem the most authoritative snapshot, but it tells you a little about how important this band were in the scheme of things. It wasn't just favourites of mine from that immediate scene and later arrivals like Billy Bragg inspired by Strummer, Jones, Simonon and Headon.

Yet, while some are happy reflecting on that era and more likely to speak about their experiences all these years on, no way does that make the story easier to write. The Clash always took on board the notion of re-imagining the past, and sometimes it's hard to pick out facts from fiction, particularly so much further down the road. Just ask the band's main chroniclers – Pat Gilbert, Marcus Gray and Chris Salewicz. While my version's more about picking out the basics to attempt a definitive slant on it all, there have been many times these last few months where I've studied past stories and seen conflicting variations on the same theme, sometimes having no idea which version was right.

There's an example in the tale about the band getting a visit in the studio from The Blockheads, dressed as policemen, post-*Top of the Pops*, carrying out a bogus drugs raid. Yet in Suggs' autobiography a similar story is attributed to Madness. Did both 'raids' happen? Then on the last weekend of January 2018, a friend asked if I'd seen BBC quiz, *Eggheads*, where a fella called Gary Dear told host Jeremy Vine he sat in for The Clash at The Vortex Club once, after their regular drummer had been arrested, his band The Unwanted having been the support. It certainly sounds feasible, judging by Topper Headon's past. But as I understood it, that Wardour Street venue only took over from The Roxy as London's prime punk hang-out in July '77, and I found no trace of that gig in the substantial print and online archives available. An omission from the records? Answers on an *End of the Trail* postcard please.

Finally, in the first week of February 2018, with the deadline for this book looming, I spoke to two more interviewees with a part in this story, in very different ways. The first was Rick Buckler, the legendary drummer of The Jam, with a few quotes from that conversation included earlier. And while his quotes didn't go down the straight-forward 'tribute' line, I can vouch for the fact that there was a lot of respect there for The Clash from their big rivals, four decades after they were first pitted against each other. In a similar but very different approach to the quotes you'll see from John Lydon on The Clash, Buckler told me, regarding the rivalry between the bands, 'It's an odd thing. They always said, 'Don't read your own press,' but we did read the press about The Clash and thought they must have been doing much better than us, as they seemed to get bigger advances from their record company, and all the rest of it. But on the other hand ... did they ever have a No.1 record in the UK?'

Erm, well, they did, I pointed out, but admittedly not until after they'd split, following that jeans commercial in 1991, the re-released, 'Should I Stay or Should I Go' topping the charts. And Rick's response?

'Yes ... well ... I won't say anything more

than that then!'

He then laughed, before adding a mischievous, 'Miaow!'

I kind of like that, and reckon Joe, Mick, Paul and Topper would appreciate it far more than some sycophantic guff. I'm putting that in the box marked, 'Respect'.

Meanwhile, the previous afternoon I spoke to comedian, broadcaster and writer Mark Steel about his love for The Clash, one going back to his formative days, having not quite reached his 17th birthday when the debut LP was released. It seems that he bought *Never Mind the Bollocks* – released six months later – before. Yet this South London-based Kentish lad still loves both albums, and it's fair to say *The Clash* proved more inspirational in his life-plan.

He wrote in his 2001 political memoir, *Reasons to be Cheerful*, 'Buying the Clash album from a Dartford record shop was like buying (my) first *Morning Star*. I waited several minutes by the 'C' section, pretending to be flicking through Johnny Cash and Creedence Clearwater Revival, before I plucked up courage, made my way to the counter and said, 'I'll have that please'. Back home came a seminal moment, the first few bars of 'Janie Jones' on side one. While the lyrics were indecipherable, the meaning boomed out of the chipboard speakers and echoed around the Swanley walls. It was all right to be angry. You be angry mate. There's a whole generation of us, expected to be grateful, well how about this for gratitude – 'Career opportunities, the ones that never knock; Every job they offer you is to keep you out the dock.' So it wasn't just me.'

He stuck by The Clash, telling me, 'I appreciated the ones who developed from there. You couldn't just stay with the punk ethic of shouting, hollering and being rubbish, just a little bit of entertainment for the evening. If you didn't develop some musical ability, you're thereby negating the philosophy of punk.'

In fact, Steel got to see the Mescaleros a few times, including their final London gig in November 2002, something – like most who were there that night – he has mixed emotions about, but maybe not for the same reason.

'It was the most humiliating experience of my life. I was asked to do this FBU benefit at Acton Town Hall, and a woman I'd known many years, a firefighter who worked full-time for the union, rang, very excited, telling me Joe Strummer had agreed to do the gig. I said, 'That's brilliant', seeing that it would now be a Strummer gig. I said I'd still come along though, and she said, 'What do you mean? Of course you'll come along – we still want you to do it'.

'I told her there was no point me being involved now she had Joe, but she persuaded me, and like an idiot I agreed, and was a complete wreck that night. It was all set up for a band and everyone there was a Strummer fan and Clash fan. I was completely written out, and when I came on ... don't ever support a band as a comic. Phill Jupitus has some awful stories about supporting Madness, including one in Cardiff in front of 5,000 or something, with people lobbing stuff.

'But it was an iconic night, the one in which Mick Jones joined him on stage. I then went backstage to get my stuff, and initially had a bit of a contretemps with the security, who hadn't let me through. When I did get back, there was Joe, sat with Mick, and I'd taken along the record I bought in 1977, in its cover. I don't know why I'd taken the actual record. I got him to sign it, and then the record fell out and landed sideways up, rolling round and round the floor while Joe, Mick and a couple of others looked at it. It just kind of rolled around Mick's foot, then came to a halt. Mick bent down, picked it up, and calmly went, 'Careful with that.' They did both sign it though, but of course, about a month later Joe died.'

I told Mark at that point how, on November 11th, 2017, Mick Jones played another FBU benefit, this time at the Maxilla in Ladbroke Grove, under the Westway, in the shadow of gutted Grenfell Tower (its survivors also beneficiaries that night), so close to where The Clash story started 40-plus years before, the date marking the 15th anniversary of that fabled night at Acton Town Hall, with Tymon Dogg, Chris Salewicz and Ray Gange also involved, Jonesy out of 'retirement' to guest on a few songs.

Six weeks later, on December 22nd, 2017, four decades after punk's most happening year and 15 years to the day after the death of The Clash's front-man, I linked on social media to the closing track of Joe Strummer's posthumously-released final LP, *Streetcore*. His version of 'Silver and Gold' seemed an apt choice to mark the end of a year in which we'd lost its co-writer, Fats Domino, who at least reached the grand age of 87 before bowing out.

That was three days before my 50th, and that was the rub really. On that latest anniversary of Strummer's passing, I was barely two months younger than Joe reached in 2002, the year my second daughter was born. Putting finishing touches to this book I've revisited the Mescaleros as well as The Clash's catalogue, and what a joy, perhaps making it all the more poignant that he went out when he did. I'm with former *Record Mirror* writer and *Flexipop* co-founder Barry Cain in *Sulphate Strip 77* when he mentions how – after Joe succumbed to his heart attack – 'my immortality died with him', explaining, 'For the first time in my life I felt vulnerable ... it was time to start thinking about dying.'

I'll add my own slant, saying how it makes you appreciate how much you still want to achieve, and at the same time not take your own limited time for granted. Nothing's nailed on in this world, and I wonder what fellow father-of-two-girls John Graham Mellor might have achieved given more time.

When Bono spoke of his anger on Julien Temple's 2007 *Joe Strummer: The Future is Unwritten* documentary at the band stopping when they did, I wondered if he'd missed the point. I'm not having a go, I and many more of us would have loved the band to have stayed the course. In fact, his bandmate, The Edge, made a similar point at 2003's Rock and Roll Hall of Fame event, but then answered himself, suggesting, 'If they'd have been around 10 years later, maybe they might have been able to resolve their internal conflicts and stay the course ... we might have enjoyed a few more records and tours. But do you know what? They wouldn't have been the Clash.'

So let's just be thankful for what we've got and continue to have by way of all those wondrous audio and visual recordings of the band – in print, on record, and on screen. Thank you, Joe, and thanks too to Mick, Paul, Topper, and all those others who played their part in the amazing story of The Clash.

In Praise of The Clash

'It was never about just one person, or one attitude. You could see it on stage, the way we complemented each other.'
Mick Jones, to Chris Salewicz, 1985

'The Clash were poets. As artists working with pop music they were completely free to express and reflect their unhappiness with the world around them. They also expressed annoyance that the bands that went before – like The Who – had not been militant enough.'
Pete Townshend, to Pat Gilbert, Passion is a Fashion, 2004

'Instead of just surviving, they moved beyond punk and gave us a string of truly amazing rock'n'roll records. Looking back now, The Clash's contribution to the survival of rock'n'roll, I think, is unique. During the late '70s and early '80s when punk was starting to wane and mainstream rock had become hopelessly and awfully redundant, The Clash, along with one or two other bands, carried the torch, they broke through barriers of perception and genre and left behind them a thousand bands in 'Garageland', who caught a glimpse of what they saw and strode forth, including one from Ireland called U2.'
The Edge, Rock and Roll Hall of Fame Induction, 2003

'I loved the way they embraced what was around them. They were in West London and the reggae thing was rubbing off. The reason The Clash had the impact that they did was that they were able to move on and reinvent themselves. They didn't get hung up on that stupid label. They realised that the world would not end at the bottom of their street. They were prepared to get on a runway and take on the world.'
Don Letts

'The Clash were a major influence on my own music. They were the best rock'n'roll band.'
Bruce Springsteen

'The Kinks were a great band and sang about London, but the way The Clash did it was special. That's why to me they'll always be the greatest punk band, the most important band ever in my life. And, along with The Who, the most important London band.'
Sniffin' Glue editor Mark Perry, Uncut, 2015

'There was magic between Joe and Mick, a Lennon–McCartney thing.'
Peter Jenner, 1999

'The whole thing with The Clash – longevity was never the point. Most of the bands I like had a natural organic life for seven or eight years – The Smiths, Led Zep. When people go on too long they destroy their own myth. There are a few exceptions. Everyone else would have been better stopping earlier. There is a window of opportunity – you use that moment, then fuck off out of the way.'
Don Letts, to John Robb, 2006

'If they'd arrived 10 years earlier they would have given The Beatles, The Kinks and the Stones a run for their money. If they'd have been around 10 years later, maybe they might have been able to resolve their internal conflicts and stay the course. Either way, we might have enjoyed a few more records and tours. But do you know what? They wouldn't have been the Clash.'
The Edge, Rock and Roll Hall of Fame Induction, 2003

5

The Clash have the last word...

'It wouldn't and couldn't have worked without any one of the four of us. It was one of those brilliant moments of intuition coming together with knowledge. Once in a while something like that happens. It wasn't planned in any way. We just got lucky. I guess there were five very strong characters involved. A lot of energy, a lot of passion and a lot of caring. Being in The Clash could be chaotic and difficult, but we all remember things differently. Everybody had an opinion, we were guided by our manager at the start and then we grew into ourselves a bit more later on.'
Mick Jones, *The Ultimate Music Guide: The Clash*, 2017

'We weren't parochial. We weren't narrow-minded. We weren't little Englanders. At least we had the suss to embrace what we were presented with, which was like the world in all its varieties. Whatever the group was, it was the chemical mixture of these four people that made it work. That's a lesson everyone should learn. Don't mess with it. If it works, do whatever you have to do to bring it forward, but don't mess with it. We learned that bitterly.'
Joe Strummer, *Westway to the World, 2000*

'I think we did a fairly good job. I would've liked to have done more, if the occasion had arisen. But it never did. We gradually just got bigger and bigger, I guess, until we burst. Maybe that's all right. We came, did our bit, and it all carries on.'
Mick Jones, to Tom Lanham for online magazine *Magnet*

'If I could do it all again, I wouldn't change anything. I think it's fine as it is.'
Paul Simonon, *Westway to the World, 2000*

'Who couldn't like good tunes with such great lyrics and fantastic drumming? And it was great to be with Paul, who was just there, probably from when I first met him. We did our job and that's the story, and now we're gone. And that's it. That suits me fine.'
Mick Jones, *Westway to the World*, 2000

'You can't be a prophet in your own country ... and that is a fact! And it's still really the same today. In America or Spain or France or Sweden or Italy, anywhere in the world but here do they really know and appreciate The Clash.'
Joe Strummer, *Westway to the World*, 2000

'I think we broke down the barrier between audience and band more than any other group before us. A lot of the groups at that time were big groups, and you liked them alright, but they left you as they found you. But when people left us they were thinking differently. It's not only about music.'
Mick Jones, *The Ultimate Music Guide: The Clash*, 2017

'There was never a dull moment, whether we were fighting each other or loving each other... whatever. It was like a nuclear explosion. It was a flash. It was too intense for it to fizzle out or last any length of time.'
Topper Headon

'It was just full-on for six years. And we'd already moved so far away from each other that it just felt like a whirlwind. Everyone has a really nice memory of us because we didn't get back together again and do something less good. If you're a fatalist that's definitely part of what makes The Clash great. Before Joe died we talked about reforming, but it was never right for everybody at the same time. It was just never quite right. But that was probably meant to be as well.'
Mick Jones, *The Ultimate Music Guide: The Clash*, 2017

'What replaced punk was the Thatcherism of so-called new pop, *Brideshead Revisited* and cocktail bars. Things got too fucking cool. People stopped talking to each other. Pathetic. I think it was a reaction to punk's sense of community, and that was sad. With punk, you could be wearing a toilet seat pinned to your jacket and we could talk about the cheapest place to buy toilet seats. Ludicrous really, but at least we're communicating. Now you've got Hooray Henries rubbing the poor's noses in it. I'm kind of glad to be on the outside again.'
Joe Strummer to Sean O'Hagan, *NME*, 1997

'My happiest memories of Joe are all based around the telepathic partnership we had. He would give me a page of lyrics and the tune and the rhythm would be already right there, just suggested by the words. It was very special, and his lyrics were very special.'
Mick Jones, *The Ultimate Music Guide: The Clash*, 2017

'We were sincere! Listen, I know from the start we weren't going to achieve anything concrete, no shifts in power or anything. Our job was to state the obvious, to reflect what people were thinking. That's all a musician can do. Jerry Dammers or Billy Bragg, I admire a lot. They do more than I ever could. I'm too scatter-brain to attend committee meetings and stuff. People thought we sold out when we went to America, but I ain't into isolationism. I think people – the fans and the press – always expected too much from The Clash. We got some right slaggings in our time. Plus, the number of Clash fans who'd come along, take speed, then sit and moan about us. I'd say, 'Why are you wasting your time complaining? Get up off your arse and do something yourself. You shouldn't even waste your time thinking of Joe Strummer.' Mainly, they'd look at me with blank incomprehension. A lot of people missed the point.'
Joe Strummer to Sean O'Hagan, *NME*, 1997

'He was just there, looking fantastic... the bastard.'
Mick Jones on Paul Simonon, *3:AM* magazine, 1994

'We all had our moments with cocaine, but it never lasted too long. Me and Paul took some coke in the States and Mick had his moment over here, but he'd got real willpower. It's the worst drug. It can be used – a Bolivian tin-miner chews eight leaves to last it out down the mines, but a New York yuppie snorts a room full of leaves in one line. Same old story, Western greed. We're too greedy, and it shows in our approach to things like drug-taking. But The Clash were pretty strong-willed. Topper was different. When I first met him, he was well into mandies. He liked a

Mandrax of a weekend. When we hit the States and he had access to stronger stuff, he just jumped right in. Terrible. I think if we had to deal with it now, we would have helped him more, instead of sacking him on the spot. We should have treated him more leniently.'
Joe Strummer to Sean O'Hagan, *NME, 1997*

Afterwords

While putting finishing touches to *This Day in Music's Guide to The Clash*, news broke about the release of a LP/CD/digital project boxset tribute from Ignition Records, Joe Strummer 001, the first compilation spanning Joe's career outside The Clash, including various rarities, fan favourites recorded with the 101'ers and The Mescaleros, solo LPs, soundtrack work and unreleased songs.

It was too early to review the finished product here, but the release gave me an excuse to talk some more about Joe, and how he had become his own archivist – with 'barns full of writings and tapes stored in his back garden'. There are more than 20,000 items in the Joe Strummer Archive, the archiving of that material and compiling of 'Joe Strummer 001' being overseen by his widow, Lucinda Mellor, and Canada-born, London-based artist and long-term friend, Robert Gordon McHarg III, its tracks restored and mastered by Grammy award-winner Peter J. Moore at the E. Room in Toronto.

You can seek out full details at https://JoeStrummer.lnk.to/001, but Gordon – who previously worked on The Clash's *Sound System* boxset with Paul Simonon and also curated the Black Market Clash exhibition – said of Joe Strummer 001, 'Hopefully it's an insight into his workings'. What's more, Gordon and Lucinda – who told me 'home is Somerset and where my heart is' – were good enough to kindly answer my questions on the project and Joe's enduring legacy, nearly 16 years after his death.

A lot of hard work went into this collection and compiling the archive. Was this project at the drawing board stage for a long time?
Gordon: "Joe did all the hard work; we've laboured. Finding a way to share the archive has taken time."
Luce: "Not really, as we were concerned primarily with the written work he left behind, having no idea of the wealth of recording material buried in the boxes and bags."

The first thing I heard from the boxset was a different treatment of 'London's Burning'/'Burnin' Streets', just one example showcasing the versatility of many great tracks in that back-catalogue. I hear Joe was one for 'hidden tracks' tucked away on tapes. Was there a fear that some of those old cassettes would snap and be lost forever after all this time?
Gordon: "Preserving all Joe's archive has been a challenge. 'London Is Burning' was Pockets' contribution to JS001 (another old friend of Joe)."
Luce: "Yes, real fear, and for this reason Gordon sought out the amazing Peter Moore in Canada, a master at repairing these precious old tapes."
Was there much gnashing of teeth, scratching of heads and arguments for arguments' sake over the track-listing?
Gordon: "Absolutely. It took months.

I worked on around seven variations. Having archived so many of Joe's set-lists, it was imperative to try and channel that dedication into trying to get it right."

Luce: "There was a little bit, as the question of why these gems never found the light of day was always prominent in our selection, and also personal preferences are subjective."

Were there occasional conversations in compiling this boxset, feeling a need to ask Joe's opinion on something?

Gordon: "Occasional? All the way through this. It's ongoing ..."

Luce: "Continual, but then I still find that today, and wonder, 'What would Joe do or say?'"

I understand there are more than 20,000 items in the Joe Strummer Archive. Were there moments when it all seemed a bit much to even contemplate sorting out?

Gordon: "It's been emotional!"

Luce: "Yes, the project has been huge, and without the input, help and enthusiasm from Gordon and Martin Bradley and his team, I would have abandoned it years ago. It really has been a mammoth undertaking."

Have there been sleepless nights thinking you shouldn't have left such and such a track off? And is there scope for a 'Joe Strummer 002'?

Gordon: "There have been many sleepless nights. I care so much about not letting Joe down. The archive is so rich in material, there is more to share. JS002 is definitely a desire."

Luce: "Many, many sleepless nights, and I'm sure there are many varying opinions out there as to what we should and shouldn't have included, but there is easily a 002 and maybe even a 003."

In an interview in 2007 with The Independent, Lucinda suggested an 'amazing book' may follow on the archive someday. Any further advanced?

Luce: "This is what we were originally planning when we realised Joe had left so many interesting and beautiful lyrics, poems and drawings. So we've put together a book to accompany the release with his handwritten lyrics, scribbles, drawings, photographs and a bio he wrote himself. In effect, we've left the book to Joe to introduce us to the album. That's not to say that sometime in the future I would love to put out a glossy coffee table book!"

I've come to appreciate in recent years the strength of the 101'ers material. Might that have been something Joe was likely to go back to and reinterpret/re-record a few songs?

Luce: "That I cannot answer, but it's interesting to note that 'Pouring Rain' was first visited in 1984 and then again in 1993, so I guess we will never know."

There were a few 'in between' projects before The Mescaleros evolved, not least the film soundtracks. What tracks from those less celebrated albums really jump out at you all these years on?

Gordon: "I've enjoyed watching and learning more about the films Joe was involved in. I Hired A Contract Killer by Aki Kaurismaki is high on my list and the track 'Burning Lights' is up there. To add to that, when Luce played me 'Generations' I thought this is one of Joe's best. It had to go on. And when he wrote 'Sandpaper Blues' for my exhibition soundtrack, that will always be a personal life highlight."

Luce: "I think my favourites are the songs

5

he did for Sara Driver's film, When Pigs Fly. But Walker is astounding too. I find myself listening to that album a lot and never tire of it."

It took Joe's departure for much of his work to be truly recognised in certain circles, but I'm convinced I don't just hold the last two albums in such reverence because of the circumstances, but because he was on a genuine career high.

Gordon: "I really enjoyed seeing Joe play with The Mescaleros. All the albums are great."

Luce: "I feel he was just getting back into his stride and had a fantastically talented bunch of musicians in The Mescaleros who reignited his passion for writing, recording and performing, so I'd agree with you."

There's a tendency to think, going back over old interviews, footage and records, we're still in late 2002 in Joe's world. But while Streetcore was perhaps his finest body of work and a couple more albums of that strength may have followed, his restless nature might have seen him move on to another band or solo project at some stage.

Gordon: "Joe was always working with different artists ..."

Luce: "Perhaps. He really enjoyed his collaborations with Horace Andy, Richard Norris, Jimmy Cliff and right at the end of his life with Dave Stewart, so I'm sure he would have branched out, and he was swapping ideas with Mick at the end too."

Inevitably, talk always returned to a Clash reformation and its likelihood. Signs and snippets of quotes suggest It was at least on a bucket-list for Joe at some point.

Gordon: "I don't have the answer ... (but) Joe loved The Clash."

Luce: "As I said, Mick and he were swapping ideas in the last few months of his life, and I guess The Clash was always unfinished business. He had enormous respect and love for Mick, so who knows."

What's (Joe and Lucinda's daughter) Eliza up to these days? Are you still in touch with (Joe's other daughters) Jazz and Lola and the rest of the family? And do you often speak to Mick, Paul and Topper?

Luce: "Eliza is a singer and producer and goes under the name of Lyza Jane. She has an EP out on Blah Records and has just finished writing her first album. Jazz and Lola are both mothers, living on the South coast, and I saw them a couple of weekends ago. Mick, Paul and Topper, not as often, as I don't come to London much these days, but we are in touch."

It's now 25 years since you met Joe, and you got to know him so much better than most. Although you both had West London links, he seemed to be just as at home in Somerset, away from the big city.

Luce: "He took to Somerset life easily and did love it down here, although he never lost his thirst for London, and indeed other cities."

Joe could outdo most of us with his 'hoarding' capabilities. I get a picture of a 'carrier-bag man' keeping hold of so many items that might one day come in handy (lyrics or whatever). Were there ever difficult 'Do you really need this, Joe?' conversations?

Luce: "Many. I couldn't understand why he kept these endless plastic bags which littered the house, especially as I am the opposite and love a good clear-out."

How important was Gordon's input in setting the right tone on this project?

Luce: "This whole project is really Gordon's baby, he has masterminded and engineered it from conception."

So how did you get to know him, Gordon? I think you suggested to BBC London's Robert Elms it involved a copy of a Hank Williams book and a pumpkin pie.

Gordon: "Back in the early '90s, my friend, Lucky Pete, drummer of Gaz Mayall's band The Trojans, left my Hank Williams book at Joe's house. I wanted my book back and lived around the corner from Joe when he was living on Lancaster Road. I remember having a Baby Belling cooker and thought I would make a pie and customise the outside of the box – 'Slim's Pumpkin Pie'. I was cooking Sunday lunch at The Globe, Talbot Road at the time.

"Anyway ... I turned up, rang the bell; Joe opened the door and I asked for my Hank book. He went and got it from the lounge and said he read it, which made me happy. Standing at the front door sporting my cowboy hat and pie in hand, I said 'I made this for you'. He immediately invited me in, with my son Hughie and Lucky Pete. He seemed happy with the pie. We chatted and my son played with his kids Lola and Jazzy. This was the beginning of our friendship."

Were you a Clash fan, growing up in Montreal? Ever dream you might get to know the band and know their London? And what did you think when Luce asked you to get involved on all this?

Gordon: "Yes. I saw The Clash in Montreal 1982. I was 18. 'The Call Up' really got into my head. I arrived in London on Carnival Monday, 1983, and knew no one. I didn't know Notting Hill Carnival was on and ended up on Portobello Road, under the Westway, listening to Aswad. Six years later I met Paul Simonon at his after-carnival party through my friend Gaz.

"And I always feel it is a great privilege to help Luce with Joe's archive."

You've paid tribute to Joe with art installations in London, Belfast and Tokyo, most famously the Edgware Road tube project. Ever try to define what it was about him that truly resonated with you?

Gordon: "The Joe Strummer Subway was my guerrilla project to rename the subway under the Marylebone flyover intersection of the Westway and the Edgware Road, where I had The Subway Gallery for 10 years.

"Joe was one of my teachers, along with Hank Williams, John Fogerty, The Beatles, Gene Clark, John Cooper Clarke, Shel Silverstein ... to name but a few. I've learned a lot through rock'n'roll, and Joe was a huge part of that."

Four years ago, you revealed that your 'seven-day pop-up shop' was to raise funds for a Strummer statue. There have been temporary murals and tributes in London, Spain and the US since 2002. Any closer to your dream?

Gordon: "I raised enough from the pop-up shop to make a 3D-printed maquette. It ended up totally different to my original idea. In Joe's archive I found a great drawing he did - a self-portrait as a cactus with a cowboy hat, boom-box and a smoke. We made a special print of this for the box-set. My dream is to make this as a life-size sculpture."

The biographers who got closest to the subject, not least Pat Gilbert, Marcus Gray and Chris Salewicz, gave honest portraits of a man who for all his faults came out as nothing less than charismatic and passionate, words that come up time and again when reference is made to Joe. Yet he remained something of an enigma. Do

you think only a few of you got to know the real John Mellor?
Gordon: "I got to meet Joe Strummer ..."
Luce: "Perhaps."
Have there been genuine moments when you've been overwhelmed by just how much love there is still out there for Joe, all around the world, where he's touched so many lives and inspired so many people?
Gordon: "Never overwhelmed. Proud to be a part of it."
Luce: "Yes, I'm continually amazed that the passion and love for the man and his music is still so strong."
The way politics has gone in recent years, particularly in the UK and US, seems to be the antithesis of everything Joe fought for – anti-poverty, anti-borders, pro-inclusion, promotion of the arts/culture, pro-cooperation and connecting. He would have plenty to rail about if he was still with us, wouldn't he?
Gordon: "Yes. Without doubt."
Luce: "Of that I am certain."
Where are we at with the Joe Strummer Foundation in 2018? And are there events taking place to mark the release of the boxset?
Gordon: "Yes, we're working on something special for the release ..."
Luce: "The Foundation is going really well and there are many projects happening. We've partnered with Kerrang Radio to create Revolution Rock, helping provide musical instruments for financially-challenged schools and music-mentoring for the homeless and/or underprivileged, helping youths find a way out of gang crime, or music therapy for mental health issues. There was also a Strummer Jam in August and a gig at Dingwall's in early September, plus support for emerging musicians in the Hastings area through a project called *DEBUT* (with all information at joestrummerfoundation.org)."
Finally, in a sense, Joe never left us - his music remains with us. Approaching 16 years after his passing, what do you both think of when Joe springs to mind today?
Gordon: "His energy and laugh. Chatting with him around his campfire at Fuji Rock Festival and Glastonbury."
Luce: "I see him in the kitchen with a half-eaten sandwich, his dog asleep on his feet, waving a piece of paper at me, asking me to fax it quick to Mick."

THEY ALSO SERVED 5

Clash Conspirators

Terry Chimes

(drums, percussion, 1976–77, 1982–83)
Born Terence Chimes on July 5, 1956, in Stepney, East London, he originally auditioned, unsuccessfully, for Mick Jones' London SS before joining Jones, Paul Simonon, Keith Levene and Joe Strummer in the original line-up of The Clash. His first spell was a short one, but he was recruited again to record the band's self-titled first album, credited on the cover as 'Tory Crimes' after leaving again, replaced by Topper Headon.

In 1982, after Headon was forced out for his drug addiction, Chimes – whose CV by then included the first of two spells with Johnny Thunders and the Heartbreakers in 1977, Cowboys International in 1979, and Generation X from 1980-81 – rejoined, playing on the 'Casbah Club' tours, both sides of the Atlantic, supporting The Who, and the following 'Combat Rock' tour in the US. He also featured in the promo video for 'Rock the Casbah', but after 1982's Jamaican World Music Festival appearance left for the final time.

Chimes took on his second spell behind the kit with Johnny Thunders & the Heartbreakers in 1984, then featured for Hanoi Rocks in 1985, The Cherry Bombz in 1986 (with ex-Hanoi Rocks members Andy McCoy and Nasty Suicide, and ex-Sham 69/Wanderers and The Lords of the New Church member Dave Tregunna), and a reformed Black Sabbath in 1987/88, as well as featuring with Billy Idol, The Crunch (with Tregunna, Diamond Dogs' Sulo Karlsson and The Cockney Rejects' Mick Geggus), and The Anita Chellemah Band. He also has the distinction of being the only non-classic line-up member inducted with The Clash into the Rock and Roll Hall of Fame in 2003, where he praised absent Topper Headon's 'genius' at the ceremony.

After 15 years in the music business, he left for a career in alternative medicine, as a chiropractor and acupuncturist. The teetotal vegetarian's change of vocation followed him being cured of serious arm pain after his first show in 1987 with Black Sabbath by that outfit's personal chiropractor. He went on to run his own Essex clinic, Chimes Chiropractic, also running seminars. Studying in the UK, with a spell of clinical practice in Nanjing, China, he developed a chain of chiropractic clinics, before turning his hand to training, running Europe's largest consulting business in alternative medicine, lecturing and leading seminars all over Europe and the USA.

Away from music, he was also nominated as a Scouting in London ambassador for a regional Scout Association body in 2008. He's also involved in charity work and was chairman of the board for the YMCA of East

5

London for eight years. In late 2013 he wrote his first book, *The Strange Case of Dr Terry and Mr Chimes*, described as 'an autobiography with a difference', including plenty about his childhood, The Clash's early years, and spiritual insights that have guided him.

Rob Harper

(drums, percussion, 1976–77)

Rob Harper-Milne, then known as Rob Harper, started rehearsing with The Clash in the first week of November 1976, having seen them play at Ilford, describing the impact of their frontline as being like 'three Eddie Cochrans'. Part of the line-up that supported the Sex Pistols on the 'Anarchy' tour, he had initially answered an advert in *Melody Maker*. Harper started out playing guitar, switching to bass in his college band, the Cafe Racers, when Mark Knopfler joined, later turning down an offer to join Knopfler's next band, Dire Straits, while studying at Sussex University. Dropping out of uni after a year, he joined The Rockettes on guitar, his bandmates including William Broad, later known as Billy Idol.

For a time he played guitar for South London R&B outfit The Marauders, set up by namesake Charlie Harper, that band becoming The UK Subs, Rob switching to drums. Along with bassist Steve Slack he left to form power-pop outfit The Dazzlers on guitar, making a few singles and a Tommy Ramone-produced LP, the group splitting before it was released.

Harper was quoted by Pat Gilbert as saying, 'My hazy, romantic notions of how pop music was put together were completely burst by being in The Clash. Because they were strong characters they were going for it. They were saying one thing to the media, but behind the scenes were saying, 'We want to be the next Rolling Stones.' Disillusioned and taking a dislike to Paul Simonon, his last gig was at The Roxy on New Year's Day, '77, with Harper soon airbrushed from the band's history.

Keith Levene

(lead guitar, 1976)

Original member, dismissed early September 1976, Strummer claiming his dwindling interest was due to his speed intake, something he always denied. Went on to form Public Image Ltd. with former Sex Pistols front-man John Lydon in 1978.

In *I Was a Teenage Guitarist 4 The Clash*, Levene detailed encounters with other central figures on that initial London punk scene, including Paul Simonon, Terry Chimes, John Lydon, Sid Vicious, Billy Idol and Viv Albertine. He wrote, 'It was a very exciting time. There was as very young, very fresh, exuberant feeling in the air – like anything was possible. And not just for those of us involved in music. It wasn't just about expressing oneself through music, although the music was certainly very important. If you had a standpoint you wanted to express, whether the vehicle was through fashion, art, the written word, or even how you presented yourself to the world – the emerging scene in West London welcomed you.'

Pete Howard

(drums, percussion, 1983–86)

Previously with Bath-based outfit Cold Fish, joining The Clash at the age of 23, replacing Terry Chimes, making his live debut at the Us Festival in California, in what would turn out to be Mick Jones' final show with the band. Remained with the band until they finally split in late 1985, going on to drum for London outfit Eat, who were with The Cure's label,

5

Fiction Records, then forming Vent 414 with The Wonder Stuff front-man Miles Hunt. Also worked with former Senseless Things bass player Morgan Nicholls, as Morgan, and made three albums with indie outfit Queen Adreena between 2002 and 2008.

Nick Sheppard

(guitar/backing vocals, 1983–86)
The Clash Mk.II's first new guitar recruit, replacing the sacked Mick Jones, playing on *Cut the Crap*. Joined the band at the age of 24, having previously featured for Bristol punk band The Cortinas. Went on to join Gareth Sager in Head, then work with Koozie Johns in Shot, who signed to the IRS label in 1991. He moved to Western Australia in 1993, playing in Perth outfits Heavy Smoker and the New Egyptian Kings, while running a clothing store. In 2007 he formed the DomNicks with Dom Mariani, touring with the Hoodoo Gurus, and has also appeared in Sydney and Melbourne with at the Revolution Rock tribute show to Joe Strummer.

Vince White

(guitar/backing vocals, 1983–86)
Astronomy and physics graduate Greg White served in The Clash Mk. II. Legend has it that Paul Simonon refused to work in a band with anyone going by the name 'Greg', hence his name change. After the band split he became a mini-cab driver, then dropped out, before settling down to complete a BSc in fine art in North London. He later published an account of his playing days, *Out of Control: The Last Days of The Clash*, for Moving Target Books. Continuing to travel, he works as an artist in Notting Hill, West London. As a guitar player he's worked with a number of recognised musicians, including BB King, Dick Dale, Macy Gray, Ian Hunter, Leon Russell, and John Mayall.

The Management

Bernard Rhodes

Manager, impresario and fashion designer Bernard Rhodes was integral to the development of the UK punk rock scene, associated with the Sex Pistols as well as The Clash, working initially alongside Malcolm McLaren. He became an important force behind The Clash, handling their marketing and creative direction. Sacked in 1979, tensions in the band led to Strummer demanding his reinstatement in 1981.

He also played a part in the success of The Specials ('Gangsters' begins with the line, 'Bernie Rhodes knows – don't argue!'), Dexy's Midnight Runners ('Dance Stance' was originally released on his Oddball Productions label, and he later signed the group to EMI), The Subway Sect (1980 debut LP *What's the Matter Boy* was on Oddball) and Joboxers. Rhodes built then operated from Rehearsal Rehearsals, having persuaded the local council to provide a space for disadvantaged local youth where they could learn to play music, the location part of a former railway yard, later incorporated within Camden's Stables Market.

Born in the East End, his pregnant mother a Russian-Jewish refugee having fled her homeland after the Second World War, he was schooled in Brixton (like Mick Jones), raised in a South London orphanage, leaving at 15 (he told *Mojo* in 1999, 'I was on the streets when I was 12.'). He never knew his father, but his mother worked in the fashion trade, a Soho seamstress.

Part of London's early Mod coffee-bar scene, he claimed to know Mick Jagger from his art-school days and many more prime players on the scene, and in the late '60s won a Design Council award for a children's educational toy designed using new plastic techniques. By the early '70s he had a shop in Chelsea's Antiquarius Market selling hand-printed silk screen designs on shirts and T-shirts, plus rare vintage reggae, soon working with McLaren and his girlfriend Vivienne Westwood, operating out of the Sex boutique at 430 King's Road. Sharing a similar philosophy, they went into business, collaborating on several T-shirts sold in Sex. Later, describing the difference between them, Rhodes said, 'Malcolm likes to titillate but I get down to substance.'

In time he became fascinated by anarchist art movement, the Situationists, a politically and socially radical subdivision of Surrealism, dealing in conceptual art, calling for revolution of everyday life, playing a key part in Paris' 1968 uprising, and an influence on the UK punk scene's artwork and advertising. Johnny Green told Pat Gilbert, 'We never had any money. If you brought it up, Bernie would give you a talk about Paris '68. You'd say, 'But Bernie, I just need some guitar strings.' And Tony James told *Mojo*, 'He'd say, 'You guys are wasting my time. Have you read any Sartre?' It taught us something important – you have to have a bigger idea. That was Bernie's lesson.'

By 1975, Sex had become a hangout for a bunch of teenagers from which the Sex Pistols would emerge, Rhodes taking the group under his wing while McLaren was overseas looking after The New York Dolls. Glen Matlock described Rhodes' contribution as making them understand the importance of being clear-cut, saying, 'He had a real ability for making people decide exactly what they were trying to do.'

John Lydon said he was wearing an 'I Hate Pink Floyd' T-shirt when he was spotted by Rhodes on King's Road, insisting he met McLaren, Steve Jones and Paul Cook in the Roebuck pub that evening. Rhodes then had Lydon back to audition. Lydon said, 'He was important in so many ways. He'd indicate where the problems with the Pistols would be in the future. He'd sow a seed, wait to see if I'd pick up on it.'

After an offer to co-manage Sex Pistols was rejected by McLaren, Rhodes was instrumental in forming The Clash after meeting Mick Jones at the Nashville, inviting Paul Simonon and Keith Levene to join, then 101'ers front-man Joe Strummer, who said, 'He constructed The Clash and focused our energies and we repaid him by being really good at what we did.' Simonon added, 'He set up the whole scene, basically. He saw how non-musicians like myself and John Lydon could contribute.'

It was Rhodes who hired Guy Stevens, who he knew from his Mod days, to produce the 1977 Polydor recordings, returning in 1979 to produce *London Calling*. And it was Rhodes who, on January 25th '77, signed The Clash to CBS, dealing directly with label boss Maurice Oberstein.

After the second album, in late '78, The Clash sacked Rhodes, who felt they were drifting away from their ideals. During the early '80s he opened Club Left in Soho, the likes of Sade, Bananarama, Georgie Fame and Slim Gaillard playing, with Vic Godard and the Subway Sect as house band. Sean McLusky said Rhodes gave him a break there in 1981, then gained a deal for his band JoBoxers, mainstream success following on both sides of the Atlantic. McLusky said, 'Bernard never got the credit for things that were his. He's been the undefined force.'

Reinstated with The Clash, Rhodes' dance remix of 'The Magnificent Seven' was credited to Pepe Unidos (Strummer, Rhodes and Simonon). He also produced 'The Call Out', remixing 'The Call Up'. Mick Jones said, 'Bernie came back on the scene because people thought we'd got out of control and the first thing he wanted to do was book us for seven nights in New York'. That 1981 Bond's residency saw the band supported by Grandmaster Flash, The Sugarhill Gang, Dead Kennedys, Bad Brains, Joe Ely, Lee 'Scratch' Perry and Funkapolitan, something Rhodes insisted turned the wider public on to hip-hop, while Kosmo Vinyl felt those dates saw The Clash 'claw their way back into the Premiership'.

In 1990, he relocated from Los Angeles to Atlanta, Georgia, where black metal band Naked Truth hired him, finding them a new bass player, producing LP *Green with Rage* and getting them signed to Sony.

Two decades later, Rhodes caused controversy at Malcolm McLaren's funeral, accusing Vivienne Westwood of 'being part of the Establishment', then delivering his own eulogy, telling the assembled, 'If we're not careful we're going to turn Malcolm into John Lennon, into a saint. Malcolm was no saint.' In her later autobiography, Westwood said he was justified in what he said.

Rhodes has also featured in an exhibition at the London Jewish Museum, called 'Entertaining the Nation: Stars of Music, Stage & Screen', and designed a biker range of T-shirts for Lewis Leathers.

Caroline Coon

Leaving Kent at 16, Caroline Coon headed to Notting Hill, London, working as a model, including making a 'black and white *nouvelle vague*-influenced film about the emotions of two people making love', working as a figurative painter and getting involved in the '60s' underground movement in the capital while at art school. That included putting on gigs attended by pre-Clash Mick Jones and Joe Strummer. In 1967, she co-founded the Release agency, providing legal advice and arrange legal representation for young people charged with drug possession, remaining politically active, campaigning primarily for feminist causes, and legalisation of prostitution.

In the '70s, she became involved in London's punk scene, writing for *Melody Maker*, getting to know The Clash, shooting the cover sleeve for 'White Riot' in 1977, and designing the Global Revolution poster for *Give 'Em Enough Rope*. Living with Paul Simonon at the time, she managed the band from 1978 to 1980, after Bernie Rhodes' sacking, assisting CBS when the group's management was taken over by a team of lawyers and accountants.

Coon also provided the cover sleeve of The Police's single 'Roxanne' in 1978, and

Babyshambles' 'Janie Jones/Strummerville' in 2006, and wrote an inside account of UK punk rock, *1977/1988: The New Wave Punk Rock Explosion*' for Omnibus Press.

'Caroline Kook', a character based on her and played by Jane Asher, featured in a sketch for BBC comedy *The Goodies*. She also inspired lyrics for Robert Wyatt's 'O Caroline', The Stranglers' 'London Lady' and (according to her) Bob Dylan's 'She Belongs to Me'. An intimate memoir, *Laid Bare*, was published in 2016. According to her website, 'Caroline Coon has worked in the vanguard of cultural movements that have caused storms of social change: the hippie 'peace and love' underground, the punk rock movement and feminism'. She added that most recently she's been 'painting her Ladbroke Grove neighbourhood in a series of narrative urban landscapes.'

Pete Jenner

Manager and record producer Pete Jenner, born in 1943, was a lecturer at the London School of Economics by the age of 21, after gaining a first-class honours degree in economics from Cambridge. But after four years at the LSE he left to manage then-unknown Pink Floyd and put on a number of free concerts in London's Hyde Park, including a 1969 Rolling Stones gig witnessed up front by Mick Jones.

He first saw Floyd at the Marquee in March 1966 and was impressed by the acoustic effects Syd Barrett and Richard Wright used in their set, tracking Roger Waters and Nick Mason back to their flat and asking to take them on. Subsequently, Jenner and fellow Pink Floyd aide Andrew King formed a partnership with Pink Floyd, Blackhill Enterprises. His voice can be heard at the start of 'Astronomy Domine', the opening track of 1967's *The Piper at the Gates of Dawn*.

As well as managing The Clash, he also managed Pink Floyd's Syd Barrett, T-Rex, Ian Dury, Roy Harper, The Disposable Heroes of Hiphoprisy, Robyn Hitchcock, Baaba Maal, Eddi Reader and Clash fan Billy Bragg, among others. In more recent years he has been part of Sincere Management.

Kosmo Vinyl

Born Mark Dunk on February 9th, 1957, Kosmo Vinyl was a long-time associate and sometime manager of The Clash, also working with Ian Dury and the Blockheads and The Jam. He can be heard introducing The Clash live at Shea Stadium, New York City, as well as many bootlegged shows. He also delivers an impression of Taxi Driver's Travis Bickle on Combat Rock's 'Red Angel Dragnet'. Before working with the Clash, he acted as MC on the Stiff Records tours, and can be heard on 1978's Live Stiffs Live. He later became a record producer, including work with Jack Black, and was a consultant on Gus van Sant's 1989 film, Drugstore Cowboy. Seven years earlier he appeared with Strummer, Jones, Simonon, Don Letts and Jones' partner Ellen Foley in Martin Scorsese's The King of Comedy, all credited as 'Street Scum'. In 2013, he helped produce a major retrospective exhibition of the art of Ian Dury at London's Royal College of Art and debuted his own punk/pop inspired artwork dedicated to his beloved West Ham United FC with shows in London and Somerset during the 2014 FIFA World Cup.

An ABC of The Clash road crew

5

Barry Auguste

A backline roadie for The Clash for seven years, Barry Auguste was poached by the band after a similar role with the other band Bernie Rhodes managed, The Subway Sect, initially as Topper Headon's drum tech. Also known as Barry Glare, 'evidently inspired by his sunny disposition,' according to Marcus Gray, he was dubbed 'The Baker' by Paul Simonon, as he thought he looked like one.

Joining the entourage for 1977's 'White Riot' tour, he was a rarity in the camp, touching neither drink nor drugs. In April 1979, with Johnny Green, he scouted out Vanilla Studios and put together the reel-to-reel four-track tape sent Guy Stevens' way to entice him to produce what would become *London Calling*. Furthermore, that's The Baker's introductory atmospheric whistling on 'Jimmy Jazz'. He also starred with Green in 1980's 'Bankrobber' video, their staged bank raid leading to genuine police questioning. As others departed, he stuck around, through to Shea Stadium and beyond, having been tasked – with Digby Cleaver – to whittle down 200 or so applicants to 10 when the band sought Headon's replacement, photographing the successful candidates from the Ear Studios auditions, presenting Strummer, Jones and Simonon with dossiers to select the last four, the job eventually going to Pete Howard.

On his website, *www.thebaker77.wordpress.com*, he explains, 'Having refused all interviews and comments regarding the band for the last 30 years, I now realise the passing of time has not diminished the essential message of The Clash and that even though huge mistakes were made, the issues addressed are in many ways even more relevant today. The energy and vision of the band continue through younger generations seeking an alternative to the manufactured nonsense that assaults us from all sides today. One would think with the intelligence and technology at hand, issues of the day would be far more widely dispersed by today's leading musicians. Sadly, this is not the case. Huge endorsements and corporate sponsorship ensure all the major music stars are kept firmly in line and few dare to cross into controversial territory. The Clash had their faults as human beings (probably more than most), and contradictions in their music and their message abound. As is so often the case, heroes are held aloft and subjected to the extremes of criteria. But remember, The Clash were just common folk – not a PhD or college grad among them. So young and innocent of the trickery of the world, they struggled daily with bruised egos, excesses of hubris, and lapses of confidence. Without the luxury of a team of seasoned handlers, counsel could only be obtained from their own inner circle and perspicacity was often out of reach. It's no wonder contradictions were made and potential left unfulfilled. So judge them lightly now, in the cold light of day. Hindsight is a wonderful thing. Above all, the world is still a far better place for their existence.'

John Broad

'Johnny Green', as he was known in Clash circles (originally Johnny Greenglasses, due to his lime green specs, then the shortened version after claiming a booked but unfilled bed for a Dagenham Plastics employee of that name in a Leeds motel one night), was taken on around the time of late-'77's cancelled Belfast show, the 27-year-old tagging along with a lorry-driving friend hired to ferry their gear. By the end of the 'Get Out of Control' tour he was the band's personal driver, taking them between gigs in a rented mini-bus. Writing about his adventures from there to March 1980 in highly entertaining, well-received 1997 memoir, *A Riot of Our Own: Night and Day with The Clash*, his role was described as 'road manager and confidant for three delirious years of rock'n'roll madness.'

Broad studied at Lancaster University before his Clash odyssey, Pat Gilbert writing, 'He'd done some living in his time: 1960s' Gillingham Mod, Carnaby Street dandy, teenage husband, the Notting Hill hippy scene, Gandalf's Garden, acid, forestry, organic food production, hard drugs, a degree in Arabic studies as a mature student.' Returning to Kent in later years, he was a county education advisor on sex and drugs in the early '90s, and by 2004, 'Enjoying a ninth life as an author and family man on the Kent coast.'

On his decision to quit at the height of the band's powers, he told Rod Kitson for *The Quietus* in 2012, 'The Clash were getting a bit predictable. I preferred the chaos of the early days.' He went to work with Clash associate Joe Ely in America, and of his departure, Gilbert wrote, '*Rude Boy* may ostensibly be about Ray Gange, but it's also in some ways the story of Johnny Green. Here was a man who thrived on chaos. Once The Clash touring machine became well oiled, his anarchic energy ceased to have a valuable function. Roadent's acrimonious exit coincided with a period when the group's original entourage suddenly found themselves in the role of 'valets'. Johnny was happy to tend the group ... like a masseur in his beloved Tour de France – the guy hired to look after the physical and mental well-being of his riders. Now it seemed his personal touch was no longer required.'

Broad briefly returned in early '81, just after Rhodes' recall, lasting one day, telling the band they were 'fucking coasting'. He told Pat Gilbert, 'It just smelt bad. I sat around in the rehearsal room. I knew what bad days were. When not a lot's going on, and it was like that. It just seemed they'd drifted even further apart than when I'd gone to Texas.' Seeing them rehearse a few months later, he painted an even bleaker picture of the mood in the camp. He later saw the Us Festival show – Jones' last – and told Strummer it was 'shit', the frontman agreeing.

A later taste for the professional cycling circuit led to his next book, Broad telling Rod Kitson, 'Last time I saw Joe, I told him about my passion for the Tour de France, and he said, 'What a great idea! That sounds terrific. I'm really busy until Christmas but come and see me in January and we'll do it together.' He really encouraged me, then the bastard went and died on me. I thought fuck it, I'm going to do it anyway. Even in death what he'd said inspired me to continue. He was a bundle of energy and encouragement.'

Digby Cleaver

Mick Jones' guitar tech from the summer of 1980 until Jones' sacking in August '83, when he decided where his loyalties laid, following him. An ex-Wishbone Ash roadie, Jones made it clear on meeting him – Cleaver was hired by Rhodes on recommendations – he didn't like his long hair nor the fact that he wasn't a female, as requested (Pat Gilbert wrote, 'The idea was to challenge the tradition of having a seething mass of testosterone tuning the guitars for them.'). But Topper Headon took a shine to him, encouraging him to get his hair cut to win Jones over.

Suggesting the haphazard way Rhodes ran his operation had hardly changed by then, Cleaver told Pat Gilbert, 'We were retained on a three-way sliding scale. If the band were doing nothing we got £100 a week, in the studio we had £200, if the band were touring we got £300.' He added, 'Bernie's idea of fun would be to be completely un-findable on the telephone all day Friday until about half four. He would then phone one of us and say he'd left our cheques at Stiff's offices in Alexander Street, or at the pub next door with Kosmo. I'd arrive hot-foot at five to find I couldn't put the cheque in until Monday, which meant I couldn't draw any money out till Thursday.'

Steve Connolly

'Roadent', as he became known (as well as 'Scon'), worked for The Clash and later the Sex Pistols. Hailing from Coventry, he first saw the band at the ICA in late October '76, aged 19, not long out of prison in Birmingham, having served two weeks for burglary. He told Joe Strummer he was sleeping rough and was offered a mattress at Rehearsal Rehearsals. As Pat Gilbert put it, like Strummer he was 'fascinated by history and politics, and like Robin Banks had flirted with crime and paid for it with jail.' He gelled with Strummer, the Camden HQ becoming his home, sharing an upstairs room with Paul Simonon and sometimes the band's frontman.

Gilbert wrote in 2004, 'Roadent was one of several key Clash associates whose energy and ideas would create a sparky, challenging, edgy atmosphere around the group.' He added how Roadent, Johnny Green, Robin Banks, later arrival 'Jock Scot', and others were 'always much more than mere apostles and the term 'roadies' is ludicrously inappropriate: a bit like calling Joe Strummer a musician'. Strummer recalled, 'Bernie didn't understand why we'd hang out with the road crew. But these were the people who threw their lot in with us when we didn't have two pennies to rub together. We developed a bond. It was great to have their enthusiasm and cutting criticism.'

Roadent also introduced Bernie Rhodes to The Coventry Automatics, later renamed The Specials, and features in German documentary, *Punk in London*, interviewed upstairs at Rehearsals. He was present for the early Beaconsfield session, part of the debut LP recordings, and the 'Complete Control' session. Along with Strummer he sprayed 'White Riot' across the front of the Capital Radio building and on the wall of the BBC, also attending – with Don Letts – the June '77 reggae all-nighter that inspired '(White Man) In Hammersmith Palais'.

He left as he felt Jones 'was becoming quite demanding,' going to work for the Pistols, but was back in touch in late April '81 during the European tour preceding NYC's Bond's residency, while with an equipment hire company, in charge of their PA, their drunken night out in Barcelona including a heated row over the band's direction, leading to Strummer taking a swing at him, described by Roadent to Gilbert as 'real handbags stuff'.

Talking to a Coventry Music blog, he revealed that after the Pistols' demise, he fled abroad and had a couple of years acting for German TV, becoming the inspiration for The Passions' 'I'm in Love with a German Film Star'. His first acting role was in a TV show featuring The Adverts, soon moving to Munich, getting more roles, earning 'around £5,000 a month', including *Das Ding* (*The Heist*), directed by Uli Edel, who later went on to direct 'an equally-bad actor, Madonna,' as he put it. He added, '£5,000 a month was too much for my liver, so I drifted back to rock'n'roll as a mercenary, journeyman, technician, doing onstage sound for The Pretenders, The Undertones, Stiff Little Fingers, UB40, PIL, Elkie Brooks, Earth Wind & Fire, Bob Marley, ABC, Bob Dylan, Barbara Dickson, among others.'

Robin Crocker

Mick Jones' guitar tech and a key member of the band's entourage, known as 'Robin Banks', was born in Whitechapel in London's East End in 1953, moving with his adoptive parents to Brixton and later Crystal Palace. Crocker and Jones became close friends at their South London grammar school through a mutual love of music. Well-read and bright but easily bored and rebellious, his disruptive behaviour continued, and after being laid off from a *West London Weekly* reporter's role, he fell in with some old mates robbing betting shops. Caught in the act in late '73 in Streatham, South London, he was convicted, aged 19, of armed robbery, serving two years between Wormwood Scrubs, then becoming the youngest inmate at maximum security prison Albany on the Isle of Wight, his story and relationship with Jones inspiring *Give 'Em Enough Rope*'s revered 'Stay Free'.

Revisiting that track with Dave Simpson for *The Guardian* in 2008, Banks said, 'By the time I got out Mick had formed the Clash. One evening he came over with an acoustic and played me 'Stay Free'. Somebody once said to me it's the most outstanding heterosexual male-on-male love song. There's a lot of truth in that. It's a memento of a glorious band, a glorious time and glorious friendship. Unfortunately, I didn't 'Stay Free'. I did a wages' snatch in Stockholm and got banged up again.'

But Banks was part of The Clash entourage for the 'White Riot' tour, covered the 'Get Out of Control' dates for *Zig Zag* magazine, and was later charged for his part in the notorious 'Guns on the Roof' incident at Rehearsal Rehearsals in late March '78. Former *NME* writer Howard Fraser got to know Banks during a spell driving the band, telling Pat Gilbert he was 'mad as a hatter, mostly drunk, but ... also quite debonair, very intelligent, a great sense of humour, a boulevardier of sorts. He was the wild card element.'

Banks was also part of the select group involved in the band's Vanilla football matches between recording sessions and attended the Leicester Square gala performance of *Rude Boy* – while the band stayed away (Johnny Green and The Baker had seen the film's Berlin Film Festival premiere). In the early 2000s he was back in the public eye, travelling to Baghdad – his passage paid by Jones – to join 'human shields' protesting against the impending Iraqi invasion, as mentioned during the Rock and Roll Hall of Fame induction in 2003 but edited out of the TV version.

In the Studio

5

Mickey Foote

It's somehow fitting that a character associated with The Clash's early days should be remembered for an act of rebellion in later life, the producer of their explosive, self-titled 1977 debut LP, becoming a key figure in a community battle to fight Donald Trump's bid to build a golf course in Aberdeenshire.

Mickey Foote moved north of the border in the 2000s and was a prime mover in a campaign against Trump International Golf Course, a vanity project being built near the Menie estate, where he lived with his partner Kym, working as an engineer for sanitation firm Saniflo after retiring from the music industry.

Taking on the arrogance of money, wealth, big-shot lawyers and a billionaire property developer who would later become US President, Foote was quoted in 2009 as saying, 'We already have some of the best courses in the world in Scotland. The idea that another golf course and hotel is going to save us is absolutely grotesquely laughable. He's sold the people on the idea that it's wild, rough country and he's going to tame it, going to make it beautiful. I'm saying it's perfectly beautiful as it is.'

Foote was a member of the Sustainable Aberdeenshire group protesting against the construction of the course on protected sand dunes, and appeared in 2011 Anthony Baxter documentary, *You've Been Trumped.* Trump rejected repeated warnings from his environment experts that plans for 'the world's greatest golf course' would severely damage a rare and legally protected stretch of dunes in north-east Scotland, following a public inquiry into controversial plans to spend £1bn building a golf resort with 950 timeshare flats, a 450-bed hotel and 500 homes on the coastline north of Aberdeen.

The former Clash soundman suffered a stroke in early 2018 and died at Aberdeen Royal Infirmary, aged 66, and was hailed by John Robb in his Louder than War website tribute as 'the architect of their classic sound on the debut album ... by extension defining just what punk rock sounded like (as well as producing Subway Sect's Ambition and arguably defining the plate for underground indie rock as well).

'He was there when Strummer had his moment of epiphany seeing the Sex Pistols in 1976 and was at the heart of The Clash camp for a couple of years. When the band were signed and there was no actual blueprint for what punk rock was meant to sound like Mickey was drafted in as a producer on early demos in an attempt to capture the band's compulsive, propulsive, thin, rattling sound and caught them perfectly as a rock'n'roll band without the power chords – the stripped-down, amphetamine-impatient, rush template that became their initial sound. That urgent rush of ideas and 'no overdubs' as Strummer demanded.'

Robb added, 'Mickey's footnote in rock'n'roll history may seem small, but is absolutely crucial – his skills on the deck created the template for what punk rock actually sounded like.'

In his own website tribute, former Clash roadie The Baker added, 'The sad news that Mickey Foote has died after a short illness leaves me speechless. He was another of the band's unsung heroes. Journey on Mickey ...'

Joe Strummer first became associated with sound technician/engineer turned producer

Mickey Foote during his Vultures days, becoming part of the art school rocakabilly scene in Newport, South Wales, the then Woody Mellor briefly moving into Foote's flat. They hooked up again when the 101'ers were recording, not least during his spell on the sound-desk at The Roundhouse and was drafted in by The Clash when they started recording, with subsequent production credits on 'White Riot' and The Clash, as well as assisting Lee 'Scratch' Perry on 'Complete Control'. But Foote was sacked after taking Bernie Rhodes' advice and tinkering with fourth single, 'Clash City Rockers' while Strummer and Jones were in Jamaica.

As well as the 101'ers, The Clash and The Subway Sect, he also worked with Mick Jones' ex-partner Ellen Foley, further Clash associate Tymon Dogg, and the Black Arabs. He later moved back to his native Scotland as a Saniflo engineer, having joined the firm in London in 1993, having lived in a houseboat there for many years.

Lee 'Scratch' Perry

Born in 1936, Jamaican producer Lee 'Scratch' Perry is revered for his innovative studio techniques and pioneering work in the development of dub reggae, working with the likes of Bob Marley and the Wailers, Junior Murvin, Max Romeo, the Beastie Boys, and The Slits' Ari Up, as well as The Clash.

His career began in the late '50s with Clement Coxsone Dodd, then Joe Gibbs (whose 1976 LP, *State of Emergency*, inspired the cover photograph of the 'White Riot single), starting Upsetter Records in 1968, with early examples of sampling and the introduction of a fast, chugging beat soon identified as 'reggae'. From then until 1972 he recorded with The Upsetters while releasing recordings on a variety of labels, with songs popular in both Jamaica and the UK.

By 1973 he'd built his own backyard studio, the Black Ark (later carrying a likeness on the studio interior wall of The Clash, the only white band featured), later burned to the ground, possibly at his own hand. Dividing his time between England and the US, he put his '80s reemergence down to his decision to quit alcohol and cannabis, his earlier days having been characterised by blowing smoke into the mic. so 'the weed would get into the song'.

In 2003, he won a Grammy for Best Reggae Album with *Jamaican E.T.* and in 2004, *Rolling Stone* ranked him in their list of the 100 Greatest Artists of All Time. He later settled in Switzerland with his wife and children, and was the subject of Volker Schaner's 2015 documentary, *Lee 'Scratch' Perry's Vision of Paradise*, with a worldwide cinematic release and a premiere at London's East End Film Festival, the director spending more than 15 years filming, witnessing the building of his Secret Laboratory in Switzerland and its destruction, that 2015 blaze also seeing his stage costumes and unreleased recordings lost.

Sandy Pearlman

The New York-born producer of *Give 'Em Enough* Rope died aged 72 in the summer of 2016 in Marin County, California, described as a 'manager, songwriter, label executive and poet'. He was otherwise best known for his association with Blue Öyster Cult, having managed the band as well as producing nine of their albums, including their best-known single, 1976 hit, '(Don't Fear) The Reaper'. Pearlman was also immortalised in a Saturday Night Live sketch, 'More cowbell', Christopher Walken playing a fictionalised version of the producer. He also produced The Dictators' 'Go Girl Crazy!' and Dream Syndicate's 'The Medicine

Show', managed Ronnie James Dio-era Black Sabbath from 1979-83, was president of 415 Records and vice-president of pioneering '90s online music service eMusic.com. Pearlman also worked from 1966 at music magazine Crawdaddy, where he is often credited with coining the phrase 'heavy metal'. He was described as the 'Hunter Thompson of rock, a gonzo producer of searing intellect and vast vision,' in Billboard's Producer Directory, and was responsible for 17 gold and platinum records.

Guy Stevens

The acclaimed producer of *London Calling* died within two years of the release of lauded Clash LP, *London Calling*, aged just 38 after overdosing on prescription drugs while fighting alcoholism. But he certainly made his mark in music, having started out as a DJ in the '60s.

East Dulwich-born Stevens was influential in promoting R&B in the UK, and gave Procol Harum and Mott the Hoople their names, working in insurance while building a collection of US import blues. In 1963 he began running a weekly R&B night at Soho's Scene Club, attracting a Mod crowd, including members of the Small Faces, The Who, The Rolling Stones, The Beatles, and The Yardbirds.

He soon began compiling and annotating reissues and compilations of American records, particularly for EMI, while writing for Record Mirror, and was approached by Chris Blackwell in 1964 to run Island offshoot Sue, going on to release a string of successful singles and albums and bringing Chuck Berry to the UK for his first tour after paying his bail to get him out of jail.

He started producing at Blackwell's suggestion in 1965, working with Alex Harvey, Larry Williams and Lee Dorsey before becoming Island's head of A&R, seeing further success with Spooky Tooth and Procol Harum. In 1968, he was imprisoned for several months for drug offences, and his record collection was stolen, leading to a breakdown. But on his release, he returned to Island, producing Free's debut LP and forming Mott the Hoople, serving as their manager and producing three of their first four albums before they hit the big time.

By the mid-1970s, Stevens' activities had become increasingly erratic through chronic alcoholism, but was present for a demo session with The Clash before they were signed, three years before the band recruited him for *London Calling*, seeing his input as a major factor in its success. In 1981, The Clash wrote Midnight to Stevens in tribute to him, while Ian Hunter included a poem with 1983 LP *All of the Good Ones Are Taken* in tribute to a maverick character who once proclaimed, 'There are only two Phil Spectors in the world... and I'm one of them!'

Bill Price

Producer and engineer Bill Price was 72 when he died on the 14th anniversary of Joe Strummer's passing on December 22nd, 2016, having also worked with the Sex Pistols, Sparks, The Jesus and Mary Chain, The Waterboys, Mott the Hoople, Guns'n'Roses, and Simon Townshend, also working with the latter's brother, Pete Townshend as chief engineer on his first three solo albums.

He started out in the mid-'60s as an engineer at Decca Studios in West Hampstead, recording artists such as Tom Jones and The Marmalade before heading on to Wessex Studios, helping build AIR Studios in Oxford Street, where he spent many years. As well as his chief engineer's role with producer Guy Stevens on *London Calling* in 1979 and the band themselves as producers on *Sandinista!* in 1980, his many successes also included roles with *Never Mind the Bollocks, Here's the Sex Pistols*, and Nilsson's *Without You*. And Price was later back in league with Mick Jones for his Carbon/Silica project with Tony James.

Glyn Johns

Born in 1942 in Epsom, Surrey, producer and engineer Glyn Johns, called in to help The Clash out on *Combat Rock* in 1982, has a CV to be marveled at, working on a number of acclaimed albums and with many revered artists over the years, starting in style with engineering and mixing duties on Georgie Fame and the Blue Flames' 1964 LP, *Rhythm and Blues at the Flamingo* and soon working with The Rolling Stones and the Small Faces, and then The Beatles and Led Zeppelin – who paid tribute to him with a cover shot of actress Glynis Johns on 1969's *Led Zeppelin II* – before the decade was out.

In the 1970s, many more big names projects followed, his productions duties including those with The Faces, The Who, The Eagles (on their first two LPs) and Eric Clapton, and has been involved with many more influential artists since, including Paul McCartney. In 2008 he was credited for his original recording of The Clash's *Live at Shea Stadium* in October 1982, from their second night supporting The Who, the tape unearthed by Joe Strummer while packing for a house move.

His recording career started while working with The Presidents, as an engineer at IBC Studios in Portland Place. In 1969 he was called on to rescue The Beatles' *Get Back* sessions, compiling several versions of the album, all rejected by the band, before the project was turned over to Phil Spector. Johns memorably called that finished version, *Let It Be*, 'a syrupy load of bullshit'.

In 2012, Johns was inducted into the Rock and Roll Hall of Fame in Cleveland, nine years after The Clash, honoured for 'musical excellence', two years later writing his memoir, *Sound Man*.

Joining The Clash on Record

Tymon Dogg

Born Stephen Murray in Formby, near Liverpool, in 1950, singer-songwriter/multi-instrumentalist Dogg's career started with shows at Liverpool's Cavern and Peppermint Lounge, aged 15. But after early solo success he drifted towards London's underground scene, where he met Joe Strummer, showing him the ropes as a busker, and later invited to contribute to the *Sandinista!* album – including his violin and vocal tour de force on 'Lose This Skin' – and further down the line with Strummer's band The Mescaleros.

Moving to London at 17, he signed to Pye Records as 'Timon', recording a single, 'The Bitter Thoughts of Little Jane', featuring future Led Zeppelin stars Jimmy Page and John Paul Jones. Switching to Apple, he recorded tracks produced by Peter Asher, featuring Paul McCartney on piano and James Taylor on guitar, then toured with The Moody Blues, working closely with Justin Hayward, with 'Now She Says She's Young' out as a single in 1970.

He later joined the squatting community, scratching out a living playing folk clubs and busking, then in 1978, moved to the North East with artist Helen Cherry, releasing an LP in the '80s. In 2000, he met up with Strummer again at the Poetry Olympics, the pair's impromptu set including Lily Allen's live début as backing singer. He soon joined The Mescaleros, the two working together until Strummer's death in 2002. Since then he's continued to write and record, and in 2010 Cherry Red released 1967/2009 compilation, *The Irrepressible Tymon Dogg*, while Thin Man Press produced a CD of Dogg's extracts from Louis Aragon's *A Wave of Dreams* in 2012.

Mikey Dread

Michael George Campbell, the dub producer, singer and broadcaster better known as Mikey Dread, died in March 2008, aged 53, internationally recognised as one of reggae's most influential performers and innovators.

Born in Port Antonio, Jamaica, Campbell soon showed an aptitude for engineering and electronics, as a teenager performing with the Safari and Sound of Music sound systems and working on his high school's radio station. After studying electrical engineering, he started as an engineer in 1976 with the Jamaica Broadcasting Corporation, soon rebelling at the JBC playlist of bland, foreign pop music while so much great reggae was being recorded at home, convincing his bosses to give him his own programme, *Dread at the Controls*, playing almost exclusively reggae.

Using his DJ name, the show became a hit, fellow Clash associate Lee 'Scratch' Perry producing his signature tune. He began recording for Sonia Pottinger and Joe Gibbs, while performing with the Socialist Roots sound system. When Campbell quit JBC in 1978 after a fall-out, he became an engineer at the Treasure Isle studio, working with producer Carlton Patterson, the pair co-producing on his and other projects. By the late '70s he had his own DATC label, working with artists such as Edi Fitzroy, Sugar Minott and Earl Sixteen, and releasing Dread's LPs *Evolutionary Rockers* (*Dread at the Controls* in the UK) and *World War III*.

Attracting the attention of The Clash, he was invited to tour with them in 1980, going on to produce some of their music, becoming friends with the band, producing 'Bankrobber', performing on several *Sandinista!* tracks, and touring with them across Britain, Europe and the US.

He studied at London's National Broadcasting School in 1980 and North London Polytechnic in 1984, while singing with reggae collective Singers and Players on Adrian Sherwood's On-U Sound label and producing dub tracks for UB40, touring Europe and Scandinavia as their support. Campbell also hosted *Rockers Roadshow* and narrated Channel 4 reggae documentary series *Deep Roots Music*, and recorded *Profile* and *African Anthem Revisited*. In 1991 he toured Europe and the US with Freddie McGregor and others, and there was even a 1992 collaboration with ex-Guns n'Roses guitarist Izzy Stradlin, with several awards en route, not least for 1990 compilation album *Mikey Dread's Best Sellers*.

That decade he also toured the album *Obsession* and was a director, presenter and producer for Miami TV station Caribbean Satellite Network (CSN), and a radio DJ in Florida too, while working towards degrees in TV/Video Production and international communications. As well as The Clash and UB40, he performed live with Bob Dylan and Carlos Santana before concentrating on his studies, in time regaining control of his entire catalogue, much of it re-released on his label. But there were Montreux Jazz and Glastonbury appearances in the early 2000s, and a UK tour in 2006, while his 2004 'Silicone on Sapphire' tribute to The Clash with The Blizzard of 78 on *The Sandinista! Project* was released three years later, the year it was announced he was being treated for a brain tumour. He died surrounded by his family at his sister's home in Stamford, Connecticut.

Ellen Foley

Born in June 1951 in St Louis, Missouri, Ellen Foley has released four solo albums, coming into The Clash's story for the *Sandinista!* LP, duetting with then-partner Mick Jones on 'Hitsville UK' and also featuring on 'Corner Soul', while providing backing vocals on *Combat Rock*'s 'Car-Jamming'. Meanwhile, 'Should I Stay or Should I Go' is assumed to be about her relationship with its author, Jones.

She first gained recognition duetting with US rock singer Meat Loaf on 'Paradise by the Dashboard Light' from 1977's *Bat out of Hell* LP, Karla DeVito miming to her words in the promo video. Her Ian Hunter and Mick Ronson-produced debut LP, *Night Out*, was released in 1979, including Dutch No.1, 'We Belong to the Night', and the following year she duetted with Hunter on 'We Gotta Get Outta Here'. She also featured on 1979 Blue Oyster Cult LP, *Mirrors*.

In 1981, all four members of The Clash appeared on her second album, *The Spirit of St. Louis*, Strummer and Jones co-writing several songs and Jones producing, the LP also featuring various Blockheads and Tymon Dogg. She also appeared with 'street scum' The Clash in Martin Scorsese's 1982 movie, *The King of Comedy*. In 1984 she sang backing vocals on Joe Jackson's *Body & Soul* LP, and five years later was one of four female vocalists fronting Pandora's Box, formed by Jim Steinman.

Based on the Upper West Side of Manhattan, married to writer Doug Bernstein, with two sons, she teaches voice at a local music school, and has featured on Broadway in *Me and My Girl* and the revival of *Hair*, off-Broadway in *Beehive*, and as The Witch in Stephen Sondheim's *Into the Woods*, and starred in the first series of US TV sitcom *Night Court*. There were also film roles, including 1979's adaptation of *Hair*, 1987's *Fatal Attraction*, and the following year's *Married to the Mob* and *Cocktail*.

Mick Gallagher

Hammond organ and keyboard player Mickey, born in October 1945, is best known for his role with Ian Dury and the Blockheads and contributions to The Clash's later albums, especially *Sandinista!* He also toured with the band, hence the 'Take the Fifth' title on the band's second US tour in late 1979.

Gallagher started his musical career in home city, Newcastle-upon-Tyne, with The Unknowns in the early '60s and joined The Animals in 1965, replacing founding member Alan Price. He then formed *The Chosen Few*, playing alongside Alan Hull, who later formed Lindisfarne. He's also worked with Peter Frampton.

By 1977, he was in Loving Awareness with guitarist John Turnbull, drummer Charley Charles and bass player Norman Watt-Roy, and was invited to join them in session work for Ian Dury, that band becoming The Blockheads. After 1980 LP *Laughter*, the band went their own ways, but briefly reformed to tour Japan in 1987, reuniting in 1990 after Charley Charles' death from cancer, sporadic gigs following before Dury's own cancer battle. *Mr Love-Pants* followed in 1998, the band hitting the road again, their last show with their charismatic singer in February 2000 at London Palladium, Dury dying six weeks later. Gallagher stayed with the band, occasionally touring and recording, Watt-Roy, Jankel and Turnbull all still involved.

Gallagher first featured with The Clash on 1979's *London Calling*, and was also part of the uncredited session team on final, critically-panned LP, *Cut the Crap* in 1985. His children, Luke, Ben and Maria, featured with him on *Sandinista!* He also worked with Topper Headon in short-lived band Samurai, and again when the drummer recorded his *Waking Up* album in 1986. Samurai guitarist Henry Padovani, said of him, 'He had a family, was the serious one of the group, never snorted any coke and managed to somehow control Topper a little. Playing with this talented musician was a pleasure.'

He's also performed and recorded with Paul McCartney, Roger Daltrey, Dave Stewart, Annie Lennox and Robbie Williams, featuring in recent times with John Steel's The Animals and Friends, and writing music for films such as *Extremes* (1971) and *After Midnight* (1990), and 1987 Broadway play *Serious Money*.

Norman Watt-Roy

The man behind that memorable bassline on 'The Magnificent Seven' has enjoyed a career spanning more than 40 years, coming to prominence in the late '70s with Ian Dury and The Blockheads and working more recently with ex-Dr Feelgood guitarist Wilko Johnson, while gaining a reputation for his session work, often with bandmate and fellow Clash associate Mickey Gallagher (and it's worth noting here that sax player Davey Payne also featured on several *Sandinista!* tracks).

Born in February 1951 in Bombay, by the age of three he'd moved to England, settling in Highbury, North London, then relocating to Harlow, Essex. Learning a few guitar chords from his Dad, he played in high school bands with older brother Garth. Leaving school at 15, he studied art in Harlow then moved into London, forming The Living Daylights with Garth, playing regularly and releasing a single for Philips. In 1968 the brothers formed a nine-piece soul band, touring US military bases in Germany, backing the likes of Sonny Burke, known as The Greatest Show on Earth. Winning a recording contract with Harvest, they released a single in 1970, 'Real Cool World' becoming a No.1 in Switzerland, two albums following before Norman joined Glencoe and met fellow future Blockhead, John Turnbull, that four-piece going on to release two albums and record four John Peel sessions.

In 1974 they got together with keyboardist Mick Gallagher to form the nucleus of a band which, with the addition of drummer Charlie Charles, became Loving Awareness. Two years later they met Ian Dury and Chaz Jankel, going on to play on Dury's 1977 Stiff Records LP, *New Boots and Panties*. They then joined the label's first UK package tour, billed as Ian Dury and the Blockheads, managed by Andrew King and future Clash co-manager Peter Jenner, enjoying a run of commercial success.

Watt-Roy became a regular member of Wilko Johnson's band by 1985 after the latter's spell with The Blockheads led to friendship, and over that period his session work included bass for Nick Lowe, Rachel Sweet, Jona Lewie and The Selecter. He then appeared with Mick Gallagher on The Clash's *Sandinista!*, recording at Electric Lady Studios in New York. He also played on the much-maligned *Cut the Crap*.

As well as parts on 'The Magnificent Seven', 'Hitsville UK' and 'Rock the Casbah', Watt-Roy will be remembered for his playing on Frankie Goes to Hollywood's 'Relax', also involving fellow Blockheads, Gallagher, Turnbull and Charles. He's also worked with Wreckless Eric, Roger Daltrey, Nick Cave, and members

5

of Madness, while guesting on fellow Clash associate, Viv Albertine's *The Vermillion Border* in 2012 and releasing solo LP, *Faith & Grace*, in 2013.

The Barnacles

While two members of the Barnacle clan feature on Clash recordings, two more from this musical family played a part in the band's story, thanks to the infamous 'Guns on the Roof' incident at Rehearsal Rehearsals, Camden, in 1978.

The initial link came through fellow Dover lad Topper Headon, whose first band, Crystal Carcass, featured his mate Steve Barnacle on bass, knocking out 12-bar boogie instrumentals. Steve was one of three Barnacle brothers involved in music, along with their father Arthur, best known as Bill Barnacle, who had his own jazz band in Kent, regularly playing the Louis Armstrong pub in Dover, Headon soon sitting in with them.

At a later stage Headon, by then in London, joined Canadian band Fury and persuaded Steve to join him, Headon's exit from that outfit after a number of gigs on the London pub-rock circuit for not hitting the drums hard enough proving a key turning point in his own story. Meanwhile, Steve's brother Pete played drums and brother Gary was a saxophonist, and it's the latter who first featured with The Clash, Headon's recommendation leading to him playing on early B-sides '1-2 Crush on You', 'City of the Dead' and Booker T cover 'Time is Tight'.

In fact, while Gary was sitting in, brothers Pete and Steve joined him in Camden, bringing an air rifle Headon was interested in buying, leading to that notorious incident, Pete along with Topper and Paul Simonon taking the rap.

Gary was back as a session sax player by the time of the *Sandinista!* album, featuring on Headon's 'Ivan Meets GI Joe', plus 'Something About England'/'Mensforth Hill', 'Lose This Skin', 'The Street Parade' and 'The Crooked Beat', his father adding trumpet on all bar the latter. Bill's mate from Dover, military bandsman David Yates also features on 'Something About England'. Gary also played on 'This is Radio Clash' and *Combat Rock*'s 'Sean Flynn'.

Space doesn't allow me the chance to give more than a flavour of his CV, but born in Dover in November 1959, he's also described as a flautist, brass arranger, composer and producer, his past roles including work on various Prince's Trust shows and Nelson Mandela 70th birthday party at Wembley in 1988. He also worked on Julien Temple's *Absolute Beginners* soundtrack – including David Bowie's title track – and – among others – with ABC, Bjork, The Boomtown Rats, China Crisis, The Communards, The Creatures, The Damned, Del Amitri, Elvis Costello, Erasure, General Public, Holly Johnson, Hothouse Flowers, Jamiroquai, Jools Holland, Kim Wilde, Kirsty MacColl, Level 42, Lloyd Cole, Madness, Marc Almond (and Soft Cell), Paul McCartney, Pet Shop Boys, PIL, Prefab Sprout, Rick Astley, Roger Daltrey, The Ruts, Soul II Soul, Swing Out Sister, Tim Finn, Tina Turner, Ultravox, and Visage.

Meanwhile, Steve Barnacle featured on bass for Visage from 1982/85 and 2012/15, and Kirk Brandon's Spear of Destiny in 1987. He was also on hand in Fulham between engagements to try to keep an eye on Topper Headon during the worst spells of his drug addiction. As for Pete Barnacle, his drumming CV included stints with Gillan, Spear of Destiny and fellow Kirk Brandon outfit Theatre of Hate, later moving to Japan, teaching English and occasionally still playing.

The Irish Horns/ The Rumour Brass

Not only did Bob Andrews play keyboards on Mick Jones' wondrous 'Stay Free' on *Give 'Em Enough Rope* (uncredited), but there was a further link to Graham Parker's band The Rumour on the mighty double LP that followed, *London Calling*. Going under the pseudonym, The Irish Horns (Strummer's competitive spirit ruling out a credit for 'GP' through their usual Rumour Brass tag) were in fact baritone/tenor sax player John 'Irish' Earle, tenor sax player Ray Beavis, and trumpet player Dick Hanson, three-quarters of the brass section that appeared with Parker. Trombonist Chris Gower missed out, as Bill Price, who ran the session in Stevens' absence (with Headon and Simonon also missing), explained to Marcus Gray in the tremendously-detailed *Route 19 Revisited: The Clash and London Calling*, saying, 'Trumpet and two tenors is the classic Stax brass line-up.'

The trio featured on five tracks on that acclaimed Wessex Studios record – 'Jimmy Jazz', 'Revolution Rock', 'The Right Profile', 'Rudy Can't Fail', and 'Wrong 'Em Boyo'. What's more, The Irish Horns – Strummer's nickname purely down to them including John 'Irish' Earle – laid down all their parts in one go. Strummer revealed, 'They made up their own arrangements on the spot. We'd suggest the way it should go, they'd fill it out. They hit five songs from scratch.'

Former Kilburn and the High Roads' member Earle, from Dublin, died in 2008, aged 63, and Beavis and Hanson gave differing versions of those sessions in Gray's book about the LP, wherein it's also revealed that Hanson was previously on the staff at Trojan Records, including work with The Pioneers and Desmond Dekker. But by the time they came to Wessex – probably booked by Kosmo Vinyl – they'd more or less become Dave Robinson's in-house brass section at Stiff.

Other Rumour Brass credits include work with Carlene Carter, Katrina and the Waves (including their big hit, 'Walking on Sunshine'), The Undertones ('Conscious') and Orange Juice's Zeke Manyika. Hanson also played in the Watt-Roy brothers' soul band, The Greatest Show on Earth, as well as with Shakin' Stevens, albeit long after that October '76 University of London show with The Clash. But between Beavis, Earle and Hanson, you can also add The Blues Band, The Boomtown Rats, Dave Edmunds, Kirsty MacColl, Randy Crawford, Rory Gallagher, Suzi Quatro, Thin Lizzy (including 'Dancing in the Moonlight'), and U2 (including 'Angel of Harlem') to that esteemed list.

Behind the Lens

Don Letts

Born in January 1956 in London, Donovan Letts' parents had newly arrived from the Caribbean in the late '50s, with their son the only black pupil at his Kennington grammar school in the late '60s. A big Beatles memorabilia collector at an early age, he was politicised by racism suffered at school but turned on by the 'better aspects of white popular culture', not just his parents' love of blues, ska and reggae.

By the mid-70s he was selling clothes for Chelsea clothing store Acme Attractions, a rival to Malcolm McLaren's fellow King's Road business, selling 'electric-blue zoot suits and jukeboxes, and pumping dub reggae all day long', as he put it in *The Guardian* in 2007, while compiling reggae tapes for the likes of the visiting Debbie Harry, Lenny Kaye, Patti Smith and the Sex Pistols, and selling weed under the counter to passing luminaries such as Bob Marley.

Making his name as a DJ and later a film director and musician, he came to prominence as The Clash's videographer. After Mick Jones' sacking, he joined the guitarist in Big Audio Dynamite, with a 'vocals and samples' role from 1984 to 1990, leaving to form Screaming Target, who released acclaimed album, *Hometown Hi-Fi*.

Seeing Bob Marley at Hammersmith Odeon in June '76, he sneaked into the Jamaican's hotel and spent the night talking to and befriending him. And when promoter Andy Czezowski opened London nightclub The Roxy at the beginning of 1977, he not only booked The Clash as the first band but took on Letts as DJ, his choice to play plenty of dub and reggae in his sets helping forge that link between punk and reggae. He's also pictured on the cover of early Clash compilation, *Black Market Clash*, and later version, *Super Black Market Clash*.

Letts quit the retail business to manage The Slits, who opened for The Clash on the 'White Riot' tour, but quickly decided that role wasn't for him, although he continued to shoot material for *The Punk Rock Movie*. He soon visited Jamaica for the first time, joining John Lydon, fresh out of the Pistols and out to escape the media frenzy, Virgin label boss Richard Branson also travelling. Letts later recalled for *The Guardian*, 'I guess (Branson) thought that since I was black and Jamaican – well, sort of – he'd be in good hands. Little did he know the closest I'd been to Jamaica was watching *The Harder They Come* at the Classic Cinema in Brixton.'

His promo videos included those for 'White Riot', 'Tommy Gun', 'London Calling', 'Bankrobber', 'The Call-Up', 'This is Radio Clash', 'Rock the Casbah', and 'Should I Stay Or Should I Go', also directing videos for Musical Youth, The Psychedelic Furs, The Pretenders, Elvis Costello, The Fun Boy 3, The Undertones, Eddy Grant, The Gap Band, and Black Grape.

Letts' documentary films include 1977's *The Punk Rock Movie*, 1997's Jamaica-based *Dancehall Queen* and 2000's *The Clash: Westway to the World*. His Clash-related works also include work on *The Essential Clash*, *Making of London Calling: Last Testament*, *The Clash Live: Revolution Rock*, and *Strummerville*.

There have also been documentaries on Gil Scott-Heron, Sun Ra, George Clinton, Franz Ferdinand, rock photographer Bob Gruen, and The Jam's *All Mod Cons*, while his features include *Soul Britannia*, *Carnival!*, *Subculture*, and *The Story of Skinhead*. Letts has released several compilation LPs for Heavenly Records and Sanctuary Records. In 2007, he published autobiography, *Culture Clash: Dread Meets Punk Rockers*, and by 2009 was presenting a weekly BBC Radio 6 Music show.

Julien Temple

Born in November 1952 in Kensington, West London, revered film, documentary and music video director Julien Temple started out making films featuring the Sex Pistols, soon carving out a reputation for off-beat projects.

It was Temple who helped get The Clash in for free at Beaconsfield's National Film and Television School in early '77 to record, the version of 'White Riot' put down that day making it on to the debut LP. His love of film was sparked at Cambridge University, discovering French anarchist director Jean Vigo, who he later made a film about, while his interest in the London punk scene led to friendship with the Pistols, documenting their early gigs, eventually resulting in 1979's *The Great Rock'n'Roll Swindle* and 2004's *The Filth and the Fury*. And while the story of the original film was from Malcolm McLaren's viewpoint and somewhat contentious, Temple was praised for his innovative mix of animated scenes, documentary film, and specially-shot footage to tell the story, something of a template for his future work, while helping him launch a career in music video production.

Explaining his cinematic vision, he added, 'I like the idea of using almost fiction to create the story of a real story, so you're kind of blurring the boundaries a bit, and though you're making a documentary, you're trying to create it as a very tight narrative, so people can emotionally be taken on a ride, like it's a narrative drama film.'

His Clash-related work also included *The Clash: New Year's Day '77* in 2015, while in late 2007 – the year he directed *Joe Strummer: The Future is Unwritten* – he shot the Pistols' comeback dates at Brixton Academy and filmed the band re-visiting old London haunts, leading to, *The Sex Pistols: There'll Always Be An England*. That came 25 years after his early '80s commercial breakthrough, including 1982's *The Secret Policeman's Other Ball* and 1984's *Jazzin' for Blue Jean* for David Bowie. But his first major film, 1986's adaptation of Colin MacInnes' acclaimed '50s London novel, *Absolute Beginners*, was critically panned.

Temple, whose early work also included a film project with The UK Subs, soon headed to America, making 1988's *Earth Girls are Easy* film and promo videos for Duran Duran, Janet Jackson, Neil Young and Tom Petty, returning in the late '90s. By the time of 2001's *Pandaemonium*, about the friendship between Romantic poets Coleridge and Wordsworth, reviews were better, and after his return to the subject of the Pistols, he made feature-length documentary *Glastonbury*, shooting festival footage and drawing on archive film, that project followed by his tribute to close friend and Somerset neighbour, Joe Strummer.

His music video subjects have also included Gary Numan, Jean Michel Jarre, Judas Priest, Stray Cats, The Beat, ABC, Culture Club, Depeche Mode, Dexy's Midnight Runners, The Rolling Stones, Sade, Billy Idol, Kenny Rogers, Tin Machine, Swing Out Sister, Whitney Houston, Roger McGuinn, Bryan Adams, Blur, Maria McKee, Enigma, Paul McCartney, S Club 7, Scissor Sisters, and Babyshambles. And since his Strummer tribute, Temple's impressive body of work has included *The Liberty Of Norton Folgate* with Madness, *Oil City Confidential* about Dr Feelgood, the similarly-brilliant *The Ecstasy of Wilko Johnson*, Motown tribute, *Requiem For Detroit*, Kinks-related documentaries, *Ray Davies: Imaginary Man* and *Dave Davies: Kinkdom Come*, having previously directed several videos for the legendary Londoners, and 2012's *London: the Modern Babylon*.

Temple, married with three children, told Edward Douglas at *ComingSoon.net*, on 2007's release of his Joe Strummer documentary, 'Like others who knew him pretty well towards the end, I was still shaken up by what had happened. A bit disoriented, a bit like something was missing in my life, and a feeling also that we hadn't done a memorial for Joe, had a concert or whatever, and a lot of his friends were feeling still very close to the pain of losing him.

'I was editing another film, *Glastonbury*, and there was a sequence Joe was featured in. I just thought, 'Here's this great guy and this great little sequence. Maybe I can get everyone back around a campfire and we can say what was special about Joe, kind of hand it on. Also, maybe help ourselves, in a personal way I was feeling for other people that maybe it would help everybody feel a bit better, having lost him.'

He knew Strummer in his 101'ers days, the then-rookie filmmaker – also involved in the squat scene – seeing him at Orsett Terrace. On the link between his Pistols work and his Strummer film, he added, 'This is a slightly different feel, more personal and more emotionally involving, maybe less fireworks in the sense the Pistols one was really pulling random things out of a hat, making them work together. There is a bit of that, but it's slightly different. It was certainly harder to make a film in a sense about a close friend, because you're worried how you're portraying him, second-guessing what he'd think. I did kind of know I was on safe ground showing some of the flaws, warts and contradictions of the guy, because he would have strangled me if I didn't do that.'

Index

100 Club 49, 55, 59, 61, 63, 66, 67, 74, 89, 90, 101, 127
101'ers, The 20, 32, 34–42, 47–50, 56, 64, 116, 119, 151, 154, 192, 211, 222, 238, 336, 344, 354
999 17, 51

A

Adam and the Ants 60
Albertine, Viv 46, 49, 51, 86, 151, 152, 277, 334, 350

B

Banks, Robin 22, 23, 25, 28, 96, 132, 185, 341, 342
Barnacle, Gary 132, 155, 157, 160, 169, 250, 258
Belfast 9, 194, 196, 107, 108, 109, 110, 340, 195, 197, 212, 238, 342
Big Audio Dynamite 184, 189, 199, 214–217, 219, 220, 223, 227, 228, 231, 247, 266, 267, 268, 281, 314, 315, 317, 352
Bono 201, 110, 111, 200, 202, 210, 211, 256, 285
Boon, Clint 75, 120, 165, 242
Bowie, David 25, 31, 78, 91, 117, 123, 133, 147, 153, 172, 221, 235, 245, 350, 353
Bragg, Billy 124, 185, 186, 338, 202, 203, 213, 285, 340
Buckler, Rick 19, 61, 64, 66, 97, 98, 101, 103
Buck, Paul 17, 19
Burchill, Julie 61, 63, 83
Burnel, Jean-Jaques 57
Buzzcocks, The 5, 6, 59, 75, 81, 89, 96, 97, 101, 102, 117, 123, 127, 164, 224, 226, 239, 244, 270

C

Central School of Art and Design 19
Chimes, Terry 16, 32, 44, 45, 47,

51, 54, 63, 67, 68, 70, 76, 82, 88, 91, 92, 165, 171, 172, 184, 185, 235, 236, 238, 239, 270, 333, 334
Chiswick Records 36, 39, 40, 147
Clash, The (album) 88–92, 94, 98, 133
Combat Rock (album) 15, 195, 161, 162, 163, 166, 168, 170, 171, 173, 176, 178, 258, 217, 228, 333, 338, 258, 259, 260, 261, 262, 263, 280, 281, 346, 348, 350, 352
Cook, Norman 120, 150, 165, 244, 251
Coon, Caroline 17, 19–24, 31, 49, 59, 66, 68, 70, 82, 83, 94, 114, 134, 337, 285, 337, 338, 340
Cost of Loving EP 34
Cut The Crap (album) 15, 220, 181, 182, 186, 221, 263–268, 337, 349, 335, 351

D

Damned, The 45, 46, 48, 55, 57, 70, 73, 74, 75, 94, 96, 103, 350, 235
Dekker, Desmond 148, 351
Diddley, Bo 20, 23, 40, 85, 117, 136, 156, 217
Donovan, Dan 217, 300, 351
Dread, Mikey 153–156, 160, 249, 250, 252, 253, 278, 347
Dr Feelgood 6, 37, 39, 42, 55, 56, 103, 349, 353
Dudanski, Richard 35, 36, 37, 38, 39, 50, 211

E

Eddie and the Hot Rods 37
Equals, The 157, 249, 279

F

Foote, Mickey 21, 39, 78, 82, 104, 117, 235, 236, 343, 344

G

Gibbs, Joe 76, 82, 344, 347
Give 'Em Enough Rope (album) 4, 5, 7, 15, 112, 129, 130, 132, 144, 152, 156, 176, 240–244, 247, 248, 268, 273, 274, 282, 337, 342, 344, 351

Green, Johnny 7, 8, 29, 30, 53, 193, 103, 107, 116–118, 121, 125, 126, 133, 134, 136, 148, 149, 153, 161, 162, 179, 185, 191, 194, 199, 200, 207, 208, 210, 230, 336, 339–342, 343, 344

Grundy, Bill 73, 74

H

Headon, Topper 6, 7, 9, 10, 12, 15, 32, 44, 45, 53, 80, 92, 94, 103, 114, 116, 117, 118, 119, 131, 134, 142, 144, 147, 148, 155, 156, 160, 161, 162, 164, 165, 166, 172, 173, 174, 175, 183, 184, 185, 186, 195, 196, 198, 207, 208, 217, 222, 227, 228, 229, 230, 333, 238, 339, 341, 242, 245, 349, 249, 350, 252, 253, 254, 258, 335, 341, 343, 350, 351, 352

joins The Clash 92–95

post-Clash career 228–232

Heartbreakers, The 73, 75, 129, 333, 333

Hollywood Brats 27, 43, 44

Hot, Roland 32, 44, 45

Hunter, Ian 26, 41, 80, 133, 221, 335, 345, 348, 170

Hynde, Chrissie 43, 46, 47, 48, 90, 200, 201

I

Irish Horns, The 147, 148, 151, 218, 245, 275, 351

J

James, Brian 43, 44, 45, 46, 55

James, Tony 28, 32, 41, 43, 45, 46, 47, 51, 185, 220, 221, 336, 346, 338

Jam, The 5, 6, 37, 48, 61, 64, 66, 76, 81, 92, 96, 97, 100, 102, 103, 108, 119, 133, 160, 203, 338, 352, 254, 340, 354

Jones, Mick 15, 16, 31, 32, 36–38, 40–60, 63–68, 74–76, 78, 80–83, 86–90, 93, 95, 96, 100–106, 112, 114, 116–120, 122, 124, 125, 127–133, 136–138, 142, 144, 146–160, 162, 164–166, 168, 169, 171–180, 183–186, 189, 190, 197–200, 208, 213–232, 247–250, 252–254, 258, 259–266, 333–342, 344–346, 348, 351, 352, 335, 337, 340–344, 346, 347, 348

boyhood 22–28

with The London SS 41–45

solo career 213–222

Jones, Steve 32, 56, 73, 127, 183, 223, 336

K

Kelleher, Dan 36, 37, 38, 40, 50
Kosmo Vinyl 29, 153, 157, 163, 165, 169, 176, 178, 185, 337, 258, 338, 351, 170

L

LaBritain, Pablo 17, 51
Letts, Don 23, 29, 58, 60, 63, 76, 77, 85, 102, 105, 118, 119, 122, 126, 128, 131, 140, 144, 148, 150, 152, 158, 164, 165, 168, 171, 184, 186, 200, 213, 214, 217, 218, 219, 338, 341, 351, 352, 354, 170
Levene, Keith 44, 47, 48, 49, 50, 51, 54, 55, 56, 60, 61, 63, 101, 333, 334, 336
Little Queenie 27, 42, 43, 44
London Calling (album) 136, 137, 145
London SS, The 32, 41, 42, 43, 54, 55, 91, 94, 132, 185, 221, 333
Lydon, John 37, 43, 46, 47, 49, 51, 55, 56, 57, 59, 73, 75, 76, 81, 90, 111, 159, 238, 334, 336, 352, 354

M

Matlock, Glen 32, 46, 48, 49, 59, 73, 90, 213, 336
McLaren, Malcolm 32, 42, 45, 46, 54, 57, 59, 78, 180, 335, 337, 352, 353
Mellor, Ronald 16, 19, 176, 177
Mescaleros, The 5, 64, 147, 159, 168, 181, 184, 189, 192, 193, 194, 195, 197, 198, 199, 346, 347, 201, 202, 203, 204, 205, 206, 207, 208, 210, 212, 213, 220, 221, 222, 186, 280, 281, 186, 348, 349
Mods 28, 29, 59, 67, 101, 336, 340, 345, 352
Morrissey 44, 75
Mott the Hoople 19, 25, 28, 32, 43, 47, 64, 92, 127, 128, 133, 151, 152, 221, 345, 248, 273, 345, 347
Murray, Charles Shaar 60, 92, 194, 200, 201, 211, 245, 247
Murvin, Junior 61, 91, 95, 104, 237, 239, 240, 272, 344

N

New York Dolls, The 26, 27, 28, 32, 37, 42, 43, 46, 129, 130, 336, 338

Northern Ireland 8, 107, 108, 110, 111, 141, 142

O

O'Neill, Damian 7, 8

P

Parsons, Tony 9, 52, 61, 63, 76, 81, 83, 85, 90, 236

Pearlman, Sandy 5, 112, 114, 128, 129, 133, 144, 242, 344

Peel, John 5, 9, 74, 349, 118, 142, 351

Perry, Mark 59, 67, 78, 85, 105, 121, 145

Pirroni, Marco 57, 60, 63

Pogues 66, 189, 190, 195, 211, 213

Pogues, The 5, 66, 134, 160, 168

Public Image Ltd 37, 55, 334

R

Raincoats, The 37

Ramones, The 6, 53, 57, 60, 66, 197, 89, 91, 100, 198, 203, 285

Reid, Jamie 59, 236

Rhodes, Bernie 16, 32, 37, 38, 41–43, 45, 47, 48, 49, 50, 52, 53, 54, 55, 57, 58, 59, 60, 61, 63, 64, 67, 76, 78, 82, 87, 89, 90, 96, 97, 214, 104, 107, 112, 114, 116, 125, 126, 127, 128, 136, 137, 152, 153, 160, 161, 162, 165, 167, 173–176, 178, 179–183, 185, 189, 215, 227, 335, 244, 260, 261, 263, 264, 336, 337, 339, 340, 341, 343, 344, 346

Rock Against Racism 66, 114, 122, 123, 125, 152, 203, 224, 285

Rolling Stones, The 6, 11, 17, 18, 22, 39, 40, 45, 63, 70, 85, 205, 144, 157, 206, 219, 334, 338, 249, 254, 345, 346, 348, 353, 355

Roundhouse, The 23, 24, 30, 39, 40, 56, 57, 61, 66, 94, 112, 344

Rude Boy (film) 114, 122, 124, 126, 127, 133, 134, 147, 148, 151, 152, 222, 256, 340, 342

S

Sam & Dave 136
Sandinista! (album) 15, 37, 40, 154–162, 178, 345, 245, 346, 347, 249, 250, 251, 252, 253, 255, 256, 257, 258, 260, 262, 263, 266, 278, 279, 280, 285, 348, 349, 350, 351, 352
Schoolgirl 25, 26, 27
Sex Pistols 4, 5, 6, 31, 32, 37, 38, 45, 48, 54, 55, 56, 57, 58, 59, 63, 67, 68, 70, 75, 82, 202, 88, 90, 92, 107, 111, 121, 127, 144, 149, 168, 185, 203, 222, 223, 225, 334, 335, 336, 236, 73, 336, 341, 343, 345, 346, 348, 352, 353, 354, 355
Simonon, Paul 4–8, 10, 15, 16, 29, 30–32, 44–55, 57–61, 63, 66–68, 70, 75, 76, 80, 83, 85, 88–91, 94, 95, 100, 101, 104, 107, 110, 114, 116–119, 124, 125, 128, 129, 130, 134, 138, 140, 141, 142, 147, 149, 150, 151, 153, 155, 157, 158, 160–162, 166, 173–176, 179–186, 189, 198, 201, 216, 217, 222–228, 235, 236, 238, 241, 242, 245, 246, 249, 252, 253, 256, 258, 260, 261, 262, 263, 333–335, 337–341, 350, 351
boyhood 29–32
post-Clash career and art 223–228
Siouxsie and the Banshees 63, 64, 73, 81, 244
Slits, The 34, 49, 51, 59, 96, 97, 100, 102, 148, 152, 212, 244, 344, 352
Smith, Patti 34, 41, 57, 66, 111, 352
Sniffin' Glue 59, 67, 78, 85
Stevens, Guy 24, 25, 27, 76, 137, 144, 145, 146, 147, 148, 151, 185, 336, 245, 247, 248, 275, 339, 345
Stewart, Mark 66
Stiff Little Fingers 109, 110, 123, 212, 235, 238, 342
Stranglers, The 5, 6, 57, 94, 98, 203, 338
Strummer, Joe 4–12, 15–17, 19, 20, 24, 29, 32, 34–43, 47–61, 63, 64, 66–68, 70, 76, 78, 80–83, 85–92, 94–96, 98, 100–103, 110, 112, 114, 116, 119–121, 124, 125–131, 133, 134, 136, 137, 140–142, 145–166, 168, 169, 170–185, 189–195, 197–208, 211–223, 225–230, 235, 240–242, 245, 248–252, 246,

254, 256–266, 280, 281, 285, 286, 336, 337, 237, 338, 340, 343, 344, 345, 346, 347, 348, 353, 253, 354, 356
boyhood 16–22
with The 101'ers 34–41
solo career 109–199
death of 199–203
Subway Sect 57, 58, 63, 94, 96, 97, 100, 102, 125, 335, 337, 339, 343, 344

T

Take the Fifth tour 8
Taylor, Vince 146, 245, 248, 275
Temple, Julien 7, 53, 74, 192, 76, 78, 186, 193, 199, 350, 229, 352, 353, 355
The Who 28, 31, 67, 195, 197, 90, 101, 102, 116, 125, 133, 136, 171, 333, 198, 220, 230, 231, 345, 346, 335, 347, 348
Thunders, Johnny 26, 28, 45, 75, 130, 333
Timperley, Clive 20, 34, 36, 37, 38
Toots and the Maytals 116, 130
Townshend, Pete 19, 26, 29, 54, 230, 345, 231, 347
Tymon Dogg 20, 21, 159, 197, 205, 206, 211, 212, 221, 222, 223, 344, 249, 252, 253, 258, 278, 280, 346, 347, 348, 350

U

Undertones, The 6, 7, 8, 9, 11, 12, 110, 117, 140, 142, 342, 351, 352, 142, 144, 344, 353, 354
Up, Ari 59, 212, 344

V

Vanilla Tapes, The (album) 137, 138, 275
Vultures, The 21, 34

W

Weller, Paul 85, 96, 101, 133, 149, 212, 276, 286
Wylie, Pete 98, 104, 114, 120, 144, 210, 222, 238, 244

Z

Zukie, Tapper 53

BRUCE SPRINGSTEEN
THE DAY I WAS THERE

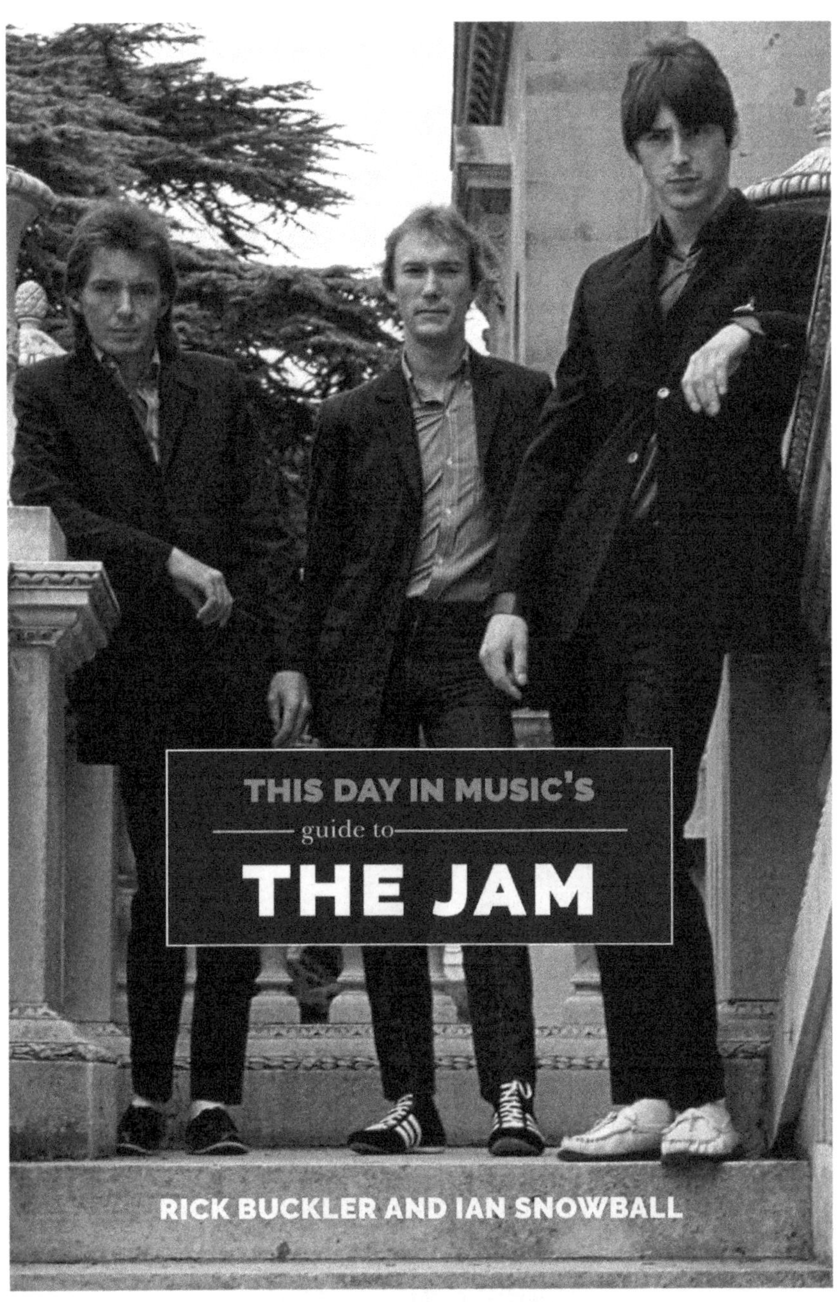

For more info, visit www.thisdayinmusic.com

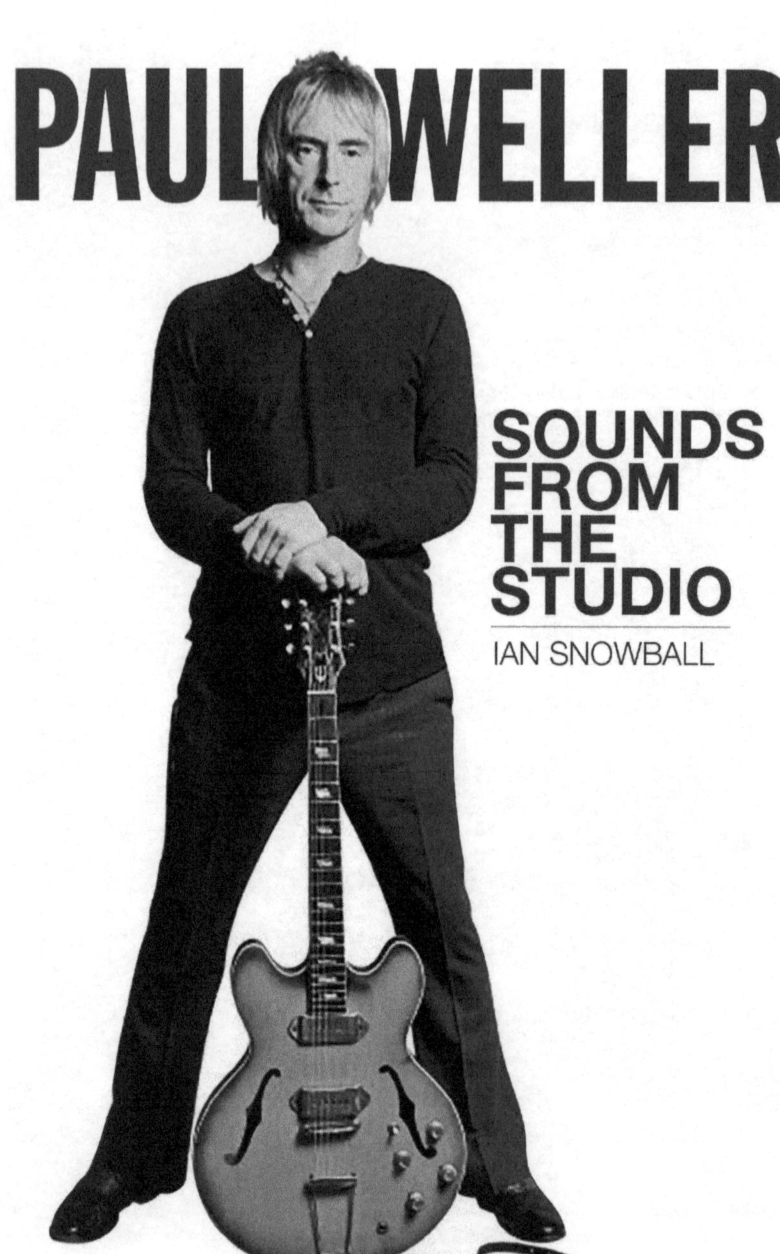
PAUL WELLER
SOUNDS FROM THE STUDIO
IAN SNOWBALL

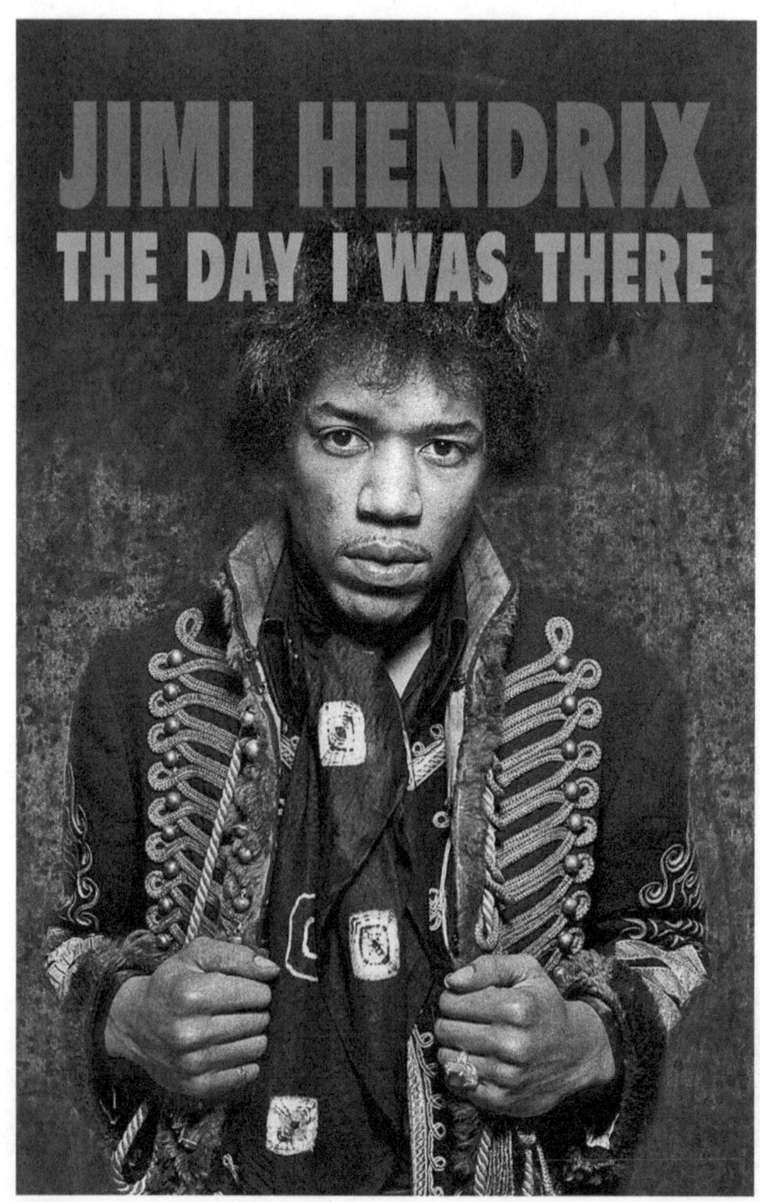
JIMI HENDRIX
THE DAY I WAS THERE